RELATED TITLES

- *Conducting Research in Psychology: Measuring the Weight of Smoke* by Brett W. Pelham
- *Culture and Psychology: People Around the World*, 2nd edition, by David Matsumoto
- *Experimental Design*, 3rd edition, by Roger Kirk
- *Group Dynamics*, 3rd edition, by Donelson Forsyth
- *Health Psychology*, 4th edition, by Linda Brannon and Jess Feist
- *Health Psychology* by Phillip Rice
- *A Lifetime of Relationships* by Nelly Vanzetti and Steve Duck
- *Our Voices: Psychology of Women* by Elizabeth Rider
- *Psychological Testing*, 3rd edition, by Robert Kaplan and Dennis Saccuzzo
- *Psychology and the Legal System*, 4th edition, by Larry Wrightsman, Michael Nietzel and William Fortune
- *Social Psychology* by Stephen Worchel, Joel Cooper, Al Goethals, and James Olson
- *Stress and Health*, 3rd edition, by Phillip Rice
- *Training in Organizations*, 3rd edition, by Irwin L. Goldstein

ADVANCED SOCIAL PSYCHOLOGY TITLES

- *Group Process, Group Decision, Group Action* by Robert S. Baron, Norbert Kerr, and Norman Miller
- *Human Aggression* by Russell Geen
- *Intergroup Relations* by Marilynn Brewer and Norman Miller
- *Negotiation in Social Conflict* by Dean G. Pruitt and Peter J. Carnevale
- *Social Psychology and Health* by Wolfgang Stroebe and Margaret S. Stroebe
- *Social Influence* by John Turner
- *Social Perception* by Leslie A. Zebrowitz
- *Relating to Others* by Steve Duck

FORTHCOMING TITLES

- *The Many Faces of Prejudice* by Russell Spears and Nyla Branscomb

Psychology Applied to Work

SIXTH EDITION

10 - 5/5

13 - 4/5
14 - 4/5
15 - 4/5

Psychology Applied to Work

AN INTRODUCTION TO INDUSTRIAL AND ORGANIZATIONAL PSYCHOLOGY

SIXTH EDITION

PAUL M. MUCHINSKY

University of North Carolina at Greensboro

Wadsworth
Thomson Learning

Australia • Canada • Denmark • Japan • Mexico • New Zealand • Philippines
Puerto Rico • Singapore • South Africa • Spain • United Kingdom • United States

Psychology Editor: *Marianne Taflinger*
Editorial Assistant: *Suzanne Wood*
Marketing Manager: *Jenna Opp*
Project Editor: *John Walker*
Print Buyer: *Karen Hunt*
Permissions Editor: *Bob Kauser*
Production Service: *New Leaf Publishing Services*

Text Designer: *E. Kelly Shoemaker*
Copy Editor: *Carol Reitz*
Compositor: *Graphic Arts Center/Indianapolis*
Cover Designer: *Rob Hugel*
Cover Printer: *Phoenix Color*
Printer/Binder: *R.R. Donnelley & Sons/Crawfordsville*

Printed in the United States of America

1 2 3 4 5 6 7 03 02 01 00 99

Library of Congress Cataloging-in-Publication Data
Muchinsky, Paul M.
    Psychology applied to work : an introduction to industrial and organizational psychology / Paul M. Muchinsky. — 6th ed.
      p.   cm.
    Includes bibliographical references and index.
    ISBN 0-534-36252-4
    1. Psychology, Industrial.
    2. Organizational behavior.
    I. Title.
    HF5548.8.M756 1999
158.7—dc21   99-26100

For more information, contact
Wadsworth/Thomson Learning
10 Davis Drive
Belmont, CA 94002-3098
USA
www.wadsworth.com

International Headquarters
Thomson Learning
290 Harbor Drive, 2nd Floor
Stamford, CT 06902-7477
USA

UK/Europe/Middle East
Thomson Learning
Berkshire House
168-173 High Holborn
London WC1V 7AA
United Kingdom

Asia
Thomson Learning
60 Albert Street #15-01
Albert Complex
Singapore 189969

Canada
Nelson/Thomson Learning
1120 Birchmount Road
Scarborough, Ontario M1K 5G4
Canada

○ This book is printed on acid-free recycled paper.

Photo Credits: pp. 1, 235, PhotoDisc, Inc.; p. 57
© Tony Freeman/PhotoEdit; p. 393, PhotoDisc, Inc.
and Gazelle Technologies, Inc. "People in Business"
photo CD collection.

To Noël

Whose Love and Support Made This Book Possible

ABOUT THE AUTHOR

Paul M. Muchinsky was born and raised in Connecticut. He received his B.A. degree in psychology from Gettysburg College, his M.S. degree in industrial/organizational psychology from Kansas State University, and his Ph.D. from Purdue University. He was a faculty member of Iowa State University for twenty years. In 1993 he was appointed the Joseph M. Bryan Distinguished Professor of Business at the University of North Carolina at Greensboro. Throughout his career, Dr. Muchinsky has been very active in a wide range of professional activities within the field of industrial/organizational psychology. Many of the cases and examples of concepts presented in this book come directly from his professional experiences. When not engaged as an I/O psychologist, Dr. Muchinsky fantasizes about playing baseball for the New York Yankees.

BRIEF CONTENTS

C O N T E N T S

It is with great delight that an author has the opportunity to recraft a book into a new edition. This 6th edition of *Psychology Applied to Work: An Introduction to Industrial and Organizational Psychology* represents the most comprehensive portrayal of our discipline to date. Since the basic structure has worked well for teachers and students alike, I have retained the same 4-section and 16-chapter format. When I began this edition I did not anticipate how much new material had entered our field since the previous edition, most notably in the area of international I/O psychology. Given expanding interest in cross-cultural issues and the development of new areas of interest, the knowledge base in I/O psychology is mushrooming. I/O is a growing, exciting, and changing field, and I've tried to capture some of that excitement and flavor in the three general themes to this revision:

+ Infusing cross-cultural I/O psychological issues in nearly all chapters. For example, you'll find material on the Asian concept of *face* as a motivational basis, the universality versus cultural-specific viewpoints of leadership, and cultural differences in the social acceptability of personnel selection methods.
+ Repositioning job attitudes (job satisfaction, job involvement, and organizational commitment) in a specific section of the book (Chapter 9), as well as including the subject of job attitudes in nearly all chapters.
+ Updating all content areas within the book, reflected by more than 250 new references that were written in the past three years.

Some of the specific revisions deal with the following topics:

+ The distinction between primary and secondary research methods as means of conducting scientific investigations.
+ Expansion of Functional Job Analysis and Fleishman's Taxonomy of Human Abilities as methods of understanding jobs.

♦ Discussion of the newly created Occupational Information Network (O*NET) by the U.S. Department of Labor.
♦ Sternberg's theory of intelligence and how it relates to I/O psychology.
♦ Discussion of changing societal views of affirmative action and how they influence personnel recruitment and selection.
♦ Emotional intelligence as an emerging construct of interest.
♦ HIV disease as a source of stress among coworkers.
♦ Antisocial behavior in organizations that can culminate in workplace violence.
♦ The practical implications of using various motivational strategies to enhance performance.
♦ The emerging area of emotions in the workplace as a topic of interest among I/O psychologists.

Learning Aides

I've had the good fortune to be able to draw upon my professional experiences to highlight and exemplify the text material. I present three Field Notes per chapter that personalize the material for students and often reveal how theory and practice can depart. I've added a brief descriptive title to each Field Note to facilitate its retention. One-third of the Field Notes are new to this edition.

The case studies presented at the end of each chapter are open-ended real dilemmas that involve making tough but necessary decisions, such as how to deal with poor performers and how to make layoff decisions. These cases are designed to involve the students in the practice side of I/O psychology, which draws upon the knowledge learned from the research side.

Over the years I've heard from students and teachers alike that the cartoons serve to enlighten the more technical aspects of I/O psychology with some humor. Six new cartoons were selected that will be familiar to today's student.

Ancillaries for Students and Teachers

As with the previous edition, a *Study Guide and Exercise Workbook* and an *Instructor's Manual/Test Bank* are both available. The *Study Guide and Exercise Workbook* consists of further examples and practical applications that reveal the potency of I/O psychological concepts in the contemporary work world. The *Instructor's Manual/Test Bank* presents multiple-choice, true-false, fill-in, short-answer, and essay questions for the teachers. Topics are also presented for class discussion as well as instructor tips on how to make the best use of the exercises in the *Study Guide and Exercise Workbook*.

Two new ancillaries have been added with this edition. Instructors adopting this edition can give their students *free* access to InfoTrac College Edition, a world-class, on-line library that offers the full text of articles from hundreds of scholarly and popular publications. Both instructors and their students receive unlimited access for one academic semester (four months) if the instructor chooses to couple InfoTrac College Edition with the textbook. InfoTrac is a virtual university library that is updated daily and has 24-hour access. Hot-linked, expertly indexed, and ready to use, InfoTrac College Edition presents articles going back as far as four years. A simple interface quickly and seamlessly gives the instructor and students access to user-oriented applications of I/O psychology. You can also print complete articles whenever you wish. While hundreds of articles are available, I have identified eight articles per chapter (along with a brief summary of each article) that discuss and expand the text material in nontechnical publications.

Finally, instructors who adopt this text have access to a special, *free* videotape: *CNN Today: Industrial/Organizational Psychology Video Series*. The video allows the instructor to integrate the news gathering and programming power of CNN into the classroom to demonstrate the relevance of I/O psychology to students' everyday lives. Organized by topics covered in a typical I/O psychology course, these videos are divided into short segments (2 to 7 minutes in length) that are highly effective for introducing key concepts. Among the issues covered are worker empowerment, job-related stress, and human performance. Instructors can use the motivating and attention-getting perspectives of this medium to initiate lectures.

Collectively, I have tried to establish more linkages between the science and practice of I/O psychology using a variety of media and sources. I feel this is critical given the extensiveness of both the science and practice of our field. I hope you are pleased with the finished product.

Acknowledgments

With great sadness I note the passing of Elliott in my life. He somehow endured five editions with me. With great joy I welcome the entrance of Ernie into my life. May he inspire me through many future editions.

The revisions for this edition were guided by a particularly fine set of critical reviews. I would like to express my sincere gratitude to the reviewers for their time and effort. They were:

Eric Braverman, Louisiana State University
Tim Buckley, Louisiana State University
David Day, Pennsylvania State University
Richard Goffin, University of Western Ontario
Leslie Hammer, Portland State University
Rebecca Henry, Purdue University
Teresa Lyons, Salem State College
Duane Miller, Mississippi State University
Jonathan Springer, Kean University of New Jersey
Holly Traver, Rensselaer Polytechnic Institute
C. York, Georgia Institute of Technology

Previous editions were similarly enhanced by the insights of the following reviewers:

Terry Beehr, Central Michigan University
John Binning, Illinois State University
Kim Buch, University of North Carolina

Leslie Hammer, Portland State University
Bruce H. Johnson, Gustavus Adolphus College
Howard J. Klein, Ohio State University
Michael McCall, Ithaca College
Tom Mitchell, University of Baltimore
Craig D. Parks, Washington State University
Steven G. Rogelberg, Bowling Green State University
Howard Tokunaga, San Jose State University

Finally, a previous employer of my secretary, Lynn Southard, once told her she was the "second best secretary in the world." When Lynn inquired as to the identity of the best secretary, she was told, "there has to be someone out there better than you, but I haven't met the person." Neither have I.

Paul M. Muchinsky

THE FOUNDATIONS OF INDUSTRIAL/ ORGANIZATIONAL (I/O) PSYCHOLOGY

The Historical Background of I/O Psychology

MAJOR CHAPTER OBJECTIVES

- ◆ Explain how I/O psychology relates to the profession of psychology as a whole.
- ◆ Be able to identify the major fields of I/O psychology.
- ◆ Understand how and why psychologists are licensed and certified.
- ◆ Learn the history of I/O psychology, including major people, events, and eras.
- ◆ Give the reasons for cross-cultural interest in I/O psychology.

Psychology is defined as the scientific study of thinking and behavior. It is a science because psychologists use the same rigorous methods of research found in other areas of scientific investigation. Some of their research is more biological in nature (such as the effects of brain lesions on a rat's food consumption); other research is more social in nature (such as identifying the factors that lead to bystander apathy). Because psychology covers such a broad spectrum of content areas, it is difficult to have a clear and accurate image of what a psychologist does. Many people think that every psychologist "is a shrink," "has a black couch," "likes to discover what makes people tick," and so on. In fact, these descriptions usually refer to the specialty of clinical psychology—the diagnosis and treatment of mental illness or abnormal behavior. Most psychologists do not treat mental disorders, nor do they practice psychotherapy. In reality, psychologists are a very diversified lot with many specialized interests.

Many psychologists are united professionally through membership in the American Psychological Association (APA), founded in 1892. As of 1998, the APA had more than 82,000 members, 53% men and 47% women. The broad diversification of interests among psychologists is reflected by the fact that the APA has 50 divisions representing special-interest subgroups. Matarazzo (1987) noted there are not really so many different specialty areas of psychology, just many fields in which the same basic psychological principles are applied. Though some APA members have no divisional affiliation, others belong to more than one. The APA publishes several journals—vehicles through which psychologists can communicate their research findings to other scholars. The APA also holds regional and national conventions, sets standards for graduate training in certain areas of psychology (that is, clinical, counseling, and school), develops and enforces a code of professional ethics, and helps psychologists find employment.

INDUSTRIAL/ORGANIZATIONAL PSYCHOLOGY

One of the specialty areas of psychology is industrial/organizational (I/O) psychology (represented by Division 14 of the APA, the **Society for Industrial-Organizational Psychology, or SIOP**). In 1998 SIOP had about 3,250 professional members and approximately 2,000 student members. The percentage of women entering the field has greatly accelerated in recent years. For example, in 1989 almost half (46%) of those receiving doctorates in I/O psychology were women (Howard, 1990). SIOP is the primary professional organization for I/O psychologists in this nation. SIOP has developed a website on the Internet, *www.siop.org,* which can be accessed to learn more about careers in I/O psychology. In other countries what we call *I/O psychology* is referenced by other names. In the United Kingdom it is referred to as *occupational psychology,* in many European countries as *work and organizational psychology,* and in South Africa as *industrial psychology.* While the terminology may vary around the world, the members of our profession share common interests.

Approximately 4% of all psychologists are in the I/O area. Our relatively small representation in the total population of psychologists probably contributes to why some people are unaware of the I/O area. About half of all psychologists work in the specialty areas of clinical and counseling psychology, which probably contributes to the stereotype of psychologists in general.

As a specialty area, **I/O psychology** has a more restricted definition than psychology as a whole. Many years ago Blum and Naylor (1968) defined it as "simply the application or extension of psychological facts and principles to the problems concerning human beings operating within the context of business and industry" (p. 4). In broad terms, the I/O psychologist is concerned with behavior in work situations. There are two sides of I/O psychology: science and practice. I/O psychology is a legitimate field of scientific inquiry, concerned with advancing knowledge about people at work. As in any area of science, questions are posed by I/O psychologists to guide their investigation, and scientific methods are used to obtain answers. Psychologists try to form the results of studies into meaningful patterns that will be useful in explaining behavior and to replicate findings to make generalizations about behavior. In this respect, I/O psychology is an academic discipline.

The other side of I/O psychology—the professional side—is concerned with the application of knowledge to solve real problems in the world of work. I/O psychological research findings can be used to hire better employees, reduce absenteeism, improve communication, increase job satisfaction, and solve countless other problems. Most I/O psychologists feel a sense of kinship with both sides: science and practice. Accordingly, the education of I/O psychologists is founded on the **scientist–practitioner model,** which trains them in both scientific inquiry and practical application.

As an I/O psychologist, I am pleased that the results of my research can be put to some practical use. But by the same token, I am more than a technician—someone who goes through the motions of finding solutions to problems without knowing why they "work" and what their consequences will be. I/O psychology is more than just a tool for business leaders to use to make their companies more efficient. So the I/O psychologist has a dual existence. Well-trained I/O psychologists realize that the good application of knowledge can come only from sound knowledge, and they can therefore both contribute to knowledge and apply it.

Figure 1–1 shows the main work settings of I/O psychologists. They fall into four main areas, with universities and consulting firms being the primary employers. Across these four areas, I/O psychologists are unevenly split in their scientist–practitioner orientation. Universities employ more scientists; consulting firms employ more practitioners; business and government have a good mix of both. As of 1997 the median annual income for M.S.-level graduates in I/O psychology was $55,000, whereas for Ph.D.-level graduates it was $80,000. Some members of our profession who work in consulting firms earn more than $1,000,000 annually.

Fields of I/O Psychology

Like psychology in general, I/O psychology is a diversified science containing several subspecialties. The professional activities of I/O psychologists can be grouped into six general fields.

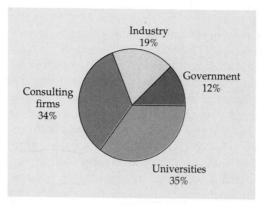

FIGURE 1–1 *Principal work settings of I/O psychologists*

SOURCE: APA, "Profile of Division 14 Members: 1993." Reprinted by permission of the author.

Selection and Placement. I/O psychologists working in this field are concerned with developing assessment methods for the selection, placement, and promotion of employees. They are involved in studying jobs and determining to what degree tests can predict performance in those jobs. They are also concerned with the placement of employees, which is directed toward identifying those jobs that are most compatible with the individual's skills and interests.

Training and Development. This field is concerned with the identification of employee skills that need to be enhanced to improve job performance. The areas of training include technical skills enhancement (e.g., computer operations), managerial development programs, and training of all employees to work together effectively. I/O psychologists who work in this field must design ways to determine whether training and development programs have been successful.

Performance Management. Performance management is the process of identifying criteria or standards for determining how well employees are performing their jobs. I/O psychologists working in this field are also concerned with determining the utility or value of job performance to the organization. They may be involved with measuring the performance of work teams, units within the organization, or the organization itself.

Organization Development. Organization development is the process of analyzing the structure of an organization to maximize the satisfaction and effectiveness of individuals, work groups, and customers. Organizations grow and mature just as people do; thus, the field of organization development is directed toward facilitating the organizational growth process. I/O psychologists who work in this field are sensitized to the wide array of factors that influence behavior in organizations.

Quality of Worklife. I/O psychologists who work in this field are concerned with factors that contribute to a healthy and productive workforce. They may be

DILBERT   by Scott Adams

SOURCE: Dilbert® reprinted by permission of United Feature Syndicate, Inc.

involved in redesigning jobs to make them more meaningful and satisfying to the people who perform them. A high-quality worklife contributes to greater productivity of the organization and to the emotional health of the individual.

Ergonomics.   Ergonomics is a multidisciplinary field that includes I/O psychologists. It is concerned with designing tools, equipment, and machines that are compatible with human skills. I/O psychologists working in this field draw upon knowledge derived from physiology, industrial medicine, and perception to design work systems that humans can effectively operate.

In summary, psychology as a discipline is composed of many specialty areas, one of which is I/O psychology. And I/O psychology consists of several subspecialties. Although some of these subspecialties overlap, many are quite distinct from one another. Thus, I/O psychology is not really a single discipline; it is a mix of subspecialties bonded together by a concern for people at work. Each of the subspecialties of I/O psychology will be explored to various degrees in this book.

LICENSING AND CERTIFICATION OF PSYCHOLOGISTS

What makes a psychologist a psychologist? What prevents people with no psychological training from passing themselves off as psychologists? One way professions offer high-quality service to the public is by regulating their own membership. Selective admission into the profession helps protect the public against quacks and charlatans who risk great damage not only to their clients but also to the profession they allegedly represent.

The practice of professional psychology is regulated by law in every state. When both the title and practice of psychology are regulated, the law is called a **licensing law.** When only the title of psychologist is regulated, the law is called a **certification law** (Hess, 1977). Laws limit licensure to those qualified to practice psychology as defined by state law. Each state has its own standards for licensure, and these are governed by regulatory boards. The major functions of any professional board are to determine the standards for admission into the profession and to conduct disciplinary actions when professional standards are violated.

Typically, licensure involves education, experience, examination, and administrative requirements. A doctoral degree in psychology from an approved program is usually required, as well as one or two years of supervised experience. Applicants must also pass an objective, written examination covering all areas of psychology. Specialty examinations (for example, in I/O psychology) usually are not given. Currently, psychologists must pass a uniform national examination to obtain a license (Hoffman, 1980). Finally, the applicant must meet citizenship and residency requirements and be of good moral character.

Licensing and certification are intended to ensure that clients receive services from qualified practitioners (Fretz & Mills, 1980). However, scrupulous I/O psychologists can never guarantee results, and they should never try. Companies have been duped by consulting firms and individuals into believing a wide range of claims that simply cannot be substantiated. The problems that the I/O psychologist faces are too complex for guarantees. Reasonable expectations on the part of both the I/O psychologist and the company are the best way to avoid such difficulties.

There is a controversy regarding the licensure of I/O psychologists. The original purpose of licensure was to protect the public in the health care areas of psychology, such as clinical and counseling. Because I/O psychologists are not health care providers, there is not as pressing a need for licensure to protect the public (Howard & Lowman, 1985). Most states regard I/O psychologists as they do other types of applied psychologists who offer services to the public, however, and thus require them to be licensed. Some states regard I/O psychologists as having a sufficiently different mandate to exempt them from requiring licensure.

THE HISTORY OF I/O PSYCHOLOGY

It is always difficult to write *the* history of anything; there are different perspectives with different emphases. It is also a challenge to divide the historical evolution of a discipline into units of time. In some cases, time itself is a convenient watershed (decades or centuries); in others, major events serve as landmarks. In the case of I/O psychology, the two world wars were major catalysts for changing the discipline. This historical overview will show how the field of I/O psychology came to be what it is and how some key individuals and events helped shape it.[1]

The Early Years (1900–1916)

In its beginnings, what we know today as I/O psychology didn't even have a name; it was a merging of two forces that gathered momentum before 1900. One force was the pragmatic nature of some basic psychological research. Most psychologists at this time were strictly scientific and deliberately avoided studying

---

[1]A more detailed treatment of the history of I/O psychology can be found in the excellent books by Ferguson (1962) and Napoli (1981) and in the article by Katzell and Austin (1992).

problems that strayed outside the boundaries of pure research. However, a psychologist named W. L. Bryan published a paper (Bryan & Harter, 1897) about how professional telegraphers develop skill in sending and receiving Morse code. A few years later in 1903, Bryan's presidential address to the American Psychological Association (Bryan, 1904) touched on having psychologists study "concrete activities and functions as they appear in everyday life" (p. 80). Bryan did not advocate studying problems found in industry per se, but he stressed examining real skills as a base upon which to develop scientific psychology. Bryan is not considered the father of I/O psychology but rather a precursor.[2]

The second major force in the evolution of the discipline came from the desire of industrial engineers to improve efficiency. They were concerned mainly with the economics of manufacturing and thus the productivity of industrial employees. A husband and wife team, Frank and Lillian Gilbreth, contributed pioneering knowledge about time and motion in industrial production. They are perhaps best known for their research on the elements of human motion, which they called "therbligs" (*Gilbreth* spelled backward, almost). Koppes (1997) reported that Lillian Gilbreth was one of several female psychologists who made substantial contributions in the early era of I/O psychology. Koppes noted that Gilbreth made a historic speech at a meeting of industrial engineers in 1908. She was asked for her opinion because she was the only woman attending the meeting. According to Yost (1943), Lillian Gilbreth "rose to her feet and remarked that the human being, of course, was the most important element in industry, and that it seemed to her this element had not been receiving the attention it warranted. The engineer's scientific training, she said, was all for the handling of inanimate objects. She called attention to the fact that psychology was fast becoming a science and that it had much to offer that was being ignored by management engineers. The plea in her impromptu remarks was for the new profession of scientific management to open its eyes to the necessary place psychology had in any program industrial engineers worked out" (Koppes, 1997, p. 511).

Thus, the merging of psychology with applied interests and concern for increasing industrial efficiency was the ingredient for the emergence of I/O psychology. By 1910 "industrial psychology" (the "organizational" appendage did not become official until 1970) was a legitimate specialty area of psychology.

Three individuals stand out as the founding fathers of I/O psychology. They worked independently; in fact, their work barely overlapped. The major contributions of these individuals deserve a brief review.

Walter Dill Scott.   Scott, a psychologist, was persuaded to give a talk to some Chicago business leaders on the need for applying psychology to advertising. His talk was well received and led to the publication of two books: *The Theory of Advertising* (1903) and *The Psychology of Advertising* (1908). The first book dealt with suggestion and argument as means of influencing people. The second book was aimed at improving human efficiency with such tactics as imitation, competition,

---

[2]The term *industrial psychology* was apparently used for the first time in Bryan's 1904 article. Ironically, it appeared in print only as a typographical error. Bryan was quoting a sentence he had written five years earlier (Bryan & Harter, 1899) in which he spoke of the need for more research in individual psychology. Instead, Bryan wrote "industrial psychology" and did not catch his mistake.

Walter Dill Scott
SOURCE: Archives of the History of American Psychology

loyalty, and concentration. By 1911 Scott had expanded his areas of interest and published two more books: *Influencing Men in Business* and *Increasing Human Efficiency in Business.* During World War I, Scott was instrumental in the application of personnel procedures within the army. Landy (1997) described Scott as the consummate scientist–practitioner who was highly respected in both spheres of professional activity. Scott had a substantial influence on increasing public awareness and the credibility of industrial psychology.

Frederick W. Taylor.   Taylor was an engineer by profession. His formal schooling was limited, but through experience and self-training in engineering he went on to obtain many patents. As he worked himself up through one company as a worker, supervisor, and finally plant manager, Taylor realized the value of redesigning the work situation to achieve both higher output for the company and a higher wage for the worker. His best-known work is his book *The Principles of Scientific Management* (1911). Van De Water (1997) reported these principles as: (1) science over rule of thumb, (2) scientific selection and training, (3) cooperation over individualism, and (4) equal division of work best suited to management and employees. In perhaps the most famous example of his methods, Taylor showed that workers who handled heavy iron ingots (pig iron) could be more productive if they had work rests. Training employees when to work and when to rest increased average worker productivity from 12.5 to 47.0 tons moved per day (with less reported fatigue), which resulted in increased wages for them. The company also drastically increased efficiency by reducing costs from 9.2 cents per ton to 3.9 cents per ton.

As a consequence of this method, it was charged that Taylor inhumanely exploited workers for a higher wage and that great numbers of workers would be

Frederick W. Taylor
SOURCE: Stevens Institute of Technology

unemployed because fewer were needed. Because there was rampant unemployment at this time, the attacks on Taylor were virulent. His methods were eventually investigated by the Interstate Commerce Commission (ICC) and the U.S. House of Representatives. Taylor replied that increased efficiency led to greater, not less, prosperity and that workers not hired for one job would be placed in another that would better use their potential. The arguments were never really resolved—World War I broke out, and the controversy faded.

Hugo Münsterberg.   Münsterberg was a German psychologist with traditional academic training. The noted American psychologist William James invited Münsterberg to Harvard University, where he applied his experimental methods to a variety of problems, including perception and attention. He was a popular figure in American education, a gifted public speaker, and a personal friend of President Theodore Roosevelt. Münsterberg was interested in applying traditional psychological methods to practical industrial problems. His book *Psychology and Industrial Efficiency* (1913) was divided into three parts: selecting workers, designing work situations, and using psychology in sales. One of Münsterberg's most renowned studies involved determining what makes a safe trolley car operator. He systematically studied all aspects of the job, developed an ingenious laboratory simulation of a trolley car, and concluded that a good operator could comprehend simultaneously all of the influences that bear on the car's progress. Some writers consider Münsterberg the father of industrial psychology. Landy (1992) reported that many prominent I/O psychologists throughout the 20th century can trace their professional roots back to Münsterberg. Münsterberg's influence in the history of the field is well evidenced by the coterie of I/O psychologists who were guided by his teachings.

Hugo Münsterberg
SOURCE: Archives of the History of American Psychology

When World War I broke out in Europe, Münsterberg supported the German cause. He was ostracized for his allegiance, and the emotional strain probably contributed to his death in 1916. Münsterberg's sudden departure from the field of industrial psychology created a scientific vacuum because he left few colleagues behind to continue his work. Only the U.S. involvement in the war gave some unity to the profession. The primary emphasis of the early work in I/O psychology was on the economic gains that could be accrued by applying the ideas and methods of psychology to problems in business and industry. Business leaders began to employ psychologists, and some psychologists entered applied research. However, World War I caused a shift in the direction of industrial psychological research.

World War I (1917–1918)

World War I was a potent impetus to psychology's rise to respectability. Psychologists believed they could provide a valuable service to the nation, and some saw the war as a means of accelerating the profession's progress. Robert Yerkes was the psychologist most instrumental in involving psychology in the war. As president of the APA, he maneuvered the profession into assignments in the war effort. The APA made many proposals, including ways of screening recruits for mental deficiency and of assigning selected recruits to jobs in the army. Committees of psychologists investigated soldier motivation, morale, psychological problems of physical incapacity, and discipline. Yerkes continued to press his point that psychology could be of great help to our nation in wartime.

The army, in turn, was somewhat skeptical of the psychologists' claims. It eventually approved only a modest number of proposals, mostly those involving the assessment of recruits. Yerkes and other psychologists reviewed a series of general intelligence tests and eventually developed one that they called the Army

Alpha. When they discovered that 30% of the recruits were illiterate, they developed the Army Beta, a special test for those who couldn't read English. Meanwhile, Walter Scott was doing research on the best placement of soldiers in the army. He classified and placed enlisted soldiers, conducted performance ratings of officers, and developed and prepared job duties and qualifications for over 500 jobs.

Plans for testing recruits proceeded at a slow pace. The army built special testing sites at its camps and ordered all existing officers, officer candidates, and newly drafted recruits to be tested. Both the Army Alpha and Beta group intelligence tests were used, as were a few individual tests. The final order authorizing the testing program came from the adjutant general's office in August 1918. However, the Armistice was signed only three months later, and World War I was over. Testing was terminated just as it was finally organized and authorized. As a result, the intelligence testing program didn't contribute as much to the war as Yerkes would have liked. Even though 1,726,000 individuals were ultimately tested in the program, actual use of the results was minimal.

Although psychology's impact on the war effort was not substantial, the very process of giving psychologists so much recognition and authority was a great impetus to the profession. Psychologists were regarded as capable of making valuable contributions to society and of adding to a company's (and in war, a nation's) prosperity. Also in 1917 the oldest and most representative journal in the field of I/O psychology—the *Journal of Applied Psychology*—began publication. Some of the articles in the first volume were "Practical Relations Between Psychology and the War" by Hall, "Mentality Testing of College Students" by Bingham, and "The Moron as a War Problem" by Mateer. The first article published in the *Journal of Applied Psychology* not only summarized the prevailing state of industrial psychology at the time but also addressed the science-versus-practice issue that still faces I/O psychologists today.

> The past few years have witnessed an unprecedented interest in the extension of the application of psychology to various fields of human activity. . . . But perhaps the most strikingly original endeavor to utilize the methods and the results of psychological investigation has been in the realm of business. This movement began with the psychology of advertising. . . . Thence the attention of the applied psychologist turned to the more comprehensive and fundamental problem of vocational selection—the question, namely, of making a detailed inventory of the equipment of mental qualities possessed by a given individual, of discovering what qualities are essential to successful achievement in a given vocation, and thus of directing the individual to the vocational niche which he is best fitted to fill. . . . Every psychologist who besides being a "pure scientist" also cherishes the hope that in addition to throwing light upon the problems of his science, his findings may also contribute their quota to the sum-total of human happiness; and it must appeal to every human being who is interested in increasing human efficiency and human happiness by the more direct method of decreasing the number of cases where a square peg is condemned to a life of fruitless endeavor to fit itself comfortably into a round hole. (Hall, Baird, & Geissler, 1917, pp. 5–6)

After the war, there was a boom in the number of psychological consulting firms and research bureaus. The birth of these agencies ushered in the next era in I/O psychology.

Between the Wars (1919–1940)

Applied psychology emerged from the war as a recognized discipline. Society was beginning to realize that industrial psychology could solve practical problems. Following the war, several psychological research bureaus came into full bloom. The Bureau of Salesmanship Research was developed by Walter Bingham at the Carnegie Institute of Technology. There was little precedent for this kind of cooperation between college and industry. The bureau intended to solve problems with psychological research techniques, problems that had never been examined scientifically. Twenty-seven companies cooperated with Bingham, each contributing $500 annually to finance applied psychological research. One of the early products of the bureau was the book *Aids in Selecting Salesmen*. For several years the bureau concentrated on the selection, classification, and development of clerical and executive personnel as well as salespeople. When the Carnegie Institute stopped offering graduate work in psychology, the bureau was disbanded.

Another influential company during the period was the Psychological Corporation, founded by James Cattell in 1921. Cattell formed it as a business corporation and asked psychologists to buy stock in it. Its purpose was to advance psychology and promote its usefulness to industry. The corporation also served as a clearinghouse for information. As protection against quacks and charlatans, who were becoming increasingly prevalent, it provided companies with reference checks on prospective psychologists. Unlike many agencies that began at the time, the Psychological Corporation has remained in business. Over the years it has changed its early mission, and today it is one of the country's largest publishers of psychological tests.

In 1924 a series of experiments began at the Hawthorne Works of the Western Electric Company. Although initially they seemed to be of minor scientific significance, they became classics in industrial psychology. In the opinion of many writers, the Hawthorne studies "represent the most significant research program undertaken to show the enormous complexity of the problem of production in relation to efficiency" (Blum & Naylor, 1968, p. 306).

The Hawthorne studies were a joint venture between Western Electric and several researchers from Harvard University (none of whom were industrial psychologists by training). The original study attempted to find the relationship between lighting and efficiency. The researchers installed various sets of lights in workrooms where electrical equipment was being produced. In some cases, the light was intense; in other cases, it was reduced to the equivalent of moonlight. Much to the researchers' surprise, productivity seemed to have no relationship to the level of illumination. The workers' productivity increased whether the illumination was decreased, increased, or held constant. The results of the study were so bizarre that the researchers hypothesized some other factors as being responsible for productivity.

The results of the first study initiated four other major studies that were conducted over a 12-year period: (1) relay assembly test room, (2) mass interviewing program, (3) bank wiring observation room, and (4) personnel counseling. (For more information on these studies, see the original text by Roethlisberger and

Dickson, 1939.) In essence, the Hawthorne studies revealed many previously unrecognized aspects of human behavior in a workplace. Researchers hypothesized that the study's results were caused by the employees' desire to please them. Flattered at having distinguished investigators from Harvard University take the time to study them, the workers had gone out of their way to do what they thought would impress them—namely, to be highly productive. They therefore had produced at a high level whether the room was too light or too dark. The researchers learned that factors other than purely technical ones (for example, illumination) influence productivity.

One of the major findings from the studies was a phenomenon labeled the **Hawthorne effect.** The workers' job performance began to improve following the start of the researchers' intervention and continued to improve because of the novelty of the situation; that is, the employees responded positively to the novel treatment they were getting from the researchers. Eventually, however, the novelty began to wear off, and productivity returned to its earlier level. This phenomenon of a change in behavior following the onset of novel treatment, with a gradual return to the previous level of behavior as the effect of the novelty wears off, is the Hawthorne effect.

As Adair (1984) observed, however, the precise reason for the change in behavior (for example, the novelty of the situation, special attention, or prestige from being selected for study) is not always clear. Sometimes behavior change is due just to a change in the environment (for example, the presence of the researchers) and not to the effect of some experimentally manipulated variable (for example, the amount of illumination). The psychological literature indicates that Hawthorne effects may last anywhere from a few days to two years, depending on the situation. Throughout this book, research findings that appear attributable to Hawthorne effects will be cited.

The Hawthorne studies also revealed the existence of informal employee work groups and their controls on production, as well as the importance of employee attitudes, the value of having a sympathetic and understanding supervisor, and the need to treat workers as people instead of merely as human capital. Their revelation of the complexity of human behavior opened up new vistas for industrial psychology, which for nearly 40 years had been dominated by the desire to improve company efficiency. Today the Hawthorne studies, while regarded by some contemporary psychologists as having been based on flawed research methods (e.g., Bramel & Friend, 1981), are considered to be the greatest single episode in the formation of industrial psychology. They also showed that researchers sometimes obtain totally unexpected results. Because the investigators were not tied to any one explanation, their studies took them into areas never before studied by industrial psychology and raised questions that otherwise might never have been asked. Industrial psychology was never the same again.

This era in industrial psychology ended with the coincidental conclusion of the Hawthorne studies and the outbreak of World War II. Industrial psychologists were now faced with an immense task: helping to mobilize a nation for a two-continent war.

World War II (1941–1945)

When the United States entered World War II, industrial psychologists were more prepared for their role in the war effort than they had been in 1917. By this time, psychologists had studied the problems of employee selection and placement and had refined their techniques considerably.

Walter Bingham chaired the advisory committee on classification of military personnel that had been formed in response to the army's need for classification and training. Unlike in World War I, this time the army approached the psychologists first. One of the committee's earliest assignments was to develop a test that could sort new recruits into five categories based on their ability to learn the duties and responsibilities of a soldier. The test that was finally developed was the Army General Classification Test (AGCT), a benchmark in the history of group testing. Harrell (1992), in reflecting on his own involvement in developing the AGCT 50 years earlier, reported that 12 million soldiers were classified into military jobs on the basis of the test. The committee also worked on other projects, such as methods of selecting people for officer training, trade proficiency tests, and supplemental aptitude tests.

Psychologists also worked on the development and use of situational stress tests, a project undertaken by the U.S. Office of Strategic Services (OSS) (Murray & MacKinnon, 1946). The purpose of this testing program was to assess candidates for assignment to military intelligence units. During a three-day session of extremely intensive testing and observation, the candidates lived together in small groups under almost continuous observation by the assessment staff. Specially constructed situational tests, many modeled after techniques developed in the German and British armies, were used to assess candidates in nontraditional ways. One test, for example, involved constructing a 5-foot cube from a collection of wooden poles, pegs, and blocks. It was impossible for one person to assemble the cube in the allotted time, so two "helpers" were provided. These were actually psychologists who played prearranged roles. One helper acted very passive and contributed little; the other obstructed work by making impractical suggestions and ridiculing and criticizing the candidate. Of course, no candidate could complete the project with this kind of "help." The real purpose of the test was not to see whether the candidates could construct the cube but to assess their emotional and interpersonal reactions to stress and frustration. In general, the OSS assessment program was judged to be quite successful.

Another area of work was the selection and training of pilots to fly warplanes. The committee formed for this purpose consisted of psychologists, military personnel, and civilian pilots. The committee's policy was to move the traditional experimental test setting from the laboratory to the cockpit. Airplanes were outfitted with recording and monitoring devices to assess the problems and reactions of student pilots. This research resulted in two products. First, good candidates were selected and trained as pilots (the traditional domain of personnel psychology). Second, equipment was designed to make the pilot's job easier and safer (a contribution of the new field of engineering psychology).

Throughout the war, industrial psychology was also being used in civilian life. The use of employment tests in industry increased greatly. Because the nation needed a productive workforce, psychologists were called on to help reduce employee absenteeism (Pickard, 1945). Industry discovered that many of the techniques of industrial psychologists were useful, especially in the areas of selection, training, and machine design, and industrial leaders were particularly interested in the applications of social psychology. New methods of measuring soldier attitude and morale could also be used in industry. In short, the techniques developed during the war could be applied to business and industry in peacetime. World War II was a springboard for refining industrial psychological techniques and honing the skills of applied psychologists.

Each of the two world wars had a major effect on industrial psychology but in a somewhat different way. World War I helped form the profession and give it social acceptance. World War II helped develop and refine it. The next era in the history of I/O psychology saw the discipline evolve into subspecialties and attain higher levels of academic and scientific rigor.

Toward Specialization (1946–1963)

In this era, industrial psychology evolved into a legitimate field of scientific inquiry, having already established itself as an accepted professional practice. More colleges and universities began to offer courses in "industrial psychology," and graduate degrees (both M.S. and Ph.D.) were soon given. The Division of Industrial Psychology of the American Psychological Association was created in 1946. Benjamin (1997) reported that earlier I/O psychologists had less professional identity, being represented in the family of "applied psychologists."

As with any evolving discipline, subspecialties of interest began to crystallize, and industrial psychology became splintered. New journals emerged along with new professional associations. Engineering psychology, born during World War II, was recognized as a separate area, in part due to such seminal books as *Applied Experimental Psychology* (Chapanis, Garner, & Morgan, 1949) and the *Handbook of Human Engineering Data* (1949). Engineering psychology entered an explosive period of growth from 1950 to 1960. This was due mainly to research done in affiliation with the defense industries (Grether, 1968). Engineering psychology's heritage was a mixture of both experimental and industrial psychology, as seen in its early label, "applied experimental psychology." That part of industrial psychology specializing in personnel selection, classification, and training also got its own identity, "personnel psychology." Sometime in the 1950s, interest grew in the study of organizations. Long the province of sociologists, this area caught the interest of psychologists. In the 1960s, industrial psychology research took on a stronger organizational flavor. Investigators gave more attention to social influences that impinge on behavior in organizations. Terms such as *organizational change* and *organization development* appeared in the literature regularly. Industrial psychology addressed a broader range of topics. Classic textbooks of the 1950s, such as *Personnel and Industrial Psychology* by Ghiselli and Brown (1955), gave way in title (as well as in substance) to books with more of an organizational thrust. Traditional academic boundaries between disciplines began to blur in this postwar period. Engineering psychology was a fusion of experimental and industrial psychology; organizational behavior was a mix of industrial psychology, social psychology, and sociology. This melding of disciplines was healthy because it decreased the use of narrow, parochial attempts to address complex areas of research.

Government Intervention (1964–Present)

In the late 1950s and early 1960s, the nation was swept up in what became known as the "civil rights movement." As a nation we became more sensitized to the plight of minorities who had systematically been denied equal opportunities to various sectors of life, including housing, education, and employment. In 1964 Congress passed the Civil Rights Act, a far-reaching piece of legislation designed to reduce unfair discrimination against minorities. One component of the Civil Rights Act, Title VII, addressed the issue of discrimination in employment. The significance of the law to I/O psychologists is explained as follows: For years I/O psychologists were given a relatively free rein to use a wide variety of psychological assessment devices (that is, tests, interviews, and so on) to make employment decisions. The result of these employment decisions was the disproportionately small representation of minorities (most notably Blacks and women) in the workplace, particularly in positions above lower-level jobs. Since historically these decisions seemed to result in discrimination against minorities, the government entered the picture to monitor (and, if necessary, remedy) employers' personnel practices.

By 1978 the government had drafted a uniform set of employment guidelines to which employers were bound. Companies were legally mandated to demonstrate that their employment tests did not uniformly discriminate against any minority group. In addition, the new government standards were not limited to just paper-and-pencil tests or the personnel function of selection; they addressed all devices (interviews, tests, application blanks) used to make all types of personnel decisions (selection, placement, promotion, discharge, and so on).

The discipline of I/O psychology now had to serve two ultimate authorities. The first authority is what all disciplines must serve—namely, to perform high-quality work, be it conducting scientific research or providing services to clients. The second authority added was government scrutiny and evaluation. I/O psychologists now had to accept the consequences of being legally accountable for their actions. As a profession, we would continue to evaluate ourselves, but government policies and agencies would also judge our actions. In 1990 President George Bush signed into law the Americans with Disabilities Act and in 1991 an updated version of the Civil Rights Act. Both acts were designed to remedy further inequities in the workplace.

Much has been discussed about the overall effect of government intervention on the profession of I/O psychology. Some people believe it has been an impetus to the profession, compelling us to address issues and develop solutions that we might otherwise have ignored. Others believe that the profession has been compromised by the intrusion of political and legal influences that serve to deflect activities into areas beyond our traditional domain. Some of the greatest advances in I/O psychology have been made in the past 15 to 20 years, and I attribute these advances, in part, to our being accountable to forces beyond our own profession.

Legal oversight has, in my opinion, prompted I/O psychologists to broaden their horizons in terms of the problems they address and the solutions they propose. In any case, the reality of being an I/O psychologist in the 1990s involves attentiveness to legal standards, parameters that our professional predecessors never had to deal with.

I/O psychology also made a major contribution to the military during this era of our history. Campbell (1990a) described the efforts of I/O psychologists to develop a test for the selection and classification of military personnel. This project involved many psychologists and took almost 10 years to complete. Called "Project A," it involved developing the Armed Services Vocational Aptitude Battery (ASVAB). Every year the ASVAB is administered to 300,000–400,000 people; of that number, 120,000–140,000 individuals are selected.

The history of I/O psychology is rich and diverse. The field was born at the confluence of several forces, developed and grew through global conflict, and was woven into the societal fabric of which it is a part. Our history is relatively brief and our members are not great in number, but I believe I/O psychologists have contributed greatly to both economic and personal welfare. The year 1992 marked the 100th anniversary of the American Psychological Association. In celebration of our centennial, Katzell and Austin (1992) wrote a major review of the history of I/O psychology. They noted that our history is marked by a continuous interweaving of scientific and professional contributions. At certain points in our history the practice of I/O psychology has been at the vanguard of our professional efforts (particularly during wars). At other times, our scientific advances have been more noteworthy. For example, in the past decade we have witnessed what some scholars refer to as the "cognitive revolution" in psychology, reflecting an emphasis on cognitive processes in understanding human behavior. However, as stated previously in this chapter, the science and practice of I/O psychology can never be too far apart from each other. Katzell and Austin quoted a memorable statement by Morris Viteles, one of the early pioneers of our field, who aptly summarized the two domains of I/O psychology: "If it isn't scientific, it's not good practice, and if it isn't practical, it's not good science" (p. 826). Likewise, Farr and Tesluk (1997) cited the comment by the first president of Division 14, Bruce Moore, on the duality of the science and practice of I/O psychology: "The extreme applied practitioner is in danger of narrow, myopic thinking, but the extreme pure scientist is in danger of being isolated from facts" (p. 484). In 1990 the *Handbook of Industrial and Organizational Psychology* was published (Dunnette & Hough), the first of a four-volume set that documents some of our profession's finest scientific achievements. Today I/O psychology is multidisciplinary with regard to both its content and its methods of inquiry. On reflection, it was the same at the turn of the century—a confluence of interest in advertising research, industrial efficiency, and mental testing. In a sense, the evolution of I/O psychology is the chronicle of mushrooming interests along certain common dimensions as molded by a few seismic events. As we enter what some call the "global era" of civilization, where national and cultural boundaries are less confining, so too has I/O psychology expanded its domains of interest and involvement.

CROSS-CULTURAL I/O PSYCHOLOGY

Cross-cultural psychology studies "similarities and differences in individual psychological and social functioning in various cultures and ethnic groups" (Kagitcibasi & Berry, 1989, p. 494). Given the central role that work plays in our lives, it is not surprising that I/O psychologists are being compelled to examine cross-cultural factors in work behavior. Erez (1994) described the following significant changes in world conditions that affect our worklives.

Cultural Diversity of the Labor Force.   Demographic trends in the United States suggest that by the year 2000 about one-third of the labor force will be Black and Hispanic. The unification of Europe and the political changes in the former Soviet republics have resulted in waves of immigrants across cultural boundaries.

Scope of the Work Environment.   More than 100,000 U.S. companies do business overseas. It is estimated that one-third of the profit of U.S. companies is derived from international business, along with one-sixth of the nation's jobs. The competitive global market requires greater knowledge of cultures, values, and business practices other than our own.

Mergers and Acquisitions.   In recent years a substantial number of companies have gone through the processes of mergers, acquisitions, and downsizing. More U.S. companies were acquired by foreign businesses than vice versa. Mergers and acquisitions have resulted in organizational downsizing and massive layoffs; from 1985 to 1988 approximately 15 million workers were affected. Very often a confrontation between organizational cultures results when two or more companies are merged.

Emergence of High Technology and Telecommunication Systems.   The revolution in telecommunication systems has introduced electronic mail, fax machines, cellular phones, and teleconferences. New technology has facilitated communication globally and reduced the time needed for communication. Such changes have accelerated cross-cultural communication and exposure to different values, norms, and behaviors.

Erez (1994) sounded a warning note about why I/O psychologists must be aware of cultural differences in proposing solutions to problems of work behavior. "The successful implementation of managerial techniques depends on their congruence with cultural values. Cultural values serve as criteria for evaluating the contributions of various managerial practices to employee well-being" (p. 601). Triandis (1994) described several practical examples of work-related problems that arise from insensitivity to cultural differences. For example, 25%–40% of U.S. managers selected for overseas assignments have failed because of "culture shock" associated with their new assignment. Values and customs prevalent in our society do not necessarily generalize to other cultures. Additionally, what constitutes satisfying work differs across cultures. Jobs that provide a sense of challenge are more appealing in Western cultures, whereas jobs that provide opportunities for affiliation are more appealing in other cultures. There is also evidence that cultural differences are not limited by geographic boundaries. Ronen (1997) observed that culture does not differ by country, per se, because there are often subcultures within nations influenced by level of industrialization, religious affiliation, and economic wealth. Furthermore, Earley and Randel (1997) noted that there can be both intracultural and intercultural variation in topics of interest to I/O psychologists, and that culture is loosely and incompletely shared across individuals.

It is abundantly clear that the very meaning and nature of work are not universal. I/O psychologists are called upon to assist in the process of developing work procedures that span diverse cultural groups to produce a uniformly desired outcome—our economic and personal well-being.

THE MANDATE OF I/O PSYCHOLOGY

I/O psychology is confronted with a daunting task—to increase the fit between the workforce and the workplace at a time when the composition of both is rapidly changing. Today's workforce is unlike any other in our history. More people are seeking employment than ever before, and they have higher levels of education. There are more women entering the workforce seeking full-time careers, more dual-income couples, and more individuals whose native language is not English. Likewise, the nature of work is changing. There are an increasing number of jobs in service industries, jobs that require computer literacy, and part-time jobs. Rapid economic changes are forcing large-scale layoffs, often requiring individuals to learn new job skills at midlife. Societal changes also influence employment, as evidenced by the growing problem of drugs in the workplace.

Another feature of the employment picture is the rate or speed of change. Although work has always had a sense of urgency, time pressures are seemingly becoming more acute. Rapid large-scale changes in automation and computerization are changing the skill levels needed by employees. Life expectancy is increasing, and many once-retired people are returning to the workforce. Medical costs are escalating at an alarming rate, and employers feel compelled to find ways to limit their liability for employee health-related expenses. Business mergers and acquisitions are at an all-time high, and the affected employees must find ways to address the trauma of job loss, transfers, and reassignments. Factors and conditions such as these add to the pressures of designing work that is both economically efficient and personally satisfying. The year 2000 was once held out as a futuristic date and symbolized an era when life would be very different than it is today. Whether I/O psychology is ready for it or not, the new millennium has arrived.

I/O psychologists have a growing realization that our worklives are intimately tied to our personal lives. It is just not realistic to try to segment our work and personal lives. We take our work problems home with us, and our personal problems can and sometimes do affect our worklives. We are now witnessing more of an integrated, holistic approach to the psychology of work and its impact on our total well-being. I/O psychologists are currently studying such topics as leisure, emotional support provided by family members, and how job stress is dealt with at home. We have learned that our scope of concern as I/O psychologists extends beyond the traditional 8:00 a.m. to 5:00 p.m. hours of employment.

I/O psychology is concerned with the worklives of people, and because those worklives are changing, so too is I/O psychology. As a profession, we find ourselves on the threshold of some areas where we have little prior experience. We would be remiss if we did not venture into these new territories, for they are legitimate and important concerns within the world of work. Furthermore, all of our work must be conducted according to our professional code of ethics (American Psychological Association, 1992). I find the mandate of I/O psychology to be very challenging, with the unending variety of issues we address being a great source of stimulation. While some disciplines rarely change their content, I/O psychology most certainly is not the "same old stuff."

I can think of few other fields of work that are as critical to human welfare as I/O psychology. We spend more of our lifetimes engaged in working than in any other activity. Thus, I/O psychology is devoted to understanding our major mission in life. As our nation faces increasing problems of economic productivity, the field of I/O psychology continues to contribute to making our world a better place in which to live. Indeed, Katzell and Guzzo (1983) reported that 87% of the psychological approaches to improving employee productivity have been successful. Additionally, the scientific contributions that I/O psychologists have made are regarded as sufficiently noteworthy to occasion the revision of federal laws governing fair employment practices.

In general, we as professionals are striving to gain a complete understanding of the problems and issues associated with the world of work, embracing both its quantitative and humanistic dimensions (Stagner, 1982). When you have finished reading this book, you should have a much better understanding of human behavior in the workplace. Perhaps some of you will be stimulated enough to continue your work in I/O psychology. It is a most challenging, rewarding, and useful profession.

Research Methods in I/O Psychology

2

MAJOR CHAPTER OBJECTIVES

◆ Understand the empirical research cycle.

◆ Know the relative advantages and disadvantages of laboratory experiments, quasi-experiments, questionnaires, observations, and computer simulations.

◆ Understand meta-analysis and qualitative research methods.

◆ Explain the statistical concepts of central tendency and variability.

◆ Understand the concept of correlation and its interpretation.

◆ Have an awareness and appreciation of the ethical issues associated with research.

We all have hunches or beliefs about the nature of human behavior. Some of us believe that red-haired people are temperamental, dynamic leaders are big and tall, blue-collar workers prefer beer to wine, the only reason people work is to make money, and the like. The list is endless. Which of these beliefs are true? The only way to find out is to conduct **research,** or the systematic study of phenomena according to scientific principles. Much of this chapter is devoted to a discussion of research methods used in I/O psychology. Understanding the research process helps people solve practical problems, apply the results of studies reported by others, and assess the accuracy of claims made about new practices, equipment, and so on.

I/O psychologists are continuously faced with a host of practical problems. Knowledge of research methods makes us better able to find useful solutions to problems rather than merely stumbling across them by chance. An understanding of research methods also helps us apply the results of studies reported by others. Some factors promote the generalizability of research findings; others retard it. Finally, people often assert the superiority of some new technique or method; a knowledge of research methods helps us determine which ones are merely cheap gimmicks. It has been suggested that science has three goals: description, prediction, and explanation. The descriptive function is like taking a photograph—a picture of a state of events. Researchers may describe levels of productivity, numbers of employees who quit during the year, average levels of job satisfaction, and so on. The second function is prediction. Researchers try to predict which employees will be productive, which ones are likely to quit, and which ones will be dissatisfied. This information is then used to select applicants who will be better employees. The explanatory function is perhaps the most difficult to unravel; it is a statement of why events occur as they do. It tries to find causes: why production is at a certain level, why employees quit, why they are dissatisfied, and so forth.

This chapter will give you some insight into the research process in I/O psychology. The process begins with a statement of the problem and ends with the conclusions drawn from the research. This chapter should help you become a knowledgeable consumer of I/O psychological research.

THE EMPIRICAL RESEARCH PROCESS

Figure 2–1 shows the steps that scientists take in conducting empirical research. The research process is basically a five-step procedure with an important feedback factor; that is, the results of the fifth step influence the first step in future research studies. First, the research process begins with a statement of the problem: What question or problem needs to be answered? Second, how do you design a study to answer the question? Third, how do you measure the variables and collect the necessary data? Fourth, how do you apply statistical procedures to analyze the data? (In other words, how do you make some sense out of all the information collected?) Finally, how do you draw conclusions from analyzing the data? Let's look at each of these steps in more detail.

FIGURE 2–1   *The empirical research cycle*

Statement of the Problem

Questions that initiate research don't arise out of thin air. They are based on existing knowledge—your own and others' experiences with the problem, personal intuition or insight, or some formal theory. Most research begins with personal insight or intuition. As researchers conduct their studies, they become more familiar with the problem and may expand the scope of their questions. One person's research may stimulate similar research by someone else; thus, researchers often benefit from their colleagues' studies. After conducting much research on a topic, researchers may propose a theory about why the behavior occurs. The sequence that starts with data and culminates in theory is the **inductive** method of science. The opposite sequence is the deductive method. In the **deductive** method, a researcher first forms a theory (perhaps by intuition or by studying previous research) and then tests the theory by collecting data. If the theory is accurate, the data will support it; if it is inaccurate, they will not.

The value of theory in science is that it integrates and summarizes large amounts of information and provides a framework for the research. Campbell (1990b) noted, however, that as a scientific discipline, psychology is much more difficult to investigate than physics or chemistry. People are far too variable, both across individuals and from day to day within one person, to be defined by a singular structure. The situation is not the same in physics or chemistry. A molecule of water has the same structure no matter where in the world it might be. Psychology has no equivalent of universal natural laws, such as Newton's three laws of motion. Accordingly, the role of theory as a guide for research in psychology is somewhat more controversial than in other disciplines. The following quotes illustrate three different yet valid views on theory:

- ♦ "There is nothing quite so practical as a good theory."—Kurt Lewin, noted social psychologist
- ♦ "Research designed with respect to theory is likely to be wasteful."— B. F. Skinner, noted experimental psychologist
- ♦ "Theory, like mist on eyeglasses, obscures facts."—Charlie Chan, noted fictional detective

Lewin's statement is often cited in psychology. Its essence is that a theory is useful for conducting research. A theory synthesizes information, organizes it into logical components, and directs the researcher's efforts in future studies. But Skinner believes that too much effort is spent on "proving" theories; that is, the theory is master of the research. Skinner feels that most theories eventually fall out of favor and that productive research does not require a theory. His position is an extreme case of empiricism. Charlie Chan thinks that researchers become too committed to proving their theories and become blinded to information that doesn't conform to what they want to believe. A good researcher doesn't let the theory obscure the facts. Rather than thinking of theories as "right" or "wrong," we try to think of them in terms of their usefulness. A useful theory helps give meaning to the problem; it helps the subject matter make more sense.

Campbell (1990b) believes that theories are only a means to an end and thus have no inherent value. He stated that theories should "help us develop better research questions, provide more useful interpretation of data, or guide the future investment of research resources" (pp. 66–67). Webster and Starbuck (1988) noted that scientists would be better off with no theories at all than with theories that lead them nowhere or in incompatible directions. Theory is only one way to formulate a research problem; other methods can also result in high-quality research. This is especially true in a pragmatic area like I/O psychology, where some research problems come from everyday experiences in industry. If 50% of a company's workforce quit every year, one doesn't need a theory to realize that this is a serious problem. Developing a carefully-thought-out research problem is far more important than determining which source (experience, theory, intuition) it came from. I believe the value of theory in I/O psychology is to provide a useful explanation for work-related behaviors as opposed to being the sole source of a research idea.

Design of the Research Study

A **research design** is a plan for conducting a study. A researcher can use many strategies; the choice of method depends on the nature of the problem being studied as well as cost and feasibility. Research strategies may be compared along several dimensions, but the two most important are (1) the naturalness of the research setting and (2) the investigator's degree of control over the study. No one strategy is the best under all conditions; there are always tradeoffs.

Naturalness of the Research Setting.   In some research strategies, the problem can be studied in the environment in which it naturally occurs. This is desirable because we don't want the research strategy to destroy or distort the phenomenon under study. Some research strategies appear phony because the problem is studied in unnatural ways. For example, the Hawthorne studies were conducted right in the plant with actual employees performing their normal jobs. However, some studies do not need to be conducted in a natural environment because the behavior under investigation is assumed to be independent of the setting. For example, an engineering psychology study to test whether people react faster to red or green lights could be conducted as appropriately in a laboratory as in a natural field setting.

Degree of Control.   In some research strategies, the researcher has a high degree of control over the conduct of the study. In others, very little control is possible. In the Hawthorne studies, the researchers could control the exact amount of lighting in the work area by installing (or removing) lights, although it turned out that factors other than lighting affected the workers' performance. But suppose you want to study the relationship between people's ages and their attitudes toward I/O psychology. You are particularly interested in comparing the attitudes of people over age 40 with those under 40. You develop a questionnaire that asks their opinions about I/O psychology (is it interesting, difficult to understand, and so on) and distribute it to your classmates. It turns out that every person in the class is under 40. Now you have no information on the over-40 group, so you can't answer your research question. This is an example of a low degree of control (you cannot control the age of the people in the study). Low control is particularly endemic to the questionnaire research method.

Primary Research Methods

This section is a discussion of five primary research methods used in I/O psychology. A **primary research method** is one that provides an original or principal source of data bearing on a particular research question. No one method is perfect; that is, none offers a high degree of both naturalism and control. Each method will be described and illustrated with an example.

Laboratory Experiment.   **Laboratory experiments** are conducted in contrived settings as opposed to naturally occurring organizational settings. In a laboratory, the researcher has a high degree of control over the conduct of the study, especially over those conditions associated with the observations of behavior. The experimenter designs the study to test how certain aspects of an actual environment affect behavior. The laboratory setting must mirror certain dimensions of the natural environment where the behavior normally occurs. A well-designed laboratory experiment will have some of the conditions found in the natural environment but will omit those that would never be present. Furthermore, in a laboratory experiment, the researcher randomly assigns the study participants to the various treatment conditions, which serves to enhance control and facilitates drawing causal inferences.

Streufert et al. (1992) conducted a laboratory experiment on the effects of alcohol intoxication on visual-motor performance. A sample of adult men participated for two days; one day they consumed alcohol and the other they consumed mineral water (disguised with a mild ethanol spray to provide the odor of alcohol). The alcohol dosage was designed to produce breath alcohol levels of .05 and .10 (the conventional legal standard for alcohol intoxication). Visual-motor performance was measured on a task similar to the PacMan video game. The researchers studied several aspects of performance, including risk taking and errors. They compared performance under alcohol intoxication to performance under the control conditions for each person. The results showed that error rates were dramatically higher under conditions of alcohol consumption. Serious performance deterioration was found to occur even at the lower (.05) intoxication level. Under the effects of alcohol, some individuals exhibited greater cautiousness (i.e., slower reaction time) to the visual-motor task, trading off speed of response for fewer errors. The researchers regarded errors in the task to be equivalent to an air traffic controller's failure to ward off aircraft that have come too close to each other. Additionally, although reduced speed of response may decrease errors, it also may prevent engaging in needed defense maneuvers.

This study illustrates the defining characteristics of a laboratory experiment. By controlling for other factors, the researchers were able to determine the causal link between alcohol consumption and performance on a visual-motor task. They could also control the dosage of alcohol to produce precise breath alcohol levels of .05 and .10, typical levels of intoxication associated with drinking alcohol in naturalistic settings. Nevertheless, one can question the generalizability of the skills needed to perform the selected visual-motor task to real jobs. Some jobs, such as a surgeon, require even greater concentration and coordination. In such a case, the magnitude of the "errors" caused by alcohol intoxication would be greater. Other jobs, such as a manual laborer, have fewer visual-motor skill requirements, in which case the errors would be less. In short, the findings from the study pertain to the effects of alcohol on visual-motor performance, not the total spectrum of skills needed for performance across many jobs. Nevertheless, the laboratory experiment is a classic research method for addressing highly specific research questions, and the results from such experiments can often be interpreted with a high degree of clarity.

Quasi-Experiment.   *Quasi* is defined as "seemingly but not actually"; therefore, a **quasi-experiment** resembles an experiment but actually offers less control over the variables under investigation. Another term for a quasi-experiment is a **field experiment.** A quasi-experiment is a research strategy in which independent variables are manipulated in a natural setting (that is, the people in the study do not perceive the setting as having been created to conduct the research). As in a laboratory experiment, the researcher tests the effects of a few variables on the subjects' behavior. But there is also less control. In a laboratory experiment, all the variables are manipulated at the researcher's discretion and can be included or excluded according to the design of the study. However, in a quasi-experiment, variables that occur in the natural setting are also part of the investigation. Though they add to the richness and realism of the study, they also lessen the researcher's control.

Furthermore, random assignment of study participants is often not possible in a field setting, which leads to less generalizable conclusions by the researcher.

Latham and Kinne (1974) reported a study that used the quasi-experiment as a research method. It examined how a one-day training program on goal setting affected the job performance of pulpwood workers. The subjects in the study were 20 pulpwood logging crews. Their behavior was observed as they performed their normal job duties harvesting lumber in a forest. The experimenters split the subjects into two groups of 10 crews each. They matched the two groups on a number of factors so that they would be equal in terms of ability and experience. One group was given a one-day course on how to set production goals—that is, how many cords of wood to harvest per hour. The other group was not given any special instructions and worked in the usual way. The experimenters then monitored the job performance of the wood crews over the next three months. Results showed that the crews who were trained to set production goals for themselves harvested significantly more wood than the other crews. The study supported the use of goal setting in an industrial context.

The major strength of this study in terms of demonstrating the quasi-experiment method is that the context was very real. Actual workers were used in the context of their everyday jobs. The setting was a forest, not a laboratory where the crews would have been pretending. Although the study's design was not complex enough to rule out competing explanations for the observed behavior, it did allow the researchers to conclude that the goal-setting technique probably caused the increase in job performance. This study also illustrates some weaknesses of the quasi-experiment method. Some workers who were supposed to participate in the goal-setting group decided not to. This forced the researchers to redesign part of the study. Also, few I/O psychologists are able to influence a company to change its work operations for research purposes. (In fact, one of the authors of this study was employed by the lumber company, which undoubtedly had some effect on the company's willingness to participate.)

Questionnaire.   Questionnaires rely on individuals' self-reports as the basis for obtaining information. They can be constructed to match the reading ability level of the individuals being surveyed. They represent a means of maintaining respondent anonymity if the subject matter being covered is sensitive. Furthermore, questionnaires are a highly effective means of data collection.

Murphy, Thornton, and Prue (1991) used the questionnaire method to ascertain the acceptability of employee drug testing. The authors asked two samples of individuals (college-aged students and older nontraditional students) to indicate the degree to which they view testing for illicit drug use as justified in each of 35 jobs (such as salesperson, surgeon, mechanic, and airline pilot). The students rated each job on a 7-point scale from low to high acceptance of drug testing. The jobs were carefully selected to represent different types of skills and temperaments needed for their successful conduct, as well as physical conditions under which the jobs are performed. The results indicated that the degree to which different jobs involved danger to the worker, coworkers, or the public was most strongly related to the acceptability of employee drug testing. The authors concluded that it would be relatively easy to justify drug testing for some jobs, whereas substantial efforts may be necessary to overcome resistance to drug testing for other jobs. Furthermore, the responses by both sets of students were virtually the same; that is, the attitudes of college-aged students were the same as those of older individuals (average age of 35). However, the results also revealed a high degree of variability in attitudes toward drug testing among members of both groups. Some individuals were in favor of drug testing across all jobs, whereas other individuals were opposed to drug testing for any job.

Questionnaires are a very popular method of research in I/O psychology; however, they do suffer from several practical limitations. Some people are not willing to complete a questionnaire and return it to the researcher. The return rate of mailed questionnaires is often less than 50%. For example, in the Murphy et al. (1991) study, the return rate of questionnaires mailed to the homes of the nontraditional students was 31%. Such a low response rate raises the question of how representative or unbiased the responses are for the group as a whole. Rising postal rates are also a concern for mail surveys. Researchers usually pay the postage both ways. At a conceptual level, there is also some debate about how accurate self-report measures are. The tendency to slant responses in socially desirable directions is an issue for some topics. Despite these limitations, questionnaires are used extensively in I/O psychology to address a broad range of research questions.

Observation.   Observation is a method that can be used when the research is examining overt behaviors. In natural field settings, behavior may be observed over extended periods of time and then recorded and categorized. As a research method, observation is not used very frequently in I/O psychology, primarily because it requires substantial amounts of time and energy.

Komaki (1986) sought to identify the behaviors that differentiate effective and ineffective work supervisors. She had observers record the behaviors of 24 managers: 12 previously had been judged as effective in motivating others and 12 judged as relatively ineffective. Approximately twenty 30-minute observations were made of each manager's behavior over a seven-month period (232 hours of observation in total). The managers were observed as they conducted their normal day-to-day job duties. The observer stood out of sight but within hearing distance of the manager and used a specially designed form for recording and coding the observations. Komaki found the primary behavior that differentiated the effective and ineffective managers was the frequency with which they monitored their employees' performance. Compared to ineffective managers, effective managers spent more time sampling their employees' work. The findings were interpreted as underscoring the importance of monitoring critical behaviors in producing effective supervisors. However, this conclusion requires corroborating empirical evidence because the two groups of managers were merely observed with no attempt to control for other variables that might account for the results.

Observation is often a fruitful method for generating ideas that can be further tested with other research methods. The observation method is rich in providing data from environments where the behavior in question occurs. But how successful can observers be in acting like "flies on the wall," observing behavior but not influencing it? In this study, the managers were highly aware that they were being observed. Given this, to what degree did the managers modify their conduct to project socially desirable behaviors (e.g., monitoring of their subordinates)? Perhaps effective managers are more sensitive to social cues than ineffective managers and thus are better able to be perceived in a positive fashion. Note that we are dealing with interpretations of the behavior (the "why"), not merely the behavior itself (the "what"). It has been suggested that acceptance and trust of the observers by the study participants are critical to the success of this research method.

Computer Simulation.   Computer simulation is a method for modeling (i.e., simulating) various aspects of an environment to assess their effect on behavior in a comprehensive manner. The closer the simulation is to real life, the more veridical are the conclusions drawn from the method.

Computer simulation is used increasingly as a research method, but to date it is not used as frequently in I/O psychology as other methods are. Seymour et al. (1994) described several computer-controlled simulations used to train law enforcement and military personnel in how to employ good judgment in the use of firearms under threatening situations. The simulations use computer-controlled, life-sized, projected video images of scenarios that may or may not present a threat. The trainee is required to shoot or not shoot a firearm in each scenario. Actual firearms are used, either with real ammunition or with a laser or infrared-light-emitting device. For realism, the laser and infrared-light systems have been developed with the balance, weight, and feel of actual firearms loaded with live ammunition. Some simulators are portable, whereas those that use live ammunition requiring a bullet trap are not. The trainee responds to a sequence of "shoot/no-shoot" judgment scenarios to provide data on three factors: judgment, reaction time, and accuracy. Most simulations can be modified to alter the parameters selected for presentation, such as the speed of the threat.

As Lewandowsky (1993) noted, the value of a simulation is to vary the levels of the parameters selected for study and to assess their corresponding effect on behavior. However, the parameters themselves are explicit and can be modified only by creating a different simulation. The degree to which the simulation parameters (e.g., degree of threat in the scenario) model the critical factors in real-life situations determines the generalizability of the conclusions drawn from the research. Some factors can be simulated faithfully, while others cannot. For example, while the video images of people in the firearm simulation may appear very life-like, those images will not return "live fire" in the simulation. In general, computer simulation offers the opportunity to study issues that do not readily or safely lend themselves to investigation in real life. Pierce and Aguinis (1997) proposed using virtual reality technology to research certain organizational topics. They stated that virtual reality technology produces *telepresence,* where the user is unaware of being present at the site of the human–computer interface and instead feels present or fully immersed in the simulated environment. Findings from simulations nevertheless should be compared with results from other research methods. As Sackett and Larson (1990) stated, "Getting caught up in making one's simulation more and more elaborate without turning to nonhypothetical data for some reality-testing is a serious mistake" (p. 466).

TABLE 2–1   *Comparison of primary research strategies*

	Laboratory Experiment	Quasi-Experiment	Questionnaire	Observation	Computer Simulation
Control (potential for testing causal relationships)	High	Moderate	Low	Low	High
Realism (naturalness of setting)	Low	High	Moderate	High	Moderate

Table 2–1 compares the five primary research methods on two major dimensions: researcher control and realism. No method is high on both factors. There is always a tradeoff; a researcher may sacrifice realism for control or vice versa, depending on the study's objectives. The choice of a strategy should be guided by the purpose of the research and the resources available. A well-trained I/O psychologist knows the advantages and disadvantages of each method.

Secondary Research Methods

A **secondary research method** is one that reanalyzes findings or conclusions reached from previously conducted primary research methods. One particular secondary research method, meta-analysis (Hunter & Schmidt, 1990; Rosenthal, 1991), is being used with increasing frequency in I/O psychology. **Meta-analysis** is a statistical procedure designed to combine the results of many individual, independently conducted empirical studies into a single result or outcome. The logic behind meta-analysis is that we can arrive at a more accurate conclusion regarding a particular research topic if we combine or aggregate the results of many studies that address the topic, instead of relying on the findings of a single study. The result of a meta-analysis study is often referred to as an "estimate of the true relationship" among the variables examined because we believe such a result is a better approximation of the "truth" than would be found in any one study. A typical meta-analysis study might combine the results from perhaps 25 or more individual empirical studies. As such, a meta-analysis investigation is sometimes referred to as "a study of studies." Although the nature of the statistical equations performed in meta-analysis is beyond the scope of this book, they often entail adjusting for characteristics of a research study (for example, the quality of the measurements used in the study and the sample size) that are known to influence the study's results.

Despite the apparent objectivity of this method, the researcher must make a number of subjective decisions in conducting a meta-analysis. For example, one decision involves determining which empirical studies to include in a meta-analysis. Every known study ever conducted on the topic could be included or only those studies that meet some criteria of empirical quality or rigor. The latter approach can be justified on the grounds that the results of a meta-analysis are only as good as the quality of the original studies used. The indiscriminate inclusion of low-quality empirical studies lowers the quality of the conclusion reached.

Another issue is referred to as the "file drawer effect." Research studies that yield negative or nonsupportive results are not published (and thus not made widely available to other researchers) as often as studies that have supportive findings. The nonpublished studies are "filed away" by researchers, resulting in published studies being biased in the direction of positive outcomes. Thus, a meta-analysis of published studies could lead to a conclusion distorted because of the relative absence of (unpublished) studies reporting negative results. These are two examples of the issues that must be addressed in conducting a meta-analysis (Wanous, Sullivan, & Malinak, 1989).

Despite the difficulty in making some of these decisions, meta-analysis is a popular research procedure in I/O psychology. Refinements and theoretical extensions in meta-analytic techniques (Raju, Burke, Normand, & Langlois, 1991) attest to the sustained interest in this method across the areas of psychology. For example, many companies have sponsored smoking cessation programs for their employees to promote health and reduce medical costs. Viswesvaran and Schmidt (1992) meta-analyzed the results from 633 studies of smoking cessation involving more than 70,000 individual smokers. They found that 18.6% of smokers quit after participation in a cessation program, but the results differed by type of program. Instructional programs were found to be twice as effective as drug-based programs. The results of this meta-analysis can be of considerable practical value in assisting organizations to develop effective smoking cessation programs for their employees.

Hunter and Schmidt (1996) are very optimistic about the scientific value of meta-analysis. They believe it has the power to change how we conduct our research and to provide guidance on major social policy issues. Shadish (1996) contended that meta-analysis can also be used to infer causality through selected statistical and research design procedures. It is clear that meta-analysis has become a prominent data-analytic method for researchers and will undoubtedly continue to be so in the future.

Qualitative Research

In recent years there has been an increase in interest among some disciplines in what is called "qualitative" research. The name is somewhat of a misnomer because it implies the absence of any quantitative procedures (i.e., statistical analyses), which is not true. **Qualitative research** involves new ways of understanding research questions and how these ways influence the conclusions we reach about the topic under investigation. Qualitative research (compared to traditional research methods) requires the investigator to become more personally immersed in the entire research process, as opposed to being just a detached, objective investigator.

Maxwell (1998) stated that qualitative research often begins with an examination of why the investigator is interested in conducting the research in the first place. He proposed three kinds of purposes for conducting a scientific study: personal, practical, and research. Personal purposes are those that motivate *you* to conduct a study; they can include a desire to change some existing situation or simply to advance your career as a researcher. Such personal purposes often overlap with the practical and research purposes. It is critical that you be aware of your personal purposes and how they may shape your research. To the extent that data analysis procedures are based on personal desires and you have not made a careful assessment of their implications for your methods and results, you are in danger of arriving at invalid conclusions. Practical purposes focus on accomplishing something—meeting some need, changing some situation, or achieving some goal. Research purposes, on the other hand, focus on understanding something, gaining some insight into what is going on and why it is happening. Maxwell advised researchers to be fully cognizant of the multiple purposes for doing a study, and of how these purposes can interact to influence the conclusions we reach in our research.

The essence of qualitative research is to recognize the number of different ways we can attain an understanding of a phenomenon. We can learn through watching, listening, and in some cases participating in the phenomenon we seek to understand. One qualitative research approach is ethnography. Fetterman (1998) described **ethnography** as the art and science of describing a group or culture. The description may be of any group, such as a work group or an organization. An ethnographer details the routine daily lives of people in the group, focusing on the more predictable patterns of behavior. Ethnographers try to keep an open mind about the group they are studying. Preconceived notions about how members of the group behave and what they think can severely bias the research findings. It is difficult, if not impossible, however, for a researcher to enter into a line of inquiry without having some existing problem or theory in mind. Ethnographers believe that both the group member's perspective and the external researcher's perspective of what is happening can be melded to yield an insightful portrayal of the group. The insider's view is called the **emic perspective,** whereas the external, scientific view is the **etic perspective.** Since a group has multiple members, there are multiple emic views of how group insiders think and behave in the different ways they do. Differing perceptions of what is going on in the group can help a researcher understand maladaptive behavior patterns. Most ethnographers begin their research process from the emic perspective, and then try to understand their data from the scientific or etic perspective. High-quality ethnographic research requires both perspectives: an insightful and sensitive interpretation of group processes combined with data collection techniques.

The field of I/O psychology has been relatively slow to adopt qualitative research methods. Historically our discipline has taken a quantitative approach to understanding phenomenon; meta-analysis is an example. However, I/O psychology is relying increasingly on more qualitative methods to facilitate our understanding of organizational issues. One example is researchers attempting to understand the processes of recruitment and selection from the perspective of the job applicant, not just the organization. With the growing use of work teams in organizations, ethnographic research methods may well aid us in understanding the complex interactions within a group (Brett, Tinsley, Janssens, Barsness, & Lytle, 1997). In the final analysis, there is no need to choose between qualitative and traditional research methods, but rather to realize that both approaches can help us understand topics of interest to us. In this book, case studies and field notes are used along with empirical research findings to facilitate an understanding of issues in I/O psychology.

Measurement of Variables

After developing a study design, the researcher must next enact it and measure the variables of interest. A **variable** is a symbol that can assume a range of numerical values. **Quantitative variables** (age, time) are those that are inherently numerical (21 years or 16 minutes). **Qualitative variables** (gender, race) are not inherently numerical, but they can be "coded" to have numerical meaning: female = 0, male = 1, or White = 0, Black = 1, Hispanic = 2, Asian = 3, and so forth. For research purposes, it doesn't matter what numerical values are given to the qualitative variables because they merely identify these variables for measurement purposes.

Variables Used in I/O Psychological Research.   The term *variable* is often used in conjunction with other terms in I/O psychological research. Four such terms that will be used throughout this book are *independent, dependent, predictor,* and *criterion.* Independent and dependent variables are associated in particular with experimental (laboratory or field) research strategies. **Independent variables** are those that are manipulated or controlled by the researcher. They are chosen by the experimenter, set or manipulated to occur at a certain level, and then examined to assess their effect on some other variable. In the laboratory experiment by Streufert et al. (1992), the independent variable was the level of alcohol intoxication. In the field experiment by Latham and Kinne (1974), the independent variable was the one-day training program on goal setting.

Experiments assess the effects of independent variables on the dependent variable. The **dependent variable** is most often the object of the researcher's interest. It is usually some aspect of behavior (or, in some cases, attitudes). In the Streufert et al. study, the dependent variable was the subjects' performance on a visual-motor task. In the Latham and Kinne study, the dependent variable was the number of cords of wood harvested by the lumber crews.

The same variable can be selected as the dependent or the independent variable depending on the goals of the study. Figure 2–2 shows how a variable (employee performance) can be either dependent or independent. In the former case, the researcher wants to study the effect of various leadership styles (independent variable) on employee performance (dependent variable). The researcher might select two types of leadership styles (a stern taskmaster approach versus a relaxed, easygoing one) and then assess their effects on job performance. In the latter case, the researcher wants to know what effect employee performance (independent variable) has on the ability to be trained (dependent variable). The employees are divided into "high-performer" and "low-performer" groups. Both groups then attend a training program to assess whether the high performers learn faster than the low performers. Note that variables are never inherently independent or dependent. Whether they are one or the other is up to the researcher's discretion.

Predictor and criterion variables are often used in I/O psychology. When scores on one variable are used to predict scores on a second, the variables are called **predictor** and **criterion** variables, respectively. For example, a student's high school grade point average might be used to predict his or her college grade point

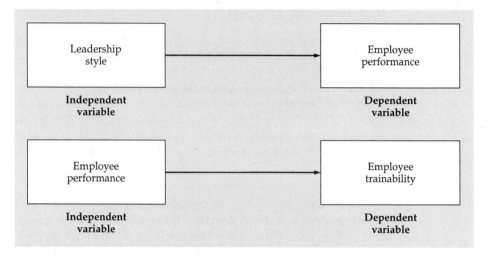

FIGURE 2–2   *Employee performance used as either a dependent or an independent variable*

average. Then high school grades are the predictor variable; college grades are the criterion variable.

As a rule, criterion variables are the focal point of our study. Predictor variables may or may not be successful in predicting what we want to know (the criterion). Predictor variables are similar to independent variables; criterion variables are similar to dependent variables. The distinction between the two is a function of the research strategy. Independent and dependent variables are used in the context of experimentation. Predictor and criterion variables are used in any research strategy where the goal is to determine the status of subjects on one variable (the criterion) as a function of their status on another variable (the predictor). Independent variables are associated with making causal inferences; predictor variables may not be.

Levels of Measurement.   Variables must be measured as accurately as possible. Some variables can be measured precisely, but others can be measured only in a coarse way. A scale is a measuring device to assess a person's score or status on some variable. Although there are many scales, there are only four basic types: nominal, ordinal, interval, and ratio.

A **nominal scale,** the crudest type, classifies objects or people into categories. It simply shows that a person (or object) is a member of one of these categories. For example, a nominal scale could classify people by gender into one of two categories (male or female). Racial groups (White, Asian, and the like) can also be categorized on a nominal scale. Note that a nominal scale does not arrange people or objects in any order or sequence.

An **ordinal scale** orders objects along some dimension. The most common type of ordinal scale is a rank order. If you were asked to rank order three foods—pizza, chicken, and steak—along a dimension of taste preference, you might rank them steak, pizza, and chicken. We know you like pizza better than chicken and steak better than both pizza and chicken. But we don't know how much you like these foods. You may like all three or despise all three, or you may like only one. So an ordinal scale shows how things are ranked along a dimension but not the distance between the ranked items.

An **interval scale** measures how much of a variable is present (using equal distances between scale units). A thermometer represents an interval scale. The distance between 10 degrees and 15 degrees (5 degrees) is the same as the distance between 87 degrees and 92 degrees (5 degrees). An interval scale is more precise than an ordinal scale because it shows not only relative preference (that is, rank order) but also how much the objects are preferred. Suppose you rated the three foods on a 10-point scale (where a rating of 10 is high and 1 is low) as steak 9, pizza 2, and chicken 1. The scale shows that you like steak a lot but not pizza or chicken. A person who had the same rank order but rated the foods as steak 10, pizza 9, and chicken 8 obviously feels different.

A **ratio scale** is the most precise type of scale. It has all the properties of the other three scales and one more: a true zero point. Measures such as length, weight, and age are all ratio scales. The true zero point in the scale means that nothing can be shorter than 0 inches (or centimeters), lighter than 0 ounces (or grams), or younger than 0 seconds. A Fahrenheit or Celsius thermometer is not a ratio scale because it has no true zero point (minus 25 degrees is a negative temperature).[1] The term *ratio* means that a ratio can be formed between two values; for example, a 20-year-old is twice as old as a 10-year-old. But we cannot say that 20 degrees is twice as warm as 10 degrees.

Analysis of Data

After the data have been collected, the researcher has to make some sense out of them. This is where statistics come in. Many students get anxious over the topic of statistics. Although some statistical analytic methods are quite complex, most are reasonably straightforward. I like to think of statistical methods as golf clubs—tools for helping do a job better. Just as some golf shots call for different clubs, different research problems require different statistical analyses. Knowing a full range of statistical methods will help you better understand the research problem. It is impossible to understand the research process without some knowledge of statistics. A brief exposure to statistics follows.

Descriptive statistics simply describe data. They are the starting point in the data analysis process; they give the researcher a general idea of what the data are like. Descriptive statistics can show the shape of a distribution of numbers, measure the central tendency of the distribution, and measure the spread or variability in the numbers.

Distributions and Their Shape.   Suppose a researcher measures the intelligence of 100 people with a traditional IQ test. Table 2–2 is a list of those 100 scores. To

---

[1]Temperature recorded on a Kelvin thermometer is a ratio scale.

TABLE 2–2   *One hundred IQ scores*

133	141	108	124	117
110	92	88	110	79
143	101	120	104	94
117	128	102	126	84
105	143	114	70	103
151	114	87	134	81
87	120	145	98	95
97	157	99	79	107
108	107	147	156	144
118	127	96	138	102
141	113	112	94	114
133	122	89	128	112
119	99	110	118	142
123	67	120	89	118
90	114	121	146	94
128	125	114	91	124
121	125	83	99	76
120	102	129	108	98
110	144	89	122	119
117	127	134	127	112

make some sense out of all these numbers, the researcher arranges the numbers according to size and then plots them in a scatter diagram. Figure 2–3 shows what those 100 test scores look like in a frequency distribution. Because so many scores are involved, they are grouped into categories of equal size, with each interval containing 10 possible scores.

The figure tells us something about the IQ data. We can see that the most frequently occurring scores are in the middle of the distribution; extreme scores (both high and low) taper off as we move away from the center. The general shape of the distribution in Figure 2–3 is called **normal** or **bell shaped.** Many variables in psychological research are distributed normally—that is, with the most frequently occurring scores in the middle of the distribution and progressively fewer scores at the extreme ends. Figure 2–4a shows a classic normal distribution. The curve in Figure 2–4a is smooth compared to the distribution in Figure 2–3 because the occurrence of many test scores takes the "kinks" out of the distribution.

Not all distributions of scores are normal in shape; some are lopsided or pointed. If a professor gives an easy test, a larger proportion of high scores results in a pointed or **skewed** distribution. Figure 2–4b shows a negatively skewed distribution (the tail of the distribution is in the negative direction). The opposite occurs if the professor gives a difficult test; the result is a positively skewed distribution (the tail points in the positive direction), as in Figure 2–4c. Thus, plotting the distribution of data is one way to understand it. We can make inferences based on the shape of the distribution. (In the case of the negatively skewed distribution of test scores, we infer that the test was easy.)

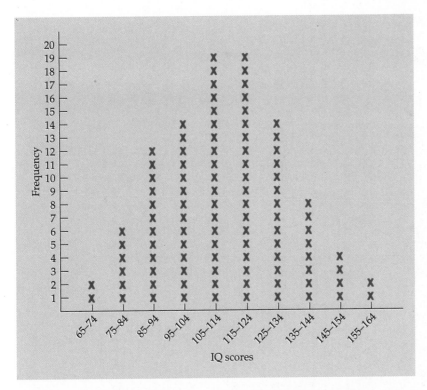

FIGURE 2–3   *Frequency distribution of 100 IQ scores (grouped data)*

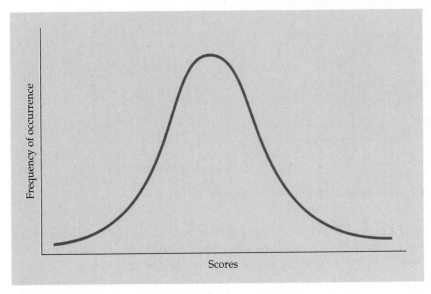

FIGURE 2–4a   *A normal or bell-shaped distribution of scores*

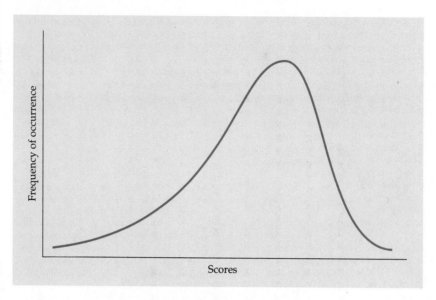

FIGURE 2–4b   *A negatively skewed distribution of scores*

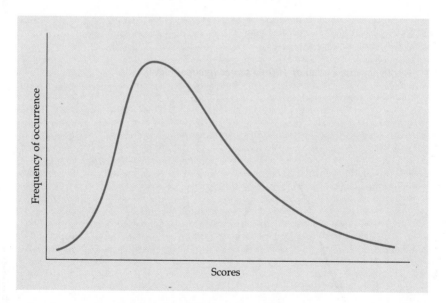

FIGURE 2–4c   *A positively skewed distribution of scores*

Measures of Central Tendency.   After we learn the shape of the distribution, the next step is to find the typical score. One of three measures of central tendency is usually used for this, depending on the shape of the distribution.

The **mean** is the most common measure of central tendency. The mean is the arithmetic average score in the distribution. It is computed by adding all of the in-

FRANK AND ERNEST   by Bob Thaves

SOURCE: Reprinted by permission of Newspaper Enterprise Association, Inc.

dividual scores and then dividing the sum by the total number of scores in the distribution. The formula for computing the mean is

$$\overline{X} = \frac{\Sigma X}{N}$$ [Formula 2–1]

where $\overline{X}$ is the symbol for the mean, Σ is the symbol for summation, X is the symbol for each individual score, and N is the total number of scores in the distribution. The mean for the data in Table 2–2 is found as follows:

$$\overline{X} = \frac{11,322}{100} = 113.22$$ [Formula 2–2]

The average IQ in the sample of people tested is 113.22 (or 113 rounded off). The entire distribution of 100 scores can be described by one number: the mean. The mean is a useful measure of central tendency and is most appropriately used with normally distributed variables.

The **median** is the midpoint of all the scores in the distribution. So 50% of all scores are above the median and 50% are below. If we have a distribution of four scores, 1, 2, 3, and 4, the median is 2.5; that is, half the scores (3 and 4) are above this point and half (1 and 2) are below it. (The statistical procedure used to compute the median for graphed data is quite lengthy and will not be presented here. For your information, the median of the data presented in Table 2–2 is 112.9.) The median is the best measure of central tendency for skewed distributions that contain some extreme scores. The median is relatively insensitive to these scores, whereas the mean is affected by them.

The **mode** is the least common measure of central tendency. The mode is defined as the most frequently occurring score in a distribution. The mode is not used for many statistical analyses, but it may have a practical purpose. Some concepts are best understood in whole numbers (that is, integers), not in fractions or decimals. For example, it makes more sense to say "The modal number of children in a family is 3" rather than "The mean number of children in a family is 2.75." It is difficult to imagine three-fourths of a child. In cases such as this, the mode is the preferred measure of central tendency. Although the mean is more appropriate than the mode for describing the data in Table 2–2, the mode is 114.

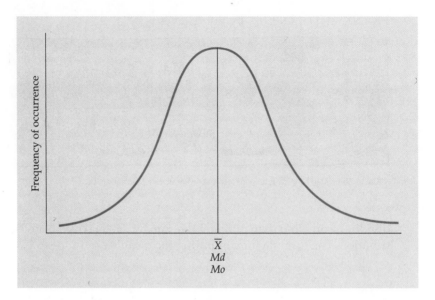

FIGURE 2–5a   *Position of the mean, median, and mode in a normal distribution*

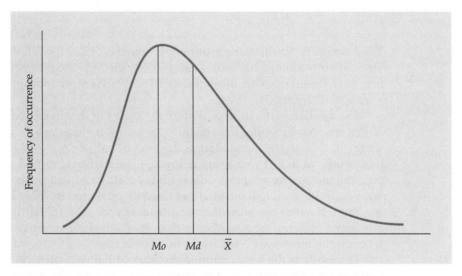

FIGURE 2–5b   *Positions of the mean, median, and mode in a skewed distribution*

In the normal distribution, the mean ($\overline{X}$), median (*Md*), and mode (*Mo*) are equal, as shown in Figure 2–5a. In a skewed distribution, the mean and median are pulled toward the tail of the distribution, as shown in Figure 2–5b.

One of the three measures of central tendency can be used to describe a typical score in a distribution.

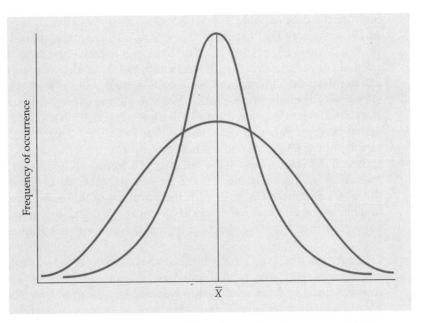

FIGURE 2–6 *Two distributions with the same mean but different variability*

Measures of Variability. In addition to describing a set of scores by the shape of their distribution and central tendency, we can talk about the spread of the scores or their variability. The scores' **variability** is an indication of how representative the mean is as a measure of central tendency. There are several numerical indices to describe variability in scores. The simplest index, the **range,** is obtained by subtracting the lowest score from the highest. The range of the data in Table 2–2 is $157 - 67 = 90$.

Consider Figure 2–6. The two normal distributions have equal means but unequal variability. One distribution is very peaked with a small range; the other is quite flat with a large range. In addition to having different ranges, these distributions differ with regard to another measure of variability, the standard deviation. The **standard deviation** is a measure of the spread of scores around the mean. The formula for the standard deviation is

$$S = \frac{\sqrt{\Sigma(X - \overline{\overline{X}})^2}}{N}$$
[Formula 2–3]

where s is the standard deviation, X is each individual score, Σ is the symbol for summation, $\overline{X}$ is the mean of the distribution, and N is the total number of scores in the distribution. To compute the standard deviation, subtract the mean $(\overline{X})$ from each individual score (X) in the distribution, square that number, add up all the numbers, divide that total by the number of scores in the distribution, and then take the square root of the figure. By applying this formula to the data in Table 2–2, we find the standard deviation for that distribution is 19.96 (or 20 rounded off).

The standard deviation is particularly important when used with the normal distribution. Given the mathematical properties of the normal curve, we know that theoretically 68% of all scores fall within ± 1 standard deviation of the mean.

So from the data in Table 2–2 (which has a mean of 113 and a standard deviation of 20), we know that theoretically 68% of all the scores should fall between 93 (113 − 20) and 133 (113 + 20). Furthermore, the mathematical derivation of the normal curve indicates that theoretically 95% of all the scores should fall within ±2 standard deviations from the mean—that is, between 73 (113 − 40) and 153 (113 + 40). Finally, theoretically 99% of all the scores should fall within ±3 standard deviations from the mean, between 53 (113 − 60) and 173 (113 + 60). The actual percentages of scores from the data in Table 2–2 are very close to the theoretical values; 69% of the scores fall within 1 standard deviation, 96% fall within 2 standard deviations, and 100% fall within 3 standard deviations. Although other measures of variability besides the range and standard deviation are also used, these two measures will suffice for the purposes of this book. Variability is important because it tells about the spread of scores in a distribution. And this can be just as important as knowing the most typical score in a distribution.

Correlation.   So far we have been concerned with the statistical analysis of only one variable: its shape, typical score, and dispersion. But most I/O psychological research deals with the relationship between two (or more) variables. In particular, we are usually interested in the extent that we can understand one variable (the criterion or dependent variable) on the basis of our knowledge about another (the predictor or independent variable). A statistical procedure useful in determining this relationship is called the correlation coefficient. A **correlation coefficient** reflects the degree of linear relationship between two variables, which we shall refer to as X and Y. The symbol for a correlation coefficient is r, and its range is from −1.00 to +1.00. A correlation coefficient tells two things about the relationship between two variables: the direction of the relationship and its magnitude.

The direction of a relationship is either positive or negative. A positive relationship means that as one variable increases in magnitude, so does the other. An example of a positive correlation is between height and weight. As a rule, the taller a person is, the more he or she weighs; increasing height is associated with increasing weight. A negative relationship means that as one variable increases in magnitude, the other gets smaller. An example of a negative correlation is between production workers' efficiency and scrap rate. The more efficient workers are, the less scrap is left. The less efficient they are, the more scrap is left.

The magnitude of the correlation is an index of the strength of the relationship. Large correlations indicate greater strength than small correlations. A correlation of .80 indicates a very strong relationship between the variables, whereas a correlation of .10 indicates a very weak relationship. Magnitude and direction are independent; a correlation of −.80 is just as strong as one of +.80.

The four parts of Figure 2–7 are graphic portrayals of correlation coefficients. The first step in illustrating a correlation is to plot all pairs of variables in the study. For a sample of 100 people, record the height and weight of each person. Then plot the pairs of data points (height and weight) for each person. The stronger the relationship between the two variables, the tighter is the spread of data points around the line of best fit that runs through the scatterplot.

Figure 2–7a shows a scatterplot for two variables that have a high positive correlation. Notice that the line through the data points slants in the positive direction, and most of the data points are packed tightly around the line. Figure

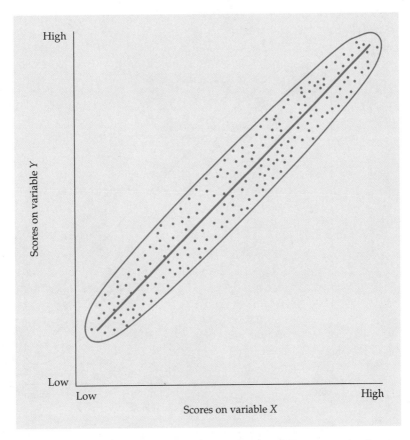

FIGURE 2–7a *Scatterplot of two variables that have a high positive correlation*

2–7b shows a scatterplot for two variables that have a high negative correlation. Again, notice that the data points are packed tightly around the line, but in this case, the line slants in the negative direction. Figure 2–7c shows a scatterplot for two variables that have a low positive correlation. Although the line slants in the positive direction, the data points in the scatterplot are spread out quite widely around the line of best fit. Finally, Figure 2–7d shows a scatterplot for two variables that have a low negative correlation. The line of best fit slants in the negative direction, and the data points are not packed tightly around the line.

The stronger the correlation between two variables (either positive or negative), the more accurately we can predict one variable from the other. The statistical formula used to compute a correlation will not be presented in this book because it is available in statistics books and it will not be necessary for you, as you read this book, to compute any correlations. However, it is important that you know what a correlation is and how to interpret one. The only way to derive the exact numerical value of a correlation is to apply the statistical formula. Although the eyeball-inspection method of looking at a scatterplot gives some idea of what the correlation is, research has shown that people are generally not very good at inferring the magnitude of correlations by using this method (Bobko & Karren, 1979).

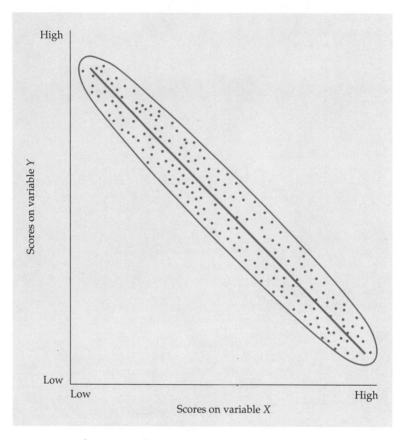

FIGURE 2–7b *Scatterplot of two variables that have a high negative correlation*

The correlation coefficient does not permit any inferences to be made about causality—that is, whether one variable caused the other to occur. Even though a causal relationship may exist between two variables, just computing a correlation will not reveal this fact.

Suppose you wish to compute the correlation between the amount of alcohol consumed in a town and the number of people who attend church there. You collect data on each of these variables in many towns in your area. The correlation coefficient turns out to be .85. On the basis of this high correlation, you conclude that because people drink all week, they go to church to repent (alcohol consumption causes church attendance). Your friends take the opposite point of view. They say that because people have to sit cramped together on hard wooden pews, after church they "unwind" by drinking (church attendance causes alcohol consumption). Who is correct? On the basis of the existing data, no one is correct because causality cannot be inferred from a single correlation coefficient. Proof of causality must await experimental research. In point of fact, the causal basis of this correlation is undoubtedly neither of the opinions offered. It is due to the fact that the various towns in the study have different populations, which produces a systematic relationship between these two variables along with many others, such as the number of people who eat out in

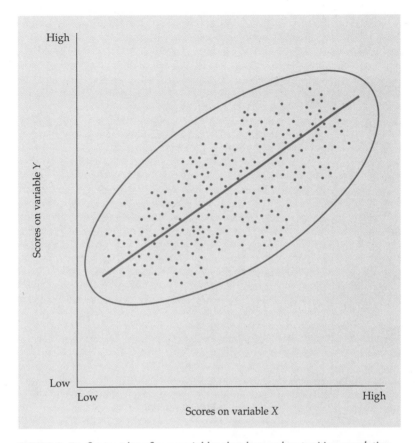

FIGURE 2–7c *Scatterplot of two variables that have a low positive correlation*

restaurants or attend movies. Just the computation of a correlation in this example does not even determine whether the churchgoers are the drinkers. The effect of a third variable on the two variables being correlated can cloud our ability to understand the relationship among the variables in purely correlational research.

To what degree can we determine causality in I/O research? Making a clear determination of causality in research is never easy, but two basic approaches have been developed. Both involve the critical factor of control—to control for other explanations for the obtained results. The classic approach is the laboratory experiment. In this case, a small number of factors are selected for study, the experiment is carefully designed to control other variables, and the causal-based conclusions are limited to only the variables examined in the study. The Streufert et al. (1992) study on the effects of alcohol intoxication on visual-motor performance is one example. The second approach to assessing causality is more recent. It is based on advances in mathematical techniques for abstracting causal information from nonexperimental data. These mathematical approaches require restrictive assumptions, such as the availability of well-developed theoretical formulations, the measurement of all critical variables, and high precision of measurement. Under these conditions, assessments of causality are permissible. Answering the question "why" is not only the ultimate objective of

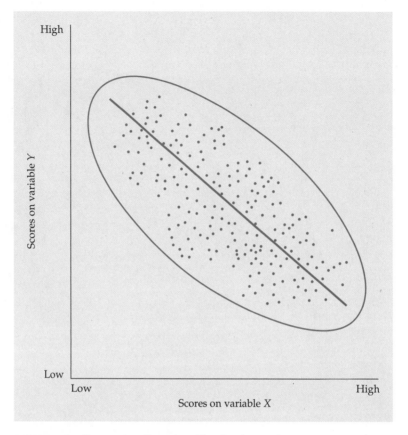

FIGURE 2–7d *Scatterplot of two variables that have a low negative correlation*

scientific research but also the means by which we make sense out of the events in our environment (Silvester & Chapman, 1997).

Because correlation is a common analytical technique in I/O psychological research, many of the empirical findings in this book will be expressed in those terms. However, the concept of correlation will not magically yield accurate inferences in I/O psychological research. As Mitchell (1985) noted, a poorly designed research study cannot be "saved" by the use of correlation to draw valid conclusions. Researchers must plan studies carefully, use sound methodological procedures, and use appropriate statistical analyses to arrive at meaningful conclusions. Kirk (1996) added that statistical results must also be judged in terms of their practical significance—that is, whether the result is useful in the real world. Practical significance is a most reasonable standard to judge research findings in I/O psychology.

Conclusions from Research

After analyzing the data, the researcher draws conclusions. A conclusion may be that alcohol intoxication impairs certain skills more than others, or jobs that require skills more adversely impaired by alcohol consumption warrant more restrictive standards than other jobs. Latham and Kinne's study (1974) concluded that goal setting increased the rate of wood harvesting. So a company might decide to implement the goal-setting procedure throughout the firm. Generally, it is unwise to implement any major changes based on the results of only one study. As a rule, we prefer to know the results from several studies. We want to be as certain as possible that any organizational changes are grounded in repeatable, generalizable results.

Sometimes the conclusions drawn from a study modify beliefs about a problem. Note in Figure 2–1 that a feedback loop extends from "Conclusions from research" to "Statement of the problem." The findings from one study influence research problems in future studies. Theories may be altered if empirical research fails to confirm some of the hypotheses put forth. One of the most critical issues in conducting research is the quality of the generalizations that can be drawn from the conclusions. A number of factors determine the boundary conditions for generalizing the conclusions from a research study to a broader population or setting. One is the representativeness of individuals who serve as the research subjects. The generalizability of conclusions drawn from research on college students has been questioned on the grounds that college-aged students are not representative of the population. This is why it is advisable to explicitly assess the generalizability of findings across groups, as was done in the Murphy et al. (1991) study on attitudes toward drug testing. A second factor is the degree of fit between the subjects and the research task. Studying what college students believe is important in finding a job is a reasonable fit between subjects and the task. Studying what leisure activities college students will engage in after they retire from the workforce is not. A third factor that determines the generalizability of conclusions is the research method. Dipboye (1990) argued that research topics get studied in either laboratory *or* field settings. He suggested that laboratory *and* field research strategies should be used in coordination with each other rather than in competition. Dipboye believes that each basic strategy has something to offer and that researchers can gain understanding by studying the problem with both methods. Laboratory research has traditionally been regarded as more scientifically rigorous, whereas field research is seen as more representative of real-world conditions. Locke (1985) reached the conclusion that most findings from laboratory experiments can be generalized beyond the lab, but other individuals (for example, Mook, 1983) are more skeptical.

Research is a cumulative process. Researchers build on one another's work in formulating new research questions. They communicate their results by publishing articles in journals. A competent researcher must keep up to date in his or her area of expertise to avoid repeating someone else's study. The conclusions drawn from research can affect many aspects of our lives. Research is a vital part of industry; it is the basis for changes in products and services. Research can be a truly exciting activity, although it is seemingly tedious if you approach it only from the perspective of testing stuffy theories, using sterile statistics, and inevitably reaching dry conclusions. Daft (1983) suggested that research is a craft, and a researcher, like an artist or craftsperson, has to pull together a wide variety of human experiences to produce a superior product. Being a researcher is more like unraveling a mystery than following a cookbook (see Field Note 1). However, research is not flash-in-the-pan thrill seeking; it involves perseverance, mental discipline, and

Field Note I *Researcher as Detective*

Being a good researcher is a lot like being a good detective. You have to use all of your senses to buttress information collected by traditional research methods. I often administer and interpret attitude surveys for my industrial clients. The results of these surveys reveal a wealth of information about the companies. However, if it is judged only in statistical terms, this information often seems somewhat dry and bland. Therefore, I decided to experience the organizations in person to better understand and appreciate the statistical results. I have smelled acid fumes in a metal fabricating company that burned my nose and eyes after only a few minutes of exposure. I have tasted a rancid bologna sandwich from a vending machine situated by a big window in the company cafeteria (the sun shining through the window heated the machine and spoiled the food). I have walked (and slipped) across a company parking lot that was a solid 2- to 3-inch sheet of ice during the months of January and February. I have been in a "sound-sensitive" room that was so quiet I could hear my heartbeat. And in the president's office of one status-conscious organization, I have seen a white llama-wool carpet thick enough to swallow most of your shoes as you walked across it. In and of themselves, these events have little meaning, but when considered as part of the total organizational fabric, they provide a rich texture to I/O research findings.

patience. There is also no substitute for hard work. I can recall many times when I anxiously anticipated seeing computer analyses that would foretell the results of a lengthy research study. This sense of anticipation is the fun of doing research—and research, in the spirit of Daft's view of researchers being craftspersons, is a craft I try to pass on to my students. McCall and Bobko (1990) also noted the importance of serendipity in scientific research. *Serendipity* refers to a chance occurrence or happening that influences the research process. The history of science is filled with chance discoveries. For example, a contaminated culture eventually led Alexander Fleming to learn about and recognize the properties of penicillin. Rather than discarding the culture because it was contaminated, Fleming sought to understand how it had become so. The lesson is we should allow room for lucky accidents and unexpected observations to occur and be prepared to pursue them when we do.

ETHICAL PROBLEMS IN RESEARCH

Research participants have certain legal rights pertaining to physical treatment during a study, confidentiality of information, privacy, and voluntary consent (no one can be forced to take part in a study). Researchers who violate these rights, particularly in studies that involve physical or psychological risk, can be subject to professional censure and possible litigation. The American Psychological Association (1992) has a code of ethics that must be honored by all APA members who conduct research. Among the researcher responsibilities covered by the code of ethics are the accurate advertising of psychological services, the confidentiality of information collected during the research, and the rights of human participants. The code of ethics was created to protect the rights of subjects and to avoid the possibility of having research conducted by unqualified people. It is the responsibility of the researcher to balance ethical accountability and the technical demands of scientific research practices (Rosnow, 1997).

The researcher is faced with additional problems with employees of companies. Even when managers authorize research, it can cause problems in an industrial context. Employees who are naive about the purpose of research are often suspicious when asked to participate. They wonder how they were "picked" for inclusion in the study and whether they will be asked difficult questions. Some

---

Field Note 2 *An Ethical Dilemma*

Most ethical problems do not have clear-cut solutions. Here is one I ran into. I was trying to identify some psychological tests that would be useful in selecting future salespeople for a company. As part of my research, I administered the tests in question to all the employees in the sales department. With the company's consent, I assured the employees that the test results would be confidential. I explained that my purpose in giving the tests was to test the tests—that is, to assess the value of the tests—and that no one in the company would ever use the test results to evaluate the employees. In fact, no one in the company would even know the test scores. The results of my research were highly successful. I was able to identify which tests were useful in selecting potentially successful salespeople.

A few weeks later the same company's management approached me and said they now wanted to look into the value of using psychological tests to promote salespeople to the next higher job in the department, sales manager. In fact, they were so impressed with the test results for selecting new salespeople that they wanted to assess the value of these very same tests for identifying good sales managers. And since I had already given the tests to their salespeople and had the scores, all I would have to do is turn over the scores to the company, and they would determine whether there was any relationship between the scores and promotability to sales manager. I said I couldn't turn over the test results because that would violate my statement that the results were confidential and that no one in the company would ever know how well the employees did on the tests. I offered two

alternatives. One was to readminister the same tests to the employees under a different set of test conditions—namely, that the company would see the test results, and in fact the results could be used to make promotion decisions. The second alternative was for me (not the company) to determine the value of these tests to make promotion decisions. In that way I would maintain the confidentiality of the test scores.

Management totally rejected the first alternative, saying it made no sense to readminister the same tests to the same people. I already had the test results, so why go back and get them a second time? The second alternative was also not approved. They said I was deliberately creating a need for the company to pay me for a second consulting project when they were perfectly capable of doing the work, with no outside help and at no extra cost. They said, in effect, I was holding the test results "hostage" and would not release them. In my opinion, the company's management was asking me to compromise my professional integrity by using the test results in a way that violated the agreement under which the tests were originally administered.

The issue was never really resolved. The company soon faced some major sales problems caused by competitors and lost interest in the idea of using psychological tests for identifying sales managers. The management is still angered by my decision, asserting that I am assuming ownership of "their" test results. I have not been asked to do any more consulting work for them, but it is also quite possible that they would no longer have needed my services even if I had turned the test results over.

people even think a psychologist can read their minds and thus discover all sorts of private thoughts. Research projects that arouse emotional responses may place managers in an uncomfortable interpersonal situation.

Mirvis and Seashore (1979) described some of the problems facing those who conduct research with employees. Most problems involve role conflict, the dilemma of being trained to be a good researcher yet having to comply with both company and professional standards (London & Bray, 1980). For example, consider a role-conflict problem I faced in doing research with industrial employees. I used a questionnaire to assess the employees' opinions and morale. Management had commissioned the study. As part of the research design, all employees were told that their responses would be confidential. One survey response revealed the existence of employee theft. Although I did not know the identity of the employee, with the information given and a little help from management, that person could have been identified. Was I to violate my promise and turn over the information to management? Should I tell management that some theft had occurred but I had no way to find out who had done it (which would not have been true)? Or was I to ignore what I knew and fail to tell management about a serious problem in the company? In this case, I informed the company of the theft, but I refused to supply any information about the personal identity of the thief. This was an uneasy compromise between serving the needs of my client and maintaining the confidentiality of the information source. These types of problems are not unique to my study (Williams, Seybolt, & Pinder, 1975).

Lowman (1998) presented a series of cases on ethical problems for I/O psychologists. Taken from real-life experiences, the multitude of ethical dilemmas cover such issues as conflict of interest, plagiarizing, and "overselling" research results. The pressures to conduct high-quality research, the need to be ethical, and the reality of organizational life sometimes place the researcher in a difficult situation (see Field Note 2). These demands place constraints on the I/O psychologist that researchers in other areas do not always face. Freeman (1990) noted a trend of increasing concern for ethics in all facets of I/O psychological research, including drug testing and the moral rights of employees.

RESEARCH IN INDUSTRY

Although the empirical research steps in Figure 2–1 are followed in most I/O psychological research, research conducted in industry (as opposed to universities or research centers) often has some additional distinguishing features. First, Boehm (1980) observed that research questions in industry inevitably arise from organizational problems. For example, problems of excessive employee absenteeism, turnover, job dissatisfaction, and so on may prompt a research study designed to reduce their severity. Rarely are research questions posed just to "test a theory." In fact, a study by Flanagan and Dipboye (1981) revealed that psychologists who view organizations simply as laboratories to test theories are not looked on favorably.

A second major difference is how the results will be used. In industry, if the results of the study turn out to be positive and useful, the research unit of the organization will then try to "sell" (that is, gain acceptance of) the findings throughout the rest of the organization. For example, if providing job applicants with a very candid and realistic preview of the organization reduces turnover, then the researchers will try to persuade the rest of the organization to use such procedures in recruiting new employees. If the results of a study turn out negative, then the organization will look for side products or secondary ideas that will be of value. In research outside industry, less attention is given to implementing the findings and convincing other people of their utility.

Third, industry has different motives for conducting research. Industrial research is conducted to enhance the organization's efficiency. Among private-sector employers, this usually translates into greater profitability. For example, research can be of vital importance in finding out consumer responses to new products and services, identifying ways to reduce waste, and making better use of employees. In university settings, research may not have such an instrumental purpose. The research questions have relevance to industry, but the link between the findings and their implementation may not be as direct (see Field Note 3).

I am reminded of a student who approached an organization with a research idea. The student needed a sample of managers to test a particular hypothesis. After patiently listening to the student's request, the organizations representative asked, "Why should we participate in this study? How can this study help us?"

Field Note 3 *Win the Battle but Lose the War*

Industrial research is always embedded in a larger context; that is, it is conducted for a specific reason. Sometimes the research is successful, sometimes it isn't, and sometimes you can win the battle but lose the war. A client of mine gave promotional tests—tests that current employees take to be advanced to higher positions in the company at higher rates of pay. These tests were important to the employees because only through the tests could they be promoted. The company gave an attitude survey and discovered that many employees did not like the tests. They said many test questions were outdated, there were no correct answers to some questions, and most questions were poorly worded. As a result of all these "bad" questions, employees were failing the tests and not getting promoted. I was hired to update and improve the promotional tests (there were 75 of them). Using the full complement of psychological research procedures, I analyzed every question on every test, eliminated the poor questions, had new questions developed, and in general "cleaned up"

each of the tests. By every known standard the tests were now of very high quality. Both the company's management and I felt confident the employees would be delighted with these revised tests. We were wrong. In the next attitude survey given by the company, the employees still thought poorly of the (new) tests, but their reasons were different than before. Now they complained that the tests were too hard and too technical and required too much expertise to pass. The employees failed the new tests with the same frequency as they had failed the old tests and were just as unhappy. In fact, they may have been even more unhappy; their expectations about the tests had been elevated because the company had hired me to revise them. I felt I had done as good a job in revising the tests as I possibly could have, but in the final analysis I didn't really solve the company's problem. I was hired to revise the tests, but what the management really wanted was to have the employees be satisfied with the tests, which didn't occur.

Industries that sponsor and participate in research do so for a reason: to enhance their welfare. Universities also conduct research for a reason, but it may be nothing more than intellectual curiosity. Some studies have examined the extent to which research influences policy makers—that is, how much the results of research studies influence important decisions. Hogan and Sinclair (1996) reported that organizations are generally reluctant to alter their practices based on the results of empirical research. Argyris (1996) noted that we need to acquire more **actionable knowledge**—knowledge that helps implement relevant research findings in organizations. Ruback and Innes (1988) concluded that to have the greatest impact, we need to study dependent variables that are important to decision makers, such as human lives and dollars saved. They also believe we should focus our attention on independent variables that policy makers have the power to change.

Although academic and industrial research may be guided by somewhat different factors, both have contributed heavily to the I/O psychological literature. The infusion of research from both sectors has in fact been very healthy and stimulating for the profession. Jahoda (1981) commented that more psychological research needs to be done in anticipation of future work problems rather than as a reaction to current problems. Industrial researchers seem to be in the best position to forecast future organizational concerns. Thus, they may be able to find answers to problems before they become crises.

What should I/O psychologists study? Strasser and Bateman (1984) surveyed both managers and nonmanagers as to what they would like to see researched. The predominant answer from both groups related to how people can learn to get along with one another in a work context. As one respondent in their survey said, "People all have different personalities and some people we just can't get along with. How can we avoid personality conflicts and still have a good working relationship?" (p. 87). The second most pressing research need was communication among people.

Thomas and Tymon (1982) believe there is an unhealthy split between academicians who research topics (the "knowledge producers") and practitioners who want to implement research findings (the "knowledge users"). Those authors feel that individuals tend to fall into one of the camps, and we need a closer interplay between producing knowledge and using it. Other researchers have echoed these same thoughts (e.g., Harmon, 1991). While it may be tempting to say that researchers should tackle big, socially important problems, such problems are usually very complex and difficult to research. However, the contributions that I/O psychologists have made to such areas are among our profession's proudest achievements. I/O psychological research has been instrumental in enhancing our nation's productivity (Guzzo, Jette, & Katzell, 1985) and the quality of our work-life (Lawler, 1982). An understanding of research methods is vital for psychologists to resolve problems that confront humankind in an increasingly complex world.

CASE STUDY ◆ How Should I Study This?

Robin Mosier had just returned from her psychology class and was eager to tell her roommate about an idea she had. Julie Hansen had taken the same class the previous semester, so Robin was hopeful that Julie could help her out. The psychology professor gave the class an assignment to come up with a research design to test some hypothesis. Robin's idea stemmed from the job she had held the past summer.

Robin began to describe her idea. "Last summer I worked as a clerk in the bookkeeping department of a bank. Sometimes it wasn't always clear how we should fill out certain reports and forms. I was always pretty reluctant to go to my supervisor, Mr. Kast, and ask for help. So were the other female workers. But I noticed the guys didn't seem to be reluctant at all to ask him for help. So I got this idea; see, I think women are more reluctant than men to ask a male superior for help."

"Okay," replied Julie. "So now you have to come up with a way to test that idea?"

"Right," said Robin. "I was thinking maybe I could make up a questionnaire and ask students in my class about it. I think people would know if they felt that way or not."

"Maybe so," Julie said, "but maybe they wouldn't want to admit it. You know, it could be one of those things that either you don't realize about yourself, or if you do, you just don't want to say so."

"Well, if I can't just ask people about it, maybe I could do some sort of experiment," Robin commented. "What if I gave students some tasks to do, but the instructions weren't too clear? If I'm right, more men than women will ask a male experimenter for help."

"Do you think you'd get the opposite effect with a female experimenter?" asked Julie.

"You mean, would more women than men ask a female experimenter for help? I don't know. Maybe," answered Robin.

"If that's the case," said Julie, "you might want to test both male and female experimenters with both male and female subjects."

Robin scratched some notes on a pad. Then she said, "Do you think an experimenter in a study is the same thing as a boss on a job? You see your boss every day, but you may only be in an experiment for about an hour. Maybe that would make a difference in whether you sought help."

"I'm sure it could," replied Julie. "I know I would act differently toward someone I might not see again than toward someone I'd have to work with a long time."

"I know what I'll do," Robin responded. "I won't do the experiment in a lab setting, but I'll go back to the company where I worked last summer. I'll ask the male and female office workers how they feel about asking Mr. Kast for help. I saw the way they acted last summer, and I'd bet they tell me the truth."

"Wait a minute," cautioned Julie. "Just because some women may be intimidated by Mr. Kast doesn't mean that effect holds for all male supervisors. Mr. Kast is just one man. How do you know it holds for all men? That's what you want to test, right?"

Robin looked disconsolate. "There's got to be a good way to test this, although I guess it's more complicated than I thought."

Questions   1. What research method should Robin use to test her idea? How would you design the study?
2. What other variables might explain the employees' attitude toward Mr. Kast?
3. If this idea were tested in a laboratory or field experiment, what variables should be eliminated or controlled in the research design?
4. If this idea were tested with a questionnaire, what questions should be asked?
5. If this idea were tested with the observation method, what behaviors would you look for?

INFOTRAC ARTICLES

1. *Discover,* November 1997 v18 n11 p129(5)
   Fall guys: A researcher in ergonomics asks the elderly to volunteer to take a trip. Mark Wheeler
   An entertaining account of being a subject in a research study on accidental falls.
2. *The Ecologist,* March–April 1998 v28 n2 pS1(2)
   The cost of objectivity.
   A commentary on the potential ethical dilemmas associated with corporate funding for scientific research, and how the source of the funding can influence the research.
3. *Flight International,* Nov 8, 1995 v148 n4497 p80(2)
   Virtual combat. Graham Warwick
   How the military uses an integrated electronic-combat computer simulation system for training in a virtual environment in which a trainee who uses the wrong tactics or countermeasures is shot down.
4. *The British Journal for the Philosophy of Science,* June 1996 v47 n2 p249(22)
   Can causes be reduced to correlations? Gurol Irzik
   An article that questions the degree to which causality can be inferred from correlational data.
5. *Across the Board,* Jan 1997 v34 n1 p51(2)
   Playing with numbers. George Newman
   An article that cautions that quantitative information should always be examined because it may be misleading despite the appearance of objectivity.
6. *British Medical Journal,* Sep 20, 1997 v315 n7110 p740(4)
   Papers that go beyond numbers. Trisha Greenhalgh & Rod Taylor
   A discussion of situations and conditions where qualitative research methods may be more useful than traditional quantitative methods in answering certain questions.
7. *Human Factors,* June 1997 v39 n2 p323(6)
   Heeding the legacy of Meister, Brunswick, & Gibson: Toward a broader view of human factors research. Kim J. Vicente
   A discussion of the relative merits of two research methods (laboratory experiments and field observations) in human factors psychology.
8. *Science,* Dec 6, 1996 v274 n5293 p1604(1)
   Draft research code raises hackles. Constance Holden
   A discussion of the controversy surrounding the drafting of a code of research ethics involving human subjects in Canada.

PERSONNEL PSYCHOLOGY

Criteria: Standards for Decision Making

MAJOR CHAPTER OBJECTIVES

◆ Understand the distinction between
conceptual and actual criteria.

◆ Understand the meaning of criterion
deficiency, relevance, and contamination.

◆ Explain the purpose of a job analysis and the
various methods of conducting one.

◆ Explain the purpose of a job evaluation and
the issues associated with determining the
worth of a job.

◆ Identify the major types of criteria examined
by I/O psychologists.

Each time you evaluate someone or something, you use criteria. **Criteria** (the plural of *criterion*) are best defined as evaluative standards; they are used as reference points in making judgments. We may not be consciously aware of the criteria that affect our judgments, but they do exist. We use different criteria to evaluate different kinds of objects or people; that is, we use different standards to determine what makes a good (or bad) movie, dinner, ball game, friend, spouse, or teacher. In the context of I/O psychology, criteria are most important for defining the "goodness" of employees, programs, and units in the organization as well as the organization itself.

When you and some of your associates disagree in your evaluations of something, what is the cause? Chances are good the disagreement is caused by one of two types of criterion-related problems. For example, take the case of rating Professor Jones as a teacher. One student thinks he is a good teacher; another disagrees. The first student defines "goodness in teaching" as (1) preparedness, (2) course relevance, and (3) clarity of instruction. In the eyes of the first student, Jones scores very high on these criteria and receives a positive evaluation. The second student defines "goodness" as (1) enthusiasm, (2) capacity to inspire students, and (3) ability to relate to students on a personal basis. This student scores Jones low on these criteria and thus gives him a negative evaluation. Why the disagreement? Because the two students have different criteria for defining goodness in teaching.

Disagreements over the proper criteria to use in decision making are quite common. Values and tastes also dictate people's choice of criteria. For someone with limited funds, a good car may be one that gets high gas mileage. But for a wealthy person, the main criterion may be physical comfort. Not all disagreements are caused by using different criteria, however. Suppose that both students in our teaching example define goodness in teaching as preparedness, course relevance, and clarity of instruction. The first student thinks Professor Jones is ill-prepared, teaches an irrelevant course, and gives unclear instruction. But the second student thinks he is well-prepared, teaches a relevant course, and gives clear instruction. Both students are using the same evaluative standards, but they do not reach the same judgment. The difference of opinion in this case is due to the discrepancies in the meanings attached to Professor Jones's behavior. These discrepancies may be due to perceptual biases, differential expectations, or operational definitions associated with the criteria that cause them. Thus, even people who use the same standards in making judgments do not always reach the same conclusion.

The profession of I/O psychology does not have a monopoly on criterion-related issues and problems. They occur in all walks of life, ranging from the criteria used to judge interpersonal relationships (for example, communication, trust, respect) to the welfare of nations (for example, literacy rates, per capita income, infant mortality rates). Since many important decisions are made on the basis of criteria, it is difficult to overstate their significance in the decision-making process. Because criteria are used to render a wide range of judgments, I define them as the evaluative standards by which objects, individuals, procedures, or collectivities are assessed for the purpose of ascertaining their quality. Criterion issues have major significance in the field of I/O psychology.

CONCEPTUAL VERSUS ACTUAL CRITERIA

Psychologists have not always felt that criteria are of prime importance. Before World War II, they were inclined to believe that "criteria were either given of God or just to be found lying about" (Jenkins, 1946, p. 93). Unfortunately, this is not so. We must carefully consider what is meant by a "successful" worker, student, parent, and so forth. We cannot plunge headlong into measuring success, goodness, or quality until we have a fairly good idea of what (in theory, at least) we are looking for.

A good beginning point is the notion of a conceptual criterion. The **conceptual criterion** is a theoretical construct, an abstract idea that can never actually be measured. It is an ideal set of factors that constitute a successful person (or object or collectivity) as conceived in the psychologist's mind. Let's say we want to define a successful college student. We might start off with intellectual growth; that is, capable students should experience more intellectual growth than less capable students. Another dimension might be emotional growth. A college education should help students clarify their own values and beliefs, and this should aid in emotional development and stability. Finally, we might say that a good college student should want to have some voice in civic activities, be a "good citizen," and contribute to the well-being of his or her community. As an educated person, the good college student will assume an active role in helping to make society a better place in which to live. We might call this dimension a citizenship factor.

Thus, these three factors become the conceptual criteria for defining a "good college student." We could apply this same process to defining a "good worker," "good parent," or "good organization." However, because conceptual criteria are theoretical abstractions, we have to find some way to turn them into measurable, real factors. That is, we have to obtain **actual criteria** to serve as measures of the conceptual criteria that we would prefer to (but cannot) assess. The decision is then which variables to select as the actual criteria.

A psychologist might choose grade point average as a measure of intellectual growth. Of course, a grade point average is not equivalent to intellectual growth, but it probably reflects some degree of growth. To measure emotional growth, a psychologist might ask a student's adviser to judge how much the student has matured over his or her college career. Again, maturation is not exactly the same as emotional growth, but it is probably an easier concept to grasp and evaluate than the more abstract notion of emotional growth. Finally, as a measure of citizenship, a psychologist might count the number of volunteer organizations (student government, charitable clubs, and so on) the student has joined over his or her college career. It could again be argued that the sheer number (quantity) of joined organizations is not equivalent to the quality of participation in these activities, and that "good citizenship" is more appropriately defined by quality rather than quantity of participation. Nevertheless, because of the difficulties inherent in measuring quality of participation, plus the fact that one cannot speak of quality unless there is some quantity, the psychologist decides to use this measure. Table 3–1 shows the relationship between the conceptual criteria and the actual criteria of success as a college student.

TABLE 3–1   *Conceptual and actual criteria for a successful college student*

Conceptual Criteria	Actual Criteria
Intellectual growth	Grade point average
Emotional growth	Adviser rating of emotional maturity
Citizenship	Number of volunteer organizations joined in college

How do we define a "good" college student in theory? With the conceptual criteria as the evaluative standard, a good college student should display a high degree of intellectual and emotional growth and should be a responsible citizen in the community. How do we operationalize a good college student in practice? Using the actual criteria as the evaluative standard, we say a good college student has earned high grades, is judged by an academic adviser to be emotionally mature, and has joined many volunteer organizations throughout his or her college career. In a review of the relationship between the two sets of criteria (conceptual and actual), remember that the goal is to obtain an approximate estimate of the conceptual criterion by selecting one or more actual criteria that we think are appropriate.

CRITERION DEFICIENCY, RELEVANCE, AND CONTAMINATION

We can express the relationship between conceptual and actual criteria in terms of three concepts: deficiency, relevance, and contamination. Figure 3–1 shows the overlap between conceptual and actual criteria. The circles represent the contents of each type of criterion. Because the conceptual criterion is a theoretical abstraction, we can never know exactly how much overlap occurs. The actual criteria selected are never totally equivalent to the conceptual criteria we have in mind, so there is always a certain amount (though unspecified) of deficiency, relevance, and contamination.

Criterion Deficiency.   **Criterion deficiency** is the degree to which the actual criteria fail to overlap the conceptual criteria—that is, how deficient the actual criteria are in representing the conceptual ones. There is always some degree of deficiency in the actual criteria. By careful selection of the actual criteria, we can reduce (but never eliminate) criterion deficiency. Conversely, criteria that are selected because they are simply expedient, without much thought given to their match to conceptual criteria, will be grossly deficient.

Criterion Relevance.   **Criterion relevance** is the degree to which the actual criteria and the conceptual criteria coincide. The greater the match between the conceptual and the actual criteria, the greater is the criterion relevance. Again, because the conceptual criteria are theoretical abstractions, we cannot know the exact amount of relevance.

Criterion Contamination.   **Criterion contamination** is that part of the actual criteria that is unrelated to the conceptual criteria. It is the extent to which the

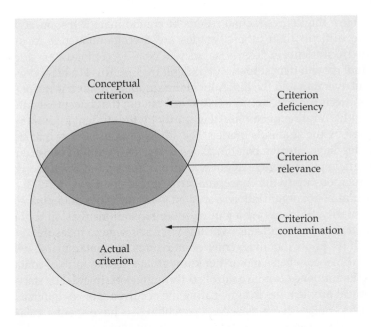

FIGURE 3–1   *Criterion deficiency, relevance, and contamination*

actual criteria measure something other than the conceptual criteria. Contamination consists of two parts. One part, called **bias,** is the extent to which the actual criteria systematically or consistently measure something other than the conceptual criteria. The second part, called **error,** is the extent to which the actual criteria are not related to anything at all.

Both contamination and deficiency are undesirable in the actual criterion, and together they distort the conceptual criterion. Criterion contamination distorts the actual criterion because certain factors are included that don't belong (that is, they are not present in the conceptual criterion). Criterion deficiency distorts the actual criterion because certain important dimensions of the conceptual criterion are not included in the actual criterion.

Let us consider criterion deficiency and contamination in the example of setting criteria for a good college student. How might the actual criteria we chose be deficient in representing the conceptual criteria? Students typically begin a class with differing amounts of prior knowledge of the subject matter. One student may know nothing of the material, while another student may be very familiar with it. At the end of the term, the former student might have grown more intellectually than the latter student, but the latter student might get a higher grade in the course. By using the grade point average as our criterion, we would (falsely) conclude that the latter student grew more intellectually. So the relationship between grades and intellectual growth is not perfect (that is, it is deficient). A rating of emotional maturity by an academic adviser might be deficient because the adviser is not an ideal judge. He or she might have only a limited perspective of the student. Finally, it is not enough to just count how many volunteer groups a student belongs to. Quality of participation is as important as (if not more important than) quantity.

How might these actual criteria be contaminated? If some academic majors are more difficult than others, grades are a contaminated measure of intellectual growth; students in "easy" majors will be judged to have experienced more intellectual growth than students in difficult majors. This is a bias between earned grade point averages and the difficulty of the student's academic major. The source of the bias affects the actual criterion (grades) but not the conceptual criterion (intellectual growth). A rating of emotional maturity by the student's adviser could be contaminated by the student's grades. The adviser might believe that students with high grades have greater emotional maturity than students with low grades. Thus, the grade point average might bias an adviser's rating even though it probably has no relationship to the conceptual criterion of emotional growth. Finally, counting the number of organizations a student joins might be contaminated by the student's popularity. Students who join many organizations may simply be more popular rather than better citizens (which is what we want to measure).

If we know that these criterion measures are contaminated, why would we use them? In fact, when a researcher knows that a certain form of contamination is present, its influence can be controlled through experimental or statistical procedures. The real problem lies in anticipating the occurrence of contaminating factors.

As Wallace (1965) observed, psychologists have spent a great deal of time trying to discover new and better ways to measure actual criteria. They have used various analytical and computational procedures to get more precise assessments. Wallace recommended that rather than dwelling on finding new ways to measure actual criteria, psychologists should spend more time choosing actual criteria that will be adequate measures of the conceptual criteria that they really seek to understand. The adequacy of the actual criterion as a measure of the conceptual criterion is always a matter of professional judgment—no equation or formula will determine it. As Wherry (1957) said in a classic statement, "If we are measuring the wrong thing, it will not help us to measure it better" (p. 5).

CRITERION DEVELOPMENT

I/O psychologists use several different means to identify or develop criteria because it is vital to determine the appropriate evaluative standards for making judgments. The adequacy and appropriateness of criteria set the limits for the quality of the judgments. Poor criteria beget poor judgments. But the issue of appropriate criteria is made more difficult by a time dimension. Short-term criteria for defining the goodness or quality of something may not be the same as long-term criteria. In the decision to buy a car, a short-term criterion may be initial cost and a long-term standard may be its resale value. Standards used to make short-term decisions about quality are called **proximal criteria.** Standards used to make long-term decisions about quality are called **distal criteria.** This section will describe two studies of criterion development that show different approaches to this topic.

Criteria may be developed deductively (from theory to data) or inductively (from data to theory). An example of the *deductive approach* was reported by Freeberg (1976), who wanted to define the relevant criteria for judging the quality of a youth work-training program. The program's purpose was to train hard-to-employ teenagers in certain skills so they could get full-time jobs. Freeberg carefully examined the existing literature on training programs and found 32 variables that were indicative of performance in the training program (proximal criteria) and 40 variables for postprogram job performance (distal criteria). Trainees rated themselves on the 32 program-completion variables (for example, their degree of vocational awareness and confidence, personal adjustment, and motivation). Former trainees who held jobs rated themselves on the 40 postprogram variables (for example, their level of job performance, extent and level of employment, and vocational planning). Freeberg used a statistical procedure called *factor analysis* to identify the major dimensions of training and posttraining success based on these ratings. The results showed that the 32 program-completion variables could be reduced to four major criteria of success in the training program: work motivation and social attitudes, social-community adjustment, training-program adjustment, and competence in vocational planning. The 40 postprogram variables were reduced to five major criteria of success on the job: overall social and vocational adjustment, on-the-job success and satisfaction, job-search motivation, competence in job planning, and short-range job orientation. This study is a good example of the deductive approach to criterion development. It starts with a careful and rational identification of possible criterion variables, followed by an empirical assessment of their value.

One of my own studies (Muchinsky, 1975) is an example of the *inductive approach* to criterion development. I was interested in establishing the criteria of consumer credit risk. I wanted to learn how people were judged to be good or poor credit risks. Unlike the author of the previous study, I had no prior theoretical notions as to what constitutes credit risk. I used the inductive approach—starting with data and reaching some conceptual ideas—to establish the criteria of credit risk. I obtained the financial records of many people who had borrowed money from loan companies. Half of them were judged poor credit risks on the basis of how they repaid their loans and had been denied further credit. The other half were judged good credit risks and would be granted another loan by the company. I wanted to find out which aspects of loan repayment affect people's credit ratings. After comparing the two groups on several variables associated with loan repayment, I found two critical dimensions: how delinquent the people were in making their monthly loan payments and whether they missed payments. The poor credit risks either missed several payments or were often late making them. So I determined that credit risk is defined by two criteria: missed payments and delinquency of payments.

What do we "do" with criteria once we have established them? They serve many purposes, both theoretical and applied. From a theoretical viewpoint, criteria are the basis for understanding a concept. In fact, the concept is best defined by the interrelationships among the criteria used to assess it. I was able to define the concept of credit risk after identifying its criterion dimensions. This procedure, called *construct validation*, will be discussed in more detail in a later chapter.

From a practical standpoint, the identification of criteria provides a rational basis for "treating" people, programs, or social collectivities. For example, as a loan company official, you would not give a loan to someone who has a history of missing payments or of being delinquent. As a training program director, you would want the program to enhance trainee motivation and increase competence

DILBERT   by Scott Adams

SOURCE: Dilbert® reprinted by permission of United Feature Syndicate, Inc.

in vocational planning. Identifying criteria is the first step in initiating action (for example, selecting, training, assisting), which is part of an organization's goals.

JOB ANALYSIS

I/O psychologists must often identify the criteria of effective job performance. These criteria then become the basis for hiring people (choosing them according to their ability to meet the criteria of job performance), training them (to perform those aspects of the job that are important), paying them (high levels of performance warrant higher pay), and classifying jobs (jobs with similar performance criteria are grouped together). A procedure useful in identifying the criteria or performance dimensions of a job is called job analysis; it is conducted by a job analyst. Harvey (1991) defined **job analysis** as "the collection of data describing (a) observable (or otherwise verifiable) job behaviors performed by workers, including both *what is accomplished* as well as *what technologies are employed* to accomplish the end results, and (b) verifiable characteristics of the job environment with which workers interact, including physical, mechanical, social, and informational elements" (p. 71). A thorough job analysis documents the tasks that are performed on the job, the situation in which the work is performed (for example, tools and equipment present, working conditions), and the human attributes needed to perform the work. These data are the basic information needed to make many personnel decisions. Their use is mandated by legal requirements, and estimated annual costs for job analyses have ranged from $150,000 to $4,000,000 in a large organization (Levine, Sistrunk, McNutt, & Gael, 1988).

Sources of Job Information

The most critical issue in job analysis is the accuracy and completeness of the information about the job. There are three major sources of job information, and each source is a **subject matter expert** (SME). The qualifications for being termed a SME are not precise, but a minimum condition is that the person has direct, up-to-date experience with the job for a long enough time to be familiar with all of its tasks (Thompson & Thompson, 1982).

The most common source of information is the *job incumbent*—that is, the holder of the job. The use of job incumbents as SMEs is predicated upon their implicit understanding of their own jobs. Landy and Vasey (1991) believe that the sampling method used to select SMEs is very important. They found that experienced job incumbents provide the most valuable job information. A second source of information is the *supervisor* of the job incumbent. Supervisors play a major role in determining what job incumbents do on their jobs, and thus they are a credible source of information. While supervisors may describe jobs somewhat more objectively than incumbents, there can be legitimate differences of opinion between incumbents and supervisors. It has been my experience that most differences occur not in what is accomplished in a job, but in the critical abilities actually needed to perform the job. The third source of job information is a trained *job analyst*. Job analysts are used as SMEs when comparisons are needed across many jobs. Because of their familiarity with job analysis methods, analysts often provide the most consistent across-job ratings. Job analyst expertise lies not in the subject matter of various jobs per se, but in their ability to understand similarities and differences across jobs in terms of the tasks performed and abilities needed.

In general, incumbents and supervisors are the best sources of descriptive job information, whereas job analysts are best qualified to comprehend the relationships among a set of jobs. The most desirable strategy in understanding a job is to collect information from as many qualified sources as possible, as opposed to exclusive reliance on just one source.

Job Analysis Procedures

The purpose of job analysis is to explain the tasks that are performed on the job and the human attributes needed to perform the job. A clear understanding of job analysis requires knowledge of four job-related concepts, as shown in Figure 3–2. At the lowest level of aggregation we have tasks. *Tasks* are the basic units of work that are directed toward specific job objectives. A *position* is defined as a set of tasks performed by a single employee. There are usually as many positions in an organization as there are employees. However, many positions may be similar to one another. In such a case, similar positions are grouped or aggregated to form a *job*. An example is the job of secretary; another job is that of bookkeeper. Similar jobs may be further aggregated based on general similarity of content to form a *job family*—in this case, the clerical job family.

It is possible to understand jobs from either a task-oriented or a worker-oriented perspective. Both procedures are used in conducting job analyses.

Task-Oriented Procedures.   A **task-oriented procedure** seeks to understand a job by examining the tasks performed, usually in terms of *what* is accomplished. The procedure begins with a consideration of job duties, responsibilities, or function. Williams and Crafts (1997) defined a job duty as "a major part of the work

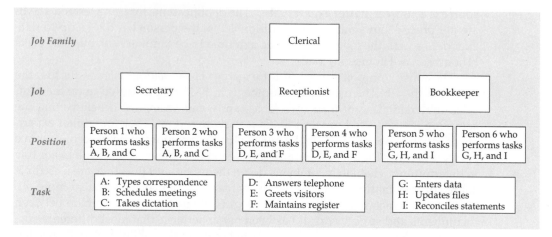

FIGURE 3–2   *Relationships among tasks, positions, jobs, and job families*

that an incumbent performs, comprised of a series of tasks, which together accomplish a job objective" (p. 57). Tasks thus become the basic unit of analysis for understanding a job using task-oriented procedures. The job analyst develops a series of **task statements,** which are concise expressions of tasks performed. Examples include "splice high-voltage cables," "order materials and supplies," and "grade tests." Task statements should not be written in too general terminology, nor should they be written in a very fine level of detail. They should reflect a discrete unit of work with appropriate specificity. Clifford (1994) estimated that the number of tasks required to describe most jobs typically is between 300 and 500.

Following the development of task statements, SMEs (most often incumbents) are asked to rate the task statements on a series of scales dimensions. The scales reflect important dimensions that facilitate understanding the job. Among the common scales used to rate task statements are frequency, importance, difficulty, and consequences of error. An example of the frequency scale is shown in Table 3–2. Based on an analysis of the ratings (especially with regard to the mean and standard deviation), we acquire a level of understanding of a job in terms of the rated frequency, importance, difficulty, and so on of the tasks that make up the job.

A classic example of a task-oriented method of job analysis is Functional Job Analysis (FJA), developed by Fine and his associates (1989). Two types of task information are obtained from FJA: (1) *what a worker does*—the procedures and processes engaged in by a worker as a task is performed, and (2) *how a task is performed*—the physical, mental, and interpersonal involvement of the worker with the task. These types of information are used to identify what a worker does and the results of those job behaviors. The critical component in analyzing a job is the proper development of task statements. These task statements are then rated by SMEs using specific rating scales. The ratings serve as a basis for inferring worker specifications needed to perform the tasks.

Perhaps the most notable characteristic of FJA is that tasks are specified in terms of three dimensions: People, Data, and Things. When a task requires involvement with People, the worker needs interpersonal resources (sensitivity, compassion, etc.).

TABLE 3–2   *Frequency scale for rating tasks*

Frequency—How often do you perform this task?

Rate the task from 0 to 5 using the following scale:

0—*Never perform.* Use this rating for tasks you do not perform.

1—*A few times per year or less.* Use this rating for tasks that are performed less frequently than any other tasks. You may perform these tasks a few times per year (up to six), or even less.

2—*Once a month.* Use this rating for tasks that you usually perform about once a month, or at least every other month, but not every week.

3—*Once a week.* Use this rating for tasks that you perform several times a month, usually every week, but not every day.

4—*Once a day.* Use this rating for tasks that you usually perform every day.

5—*More than once a day.* Use this rating for tasks you perform most frequently. On most days, you perform these tasks more than once.

SOURCE: From "Inductive Job Analysis" by K. M. Williams and J. L. Crafts, 1997, in *Applied Measurement Methods in Industrial Psychology* (pp. 51–88), edited by D. L. Whetzel and G. R. Wheaton, Palo Alto, CA: Consulting Psychologists Press.

When a task requires involvement with Data, the worker needs mental resources (knowledge, reasoning, etc.). When a task is defined primarily in relation to Things, the worker needs physical resources (strength, coordination, etc.). Each of these three dimensions (People, Data, Things) is presented in a hierarchy ranging from high to low. Thus, a given job may be defined as requiring a medium level of People, a high level of Data, and a low level of Things, for example. Figure 3–3 portrays the three dimensions and their associated levels. FJA has been used to analyze jobs in many sectors of society, but most frequently in the federal government. The method is regarded as one of the major systematic approaches to the study of jobs.

Worker-Oriented Procedures.   A **worker-oriented procedure** seeks to understand a job by examining the human attributes needed to perform it successfully. The human attributes are classified into four categories: knowledges (K), skills (S), abilities (A), and other (O) characteristics. *Knowledges* are specific types of information people need in order to perform a job. Some knowledges are required of workers before they can be hired to perform a job, while other knowledges may be acquired on the job. *Skills* are defined as the proficiencies needed to perform a task. Skills are usually enhanced through practice—for example, skill at typing and skill at driving an automobile. *Abilities* are defined as relatively enduring attributes that generally are stable over time. Examples are cognitive ability, physical ability, and spatial ability. Skills and abilities are confused often and easily, and the distinction is not always clear. It is useful to think of skills as cultivations of innate abilities. Generally speaking, high levels of (innate) ability can be cultivated into high skill levels. For example, a person with high musical ability could become highly proficient in playing a musical instrument. However, low levels of (innate) ability preclude the development of high skill levels. *Other* characteristics are all other personal attributes, most often personality factors (e.g., remaining calm in emergency situations) or capacities (e.g., withstanding extreme temperature conditions). Collectively these four types of attributes,

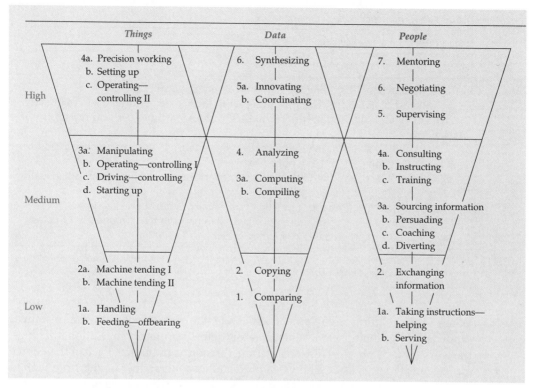

FIGURE 3–3   *Hierarchy of Things, Data, and People dimensions of work*

SOURCE: From *Functional Job Analysis Scales: A Desk Aid* (rev. ed.) by S. Fine, 1989, Orlando, FL: Dryden.

referenced as *KSAOs*, reflect an approach to understanding jobs by analyzing the human attributes needed to perform them.

Similar to task statements, KSAO statements are written to serve as a means of understanding the human attributes needed to perform a job. They are written in standard format, using the wording "Knowledge of," "Skill in," or "Ability to." Examples include "Knowledge of city building codes," "Skill in operating a pneumatic drill," and "Ability to lift a 50-pound object over your head." The KSAO statements are also rated by SMEs. An example of an importance scale for rating KSAOs for the job of electrician is shown in Table 3–3. Similar to analyzing the ratings of task statements, the ratings of KSAO statements are analyzed (i.e., mean and standard deviation) to provide an understanding of a job based on the human attributes needed to successfully perform the job.

Other analytic procedures can be followed to gain further understanding of a job. A *linkage analysis* unites the two basic types of job analysis information: task-oriented and worker-oriented. A linkage analysis examines the relationship between KSAOs and tasks performed. The results of this analysis reveal which particular KSAOs are linked to the performance of many important and frequently performed tasks. For example, a knowledge that is linked to many important and frequently performed tasks would be included in an employee selection test, while knowledges of lesser importance may not be included.

TABLE 3–3 *Importance scale for rating KSAOs for electrician tasks*

Importance—How important is this knowledge, skill, ability, or other characteristic for performing the job tasks of an electrician?

Rate the KSAOs from 0 to 5 using the following scale:

0—*Of no importance.* Use this rating for knowledge that is unnecessary for performing the job, skills that are unnecessary, or abilities and other characteristics that an electrician does not need.

1—*Of little importance.* Use this rating for knowledge that is nice to have but not really necessary, skills that are rarely used, or abilities and other characteristics that are of little importance in relationship to the job.

2—*Of some importance.* Use this rating for knowledge, skills, or abilities and other characteristics that have some importance, but still would be ranked below average in relation to others.

3—*Moderately important.* Use this rating for knowledge, skills, or abilities and other characteristics that are of average importance in terms of successful completion of the job. These KSAOs are not the most critical, but still are needed to be successful on the job.

4—*Very important.* Use this rating for knowledges, skills, or abilities and other characteristics that are very important for successful job performance. These knowledges, skills, abilities, and other characteristics are essential, but are not the most critical.

5—*Extremely important.* Use this rating for knowledge that is critical for an electrician to have in order to perform safely and correctly, skills that are essential and are used throughout the job, and abilities and other characteristics that all electricians must possess for successful completion of job tasks.

SOURCE: From "Inductive Job Analysis" by K. M. Williams and J. L. Crafts, 1997, in *Applied Measurement Methods in Industrial Psychology* (pp. 51–88), edited by D. L. Whetzel and G. R. Wheaton, Palo Alto, CA: Consulting Psychologists Press

How to Collect Job Analysis Information

The first step in conducting job analyses is to review written materials that contain information about the job. Such materials may include position descriptions, training manuals, and other information provided by the organization. Upon reading these materials, the job analyst is prepared to collect more extensive information about the job to be analyzed. Three procedures are typically followed: the interview, direct observation, and a questionnaire.

Procedures for Collecting Information.   In the first procedure, the interview, employees are asked questions by the job analyst about the nature of their work. They may be interviewed individually, in small groups, or through a series of panel discussions. The job analyst questions the employees to get an understanding of the tasks performed on the job and the KSAOs needed to perform them. The incumbents selected to be interviewed are regarded as SMEs, people qualified to render informed judgments about their work. Desirable characteristics in SMEs include verbal ability, a good memory, and cooperativeness. Also, if incumbents are suspicious of the motives behind a job analysis, they are inclined to magnify the importance or difficulty of their abilities as a self-protective tactic (see Field Note 1).

The second method is called direct observation: Employees are observed as they perform their jobs. Observers try to be unobtrusive, observing the jobs but not getting in the workers' way (see Field Note 2). Observers generally do not talk to the employees because it interferes with the conduct of work. They sometimes use cameras or videotape equipment to facilitate the observation. Direct observation is an excellent method for appreciating and understanding the adverse conditions (such as noise or heat) under which some jobs are performed; however, it is a poor method for understanding *why* certain behaviors occur on the job.

The third procedure for collecting job information is a structured questionnaire or inventory. The analyst uses already existing knowledge or taxonomies of job information to analyze a job. A **taxonomy** is a classification scheme useful in organizing information—in this case, information about jobs. The information collected about the job is automatically organized within the already existing system of measurement and can be integrated into a database of scores describing other jobs previously analyzed. Peterson and Jeanneret (1997) referred to this procedure as being *deductive* in nature because the job analyst can deduce an understanding of a job from a preexisting framework for analyzing jobs. Alternatively, the interview and direct observation procedures are *inductive* in nature because the job analyst has to rely on newly created information about the job being analyzed.

Field Note 1 *A Memorable Lesson*

When interviewing employees about their jobs, job analysts should explain what they are doing (and why they are doing it). If they do not fully explain their role, employees may feel threatened, fearing the analysts may somehow jeopardize their position by giving a negative evaluation of their performance, lowering their wages, firing them, and so on. Although job analysts do not have the power to do these things, some employees assume the worst. When employees feel threatened, they usually magnify the importance or difficulty of their contributions to the organization in an attempt to protect themselves. Therefore, to ensure accurate and honest responses, all job analysts should go out of their way to disarm any possible suspicions or fears.

I learned the importance of this point early in my career. One of my first job analyses focused on the job of a sewer cleaner. I had arranged to interview three sewer cleaners about their work. However, I had neglected to provide much advance notice about myself, why I would be talking to them, or what I was trying to do. I simply arrived at the work site, introduced myself, and told the sewer cleaners that I wanted to talk to them about their jobs. Smelling trouble, the sewer cleaners proceeded to give me a memorable lesson on the importance of first establishing a nonthreatening atmosphere. One sewer cleaner turned to me and said: "Let me tell you what happens if we don't do our job. If we don't clean out the sewers of stuff like tree limbs, rusted hubcaps, and old tires, the sewers get clogged up. If they get clogged up, the sewage won't flow. If the sewage won't flow, it backs up. People will have sewage backed up into the basements of their homes. Manhole covers will pop open, flooding the streets with sewage. Sewage will eventually cover the highways, airport runways, and train tracks. People will be trapped in their homes surrounded by sewage. The entire city will be covered with sewage, with nobody being able to get in or out of the city. And that's what happens if we don't do our job of cleaning the sewers." Sadder but wiser, I learned the importance of not giving employees any reason to overstate their case.

Because job analysts are often interested in understanding more than one job, the structured inventory is a very useful way to examine the relationships among a set of jobs. Most of the recent professional advances in job analysis within the field of I/O psychology have occurred with deductive procedures.

Taxonomic Information.   There are several examples of taxonomic information for job analysis. The first is the Position Analysis Questionnaire (PAQ) (McCormick & Jeanneret, 1988), which consists of 195 statements used to describe the human attributes needed to perform a job. The statements are organized into six major categories: information input, mental processes, work output, relationships with other persons, job context, and other requirements. Some sample statements from the Relationships with Other Persons category are shown in Figure 3–4. Based on a database of thousands of similar jobs that have been previously analyzed with the PAQ, the job analyst can come to understand the focal job.

A second example of this approach is the research of Fleishman and his associates in developing a taxonomy of human abilities needed to perform tasks (Fleishman & Quaintance, 1984). Fleishman identified 52 abilities required in the conduct of a broad spectrum of tasks. Examples of these abilities are oral expression, arm-hand steadiness, multilimb coordination, reaction time, selective attention, and night vision. Fleishman calibrated the amount of each ability needed to perform tasks. For example, with a scale of 1 (low) to 7 (high), the following amounts of *arm-hand steadiness* are needed to perform these tasks:

Cut facets in diamonds	6.32
Thread a needle	4.14
Light a cigarette	1.71

Field Note 2 *Unintentional Obstruction of Work*

Although logically it may not seem so, it takes talent to watch people at work. Observation is one of the methods job analysts use to study jobs. The object is to unobtrusively observe the employee at work. The analyst doesn't need to hide; he or she simply needs to blend in. In attempts to avoid interfering with employees, I have inadvertently positioned myself too far away to see what was really happening. I have also learned to bring earplugs and goggles to work sites because, when watching people at work, the observer is exposed to the same environmental conditions they are. Although you can be "too far" from a worker to make accurate observations, you can also get "too close." Cascio (1982) described this true story:

> While riding along in a police patrol car as part of a job analysis of police officers, an analyst and an officer were chatting away when a call came over the radio regarding a robbery in progress. Upon arriving at the scene the analyst and the officer both jumped out of the patrol car, but in the process the overzealous analyst managed to position himself between the robbers and the police. Although the robbers were later apprehended, they used the analyst as a decoy to make their getaway from the scene of the crime. (p. 56)

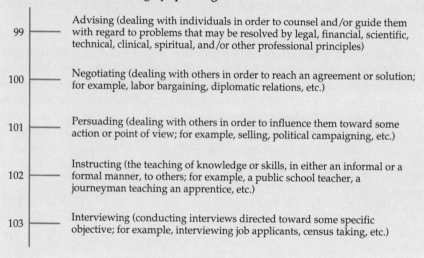

Relationships with Other Persons

This section deals with different aspects of interaction between people involved in various kinds of work.

Code	Importance to this job
DNA	Does not apply
1	Very minor
2	Low
3	Average
4	High
5	Extreme

4.1 Communications

Rate the following in terms of how *important* the activity is to the completion of the job. Some jobs may involve several or all of the items in this section.

4.1.1 Oral (communicating by speaking)

99 —— Advising (dealing with individuals in order to counsel and/or guide them with regard to problems that may be resolved by legal, financial, scientific, technical, clinical, spiritual, and/or other professional principles)

100 —— Negotiating (dealing with others in order to reach an agreement or solution; for example, labor bargaining, diplomatic relations, etc.)

101 —— Persuading (dealing with others in order to influence them toward some action or point of view; for example, selling, political campaigning, etc.)

102 —— Instructing (the teaching of knowledge or skills, in either an informal or a formal manner, to others; for example, a public school teacher, a journeyman teaching an apprentice, etc.)

103 —— Interviewing (conducting interviews directed toward some specific objective; for example, interviewing job applicants, census taking, etc.)

FIGURE 3–4   *Sample items from the PAQ*

SOURCE: From Position Analysis Questionnaire. Copyright 1969 by Purdue Research Foundation. All rights reserved. Reprinted by permission.

Fleishman's method permits jobs to be described in terms of the tasks performed and the corresponding abilities and levels of those abilities needed to perform them. Such a taxonomic approach classifies jobs on the basis of requisite human abilities.

The third example of taxonomic information available for job analyses is provided by the U.S. Department of Labor. Based on job analyses of millions of incumbents, these massive compilations of information provide users with broad job and occupational assessments. Two such resources are available. The first is the *Dictionary of Occupational Titles* (DOT) (U.S. Department of Labor, 1991). The DOT describes thousands of jobs in terms of the worker traits needed to perform each job. The DOT is based, in part, on the framework of Functional Job Analysis with regard to the People, Data, and Things dimensions of work. Eleven worker traits are given, including intelligence, verbal ability, numerical ability, finger dexterity, and motor coordination. Job analysts compiled the trait requirement ratings by estimating how much of each of the 11 traits were needed for each job. Made on a 5-point scale, the ratings showed the amount of each trait possessed by various segments of the working population, ranging from 1 (the top 10% of the population) to 5 (the lowest 10%). The DOT also describes jobs in terms of occupational groups, based on similarity of job content.

The second resource is the Occupational Information Network (O*NET), which is being developed by the U.S. Department of Labor. It is intended to become a comprehensive national database of worker attributes and job characteristics. It is designed to replace the DOT and will be the primary source of occupational information. The initial version of O*NET has been developed, with a more complete database scheduled for completion in 2000. The database contains information about KSAOs, interests, general work activities, and work context. It provides the essential foundation for facilitating career counseling, education, employment, and training activities. Additional information about the O*NET can be found at *www.onetcenter.org*.

Figure 3–5 shows the conceptual model upon which the O*NET is based. There are six domains of descriptions (e. g., worker requirements) containing more refined information within each domain (e.g., basic skills within worker requirements). The worker requirements and worker characteristics of the O*NET contain the kind of descriptions called "worker-oriented," while the occupational requirements, occupational-specific requirements, and organizational characteristics contain the kind of descriptions referenced as "task-oriented." The experience requirements domain presents descriptions that are positioned between the worker- and task-oriented domains.

It is intended that a large number of applications will be developed that utilize the O*NET data, including job descriptions, job classification schemes, selection, training, and vocational counseling. The O*NET is anticipated to be a major contribution of I/O psychology to enhancing our knowledge and use of job-related information (Peterson, Mumford, Borman, Jeanneret, & Fleishman, 1999).

Uses of Job Analysis Information

Job analysis information produces the criteria needed for a wide range of applications in I/O psychology, as the ensuing chapters will show. A brief introduction to its uses is instructive.

First, an analysis of KSAOs reveals those attributes that are needed for successful job performance, including those needed upon entry into the job. The identification of these attributes provides an empirical basis to determine what personnel selection tests should assess. Thus, rather than selection tests being based on hunches or assumptions, job analytic information offers a rational approach to test selection. This topic will be described in Chapter 4. Second, job analytic information provides a basis to organize different positions into a job, and different jobs into a job family. Such groupings provide a basis for determining levels of compensation because one basis of compensation is the attributes needed to perform the work. This topic will be discussed in the next section on job evaluation. Third, job analytic information contributes to a determination of the content of training needed to perform the job. The tasks identified as most frequently performed or most important become the primary content of training. This topic

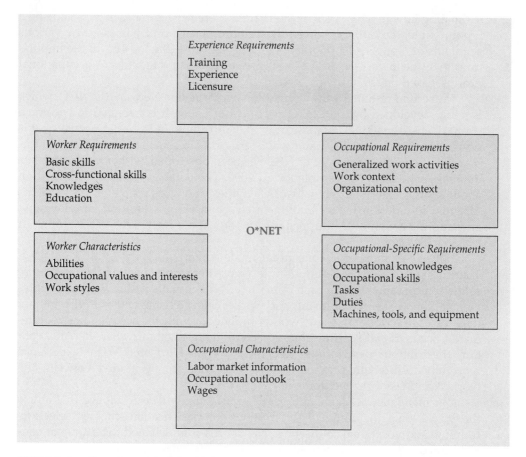

FIGURE 3–5 *Content model of the O*NET*

SOURCE: From "The O*NET Content Model: Structural Considerations in Describing Jobs" by M. D. Mumford and N. G. Peterson, 1999, in *An Occupational Information System for the 21st Century: The Development of O*NET,* edited by N. G. Peterson, M. D. Mumford, W. C. Borman, P. R. Jeanneret, and E. A. Fleishman, Washington, DC: American Psychological Association. © 1999. Reprinted by permission.

will be discussed in Chapter 6. Finally, job analytic information provides one basis to determine the content of performance evaluation or appraisal. A job analysis reveals the tasks most critical to job success, so the performance appraisal is directed at assessing how well the employee performs those tasks. This topic will be discussed in Chapter 7. In addition to these uses of job analytic information, the information can also be used in vocational counseling, offering insight into the KSAOs needed to perform successfully in various occupations. Although not discussed in this book, the application of job analytic information in vocational counseling provides guidance in career selection. It is anticipated that one of the major uses of O*NET will be for vocational counseling.

Evaluating Job Analysis Methods

It should be evident that there are multiple ways of analyzing jobs. Are some methods better than others? Most of what we know about the relative merits of job analysis methods comes from questionnaires. For example, Arvey, Passino, and Lounsbury (1977) showed that the PAQ gave job analysis information that was not strongly biased by the gender of either the employee or the analyst. Conley and Sackett (1987) demonstrated that high-performing and low-performing job incumbents gave equivalent descriptions of their job; that is, job analytic information was not biased by the performance level of the incumbent. Cornelius, DeNisi, and Blencoe (1984) reported differences in the PAQ conclusions reached by expert job analysts and college students. As with most sophisticated measuring instruments, PAQ conclusions are influenced by the qualifications of the user.

The results of a study by Levine, Ash, Hall, and Sistrunk (1983), comparing seven major questionnaire methods of job analysis, reflect what the I/O profession as a whole has come to understand about job analysis methods. The authors found that different methods are regarded as differentially effective and practical depending on the purposes for which they may be used. No one method consistently surfaces as the best across the board. I believe that a well-trained job analyst could draw accurate inferences and conclusions using any one of several questionnaire methods. The converse is also true. No method can ensure accurate results when used by someone who is inexperienced with job analysis. A related opinion was reached by Harvey and Lozada-Larsen (1988), who concluded that the most accurate job analysis ratings are provided by raters who are highly knowledgeable about the job. Spector, Brannick, and Coovert (1989) described using computers to develop an artificial intelligence system to perform a job analysis. If successful, the computer would model the human judgment process in assembling information about jobs, and thereby remove the human job analyst from the process of analyzing jobs. Finally, Morgeson and Campion (1997) outlined a series of potential inaccuracies in job analytic information caused by such factors as biases in how job analysts process information about the jobs they are analyzing, and loss of motivation among SMEs who are less than enthusiastic about participating in job analyses. Morgeson and Campion believe the chances for inaccuracies are considerably less in task-oriented job analysis than in worker-oriented job analysis. That is, the ratings of observable and discrete tasks are less subject to error than the ratings of some abstract KSAOs.

JOB EVALUATION

Different jobs have different degrees of importance or value to organizations. Some jobs are critically important, such as company president, and command the highest salary in the organization. Other jobs are less important to the organization's success and thus pay lower salaries. **Job evaluation** is a procedure that is useful for determining the relative value of jobs in the organization, which in turn helps determine the level of compensation. It is beyond the scope of this book to present a complete discourse on compensation. An excellent analysis of compensation from an I/O psychology perspective has been written by Gerhart and Milkovich (1992). This section will simply review one component of the compensation process: job evaluation.

Organizations that wish to attract and retain competent employees have to pay competitive wages. If wages are set too low, competent people will obtain better-paying jobs elsewhere. Similarly, if wages are set too high, the organization will pay more than is necessary to staff itself. How, then, does an organization determine what is a fair and appropriate wage? Basically, two different operations are required. One is to determine external equity. Equity means fairness, so **external equity** is a fair wage in comparison to what other employers are paying. A wage survey (that is, a survey that reveals what other companies pay employees for performing their jobs) is used to determine the "going rate" for jobs in the business community. The second operation is to determine **internal equity,** or the fairness of compensation levels within the organization. Job evaluation is used to determine the relative positions (from highest paid to lowest paid) of the jobs in the organization; thus, it is used to assess internal equity.

Methods of Job Evaluation

The several methods of job evaluation all rely heavily, either implicitly or explicitly, on using criteria to assess the relative worth of jobs. Their differences rest primarily on the degree of specificity involved in the comparison process; that is, jobs may be compared either in some global fashion (as in their overall value to the company's success) or along certain specific dimensions (as in how much effort they require and the working conditions under which they are performed).

In practice, most organizations use job evaluation methods that examine several dimensions or factors of work. These dimensions are called **compensable factors,** or those factors for which employers pay compensation; that is, various levels of compensation are paid for jobs depending on "how much" of these compensable factors are present in each. Please note a fine distinction here that people often confuse. With a few notable exceptions, organizations do not pay individuals; organizations pay jobs, which individuals fill. The jobs determine the level of compensation, not the people in them.

There is no one fixed set of compensable factors. In theory, organizations can pay jobs for whatever reasons they want. In practice, however, *effort, skill, responsibility,* and *working conditions* are typical compensable factors.

Another related set of four compensable factors, often used in the compensation of managers and executives, is the Hay Plan (named after the Hay Group consulting firm). The first, *know-how,* is the total of all skills and knowledge required to do the job. The second factor, *problem solving,* is the amount of original thinking required to arrive at decisions in the job. The third factor, *accountability,* is answerability for actions taken on the job. The fourth factor, *additional compensable elements,* addresses exceptional contexts in which the jobs are performed.

Here is one way in which job evaluation works. Let us say the organization has selected these four compensable factors: skill, effort, responsibility, and working conditions. Although most or all of the jobs in the organization would be evaluated, our discussion will be limited to two jobs: office secretary and security officer. The results of a job analysis might reveal that the major criteria for a secretary's performance are typing, filing, and supervising a clerk. For the security officer, the criteria of job performance might be physically patrolling the office

TABLE 3–4 *Factor description table for factor evaluation system*

Factor	Possible Points for Factor	Value of Factor as Percentage of Total (Weight of Factor)	Number of Levels	Points for Each Level
Knowledge required by the position	1,850	41.3%	9	50, 200, 350, 550, 750, 950, 1250, 1550, 1850
Supervisory control	650	14.5%	5	25, 125, 275, 450, 650
Guidelines	650	14.5%	5	25, 125, 275, 450, 650
Complexity	450	10.0%	6	25, 75, 150, 225, 325, 450
Scope and effect	450	10.0%	6	25, 75, 150, 225, 325, 450
Personal contact	110	2.5%	4	10, 25, 60, 110
Purpose of contact	220	4.9%	4	20, 50, 120, 220
Physical demand	50	1.1%	3	5, 20, 50
Work environment	50	1.1%	3	5, 20, 50
Total	4,480	99.9%		

SOURCE: From U.S. Civil Service Commission, *Instructions for the Factor Evaluation System*, May 1977, Washington, DC: U.S. Government Printing Office.

building, remaining vigilant, and maintaining security records. The criteria for both jobs would be evaluated or scored in terms of the degree to which the compensable factors are present. For example, the secretary's job might be evaluated as requiring considerable skill, little effort, modest responsibility, and performance under temperate working conditions. The security officer's job might be evaluated as requiring little skill, modest effort, considerable responsibility, and performance under potentially hazardous working conditions.

Thus, the level of compensation paid for jobs is a function of their status on the compensable factors. Jobs that have high levels of the compensable factors (for example, high effort, great skill) receive higher rates of pay than jobs that have low levels of these factors. All the jobs in the company would be evaluated in this fashion and then arranged in a hierarchy from high to low. A job evaluation method called the Factor Evaluation System (FES) developed by the U.S. Civil Service Commission (1977) is used to evaluate jobs in the federal government. The method is based on assessing nine factors (or criteria). Each factor is broken down into levels (as low, medium, and high), with a corresponding point value for each level. Every job is evaluated using this method, with the result that every job is assigned a point total based on the scores from the nine factors. The point total is then used to set the salary paid to the job. Table 3–4 shows the nine factors and their corresponding points.

Other methods of job evaluation do not require the use of compensable factors, but all methods require that jobs be evaluated on one or more criteria. A (dollar) value is then ultimately attached to the relative position of every job in the hierarchy. Job evaluation attempts to ensure some correspondence between the compensation paid for the job and the value of the job to the organization.

Obviously a key to any job evaluation system is whether the "right factors" are being considered. The evaluations should be made on the basis of factors that truly reflect the jobs' worth, importance, or value. Also, unlike job analysis, which is basically a value-free operation (that is, an analysis), job evaluation is heavily loaded with values (that is, an evaluation). Values are evidenced in the selection of job factors to be evaluated and whether certain factors are considered more important than others. Therefore, job evaluation is an extension of job analysis applied to determining the relative worth of jobs in an organization for the purpose of providing equitable pay.

Research on Job Evaluation

I/O psychological research on job evaluation is not as extensive as the research on job analysis. However, a few studies will be described. Gomez-Mejia, Page, and Tornow (1982) compared the relative accuracy and practical utility of seven different job evaluation approaches. Their results indicated that although several methods provided useful information, a critical factor was the job analysis data on which the job evaluation system was based. If the job analysis data are of poor quality, their use in job evaluation makes that process suffer. Hahn and Dipboye (1988) reported that the most accurate and reliable job evaluation ratings were provided by people who received training in how to evaluate as well as extensive information about the jobs to be evaluated. Collins and Muchinsky (1993) reported that job evaluation ratings provided consistent assessments of job worth *within* a job family (e.g., secretary vs. clerk) but produced considerable disagreements about job worth *across* job families (e.g., secretary vs. electrician). Since large companies often organize their jobs into multiple job families, the finding suggests that it will be unlikely to find a single job evaluation instrument to provide consistent and accurate assessments of worth across all jobs in a company.

I/O psychologists typically regard agreement among people in describing work-related issues as evidence of the "correctness" of their opinions. However, research on job evaluation reveals the potential fallibility of this perspective. Schwab and Wichern (1983) suggested that systematic bias may be operating in the determination of compensation. For example, let us assume that most secretaries are women and that society as a whole does not highly value the work that women typically perform. Therefore, the wages paid to female secretaries are lower than they "should" be. Additionally, this same bias operates to uniformly suppress the judged value of a secretarial job vis-à-vis the compensable factors; that is, secretarial jobs are judged to be relatively low in required effort, skill, and responsibility. Therefore, what looks like a "fair" relationship between the value of the job and the wages paid for it is actually the product of linking biased job evaluation results with biased wages. In other words, as Schwab and Wichern indicated, agreement may masquerade as truth or fairness when it is actually indicating systematic bias. Rynes and Milkovich (1986) concluded that market wages, which often serve as criteria in job evaluation, can be biased by many factors. For example, geographical differences and company pay practices influence market wages, as does the supply and demand of labor, thus dispelling the myth that market wages reflect the true worth of a job.

Comparable Worth. The issue of systematic bias in job evaluation also relates to the doctrine of comparable worth. It is called a "doctrine" because it represents a philosophy of how jobs should be paid. **Comparable worth** means giving people equal pay for performing comparable work (Mahoney, 1983). This is in contrast to giving equal pay for equal work, which is the doctrine underlying the Equal Pay Act, a federal law regarding compensation. The Equal Pay Act states that men and women who perform equal work are to receive equal pay. Proponents of comparable worth believe that two jobs are rarely ever truly equal. They believe it is more reasonable to speak of jobs as having comparable or equivalent worth. Jobs that are of comparable worth should be paid the same.

To determine the worth of all jobs would require a common measuring device, such as job evaluation. However, comparable worth proponents believe that many current job evaluation methods are inherently biased against the work typically performed by women. These people point to labor statistics indicating that women on the average earn about 60 cents for every $1 earned by men. This, they assert, is de facto evidence that women are the victims of discrimination caused by job evaluation methods that unfairly undervalue the work they perform. Indeed, Arvey (1986) suggested that the factors selected for consideration in job evaluation may be biased against women. For example, the physical strength exerted in a job is often used as one factor in job evaluation. Since most men are physically stronger than most women, the rated value of female-dominated jobs may suffer on this

---

Field Note 3 *What to Compensate?*

At the core of the debate on comparable worth is the question of how the worth of a job is determined. A traditional way of determining job worth is through job evaluation. It is common to rate jobs on certain factors (such as effort and working conditions), with each rating being worth a certain number of points. The points are then summed, and the total point value of the job becomes the measure of its relative worth. Comparable worth advocates believe that the very factors on which jobs are evaluated often slant the final results in favor of jobs traditionally held by men.

For example, on the effort factor, jobs that involve heavy lifting are worth more than jobs that involve light lifting. On the working conditions factor, jobs that are performed under adverse physical conditions (such as outdoor work) are worth more than jobs performed under temperate conditions (such as an air-conditioned or heated office). Who is more likely to fill a job requiring heavy lifting—men or women? Typically men. Who is more likely to work outdoors? Typically men. Therefore, men's jobs are

more likely to be worth more points, and thus receive higher wages, than jobs traditionally filled by women. But what if we changed the very factors on which jobs are rated? Two possible factors are mental stress and the handling of sensitive/confidential information. Jobs that subject workers to high mental stress and the handling of confidential information would be worth more than jobs that don't. Secretaries often work under stressful conditions (that is, a hectic work pace and continual deadlines) and deal with confidential information. Most secretarial jobs are held by women. Therefore, depending on the job factors you wish to consider (effort and working conditions versus mental stress and confidential information), you could arrive at two quite different conclusions regarding the worth of a secretary's job. Job factors are nothing more than criteria, the criteria by which the worth of a job is determined. As stated earlier in this chapter, differences of opinion about criteria are often at the heart of many disputes. Such is certainly the case regarding comparable worth.

factor. Alternatively, many women work in jobs in which eyestrain is a problem, yet amount of eyestrain is typically not a factor included in job evaluation (see Field Note 3). Proponents of comparable worth propose the need for a bias-free system to evaluate jobs that would serve to reduce the male/female pay differential by increasing the wages paid to women.

Opponents of the doctrine of comparable worth believe there is no systematic bias operating against "female" jobs. They believe that women are as free to choose whatever jobs they want as are men; they simply settle for lower-paying jobs that allow them more latitude for other obligations, such as family duties. Economic forces are always operating in a free society. Companies that implement a comparable worth policy would be at a disadvantage for hiring some types of employees. In short, the opponents believe the job evaluation system is not at fault; rather, society has socialized men and women to pursue different types of jobs. They further believe there is no way to ever measure jobs in a way that is totally free of any values—that is, to have a totally bias-free assessment.

Most discussions of comparable worth are presented by people who feel strongly about the topic, one way or the other (England, 1992). There are currently no correct answers to this heated debate. At its core is the issue of values applied to job evaluation.

JOB PERFORMANCE CRITERIA

Desirable job performance criteria can be defined by three general characteristics; the criteria must be appropriate, stable, and practical. The criteria should be relevant and representative of the job. They must endure over time or across situations. Finally, they should not be too expensive or hard to measure. Other authors think that different issues are important—for example, the time at which criterion measures are taken (after one month on the job, six months, and so on), the type of criterion measure taken (performance, errors, accidents), and the level of performance chosen to represent success or failure on the job (college students must perform at a C level in order to graduate). Criteria are often chosen by either history or precedent; unfortunately, sometimes criteria are chosen because they are merely expedient or available.

Job performance criteria may be objective or subjective. *Objective criteria* are taken from organizational records (payroll or personnel) and supposedly do not involve any subjective evaluation. *Subjective criteria* are judgmental evaluations of a person's performance (such as a supervisor might render). Although objective criteria may involve no subjective judgment, some degree of assessment must be applied to them to give them meaning. Just knowing that an employee produced 18 units a day is not informative; this output must be compared with what other workers produce. If the average is 10 units a day, 18 units clearly represents "good" performance. If the average is 25 units a day, 18 units is not good.

Objective Criteria

Production.   Using units of production as a criterion is most common in manufacturing jobs. If an organization has only one type of job, then setting production

CNN PHOTO

A production worker making parts for a Harley-Davidson motorcycle.

SOURCE: CNN

criteria is easy. But most companies have many types of production jobs, so productivity must be compared fairly. That is, if average productivity in one job is 6 units a day and in another job it is 300 units a day, then productivities must be equated to adjust for these differences. Statistical procedures are usually used for this. Other factors can diminish the value of production as a criterion of performance. In an assembly-line job, the speed of the line determines how many units are produced per day. Increasing the speed of the line increases production. Furthermore, everyone working on the line has the same level of production. In a case like this, units of production are determined by factors outside of the individual worker. So errors that are under the worker's control may be the criterion of job performance. However, this is no cure-all for the criterion problem either. Errors are not fair criteria if they are more likely in some jobs than others. Due to automation and work simplification, some jobs are almost "goof-proof." In such jobs error-free work has nothing to do with the human factor.

Sales.   Sales are a commonly used performance criterion for wholesale and retail sales work, but variations must be considered. Using the sheer number of sales as a criterion is appropriate only if everyone is selling the same product(s) in comparable territories. A person who sells toothbrushes should sell more units than a person who sells houses. Also, someone selling tractors in Iowa should sell more than a person whose sales territory is Rhode Island. Not only is Iowa bigger than Rhode Island but also more farming is done proportionately in Iowa than in Rhode Island. Total sales volume is equally fallible as a criterion. A real estate salesperson can sell a $100,000 house in one afternoon, but how long would it take to sell $100,000 worth of toothbrushes?

The solution to these types of problems is to use norm groups for judging success. A real estate salesperson should be compared to other real estate salespeople in the same sales territory. The same holds for other sales work. If comparisons have to be drawn across sales territories or across product lines, statistical adjustments are needed. Ideally, any differences in sales performance would then be due to the ability of the salesperson, which is the basis for using sales as a criterion of job performance.

Tenure or Turnover.   Length of service is a very popular criterion in I/O psychological research. Turnover not only has a theoretical appeal (for example, Hom & Griffeth, 1995) but also is a practical concern. Employers want to hire people who will stay with the company. For obvious practical reasons, employers don't want to hire chronic job-hoppers. The costs of recruiting, selecting, and training new hires can be extremely high. Turnover is perhaps the most frequently used nonperformance criterion in the psychological literature. It is a valuable and useful criterion because it measures employment stability.

Campion (1991) suggested that many factors should be considered in the measurement of turnover. One is *voluntariness* (whether the employee was fired, quit to take another job with better promotional opportunities, or quit because of dissatisfaction with a supervisor). Another factor is *functionality* (whether the employee was performing the job effectively or ineffectively). Williams and Livingstone (1994) meta-analyzed studies that examined the relationship between turnover and performance, and concluded that poor performers were more likely to voluntarily quit their jobs than good performers.

Absenteeism. Absence from work, like turnover, is an index of employee stability. Although some degree of employee turnover is good for organizations, employee absenteeism always has bad consequences. Rhodes and Steers (1990) and Martocchio and Harrison (1993) reviewed many studies on why people are absent from work. Absence appears to be the product of many factors, including family conflicts, feelings of job dissatisfaction, alcohol and drug abuse, and personality. However, as Johns (1994) noted, employees are likely to give self-serving justifications for their absence. For example, being absent from work to care for a sick child is more socially acceptable than acknowledging deviant behavior such as drug use. Accordingly, relying on self-reports of why employees are absent can be highly inaccurate.

Absenteeism is a pervasive problem in industry; it costs employers billions of dollars a year in decreased efficiency and increased benefit payments (for example, sick leave) and payroll costs. Absenteeism has social, individual, and organizational causes, and it affects individuals, companies, and even entire industrial societies.

Accidents. Accidents are sometimes used as a criterion of job performance, although they have a number of limitations. First, accidents are used as a measure mainly for blue-collar jobs. (While white-collar workers can be injured at work, the frequency of such accidents is small.) Thus, accidents are a measure of job performance for only a limited sample of employees. Second, accidents are difficult to predict, and there is little stability or consistency across individuals in their occurrence (Senders & Moray, 1991). Third, accidents can be measured in many ways: number of accidents per hours worked, miles driven, trips taken, and so on. Different conclusions can be drawn depending on how accident statistics are calculated. Employers do not want to hire people who, for whatever reason, will incur job-related accidents. But in the total picture of job performance, accidents are not used as a criterion as often as production, turnover, or absence.

Theft. Employee theft is a major problem facing organizations, with annual losses estimated to be $200 billion annually by the year 2000 (Greenberg & Scott, 1996). Hollinger and Clark (1983) administered an anonymous questionnaire about theft to employees at three types of organizations. The percentages of employees who admitted to stealing from their employer were 42% in retail stores, 32% in hospitals, and 26% in manufacturing firms. Thus, employee theft is a pervasive and serious problem. From an I/O psychologist's perspective, the goal is to hire people who are unlikely to steal from the company, just as it is desirable to hire people who have a low probability of having accidents. The problem with theft as a criterion is that we know very little about the individual identity of employees who do steal. Hollinger and Clark based their survey results on anonymous responses. Furthermore, those responses came from people who were willing to admit they stole from the company. Those employees who were stealing but chose not to respond to the survey or who did not admit they stole were not included in the theft results. Greenberg and Scott (1996) asserted that some employees resort to theft as a means of offsetting perceived unfairness in how their employer treats them.

A drawback in using theft as a job performance criterion is that only a small percentage of employees are ever caught stealing. The occurrence of theft often has to be deduced on the basis of calculated shortages from company inventories of supplies and products. In addition, many companies will not divulge any information about theft to outside individuals. Although companies often share information on such criteria as absenteeism and turnover, theft records are too sensitive to reveal. Despite these limitations, I/O psychologists regard theft as an index of employment suitability, and we will probably witness much more research on theft in the years ahead.

Subjective Criteria

Subjective criteria are judgments made of an employee's performance. The judgment is usually a rating or ranking. For example, a supervisor might rate the employees in a department on the basis of overall effectiveness. This rating would then be the standard of job performance. Supervisor ratings are by far the most frequently used judgmental criteria; however, ratings may also be supplied by peers, subordinates, and workers themselves. The ratings may be on a general factor, such as overall effectiveness, or specific factors, such as quantity of work, quality of work, creativity, practical judgment, and so forth. Some studies have even compared judgments made by two or more sets of raters (for example, supervisors and peers) who evaluate several dimensions of behavior. Such studies normally show that certain raters are more consistent in rating certain aspects of job performance. Supervisors may agree in rating the quality of work; peers agree in rating interpersonal relations. Chapter 7 will discuss this issue in greater detail.

Because judgmental criteria are used so often, a great deal of attention has been given to improving the quality of these judgments. If the people doing the judging don't know how to make such decisions, the quality of their decisions will be very poor. Spool (1978) reviewed the research on training people to make more accurate judgments of behavior. He found that people can indeed learn to be accurate evaluators. People who are more involved and interested in evaluating behavior make more careful and accurate judgments. Research (for example, Pursell, Dossett, & Latham, 1980) revealed that a one-day training program can greatly enhance people's skills in observing and interpreting behavior.

From this discussion, it is clear that no single measure of job performance is totally adequate. While each criterion may have merit, each can also suffer from weakness along other dimensions. For instance, few people would say that an employee's absence has no bearing on overall job performance, but no one would say that absence is a complete measure of job performance. Absence, like production or job level, is but one piece of the broader picture. Don't be discouraged that no one criterion meets all our standards. It is precisely because job performance is multidimensional (and each single dimension is a fallible index of overall performance) that we are compelled to include many relevant aspects of work in establishing criteria.

Wine tasters at a California winery. What are the criteria for judging wine?
SOURCE: Courtesy of Chateau Julien Winery

Relationships Among Job Performance Criteria

Several job performance criteria can be identified for many jobs, and each criterion frequently assesses a different aspect of performance. These criteria are usually independent of one another. If they were all highly positively intercorrelated—say, $r = .80$ or $r = .90$—there would be no point in measuring them all. Knowing an employee's status on one criterion would give his or her status on the others. Several studies have tried to identify interrelationships among criteria.

A classic study by Seashore, Indik, and Georgopoulos (1960) revealed multiple job performance criteria and also showed that the criteria were relatively independent of one another. For example, Seashore and associates studied delivery men on whom five job performance criteria were available: productivity (objectively measured by time standards), effectiveness (subjectively rated based on quality of performance), accidents, unexcused absences, and errors (based on the number of packages not delivered). The correlations among these five criteria appear in Table 3–5. The data show that the five criteria were relatively independent of one another. The highest correlations were found among the variables of productivity, effectiveness, and errors (.28, $-.26$, and $-.32$). These results demonstrate that there really is no single measure of overall performance on the job; each criterion measures a different facet.

Bommer, Johnson, Rich, Podsakoff, and MacKenzie (1995) conducted a meta-analytic study examining the relationship between subjective ratings of job performance and objective measures of job performance. They reported an aver-

TABLE 3–5 *Intercorrelations among five criterion variables*

	Productivity	Accidents	Absences	Errors
Effectiveness	.28	−.02	−.08	−.32
Productivity	.12	−.01	−.26	
Accidents	.03	−.18		
Absences	.15			

SOURCE: Adapted from "Relationship Among Criteria of Job Performance" by S. E. Seashore, B. P. Indik, and B. S. Georgopoulos, 1960, *Journal of Applied Psychology, 44*, pp. 195–202.

age correlation of .39 between these two types of assessment. Quite clearly, you can arrive at different conclusions about a person's job performance depending on how you choose to assess it.

There is also a relationship between job level and the number of criteria needed to define job performance. Lower-level, relatively simple jobs do not have many dimensions of performance; more complex jobs have many. In fact, the number of job performance criteria can separate simple jobs from complex ones. Manual laborers who unload trucks might be measured by only three criteria: attendance (they have to show up for work), errors (they have to know how to stack the material), and speed. More complex jobs, as in the medical field, might be defined by as many as 15 independent criteria. The more complex the job, the more criteria are needed to define it and the more skill or talent a person has to have to be successful.

Dynamic Criteria

The concept of **dynamic criteria** refers to levels of job performance criteria that change over time. Its significance is that job performance is not stable or consistent over time, and this dynamic quality of criteria adds to the complexity of making personnel decisions.

Consider Figure 3–6, which shows the levels of three job performance criteria—productivity, absence, and accidents—over an eight-year period. The time period represents a person's eight-year performance record on a job. You will notice that the patterns of behavior for the three criteria differ over time. The individual's level of accidents is stable over time. In this case, accidents is not a dynamic criterion because of its stability over time. However, a very different pattern emerges for the other two criteria. The individual's level of productivity increases over the years, more gradually in the early years and then more dramatically in the later years. Absence, on the other hand, follows the opposite pattern. The employee's absence was greatest in the first year of employment and progressively declined over time. Absence and productivity are dynamic criteria, while accidents is a static criterion.

When a job applicant is considered for employment, the organization attempts to predict how well that person will perform on the job. A hire/no hire decision is then made on the basis of this prediction. If job performance criteria are static (like

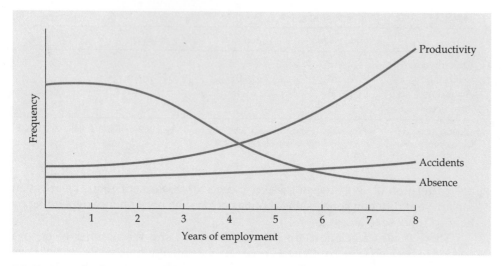

FIGURE 3–6   *Performance variation in three criteria over an eight-year period*

accidents in Figure 3–6), the accuracy of the prediction is aided by the stability of the behavior. However, if job performance criteria are dynamic, a critical new element is added to the decision, *time*. It may be that initially productivity would not be very impressive, but over time the employee's performance would rise to and then surpass a satisfactory level. The concept of dynamic criteria is equivalent to "hitting a moving target," as the level of the behavior being predicted is continuously changing. Furthermore, the pattern of change may be different *across* individuals. That is, for some people productivity may start off low and then get progressively higher, while for others the pattern may be the reverse.

To what degree are dynamic criteria an issue in I/O psychology? The profession is divided. Some researchers (e.g., Barrett, Alexander, & Doverspike, 1992; Barrett, Caldwell, & Alexander, 1985) contend that job performance criteria aren't very dynamic at all, and the problem is not severe. Others (Deadrick & Madigan, 1990; Hofmann, Jacobs, & Baratta, 1993) provide research findings indicating that various criteria of job performance do change over time, as does their predictability. Hulin, Henry, and Noon (1990) believe that time is an under-researched topic in understanding the relationship between concepts. They assert that over time some criteria become more predictable while others decline in predictability. The investigation into dynamic criteria requires examining complex research questions that do not lend themselves to simple answers. In general, if criteria operate in a dynamic fashion over time, this underscores our need to be sensitive to the difference between prediction of behavior in the short term versus the long term.

EXPANDING OUR VIEW OF CRITERIA

Throughout the history of I/O psychology, our concept of criteria has been primarily *job-related*. That is, we have defined the successful employee primarily in terms of how well he or she meets the criteria for performance on the job.

However, as Borman (1991) noted, it is possible to consider ways employees contribute to the success of the work group or organization that are not tied directly to *job* performance criteria. One example is being a "good soldier"—demonstrating conscientious behaviors that demonstrate concern for doing things properly for the good of the organization. Another example is prosocial behavior—doing little things that help other people perform their jobs more effectively.

Brief and Motowidlo (1986) found that in some organizations it is explicitly stated that part of an employee's own job performance is to support and provide guidance to other individuals. A military combat unit is one such example. However, in many other organizations, going beyond the call of duty to help out a fellow employee or the organization is outside the formally *required* job responsibilities. The proclivity of some individuals in a group to help out others can at times be detrimental to the organization, as when a group member helps a co-worker with a problem and in the process fails to complete an important job-related task. Nevertheless, Borman concluded, in most cases the welfare of the organization is enhanced by prosocial behavior. The topic of prosocial behavior will be discussed in more detail in Chapter 9.

Research on prosocial behavior shows that the criteria for a successful employee may transcend performance on job tasks. It is thus conceivable that some employees may be regarded as valuable members of the organization because they are quick to assist others and be "good soldiers"—and not because they perform their own job tasks very well. The concept of a "job" has historically been a useful framework for understanding one's duties and responsibilities, and accordingly for employees to be held accountable for meeting job performance criteria. However, there are circumstances and conditions (such as demonstrating prosocial behavior) that lead I/O psychologists to question the value of criteria strictly from a job perspective. Some researchers believe it is more beneficial to think of employees as performing a series of roles for the organization, as opposed to one job. The relationship between roles and jobs will be discussed in Chapter 8.

CONCLUDING COMMENTS

Austin and Villanova (1992) traced the history of criterion measurement in I/O psychology over the past 75 years. The conceptual problems associated with accurate criterion representation and measurement of today are not all that different from those faced at the birth of I/O psychology. However, I believe I/O psychology may be at the dawn of a new criterion for determining the successful employee. Actually, it is not a *new* criterion as much as a reemphasis and generalization of a criterion that has always been with us. The growing importance of this criterion results from the changing conditions of contemporary work, the subject of Chapter 16. The criterion has two components: the ability to learn and grow, and the willingness to do so. The world of work is constantly changing, and the rate of change is accelerating. Few things are as they used to be. Technological advances in communication and production have revolutionized the way we work. The means by which organizations utilize their employees has changed likewise. No longer are we in static, stable environments. New employees are required to be able to learn quickly on the job. Older employees are expected (and in some cases required) to learn new systems and ways of conducting business. We have entered an era of required growth and learning. The successful employee must have not only the capacity to learn and grow, but also the desire and willingness to do so. As our work environment continues to change, so too must employees change with them. Offices and factories are becoming learning sites, and employees must engage in "learning a living." Ways of measuring both the capacity to learn and the willingness to learn will be discussed in the next chapter.

CASE STUDY ◆ Who Gets the Scholarship?

The Rippowam High School principal convened a panel of three teachers to make a most important decision. A local company wanted to award a $10,000 college scholarship to "the most outstanding senior" in the class, with the recipient to be determined by the high school. Walter Plant, Sandra Meltzer, and Jerry Driscoll were given the assignment to select the scholarship recipient. They agreed to meet at 2:30 to discuss their assignment.

Driscoll opened the meeting: "I wish we had more to go on than what they gave us. A student can be outstanding in many ways."

"Well, I assume grades are the most important factor," said Meltzer. "Why don't we start out with the ranking of all students based on their grade point averages? I'd be hard pressed to award ten thousand dollars to any student other than the class valedictorian."

"I don't think it's that easy," said Plant. "I am far more impressed with a student who gets a B+ in honors physics than someone who gets an A in basket weaving. While a student's grade point average is certainly a good measure of academic accomplishments, it's tainted by the difficulty of the courses taken."

"That's not the only problem with the grade point average," Driscoll warned. "I've got some students in my homeroom who will graduate with the minimum number of hours, and I've got some others who branched out and took more than the minimum. I think we should give some consideration to the total number of hours taken in the curriculum."

A deep frown appeared on Plant's face. "I don't see why we should penalize the student who did only what was required by the school. We specify what is needed for graduation, and the students have to comply. I never discourage a student from sticking to the minimum, and I don't think we should devalue their performance for having done so."

"Maybe we're getting too hung up with grades and hours," said Meltzer. "Suzanne Millord won first prize in the regional science fair competition. Shouldn't something like that count, too? I'm more impressed with that than with an A in any class."

"You know," Plant commented, "we are forgetting about some other things, too. How about civic activities, such as participation in student government or interest clubs? We encourage student involvement in these activities to make for a more well-rounded education. I don't feel we should ignore them when it comes time to make an award."

"I feel those activities have their own rewards," said Driscoll. "We want to give this scholarship to the best student, not the most socially active one."

"While we're at it," mused Plant, "how about athletic participation? We stress physical education as well as social and intellectual development. Maybe we should also include interscholastic athletics. We've got some outstanding athletes in this school, and who's to say that 'most outstanding' can't be defined in terms of athletics?"

"I hardly think this was designed to be an athletic scholarship," Meltzer grumbled. "If you want to make it more complicated, why not throw in financial need; ten thousand dollars is a lot of money, and some families could use it more than others."

Driscoll stared out the window. He knew it would be a long afternoon.

Questions
1. What do you think the conceptual criteria should be in making a scholarship determination?
2. What are some sources of criterion deficiency and contamination in the actual criteria being discussed?
3. Would the criteria for selecting the "most outstanding student" be more biased or less biased by the inclusion of financial need? Why?
4. Do you think it's more difficult to identify what the appropriate criteria are, or to determine how to weight the criteria once they have been identified? Why?
5. If you had been invited to this meeting, what suggestions would you make to help the teachers reach a decision?

INFOTRAC ARTICLES

1. *Success*, August 1998 v45 n8 p24(2)
   Close the steal mill: 12 surefire ways to stop wayward employees from swiping your profits.
   A discussion of employee theft in the workplace and recommended ways to reduce the problem.
2. *The Journal of Psychology*, July 1997 v 131 n4 p417(9)
   Rational or symbolic: A field study of the impact of group discussion on job evaluation ratings. Edilberto F. Montemayor & John A. Fossum
   A study that compares job evaluation scores based on group discussions and scores from individual evaluators.
3. *Across the Board*, July–August 1998 v35 n7 p16(8)
   You're hired.
   An article that explains the high cost of employee turnover and the associated repercussions of turnover throughout the company.
4. *British Medical Journal*, Oct 5, 1996 v313 n7061 p874(4)
   Absence from work. Rob B. Briner
   An article that explains the causes of employee absenteeism, including cultural, occupational, and cross-industrial differences.
5. *Executive Female*, Jan–Feb 1995 v18 n1 p46(5)

How to get paid + more really. Martha Burke & Josh Feltman
A discussion of the salary differential between male and female managers, addressing the gender-based pay inequities in society.

6. *The Quill*, May 1997 v 85 n4 p40(7)
   To print or not. Charles M. Mayo, Judith Sylvester, & LeAnne Daniels
   A case study of the criteria 16 top media managers used to decide to publish a story about a controversial subject.

7. *Success*, Oct 1997 v45 i10 p52(1)
   GOOD REP. Arthur R. Pell
   A discussion of the criteria for hiring successful sales representatives.

8. *Sex Roles: A Journal of Research*, June 1996 v34 n11–12 p878(3)
   Masculinity reconstructed: Changing the rules of manhood—at work, in relationships, and in family life. Denise Twohey
   A review of a book that addresses the changing criteria by which men and women evaluate each other in personal relationships.

Predictors: Psychological Assessments

4

MAJOR CHAPTER OBJECTIVES

◆ Identify the major types of reliability and
 what they measure.

◆ Understand the major representations of
 validity and what they measure.

◆ Know the major types of psychological tests
 categorized by administration and content.

◆ Explain the role of psychological testing in
 making assessments of people, including
 ethical issues and predictive accuracy.

◆ Explain nontest predictors such as
 interviews, assessment centers, work
 samples, biographical information, and letters
 of recommendation.

◆ Understand the new and controversial
 methods of assessment.

A **predictor** is any variable used to forecast a criterion. In weather prediction, barometric pressure can be used to forecast rainfall. In medical prediction, body temperature can be used to predict (or diagnose) illness. In I/O psychology, we seek predictors of job performance criteria as indexed by productivity, absenteeism, turnover, and so forth. There is no limit to the variables we can use for this purpose. Although we do not use tea leaves and astrological signs as fortune-tellers do, we have explored a multitude of devices as potential predictors of job performance criteria. This chapter will review the variables traditionally used, examine their success, and discuss some professional problems inherent in their application.

ASSESSING THE QUALITY OF PREDICTORS

All predictor variables, like other measuring devices, can be assessed in terms of their quality or goodness. We can think of several features of a good measuring device. We would like it to be consistent and accurate; that is, it should repeatedly yield precise measurements. In psychology we judge the goodness of our measuring devices by two psychometric criteria: reliability and validity. If a predictor is not both reliable and valid, it is useless.

Reliability

Reliability is the consistency or stability of a measure. A measure should yield the same estimate on repeated use when the measured trait has not changed. Even though that estimate may be inaccurate, a reliable measure will always be consistent. Three major types of reliability are used in psychology to assess the consistency or stability of the measuring device, and a fourth assessment of reliability is often used in I/O psychology.

Test-Retest Reliability.   **Test-retest reliability** is perhaps the simplest assessment of a measuring device's reliability. We measure something at two points in time and compare the scores. We can give an IQ test to the same group of people at two different times and then correlate the two sets of scores. This correlation is called a **coefficient of stability** because it reflects the stability of the test over time. If the test is reliable, those who scored high the first time will also score high the second time, and vice versa. If the test is unreliable, the scores will "bounce around" in such a way that there is no similarity in individuals' scores between the two trials.

When we say a test (or any measure) is *reliable*, how high should the reliability coefficient be? The answer is the higher the better. A test cannot be too reliable. As a rule, reliability coefficients around +.70 are professionally acceptable, though some frequently used tests have test-retest reliabilities only in the +.50 range. "Acceptable" reliability is also a function of the test's use. A test used for individual prediction (to diagnose brain impairment) should be much more reliable than a test used for group prediction (to measure the attitudes of a work group).

Equivalent-Form Reliability.   A second type of reliability is parallel or **equivalent-form reliability.** Here a psychologist develops two forms of a test to measure the same attribute and gives both forms to a group of people. He or she then correlates the two scores for each person. The resulting correlation, called a **coefficient of equivalence,** reflects the extent to which the two forms are equivalent measures of the same concept. Of the three major types of reliability, this type is the least popular because it is usually challenging to come up with one good test, let alone two. Many tests do not have a "parallel form." However, in intelligence and achievement testing (to be discussed shortly), equivalent forms of the same test are sometimes available. If the resulting coefficient of equivalence is high, the tests are equivalent and reliable measures of the same concept. If it is low, they are not.

Internal-Consistency Reliability.   The third major assessment is the **internal-consistency reliability** of the test—the extent to which it has homogeneous content. Two types of internal-consistency reliability are typically computed. One is called split-half reliability. Here a test is given to a group of people, but in scoring the test (though not administering it), the researcher divides the items in half, into odd- and even-numbered items. Each person thus gets two sets of scores (one for each half), which are correlated. If the test is internally consistent, there should be a high degree of similarity in the responses (that is, right or wrong) to the odd- and even-numbered items. All other things being equal, the longer a test is, the greater is its reliability.

A second technique for assessing internal-consistency reliability is to compute one of two coefficients: Cronbach's alpha or Kuder-Richardson 20 (KR20). Both procedures are similar, though not statistically identical. Conceptually, each test item is treated as a minitest. Thus, a 100-item test consists of 100 minitests. The response to each item is correlated with the response to every other item. A matrix of interitem correlations is formed whose average is related to the homogeneity of the test. If the test is homogeneous (the item content is similar), it will have a high internal-consistency reliability. If the test is heterogeneous (the items cover a wide variety of concepts), it is not internally consistent and the resulting coefficient will be low. Internal-consistency reliability is frequently used to assess a test's homogeneity of content in I/O psychology.

Inter-Rater Reliability.   When assessments are made on the basis of raters' judgments, it is possible for the raters to disagree in their evaluations. Two different raters may observe the same behavior yet evaluate it differently. The degree of correspondence between judgments or scores assigned by different raters is most commonly referred to as **inter-rater reliability,** although it has also been called *conspect reliability.* There are some situations in which raters must exercise judgment in arriving at a score. Two examples are multiple raters analyzing a job and multiple interviewers evaluating job candidates. The score or rating depends not only on the job or candidate but also on the persons doing the rating. The raters' characteristics may produce distortions or errors in their judgments. Estimation of inter-rater reliability is usually expressed as a correlation and reflects the degree of agreement among the ratings. Evidence of high inter-rater agreement establishes a basis to conclude that the behavior was reliably observed, and in turn we conclude that such observations are accurate. It is a frequently assessed type of reliability in I/O psychology.

Validity

Reliability refers to consistency and stability of measurement; validity refers to accuracy. A valid measure is one that yields "correct" estimates of what is being assessed. However, another factor distinguishes validity from reliability. Reliability is inherent in a measuring device, but validity depends on the use of a test. **Validity** refers to the test's appropriateness for predicting or drawing inferences about criteria. A given test may be highly valid for predicting employee productivity but totally invalid for predicting employee absenteeism. In other words, it would be appropriate to draw inferences about employee productivity from the test but inappropriate to draw inferences about absenteeism.

There are several different ways of assessing validity, and they all involve determining the appropriateness of a measure (test) for drawing inferences.

Criterion-Related Validity.

As its name suggests, **criterion-related validity** refers to how much a predictor relates to a criterion. It is a frequently used and important type of validity in I/O psychology. The two major kinds of criterion-related validity are concurrent and predictive.

In measuring *concurrent* criterion-related validity, we are concerned with how well a predictor can predict a criterion at the same time, or concurrently. Examples abound. We may wish to predict a student's grade point average on the basis of a test score. So we collect data on the grade point averages of many students, and then we give them a predictor test. If the predictor test is a valid measure of grades, there will be a substantial correlation between test scores and school grades. We can use the same method in an industrial setting. We can predict a worker's level of productivity (the criterion) on the basis of a test (the predictor). We collect productivity data on a current group of workers, give them a test, and then correlate their scores with their productivity records. If the test is of value, we can draw an inference about a worker's productivity on the basis of the test score. In measurements of concurrent validity, there is no time interval between collecting the predictor and criterion data. The two variables are assessed concurrently, which is how the method gets it name.

Because the criterion for concurrent validity is always available at the time of using the predictor, why bother to collect predictor data at all? Because predictors usually provide a simpler, quicker, or less expensive substitute for criterion data. For example, say the criterion is a salesperson's yearly dollar volume. A predictor that could predict a certain level of sales volume would be much more efficient than having all job applicants serve as salespeople for a year.

In measuring *predictive* criterion-related validity, we collect predictor information and use it to forecast future criterion performance. A college might use a student's high school class rank to predict the criterion of overall college grade point average four years later. A company could use a test to predict whether job applicants will complete a six-month training program.

Concurrent validity is used to diagnose existing status on some criterion, and predictive validity is used to forecast future status. The primary distinction is the time interval between collecting the predictor and criterion data. The conceptual significance of predictive and concurrent validity in the context of personnel selection will be discussed in the next chapter. The logic of criterion-related validity is straightforward. We determine whether there is a relationship between predictor scores and criterion scores based on a sample of employees for whom we have both sets of scores. If there is a relationship, we use scores on those predictor variables to select applicants on whom there are no criterion scores. Therefore, we can predict the applicants' future (and thus unknown) criterion performance from their known test scores based on the relationship established through criterion-related validity.

When predictor scores are correlated with criterion data, the resulting correlation is called a **validity coefficient.** Although an acceptable reliability coefficient is in the .70–.80 range, a desirable validity coefficient is in the .30–.40 range. Validity coefficients less than .30 are not uncommon, but those over .50 are rare. Just as a predictor cannot be too reliable, it also cannot be too valid. The greater the correlation between the predictor and the criterion, the more we know about the criterion on the basis of the predictor. By squaring the correlation coefficient (r), we can calculate how much variance in the criterion we can account for by using the predictor. For example, if a predictor correlates .40 with a criterion, we can explain 16% (r^2) of the variance in the criterion by knowing the predictor. A correlation of 1.0 indicates perfect prediction (and complete knowledge). However, as Lubinski and Dawis (1992) noted, tests with moderate validity coefficients are not necessarily flawed or inadequate. The results attest to the complexity of human behavior. Our behavior is influenced by factors not measured by tests, such as motivation and luck. We should thus have realistic expectations regarding the validity of our tests.

Some criteria are difficult to predict no matter what predictors are used; other criteria are fairly predictable. Similarly, some predictors are consistently valid and are thus used quite often. Other predictors do not seem to be of much predictive value no matter what the criteria are, and thus they fall out of use. Usually, however, certain predictors are valid for predicting only certain criteria. Later in this chapter there will be a review of the predictors typically used in I/O psychology and an examination of how valid they are for predicting criteria.

Content Validity. **Content validity** involves the degree to which a predictor covers a representative sample of the behavior being assessed. It is limited mainly to psychological tests, but it could also be extended to interviews or other predictors. Historically, content validity was most relevant in achievement testing. Achievement tests are designed to indicate how well a person has mastered a specific skill or area of content. In order to be "content valid," an achievement test on Civil War history, for example, must contain a representative sample or mix of test items covering the domain of Civil War history, such as battles, military and political figures, and so on. If all of the questions were about the dates of famous battles, the test would not be a balanced representation of the content of Civil War history. If a person scores high on a content-valid test of Civil War history, we can infer that he or she is very knowledgeable about the Civil War.

How do we assess content validity? Unlike criterion-related validity, we do not compute a correlation coefficient. Content validity is assessed by subject matter experts in the field the test covers. Civil War historians would first define the domain of the Civil War and then write test questions covering it. These experts would then decide how content valid the test is. Their judgments could range from "not at all" to "highly valid." Presumably, the test would be revised until it showed a high degree of content validity.

A similar type of validity based on people's judgments is called **face validity.** This is concerned with the appearance of the test items: Do they look appropriate for such a test? Estimates of content validity are made by test developers; estimates of face validity are made by test takers. Because test developers are more knowledgeable, content validity is far more important than face validity. It is possible for a test item to be content valid but not face valid, and vice versa. In such a case, the test developers and test takers would disagree over the relevance or appropriateness of the item for the domain being assessed.

Content validity has importance for I/O psychology. Once used mainly for academic achievement testing, it is also relevant for employment testing. There is a strong and obvious link between the process of job analysis (discussed in Chapter 3) and the concept of content validity. Employers develop tests that assess the knowledge, skills, and abilities needed to perform a job. How much the content of these tests is related to the actual job is assessed by content-validation procedures. First, the domain of job behavior is specified by employees and supervisors. Then test items are developed to assess the factors needed for success on the job. The content validity of employment tests is thus a function of the extent to which the content of the job is reflected in the content of the test. Goldstein, Zedeck, and Schneider (1993) asserted that content validity is established by the careful linkage between the information derived from job analysis and its associated use in test construction. Content validity purports to reveal that the knowledges and skills required to perform well on the job and on the employment test are interchangeable.

Construct Validity.   Construct validity is the most theoretical and complex type of validity. A **construct** is a theoretical concept we propose to explain aspects of behavior. Examples of constructs in I/O psychology are intelligence, motivation, anxiety, and mechanical comprehension. Because constructs are abstractions (ideas), we must have some real, tangible ways to assess them; that is, we need an actual measure of the proposed construct. A paper-and-pencil test of intelligence is one way to measure the psychological construct of intelligence. **Construct validity,** in turn, refers to the extent our measure of intelligence (the test) is an accurate representation of the theoretical construct of intelligence. A test that manifests a high degree of construct validity is regarded as faithfully assessing the construct in question.

The construct validity process is the quest to ascertain the linkage between what is measured by the test and the theoretical construct. Let us assume we wish to understand the construct of intelligence, and to do so we develop a paper-and-pencil test that we believe assesses that construct. To establish the degree of construct validity of our test, we want to compare scores on our test with known measures of intelligence, such as verbal, numerical, and problem-solving ability. If our test is a faithful assessment of intelligence, then the scores on our test should converge with these other known measures of intelligence. More technically, there should be a high correlation between the scores from our new test of intelligence

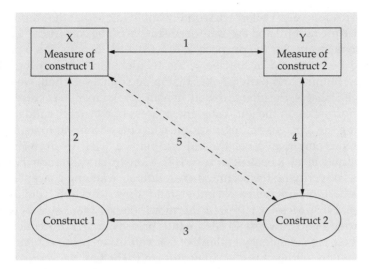

FIGURE 4–1   *Inferential linkages in construct validation*

SOURCE: From "Validity of Personnel Decisions: A Conceptual Analysis of the Inferential and Evidential Bases" by J. F. Binning and G. V. Barrett, 1989, *Journal of Applied Psychology, 74*, p. 480.

and the existing measures of intelligence. These correlation coefficients are referred to as *convergent validity coefficients* because they reflect the degree to which these scores converge (or come together) in assessing a common concept, intelligence. Likewise, scores on our test should not be related to concepts that we know are not related to intelligence, such as physical strength, eye color, and gender. That is, scores on our test should diverge (or be separate) from these concepts that are un-related to intelligence. More technically, there should be very low correlations be-tween the scores from our new test of intelligence and these concepts. These correlation coefficients are referred to as *divergent validity coefficients* because they reflect the degree to which these scores diverge from each other in assessing unre-lated concepts. Other statistical procedures may also be used to establish the con-struct validity of a test. After collecting and evaluating much information about the test, we accumulate a body of evidence supporting the notion that the test measures a psychological construct. In turn, we say the tests manifest a high de-gree of construct validity. Tests that manifest a high degree of construct validity are among the most widely respected and frequently used assessment instruments in I/O psychology.

Binning and Barrett (1989) described construct validation as the process of demonstrating evidence for five linkages or inferences, as illustrated in Figure 4–1. Figure 4–1 shows two empirical measures and two constructs. *X* is a measure of construct 1, as a test of intelligence purports to measure the psychological con-struct of intelligence. *Y* is a measure of construct 2, as a supervisor assessment of an employee's performance purports to measure the construct of job performance. Linkage 1 is the only one that can be tested directly because it is the only inference involving two variables that are directly measured (*X* and *Y*). In assessing the con-struct validity of *X* and *Y*, one would be most interested in assessing linkages 2 and 4, respectively. That is, we would want to know that the empirical measures of X and Y are faithful and accurate assessments of the constructs (1 and 2) they purport to measure. For the purpose of constructing theories of job performance, one would be interested in linkage 3, the relationship between the two constructs. Finally, Binning and Barrett noted that in personnel selection, we are interested in linkage 5; that is, the inference between an employment test score and the domain of performance on the job. Thus, the process of construct validation involves examining the linkages among multiple concepts of interest to us. We always operate at the empirical level (X and Y), yet we wish to draw inferences at the conceptual level (constructs 1 and 2). Construct validation is the continuous process of verifying the accuracy of an inference among concepts for the purpose of furthering our ability to understand those concepts (Pulakos, Borman, & Hough, 1988). Messick (1995) furthermore believes that issues of construct validation extend into how test scores are interpreted and the consequences of test use.

There is the tendency to think of test validity as being equivalent to an on/off light switch—either a test is valid or it isn't. The temptation to do so is probably based on other uses of the word *valid* in our language, such as whether or not a person has a valid driver's license. However, this either/or type of thinking about test validity is not correct. It is more accurate to think of test validity as a dimmer light switch. Tests manifest various degrees of validity, ranging from none at all to a great deal. At some point along the continuum of validity, practical decisions have to be made about whether a test manifests "enough" validity to warrant its use. To carry the light switch analogy further, a highly valid test sheds much light on the object (construct) we seek to understand. Thus, the test validation process is the ongoing act of determining the amount of "illumination" the test projects on the construct.

PSYCHOLOGICAL TESTS AND INVENTORIES

Psychological tests and inventories have been the most frequently used predictors in I/O psychology. The difference between the two is that in a **test** the answers are either right or wrong; in an **inventory** there are no right or wrong answers. Usually, though, the terms *tests* and *psychological testing* refer to the family of tests and inventories.

History of Psychological Testing

Testing has a long multinational history in the field of psychology. Sir Francis Galton, an English biologist, was interested in human heredity. During the course of his research, he realized the need for measuring the characteristics of biologically related and unrelated persons. He began to keep records of people on such factors as keenness of vision and hearing, muscular strength, and reaction time. By 1880, he had accumulated the first large-scale body of information on individual differences. He was probably the first scientist to devise systematic ways of measuring people. In 1890 the American psychologist James Cattell introduced the term *mental test*. He devised an early test of intelligence based on sensory discrimination and reaction time. Hermann Ebbinghaus, a German psychologist, developed math and sentence-completion tests and gave them to schoolchildren. In 1897 he reported that the sentence-completion test was related to the children's scholastic achievement.

The biggest advances in the early years of testing were made by the French psychologist Alfred Binet. In 1904 the French government appointed Binet to study procedures for the education of retarded children. To assess mental retardation, Binet (in collaboration with Theodore Simon) developed a test of intelligence. It consisted of 30 problems covering such areas as judgment, comprehension, and reasoning, which Binet regarded as essential components of intelligence. Later revisions of this test had a larger sampling of items from different areas. Binet's research on intelligence testing was continued by the American psychologist Lewis Terman, who in 1916 developed the concept of IQ (intelligence quotient). These early pioneers paved the way for a wide variety of tests that would be developed in the years to come, many of which were used by industrial psychologists to predict job performance. Although most of the early work in testing was directed at assessing intellect, testing horizons expanded to include aptitude, ability, interest, and personality.

Types of Tests

Tests can be classified either by their administration or by their content. Both methods will be used here.

Speed versus Power Tests.   **Speed tests** have a large number of easy questions; the questions are so easy that the test taker will always get them right. The test is timed (for example, 5-minute limit) and has more items than can possibly be answered in the allotted time period. The total score on such a test is the number of items answered and reflects the test taker's speed of work.

Power tests have questions that are fairly difficult; that is, the test taker cannot get them all right. Usually there is no time limit. The total score on such a test is the number of items answered correctly. Most tests given in college are power tests. If time limits are imposed, they are mostly for the convenience of the test administrator.

Individual versus Group Tests.   **Individual tests** are given to only one person at a time. Such tests are not common because of the amount of time needed to administer them to all applicants. For example, if a test takes one hour and ten people are to take it, ten hours of administration time will be required. The benefits of giving such a test must be balanced against the costs. Certain types of IQ tests are individually administered, as are certain tests for evaluating high-level executives. In these tests the administrator has to play an active part (for example, asking questions, demonstrating an object) as opposed to just monitoring them.

Group tests are administered to several people simultaneously and are the most common type of test. They do not involve the active participation of an administrator. The Army Alpha and Beta tests were early group intelligence tests used in World War I. Most tests used in educational and industrial organizations are group tests because they are efficient in terms of time and cost.

Paper-and-Pencil versus Performance Tests.   **Paper-and-pencil tests** are the most common type of test used in industrial and educational organizations. They do not involve the physical manipulation of objects or pieces of equipment. The questions asked may require answers in either multiple-choice or essay form. The individual's physical ability to handle a pencil should not influence his or her score on the test. The pencil is just the means by which the response is recorded on a sheet of paper.

In a **performance test** the individual has to manipulate an object or a piece of equipment. The score is a measure of the person's ability to perform the manipulation. A typing test and a test of finger dexterity are examples of performance tests. Sometimes paper-and-pencil and performance tests are used jointly. To get a driver's license, for example, most people have to pass both a written and a behind-the-wheel performance test.

ETHICAL STANDARDS IN TESTING

To prevent the misuse of psychological tests, the American Psychological Association has developed guidelines. The ethics of psychological testing are a major responsibility of psychologists, as seen in the APA code of professional ethics (*Standards for Educational and Psychological Testing*, 1985). Maintaining ethical standards in testing is one of the more important ethical issues confronting the entire profession of psychology (American Psychological Association, 1992).

Depending on the purpose of the testing, test users must have certain qualifications. Sometimes the user must be a licensed professional psychologist, particularly in clinical psychology. But in industry fewer qualifications are required to administer employment tests. To prevent their misuse and to maintain test security, restrictions are also placed on who can buy the tests. However, Moreland et al. (1995) concluded that educational efforts will ultimately be more effective in promoting good testing practices than efforts to limit the use of tests. Test publishers are discouraged from giving away free samples or printing detailed examples of test questions as sales promotions, which could invalidate future test results.

Other ethical issues are the invasion of privacy and confidentiality. **Invasion of privacy** occurs when a psychological test reveals more information about a person than is needed to make an informed decision. Tests should be used for precise purposes; they should not be used to learn information irrelevant to performing the job. For example, if a mechanical comprehension test is used to hire mechanics, the company should not also give an interest inventory just to learn about potential employees' hobbies and recreational activities. Using an interest inventory that has no relationship to job performance could be an invasion of the applicant's privacy.

Confidentiality refers to who should have access to test results. When a person takes an employment test, he or she should be told the purpose of the test, how the results will be used, and which people in the company will see the results. Problems arise if a third party (another prospective employer, for example) wants to know the test results. The scores should be confidential, unless the test taker gives a written release.

Another problem in this area is the retention of records. Advances in computer technology have made it possible to store large quantities of information about people. Who should have access to this information, and what guarantees are there that it will not be misused? The results of an intelligence test taken in sixth grade may become part of a student's permanent academic record. Should a potential employer get the results of this elementary school test? Furthermore, the test probably couldn't predict job performance, so why would anyone want the results? These types of questions are central to problems of confidentiality.

SOURCES OF INFORMATION ABOUT TESTING

Because testing is a rapidly changing area, it is important to keep up with current developments in the field. Old tests are revised, new tests are introduced, and some tests are discontinued. Fortunately, several key references are available. Perhaps the most important source is the series of *Mental Measurement Yearbooks* (MMY). The MMY was first published in 1938, and it has been revised in roughly a five-year cycle. Each yearbook includes tests published during a specified period, thus supplementing the tests reported in previous yearbooks. The *Thirteenth Mental Measurements Yearbook* (Impara & Plake, 1998), for example, deals mainly with tests that appeared between 1993 and 1996. Each test is critically reviewed by an expert in the field and documented with a complete list of references. Information about price, publisher, and versions of the test is also given. The MMY series is the most comprehensive review of psychological tests available in the field.

Less-detailed books, such as *Tests in Print* (Murphy, Conoley, & Impara, 1994), resemble bibliographies and help locate tests in the MMY. Other resource books review tests relevant for more restricted applications, as in business and industry (Hogan & Hogan, 1990; Sweetland & Keyser, 1991). Some psychological journals review specific tests, and various professional test developers publish test manuals. The test manual should give the information needed to administer, score, and evaluate a particular test, as well as data on the test's reliability and validity. Although these manuals are useful, they are usually not as complete and critical as reviews in the MMY.

The test user has an obligation to use the test in a professional and competent manner. Tests should be chosen with extreme care and concern for the consequences of their use. Important decisions are based on test scores, and the choice of test is equally important. A test should be thoroughly analyzed before it is considered for use.

TEST CONTENT

Tests can be classified according to their content. The next sections will discuss the major types of constructs assessed by tests used in industry. Also presented will be information on how valid the various types of tests have been in personnel selection as documented from their use in the psychological literature.

Intelligence Tests

Intelligence or cognitive ability is perhaps the most heavily researched construct in all of psychology. Interest in the assessment of intelligence began more than 100 years ago. Despite the length of time the construct of intelligence has been assessed, however, there remains no singular or standard means to assess it. Furthermore, recent research suggests intelligence is even more complex than we have believed.

What is generally agreed upon regarding intelligence? Intelligence traditionally has been conceptualized as having a singular, primary basis. This concept is known as **general mental ability** and is symbolized by g. By assessing g, we gain an understanding of a person's general level of intellectual capability. Tests that measure g have been found to be predictive of performance across a wide range of occupations (e.g., Ree, Earles, & Teachout, 1994). The criterion-related validity of g is impressive, oftentimes in the range of .40–.60. Many researchers believe it is the single most diagnostic predictor of future job performance. Simply put, if we could know only one attribute of a job candidate upon which to make a prediction, we would want an assessment of intelligence. General intelligence is regarded to be a ubiquitous predictor of a wide variety of performance criteria, prompting Brand (1987) to observe: "g is to psychology what carbon is to chemistry" (p. 257). Furthermore, Hunter (1986) showed that the predictive power of intelligence *increases* with higher degrees of job complexity.

However, while research clearly supports the validity of general intelligence as a predictor, some researchers believe that conceptualizing intelligence merely as g encourages oversimplification of the inherent complexity of intelligence. Murphy (1996) asserted that intelligence is not a unitary phenomenon, and other dimensions of intelligence are also worthy of our consideration. Ackerman (1992), for example, reported superior predictive power of multiple abilities over general intelligence in complex information-processing tasks, as in the job of air traffic controller. Ackerman and Kanfer (1993) developed a useful selection test for air traffic controllers based in large part on the assessment of spatial ability. From an I/O psychology perspective, therefore, the controversy regarding the assessment of intelligence rests primarily on the adequacy of measuring (just) general intelligence (g) or assessing multiple cognitive abilities in forecasting job behavior.

In a recent development, Sternberg (1997a) proposes a triarchic (or three-part) theory of intelligence. Sternberg contends that there are multiple kinds of intelligence. He posits academic intelligence as representing what intelligence tests typically measure, such as fluency with words and numbers. Table 4–1 shows some sample test questions from a typical intelligence test. However, Sternberg proposes two other important kinds of intelligence that conventional intelligence tests don't measure. One is *practical intelligence,* which he states is the intelligence needed to be competent in the everyday world and is not highly related to academic intelligence. The second (nontraditional) kind of intelligence Sternberg calls *creative intelligence,* which pertains to the ability to produce work that is both novel (i.e., original or unexpected) and appropriate (i.e., useful). Manifestations of this kind of intelligence are critical in writing, art, and advertising. Sternberg believes that all three kinds of intelligence may be necessary for lifelong learning and success, depending upon the nature of our vocation. As Daniel (1997) stated, our means of assessing intelligence (i.e., a test) are heavily guided by how we view what we are trying to assess (see Field Note 1). A view of intelligence dominated by academic intelligence will lead us to assess that particular kind to the relative exclusion of

TABLE 4–1 *Sample test questions for a typical intelligence test*

1. What number is missing in this series?
   3–8–14–21–29–(?)

2. SHOVEL is to DITCHDIGGER as SCALPEL is to:
   (a) knife (b) sharp (c) butcher (d) surgeon (e) cut

practical and creative intelligence. Wagner (1997) asserted we need to expand our criteria to show the various manifestations of intelligence, such as over time and over different aspects of job performance (e.g., task proficiency versus successfully interacting with other people).

Finally, Sternberg (1997b) proposes the concept of *thinking styles*. A style is not an ability, but rather a preferred way of using the abilities one has. Whereas an ability reflects how well someone can do something, a style reflects how someone *likes* to do something. Sternberg asserts that schools and employers value certain ways of thinking more than others. People whose ways of thinking do not match those valued by the organization are usually penalized. Individuals may be practically identical in their mental ability and yet have very different styles. "People whose styles match those expected in certain situations are judged as having higher levels of mental ability, despite the fact that what is present is not ability, but fit between those people's styles and the tasks they are confronting" (p. 19).

Sternberg proposed a theory of mental self-government that mirrors the mechanisms government uses to organize society. Just as government has three branches (legislative, executive, and judicial), people have the equivalent

---

Field Note I *What Is Intelligence?*

The construct of intelligence is highly complex, perhaps more complex than researchers have previously realized. Theorists have long debated whether intelligence is a unitary concept or whether there are various forms of intelligence, such as verbal and quantitative. Tests of intelligence are designed and interpreted based on these theoretical formulations. The questions on traditional tests of intelligence have a correct answer and only one correct answer. Examples include the answers to questions about mathematics and vocabulary. However, recent research by Sternberg suggests that there are other manifestations of intelligence. Many problems in life do not have a single correct answer; other problems may have more than one correct answer. Furthermore, in real life, solutions to problems are not so much "correct" and

"incorrect" as they are "feasible" and "acceptable." Examples include dealing with interpersonal problems at the individual level and with global problems at the national level. It takes intelligence to solve such problems, but these types of questions do not appear on typical tests of intelligence. There is an adage that "young people are smart and old people are wise." Perhaps wisdom is a form of intelligence that is derived through many years of successfully dealing with problems that lack single correct solutions. The capacity to derive feasible and acceptable solutions to complex problems that have no single correct answers is, as current research supports, a legitimate form of intelligence. Accordingly, tests of intelligence should be modified to also permit assessments of this form of intelligence.

"Let's put it this way—if you can find a village without an idiot, you've got yourself a job."

SOURCE: Reprinted from *The Industrial-Organizational Psychologist.*

"branches" (or styles) of their thinking and working. Legislative people like to come up with their own ways of doing things and prefer to decide for themselves what they will do and how they will do it. The legislative style is particularly conducive to creativity. Executive people like to follow rules and prefer problems that are highly structured. The executive style tends to be valued both in school and in business because executive styles generally do what they are told. Judicial people like to evaluate rules and procedures, and they prefer problems in which one analyzes and evaluates things and ideas. Some of their preferred occupations are judge, critic, and consultant. According to Sternberg, success in life is a function of not only ability but also the match between how you use your abilities and the demands of your environment. He has developed paper-and-pencil tests for assessing one's preferred style.

As can be inferred from the foregoing discussion, the construct of intelligence is highly complex. From an I/O psychology perspective, we are concerned with the degree to which cognitive ability forecasts job performance. Murphy (1996) stated: "Research on the validity of measures of cognitive ability as predictors of job performance represents one of the 'success stories' in I/O psychology" (p. 6). The question becomes, Can we enhance predictive power by considering cognitive abilities beyond g? Furthermore, if Sternberg's theory of thinking styles is useful, we should assess not only cognitive abilities but also how we prefer to use those abilities. The future of intelligence for personnel selection may thus involve not only assessments of how much ability we have but also how we use it.

FIGURE 4–2   *Sample test questions from the Bennett Test of Mechanical Comprehension*

SOURCE: From Bennett Mechanical Comprehension Test. Copyright 1942, 1967–1970, 1980 by the Psychological Corporation. Reproduced by permission. All rights reserved.

Mechanical Aptitude Tests

Mechanical aptitude tests require a person to recognize which mechanical principle is suggested by a test item. One of the more popular tests of mechanical reasoning is the Bennett Test of Mechanical Comprehension (Bennett, 1980). The test is a series of pictures reflecting various mechanical facts and principles. Sample questions from the Bennett Test are shown in Figure 4–2. Other tests of mechanical comprehension have also been developed.

Muchinsky (1993) reported that the Bennett Test was most effective in predicting job performance of manufacturing employees who produce electromechanical components. A concurrent criterion-related validity coefficient of .38 was reported in the study. Schmitt, Gooding, Noe, and Kirsch (1984) reported an average validity coefficient of .27 for mechanical aptitude tests across many studies. The highest validity coefficients are typically found for vehicle operators as well as trade and craft employees.

Sensory/Motor Ability Tests

Sensory ability tests assess visual acuity, color vision, and hearing sensitivity. These abilities are related to success in certain types of jobs. Perhaps the best-known test of visual acuity is the Snellen Eye Chart, a display with rows of letters that get increasingly smaller. The test taker stands 20 feet away from the chart and reads each row until the letters are indistinguishable. A ratio is then computed to express acuity:

$$\text{Acuity} = \frac{\text{Distance at which a person can read a certain line of print (usually 20 feet)}}{\text{Distance at which the average person can read the same line of print}}$$

For example, if the smallest line of print a person can read from 20 feet is the line most people can read from 40 feet, then the person's score is 20/40. Each eye is tested separately, and normal vision is 20/20.

The most common way to measure hearing sensitivity is with an instrument called an *audiometer*. An audiometer produces tones of different frequencies and loudness. The tone is gradually raised in intensity. When the test taker signals that the note has been heard, the examiner records the level of intensity on an audiogram, which shows the intensity of sound needed to hear tones of different frequency. An audiogram is prepared for each ear. Hearing loss is detected by comparing one person's audiogram with the results from a tested population.

Researchers have also devised paper-and-pencil tests of perceptual accuracy. In these tests two stimuli are presented, and the test taker must judge whether they are the same or different. The stimuli may be numbers or names. Table 4–2 shows the types of items in a perceptual accuracy test.

Tests of motor ability assess fine or gross motor coordination. Two frequently used motor ability tests are the Purdue Pegboard and the Crawford Small Parts Dexterity Test. In the first part of the Purdue Pegboard, the test taker places pins into small holes in a pegboard using the right hand first, then the left hand, and then both hands together. In the second part, the pins are again placed in the holes but with the addition of collars and washers. The first part of the test measures manual dexterity; the second part measures finger dexterity. In the Crawford Small Parts Dexterity Test, the test taker first places pins in holes in the board and then places metal collars over the pins. In the second part of the test, a screwdriver is used to insert small screws after they have been placed by hand into threaded holes.

Sensory/motor ability tests manifest a typical validity coefficient between .20 and .25. They are most predictive of job success in clerical occupations.

Personality Inventories

Unlike the previously cited tests, which have objective answers, personality inventories do not have right or wrong answers. Test takers answer how much they agree with certain statements ("People who work hard get ahead"). In personality inventories similar types of questions normally make up a scale, which reflects a person's introversion, dominance, confidence, and so on. Items are scored according to a

TABLE 4–2 *Sample test question from a typical perceptual accuracy test*

Which pairs of items are identical?
    17345290—17342590
    2033220638—2033220638
    WPBRAEGGER—WPBREAGGER
    CLAFDAPKA26—CLAPDAFKA26

predetermined key such that responding one way or another to an item results in a higher or lower score on a respective scale. These scale scores are then used to predict job success. The basic rationale is that successful employees possess a particular personality structure, and scales reflective of that structure become the basis for selecting new employees.

The use of personality inventories for predicting job success has undergone a complete cycle. Originally, psychologists thought personality variables were related to job performance. At least on logical grounds, this perspective makes a lot of sense because some people seemingly have the "wrong personality" for a job. Psychologists used large omnibus personality inventories developed by clinical psychologists to forecast job success. The classic personality inventory of this type is the Minnesota Multiphasic Personality Inventory (MMPI) developed in 1943. The MMPI consists of 550 statements that must be answered "true," "false," or "cannot say." The inventory is scored in terms of ten clinical scales (for example, depression or schizophrenia). The inventory has since been revised (MMPI-2) to reflect advances in personality theory and measurement.

Personality inventories such as the original MMPI were used for many years for personnel selection; in fact, they were overused or misused. They were used indiscriminately to assess a candidate's personality, even when there was no established relationship between test scores and job performance. Soon personality inventories came under attack for invading the test taker's privacy. Some scales of a personality inventory may be useful for personnel selection decisions, but information unrelated to employment success may be revealed in the other scales. Guion and Gottier (1965) concluded that the evidence on personality inventories did not support their use for selecting personnel. Furthermore, influential psychologists questioned the value of personality assessments in understanding and predicting behavior. The upshot of these criticisms was a marked curtailment in the use of personality inventories for personnel selection.

However, psychologists continued to believe that personality variables were influential in job performance. Previously, they had predicted job performance with conventional personality inventories that were never really intended for industrial use with "normal" adults. Personality inventories like the original MMPI were developed to make clinical diagnoses and to differentiate normal from abnormal personalities. Consequently, the scales weren't refined enough to make accurate predictions about job candidates. Accordingly, I/O psychologists have recently begun developing new personality inventories designed exclusively for use with working populations. The results have been far more impressive than the previous research on clinical personality inventories. For example, Gough (1984) successfully developed a personality scale to measure managerial potential, as defined by such factors as being organized, capable, mature, and self-confident. Hogan, Hogan, and Busch (1984) created a personality scale designed to measure the disposition that is helpful in dealing with other people, as indexed by such factors as being thoughtful, considerate, and cooperative. Today personality assessment is one of the fastest growing areas in personnel selection.

A comprehensive five-factor model of personality structure was proposed as being useful for predicting job performance. It is often referred to as the "Big 5" theory of personality. Extensive empirical support for its validity was provided by McCrae and Costa (1987) and R. T. Hogan (1991). Personality inventories have also been developed based upon this model—for example, the NEO-PI (P. T. Costa, 1996) and the Hogan Personality Inventory (Hogan & Hogan, 1992). The five factors are extraversion, emotional stability, agreeableness, conscientiousness, and openness to experience. Barrick and Mount (1991) concluded from a meta-analysis that extraversion is a valid predictor of performance in occupations involving social interactions, such as managers and salespeople. Conscientiousness shows consistent correlation with job performance criteria for all occupations and across different cultures (Salgado, 1997). These five factors are a durable framework for considering personality structure among people of many nations, and they have prompted McCrae and Costa (1997) to refer to their pattern of interrelationships as a "human universal." Similar empirical support for personality measures as predictors of job performance have been reported by Tett, Jackson, and Rothstein (1991) and Schmit and Ryan (1993). Furthermore, such personality measures provide *incremental* predictive validity beyond measures of intelligence.

A long-standing concern with personality tests for personnel selection is that job applicants might not give truthful responses. Rather, applicants may fake their responses to give what they believe are socially desirable responses. Ones, Viswesvaran, and Reiss (1996) examined this issue through a meta-analysis of research studies and concluded that faking does not have a significant influence on the validity of personality tests for personnel selection. They believe a person who would attempt to "fake" a personality selection test would also be inclined to "fake" job performance. Hogan, Hogan, and Roberts (1996) concluded that personality tests should be used in conjunction with other information, particularly the applicant's technical skills, job experience, and ability to learn. More specifically, Ackerman and Heggestad (1997) believe "abilities, interests, and personality develop in tandem, such that ability level and personality dispositions determine the probability of success in a particular task domain, and interests determine the motivation to attempt the task" (p. 239). Simply put, the influence of personality in job performance should not be overestimated, but it should also not be underestimated.

Integrity Tests

The reemergence of personality assessment for personnel selection is also demonstrated by the recent development and growing use of honesty or integrity tests. Honesty tests are designed to identify job applicants who will not steal from their employer or otherwise engage in counterproductive behavior on the job. These tests are paper-and-pencil tests and generally fall into one of two types (Sackett & Wanek, 1996). In the first type, an *overt integrity test*, the job applicant clearly understands that the intent of the test is to assess integrity. The test typically has two sections: One deals with attitudes toward theft and other forms of dishonesty (namely, beliefs about the frequency and extent of employee theft, punitiveness toward theft, perceived ease of theft, and endorsement of common rationalizations about theft), and a second section deals with admissions of theft and other illegal activities (such as dollar amounts stolen in the past year, drug use, gambling). There is some evidence (Cunningham, Wong, & Barbee, 1994) that the responses to such tests are distorted by the applicants' desire to create a favorable impression. The second type of test, called a *personality-based measure,* makes no reference to theft. These tests contain conventional personality assessment items that have been found to be predictive of theft. Because this type of test does not contain obvious references to theft, it is less likely to offend job applicants. These tests are primarily assessments of conscientiousness and emotional stability personality factors (Hogan & Brinkmeyer, 1997).

The research findings on the validity of integrity tests is positive. Bernardin and Cooke (1993) found that scores on an honesty test successfully predicted theft among convenience store employees. Collins and Schmitt (1993) conducted a study of incarcerated offenders convicted of white-collar crimes, such as embezzlement and fraud. Compared to a control sample of employees in upper-level positions of authority, offenders had greater tendencies toward irresponsibility, lack of dependability, and disregard of rules and social norms. In a meta-analytic review, Ones, Viswesvaran, and Schmidt (1993) concluded that integrity tests effectively predict the broad criterion of organizationally disruptive behaviors like theft, disciplinary problems, and absenteeism. Self-reported measures of counterproductive behavior were found to be more predictable than objective measures (such as detected workplace theft). However, Ones and Viswesvaran (1998) found gender differences in integrity tests, with women scoring higher than men. Differences in honesty scores by race and age were negligible.

Problems are inherent in validating tests designed to predict employee theft. First, the issue is very sensitive, and many organizations don't care to make information public. Organizations may readily exchange information on employee absenteeism, but employee theft statistics are often confidential. Second, the criterion isn't really theft as much as being caught stealing, because many thefts go undetected. Third, the percentage of employees caught stealing in an organization is usually very small—2% to 3% is the norm. Consequently, there are statistical difficulties in trying to predict what is essentially a rare event. Furthermore, Camara and Schneider (1994) noted that test publishers classify integrity tests as proprietary, meaning that access to these tests is not provided to researchers interested in assessing their validity. Some people argue that the value of integrity tests for personnel selection is greater than the typical validity coefficient suggests. They argue that applicants who pass an integrity test are sensitized to the organization's concern for honesty and that other theft-reducing measures (such as internal surveillance systems) may well be used to monitor employees. Such procedures reduce the occurrence of employee theft but are not evidenced in the predictive accuracy of the honesty test.

Physical Abilities Testing

Psychological assessment has long been directed toward cognitive abilities and personality characteristics. However, research (e.g., Fleishman & Quaintance,

1984) has also examined the assessment of physical abilities, and in particular how these physical abilities relate to performance in some jobs. J. Hogan (1991a) presented the set of physical abilities relevant to work performance. These are some of the abilities:

- *Static strength*—the ability to use muscle force to lift, push, pull, or carry objects
- *Explosive strength*—the ability to use short bursts of muscle force to propel oneself or an object
- *Gross body coordination*—the ability to coordinate the movement of the arms, legs, and torso in activities where the whole body is in motion
- *Stamina*—the ability of the lungs and circulatory (blood) systems of the body to perform efficiently over time

An analysis (J. Hogan, 1991b) revealed that the total set of physical abilities could be reduced to three major constructs: strength, endurance, and movement quality. These three constructs account for most of the variation in individual capacity to perform strenuous activities. Arvey, Landon, Nutting, and Maxwell (1992) established the construct validity of a set of physical ability tests for use in the selection of entry-level police officers. The findings suggested that two factors—strength and endurance—underlie performance on the physical ability tests and performance on the job of police officers. The results further showed that women scored considerably lower than men on the physical ability tests. However, the findings did not suggest how much importance physical abilities compared to cognitive abilities should be accorded in the selection decision.

In general the research on physical abilities reveals they are related to successful job performance in physically demanding jobs, such as firefighters, police officers, and factory workers. Future research needs to consider the effects of aging on the decline of physical abilities and the legal implications of differences in physical abilities across groups.

Multiple-Aptitude Test Batteries

Tests may also be categorized on the basis of their structural composition rather than their item content. Test "batteries" consist of many of the types of tests already discussed: intelligence, mechanical aptitude, personality, and so on. These tests are usually quite long, often taking several hours to complete. Each part of the test measures such factors as intellectual ability and mechanical reasoning. The tests are useful because they yield a great deal of information that can be used later for hiring, placement, training, and so forth. The major disadvantages of the tests are the cost and time involved. The two most widely known multiple-aptitude batteries are the Armed Services Vocational Aptitude Battery (ASVAB) and the Differential Aptitude Test (DAT).

Computerized Adaptive Testing

One of the major advances in psychological testing is called Computerized Adaptive Testing (CAT), or "tailored testing" (Weiss & Vale, 1987). Here is how it works: CAT is an automated test administration system that uses a computer. The test items appear on the video display screen of the computer terminal, and the examinee answers using the keyboard. Each test question presented is prompted by the response to the previous question. The first question given to the examinee is of medium difficulty. If the answer given is correct, the next question selected from the item bank of questions has been precalibrated to be slightly more difficult. If the answer given to that question is wrong, the next question selected by the computer is somewhat easier. And so on.

The purpose of the CAT system is to get as close a match as possible between the question-difficulty level and the examinee's demonstrated ability level. In fact, by the careful calibration of question difficulty, one can infer ability level on the basis of the difficulty level of the questions answered correctly. CAT systems are based on complex mathematical models. Proponents believe that tests can be shorter (because of higher precision of measurement) and less expensive and have greater security than traditional paper-and-pencil tests. The military is the largest user of CAT systems, testing thousands of examinees monthly. In a rare example of CAT being used in the private sector, Overton, Harms, Taylor, and Zickar (1997) found their CAT system did achieve greater test security than traditional paper-and-pencil tests. However, the amount of testing time required was actually greater than with traditional methods.

Although CAT systems represent the high-tech approach to psychological assessment, I doubt that they will soon make all paper-and-pencil tests obsolete. In fact, Bartram (1993) suggested that advances in computer technology have outpaced advances in psychological test theory. First, CAT systems were designed to assess abilities and aptitudes. They are not typically used for personality or interest measurement. Second, they obviously require elaborate computer programs, which not all organizations possess. Third, they are most cost efficient for very large employers like the military. And fourth, the mathematical foundations of such systems (called "Item Response Theory") are still a matter of professional debate. CAT systems will never completely replace traditional testing, but they do represent the cutting edge of psychological assessment. Computers have made possible great advances in science, as evidenced in I/O psychology by this major breakthrough in testing. Furthermore, with the creation of national information networks the traditional practice of using psychological tests late in the selection process may change as it becomes possible to have access to test results at the time a job application is made. There have also been recent technical advances in the use of pen-based notebook computer testing (Overton, Taylor, Zickar, & Harms, 1996).

The Value of Testing

As Haney (1981) observed, society has tended to imbue psychological tests with some arcane mystical powers, which, as the evidence reviewed in this chapter indicates, is totally unwarranted. There is nothing mysterious about psychological tests; they are merely tools to help us make better decisions than could be made without them. The psychological testing profession has a large share of critics. Criticism relates more to the inappropriate use of good tests than to poor quality. For example, since the MMPI was never originally intended to predict managerial success, we really shouldn't be too surprised or unhappy when we find it does not. Testing has been oversold as a solution to problems. Many people have decried the "tyranny of testing"—the fact that critical decisions (say, entrance into a college or professional school) that affect an entire lifetime are based on a single test. Testing has its place in our repertoire of diagnostic instruments; tests should help us meet our needs and not be the master of our decisions. This is sound advice that psychologists have long advocated. However, it is advice that both the developers and users of psychological tests have occasionally ignored or forgotten.

What we have learned about psychological tests from an I/O perspective is that some tests are useful in forecasting job success and others are not. As an entire class of predictors, psychological tests have been modestly predictive of job performance. Yet some authors (for example, Hunter & Hunter, 1984) believe that, all things considered, psychological tests have outperformed all other types of predictors across the full spectrum of jobs. Single-validity coefficients in excess of .50 are as unusual today as they were in the early years of testing. While test validity coefficients are not as high as we would like, it is unfair to condemn tests as useless. Also, keep in mind that validity coefficients are a function of both the predictor and the criterion. A poorly defined and constructed criterion will produce low-validity coefficients no matter what the predictor is like. Because of the limited predictive power of tests, psychologists have had to look elsewhere for forecasters of job performance. The balance of this chapter will examine other predictors that psychologists have investigated.

INTERVIEWS

In terms of sheer frequency, interviews are the most popular method of selecting employees. The popularity of the employment interview may be enhanced by legal problems with paper-and-pencil tests. Although most court cases regarding discrimination have involved paper-and-pencil tests, interviews along with other predictors are still regarded as a test by the government and, as such, are subject to the same judicial review. Interviews are more subjective than tests, so chances for unfair discrimination seem to be greater. Because interviews are used so often in employment decisions, many research studies on them have been conducted. Some of the major issues related to the employment interview will be discussed next.

Degree of Structure

Interviews can be classified along a continuum of structure, where **structure** is defined as the amount of procedural variability across job applicants. In a highly unstructured interview, the interviewer typically asks the applicant to "tell me about yourself" and the applicant can provide responses ranging from hobbies and goals to previous work experience. The interviewer may or may not ask follow-up questions and has a great deal of discretion in what questions are asked (Whetzel & McDaniel, 1997).

Highly structured interviews have predetermined procedures for eliciting, observing, and evaluating responses. The questions to be asked have been determined in advance, and all applicants are asked the same questions. It is not unusual for the interviewer to use a standardized rating scale to assess the answers given by each candidate. In reality, most employment interviews rest somewhere along the continuum between the "highly unstructured" and the "highly structured" interview. However, research results indicate the preferability of the structured interview over the unstructured type.

Campion, Palmer, and Campion (1997) examined procedures to increase the degree of structure in the interview. Among the suggestions are to base the questions on an analysis of the job, to limit prompting by the interviewer, to rate the answers given to each question asked, and to use multiple interviewers per candidate. Campion et al. reported that while some techniques increase structure, such as limiting prompting and not accepting any questions from the applicant, neither the interviewer nor the applicant likes being so constrained. Thus, while these procedures reduce the likelihood that different applicants are treated unequally in the interview, they also produce negative reactions among the participants. In a study that examined interview structure and litigation outcomes, Williamson et al. (1997) reported that organizations were more likely to win when their interviews were job related (e.g., the interviewer was familiar with the job requirements) and based on standardized administration (e.g., minimal interviewer discretion) and the interviewer's decision was reviewed by a superior.

Despite these reasons for supporting the use of the structured interview, Dipboye (1997) reported there are also reasons that unstructured interviews have value to the organization. A primary reason is that interviews can serve purposes besides assessing the candidate's suitability for a job. They also provide an opportunity for the interviewer to convey information about the organization, its values, and its culture. The unstructured interview can be akin to a ritual conveying to others the important attributes of the organization and sending the message that great care is being taken to select a qualified applicant. Dipboye concluded that perhaps a semistructured interview procedure may be the best compromise for meeting the multiple purposes of the employment interviews.

Situational Interviews

Situational interviews present the applicant with a situation and ask for a description of the actions he or she would take in that situation. Some situational interviews focus on hypothetical, future-oriented contexts in which the applicants are asked how they would respond if they were confronted with these problems. Other situational interviews focus on how the applicants have handled situations in the past that required the skills and abilities necessary for effective performance on the job. Pulakos and Schmitt (1995) referred to the latter type of interviews as "experienced-based," and they offered the following examples to illustrate the difference in focus (p. 292):

- *Experience-based question:* Think about a time when you had to motivate an employee to perform a job task that he or she disliked but that you needed the individual to do. How did you handle that situation?

♦ *Situational question:* Suppose you were working with an employee who you knew greatly disliked performing a particular job task. You were in a situation where you needed this task completed, and this employee was the only one available to assist you. What would you do to motivate the employee to perform the task?

The candidate's responses to such questions are typically scored on the type of scale shown in Figure 4–3. The interviewer has to use his or her best judgment to evaluate the candidate's response because there is clearly no one correct answer to the question. Each candidate responds to several such situational questions, and the answers to each question might be evaluated on different dimensions, such as "Taking Initiative" and "Problem Diagnosis."

The situational interview grows in frequency of use and has been found particularly helpful in evaluating candidates for supervisory jobs. Latham and Finnegan (1993) reported that the use of the situational interview as a selection method was a source of pride among those who passed and were hired. The current employees who had gone through it themselves believed the people being hired were well qualified for the job. There is also recent evidence (Weekley & Jones, 1997) that situational judgments can be assessed through video-based tests. Thus, the use of situational contexts, which was originally developed through the interview format, is now being expanded with different technologies.

The interview remains one of the most (if not the most) commonly used personnel selection methods. Arvey and Campion (1982) postulated three reasons for its persistent use. First, the interview really is more valid than our research studies indicate. However, due to methodological problems and limitations in our research, we can't demonstrate how valid it actually is (Dreher, Ash, & Hancock, 1988). Second, people generally are likely to place confidence in highly fallible interview judgments; that is, we are not good judges of people, but we think we are—a phenomenon called the *illusion of validity*. Finally, although the interview may not be highly valid for selection, it serves other personnel functions unrelated to employee selection, such as selling candidates on the value of the job and of the organization as an attractive employer. Whatever the reasons for the interview's popularity, few companies are willing to do something as important as extending a job offer without first seeing a person "in the flesh."

ASSESSMENT CENTERS

Assessment centers involve evaluating job candidates, most typically for managerial-level jobs, using several methods and raters. They were originally developed by researchers at AT&T who were interested in studying the lives of managers over the full duration of their careers. **Assessment centers** are a group-oriented, standardized series of activities that provide a basis for judgments or predictions of human behaviors believed or known to be relevant to work performed in an organizational setting. They may be a physical part of some organizations, such as special rooms designed for the purpose. They may also be located in a conference center away from the normal workplace. Because these centers are expensive, they

Low	*Medium*	*High*
Responses showed limited awareness of possible problem issues likely to be confronted. Responses were relatively simplistic, without much apparent thought given to the situation.	Responses suggested considerable awareness of possible issues likely to be confronted. Responses were based on a reasonable consideration of the issues present in the situation.	Responses indicated a high level of awareness of possible issues likely to be confronted. Responses were based on extensive and thoughtful consideration of the issues present in the situation.
1	2 3 4	5

FIGURE 4–3 *Example of rating scale for scoring a situational interview*

have been used mainly by large organizations; however, private organizations now conduct assessment center appraisals for smaller companies.

Here are four characteristics of the assessment center approach:

1. Those employees selected to attend the center (the assessees) are usually management-level personnel the company wants to evaluate for possible promotion, transfer, or training. Occasionally, organizations send management applicants to the center and then use appraisal information for selection.
2. Assessees are evaluated in groups of 10 to 20. They may be divided into smaller groups for various exercises, but the basic strategy is to appraise individuals against the performance of others in the group.
3. Several raters (the assessors) do the evaluation. They work in teams and collectively or individually recommend personnel action (for example, selection, promotion). Assessors may be psychologists, but usually they are company employees unfamiliar with the assessees. They are often trained in how to appraise performance. The training may last from several hours to a few days.
4. A wide variety of performance appraisal methods are used. Many involve group interactions—for example, leaderless group discussions in which leaders "emerge" through their degree of participation in the exercise. Other methods include in-basket tests, projective personality inventories, personal history information forms, and interviews. The program typically takes from one to several days.

Given the variety of tests, the assessee provides substantial information about his or her performance. Raters evaluate the assessees on a number of performance dimensions judged relevant for the job in question. These dimensions involve leadership, decision making, practical judgment, and interpersonal relations skills—the typical performance dimensions for managerial jobs. Based on these evaluations, the assessors prepare a summary report for each assessee and then feed back portions of the report to the assessee. Raters forward their recommendations for personnel action to the organization for review and consideration.

Assessment centers offer promise for identifying persons with potential for success in management. Assessment centers seem to be successful in their major goal of selecting high-talent people. Nevertheless, not all of the research results are totally positive. Drakely, Herriot, and Jones (1988) found that biographical data predicted the success of British navy officers in training as well as the overall assessment rating of a lengthy assessment center procedure did. Pynes and Bernardin (1989) reported that paper-and-pencil tests of cognitive ability had greater validity than assessment center ratings for the selection of police officers. One critical factor seems to be the criterion against which assessment center ratings are validated. For example, Borman (1982) and Tziner and Dolan (1982) found that assessment center ratings were predictive of success in military training and far superior in validity to interviews or psychological tests. We have known for a long time that assessment center ratings predict the criterion of promotability. Thus, assessment ratings have the capacity to identify individuals who will "get ahead" in the organization. However, Turnage and Muchinsky (1984) found that assessment center ratings were not predictive of actual on-the-job performance measures, as indexed by 21 criteria of supervisory performance. Assessment ratings more strongly predict advancement than performance. In a survey of organizations that use assessment centers, Spychalski, Quinones, Gaugler, and Pohley (1997) reported that while organizations made considerable use of assessment center ratings for selection, promotion, and development programs, most organizations do not assess the validity of the ratings.

Assessment center evaluations are particularly susceptible to criterion contamination from several sources. One source is basing overall judgments of performance on many evaluation methods (tests, interviews, life history forms, and so on). The validity of the evaluations may stem from the validity of these separate appraisal methods; that is, a valid interview or test might be just as capable of forecasting later job success as the resulting evaluation. But because the incremental value of these methods is "buried" in the overall assessor judgments, it is debatable how much assessors' ratings contribute to predicting future performance beyond these separate methods. There is also evidence (Kleinmann, 1993) that assessees can fashion their behavior to impress assessors when the assessees know what dimensions of their performance are being evaluated.

Klimoski and Strickland (1977) proposed a second source of contamination that is far more subtle. They contended that assessment center evaluations are predictive because both assessors and company supervisors hold common stereotypes of the effective employee. Assessors give higher evaluations to those who "look" like good management talent, and supervisors give higher evaluations to those who "look" like good "company" people. If the two sets of stereotypes are held in common, then (biased) assessment center evaluations correlate with (biased) job performance evaluations. The danger is that organizations may hire and promote those who fit the image of the successful employee. The long-term effect is an organization staffed with people who are mirror images of one another. Opportunity is greatly limited for creative people who "don't fit the mold" but who might be effective if given the chance.

After reviewing the literature on assessment centers, Klimoski and Brickner (1987) concluded that assessment evaluations are indeed valid but I/O psychologists still do not really know why. The authors proposed five possible explanations.

1. *Actual criterion contamination.* Companies use assessment evaluations to make decisions regarding promotions, pay raises, and rated job performance, so it is hardly surprising that assessment evaluations would predict such criteria.

2. *Subtle criterion contamination.* As explained by Klimoski and Strickland (1977), both assessors and company supervisors hold common stereotypes of the successful employee, so biased assessment evaluations are related to biased performance evaluations.

3. *Self-fulfilling prophecy.* Companies designate their "up-and-coming" employees to attend assessment centers, and after assessment these same people are indeed the ones who get ahead in the company.

4. *Performance consistency.* People who succeed in work-related activities do so in many arenas—in assessment centers, in training, on the job, and so on. They are consistently good performers, so success in assessment relates to success on the job.

5. *Managerial intelligence.* The skills and abilities needed to be successful in assessment centers and on the job have much in common. Such talents as verbal skills, analytic reasoning, and well-developed plans of action are acquired and cultivated by more intellectually capable people. The authors refer to this construct as "managerial intelligence."

Research on assessment centers has been evolving. Early research addressed whether assessment evaluations were predictive of job success and found they were. More recent research addresses the limitations of this method of assessment and the reasons that assessment evaluations are predictive. As our knowledge about assessment centers continues to grow, we are beginning to address some complex and intriguing questions of both theoretical and practical significance.

WORK SAMPLES AND SITUATIONAL EXERCISES

Work Samples

Motowidlo, Hanson, and Crafts (1997) classified **work samples** as "high-fidelity simulations," where *fidelity* refers to the level of realism in the assessment. Work samples present applicants with carefully developed examples of work-related problems and require the applicant to solve the problems as if they were on the job, but without actually putting them on the job.

An excellent example of a work sample was reported by Campion (1972), who wanted to develop a predictor of job success for mechanics. Using job analysis techniques, he learned that the mechanic's job was defined by success in the use of tools, accuracy of work, and overall mechanical ability. He then designed tasks that would show an applicant's performance in these three areas. Through the cooperation of job incumbents, he designed a work sample that involved such typical tasks as installing pulleys and belts and taking apart and repairing a gearbox. The proper steps necessary to perform these tasks were identified and given numerical values according to their appropriateness (for example, 10 points for aligning a motor with a dial indicator, 1 point for aligning it by feeling the motor, 0 points for just looking at the motor). Campion used a concurrent criterion-related validity design, and each mechanic in the shop took the work sample. Their scores were correlated with the criterion of supervisor ratings of their job performance. The validity of the work sample was excellent: It had a coefficient of .66 with use of tools, .42 with accuracy of work, and .46 with overall mechanical ability.

Campion showed that there was a substantial relationship between how well mechanics did on the work sample and how well they did on the job. In general, work samples are among the most valid means of personnel selection.

But work samples do have limitations. First, they are effective primarily in blue-collar jobs that involve either the mechanical trades (for example, mechanics, carpenters, electricians) or the manipulation of objects. They are not very effective when the job involves working with people rather than things. Second, work samples assess what a person can do; they don't assess potential. They seem best suited to evaluating experienced workers rather than trainees. Finally, work samples are time-consuming and costly to administer. Because they are individual tests, they require a lot of supervision and monitoring. Few work samples are designed to be completed in less than one hour. If there are 100 applicants to fill five jobs, it may not be worthwhile to give a work sample to all applicants. Perhaps the applicant pool can be reduced with some other selection instrument (for example, a review of previous work history). Yet, despite their limitations, work samples are quite useful in personnel selection.

Robertson and Kandola (1982) reported another advantage of work samples: Applicants respond to them very favorably. Work samples engender a positive reaction from applicants because of their high face validity. Applicants perceive a direct linkage between how well they perform on a work sample and how well they would perform on the job (that is, the concept of criterion-related validity). Indeed, Cascio and Phillips (1979) reported that one major U.S. city has instituted work-sample selection tests for many city jobs, in part because of the appeal of the method to applicants.

Situational Exercises

Situational exercises are roughly the white-collar counterpart of work samples; that is, they are used mainly to select people for managerial and professional jobs. Unlike work samples, which are designed to be replicas of the job, situational exercises mirror only part of the job. Accordingly, Motowidlo et al. (1997) referred to them as "low-fidelity simulations" because they present applicants with only a description of the work problem and require them to describe how they would deal with it.

Situational exercises involve a family of tests that in one way or another assess problem-solving ability. Two examples are the In-Basket Test and the Leaderless Group Discussion. The In-Basket Test involves having applicants sort through an in-basket of things to do. The contents are carefully designed letters, memos, brief reports, and the like that require the applicant's immediate attention and response. The applicant goes through the contents of the basket and takes the appropriate action to solve the problems presented, such as making a phone call, writing a letter, or calling a meeting. A number of observers score the applicant on such factors as productivity (how much work got done) and problem-solving effectiveness (versatility in resolving problems). The In-Basket Test is predictive of the job performance of managers and executives, a traditionally difficult group of employees to select. But a major problem with the test is that it takes up to three hours and, like a work sample, is an individual test. If there are many applicants, too much time is needed to administer the test. Schippman, Prien, and Katz (1990) reported the typical validity coefficient for the In-Basket Test is approximately .25.

In a Leaderless Group Discussion (LGD), a group of applicants (normally, two to eight) engage in a job-related discussion in which no spokesperson or group leader has been named. Raters observe and assess each applicant on such factors as individual prominence, group goal facilitation, and sociability. Scores on these factors are then used as the basis for hiring. The reliability of the LGD increases with the number of people in the group. The typical validity coefficient is in the .15–.35 range.

Although neither the In-Basket Test nor the LGD has the validity of a typical work sample, remember that the criterion of success for a manager is usually more difficult to define. The lower validities usually found in the selection of managerial personnel are as attributable to problems with the criterion and its proper articulation as anything else. However, as Motowidlo et al. noted, high-fidelity simulations (like work samples) are often very expensive to develop and use. Thus, the gains in validity that come from their use might not offset their cost. Accordingly, the authors believe that low-fidelity simulations can be adapted to a wide variety of jobs and, because of their lower cost, may be a promising alternative to the high-fidelity simulations.

BIOGRAPHICAL INFORMATION

The theory of using biographical information as a method of personnel selection is based upon our development as individuals. Our lives represent a series of experiences, events, and choices that define our development. Past and current events shape our behavior patterns, attitudes, and values. Because there is consistency in our behaviors, attitudes, and values, an assessment of these factors from our past experiences should be predictive of such experiences in the future. Biographical information assesses constructs that shape our behavior, such as sociability and ambition. To the extent these constructs are predictive of future job performance, through biographical information we assess previous life experiences that were manifestations of these constructs.

Biographical information is frequently recorded on an application blank. The application blank, in turn, can be used as a selection device on the basis of the information presented. The questions asked on the application blank are predictive of job performance criteria. Mael (1991) recommended that all biographical questions pertain to historical events in the person's life, as opposed to questions about behavioral intentions or presumed behavior in a hypothetical situation. Accordingly, the following types of questions are typically found on a biographical information questionnaire.

- How old were you when you got your first job?
- Did you ever get fired from a job?
- What was your grade point average in high school?

Some biographical information questionnaires contain as few as 20 questions; others include as many as several hundred questions. To determine which questions should be asked, the following research procedure is typically used: A performance criterion of interest is chosen, usually productivity, turnover, or absenteeism. A sample of current employees who are administered the questionnaire are divided into two groups, such as high and how productivity or high and low absenteeism. The next step is to determine whether the high- and low-criterion groups differ in the characteristics of the members. If the responses to some biographical question occur far more often in one group, then that question is predictive of job performance. For instance, suppose 80% of the high-productivity group graduated from high school and only 30% of the low-productivity group did. Then answers to the item "Did you graduate from high school?" are predictive of productivity and can be used to hire employees.

There are many examples of useful applications of biographical information. Cascio (1976) reported validity coefficients of .77 and .79 for predicting the turnover of White and Black workers, respectively. While the magnitude of these validity coefficients is extremely impressive, what is also desirable is that the biographical questionnaire method was fair to members of both racial groups. Childs and Klimoski (1986) demonstrated that selected early life experiences predicted not only later success in a job but also feelings of personal and career accomplishments throughout a lifetime. Other researchers have reported the success of biographical questionnaires in predicting salary, absenteeism, and productivity. Brown and Campion (1994) reported that job recruiters found biographical information to be a useful way to assess whether applicants possessed the attributes needed to perform the job.

While this method of personnel selection has generated considerable interest on the part of researchers (e.g., Gunter, Furnham, & Drakely, 1993; Stokes, Mumford, & Owens, 1994), there are concerns about fairness, legal issues, and honesty of responses. One aspect of the fairness problem concerns equal accessibility of the behavior or experience being questioned by all respondents. For example, assume the response to a question about participation in high school football is found to be predictive of subsequent performance on a job. The strategy would then be to include this question on an application blank to evaluate job candidates. The problem is that only men are allowed to play high school football, thereby prohibiting women from having potential access to this type of experience. Female job applicants would be disadvantaged in being evaluated by this question. The problem is not that women *didn't* have this experience but that they *couldn't* have it (i.e., women didn't have equal access). The "solution" to this problem is not to ask different questions of male and female applicants because laws governing fair employment practice emphasize consistency of treatment to all job applicants.

Another concern is that the questions should not be invasive. Invasiveness addresses whether the respondent will consider the item content to be an invasion of his or her privacy. As Nickels (1994) noted, items inquiring about religious affiliations, marital status, or dating habits are potentially invasive. Mael, Connerley, and Morath (1996) reported two types of biodata questions that are regarded as intrusive: a question that refers to an event that could have been explained away if the applicant had the chance to do so and a question with a response that is not reflective of the type of person the respondent has since become. Questions that are

Field Note 2 *Inappropriate Question?*

Biographical items sometimes lack content validity for the job in question even though they manifest empirical criterion-related validity. The potential irrelevance of biographical questions is always a concern in personnel selection. Here is a case in point.

A city had developed a biographical inventory that was to be used along with some psychological tests to evaluate police officers for promotion to police detectives. All the questions in the biographical inventory were predictive of job performance as a detective, as determined by a criterion-related validity study. One of the questions on the inventory was: "Did you have sexual intercourse for the first time before the age of 16?" Some police officers who took this promotional exam and failed it sued the city for asking such a question in an employment test. The officers said the question had absolutely no relevance to the conduct of a detective's job, and furthermore it was an invasion of their privacy.

They had been denied a detective's job because of a totally inappropriate question, and therefore they wanted the entire test results thrown out.

The case was heard at the district court. The judge ruled in favor of the officers, saying that that question was totally lacking in content validity and was an invasion of their privacy. Therefore, the officers should be reconsidered for promotion to detective. The city appealed the verdict to the state supreme court. The judge there reversed the lower court ruling and allowed the test results to stand, meaning the officers would not get promoted. The state supreme court judge based his decision on the grounds that the answer to that question did correlate with job performance as a detective. From a practical and legal standpoint, it is advisable to avoid asking such invasive questions in the first place, even though in this case a lengthy legal battle ultimately resulted in a decision favorable to the city.

perceived to invade privacy invite litigation against the hiring organization by job applicants (see Field Note 2).

A final issue is the question of fakability: To what extent do individuals distort their responses to create a more socially desirable impression? Research (Kluger, Reilly, & Russell, 1991; Becker & Colquitt, 1992) reveals that faking does occur in responses to certain types of questions. The questions most likely to be faked in a socially desirable direction are those that are difficult to verify for accuracy and have the appearance of being highly job relevant.

Despite these limitations, using biographical information is a logically defensible strategy to personnel selection. Mumford and Stokes (1992) portrayed biographical information as revealing consistent patterns of behavior that are interwoven throughout our lives. By assessing what applicants have done, we can gain great insight into what they will do.

LETTERS OF RECOMMENDATION

One of the most commonly used and least valid of all predictors is the letter of recommendation. Letters of recommendation and reference checks are as widespread in personnel selection as the interview and the application blank. Unfortunately, they usually lack comparable validity. Letters of recommendation are usually written on behalf of an applicant by a current employer, professional associate, or personal friend. The respondent rates the applicant on such dimensions as leadership ability and written and oral communication skills. The responses are then used as a basis for hiring.

One review of letters of recommendation (Muchinsky, 1979) reported an average validity coefficient of .13. Some people even make recommendations that have an inverse relationship with the criterion; that is, if the applicant is recommended for hire, the company would do best to reject him or her! One of the biggest problems with letters of recommendation is their restricted range. As you might expect, almost all letters of recommendation are positive. Most often, the applicants themselves choose who will write the letters, so it isn't surprising that they pick people who will make them look good. Because of this restriction (that is, almost all applicants are described positively), the lack of predictive ability of the letter of recommendation is not unexpected.

While a few studies using specially constructed evaluation forms have reported moderate validity coefficients, the typical validity coefficient is very low. Because of their limited validity, letters of recommendation should not be taken too seriously in making personnel selection decisions. The only major exception to this statement is the following condition: When applicants are described in positive terms, you will not know that they will be successful on the job. However, on those rare occasions when the applicant is described in negative terms (even if only mildly), such an assessment is usually indicative of future problems on the job. Those types of letters should be taken seriously. On average, though, very few

---

Field Note 3 *Intentional Deception in Letters of Recommendation*

I was the director of a graduate program to which about 100 students seek admission annually. One of the requirements for admission is a letter of recommendation. Over the years I received several memorable letters of recommendation, but on one occasion I received a letter (actually, two) that clearly illustrates why such letters have little predictive value. This letter came from the president of a foreign university where the student was enrolled. It made the student sound incredibly strong academically: the class valedictorian, the only recipient of the native king's fellowship program, the only student who received a special citation from the university, and so forth. Needless to say, I was most impressed by this letter.

About two weeks later I got another application for admission from a second student from that same university. Accompanying this application was another letter supposedly written by the university president. This letter was identical to the first. The only difference was the name of the student typed at the top of the letter. Thus, both students had been the class valedictorian, both were the only recipient of the fellowship, and so on.

I then called a different academic department and discovered that it had received the identical letter on yet a third student from that university who was applying for graduate work in that department. What we had was literally a form letter in which every student in the university was being described, word for word, as the best. The university apparently provided this "service" to its students seeking admission to graduate schools in the United States. Such attempts at deception do nothing to portray fairly a candidate's strengths and weaknesses—and most certainly do not enhance the validity of the letter of recommendation as a personnel selection method.

letters of recommendation contain nonsupportive information about an applicant (see Field Note 3).

NEW AND CONTROVERSIAL METHODS OF ASSESSMENT

This final category is reserved for four new and controversial methods of assessing job applicants.

Drug Testing

Drug testing is the popular term for efforts to detect *substance abuse,* the use of illegal drugs and the improper and illegal use of prescription and over-the-counter medications, alcohol, and other chemical compounds. Substance abuse is a major global problem with far-reaching societal, moral, and economic consequences. The role that I/O psychology plays in this vast and complex picture is to detect substance abuse in the workplace. Employees who engage in substance abuse jeopardize not only their own welfare but also potentially the welfare of fellow employees and other individuals. I/O psychologists are involved in screening out substance abusers among both job applicants and current employees.

Unlike other forms of assessment used by I/O psychologists that involve estimates of cognitive or motor abilities, drug testing embraces chemical assessments. The method of assessment is typically based on a urine sample (hair samples can also be used). The rationale is that the presence of drugs will be revealed in a person's urine. Therefore, a sample of urine is treated with chemicals that will reveal the presence of drugs if they have been ingested by the person. There are two basic types of assessments. A *screening test* assures the potential presence of a wide variety of chemicals. A *confirmation test* on the same sample identifies the presence of chemicals suggested by the initial screening test. I/O psychologists are not directly involved with these tests because they are performed in chemical laboratories by individuals with special technical training. The profession of I/O psychology does become involved in drug testing because it assesses suitability for employment, with concomitant concern about the reliability, validity, legality, and cost of these tests.

The issues are very complex, and there are some real concerns. The reliability of the chemical tests is much higher than the reliability of traditional paper-and-pencil psychological assessments. However, the reliability is not perfect, which means that different conclusions can be drawn about substance abuse depending on the laboratory conducting the testing. Questions of validity are much more problematic. The accurate detection of drug use varies as a function of the type of drug involved, because some drugs remain in our systems for days and others remain for weeks. Thus, the timing of taking the urine sample is critical. It is also possible that diet can falsely influence the results of a drug test. For example, eating poppy-seed cake may trigger a confirmatory response to heroin tests because heroin is derived from poppy seeds. The legality of drug testing is also highly controversial. Critics of drug testing contend it violates the U.S. Constitution with regard to unreasonable search and seizure, self-incrimination, and the right to privacy. It is also a matter of debate which jobs should be subject to drug testing. Some people argue for routine drug testing; others say drug testing should be limited to jobs that potentially affect the lives of others (for example, transportation workers). Yet another issue is the criteria for intoxication and performance impairment. What dosage of a drug constitutes a level that would impair job performance? Finally, there is the matter of cost. Screening tests cost about $10 per specimen, but confirmatory tests can cost up to $100 per specimen. These costs will eventually have to be passed on to consumers as part of the price they pay for having their goods and services rendered by a drug-free workforce. A major investigation by the National Research Council (Normand, Lempert, & O'Brien, 1994) on drug testing underscored the particular danger of unfairness to job applicants who are falsely classified as drug users. Drug testing thus must balance the economic goals of workforce productivity with individual rights to fair treatment in the workplace.

Some recent research on drug testing has revealed applicant reactions to such testing and its effectiveness. Murphy, Thornton, and Prue (1991) found that drug testing was judged most acceptable for jobs in which there was the potential for danger to others. Uniform drug testing for all jobs was not viewed favorably. Stone and Kotch (1989) reported that the negative reaction to drug testing by companies can be reduced by giving employees advance notice of scheduled drug tests and responding to detected drug use with treatment programs rather than the discharge of employees. Normand, Salyards, and Mahoney (1990) conducted a study on the effects of drug testing and reported sobering results. A total of 5,465 job applicants were tested for use of illicit drugs. After 1.3 years of employment, employees who tested positive for illicit drugs had an absenteeism rate 59.3% higher than employees who tested negative. The involuntary turnover rate (namely, employees who were fired) was 47% higher among drug users than nonusers. The estimated cost savings of screening out drug users in reducing absenteeism and turnover costs for one cohort of new employees was $52,750,000. This figure does not reflect the compounded savings derived by cohorts of new employees added each year the drug-testing program is in existence.

As can be seen, drug testing is an exceedingly complex and controversial issue. While the analysis of urine is beyond the purview of I/O psychology, making decisions about an applicant's suitability for employment is not. I/O psychology is being drawn into a complicated web of issues that affects all of society. Our profession may be asked to provide solutions to problems we couldn't even have imagined 20 years ago.

Polygraphy or Lie Detection

A **polygraph** is an instrument that measures aspects of the autonomic nervous system—physiological reactions of the body such as heart rate and perspiration. In theory these autonomic responses will "give you away" when you are telling a lie. The polygraph is attached to the body with electronic sensors for detecting the physiological reactions. Polygraphs are used more to evaluate people charged with criminal activity in a post hoc fashion (for example, after a robbery within a company has occurred) than to select people for a job, although it is used in the latter capacity as well.

Is a polygraph foolproof? No. People can appear to be innocent of any wrong-doing according to the polygraph but in fact be guilty of misconduct. Research conducted by the Federal Bureau of Investigation (Podlesny & Truslow, 1993) based on a crime simulation reported that the polygraph correctly identified 84.7% of the guilty group and 94.7% of the innocent group. Bashore and Rapp (1993) suggested that alternative methods that measure brain electrical activity can be used to complement the polygraph and would be particularly effective in revealing the possession of information in persons attempting to conceal it (i.e., the guilty group). Many psychologists are skeptical of the scientific value of the polygraph, believing people can readily learn countermeasures to invalidate the results (Iacono & Lykken, 1997). In 1988 President Reagan signed into law a bill banning the widespread use of polygraphs for preemployment screening among private-sector employers. However, as Honts (1991) reported, polygraph use by the federal government continues to grow. It is used extensively in the hiring process of government agencies involved in national security, as well as in the area of law enforcement.

Graphology

Graphology or handwriting analysis is very popular in Europe as a selection method. Here is how it works: A person trained in handwriting analysis (called a *graphologist*) examines a sample of a candidate's handwriting. Based on such factors as the specific formation of letters, the slant and size of the writing, and how hard the person presses the pen or pencil on the paper, the graphologist makes an assessment of the candidate's personality. This personality assessment is then correlated with criteria of job success.

Rafaeli and Klimoski (1983) had 20 graphologists analyze handwriting and then correlated their assessments with three types of criteria: supervisory ratings, self-ratings, and sales production. Although the authors found some evidence of inter-rater agreement (meaning the graphologists tended to base their assessments on the same facets of handwriting), the handwriting assessments did not correlate with any criteria. Ben-Shakhar et al. (1986) reported that graphologists did not perform significantly better than chance in predicting the job performance of bank employees. Graphology has been found to be predictive of affective states such as stress (Keinan & Eilat-Greenberg, 1993), but its ability to predict job performance has not been empirically established.

Tests of Emotional Intelligence

Recently I/O psychology has begun to address what has historically been regarded as the "soft" side of individual differences, including moods, feelings, and emotions. For many years the relevance of these constructs to the world of work were denied. They were regarded as transient disturbances to the linkages between abilities (e.g., intelligence) and performance. However, we are coming to realize that moods, feelings, and emotions play a significant role in the workplace, just as they do in life in general. The concept of emotional intelligence was initially proposed by Salovey and Mayer (1990).

It is proposed that individuals differ in how they deal with their emotions, and those who effectively manage their emotions are said to be "emotionally intelligent." Some theorists believe that emotions are within the domain of intelligence, rather than viewing "emotion" and "intelligence" as independent or contradictory. Goleman (1995) proposed five dimensions to the construct of emotional intelligence. The first three are classified as intrapersonal, and the last two are interpersonal.

1. *Knowing one's emotions.* Self-awareness, recognizing a feeling as it happens, is the cornerstone of emotional intelligence. The ability to monitor feelings from moment to moment is hypothesized to be crucial to psychological insight and self-understanding.
2. *Managing one's emotions.* Handling feelings so they are appropriate is an ability that builds on self-awareness. People who are low in this ability are prone to feelings of distress, whereas those who are high are more resilient to life's setbacks and upsets.
3. *Motivating oneself.* Marshaling emotions in pursuit of a goal is essential for paying attention, for self-motivation, and for creativity. People who have this ability tend to be more productive and effective in whatever they undertake. More will be said about this topic in Chapter 11 on work motivation.
4. *Recognizing emotions in others.* Empathy is the fundamental "people skill." People who are empathetic are more attuned to the subtle social signals that indicate what others need or want. This skill makes them well suited for the caring professions such as nurses and social workers.
5. *Handling relationships.* Proficiency in social relationships is, in large part, the ability to manage emotions in others. People who excel in this ability do well in tasks that rely on interacting smoothly with others.

Goleman differentiated people who are high in traditional intelligence (i.e., cognitive ability) from those high in emotional intelligence as follows: People with high cognitive ability (alone) are ambitious and productive, unexpressive, detached, and emotionally bland and cold. In contrast, people who are high in emotional intelligence are socially poised, outgoing, and cheerful. They are sympathetic and caring in their relationships. They are comfortable with themselves, others, and the social environment they live in. These portraits are of extreme types, when in reality most of us are a mix of traditional and emotional intelligence. However, each construct adds separately to a person's attributes. Goleman (1995) believes "of the two, emotional intelligence adds far more of the qualities that make us more fully human" (p. 45).

Because the concept of emotional intelligence is very new, we don't know a great deal about it. Currently there are no well-established tests or inventories to measure it, although some initial attempts have been made (i.e., Goleman, 1998; Weisinger, 1998). Furthermore, it is a matter of professional debate whether emotional intelligence is a distinct construct, or whether it is already understood under the rubric of personality theory. There is conceptual overlap between personality and emotions, but they are not identical. While psychology has not yet reached a verdict on the scientific status of emotional intelligence, what it addresses is certainly not well understood within the field of I/O psychology. I anticipate that the relationship between emotional intelligence and job performance will be more fully explored in the near future.

OVERVIEW AND EVALUATION OF PREDICTORS

Personnel selection methods can be evaluated by many standards. I have identified four major standards that I feel are useful in organizing all the information we have gathered about predictors.

1. *Validity*, as defined in this book, refers to the ability of the predictor to forecast criterion performance accurately. Many authorities argue that validity is the predominant evaluative standard in judging selection methods; however, the relevance of the other three standards is also substantial.
2. *Fairness* refers to the ability of the predictor to render unbiased predictions of job success across applicants in various subgroups of gender, race, age, and so on. The issue of fairness will be discussed in greater detail in Chapter 5.
3. *Applicability* refers to whether the selection method can be applied across the full range of job and applicant types. Some predictors have wide applicability in that they appear well suited for a diverse range of people and jobs; other methods have particular limitations that affect their applicability.
4. The final standard is the *cost* of implementing the method. The various personnel selection methods differ markedly in their cost, which has a direct bearing on their overall value.

Table 4–3 presents the 11 personnel selection methods appraised on each of the four evaluative standards. Each standard is partitioned into three levels: low, moderate, and high. This classification scheme is admittedly oversimplified, and in some cases the evaluation of a selection method did not readily lend itself to a uniform rating. Nevertheless, this method is useful in providing a broad-brush view of all the personnel selection methods.

Average validities in the .00–.20, .21–.40, and over .40 ranges were labeled low, moderate, and high, respectively. Selection methods that have many, some, and few problems of fairness were labeled low, moderate, and high, respectively. The applicability standard, the most difficult one to appraise on a single dimension, was classified according to the ease of using the method in terms of feasibility and generalizability across jobs. Finally, direct cost estimates were made for each selection method. Methods estimated as costing less than $20 per applicant were labeled low; $20 to $50, moderate; and over $50, high. The ideal personnel selection method would be high in validity, fairness, and applicability and low in cost. Inspection of Table 4–3 reveals that no method has an ideal profile. The 11 methods produce a series of trade offs among validity, fairness, applicability, and cost. This shouldn't be surprising; if there were one uniformly ideal personnel selection method, there probably would be little need to consider ten others.

In terms of validity, the best methods are work samples, biographical information, assessment centers, and physical abilities tests. However, each of these methods is limited by some problems with fairness, applicability, or cost. Ironically,

TABLE 4–3 *Assessment of 11 personnel selection methods along 4 evaluative standards*

Selection Method	Evaluative Standards			
	Validity	Fairness	Applicability	Cost
Intelligence tests	Moderate	Moderate	High	Low
Mechanical aptitude tests	Moderate	High	Moderate	Low
Sensory/motor ability tests	Moderate	High	Low	Low
Personality inventories	Moderate	High	Moderate	Moderate
Physical abilities tests	High	Moderate	Low	Low
Interviews	Moderate	Moderate	High	Moderate
Assessment centers	High	High	Moderate	High
Work samples	High	High	Low	High
Situational exercises	Moderate	(Unknown)	Low	Moderate
Biographical information	High	Moderate	High	Low
Letters of recommendation	Low	(Unknown)	High	Low

the worst selection method in terms of validity, letters of recommendation, is one of the most frequently used. This method is characterized by high applicability and low cost, which no doubt accounts for its popularity.

Fairness refers to the likelihood that the method will have differential predictive accuracy according to membership in any group, such as gender or race. While the issue of fairness has generated a great deal of controversy, no method is classified in Table 4–3 as having low fairness. Insufficient information is available on two of the methods (situational exercises and letters of recommendation) to render an evaluation of their fairness, but it seems unlikely they would be judged as grossly unfair. Although several methods have exhibited some fairness problems (thus warranting caution in their use), the problems are not so severe as to reject any method as a means of selecting personnel.

The applicability dimension was the most difficult to assess, and evaluation of this dimension is most subject to qualification. For example, work samples are characterized by low applicability because they are highly limited to certain types of jobs (that is, jobs involving the mechanical manipulation of objects). However, this limitation appears to be more than offset by the method's high validity and fairness. Simply put, the problem with this method is its feasibility for only a selected range of jobs. In contrast, other methods have high applicability (such as the interview) and qualify as an almost universal means of selection.

The cost dimension is perhaps the most arbitrary. Indirect or hidden costs may be associated with selection methods—costs that were not included in their evaluation but perhaps could have been. The break points in the classification scheme are also subjective. For example, I considered a $40-per-applicant cost to be moderate; others might say it is low or high. These issues notwithstanding, one can see a full range of cost estimates in Table 4–3. Some methods do not cost much (for example, letters of recommendation), but they do not appear to be worth much either.

This chapter has examined several major types of predictors used in personnel selection: psychological tests, physical abilities tests, interviews, work samples and situational exercises, biographical information, and letters of recommendation. These predictors have been validated against a number of different criteria for a variety of occupational groups. Some predictors have been used more extensively than others. Furthermore, certain predictors have historically shown more validity than others. The ideal predictor would be an accurate forecaster of the criterion, equally applicable across different groups of people, and not too lengthy or costly to administer. But predictors rarely meet all these standards in practice.

CASE STUDY ◆ How Do We Hire Police Officers?

Bay Ridge, a city with a population of about 125,000, experienced remarkable growth over a short time for two major reasons. First, several large industries had been attracted to the area; with more jobs, there were more people. Second, due to a rezoning plan, several small townships were incorporated into Bay Ridge, which caused a sudden burgeoning in the city's official population. As a consequence of this growth, the city needed to expand its police force. For many years, Bay Ridge had only a relatively small force and used only a brief interview to select the officers. Recently, however, there had been several complaints about the city's selection interview. Due to the complaints and the need to hire many more officers, the city council decided to abandon the old method of hiring. The city commissioned a job analysis for police officers and determined that three major factors contributed to success on the job. The next step was to develop selection measures to assess each of the three factors. The city council called a meeting with the city personnel director to get a progress report on the selection measures being proposed. Four city council members and Ron Davenport, the city personnel director, attended.

> *Davenport:* I'm pleased to report to you that we have made substantial progress in our study. The job analysis revealed that the following factors determine success on the police force: physical agility, sensitivity to community relations, and practical judgment. We are fairly pleased with the tests developed to assess two of the factors, although one of them is causing us some problems.
>
> *Councilmember DeRosa:* Would you kindly elaborate on what these factors mean?
>
> *Davenport:* Certainly. Physical agility is important in being able to apprehend and possibly disarm a suspect. It is also important in being able to carry a wounded officer out of the line of hostile fire. Sensitivity to community relations involves knowledge of racial and ethnic problems in the city, plus an ability to work with the community in preventing crime. Practical judgment reflects knowing when it is advisable to pursue a criminal suspect and what methods of action to use in uncertain situations.
>
> *Councilmember Flory:* How do you propose to measure physical agility?
>
> *Davenport:* It looks as if we'll go with some physical standard—being able to carry a 150-pound dummy 25 yards, or something similar. We might also use some height and weight requirements. We could have some problems with gender differences in that women are not as strong as men, but I think we can work it out.
>
> *Councilmember Reddinger:* Are all of these tests going to be performance tests?
>
> *Davenport:* No, that's the only one so far. For the community relations factor, we're going to use a situational interview. We'll ask the candidates how they would go about

dealing with some hypothetical but realistic problem, such as handling a domestic argument. The interviewers will grade their answers and give them a total score.

Councilmember Hamilton: What will be a passing score in this interview?

Davenport: We haven't determined that yet. We're still trying to determine if this is the best way to measure the factor.

Councilmember Flory: How do you plan to measure practical judgment?

Davenport: That's the problem case. We really haven't figured out a good test of that yet.

Councilmember DeRosa: How about a test of general intelligence?

Davenport: It appears that practical judgment is related to intelligence, but it's not the same thing. A person can be very intelligent in terms of verbal and numerical ability but not possess a great deal of practical judgment.

Councilmember Reddinger: Hasn't some psychologist developed a test of practical judgment?

Davenport: Not that we know of. You also have to remember that the type of judgment a police officer has to demonstrate is not the same thing as the type of judgment, say, a banker has to show. I guess I'm saying there appear to be different kinds of practical judgment.

Councilmember Hamilton: Could you use some personality inventory to measure it?

Davenport: I don't think so. I doubt that practical judgment is a personality trait. At least I'm not aware of any direct measures of it.

Councilmember Flory: How about using the interview again? A police officer has to demonstrate practical judgment in handling community relations. Can't you just expand the interview a bit?

Davenport: That's a possibility we're considering. Another possibility is to put candidates in a test situation where they have to demonstrate their practical judgment. It could be a pretty expensive method, all things considered, but it may be the best way to go.

Councilmember DeRosa: I have a feeling, Mr. Davenport, that your success in measuring practical judgment will determine just how many good officers we get on the force.

Questions

1. The city will have to validate whatever predictors it develops to select police officers. What method or methods of validation do you think it should use?

2. Do you think that biographical information might be useful in predicting one's success as a police officer? If so, what types of items might be useful?

3. Describe a work sample or situational exercise that might measure practical judgment.

4. What might be a problem in using a physical ability test to select police officers?

5. The personnel department has asked you to assist in developing or selecting predictors of police officer performance. What advice would you give?

INFOTRAC ARTICLES

1. *Across the Board,* Nov–Dec 1997 v34 n10 p18(6)
   Beyond appearances. James Krohe, Jr.
   Discusses the value of using personality tests, cognitive tests, and simulations in assessing candidates for executive positions.

2. *Working Woman,* Jan 1995 v20 n1 p44(3)
   When employees lie, cheat, or steal. Wilma Randle
   Chronicles the case of an employee who embezzled funds from her employer
   and recommends assessment of integrity to reduce the frequency of such
   behavior.

3. *Working Woman,* Sep 1997 v22 n9 p28(1)
   Letters of reference.
   Graphologists interpret the handwriting of Bill Gates, Michael Eisner, and others.

4. *USA Today* (Magazine), Jan 1995 v123 n2596 p81(2)
   Drug testing is vital in the workplace. Ira A. Lipman
   Discusses magnitude of workplace drug abuse costs in U.S. businesses and recommends universal drug testing for all employees.

5. *Training & Development,* March 1997 v51 n3 p13(1)
   How to ace a job interview. Richard Koonce
   Discusses strategies job applicants can follow to be evaluated positively in a job
   interview.

6. *Insight on the News,* Sep 2, 1996 v12 n33 p38(1)
   Recommend at own risk: Employers face a new quandary: What information
   should they give out about former workers? Jeffrey R. Sipe
   Discusses issues associated with prospective employers conducting reference
   checks on job applicants and the liabilities associated with passing on information.

7. *Commentary,* Sep 1998 v106 n3 p34(4)
   The war against testing. David W. Murray
   An article critical of using standardized tests to make assessments of abilities. It
   is argued that tests are sexually, culturally, and racially biased.

8. *Working Woman,* Oct 1997 v22 n10 p74(3)
   Testing . . . 1, 2, 3. Lorie Parch
   An article supportive of using tests to make employment decisions to identify
   employees who are reliable, creative, and emotionally stable.

5

Personnel Decisions

MAJOR CHAPTER OBJECTIVES

◆ Explain the legal context for personnel decisions.

◆ Describe the process of personnel recruitment and affirmative action.

◆ Understand the statistical concepts of regression analysis and multiple regression analysis.

◆ Explain the concept and significance of validity generalization.

◆ Describe the selection of employees and the process of assessing job applicants.

◆ Identify issues pertaining to the determination of the passing score.

◆ Explain the concept and significance of test utility related to organizational efficiency.

◆ Describe the personnel functions of placement and classification.

Personnel decisions affect people's worklives. Becker and Gerhart (1996) asserted that if personnel decisions influence organizational performance, they must either improve efficiency or contribute to profitability. The amount of money organizations pay to their employees is the single largest operating cost in many organizations. Therefore, it is to the advantage of both the individual and the organization that personnel decisions be made wisely. For individual employees, it is best that they be selected for jobs that utilize their abilities. For organizations, it is best that they hire qualified individuals who will contribute to the success of the organization. This chapter will examine the process of making personnel decisions and the factors associated with determining their quality.

THE LEGAL CONTEXT FOR PERSONNEL DECISIONS

Civil Rights Act of 1964

For the first 60 years or so of I/O psychology, there was virtually no connection between psychologists and the legal community. Psychological tests were developed, administered, and interpreted by psychologists, and as a profession psychologists governed themselves. However, during the late 1950s and early 1960s, the nation was swept up in the civil rights movement. At that time civil rights concerned primarily the conditions under which Blacks lived and worked in this country. Blacks were denied access to colleges, restaurants, and jobs—in short, their civil rights were denied. Presidents Kennedy and Johnson were interested in changing this aspect of American society. In 1964 the Civil Rights Act, a major piece of federal legislation aimed at reducing discrimination in all walks of life, was passed. The section of the law pertaining to discrimination in employment is Title VII, and it is the section most relevant to I/O psychology. In essence, this was the message: Blacks were grossly underemployed throughout the country in both private- and public-sector jobs, particularly in jobs above the lower levels of organizations. To reduce discrimination in employment (one of the mandates of the Civil Rights Act), the federal government began to intervene in employment hiring; in essence, it would monitor the entire procedure to ensure fairness in selection. Thus, personnel decisions became deeply embedded within a legal context in the 1960s. As Guion (1998) asserted, previously the federal government had regulated things (e.g., food and drugs), while with this act it regulated behavior. The Civil Rights Act was expanded to cover other people as well. In fact, five groups were identified for protection: race, gender, religion, color, and national origin. They were referred to as the *protected groups*. The Civil Rights Act included all personnel functions—training, promotion, retention, and performance appraisal—in addition to selection. Furthermore, any methods used for making personnel decisions (e.g., tests, interviews, assessment centers, etc.) were subject to the same legal standards.

Title VII specifies several unlawful employment practices, including the following:

- ◆ Employers may not fail or refuse to hire, or discharge, anyone on the basis of the five protected groups.

◆ Employers may not separate or classify employees or applicants so as to de-prive anyone of employment opportunities on the basis of any of the five protected groups.

◆ Advertising employment or training opportunities may not indicate prefer-ences for any group, as witnessed, for example, in separate classified adver-tisements for "Help Wanted—Men" and "Help Wanted—Women."

Adverse Impact

Under the Civil Rights Act discrimination may be charged under two legal theo-ries. One is **adverse impact** (also called *disparate impact*), in which discrimination affects different groups (vis-à-vis the five protected groups) differently. Evidence that one group (e.g., women) as a whole is less likely to be hired is evidence of discrimination against those group members. The second theory is **disparate treat-ment,** which refers to evidence that a member of a protected group is treated dif-ferently from other job applicants in the employment process. All job applicants should receive the same treatment with regard to selection methods and hiring standards. Singling out some applicants for different employment procedures is evidence of disparate treatment.

Of the two legal bases of discrimination, adverse impact has garnered the greater attention among I/O psychologists. The definition of adverse impact was operationalized by what is known as the "80%" (or "4/5ths") rule. The rule states that adverse impact occurs if the selection ratio (that is, the number of people hired divided by the number of people who apply) for any group of applicants (such as Blacks) is less than 80% of the selection ratio for another group. Suppose 100 Whites apply for a job and 20 are selected. The selection ratio is 20/100, or .20. By multiplying .20 by 80%, we get .16. This means that if fewer than 16% of the Black applicants are hired, the selection test produces adverse impact. So if 50 Blacks ap-ply for the job and if at least 8 (50 × .16) Blacks are not selected, then the test pro-duces adverse impact.

If adverse impact is found to exist, the organization is obligated to use another selection method that does not produce adverse impact or to validate the test. If adverse impact does not result from the selection method, the organization is not required to validate it. Obviously, however, it is a sound business decision to vali-date any selection method at any time. A company would always want to know whether its method is identifying the best candidates for hire. As discussed in Chapter 4, three manifestations of validity can be shown to support the use of a test: content, construct, and criterion-related.

As part of the Civil Rights Act, the Equal Employment Opportunity Commis-sion (EEOC) was established to investigate charges of prohibited employment practices and to use conciliation and persuasion to eliminate prohibited practices. The EEOC subsequently produced a set of uniform guidelines for organizations to follow in making employment decisions. When there is a conclusion of "just cause" to believe charges of employment discrimination are true, the EEOC can file suit in federal court. If the organization cannot be persuaded to change its em-ployment practices, then the issue is brought before the court for adjudication.

Organizations that lose such cases are obligated to pay financial damages to the victims of their employment practices. The financial awards in these cases can be class-action settlements (the individual who is suing represents a class of similar people) or back-pay settlements (the organization has to pay a portion of what victims would have earned had they been hired), or both. The courts have granted multi-million-dollar awards in single cases. However, not everyone who fails an employment test automatically gets his or her day in court. A lawsuit must be predicated on just cause, and the two parties may reach an agreement without resorting to litigation.

Major Court Cases

If a case proceeds to trial, the body of facts presented and how the court ultimately evaluates those facts become the judicial interpretation of the law. The decisions rendered by the courts become part of what is called *case law*. Several landmark decisions rendered by the U.S. Supreme Court have shaped the interpretation of the Civil Rights Act. In *Griggs v. Duke Power Company*, the Court ruled in 1971 that individuals who bring suit against a company do not have to prove that the company's employment test is unfair; rather, the company has to prove that its test *is* fair. Thus, the burden of proving the fairness of the test rests with the employer. This finding was referred to as "Griggs' Burden." In *Albemarle v. Moody*, the Court ruled on just how much judicial power the employment guidelines really have. Although they were called guidelines, the Court ruled that they be granted the "deference of law," meaning they were in effect the law on employment testing. However, many I/O psychologists believe that a set of testing principles developed by the Society for Industrial-Organizational Psychology (1987) are more technically precise. In *Bakke v. University of California*, the Court ruled that Whites can be the victims of discrimination as well as Blacks. Bakke (a White man) sued the University of California on the grounds that his race had been a factor in his being denied admission to their medical school. The Court ruled in Bakke's favor and required the University of California to admit Bakke to the medical college. This case was heralded as a classic case of "reverse discrimination," which technically is incorrect. First, the name connotes that only Blacks can be discriminated against, which obviously is not true. Second, reversal of the process of discrimination results in nondiscrimination. In *Watson v. Fort Worth Bank & Trust*, the Court ruled that the *cost* of alternative selection procedures must be considered in making decisions about selection methods. Previously, matters of cost had not been a concern of the courts or the EEOC. Furthermore, the Court modified its stance regarding burden of proof. Literally thousands of cases have been adjudicated in the district, appellate, state supreme courts, and U.S. Supreme Court based on litigation spawned by employment law. These four cases (all from the U.S. Supreme Court) represent a very small sampling.

Other employment laws followed the passage of the Civil Rights Act, but none had the same far-reaching impact on employment practices. In 1967 the Age Discrimination in Employment Act (ADEA) was passed, which extends to people aged 40 and over the same type of legal protection granted to the five protected groups under the Civil Rights Act.

FRANK AND ERNEST   by Bob Thaves

SOURCE: Reprinted by permission of Newspaper Enterprise Association, Inc.

Americans with Disabilities Act

In 1990 the Americans with Disabilities Act (ADA) was signed into law by President George Bush. The ADA is the most important piece of legislation ever enacted for persons with disabilities (O'Keeffe, 1994). A *disability* is defined by ADA as "a physical or mental impairment that substantially limits one or more (of the) major life activities; a record of such impairment; or being regarded as having such an impairment." A major life activity is seeing, hearing, walking, learning, breathing, and working. An employment test that screens out an individual with a disability must be job-related and consistent with business necessity. The law states that employers must provide disabled persons *reasonable accommodation* in being evaluated for employment and in the conduct of their jobs. Employers are required to modify or accommodate their business practices in a reasonable fashion to meet the needs of disabled persons. This can include providing elevators or ramps for access to buildings for those who cannot walk, and also providing readers for those with dyslexia or who are blind. The ADA extends protection to individuals who are alcoholics and former illegal drug users (Jones, 1994) as well as to individuals with psychiatric disabilities (Carling, 1994). The fundamental premise of the law is that disabled individuals can effectively contribute to the workforce, and they cannot be discriminated against in employment decisions because of their disabilities. If a reasonable accommodation on the employer's part is needed to meld these individuals into the workforce, it is so prescribed by the ADA law. As Klimoski and Palmer (1994) noted, organizations are expected to act with good-will in responding to the ADA and be committed to make it work effectively. At this time there appear to be legitimate differences of opinion regarding the legal interpretation of the law. These interpretations will become clearer as the courts address cases brought before them regarding the employment rights of disabled persons. As with all employment laws, the ultimate goal of the ADA is to produce a more just and productive society.

Societal Values and Employment Law

Employment laws reflect our societal values as to what we regard as "fairness" in the work world. As our conceptions of fairness have changed over time, so have employment laws. Guion (1998) stated, "Changes follow or accompany (or are accompanied by) changes in the ideas and attitudes of society in general, whether emerging spontaneously or in response to leadership. Even imperfect law is an expression of, and an understanding of, social policy" (p. 205). Tenopyr (1996) asserted that there is a strong linkage between measurement issues in psychology (e.g., validity) and social policy pertaining to employment. Tenopyr argued that psychologists should have addressed many of the issues long before national policy debates practically mandated the research. She believes psychologists "should undertake an organized effort to anticipate social issues of the future and to begin the research necessary to address them" (p. 360). The Civil Rights Act of 1964 provides for equal access to employment by all protected groups. Access to employment is often gained by passing tests used to make employment decisions. Psychological research has revealed that different groups of people do not score equally on all standard employment tests. An example is a test of physical fitness for the job of firefighter. Because men have, on average, greater upper body strength than women, more men than women pass a test requiring the lifting of a heavy object. This difference between genders in upper body strength increases the likelihood that both men and women are not hired in equivalent proportions, thereby increasing the likelihood of adverse impact against women. Psychologists are thus sometimes compelled to consider two undesirable tradeoffs: Either use tests that have validity but produce adverse impact, or use tests that do not produce adverse impact but also are less valid. Selection methods that uniformly have high validity and no adverse impact are elusive, although various strategies have been proposed (e.g., Hattrup, Rock, & Scalia, 1997; Hoffman & Thornton, 1997). One strategy that had been used is to set different passing scores for various groups to avoid adverse impact. However, in 1991 President George Bush signed into law an amendment to the Civil Rights Act that prohibited test score adjustments as a means of attaining employment fairness. Specifically, the amended Civil Rights Act stated it shall be an unlawful practice for an employer "in connection with the selection or referral of applicants or candidates for employment or promotion to adjust the scores of, use different cutoffs for, or otherwise alter the results of employment related tests on the basis of race, color, religion, sex, or national origin."

Varca and Pattison (1993) presented a cogent discussion of how the amended Civil Rights Act and more recent court cases, such as *Wards Cove Packing Company v. Antonio*, have modified both the applicant's and employer's responsibilities in employment discrimination litigation, pertaining to such issues as burden of proof. Wigdor and Sackett (1993) described the development of employment laws as reflecting attempts in reaching ultimate societal goals of workforce productivity and providing opportunities for all social groups to achieve their employment potential. Our society is divided on the relative importance that should be attached to attaining these two goals (e.g., Gottfredson, 1994; Sackett & Wilk, 1994). The ensuing years will witness how the courts adjudicate the complicated interplay among the societal goals that surround employment testing. The profusion of laws and court cases testifies to the continuing debate within our country over issues of *social justice* in employment. The matter of social justice in employment will be discussed in several contexts throughout this book.

RECRUITMENT

The personnel function of **recruitment** refers to the process of attracting people to apply for a job. Organizations can select only from those candidates who apply. If few people apply for a job, the odds of finding a strong candidate are less than if many candidates apply. Likewise, organizations often have preferences for recruiting recent college graduates versus individuals with work experience. Rynes, Orlitzky, and Bretz (1997) reported that experienced hires were regarded by staffing specialists as having a stronger work ethic and more realistic expectations than recent college graduates. However, new graduates were regarded more highly than experienced hires on their willingness and ability to learn new things.

There is more to recruiting than you might think. The concept of a **recruiting yield pyramid** is useful for hiring candidates. A diagram of that pyramid is shown in Figure 5–1. Let us say that the goal is to hire 5 managers. The company has learned from past experience that for every 2 managers who are offered jobs, only 1 will accept. Therefore, the company will need to make 10 offers. Furthermore, the company has learned that to find 10 managers who are good enough to receive an offer, 40 candidates must be interviewed; that is, only 1 manager out of 4 is usually judged acceptable. However, to get 40 managers to travel to the company for an interview, the company has to invite 60 people; that is, typically only 2 out of 3 candidates are interested enough in the job to agree to be interviewed. Finally, to find 60 potentially interested managers, the company needs to get four times as many contacts or leads. Some people will not want to change jobs, others will not want to move, and still others will simply be unsuitable for further consideration. Therefore, the company has to make initial contacts with about 240 managerial candidates. Note the mushrooming effect in recruiting applicants. Stated in reverse order, 240 people are contacted to find 60 who are interested, to find 40 who agree to be interviewed, to find 10 who are acceptable, to get the 5 people who will accept the offer.

Obviously these yield ratios (that is, 240:5) differ depending on the organization and the job in question. Highly attractive employers have fewer people decline their offers, and less demanding jobs are filled with less selectivity. Also, economic conditions play a big role in whether the company must pursue the applicant, or vice versa. Nevertheless, a poor job of recruiting greatly limits the caliber of people available for hire. Also, the time from when a company realizes it needs new employees until the employees show up for work is typically measured in weeks or months rather than days.

Rynes (1993) noted that most of the emphasis on personnel decisions from an I/O perspective centers on how employers can make better decisions in assessing applicants. However, as Rynes observed, the process can be viewed from the opposite perspective—that is, the extent to which applicants consider the company to be a desirable employer. Specifically, what impressions of the company are generated by the company's recruitment and assessment practices? Schuler (1993) referred to the quality of a selection process that makes it acceptable to job applicants as "social validity." Steiner and Gilliland (1996), for example, reported that the social validity of selection procedures was the strongest correlate of applicants' favorable reactions to the organization. Furthermore, there were cultural differences

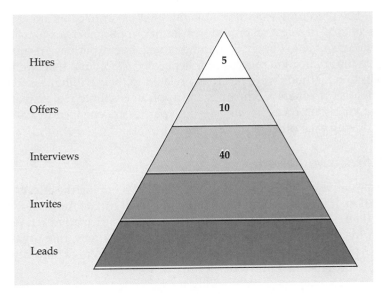

FIGURE 5–1   *Recruiting yield pyramid*

in the social validity of various selection procedures. French college students were more favorably disposed to graphology as a selection method, whereas U.S. college students were more accepting of biographical information. Ployhart and Ryan (1998) found that job applicants held negative views of an organization for using what they considered unfair selection procedures, even when the applicants were hired. Applicant reactions to assessment procedures are often vividly personal and highly emotional, and they clearly influence the applicant's decision to consider the company as a prospective employer. Rynes (1993) offered the following examples of applicant reactions to the recruiting and assessment tactics of companies:

◆ A married graduate student with a 3.9+ grade point average reported that the first three questions in a company's psychological assessment procedure involved inquiries about her personal relationship with her husband and children. Although the company asked her what she thought of the procedure before she left, she lied because she was afraid that telling the truth would eliminate her from future consideration. Because of dual-career constraints, she continued to pursue an offer, but noted that if she got one, her first on-the-job priority would be to try to get the assessor fired.

◆ A student told how he had originally planned to refuse to submit to psychological testing, but was persuaded by his girlfriend that it would be a more effective form of protest to pursue the offer and then pointedly turn it down.

◆ The first interview question asked of a female student was, "We're a pretty macho organization. . . . Does that bother you?" Unfortunately it did, and she simply wrote the company out of her future interviewing plans. (p. 242)

The preceding examples illustrate that job applicants are not merely passive "receptors" of selection procedures. Rather, applicants react to what they are asked to do or say to get a job. Sometimes a negative experience results in withdrawal from the application process. Smither et al. (1993) found that applicant reactions to selection methods were positively related to their willingness to recommend the employer to others. Companies and applicants should realize that the recruitment and selection process is *mutual*—both parties are engaged in assessing the degree of fit with each other (see Field Note 1).

Affirmative Action

Affirmative action is a social policy aimed at reducing the effects of prior discrimination. It is not a requirement under the Civil Rights Act, although it is included in the EEOC guidelines. The original intent of affirmative action was aimed primarily at the recruitment of new employees—namely, that organizations would take positive (or affirmative) action to bring members of minority groups into the workforce that had previously been excluded.

Field Note 1   The Left-Handed Dentist

One of the more unusual personnel selection consulting projects I've worked on involved hiring a dentist. A dentist in my town had just experienced an unpleasant breakup with his partner. They disagreed on many major issues surrounding dentistry, including the relative importance of preventive dental maintenance versus treatment, pain management for patients, and so on. Their parting was not amicable. The dentist who remained solicited my help in getting a new partner. He described at great length the characteristics he was looking for in a new partner. Some related to certain dentistry skills, while others dealt with attitudinal or philosophical orientations toward dentistry.

I didn't envision any major problems in picking a new partner because the desired characteristics seemed reasonable, and I knew dental schools turned out many graduates each year (thus, I would have a large applicant pool). Then came a curve ball I neither anticipated nor understood initially. The dentist said to me, "And, of course, my new partner must be left-handed." The dumb look on my face must have told the dentist I didn't quite catch the significance of left-handedness. The dentist then explained to me something I had never realized despite all

the years I have gone to dentists. Dental partners often share instruments in their practice, and there are both left-handed and right-handed dental instruments. The dentist was left-handed himself, so therefore his new partner would also have to be left-handed. I then asked the dentist what proportion of dentists were left-handed. He said he didn't know for sure, but knew it was a small percentage. Suddenly, my task had become much more difficult.

It was one thing to find a new dentist who met the specifications for the job and who would like to set up a practice in a small Iowa town. It was another thing to have the size of the potential applicant pool greatly reduced by such a limiting factor as left-handedness. There is a technical term for left-handedness in this case: "bona fide occupational qualification" (BFOQ). For a qualification to be a BFOQ, it must be "reasonably necessary to the operation of that particular business or enterprise." Thus, an employer could use left-handedness as a BFOQ in dentistry, but left-handedness would not be a BFOQ in accounting, for example. I am happy to tell you I found a dentist who met all the qualifications. The two dentists have been partners for over 15 years now, and their practice continues to thrive.

Campbell (1996) described four goals of affirmative action:

1. *Correct present inequities.* If one group has "more than its fair share" of jobs or educational opportunities because of current discriminatory practices, then the goal is to remedy the inequity and eliminate the discriminating practices.
2. *Compensate past inequities.* Even if current practices are not discriminatory, a long history of past discrimination may serve to put members of a minority group at a disadvantage.
3. *Provide role models.* Increasing the frequency of minority group members acting as role models could potentially change the career expectations, educational planning, and job-seeking behavior of younger minority group members.
4. *Promote diversity.* Increasing the minority representation in a student body or workforce may act to increase the range of ideas, skills, or values that can be brought to bear on organizational problems and goals.

As straightforward as these goals may appear, there is great variability in the operational procedures used to pursue the goals. The most passive interpretation is to follow procedures that strictly pertain to recruitment, such as extensive advertising in sources most likely to reach minority group members. A stronger interpretation of the goals is *preferential selection:* Organizations will select minority group members from the applicant pool if they are judged to have substantially equal qualifications with nonminority applicants. The most extreme interpretation is to set aside a specific number of job groups or promotions for members of specific protected groups. This is referred to as the *quota interpretation* of affirmative action: Organizations will staff themselves with explicit percentages of employees representing the various protected groups, based on local or national norms, within a specific time frame.

Affirmative action has been hotly debated by proponents and critics. In particular, over the past ten years the subject of affirmative action has been a major political issue. Criticism of the quota interpretation has been strident, claiming the strategy ignores merit or ability. Under a quota strategy it is alleged that the goal is merely "to get the numbers right." Proponents of affirmative action believe it is needed to offset the effects of many years of past discrimination against specific protected groups. The State of California recently reversed its commitment to affirmative action in the admission of students into its universities. Preliminary evidence indicates the new admission policy has resulted in less representation of some minority groups in the student population.

Has affirmative action been effective in meeting national goals of prosperity in employment for all people? Some experts (e.g., Guion, 1998; Heilman, 1996) question its overall effectiveness, asserting that unemployment rates are much higher and average incomes much lower now for some groups (particularly Blacks) than they were at the inception of affirmative action over 30 years ago. Furthermore, the perceived beneficiaries of affirmative action are often stigmatized as being incompetent, as nonbeneficiaries attribute minority employment in large part to group membership (Heilman, McCullough, & Gilbert, 1996). While there appears to be consensus that affirmative action has not produced its intended goals (Murrell &

Jones, 1996), there is considerable reluctance to discard it altogether. It is feared that its absence may produce outcomes more socially undesirable than have occurred with its presence, however flawed it might be. Dovidio and Gaertner (1996) asserted that affirmative action policies are beneficial in that they emphasize outcomes rather than intentions and they establish monitoring systems that ensure accountability.

Kravits et al. (1997) documented a large quantity of psychological and behavioral research conducted on affirmative action. Among the issues studied are reactions to individuals and by individuals hired because of affirmative action policies. Heilman and Herlihy (1984) investigated the reactions of individuals to women who got their jobs on the basis of merit or because of preferential treatment based on gender. Neither men nor women were attracted to jobs when it was believed that women in those jobs had been hired because of their gender. Heilman, Simon, and Repper (1987) examined the effects of gender-based selection. In a laboratory study they led women to believe they were selected for a group leader position because of either their gender or their ability. When selected on the basis of gender, women devalued their leadership performance, took less credit for successful outcomes, and reported less interest in persisting as leaders. The findings suggest that when individuals have doubts about their competence to perform a job effectively, gender-based preferential selection is likely to have adverse consequences on how they view themselves and their performance. Heilman, Block, and Lucas (1992) reported that individuals viewed as having been hired on an affirmative action basis were not believed to have had their qualifications given much weight in the hiring process. The stigma of incompetence was found to be fairly robust, and the authors questioned whether the stigma would dissipate in the face of disconfirming information about the individuals' presumed incompetence. Kleiman and Faley (1988) concluded that although granting preferential treatment as part of an affirmative action program may help remedy discrimination inequities in the workplace, it may also affect other important societal and organizational outcomes.

A MODEL OF PERSONNEL DECISIONS

Figure 5–2 is a model outlining the sequence of factors associated with making personnel decisions. Several of these factors have been discussed in earlier chapters. The process of job and organizational analysis initiates the sequence and was presented in Chapter 3. An analysis of the job and organization establishes the context in which the personnel decisions will be made. The results of these analyses provide information useful in determining the criteria of job performance (also discussed in Chapter 3), as well as provide insights into those predictor constructs useful in forecasting job performance (as discussed in Chapter 4). The linkage between the predictors and criteria is the essence of validity—the determination of how well our predictors forecast job performance (as also discussed in Chapter 4). We are now in a position to continue the sequence used by I/O psychologists—examining issues pertaining to recruiting, designing selection systems, and assessing the utility of those systems. However, before a discussion of these issues, the next topic is a method of statistical analysis often used by I/O

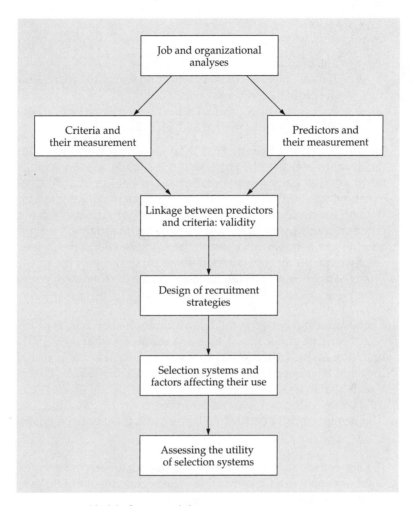

FIGURE 5–2 *Model of personnel decisions in organizations*

psychologists in assessing the linkage between predictors and criteria. It is called regression analysis.

REGRESSION ANALYSIS

The statistical technique used to predict criterion performance on the basis of a predictor score is called **regression analysis.** Although a correlation coefficient is useful for showing the degree of relationship between two variables, it is not useful for predicting one variable from the other. Regression analysis, however, does permit the prediction of a person's status on one variable (the criterion) based on his or her status on another variable (the predictor). If we assume that the relationship between the two variables is linear (as it usually is), it can be described mathematically with a regression equation:

$$\hat{Y} = a + bX \qquad\qquad \text{[Formula 5–1]}$$

where

$\hat{Y}$ = The predicted criterion score

a = A mathematical constant reflecting where the regression line intercepts the ordinate (or Y axis)

b = A mathematical constant reflecting the slope of the regression line

X = The predictor scores for a given individual

The values of a and b are derived through mathematical procedures that minimize the distance between the regression line (that is, a line useful for making predictions) and the pairs of predictor–criterion data points. To develop a regression equation, we need predictor and criterion data on a sample of people. Let us say we have a sample of 100 employees. Supervisor ratings of job performance are the criterion, and the predictor test we wish to investigate is an intelligence test. We administer the intelligence test to the workers, collect the criterion data, and then see if we can predict the criterion scores on the basis of the intelligence test scores. From the predictor–criterion data, we derive the following regression equation:

$$\hat{Y} = 1 + .5X \qquad\qquad \text{[Formula 5–2]}$$

The relationship between the two variables is shown in Figure 5–3. Note that the regression line crosses the Y axis at a value of 1 (that is, $a = 1$). Also, for every 2-unit increase in X, there is a corresponding 1-unit increase in Y. Thus, the slope of the regression line, defined as the change in Y divided by the change in X, equals $\frac{1}{2}$ or .5 (that is, $b = .5$).

For any value of X, we can now predict a corresponding Y score. For example, if someone scores 12 on the intelligence test, the predicted criterion rating is

$$\hat{Y} = 1 + .5(12) = 7 \qquad\qquad \text{[Formula 5–3]}$$

If a supervisor rating of 5 represents adequate job performance (and we do not want anyone with a lower rating), the regression equation can be worked backward to get the minimum passing score:

$$5 = 1 + .5X$$
$$X = 8$$

So, if we use the intelligence test to hire, we will not accept any applicant who scores less than 8, because those scores would result in a predicted level of job performance lower than we want. There is also another way to find the passing score. In Figure 5–3, locate the value of 5 on the Y axis (the criterion). Move horizontally to the regression line, and then drop down to the corresponding point of the X axis (the predictor). The score is 8.

Multiple Predictors

Better personnel decisions are made on the basis of more than one piece of information. How well two or more predictors combined improve the predictability of the criterion depends on their individual relationships to the criterion and their relationship to each other. Suppose two predictors both correlate with the criterion but do not correlate with each other. This relationship is illustrated by the

$$\hat{Y} = 1 + .5X$$

FIGURE 5–3   *Predictor–criterion scatterplot and regression line of best fit*

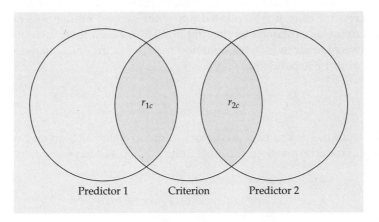

FIGURE 5–4   *Venn diagram of two uncorrelated predictors*

Venn diagram in Figure 5–4. The shaded area on the left shows how much the first predictor overlaps the criterion. The overlap area is the validity of the first predictor, symbolized by the notation r_{1c}, where the subscript 1 stands for the first predictor and the subscript c stands for the criterion. The shaded area on the right shows the extent to which the second predictor overlaps the criterion; its validity is expressed as r_{2c}. As can be seen, more of the criterion can be explained by using two predictors. Also note that the two predictors are unrelated to each other, meaning that they predict different aspects of the criterion. The combined relationship between two or more predictors and the criterion is referred to as a **multiple correlation** (R). The only conceptual difference between r and R is that the range of R is from 0 to 1.0, while r ranges from -1.0 to 1.0. When R is squared, the resulting R^2 value represents the total amount of variance in the criterion that can be explained by two or more predictors. When predictors 1 and 2 are not correlated with each other, the squared multiple correlation (R^2) is equal to the sum of the squared individual validity coefficients, or

$$R^2_{c.12} = r^2_{1c} + r^2_{2c}$$ [Formula 5–4]

For example, if $r_{1c} = .60$ and $r_{2c} = .50$, then

$$\begin{aligned} R^2_{c.12} &= (.60)^2 + (.50)^2 \\ &= .36 + .25 \\ &= .61 \end{aligned}$$ [Formula 5–5]

The notation $R^2_{c.12}$ is read "the squared multiple correlation between the criterion and two predictors." In this condition (when the two predictors are unrelated to each other), 61% of the variance in the criterion can be explained by two predictors.

In most cases, however, it is rare that two predictors related to the same criterion are unrelated to each other. Usually all three variables share some variance with one another; that is, the intercorrelation between the two predictors (r_{12}) is not zero. Such a relationship is presented graphically in Figure 5–5. In the figure each predictor correlates substantially with the criterion (r_{1c} and r_{2c}), and the two predictors also overlap each other (r_{12}). The addition of the second predictor adds more criterion variance than can be accounted for by one predictor alone. Yet all of the criterion variance accounted for by the second predictor is not new variance; part of it was explained by the first predictor. When there is a correlation between the two predictors (r_{12}), the equation for calculating the squared multiple correlation must be expanded to

$$R^2_{c.12} = \frac{r_{1c} + r_{2c} - 2r_{12}r_{1c}r_{2c}}{1 - r^2_{12}}$$ [Formula 5–6]

For example, if the two predictors intercorrelated .30, given the validity coefficients from the previous example and $r_{12} = .30$, we have

$$\begin{aligned} R^2_{c.12} &= \frac{(.60)^2 + (.50)^2 - 2(.30)(.60)(.50)}{1 - (.30)^2} \\ &= .47 \end{aligned}$$ [Formula 5–7]

As can be seen, the explanatory power of two intercorrelated predictor variables is diminished compared to the explanatory power when they are uncorrelated (.47 versus .61). This example provides a rule about multiple predictors: It is generally advisable to seek predictors that are related to the criterion but are uncorrelated with each other. However, in practice, it is very difficult to find multiple variables that are statistically related to another variable (the criterion) but at the same time statistically unrelated to each other. Usually variables that are both predictive of a criterion are also predictive of each other. Also note that the abbreviated version of the equation used to compute the squared multiple correlation with independent predictors is just a special case of the expanded equation caused by r_{12} being equal to zero.

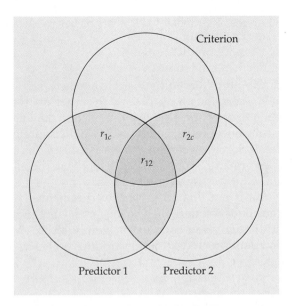

FIGURE 5–5   *Venn diagram of two correlated predictors*

Multiple Regression Analysis

The relationship between correlation and regression is the foundation for the relationship between multiple correlation and multiple regression. Just as regression permits prediction on the basis of one predictor, **multiple regression** permits prediction on the basis of multiple predictors. The logic for using multiple regression is the same as the logic for using multiple correlation: It usually enhances prediction of the criterion.

As we noted before, the formula for a regression equation with one predictor is

$$\hat{Y} = a + bX \qquad \text{[Formula 5–8]}$$

When we expand this to the case of two predictors, we have

$$\hat{Y} = a + b_1 X_1 + b_2 X_2 \qquad \text{[Formula 5–9]}$$

where X_1 and X_2 are the two predictors and b_1 and b_2 are the regression weights associated with the two predictors. As before, the b values are based in part on the correlation between the predictors and the criterion. In multiple regression the b values are also influenced by the correlation among the predictors. However, the procedure for making predictions in multiple regression is similar to that used in one-predictor (or simple) regression. Suppose we have criterion data on a sample of industrial workers who take two tests we think may be useful for hiring future workers. We analyze the data to derive the values of a, b_1, and b_2 and arrive at this regression equation:

$$\hat{Y} = 2 + .4X_1 + .7X_2 \qquad \text{[Formula 5–10]}$$

If a person scores 30 on test 1 and 40 on test 2, his or her predicted criterion performance is

$$\hat{Y} = 2 + .4(30) + .7(40) = 42$$

The degree of predictability afforded by the two predictors is measured by the multiple correlation between the predictors and the criterion. If the multiple correlation is large enough to be of some value for prediction purposes, we might use the two tests to hire future workers. The company would undoubtedly set a minimum predicted criterion score at a certain value—say, 40. In this example, the person's predicted job performance score (42) was higher than the minimum score set by the company (40), so the person would be hired.

Multiple regression is not limited to just two predictors; predictors can be added to the regression equation until they no longer enhance prediction of the criterion. The k-predictor regression equation is simply an extension of the two-predictor regression equation, and all terms are interpreted as before. Such an equation looks like this:

$$\hat{Y} = a + b_1X_1 + b_2X_2 + b_3X_3 + \cdots + b_kX_k \qquad \text{[Formula 5–11]}$$

Usually, there comes a point at which adding more predictors will not enhance the prediction of the criterion. Regression equations with four or five predictors usually do as good a job as those with more. The reason is that the shared variance among the predictors becomes very large after four to five predictors, so adding more does not add unique variance in the criterion. If we could find another predictor that was (1) uncorrelated with the other predictors and (2) correlated with the criterion, it would be a useful addition to the equation. Multiple regression is a very popular prediction strategy in I/O psychology and is used extensively.

VALIDITY GENERALIZATION

The concept of **validity generalization** refers to a predictor's validity spreading or generalizing to other jobs or contexts beyond the one in which it was validated. For example, let us say that a test is found valid for hiring secretaries in a company. If that same test is found useful in hiring secretaries in another company, we say its validity has generalized. That same test could also be useful in selecting people for a different job, such as clerks. This is another case of the test's validity generalizing. Schmitt and Landy (1993) graphically depicted the domains across which validity can generalize, as shown in Figure 5–6. Validity generalization has long been a goal of I/O psychologists because its implication would certainly make our jobs easier. However, the problem is that when we examined whether a test's validity would generalize across either companies or jobs, we often found that it did not; that is, the test's validity was specific to the situation in which it was originally validated. The implication, of course, was that we had to validate every test in every situation in which it was used. We could not assume that its validity would generalize.

Schmidt and Hunter (1978, 1980) support validity generalization as a means of selecting personnel. They argue that the problem of situational specificity of test validity is based on psychologists' erroneous belief in the "law of small numbers," which is the belief that whatever results hold for large samples will also hold for

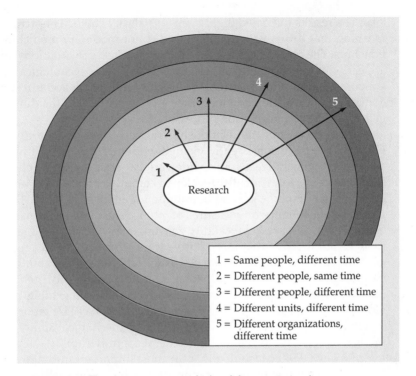

FIGURE 5–6   *The domains across which validity can generalize*

SOURCE: From *Personnel Selection in Organizations* by N. Schmitt and F. J. Landy, © 1993, San Francisco: Jossey-Bass.
All rights reserved. Reprinted by permission of the publisher.

small samples. They think this belief is incorrect—that small-sample results are highly unstable, resulting in highly variable test validities. Schmidt and Hunter believe that in most cases psychologists use small samples (40 to 50) to validate tests. Indeed, Monahan and Muchinsky (1983) found that in fewer than 10% of the personnel selection validation studies conducted over a 30-year period did the researchers use a sufficiently large sample size, according to the standards Schmidt and Hunter recommend. So test validities are situation specific. Schmidt and Hunter argue that if tests were validated in large samples, the results would generalize (not be situation specific).

Validity generalization means that there is a single "true" relationship between a test and job performance, as for a secretary. Let us say that relationship has a correlation of .40 based on validity studies involving thousands of subjects each. In theory, we could generalize the validity of these findings from huge sample sizes to more typical employment situations with small samples. Organizations with immense sample sizes (such as the military or federal government) would validate certain tests; the rest of the business world would simply "borrow" these validities as a basis for using the tests for hiring. Alternatively, appropriately large samples can be found by pooling results from many smaller studies through meta-analysis.

In support of their position, Schmidt and Hunter (1978) presented data based on a sample of more than 10,000 individuals. The sample was drawn from the army. Data were reported on ten predictors that were used to forecast success in 35 jobs. The results indicated highly similar validity coefficients across different jobs, meaning that differences among jobs did not moderate predictor–criterion relationships. The researchers concluded that the effects of situational moderators disappear with appropriately large sample sizes. One psychological construct that is supposedly common for success in all jobs (and which accounts for validity generalizing or spreading) is intelligence and, in particular, the dimension of intelligence relating to information processing.

Meta-analyses of the relationship between tests of cognitive ability and job performance have consistently yielded evidence that the validity of intelligence does indeed generalize across a wide variety of occupations. Schmidt and Hunter (1981) stated, "Professionally developed cognitive ability tests are valid predictors of performance on the job and in training for all jobs" (p. 1128). Such a conclusion increases our reliance on measures of g to forecast job performance. However, as Guion (1998) observed, the validity generalization conclusion about cognitive ability does not indicate that all cognitive tests are *equally* valid predictors across all jobs, all criteria, or all circumstances. Thus, while cognitive ability does predict job performance across many occupations, it is not comparably predictive in all cases. Even in lower-level jobs, however, cognitive ability still exhibits respectable levels of predictive validity. Borman, Hanson, and Hedge (1997) reported that some research indicates that specific abilities (such as mechanical ability) are in fact more predictive of job performance than general cognitive ability.

Murphy (1997) concluded that the most important message of validity generalization research is that "validation studies based on small samples and unreliable measures are simply a bad idea" (p. 337). Such studies are more likely to mislead us into believing validity varies greatly across situations. The impact of validity generalization research has been to improve the way researchers design validation studies. When research is designed improperly, the conclusions will most likely be erroneous. Guion (1998) believes that validity generalization is one of the major methodological advances in personnel selection research in the past 20 years. It has allowed personnel selection specialists to infer criterion-related evidence and therefore use cognitive ability tests in situations where a local validity study would have been infeasible and might therefore preclude the use of cognitive ability testing.

SELECTION

Personnel selection is the process of identifying from the pool of recruited applicants those to whom a job will be offered. As long as there are fewer job openings than applicants, some applicants will be hired and some won't. Selection is the process of separating the selected from the rejected applicants. Ideally, the selected employees will be successful on the job and contribute to the welfare of the organization. Three major factors determine the quality of the newly selected employees and the degree to which they can affect the organization: the validity of the predictor, the selection ratio, and the base rate.

Predictor Validity.   Figure 5–7 shows a predictor–criterion correlation of .80, which is reflected in the oval shape of the scatterplot of the predictor and criterion

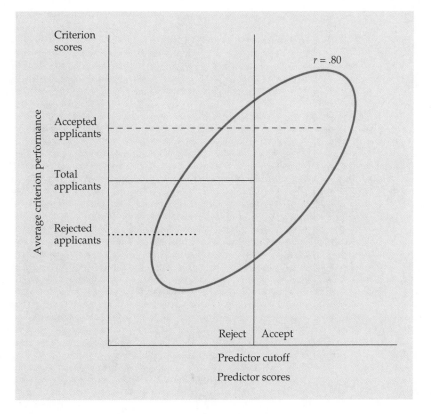

FIGURE 5–7 *Effect of a predictor with a high validity (r = .80) on test utility*

scores. Along the predictor axis is a vertical line—the **predictor cutoff**—that separates passing from failing applicants. People above the cutoff are accepted for hire; those below it are rejected. Also, observe the three horizontal lines. The solid line, representing the criterion performance of the entire group, cuts the entire distribution of scores in half. The dotted line, representing the criterion performance of the rejected group, is below the performance of the total group. Finally, the dashed line, which is the average criterion performance of the accepted group, is above the performance of the total group. The people who would be expected to perform the best on the job fall above the predictor cutoff. In a simple and straightforward sense, that is what a valid predictor does in personnel selection: It identifies the more capable people from the total pool.

A different picture emerges for a predictor that has no correlation with the criterion, as shown in Figure 5–8. Again, the predictor cutoff separates those accepted from those rejected. This time, however, the three horizontal lines are all superimposed; that is, the criterion performance of the accepted group is no better than that of the rejected group, and both are the same as the performance of the total group. The value of the predictor is measured by the difference between the average performance of the accepted group and the average performance of the total group. As can be seen, these two values are the same, so their difference equals zero. In other words, predictors that have no validity also have no value.

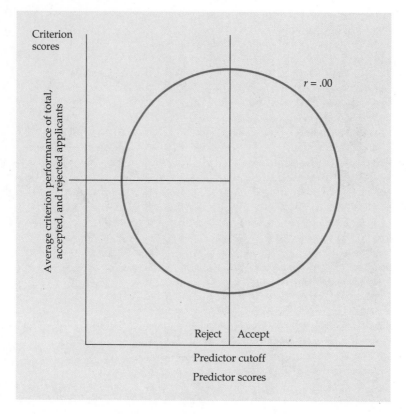

FIGURE 5–8   *Effect of a predictor test with no validity (r = .00) on test utility*

On the basis of this example, we see a direct relationship between a predictor's value and its validity: The greater the validity of the predictor, the greater its value as measured by the increase in average criterion performance for the accepted group over that for the total group.

Selection Ratio.   A second factor that determines the value of a predictor is the selection ratio (SR). The **selection ratio** is defined as the number of job openings (*n*) divided by the number of job applicants (*N*):

$$SR = \frac{n}{N}$$

[Formula 5–12]

When the SR is equal to 1 (there are as many openings as there are applicants) or greater (there are more openings than applicants), the use of any selection device has little meaning. The company can use any applicant who walks through the door. But most often, there are more applicants than openings (the SR is somewhere between 0 and 1), and the SR is meaningful for personnel selection.

The effect of the SR on a predictor's value can be seen in Figures 5–9 and 5–10. Let us assume we have a validity coefficient of .80 and the selection ratio is .75, meaning we will hire three out of every four applicants. Figure 5–9 shows the

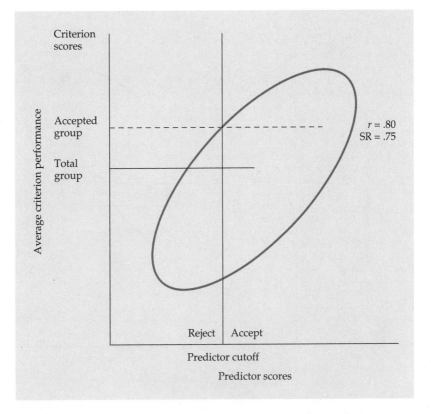

FIGURE 5–9   *Effect of a large selection ratio (SR = .75) on test utility*

predictor–criterion relationship, the predictor cutoff that results in accepting the top 75% of all applicants, and the respective average criterion performances of the total group and the accepted group. If a company hires the top 75%, the average criterion performance of that group is greater than that of the total group (which is weighted down by the bottom 25% of the applicants). Again, value is measured by this difference between average criterion scores. Further, when the bottom 25% is lopped off (the one applicant out of four who is not hired), the average criterion performance of the accepted group is greater than that of the total group.

In Figure 5–10 we have the same validity coefficient ($r = .80$), but this time the SR is .25; that is, out of every four applicants, we will hire only one. The figure shows the location of the predictor cutoff that results in hiring only the top 25% of all applicants and the respective average criterion performances of the total and accepted groups. The average criterion performance of the accepted group is not only above that of the total group as before, but the difference is also much greater. In other words, when only the top 25% are hired, their average criterion performance is greater than the performance of the top 75% of the applicants, and both of these values are greater than the average performance of the total group.

The relationship between the SR and the predictor's value should be clear: The smaller the SR, the greater the predictor's value. This should also make sense intuitively. The fussier we are in admitting people (that is, the smaller the selection

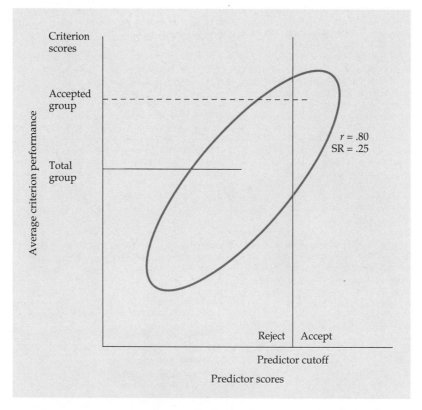

FIGURE 5–10   *Effect of a small selection ratio (SR = .25) on test utility*

ratio), the more likely it is that the people admitted (or hired) will be of the quality we desire.

Base Rate.   The third factor that influences the utility of a predictor is the percentage of present employees who are successful, called the **base rate.** Management usually decides what constitutes successful job performance. It has in mind a standard or critical value that separates successful from unsuccessful workers. This critical value is the criterion cutoff. For example, in most undergraduate colleges, the criterion cutoff separating successful from unsuccessful students is a C average (2.0/4.0).

In absolute terms, the largest gains in average criterion performance occur with a base rate of .50; that is, a new predictor produces the greatest increase in the number of people who attain satisfactory performance if the base rate is .50. As the base rate becomes more extreme (high or low), the absolute utility of the predictor decreases. In other words, it is difficult for a predictor to change the actual number of workers who are performing successfully if the current group of employees is performing extremely well or poorly. In summary, the relationship between the percentage of present employees who are performing successfully and predictor value is as follows: The closer the base rate is to .50, the greater will be the gain in the actual number of new employees who will perform successfully.

Selection Decisions

As long as the predictor used for selection has less than perfect validity ($r = 1.00$), we will always make some errors in personnel selection. The object is, of course, to make as few mistakes as possible. With the aid of the scatterplot, we can examine where the mistakes occur in making selection decisions.

Part (a) of Figure 5–11 shows a predictor–criterion relationship of about .80 where the criterion scores have been separated by a criterion cutoff. The criterion cutoff is the point that separates successful (above) from unsuccessful (below) employees. Again, management decides what constitutes successful and unsuccessful performance (see Field Note 2). Part (b) shows the same predictor–criterion relationship, except this time the predictor scores have been separated by a predictor cutoff. The predictor cutoff is the point that separates accepted (right) from rejected (left) applicants. The score that constitutes passing the predictor test is determined by the selection ratio, cost factors, or occasionally law.[1] Part (c) shows the predictor–criterion relationship intersected by both cutoffs. Each of the resulting four sections of the scatterplot is identified by a letter representing a different group of people:

Section A: Applicants who are above the predictor cutoff and above the criterion cutoff are called **true positives.** These are the people we think will succeed on the job because they passed the predictor test, and who in fact turn

[1]In some public-sector organizations (for example, state governments), the passing score for a test is determined by law. Usually a passing score is set at 70% correct.

Field Note 2 Raising the Bar

A popular expression heard in organizations is the desire to "raise the bar"—meaning to elevate the organization's standards above current levels. If the organization believes it necessary to have higher standards associated with its operations, then it will "raise the bar" regarding what it considers to be acceptable or satisfactory. A good way to visualize this metaphor (both literally and figuratively) is with regard to personnel selection. Assume an organization uses a test that manifests criterion-related validity to select employees for its sales jobs. Let us further assume that the standard of satisfactory performance (or the criterion cutoff) is selling $1,000,000 in products per year. Assume the minimum score that corresponds to that sales figure is 87 on the test. However, the company decides that $1,000,000 per year no longer represents acceptable job performance; they now decide to elevate the sales standard to $1,250,000 per year. Think of the horizontal line reflecting the criterion cutoff in Figure 5–11(a) as the "bar." By "raising the bar," or elevating the minimum standard from $1,000,000 to $1,250,000, the organization seeks a higher level of job performance. To select employees who can attain this new higher level of job performance also entails raising the passing score on the test, for example, from 87 to 92. Because the test manifests criterion-related validity, the better people perform on the test, the better they perform on the job. To perform on the job at a level of $1,250,000 in sales per year now requires scoring 92 on the test. The expression "raising the bar" in this case refers to elevating the standard, first on the criterion and then the concomitant effect of that decision on raising the standard passing score on the test.

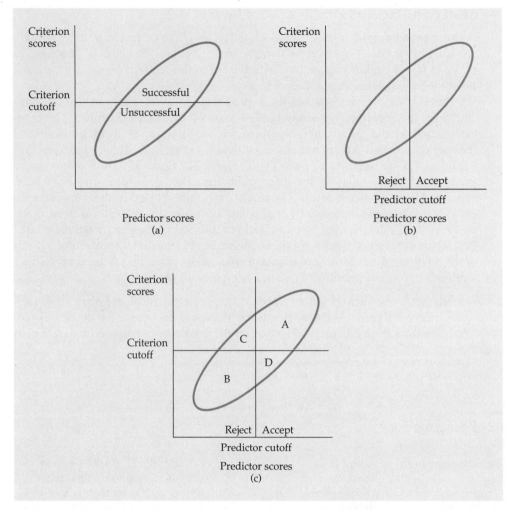

FIGURE 5–11   *Effect of establishing (a) criterion cutoff, (b) predictor cutoff, and (c) both cutoffs on a predictor–criterion scatterplot*

out to be successful employees. This group represents a correct decision: We correctly decided to hire them.

Section B: The people in this group are those we thought would not succeed on the job because they failed the predictor test and who, if hired anyway, would have performed unsatisfactorily. This group represents a correct decision: We correctly predicted they would not succeed on the job. These people are **true negatives.**

Section C: People who failed the predictor test (and are thus predicted not to succeed on the job) but who would have succeeded had they been given the chance are called **false negatives.** We have made a mistake in our decision-making process with these people. They would really turn out to be good employees, but we mistakenly decided they would not succeed. These are "the good ones we let get away."

Section D: The people who passed the predictor test (and are thus predicted to succeed on the job) but perform unsatisfactorily after being hired are called **false positives.** We have also erred with these people. They are really ineffective employees who should not have been hired, but we mistakenly thought they would succeed. They are "the bad ones we let in."

Positive/negative refers to the result of passing/failing the predictor test; *true/false* refers to the quality (good/bad) of our decision to hire the person. In personnel selection we want to minimize the false positives and false negatives.

If there is no difference between making false positive and false negative decisions (that is, letting a bad worker in is no worse than letting a good one get away), it does no good to "juggle" the predictor cutoff scores. By lowering the predictor cutoff in part (c) of Figure 5–11 (moving the line to the left), we *decrease* the size of section C, the false negatives. But by reducing the number of false negatives, we *increase* the space in section D, the false positives. The converse holds for raising the predictor cutoff (moving the line to the right). Furthermore, classification errors (false positives and false negatives) are also influenced by extreme base rates. For example, when the behavior being predicted occurs very rarely (as employees who will commit violent acts in the workplace), the differential likelihood of one type of error over the other is great (Martin & Terris, 1991). However, cutoff scores cannot be established solely for the purpose of minimizing false positives or false negatives. Cascio, Alexander, and Barrett (1988) indicated that there must be some rational relationship between the cutoff score and the purpose of the test. Issues pertaining to the cutoff score will be discussed in the next section.

For many years, employers were not indifferent between making false positive and false negative mistakes. Most employers preferred to let a good employee get away (in the belief that someone else who is good could be hired) rather than hire a bad worker. The cost of training, reduced efficiency, turnover, and so on made the false positive highly undesirable. Although most employers still want to avoid false positives, false negatives are also important. The applicant who fails the predictor test and sues the employer on the grounds of using unfair tests can be very expensive. If people do fail an employment test, employers want to be as sure as possible that they were not rejected due to unfair and discriminatory practices. Denying employment to a qualified applicant is tragic; denying employment to a qualified minority applicant can be both tragic and expensive. Both types of selection errors can be reduced by increasing the validity of the predictor test. The greater the validity of the predictor, the smaller the chance that people will be mistakenly classified.

Determination of the Cutoff Score

Have you ever wondered how certain cutoff or passing scores came to be? Why is 70% correct associated with passing a test (such as a driving test)? In educational institutions, why are the cutoffs of 90%, 80%, and 70% usually associated with the grades of A, B, and C, respectively? It has been reported that in ancient China several thousand years ago an emperor decreed that 70% correct was needed to successfully pass a test. That 70% correct figure, or relatively close approximations, has been used throughout history in a wide range of assessment contexts as representing a standard to guide pass/fail decisions. While I/O psychologists are primarily limited to assessment decisions in employment contexts, we too have had to wrestle with issues pertaining to the determination of where to set the cutoff score.

Cascio, Alexander, and Barrett (1988) addressed the legal, psychometric, and professional issues associated with setting cutoff scores. As they reported, there is a wide variation regarding the appropriate standards to use in evaluating the suitability of established cutoff scores. In general, a cutoff score should normally be set to be reasonable and consistent with the expectations of acceptable job proficiency in the workplace. Also, the cutoff should be set at a point that selects employees who are capable of learning a job and performing it in a safe and efficient manner. Thus, undesirable selection consequences are associated with setting the cutoff score "too low" (an increase in false positive selection decisions) or "too high" (an increase in false negative selection decisions).

When there is criterion-related evidence of a test's validity, it is possible to demonstrate a direct correspondence between performance on the test and performance on the criterion, which aids in selecting a reasonable cutoff score. Take, for example, the case of predicting academic success in college. The criterion of academic success is college grade point average, and the criterion cutoff is a C average, or 2.0 on a 4.0 scale. That is, students who attain a grade point average of 2.0 or higher graduate, whereas those with a grade point average of less than 2.0 do not graduate from college. Furthermore, assume the selection (admission) test for entrance into the college is a 100-point test of cognitive ability. With a criterion-related validation paradigm, it is established that there is an empirical linkage between scores on the test and college grade point average. The statistical analysis of the scores reveals the relationship shown in Figure 5–12. Because a minimum grade point average of 2.0 is needed to graduate and there is a relationship between test scores and college grade point average, we can determine (through regression analysis) the exact test score associated with a predicted grade point average of 2.0. In this example, a test score of 50 is predictive of a grade point average of 2.0. Therefore, a score of 50 becomes the cutoff score on the intellectual ability test.

The task of determining a cutoff score is much more difficult when only content-related evidence of the validity of a given test is available. In such cases it is important to consider the level of ability associated with a certain test score that is judged suitable or relevant to job performance. However, obvious subjectivity is associated with such decisions. In general, there is no such thing as a single, uniform, correct cutoff score. Nor is there a single best method of setting cutoff scores for all situations. Cascio et al. (1988) made several suggestions regarding the setting of cutoff scores. Here are three:

- The process of setting a cutoff score should begin with a job analysis that identifies relative levels of proficiency on critical knowledge, skills, and abilities (KSAs).
- When possible, data on the actual relationship of test scores to criterion measures of job performance should be considered carefully.
- Cutoff scores should be set high enough to ensure that minimum standards of job performance are met.

In summarizing the process of determining a passing score, Ebel (1972) noted: "Anyone who expects to discover the 'real' passing score . . . is doomed to disappointment, for a 'real' passing score does not exist to be discovered. All any

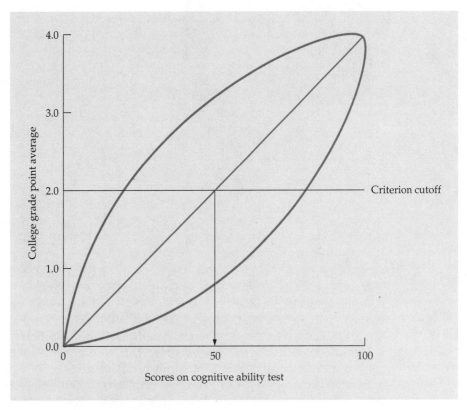

FIGURE 5–12   *Determining the cutoff score through a test's criterion-related validity*

examining authority . . . can hope for, and all any of their examinees can ask, is that the basis for defining the passing score be defined clearly, and that the definition be as rational as possible" (p. 496).

In addition to measurement issues associated with determining a cutoff score, there are legal issues to consider. Many of these legal issues pertain to adverse impact. It will be recalled that adverse impact is determined by the "80% rule"; that is, adverse impact is said to exist if the selection ratio associated with a particular passing score on a test for one subgroup of job applicants is less than four-fifths (or 80%) of the selection ratio for the largest subgroup of job applicants. Suppose, for example, the passing score on a selection test results in a selection ratio of 70% for male applicants, but only 40% for female applicants. Because 40% is less than four-fifths of 70% ($\frac{4}{5}$ × 70% = 56%), the particular passing score has an adverse impact against female applicants. Some organizations mistakenly believed that they could avoid the issue of adverse impact by setting a cutoff score so low that virtually all of the applicants pass the test (i.e., the selection ratio is extremely high). The courts have recognized this procedure to be futile, for if an organization is unable to weed out those individuals who are minimally qualified, there is no justification for using the test in the first place. Setting a very low cutoff score tends, in the opinion of the courts, to destroy the credibility of the entire testing process.

An alternative to setting low cutoff scores is a procedure called **banding** (Murphy, Osten, & Myors, 1995). The traditional approach to personnel selection is to rank applicants on the basis of their test scores and select the applicants with the highest scores. An alternative approach involves test score banding, in which some differences in test scores are ignored, and individuals whose scores fall within the same band are selected on some basis other than the test score (such as gender or race), thereby eliminating or greatly reducing adverse impact. The width of the band is a function of the reliability of the test. Highly reliable tests produce relatively narrow bands, while less reliable tests produce wider test score bands. Thus a one-point difference in test scores (e.g., a score of 90 versus 89) is not judged to be of sufficient magnitude to reflect a meaningful difference in the applicants' respective abilities. One then extends this logic to a two-point difference in test scores, a three-point difference, and so on. Eventually, a certain magnitude of differences in test scores *is* determined to reflect a meaningful difference in ability. It is at this point where this band ends, and other bands may be formed from the distribution of test scores.

Banding is a controversial interpretation of test scores. Proponents of the method (e.g., Siskin, 1995; Zedeck, Outtz, Cascio, & Goldstein, 1995) argue that banding achieves the objectives of hiring able candidates while avoiding adverse impact. Critics of the method (e.g., Schmidt, 1991; Schmidt & Hunter, 1995) contend that banding leads to the conclusion that random selection (i.e., ignoring test scores altogether) is logically defensible, which is anathema to the classic principles of measurement. There is also concern (Gottfredson, 1994; Sackett & Wilk, 1994) that banding may lead to an overemphasis on certain types of selection errors relative to others. The ultimate resolution of the question on whether banding is advisable is likely to depend on the organization's values regarding social and economic issues. The controversy also underscores the point raised by Ebel (1972) that there is no one professionally agreed-upon method to determine passing scores on tests. Furthermore, sometimes selection decisions are made for reasons having little to do with passing scores (see Field Note 3).

Field Note 3 *Dirty Politics*

This chapter is devoted to explaining how personnel decisions are made. Many factors have been identified and explained, but one has been left out. I've never seen it discussed in any book or article on personnel selection, but (unfortunately) it is sometimes a critical, if not deciding, factor. It is called politics. Consider this experience I had.

I was hired for a very important consulting project: to pick the chief of police for a large city. The job has tremendous visibility, high influence, and great responsibility. I didn't want to "blow it" as the consultant. The city recruited applicants for the opening, and a total of 50 applicants met the minimum qualifications for consideration set by the city. I was handed the 50 applications and told to identify the best candidates in the applicant pool.

My first step was to evaluate each candidate in terms of education and experience using a weighted application-blank procedure. That got the applicant pool down to 25. These 25 quarter-finalists then had to submit written answers to three essay test questions about how they would

Field Note 3   *(continued)*

handle some difficult police problems. These answers were evaluated, and the 15 best applicants proceeded to the semifinalist stage. Here the candidates took a series of personality inventories and intelligence tests. Based on those results, 10 finalists were selected and in turn were subjected to a lengthy oral interview. From all the assessment results, I rank ordered the 10 finalists and submitted the list to the city council, which had the judicial authority to approve the new chief of police. The candidate ranked first was from a different state; the candidate ranked second was the current assistant chief of police, the second in command. The candidate ranked first was clearly the best person for the job, far and away better than anyone else. I thought the city council (composed of seven people) had an easy job: to approve the top candidate as the new chief of police. It is here that politics came in, and it got rather dirty.

The assistant chief of police was a close friend of three city council members. They played cards together, as did their wives. From the very beginning, the three city council members had known the assistant chief of police would rank high in the selection process. In fact, nearly everyone had thought he would be the next chief of police. When I presented the city council with my list of the 10 candidates, things got very awkward: "Their man" was not first on the list. The press followed the selection process carefully because it was a hot news item. The media announced the rank order of the 10 finalists. The public's general reaction was to have the city council approve the candidate who had been ranked first. But the head of the city council was not about to sell out his old friend.

The head of the city council (one of the three friends) then made this startling announcement. Because every rookie cop on the force dreams about one day rising to be the chief, to award the chief's job to an "outsider" (that is, a candidate not native to the city) would

destroy the morale of the police force and take away every rookie's dream forever. Therefore, he was going to advise the city council to select as the next chief of police not the person ranked first (the outsider) but the person ranked second (the assistant chief, and his friend). This was the first time anyone had made any reference at all to the insider/outsider distinction. It was a new hurdle imposed at the eleventh hour as a means of bumping the top-ranked candidate from the list. Some members of the community howled in protest at this announcement, as did the media, declaring it was a "fix" to install the council's personal choice. All the three city council members had to do was convince a fourth member to vote for the second-ranked person and he would be in. In a highly electrified meeting of the city council in a council chamber jam-packed with reporters and camera crews, the city council members publicly cast their votes. By a 4–3 vote, the number-one-ranked candidate (the outsider) was approved and became the new chief of police.

I would like to believe the four "yes" votes came from people who recognized the quality of the top candidate, but I know better. Politics being what it is, strange things can happen. They voted the way they did not simply because they supported the stronger candidate but because they wanted to get even with the three council members against whom they had held a grudge from a previous political episode. In short, the right decision was made, but for the wrong reason.

I wish to emphasize that there was absolutely nothing in my graduate training to prepare me for this experience. Similarly, there is no section of this book titled "How to Cope with Political Intrigue." But politics is a driving force in all organizations at all levels. Given this fact, sometimes I wonder how I/O psychologists accomplish as much as they do.

TEST UTILITY AND ORGANIZATIONAL EFFICIENCY

It is important to remember that a human resources office is only one part of an organization. Each part must contribute to the organization's overall success. If the company is a profit-making firm (as many are) or just wants to improve its operating efficiency (as all organizations should), a basic question is how much improved personnel-selection techniques contribute to its overall profitability or efficiency. If more productive workers are hired as a result of a new selection technique, how much value or utility will they have to the company? Several studies have shown just how much utility a valid testing program can provide.

Schmidt, Hunter, McKenzie, and Muldrow (1979) estimated the dollar value to the company of using a valid employee-selection program. They analyzed the job of a computer programmer. They asked supervisors to estimate the "worth" (in dollars) of good, average, and poor computer programmers. Supervisors considered such factors as work speed, number of errors, and so on. The authors used the responses along with the following information they had collected: (1) a certain test useful in hiring computer programmers had a validity of .76; (2) it cost $10 to administer the test to each applicant; (3) over 4,000 computer programmers were employed by the company (which was, in this case, the federal government); (4) over 600 new programmers were hired each year; and (5) once on the job, the average programmer lasted about ten years.

Using all this information, the authors compared the expected utility of the test with other tests that had been used in the past and had validities ranging from .00 to .50. They also examined the effect of various selection ratios ranging from .05 to .80. The dollar value to the government of using the more valid test was astonishing. When the previously used test was assumed to have a validity of .50 and the selection ratio was .80, the incremental gain in efficiency (that is, the result of hiring better-quality people) was $5.6 million in one year. This was the smallest dollar gain because the previous testing conditions were quite favorable ($r = .50$). Given the poorest testing condition (a previous test with no validity) and a selection ratio of .05, the dollar gain was $97.2 million in one year.

Keep in mind that these dollar values pertain to using just one test to hire people in one job in one organization for one year. If you extend these principles to testing in general across many jobs and many companies (and also across time), the dollar value extends into the billions. Other studies have shown that the utility of valid tests enhances efficiency by reducing turnover, training time, and accidents. The key element in improved utility is test validity. The impact of test validity on subsequent job performance is dramatic; there is no substitute for using "good" selection techniques.

The concept of assessing the dollar value of using valid selection tests has also prompted some admonitions. Cascio (1993) challenged the assumption that all applicants who are offered jobs accept and are hired. In practice, lower-scoring applicants must be accepted in place of higher-scoring applicants who decline offers of employment. When unemployment is low, companies may be forced to lower their minimum hiring requirements in order to fill vacancies. Lower hiring requirements mean higher selection ratios. Smith, Farr, and Schuler (1993) discussed the difference between considering utility for a particular organization versus for society as a whole. In a single organization, the worst candidates can be selected out. In the economy as a whole, this is only marginally possible. Even in times of high unemployment (10%), 90% of the economically active population are at work. Selection merely shifts the static pool of talent toward organizations that have high selection standards, without any net gain to the economy as a whole. The underlying significance of all these findings is that while utility is a valuable concept for guiding personnel decisions, a number of factors make utility estimates inexact, or at the least contingent upon complicating issues.

Hazer and Highhouse (1997) concluded that the complexity of utility analysis makes potential users of the method skeptical, and they recommended using the simplest approaches to the method. Although Carson, Becker, and Henderson (1998) were able to make some progress in getting managers to understand utility analysis, they concluded that the acceptability of the procedure to managers was "disappointingly low." Whyte and Latham (1997) referred to the reluctance of managers to understand and accept the rational statistically-based conclusions of the procedure as the "futility of utility analysis." Cronshaw (1997) suggested that the best feature of utility analysis might be its informational value provided by psychologists to assist managers in making personnel decisions. This use is in contrast to presenting utility analysis as a sales and marketing technique to persuade managers to adopt a particular selection method.

PLACEMENT AND CLASSIFICATION

The vast majority of research in personnel psychology is on selection, the process by which applicants are hired. Another personnel function (albeit less common) involves deciding which jobs people should be assigned to after they have been hired. This personnel function is called either *placement* or *classification*, depending on the basis for the assignment. In many cases selection and placement are not separate procedures. Usually people apply for certain fixed jobs. If they are hired, they fill the jobs they were applying for. However, in some organizations (and at certain times in our nation's history), decisions about selection and placement have to be made separately.

Placement and classification decisions are usually limited to large organizations that have two or more jobs an applicant could fill. It must be decided which job best matches the person's talents and abilities. A classic example is the military. Thousands of applicants used to be selected each year, either voluntarily or through the draft. The next question was where to assign them. Placement and classification procedures are designed to get the best match between people and jobs.

Placement differs from classification on the basis of the number of predictors used to make the job assignment. **Placement** involves allocating people to two or more groups (or jobs) on the basis of a single predictor score. Many junior high school students are placed into math classes on the basis of a math aptitude test. The aptitude test is usually given during seventh grade. Students with high math aptitude are placed in an algebra class in eighth grade; students with average aptitude do not take algebra until ninth grade; students with low math aptitude do not take algebra until tenth grade, if at all. Applicants for secretarial positions may be placed into job grades (for example, secretary I, secretary II) on the basis of a typing test. The point is that placement decisions are made on the basis of one predictor factor (math aptitude, typing speed, and so on).

Classification involves allocating people to jobs on the basis of two or more valid predictor factors. For this reason, classification is more complex; however, it results in a better assignment of people to jobs than placement. Classification uses smaller selection ratios than placement, which accounts for its greater utility. The reason classification is not always used instead of placement is that it is often difficult to find more than one valid predictor to use in assigning people to jobs. The military has been the object of most classification research. Military recruits take a battery of different tests covering such areas as intelligence, ability, and aptitude. On the basis of these scores, recruits are assigned to jobs in the infantry, medical corps, military intelligence, and so on. Other organizations that have to assign large numbers of people to large numbers of jobs also use this procedure. Given this constraint, relatively few companies need to use classification procedures.

Two sets of issues are particularly important in the areas of placement and classification. The first issue is the nature of the jobs that need to be filled. Placement and classification decisions are easier when the jobs are very different. It is easier to decide whether a person should be assigned as a manager or a clerk than to decide between a secretary and a clerk. The manager and clerk jobs require very different types of skills, whereas the secretary and clerk jobs have many similar job requirements. These decisions become more complex when the jobs require successive operations (such as on an assembly line) or coordination among work units. In these cases, we are also concerned about how well all of the people in the work unit fit together to form a cohesive team.

The second issue is values. What is best in terms of satisfaction and productivity for the individual may not be best for the company, and vice versa. There can be conflicts between individuals and organizations about which values underlie manpower allocation decisions. Basically three strategies are possible; each reflects different values.

The *vocational guidance strategy* aims to maximize the values of the individual in terms of his or her wants or preferences. College students select their own majors based on the careers they wish to pursue. In other words, no college ever states that a student "must" major in a certain area; the decision is strictly an individual one.

The *pure selection strategy* maximizes organizational values. In this case only the best-qualified people are placed in a job. Although the placed people are indeed very good, the method is somewhat impractical. Large numbers of people might not be placed into any job because they are not the "best" of the applicants. The method is inherently wasteful because many applicants remain unemployed. Both the vocational guidance and pure selection strategies have weaknesses. While the vocational guidance method may work well in educational institutions, it does not work well in industry. If all the applicants wanted to be the company president, large numbers of jobs would go unfilled.

The *successive selection strategy* is a compromise between the two extremes. In this method all jobs are filled by at least minimally qualified people, and, given the available jobs, people are placed into those that will make the best use of their talents. Successive selection is a good compromise because the jobs get filled (the organization's needs are met) and the individuals get assigned to jobs for which they are suited (the individual's needs are met).

At one time, placement and classification were as important as (if not more so than) selection. During World War II, industry needed large numbers of people to produce war materiel. The question was not whether people would get a job but what kind of job they would fill. A similar situation occurred in the military as thousands of recruits were being inducted every month. It was of paramount importance to get the right people into the right jobs. Today the greatest amount of interest in classification continues in the military (Rumsey, Walker, & Harris, 1994). Researchers interested in classification have addressed many of the same issues that are confronted in selection. For example, Bobko (1994) reported that the most vexing issues facing classification decisions revolve around values, such as attaining ethnic and gender balance versus maximizing performance. The relative importance of general mental ability (*g*) versus consideration of other factors as well is also a matter of debate in making classification decisions. Zeidner and Johnson (1994) believe other factors besides *g* must be considered in efficiently assigning individuals to jobs. In addition to cognitive ability, Alley (1994) recommended the assessment of personality, interests, and knowledge. The rationale behind placement and classification remains the same: Certain people will perform better in certain jobs than others. To this end, placement and classification are aimed at assigning people to jobs in which their predicted job performance will be the greatest.

CASE STUDY ◆ Just Give Me a Chance

Hugh Casey slumped at his desk, totally dejected. He just read the letter from Fulbright University informing him that his application for admission into the school of medicine had been rejected. It had been his dream since high school to become a doctor, and in particular to be a heart surgeon. Hugh had been an excellent student in high school and was admitted to the highly selective Seymour College despite achieving only a modest score on the college admission test. His interest in medicine was sparked when his father had triple-bypass heart surgery. The surgeon who performed the operation, Dr. Charles Dressen, was a friend of the family. Dr. Dressen had graduated from Fulbright University's medical school, which was nationally renowned for its high standards. Fulbright was the premier medical school in the region. Hugh wanted to emulate Dr. Dressen, to become a heart surgeon who saved lives, just as Dr. Dressen had saved his father's life. Fulbright was not only his first choice for medical school, it was his only choice. Hugh felt it almost was his destiny to graduate with a medical degree from Fulbright and follow in Dr. Dressen's footsteps.

At Seymour College, Hugh made the dean's list the previous four semesters. His overall grade point average was 3.60. After a rough freshman year, which many first-year students experience, he settled down and performed very well in the pre-med curriculum. At the start of his senior year he took the medical college admission test and did not score extremely well. It was the same story with the admission test used by Seymour. He just didn't test well in standardized three-hour examinations. However, Hugh felt he had more than proved himself by his performance at Seymour. He believed that doing well over a four-year period should count more in his application to medical school than his performance in a three-hour test.

Furthermore, three professors at Seymour wrote what they said were very positive letters of recommendation on his behalf. Additionally, even Dr. Dressen, a graduate of Fulbright's medical school, wrote a letter to his alma mater in support of Hugh. Finally, Hugh traveled to Fulbright for an interview with the medical school's admission committee. While he was admittedly nervous, Hugh felt the interview had gone very well. He was particularly delighted to tell the committee about his coming to know Dr. Dressen, and how Dr. Dressen had become his inspirational role model. Hugh got goose bumps when he walked through the halls of the medical school during his visit to Fulbright. He just knew Fulbright was the place for him.

Hugh stared at the rejection letter feeling devastated and angry. How could Fulbright do this to him? How did the admission committee reach its decision? Hugh had earned excellent grades in high school and undergraduate school, and he just knew he would be equally good in medical school. Hugh reasoned their rejection implied they thought he wouldn't make it through medical school. What would he have to do to prove himself, to prove to the admission committee he would be a successful medical school student and then a successful heart surgeon? Hugh decided he would ask Fulbright to admit him on a conditional basis, not even knowing whether the medical school had such a policy. He would agree to be evaluated after one year in medical school. If he were performing poorly, he would leave Fulbright and accept that the admission committee's initial decision on his application was correct. But if he performed well in that year, then he would want to be fully admitted to the medical school and no longer be under their scrutiny. Hugh wanted to prove to himself, to Fulbright, and to the world that he would become as great a heart surgeon as Dr. Dressen. All he wanted was a chance.

Questions

1. Which type of selection mistake (false positive or false negative) do you think Fulbright wants to avoid? Why does Fulbright feel this way?

2. Do you believe Fulbright thinks Hugh won't be successful in medical school, and that is why they rejected his application? Or do you believe Fulbright probably concluded Hugh would be successful in medical school, but there were simply other candidates who had better credentials?

3. If organizations are faced with evaluating many qualified applicants and they have more qualified applicants than there are openings, should a personal experience of the type Hugh had with Dr. Dressen be a factor in determining admission? Why, or why not?

4. If you were on the admissions committee at Fulbright, how would you make decisions about applicants in a way that is fair and reasonable to both the medical school and the applicants?

5. What do you think about Hugh's plea to be given a chance to prove himself? Is his plea unreasonable? Given the imperfect validity of our selection methods, should organizations give applicants a chance to prove themselves in a trial period on the job (or in school)? Why, or why not?

INFOTRAC ARTICLES

1. *Policy Review,* July–August 1996 n78 p30(3)
   Smart women, foolish quotas. Sally C. Pipes & Michael Lynch
   An article that expresses a position critical of affirmative action for enhancing women's ascension in the business world.

2. *Executive Female,* Nov–Dec 1995 v18 n6 p18(1)
   Affirmative action does make a difference.
   An article that expresses a position supportive of affirmative action for enhancing women's ascension in the business world.

3. *Psychology Today,* Nov–Dec 1998 v31 n6 p14(1)
   Reality bites. Camille Chatterjee
   How companies are using realistic job previews to lower turnover rates and give new employees more realistic attitudes about their jobs.

4. *Online,* March–April 1997 v21 n2 p78(4)
   Recruiting on the Internet. Marydee Ojala
   Discusses how the Internet is being used by companies and job seekers to bring about a match between the two.

5. *Nursing Homes,* March 1995 v44 n2 p13(1)
   Staffing: The true bottom line.
   Discusses the importance of making good hiring decisions to ensure the success of the nursing care industry.

6. *Policy Review,* May–June 1997 n83 p22(6)
   The quota czars. Jessica Gavura
   Discusses the role of the American Civil Liberties Union (ACLU) in its response to legislation in California that prohibited racial- and gender-based preferences.

7. *Social Justice,* Fall 1995 v22 n3 p45(8)
   Questions and answers about affirmative action. Nancy Stein
   An article presented in question-and-answer format regarding the meaning and interpretation of affirmative action as a social policy.

8. *Training & Development,* Sep 1995 v49 n9 p49(3)
   Measuring HR for success. Nancy M. Sorenson
   Explains the logic of assessing the effectiveness in financial terms of human resource functions, including selection, turnover, and absenteeism.

Training and Development

MAJOR CHAPTER OBJECTIVES

◆ Explain the relationship between learning and task performance.

◆ Understand the strategic value of training and development to organizations.

◆ Describe the assessment of training needs through organizational, task, and person analysis.

◆ Know major methods of training and their associated strengths and weaknesses.

◆ Describe the importance of cultural diversity training, sexual harassment training, 360-degree feedback, and mentoring in management development.

◆ Explain the evaluation of training and development programs.

Organizations select employees on the basis of their predicted likelihood of succeeding on the job. Although some employees are expected to perform their jobs well immediately upon hire, the vast majority of employees are granted time to grow into their new jobs. This growth process is expedited by formal organizational training processes designed for that purpose. Goldstein (1991) referred to **training processes** as "the systematic acquisition of attitudes, concepts, knowledge, roles, or skills that result in improved performance at work" (p. 508).

Entry-level employees are hired on the basis of their ability to be successfully trained. For them, the key qualification is their predicted capability to learn how to perform the job. At other job levels, the knowledge and skill demands of work are continuously escalating. Martocchio and Baldwin (1997) expressed this perspective clearly: "In an age of technological innovation in which robots, telecommunications, artificial intelligence, software, and lasers perform routine tasks, worker skills soon become obsolete. Put bluntly, today's jobs require new and different skills at all levels of an organization" (p. 6). Accordingly, employees in these jobs must enhance their capabilities to perform their jobs satisfactorily. Training provides opportunities for people to enter the job market with needed talents and to perform in new functions.

I share the opinion of others that the relative importance of training to enhance job performance is increasing. A major reason for this emphasis is increasing reliance on computers in the conduct of work, and its associated repercussions on the human requirements of work. Computer-assisted manufacturing and computer-assisted design are two major technological innovations in production. Manufacturing employees are now often expected to have some fluency in computer-based operations. Such talents can be acquired only through additional preparation for work. There is a growing emphasis in all areas of work to operate more efficiently (i.e., work procedures must require less time or produce less waste) and to enhance the overall quality of our goods and services. Such advances are the basis for enhancing organizational performance in increasingly competitive markets. Training, therefore, is a process to enhance the fit between job demands and human attributes.

The title of this chapter is "Training and Development." Training and development are both processes for enhancing employee skills, but historically they have a somewhat different focus. The term *development* was generally reserved for skill-enhancing processes for managerial-level personnel, whereas *training* was generally applied to skill-enhancement processes in jobs lower in the organizational hierarchy. That is, managers (and above) are "developed"; nonmanagers are "trained." Today this distinction is not as meaningful as it once was. The need is acute for skill enhancement for employees at *all* organizational levels, and all employees should be engaged in the process of expanding their capabilities. Universities and colleges are no longer regarded as exclusive centers of "learning." Learning needs to occur in all organizations on a continuous basis. It might be advisable to think of your college years as "learning through education" and of your working years as "learning through training and development." Because some of the classic distinctions between training and development are still relevant, both sets of processes will be described. Recognizing the need for skill enhancement and having processes to do so are more important than the labels affixed to them.

LEARNING AND TASK PERFORMANCE

Learning can be defined as the process of encoding, retaining, and using information. This perspective of learning prompted Howell and Cooke (1989) to refer to individuals as "human information processors." The specific procedures by which we process information for both short-term and long-term use has been the subject of extensive research in cognitive psychology (Weiss, 1990). This section will examine some useful findings from this body of research that facilitate our understanding of how learning affects the training and development process.

Anderson (1985) suggested that skill acquisition be segmented into three phases: declarative knowledge, knowledge compilation, and procedural knowledge. **Declarative knowledge** is defined as knowledge about facts and things. The declarative knowledge of skill acquisition involves memorizing and reasoning processes that allow the individual to attain a basic understanding of a task. During this phase the individual may observe demonstrations of the task and learn task-sequencing rules. Individuals must devote nearly all of their attention to understanding and performing the task. Performance in the declarative knowledge stage is slow and error prone. Only after the person has acquired an adequate understanding of the task can he or she proceed to the second phase, the **knowledge compilation** phase.

During this second stage of skill acquisition, individuals integrate the sequences of cognitive and motor processes required to perform the task. Various methods for simplifying or streamlining the task are tried and evaluated. Performance then becomes faster and more accurate than in the declarative knowledge phase. The attentional demands on the individual are reduced as the task objectives and procedures are moved from short-term to long-term memory.

Procedural knowledge refers to knowledge about how to perform various cognitive activities. This final phase of skill acquisition is reached when the individual has essentially automatized the skill and the task can be performed efficiently with little attention (Kanfer & Ackerman, 1989). After considerable practice, the task can be performed with minimal impairment while attention is devoted to other tasks.

Furthermore, Ackerman (1987) proposed that three major classes of abilities are critically important for performance in the three phases of skill acquisition. *General intellectual ability* is posited to be the most important factor in acquiring declarative knowledge. When the individual first confronts a novel task, the attentional demands are high. As he or she begins to understand the demands of the task and develops a performance strategy, the attentional demands decrease and the importance of intellectual ability for task performance is lessened.

As the individual moves along the skill acquisition curve from declarative to procedural phases, *perceptual speed abilities* become important. The individual develops a basic understanding of how to perform the task but seeks a more efficient method for accomplishing the task with minimal attentional effort. Perceptual speed abilities seem most critical for processing information faster or more efficiently at this phase.

Finally, as individuals move to the final phase of skill acquisition, their performance is limited by their level of *psychomotor ability*. "Thus individual differences in final, skilled performance are not necessarily determined by the same abilities that affect the initial level of task performance or the speed of skill acquisition" (Kanfer & Ackerman, 1989, p. 664). Therefore, psychomotor abilities (such as coordination) determine the final level of task performance in the procedural knowledge phase.

It should be evident based upon these research findings from cognitive psychology that there are complex relationships between individual abilities and phases of task performance. These findings offer an explanation of why some individuals may be quick to acquire minimal competency in a task, but do not subsequently develop a high degree of task proficiency. Alternatively, other individuals may initially learn a task slowly, but gradually develop a high level of task proficiency. Research by Morrison and Brantner (1992) revealed that learning the requirements of jobs in the military occurred in stages, with plateaus in learning followed by subsequent periods of growth. It appears that the relationship between learning and task performance is more complex than many researchers have believed. These findings bear not only on why certain individuals learn at different rates of speed but also on how training and development processes have to be targeted to enhance selected individual abilities. This conclusion was also supported by the research of Kluger and DeNisi (1996). Their meta-analysis of the effects of feedback on performance revealed that learning to perform tasks depends on a complex set of factors that affect gains in performance as well as the duration of the performance. The process of how we learn to perform tasks appears more complex than we have long believed.

THE STRATEGIC VALUE OF TRAINING AND DEVELOPMENT

Organizations do not train and develop their employees for the sheer sake of doing so. Rather, it is because employees represent a competitive advantage that enhances organizational performance when managed wisely. The competitive strategy an organization uses is the means by which it competes for business in the marketplace. There is a linkage between the type of competitive strategy an organization uses and its training and development practices (Jackson & Schuler, 1990).

A **speed strategy** is designed to offer the customer a competitive value in terms of reduced time for products or services. A training practice that serves this strategic function emphasizes teamwork among employees and methods of streamlined production, designed to reduce the time it takes to meet a customer's needs. An **innovation strategy** is used to develop products or services that differ from the competition. Its primary business objective is to offer something new and different. The focus of training in this context is on developing new products, services, or technologies. A **quality-enhancement strategy** is designed to provide value by offering a product or service of higher quality than that offered by competitors. To reach that objective, employees are trained to provide a consistently high level of service quality with no defects. Finally, the objective of a **cost-reduction strategy** is to gain a competitive advantage by being a low-cost provider of services. Under this business strategy, relatively little emphasis is placed on en-hancing employee skills through training. Employees with higher skill levels war-rant higher levels of compensation, which serves to increase costs. Since this is the opposite of the desired outcome, organizations that pursue cost-reduction strate-gies tend to invest few resources in enhancing the skills of their employees.

In reality most organizations adopt a mix of competitive business strategies. Accordingly, training and development activities are directed to meeting multiple objectives. The fast-food industry is a good example. However, you should note there is an overarching pattern between what organizations are trying to accom-plish (i.e., their strategy for competing) and their philosophy toward training and development. Certain business strategies (innovation) are far more dependent on the quality of their employees than others (cost reduction). Therefore, the greatest advances and emphases in training technologies occur in those organizations that most highly value their human resources to sustain a competitive advantage.

THE PRETRAINING ENVIRONMENT

Tannenbaum and Yukl (1992) reviewed evidence suggesting that events that take place prior to training (i.e., the pretraining environment) can influence the effec-tiveness of training. Management actions and decisions provide cues that signal employee motivation for training. Employees start to learn about the way training is viewed in the organization early in the socialization process and continue to gather information with each training activity they attend. Some actions signal to trainees whether training is important (e.g., supervisory and peer support). Other actions reveal to employees the amount of control, participation, or input they have in the training process (e.g., participation in needs assessment).

Cohen (1990) found that trainees with more supportive supervisors entered training with stronger beliefs that training would be useful. Supportive supervi-sors would discuss an upcoming training course with the employees, establish training goals, provide them release time to prepare, and generally encourage the employees. Baldwin and Magjuka (1991) found that trainees who entered training expecting some form of follow-up activity or assessment afterward reported stronger intentions to transfer what they learned back on the job. The fact that their supervisor would require them to prepare a posttraining report meant they were held accountable for their own learning and apparently conveyed the message that the training was important. The converse is also true. Mathieu, Tannenbaum, and Salas (1990) found that trainees who reported many limitations in their job (e.g., lack of time, equipment, and resources) entered training with lower motivation to learn. These trainees had little incentive to learn new skills in an environment where the skills could not be applied.

Another factor that defines the pretraining environment is trainee input and choice in training. Baldwin, Magjuka, and Loher (1991) found that allowing trainees to specify what training they wanted increased their motivation to learn, provided they were given the training of their choice. However, trainees who were allowed to choose a course but were then assigned to a different course were less motivated and learned less than the trainees who did not participate at all in the choice of training. Similarly, Quinones (1995) concluded that one way employee motivation in training can be enhanced is by giving individuals the chance to choose their own training programs and ensuring that these preferences are honored.

As Tannenbaum and Yukl (1992) articulated, several factors representative of the organizational environment in which training occurs bear directly on its effectiveness. Training does not occur in a vacuum; it is but a means to an end. Factors that strengthen the linkage between training and relevant outcomes can be as critical as the training itself.

ASSESSING TRAINING NEEDS

The entire personnel training process has a rational design (see Figure 6–1) as proposed by Goldstein (1993). The design of personnel training begins with an analysis of training needs and culminates in the assessment of training results. Important steps in between involve developing objectives, choosing methods, and designing an evaluation. Training directors must keep up with the current literature on training methods because previous successes or failures can help shape the selection or design of a training program. It is equally important to determine a means of evaluating the program before it is implemented; that is, evaluative criteria must be selected to serve as the program's scorecard. The bulk of this chapter will discuss the major steps in the design of personnel training.

The assessment of training needs consists of a classic three-step process: organizational analysis, task analysis, and person analysis.

Organizational Analysis

In the evolution of thinking on training and development, the early focus of organizational analysis was on factors that provided information about where and when training could be used in the organization. More contemporary thinking has transformed **organizational analysis** into an examination of systemwide components that determine whether the training program can produce behavior that will transfer to the organization. Goldstein (1991) observed that persons who participate in training are faced with a problem: They are required to learn something in one environment—the training situation—and to use it in another—on the job. This problem requires an examination of the systemwide components of the organization that affect a trainee who arrives with newly learned skills. Training programs can fail because of organizational constraints that they were not intended to address. For example, trainees may learn a set of behaviors that are inconsistent with the way a manager prefers to have the job performed.

Michalak (1981) believes trainers overemphasize the portion of training that deals with acquisition of skill and place too little emphasis on what happens afterward. Baumgartel and Jeanpierre (1972) found that training is more effective when management provides a supportive climate that encourages trainees to explore new ideas and use their training knowledge. Rouillier and Goldstein (1990) proposed the concept of an organizational transfer climate to explain why training can

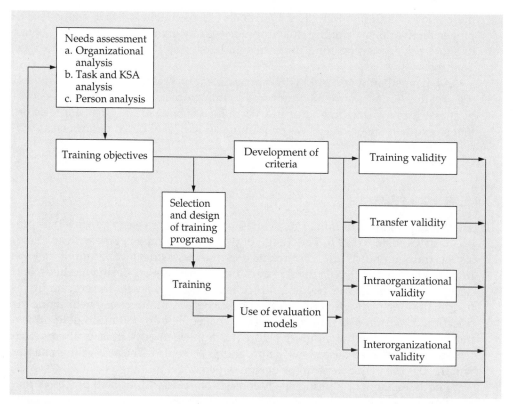

FIGURE 6–1   *The classic training system*

SOURCE: Adapted from *Training and Organizations: Needs Assessment, Development, and Evaluation* (p. 21) by I. L. Goldstein, 1993, Pacific Grove, CA: Brooks/Cole.

differ in its effectiveness. They determined that trainees demonstrated more transfer of skills from training to the job in organizational units where they were encouraged to use what they had learned and were rewarded for doing so. It was concluded that transfer climate was a potentially powerful tool that organizations should consider to facilitate training transfer.

In summary, organizational analysis examines systemwide factors that facilitate or retard the transfer of skills from training to the job. Whatever factors facilitate development of new skills in training should also be present on the job to facilitate maintenance of those skills.

Task Analysis

A **task analysis** is used to determine the training objectives that are related to the performance of particular activities or job operations. The task analysis results in a statement of the activities or work operations performed on the job and the conditions under which the job is performed. Task analysis involves four major steps as input for the design of training programs, as shown in Figure 6–2.

Development of Task Statements.   The first step in task analysis is to completely specify the tasks performed on the job. Chapter 3 discussed task analysis.

FIGURE 6–2   *Task and KSA development steps as input for the design of training systems*

SOURCE: Adapted from "Training in Work Organizations" by I. L. Goldstein, 1991, in *Handbook of Industrial and Organizational Psychology*, 2nd ed., Vol. 2, edited by M. D. Dunnette and L. M. Hough, Palo Alto, CA: Consulting Psychologists Press.

The goal is to write a sentence that conveys *what* the worker does, *how* the worker does it, to *whom* or *what*, and *why* the worker does it. The following two examples of task statements were provided by Goldstein (1991, p. 529):

> From the job of a secretary: "Sorts correspondence, forms, and reports to facilitate filing them alphabetically."
> From the job of a supervisor: "Inform next shift supervisor of departmental status through written reports so that the number of employees needed at each workstation can be determined."

It would not be unusual to have as many as 100 task statements written to describe the tasks performed in a job. The more varied the job, the greater the number of task statements.

Development of Task Clusters.   In this step task statements are grouped into homogeneous clusters to make them more usable and manageable. Subject matter experts (SMEs) are responsible for sorting the task statements into meaningful categories that reflect important dimensions of work. For example, for the job of a secretary one cluster might pertain to tasks involving maintenance of records.

Knowledge, Skill, and Ability Analysis.   A useful way for specifying the human capabilities needed to perform tasks is through knowledges, skills, and abilities (KSAs). *Knowledges* (K) refer to a body of information that, if applied, makes adequate job performance possible. *Skill* (S) refers to the capability to perform job operations with ease and precision and typically refers to psychomotor abilities. *Ability* (A) refers to cognitive capabilities necessary to perform a job function. Most often, abilities require the application of knowledge. The purpose of this analysis is to establish the KSAs needed to perform particular tasks. Most often, persons who directly supervise the job being analyzed serve as SMEs to provide this information because they often think about what a job incumbent needs to know or what skills and abilities the incumbent needs in order to perform the tasks. Among the questions asked of SMEs to elicit KSA information are these:

♦ What are the characteristics of good and poor employees on [tasks in cluster]?

♦ Think of someone you know who is better than anyone else at [tasks in cluster]. What is the reason he or she does it so well?

♦ What does a person need to know in order to [tasks in cluster]?

The researcher then develops a linkage between the tasks performed on a job and the knowledges, skills, and abilities needed to perform them.

Development of Training Programs from the KSA–Task Links.   The linkage between the KSAs and tasks provides the basis for directing training to enhance those KSAs that are critical to job performance. While the relevance of the training for KSA enhancement is established through the linkage, it has been my experience that it is difficult to disentangle what might be a K, S, or A. This seems particularly true with knowledges and abilities. One can generally train people to acquire new knowledges, but it is more difficult to train them in the ability to use that knowledge wisely.

Person Analysis

Person analysis seeks to answer two questions: Who within the organization needs training, and what kind of training do they need? Most of the assessment questions for person analysis are based on the use of performance appraisal systems because it is necessary to appraise employees to determine their training needs. Performance appraisal is the subject of Chapter 7, and the issues inherent in its use will be discussed soon. For the moment, however, realize that performance appraisal is typically conducted for two reasons. One is to diagnose the employees' strengths and weaknesses as an aid in their development. The other reason is to evaluate the employees for the purpose of making administrative decisions, such as pay raises and promotions. Person analysis is predicated upon the diagnostic purpose of performance appraisal—to provide learning experiences helpful to the employee. To the extent that person analysis is directed solely to developmental issues and not administrative ones, there is usually little employee resistance to it. There is also some evidence that self-evaluations of ability (Mabe & West, 1982) may be of value in identifying individual training needs. Finally, it is possible to direct a person analysis of training needs not only to the present but also to the future in terms of what KSAs need to be learned to reach the next level of the organization. In this case, SMEs, usually upper-level managers, articulate the KSAs needed to perform future job requirements.

In summary, Ostroff and Ford (1989) concluded that the classic tripartite approach of needs analysis (organization, task, and person) is entrenched in the literature as the basis upon which all subsequent training issues are based. While we still regard these three perspectives as a useful framework for determining training needs, the specific content of each continues to evolve over time. The most recent advances in training have demonstrated the critical importance of cues and consequences that promote the transfer of skills from training to the job. We are now more aware of the need to examine factors that enable training to be success-fully applied to the job. These factors are just as critical as (if not more so than) the specific nature of the training.

METHODS AND TECHNIQUES OF TRAINING

After an organization determines its training needs and translates them into ob-jectives, the next step is to design a training program to meet these objectives. This isn't an easy task because each training method has its own strengths, weaknesses, and costs. Ideally, we seek the "best" method—the one that meets our objectives in a cost-efficient manner. Many training methods are available. They can be classi-fied in a number of ways, though probably the best way is according to where the training takes place.

On-Site Training Methods

As the name suggests, **on-site methods** are conducted on the job site. On-site methods usually involve training in the total job, whereas off-site instruction often involves only part of the job.

On-the-Job Training.   **On-the-job training** is perhaps the oldest and most com-mon form of instruction. Usually no special equipment or space is needed because new employees are trained at the actual job location. The instructors are usually more established workers, and the employees learn by imitation. They watch an experienced worker perform a task and try to imitate the behavior. This method ensures one classic principle of training—transfer of training. Since the training content and location are the same as the job content, there are usually few prob-lems with transfer.

But on-the-job training has several limitations. It is often brief and poorly structured, often little more than "Watch me, and I'll show you how to do it." Also, many established workers find teaching a new recruit to be a nuisance, and the new employee may be pressured to master the task too quickly. On-the-job training is popular partly because it is so easy to administer. But since many new recruits make mistakes during training, the consequences of error must be evaluated.

Job Rotation.   **Job rotation** is a method of training in which workers rotate through a variety of jobs. They may be in the same job anywhere from a week to a year before they rotate. Job rotation is used with both blue-collar production work-ers and white-collar managers, and it has several organizational benefits. It ac-quaints workers with many jobs in a company and gives them the opportunity to

FRANK AND ERNEST   by Bob Thaves

SOURCE: Reprinted by permission of Newspaper Enterprise Association, Inc.

learn by doing. Job rotation creates flexibility; during worker shortages, workers have the skills to step in and fill open slots. The method also provides new and different work on a systematic basis, giving employees a variety of experiences and challenges. Employees increase their flexibility and marketability because they can perform a wide array of tasks. Campion, Cheraskin, and Stevens (1994) found that job rotation was more common for employees early in their career rather than later. One explanation for this may be that younger employees may be more interested in rotation because they see it as having greater value to their careers than do older employees. Another explanation is that senior management may view job rotation as a better investment when used with early-career employees (i.e., there is a bigger organizational payoff due to a longer payback period).

Like any method, job rotation also has its limitations. If workers are paid on a piece-rate or commission basis, they can earn more money on some jobs and less on others; that is, due to individual differences, people are not equally suited for all jobs. Workers are then reluctant to rotate out of their "best" job. Job rotation also challenges one of the basic principles of personnel placement: Assign workers to jobs that best match their talents and interests. Some employees are wary of a training system that puts them in jobs they are not good at or do not like. Workers' willingness to learn new jobs is a key factor in the success of a job-rotation system.

Apprentice Training.   The **apprentice system** is one of the oldest types of training programs. It is particularly common in the skilled trades. A new worker is "tutored" by an established worker for a long period (sometimes up to five years). The apprentice serves as an assistant and learns the craft by working with a fully skilled member of the trade called a *journeyman*. Apprenticeship programs are often used in the plumbing, carpentry, and electrical trades. At the end of the apprenticeship program, the person is "promoted" to journeyman. Training is intense, lengthy, and usually on a one-to-one basis. Generally one apprentice is assigned to one journeyman.

One weakness of the method is that the amount of time an apprenticeship lasts is predetermined by the members of the trade. Individual differences in learning time are generally not allowed for, so all apprentices have to work for a fixed time before they are upgraded. It has been argued that the apprentice program should be modified to allow more rapid rates of progress for faster learners.

Off-Site Training Methods

There is more diversity in **off-site training methods,** and they differ markedly in their content and approach to learning.

Lectures.   As all students know, the lecture method is a popular form of instruction in educational institutions. It is also used in industry. With this method, large numbers of people can be taught at the same time; in that sense, it is quite cost efficient. However, the more diversified the audience, the more general the content usually becomes. Hence, its utility for imparting specialized knowledge is more limited. A frequent reaction to a lecture on improving sales techniques is, "That idea sounds okay in principle, but how do I put it into operation in my company?" With a more homogeneous audience, a trainer (or teacher) can direct the lecture to specific topics and techniques, which is often more beneficial than using some broad-based material. Thus, lectures are an effective way to train large numbers of people at once, particularly if they have a specific training need.

On the negative side, lectures are usually one-way communication. There is little chance for dialogue, questions, or discussions of individual problems and special interests. Trainees themselves have to understand and personalize the content of the lecture. Although popular, lecturing is not the best method to use for skill acquisition.

Audiovisual Material.   Audiovisual material covers an array of training techniques, such as films, slides, and videotapes. It allows participants to see as well as hear, and it is usually quite good at capturing their interest. This underscores the importance of motivation and interest as necessary conditions for learning. After the initial expense of creating such a program, the cost of repeated use is usually minimal. Audiovisual material is particularly useful for training people in a work process or sequence. People can more readily trace the pattern of work flow when it is laid out graphically.

On the negative side, it is difficult to modify audiovisual material. If the training content changes, a whole new film has to be made. Slide presentations are more modifiable because the outdated slides can be replaced with more current ones. Also, the production cost of training films can be substantial. A half-hour color film with a soundtrack can cost $100,000 to produce. However, if the task or job is very important to the company, then the film is cost effective. With the aid of close-up images, stop action, slow motion, and instant replay, delicate and complex tasks can be broken down into discrete and understandable units.

Conferences.   The conference method of training stresses two-way communication. It is particularly effective when the ratio of trainees to trainers is not very large. This method is useful when the material needs clarification or elaboration or when a lively discussion facilitates understanding. Sometimes the lecture method can be followed with a conference discussion, giving the participants a chance to share opinions about the material. The trainer can call on people to see whether they understand the material, and participants can ask questions. An effective trainer can get all the participants involved, even the less vocal ones. The success of this method depends heavily on the skills and personality of the discussion leader. A dogmatic, abrasive leader can stifle discussion. A good leader knows when to lead the discussion and when to allow others to lead.

The conference method can draw on the learning principles of motivation and feedback. Stimulated participants readily join in the discussion and then receive feedback on their ideas from others in the group. This method is used to enhance knowledge or attitudinal development. The participants' willingness to acquire new knowledge and explore attitude change (and the trainer's ability to facilitate such learning) influences the success of the method. Perhaps because this method does not usually involve any tangible assets other than people, the attitudes, enthusiasm, and verbal communication skills of the participants affect the outcome more than in any other training method.

Programmed Instruction.   **Programmed instruction** (PI) is a method of training that originated with the research of learning theorist B. F. Skinner. PI may involve an actual piece of equipment (usually called a teaching machine) or a specially constructed paper booklet. In either case, the method has three main characteristics. First, the participants are active in the training process; in fact, they determine their own learning pace. Second, the subject to be learned involves many discrete pieces of material, and the participants get immediate feedback on whether they have learned each piece. Third, the material is divided into an organized sequence.

Developing material for PI takes considerable time. Each segment has to facilitate understanding all the material covered. Thus, the sequence of material is highly integrated and then verified to ensure that each piece contributes to understanding and that the entire process covers a unified theme.

The common features of PI follow:

- A single piece of information is presented at each stage, or frame. All of the frames taken together (however many it takes to present the material) are called a *program*. The first frame deals with the first step in some procedure; in industrial training this is usually a work procedure (like operating a piece of equipment). The frames may involve only one question, or they may involve examining some information given in a figure or diagram. A question is then asked about the diagram. The question is either true/false or multiple choice.
- The participant gives an answer to the question in the first frame. If the answer is correct, the participant proceeds to the next frame (by turning a knob on the teaching machine or turning the page in a booklet). If the answer is incorrect, the right answer is given along with an explanation of why it is correct.
- The frames are arranged in the exact sequence that occurs in the work process. This step-by-step sequence in learning matches the step-by-step sequence followed in performing the task on the job.
- The participant goes through the program at his or her own pace. Emphasis is placed on correct answers rather than work speed. Some people learn best at a slow pace; others can learn more rapidly.
- The participant proceeds through the entire program. After he or she completes it, the number of correct answers is tabulated (either automatically on the machine or by hand with the booklet). Before training, a criterion of

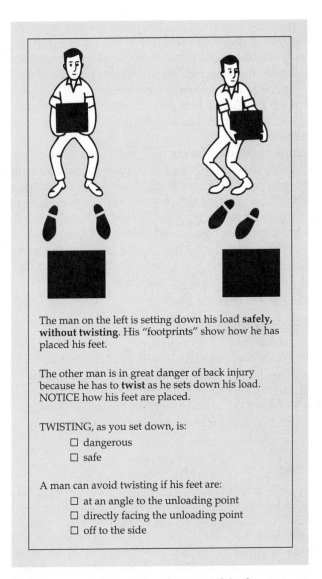

The man on the left is setting down his load **safely, without twisting**. His "footprints" show how he has placed his feet.

The other man is in great danger of back injury because he has to **twist** as he sets down his load. NOTICE how his feet are placed.

TWISTING, as you set down, is:
☐ dangerous
☐ safe

A man can avoid twisting if his feet are:
☐ at an angle to the unloading point
☐ directly facing the unloading point
☐ off to the side

FIGURE 6–3 *Sample problem from one of the first programmed instruction safety programs*

SOURCE: From "A New Approach to Management's Role in Back Safety," 1966, Hicksville, NY: Advanced Learning Systems.

mastery has been set, usually 90% or 95% correct. If the participant reaches that level, training on that program is ended. If the percentage of correct answers falls below the criterion, the participant repeats the program.

Figure 6–3 shows a sample frame from a PI program designed to train workers on the proper way to lift heavy boxes. PI is used in industry and also with schoolchildren.

PI has many advantages as a training method. Participants get immediate feedback. Because the material is presented in a precise and systematic manner, there are no gaps in the presentation. The participants are active learners; there is a constant exchange of information between themselves and the program. When participants make mistakes, they suffer no embarrassment because they are the only ones who know they erred. Fast learners do not have to wait for slow ones to catch up; slow learners do not always have to try to catch up. Finally, PI is an efficient way to train people on material that is structured and rote. It gives a trainer more time to cover unstructured and ambiguous material with a different method (usually the conference).

On the negative side, developing a PI program is time-consuming. The material has to be broken down into a logical sequence. Each frame has to be checked to be sure that it is accurate and contributes to overall learning of the material. Some work procedures are hard to break down into an exact sequence, since there may be several correct ways to perform the task. Also, the stability or consistency of a structured task must be considered before a PI program is developed. PI has its place in a rapidly changing technological area, but it is not a panacea for all training needs.

Computer-Assisted Instruction

Computer-assisted instruction (CAI) is the most recently developed training method. Once restricted in use to mainframe computers, CAI has been expanded with the advent of microcomputers. CAI has been used to teach a wide range of skills, ranging from how to speak a foreign language to how to fly a helicopter. One CAI program begins by flashing the words "Good Morning." If the trainee fails to press a key that says "Good Morning" in five seconds, the computer flashes a second message: "What's the matter—kind of grumpy today?" All this has been

---

Field Note I   *Distance Learning*

Computers are having a profound impact in the field of education at all levels. Children in the early grades of elementary school are learning how to operate a computer. High school graduates of today have a level of computer literacy that greatly exceeds that of college graduates less than a generation ago. Computer-aided instruction is changing the very nature of the educational process at the college level. An increasingly large number of students want a college education, yet they work during the day and may not have a university nearby that offers evening instruction. A solution to this problem is called *distance learning*, meaning that students can enroll in college courses yet not be physically present at the college. Course lectures offered at the college are videotaped and made available for viewing by students on their personal computers, at whatever time the students have available. Thus, a course can be offered without regard to time or space because computer technology delivers the course to the student. Some universities are now offering entire degree programs to students through this technology. A student can earn a degree from a university without ever having physically attended the university. Such degree programs are in their infancy, and they do require the technical support needed to make such an offering possible. However, their very existence attests to the power of the computer in being the dominant technological innovation in the second half of the 20th century.

programmed to make the trainee feel that the computer is not totally impersonal. This, in turn, is designed to enhance motivation.

The advantages of CAI include individualized instruction, reduced training time, and elimination of travel for training. Some advantages to the trainee are being able to work at his or her own pace, to begin and end a lesson when convenient, and to enter a program at his or her current level of achievement. Indeed, Dossett and Hulvershorn (1983) reported the average training time with CAI was less than with the lecture method for training military recruits in electronics. However, training program development lags far behind computer development, and programming for training purposes is still in its early stages. Goldstein (1991) also cautioned that successful learning in training systems is not guaranteed by the advent of a new, revolutionary technique alone. It requires careful needs assessment, careful design of training based on those needs, and evaluation efforts to fine-tune the program. Although much more work needs to be directed toward meeting the potential promise of this method, CAI appears to be a very viable technique for enhancing complex skills (see Field Note 1).

Simulation

A **simulation** is designed to replicate the essential characteristics of the real world necessary to produce learning and transfer. The purpose of the simulation is to produce *psychological fidelity*—that is, to reproduce in the training tasks those KSAs necessary to perform the job. As Goldstein (1991) noted, one important aspect of these simulators is that they permit the environment to be reproduced under the control of the trainer. Environments are created by careful design and planning to provide variation in the essential characteristics of the real situation. Simulation also permits the trainer to expand, compress, or repeat time, depending on the needs of the trainees.

The final job behavior to be learned is often too complex to be handled safely by a trainee in a real-life situation. Simulations permit the trainee to be slowly introduced to the essential task characteristics without danger to the trainee, coworkers, or expensive equipment. Simulations also permit the trainee to practice emergency procedures before being exposed to hazardous situations in real life. Flight simulations, for example, manifest a high degree of *physical fidelity*—the accurate representation of the real world of operational equipment. Flight simulations are so complex that nearly all aspects of flight training can be practiced on them. Goldberg, Mastaglio, and Johnson (1995) described the development of the Distributed Interactive Simulation (DIS) used by the military to train armor and mechanized infantry units in weapons systems. The DIS combines aviation, combat engineers, air defense, and field artillery simulators to represent the combined arms battlefield.

Many simulations use games. Business games train employees in certain skills. Within the rules of the game, participants try to meet the exercise's stated objectives. Business games can be used to train individuals or groups. Games have been developed to simulate interpersonal relations problems, financial and budgeting issues, and resource allocation decisions. Participants are told the objective (for example, to reach a certain profit level or to maximize financial return with a fixed budget), and then they are evaluated on whether they achieve it. Business games are popular for training managers and executives, particularly in financial matters.

A problem with simulations that have a game component is that the participants know it is only a game. Failing at a game is not the same as failing on the job. Participants sometimes behave differently than they would in real life. For example, in a marketing course a business game was created to simulate marketing a product. The class was divided into work teams. The team that achieved the greatest profit at the end of the semester received an award. Within the rules of the game (advertising the product, spending on research to improve the product, and so on), the "sales volume" of each work team was posted weekly. As the weeks went by, some work teams gradually fell behind in profit. So members of the losing teams began to take unnatural risks with their companies, risks they probably would not take on a real job. They did not care if their actions failed (the company went bankrupt) because it was only a game. And if their wild risks came through, they would receive the award. In this case, the game did not include some key elements of the job. Unlike a semester, the life span of a real company does not end on a predetermined date. The consequences of losing one's job (as well as destroying a company) are not the same as simply failing to win a class award. The best simulations are "best" because they provide for a high degree of transfer of training to the actual job. Needless to say, some simulations are easier than others to construct to maximize this transfer.

Role Playing.   **Role playing** is a training method often aimed at enhancing either human relations skills or sales techniques. As opposed to programmed instruction, which is deliberately aimed at the individual, role playing involves many people. Role playing originally evolved out of clinical psychology, in which problems involving human interaction, real or imaginary, are presented and then spontaneously acted out. The enactment is normally followed by a discussion to determine what happened and why. Participants suggest how the problem could be handled more effectively in the future.

Role playing is less tightly structured than acting, where performers have to say set lines on cue. Participants are assigned roles in the scenario to be enacted. For example, the scenario may be a department store. One person takes the role of an irate customer who is dissatisfied with a recently purchased product. A second person is assigned the role of the clerk who has to attend to the customer's complaint. Aside from observing some general guidelines about the product, the participants are free to act out their roles however they wish. Their performance is judged by people who do not have an active part in the role playing. In an educational setting the observers may be other students in the class; in a business setting they might be supervisors.

Many variations of role playing are possible. In some exercises participants repeat the enactment several times but switch roles. In other cases participants reverse the role they play in real life; for example, the supervisor plays a union representative. The role forces the participant to adopt the other side's position and then defend it.

Goldstein (1980) described advances with a technique called *behavioral role modeling*, which uses role playing as one of its parts. In behavioral role modeling, some points or principles to be stressed in training are identified. The participants watch a model use the principles (often on film) and then rehearse the principles by role playing. The trainer and other group members provide social reinforcement. Latham and Saari (1979) reported on a study of behavioral role modeling that was designed to increase interpersonal skills in dealing with employees. Forty first-line supervisors were assigned to either the modeling group or a control group, which received another form of training to meet the same objectives. Results showed that the supervisors trained with behavioral role modeling were more impressed with the training, scored higher on a learning test six months after training, and were judged to be performing better on the job a year later.

One advantage of role playing is that participants are highly active. By "putting their feet in the other person's shoes," participants gain some understanding of what it is like to experience interpersonal conflict in someone else's position. Interpersonal relations skills are among the more difficult ones to enhance with any method. Despite legitimate criticism that some people put more emphasis on acting than problem solving, the method has been quite useful.

MANAGEMENT DEVELOPMENT ISSUES

Management development is the process by which individuals learn to perform effectively in managerial roles. Organizations are interested in management development in large part because they recognize its value as a strategy to improve organizational performance. Kotter (1988) argued the one factor that seems to distinguish excellent companies from others is the amount of time and energy spent in the planning, design, and execution of developmental activities. Baldwin and Padgett (1993) estimated that over 90% of organizations worldwide engage in some form of development activities for managers. Tharenou (1997) reported that many managers seek advancement continuously, not just until they reach a particular level in the organization. For them, successful development activities are particularly critical because they contribute greatly to what Tharenou called "career velocity." The literature on management development tends to focus on major issues or processes managers address as part of their professional maturation. Alternatively, the literature on personnel training often tends to be more concerned with specific methods or techniques of training. However, the larger systems issues of needs assessment, skill enhancement, and transfer are equally applicable to both training and development.

Whetten and Cameron (1991) identified critical management skills and linked them to successful performance on the job. Three *personal skills* were noted: developing self-awareness, managing stress, and solving problems creatively. Four *interpersonal skills* were also identified: communicating supportively, gaining power and influence, motivating others, and managing conflict. The authors pointed out that these skills overlap and managers must draw upon all of them to perform effectively in a managerial role. Yukl, Wall, and Lepsinger (1990) developed a survey that assesses managerial practices based upon these skills. Subordinates and peers describe how much a manager uses these practices and make recommendations on whether the manager's behavioral style should be modified. Managers compare this feedback with their own self-assessment of behavior. Ratings of the importance of these behaviors for the manager's job provide additional information for identifying relevant developmental activities. Lombardo and McCauley (1988) proposed that underutilization of selected managerial skills and practices contributes to *derailment*. Derailment occurs when a manager who has been judged to have the ability to go higher fails to live up to his or her full potential and is fired, demoted, or plateaued below expected levels of achievement.

There is also considerable interest in gender differences in management development (Ragins & Sundstrom, 1989). Many organizations have created a male managerial hierarchy—one composed predominately of men—which is thought to be a critical structural feature influencing the processes that affect men's and women's managerial advancement. There is evidence that a "glass ceiling" exists for women in their professional advancement through an organization. This transparent barrier is fostered by organizations that regulate access to developmental experiences as part of a pattern that grooms men for powerful positions. Lyness and Thompson (1997) found that even women who "broke through" the glass ceiling into the highest-level executive jobs reported having less authority, fewer stock options, and less international mobility than men. Tharenou, Latimer, and Conroy (1994) reported that developmental activities had a more positive influence on the managerial advancement of men than of women. Men were more likely than women to attend company-sponsored training courses, especially between the ages of 35 and 54. Development may lead to more advancement for men than for women because men are thought to gain more skills and knowledge from professional development than women do. In turn, men gain skill and knowledge that are more relevant to managerial work, thus becoming better prepared for advancement than women. The authors believe organizations need to ensure that women's contributions of education, work experience, and development are perceived as similarly conducive to productivity as men's, and thus are rewarded with similar advancement.

Four issues of contemporary relevance to the management development process are deserving of discussion: cultural diversity, sexual harassment, 360-degree feedback, and the mentoring process.

Cultural Diversity Training

Triandis, Kurowski, and Gelfand (1994) offered an insightful analysis of the consequences of our nation's increasing cultural heterogeneity or diversity. However, dealing with diversity is not a novel issue in this country; cultural diversity has characterized this nation since its founding. What is novel about modern diversity is that managers are encountering it more frequently both within their organization (their employees) and among their customers. Changes in the composition of the workforce are driven by labor and market trends, legislation, and demographics. Multinational companies increasingly have multinational management, with some top managers who come from the companies' homelands and some from other countries. The composition of the workforce is also changing in the United States at the entry level. White men, who traditionally have constituted the majority of new entrants into the labor force, will be a minority among the new entrants by the year 2000 (Goldstein & Gilliam, 1990). Likewise, the Americans with Disabilities Act may usher in an increase in the percentages of disabled workers.

Historically, there have been two ways to approach cultural differences. One is the color-blind perspective (Ferdman, 1992), which advocates ignoring cultural differences. Its basic rationale is thus "Do not pay attention to differences." The second approach accepts the presence of cultural differences and proposes to improve relationships by teaching people from each culture to appreciate the perspectives of people from other cultures. Triandis (1995) classified these two approaches as the **melting pot conception,** where cultural differences are homogenized, versus the **multiculturalism conception,** which assumes each cultural group should maintain as much of its original culture as possible while contributing to the smooth functioning of society. Research indicates that both perspectives have merit, and an optimal approach may emphasize both what people universally have in common and what makes them different. Triandis et al. (1994) suggested that approximately half of all psychological theories are universally relevant and the other half are the products of Western cultures. The task of crosscultural psychology is to sort out the two halves.

Triandis (1975) suggested that the ideal problem-solving group is diverse, with members who have been trained to understand the others' points of view. However, diversity has a price: Communication becomes more difficult and interpersonal attraction is likely to be lower. To increase interpersonal attraction, Triandis recommended individuals be trained to view the behavior of members of other cultures as functional and reasonable within a particular environment. That is, to be able to say, "If I faced that set of circumstances, I would also behave that way." Such a process produces a sense of *similarity* across culturally diverse people, where the psychological processes of adoption are similar but the situations are different. When similarities are emphasized, attraction can be created in two ways: by showing that there are universals and by indicating that the existing cultural differences "make sense." Despite sincere attempts to understand the underlying causes of why people react negatively to cultural differences, Brief and Hayes (1997) regard racial discrimination as an enduring employment problem in the United States. They believe manifestations of racism have evolved over the past 50 years from the blatant to the subtle, but racism continues to exist.

The goal of diversity training programs is to reduce barriers, such as values, stereotypes, and managerial practices, that constrain employee contributions to organizational goals and personal development (Noe & Ford, 1992). Diversity training programs differ on whether attitude or behavior change is emphasized to achieve these goals.

Attitude change programs focus on an awareness of diversity and the personal factors that most strongly influence our behavior toward others. Many programs involve self-assessment of perceived similarities and differences between different groups of employees, and attributions for success and failure of minority employees. These programs may use videotapes and experiential exercises to increase employees' awareness of the negative effects of stereotypes on minority group members. It is assumed that this heightened awareness will result eventually in behavior change.

The *behavior change* approach emphasizes changing organizational policies and individual behaviors that limit employee productivity. Programs with the behavioral emphasis identify incidents that discourage employees from working to their potential. Perceptions regarding the degree to which the work environment and management practices are congruent with a philosophy of valuing differences among employees are often collected. Specific training programs are then directed at developing employee skills that are needed to create a workplace that supports diversity.

Rynes and Rosen (1995) conducted a major survey of human resource professionals about diversity issues in their organizations. Organizations that had successfully adopted diversity programs had strong support from top management and placed a high priority on diversity relative to other competing organizational objectives. Diversity training success was also associated with mandatory attendance for all managers, long-term evaluation of training results, managerial rewards for increasing diversity, and a broad inclusionary definition of what is meant by "diversity" in the organization. However, some critics believe that diversity training has been largely unsuccessful. Hemphill and Haines (1997) cited that Texaco paid a record settlement of $176 million in a racial discrimination suit, and the U.S. Army has been confronted with potential sexual harassment claims from over 5,000 women. Both of these organizations had previously implemented diversity training. The authors believe organizations can do little to compel changes in how people feel about each other, but organizations should adopt a zero-tolerance policy for discrimination and harassment practices.

Ronen (1989) discussed a more specialized area of cultural diversity training—the individual assigned to an international position. The need for such training has grown for two reasons. The first is the increase in the number of individuals so assigned, and the second is the relatively high failure rate of managers in such assignments. Spreitzer, McCall, and Mahoney (1997) developed an assessment for the early identification of international executive potential. It is based on rating aspiring international executives on selected competencies and the ability to learn from experience. Dotlich (1982) reported the findings from a survey of U.S. managers who lived or traveled abroad on the reasons for difficulties in overseas assignments. The following two quotes were representative of the findings:

> Time as a cultural value is something which we don't understand until we are in another culture. It took me six months to accept the fact that my staff meeting wouldn't begin on time and more often would start thirty minutes late and nobody would be bothered but me.

> Communication can be a problem. I had to learn to speak at half the speed I normally talk. (p. 28)

Another problem area is family members adjusting to a different physical or cultural environment. Arthur and Bennett (1995) determined from a study of internationally assigned managers from many countries that family support is the most critical factor in accounting for successful international assignments. The results suggest the advisability of including one's spouse and other family members in cross-cultural training and, if feasible, sending them overseas to preview their new environment. Ronen identified four abilities considered critical for successful overseas assignments: tolerance for ambiguity, behavioral flexibility, nonjudgmentalism, and cultural empathy. The selection decision for overseas assignments is usually predicated upon the candidate's technical skills in applied functional areas (such as engineering or finance), but usually the reasons for a failed assignment have little to do with deficient technical skills. Major areas recommended for enhancement through training include information about the host country's geography, political system, history, religion, and generalized customs and habits. It is also recommended that managers learn to understand their own listening ability, reaction to feedback, and predisposition toward judgmental attitudes. Black and Mendenhall (1990) suggested that cultural novelty, expected degree of interpersonal interaction in the foreign assignment, and the novelty of new jobs and tasks are situational factors that likely influence the appropriateness and effectiveness of cross-cultural training.

Hesketh and Bochner (1994) proposed that the process of cultural adjustment be viewed as a special case of being socially skilled, reflecting the more basic principle that when individuals interact, they are engaged in a mutually organized, skilled performance. Social competence is the ability to produce the desired effects on others in social situations. Thus, individuals who are socially inadequate have not mastered the conventions of their society, either because they are unaware of the prevailing rules of social behavior or because they are unwilling to abide by them. Therefore, success in international assignments is posited to be a function of one's capacity and willingness to learn new social skills. Many specific work-related social skills and attitudes are highly culture-based. For example, Adler, Doktor, and Redding (1986) reported the Japanese prefer to go from the general to the specific, whereas Westerners like to get the details out of the way before tackling the larger issues. Other cultural differences exist with regard to strategies of conflict resolution, bargaining style, and cognitive information processing. Thus, training in social skills can be developed to teach specific culturally relevant behaviors designed to enhance the person's repertoire.

The current emphasis on cultural diversity training seems attributable in part to two general factors. The first is the increasing awareness of our "differentness" as people, and the second is the reality that we all have to get along with one another to have an amicable and productive society. In a sense it is somewhat of a paradox—seeking ways to find similarities among differences. I believe the importance of addressing this paradox will intensify in the years to come.

Sexual Harassment Training

The Equal Employment Opportunity Commission (EEOC) (1980) defined sexual harassment as

> unwelcome sexual advances, requests for sexual favors, and other verbal or physical conduct of a sexual nature when submission to or rejection of this conduct explicitly or implicitly affects an individual's employment, unreasonably interferes with an individual's work performance, or creates an intimidating, hostile, or offensive work environment.

In this definition are the two kinds of sexual harassment actionable under federal law: *quid pro quo* sexual harassment and hostile-environment harassment. **Quid pro quo harassment** occurs when sexual compliance is made mandatory for promotion, favors, or retaining one's job. **Hostile-environment harassment** is less blatant than *quid pro quo* and refers to conditions in the workplace that are regarded as offensive, such as unwanted touching and off-color jokes. In the vast majority of cases on this issue, women rather than men have suffered from sexual abuse at work. Such abuse may constitute illegal sex discrimination in the form of unequal treatment on the job. More than 15,500 complaints were filed with the EEOC in 1995, and the cost of investigating and resolving claims of sexual harassment is in the millions of dollars annually. Sexual harassment is not so much about sex as about power and the power differential between managers and employees (Cleveland & Kerst, 1993). Organizations are devoting considerable training resources to deter the likelihood of sexual harassment in the workplace.

Much of the research on sexual harassment has focused on how men and women define it and whether men's definitions differ markedly from women's. Gutek (1985) reported that women consistently were more likely than men to label a behavior as sexual harassment. Men and women tend to disagree on whether uninvited sexual teasing, jokes, remarks, or questions represent sexual harassment. Generally, as an act becomes more overt and coercive, women and men are more likely to agree that it is sexual harassment. Nevertheless, Schneider, Swan, and Fitzgerald (1997) found that low-level but frequent types of sexual harassment can have significant negative consequences for working women.

Tangri, Burt, and Johnson (1982) described three models used to explain sexual harassment. The *natural/biological model* asserts that sexual harassment is simply natural sexual attraction between two people. The *organizational model* argues that sexual harassment is the result of certain opportunities created by the organizational climate, hierarchy, and specific authority relationships. The *sociocultural model* states that sexual harassment reflects the larger society's differential distribution of power and status between the genders. A test of these models revealed that all three approaches have some empirical support, which leads the authors to conclude there is no single explanation for sexual harassment. Fitzgerald, Drasgow, Hulin, Gelfand, and Magley (1997) found that sexual harassment was associated with female perceptions of the risk of reporting harassing events, the likelihood of being taken seriously, and the probability of sanctions against the alleged harasser. They also demonstrated that gender composition (ratio of men to women in a work group) is associated with sexual harassment.

Physical attractiveness has also been examined as a factor influencing third-party judgments of sexual harassment. Quinn and Lees (1984) asserted that personnel departments are less likely to take seriously sexual harassment complaints from unattractive female employees than from attractive women. Castellow, Wuensch, and Moore (1990) found that female sexual harassment victims are more likely to win lawsuits against their harassers when the victims are attractive and the harassers are unattractive.

Training in the area of sexual harassment frequently consists of teaching sensitivity to other people's values and preferences. It should not be assumed, for example, that people prefer to be touched (as on the hand or arm) when engaged in conversation. There are also broad cultural differences in the degree to which physical contact between people is regarded as acceptable. People differ in the degree to which verbal statements, including profanity, are considered offensive or inappropriate. One organizational response to fear of allegations of sexual harassment is to engage in highly defensive behavior, including having a third party present when one talks with a member of the opposite sex and interacting with people only in an open, highly visible work area. Other examples are prohibiting any comments regarding physical appearance (e.g., "those are attractive shoes you are wearing") and the reciprocal exchange of gifts among employees on special occasions (e.g., flowers or cards on birthdays). Some defensive behaviors are more personalized, such as a male manager refusing to mentor any female protégé. Lobel (1993) questioned the long-term benefit of these types of prohibitions on male/female relationships in the workplace. In an attempt to limit opportunities for potentially sexual harassing behaviors to occur, we may also be precluding opportunities for beneficial across-gender relationships to develop. Furthermore, the workplace can be a setting where people meet and mutually enter into a romantic relationship. Pierce, Byrne, and Aguinis (1996) proposed an explanation of workplace romance. They asserted that while a successful relationship can be beneficial to both parties, the breakup of a relationship can lead to charges of sexual harassment. Thus, allegations of sexual harassment can be spawned by what were once mutually positive experiences.

360-Degree Feedback

The term **360-degree feedback** refers to the practice of using multiple raters, often including self-ratings, in the assessment of individuals. Typically, feedback about a target manager is solicited from significant others, including the individual's co-workers, subordinates, and superiors. The primary purpose for 360-degree feedback is to enhance managers' awareness of their strengths and weaknesses to guide developmental planning. According to Tornow (1993), 360-degree assessment activities are usually based on two key assumptions: (1) awareness of any discrepancies between how we see ourselves and how others see us enhances self-awareness, and (2) enhanced self-awareness is a key to maximum performance as a manager and thus becomes a foundation for management and leadership development programs.

The term *360-degree feedback* derives from the geometric rationale for the multiple-rater assessment, as shown in Figure 6–4. The target manager is evaluated by other individuals who interact in a social network. The target manager also provides self-assessments. The typical assessment includes evaluations along three dimensions (Van Velsor, Ruderman, & Young, 1991):

1. *People*—dealing effectively with people, building good relationships
2. *Change*—setting, communicating, and implementing a goal or vision
3. *Structure*—structuring and organizing information, time, and work

The multiple raters make their assessments of an individual, and then the assessments are compared. Van Velsor et al. reported the following findings from their study, which are representative of most 360-degree feedback studies:

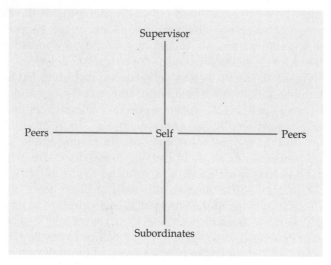

FIGURE 6–4   *360-degree feedback relationships*

- Only 10% of the managers saw themselves as others saw them; the rest had substantial discrepancies (i.e., more than half of a standard deviation) on one, two, or three of the scales.
- Overrating oneself was the most common profile across scales. This difference was especially noteworthy in the *People* scale, where overrating was almost twice as common as underrating oneself or showing self–other agreement.
- About 80% of the managers modified their self-assessment in the expected direction on one or more scales after feedback. This change was most pronounced in the area of interpersonal skills.

It is particularly instructive to understand how disagreement among raters in 360-degree feedback is interpreted. The classic measurement perspective treats disagreement among raters as error variance—that is, something undesirable that reduces inter-rater reliability. With 360-degree feedback, differences in rater perspectives are regarded as potentially valuable and useful and are not treated as variations to be reduced. Such differences provide an opportunity for professional development and personal learning, to understand why individuals are perceived as they are by others.

How important is it that managers see themselves as others see them? Nilsen and Campbell (1993) proposed that job performance is a function of an individual's aptitude, task understanding, decision about how intensely to work, decision about how long to persist in the face of obstacles, and facilitating or inhibiting conditions not under the individual's control. Self-assessments are important because individuals make judgments about themselves that are relevant to these determinants of performance. Individuals have beliefs about their level of aptitude, and whether or not they understand the task they are asked to perform. If individuals overestimate their aptitude, they will devote less effort to the task than is needed to perform it adequately. Additionally, if individuals believe that they fully understand a task, they will probably devote little or no effort to obtaining additional task-relevant information. If, however, individuals do not in fact understand what is expected, they may utilize their aptitude and devote their effort, yet still fail to perform the task correctly. Additionally, London, Smither, and Adsit (1997) believe that 360-degree feedback will have little impact on changing behaviors when (1) the ratees are not accountable for using the feedback, and (2) the raters are not accountable for the accuracy or usefulness of the feedback they provide.

In general, it appears that accurate self-assessors are better able to improve their performance than are inaccurate self-assessors. Self-awareness and self-perception are becoming recognized as critical factors in determining managerial job performance, a job that typically entails working with many other people. However, what exactly people agree or disagree on is not totally clear. Moses, Hollenbeck, and Sorcher (1993) proposed that it is not simply agreement among people's *observations* that contributes to effective job performance, but rather agreement among people's *expectations* of behavior. Thus, self-aware managers are knowledgeable of the expectations placed on them by others, including the likelihood of differential expectations held by subordinates, peers, and superiors. Dunnette (1993) concluded that 360-degree feedback offers an opportunity to enhance understanding of managerial behavior. Furthermore, it is a new method for identifying areas of individual need for improving managerial skills.

Mentoring

A method growing in use for facilitating management development is mentoring. **Mentors** are older, more experienced individuals who advise and shepherd new people in the formative years of their careers. They are professionally paternalistic and serve in a "godparent" role. Hunt and Michael (1983) discovered four states of the mentor relationship. The first is the *initiation phase,* when the more powerful and professionally recognized mentor recognizes the apprentice as a protégé. The second is the *protégé phase,* when the apprentice's work is recognized not for its own merit but as the by-product of the mentor's instruction, support, and advice. The third is the *breakup stage,* when the protégé goes off on his or her own. If the mentor–protégé relationship has not been successful, this is the final stage. However, if it has been successful, both parties continue on to the *lasting-friendship stage.* Here the mentor and the protégé have more of a peer relationship. The protégé may become a mentor but does not sever ties with the former mentor.

Noe (1988) determined two major dimensions to the mentoring relationship. One is psychosocial, where the mentor serves as a role model who provides counseling, acceptance, and coaching. The other dimension is job related, where the mentor provides exposure and visibility, sponsorship, and challenging assignments to augment the protégé's career. Most studies report positive results from mentoring. Fagenson (1989) found that mentored individuals had more satisfaction, career mobility and opportunity, recognition, and a higher promotion rate than nonmentored individuals. Similarly, Dreher and Ash (1990) found that individuals with extensive mentoring relationships had higher incomes and were more satisfied with their pay and benefits than individuals who had less extensive mentoring relationships. Chao, Walz, and Gardner (1992) demonstrated that informal mentoring programs (e.g., a senior-level and a junior-level manager share similar goals and values) produced more career-related support for the protégé than formal mentoring programs (e.g., a pool of potential protégés submit résumés for review by a "matchmaker committee"). It appears that problems such as personality conflicts and lack of mentor commitment are more likely to occur with assigned mentors than with informal mentors unless the assigned mentors are carefully selected and trained. Eby (1997) reported that mentors can be at either the same organizational level or at a higher organizational level than the protégé. Also, the mentor can give the protégé guidance on the development of job skills or career skills. Eby found that mentoring was particularly helpful in getting individuals to adapt to rapidly changing organizational conditions.

Research has also been directed to across-race and across-gender mentoring issues. Thomas (1990) reported that White protégés had almost no developmental relationships with persons of another race. Blacks were more likely than Whites to form relationships outside the formal lines of authority and their own departments. Same-race relationships were found to provide significantly more psychosocial support than across-race relationships did.

Thomas (1993) concluded that the two parties' preferred strategy for dealing with racial difference (either denying and suppressing it or discussing it openly) and whether both parties preferred the same strategy influenced the kind of relationship that developed. In some relationships, the senior person becomes merely a sponsor for the protégé, providing career support through advocacy for promotions, feedback, and coaching. In others, the senior person becomes a mentor, offering psychosocial support and friendship along with instrumental career support. Ragins and McFarlin (1990) found that across-gender protégés were less likely than same-gender protégés to report engaging in after-work social activities with their mentors. Compared to other gender combinations, female protégés with female mentors were more likely to agree with the idea that their mentors served a role-model function. Ragins and Cotton (1991) reported that women were more likely than men to report restricted access to mentors, in part because initiating a relationship with a mentor might be misinterpreted as a sexual advance.

Given the sensitivity of gender issues and the power differential between senior and junior managers, women may be more likely than men to pursue peer relationships to facilitate their career development. Kram and Isabella (1985) described how peer relationships are important. They found three types of peers. One is the *information peer,* a person with whom you can exchange information about work in the organization. You share a low level of disclosure and trust, and there is little mutual emotional support. The second type is the *collegial peer,* with whom you have a moderate level of trust and engage in some self-disclosure. Collegial peers provide increased emotional support and feedback and engage in more intimate discussions. The third type is the *special peer,* with whom there are no pretenses and formal roles. You reveal ambivalence and personal dilemmas as you would to few other people in your life. You need not limit peer relationships to members of the same gender, but special peers are most likely of your gender. The value of peer relationships to career development is not limited to women. However, because of the constraints women have in mentoring relationships, the importance of the peer relationship in career development is accentuated for women.

THE POSTTRAINING ENVIRONMENT

Tannenbaum and Yukl (1992) noted that the effectiveness of a training program can be influenced by events that occur after a trainee returns to the job. Some employees leave training with new skills and with strong intentions to apply those skills to their job, but limitations in the posttraining environment interfere with the actual transfer of training.

Transfer of training is defined as the extent to which trainees effectively apply the knowledge, skills, and attitudes gained in a training context back to the job. Baldwin and Ford (1988) noted the distinction between *generalization*, the extent to which trained skills and behaviors are exhibited in the transfer setting, and *maintenance*, the length of time that trained skills and behaviors continue to be used on the job. They believe that supervisory support is a major environmental factor that can affect the transfer process. In the posttraining environment, supervisor support includes reinforcement, modeling of trained behaviors, and goal-setting activities. Another factor that can influence transfer is the extent to which the

Field Note 2   *The Willingness to Be Trained*

When I was in graduate school, I helped a professor with a study of the coal mining industry. Many on-the-job accidents occurred in coal mines, and our assignment was to develop a safety training program to reduce them. My personal assignment was to observe and interview the coal miners about their work. While down in the mines, I noticed that the miners engaged in dangerous behaviors, such as not wearing their hard hats, leaving off their masks (which filtered out coal dust), and smoking in the mine (where an open flame could trigger an explosion). In addition to being unsafe, some of these behaviors were blatant violations of safety rules.

After the miners finished their work shifts, I interviewed them about their jobs. I was particularly interested in why they did such seemingly hazardous things. Since our goal was to develop a training program to reduce accidents, I felt that eliminating these unsafe behaviors was an obvious place to start. So I asked them why they didn't wear safety equipment at times. I did not expect their answer. They said they believed there was no relationship between what they did in the mine and what happened to them. They felt their lives were in the hands of luck, fate, or God, and it did not really matter how they

conducted themselves. They all seemed to have personal anecdotes about other miners who were extremely safety conscious (that is, always wore all the safety equipment and were exceedingly cautious people in general) yet suffered serious injuries or death in accidents through no fault of their own, such as a cave-in. In short, the miners were highly fatalistic. They believed that if "your number was up," you would get hurt or killed, and there was nothing you could do about it. While a hard hat was a fine thing to wear, it would not do much good if five tons of rock fell on you. Therefore, they were not interested in engaging in safe behavior because their behavior did not matter one way or another.

This experience taught me many lessons about training. The major one is that if people are not motivated to be trained, to learn some new behaviors, it is pointless to try. As every teacher can tell you, if students do not want to learn or just do not care, there is nothing you can do to force them to learn. The coal miners simply did not want to learn new behaviors because in their minds their lives and welfare were determined by factors beyond their control. Trainers are like chefs: They can prepare the finest meals, but they cannot make you eat if you are not hungry.

posttraining environment provides opportunities for trainees to apply what they have learned. Ford et al. (1991) studied technical trainees after they completed training and found significant differences in opportunities to apply the training and wide variations in the lengths of time before trainees first performed the tasks for which they had been trained. Tracey, Tannenbaum, and Kavanagh (1995) concluded that posttraining knowledge and behavior are more likely to perseverate in organizations that have strong social support systems. Specifically, transfer of training is enhanced in organizations that regard themselves as having a culture that recognizes the importance of continuous learning.

Some studies have examined whether transfer is facilitated by relapse-prevention training, an approach derived from research on physical addictions (Marx, 1982). Relapse-prevention training is designed to prepare trainees for the posttraining environment and to anticipate and cope with "high-risk" situations. Marx and Karren (1988) found that trainees who received relapse-prevention training after a regular training seminar demonstrated more of the trained behaviors than trainees with no relapse-prevention training.

It appears that limitations in the posttraining environment may inhibit the application of skills acquired during training. Furthermore, supervisory actions taken after one training course may become pretraining cues for subsequent training courses. Tannenbaum and Yukl (1992) recommended that the transfer environment be examined carefully to identify situational facilitators and inhibitors, and they proposed means either to prepare trainees to deal with the inhibitors or to modify the posttraining environment to encourage transfer.

EVALUATION CRITERIA OF TRAINING PROGRAMS

As is the case with any assessment or evaluation, some measure of performance must be obtained. Measures of performance refer to criteria, and the criteria used to evaluate training are just as important as those used in personnel selection. Relevance, reliability, and freedom from bias are all important considerations. One distinction between criteria used in personnel selection and criteria used to evaluate training is that training criteria are more varied and are used to evaluate multiple aspects of a training program.

Kirkpatrick (1976) identified four criteria used to evaluate training programs: reaction, learning, behavioral, and results. **Reaction criteria** are the participants' reactions to the program. These criteria measure impressions and feelings about the training; for example, did they believe it was useful or add to their knowledge? Reaction criteria are treated as a measure of the face validity of the training program. Most trainers believe that initial receptivity provides a good atmosphere for learning in the instructional program, but as Goldstein (1991) cautioned, it does not necessarily cause high levels of learning. An evaluation form used to assess participants' reactions is shown in Figure 6–5. Alliger, Tannenbaum, Bennett, Traver, and Shotland (1997) concluded that we know the most about reaction criteria because they are assessed most frequently by organizations.

Learning criteria evaluate how much has been learned in the training program. A final exam given at the end of a training program is an example of a learning

The following evaluation form was established for use by the Training Department. Your cooperation will be appreciated and will help us to improve existing training courses.

At the end of each statement below, please fill in the blank with the number (according to the scale) that most accurately describes your reactions

Strongly Agree	Agree	Slightly Agree	Neutral	Slightly Disagree	Disagree	Strongly Disagree
7	6	5	4	3	2	1

Response

Course, Purpose, Objectives, and Structure

1. The purpose of the session was stated. _____
2. The session's objectives were stated. _____
3. An outline was provided to participants. _____

Course Content

4. The material covered was important. _____
5. The material covered was adequate to meet my job needs. _____
6. The session was valuable for the information it contained. _____
7. The material should be covered in the future, with others bearing my job title. _____

Course Delivery

8. The training leader(s) knew the subject well. _____
9. Training methods helped meet course objectives. _____
10. Presentations were effectively delivered. _____
11. The course helped me understand important ideas. _____
12. Instructional aids (e.g., overhead projector, slides, videotapes) were used effectively to emphasize key ideas. _____
13. The training leader(s) maintained a positive attitude toward participants. _____
14. Participants felt free to talk among themselves. _____
15. I was free to discuss areas I had difficulty understanding before the course. _____
16. The training leader(s) showed sensitivity to participant feedback. _____
17. The presentation methods helped to hold my interest. _____

Use of Time

18. Time was effectively used. _____

Overall Course Evaluation

19. The session's objectives were accomplished. _____
20. I recommend this training program to others. _____

FIGURE 6–5   *Participant evaluation form*

SOURCE: From *Professional Training Roles and Competencies*, Vol. II, by H. J. Sredl & W. J. Rothwell, 1987, Amherst, MA: HRD Press.

criterion. With some training methods, such as programmed instruction, the learning criterion is built right into the program; the participant must reach a certain level of proficiency (for example, 90% correct) before training is complete. With other methods, such as role playing directed at improving attitudinal skills, there may be no formal evaluation of how much was learned, or participants may simply be asked whether they changed their attitudes because of the training. Collectively, reaction and learning criteria are called *internal criteria*; that is, they refer to assessments internal to the training program itself.

Behavioral criteria refer to actual changes in performance once the employee is back on the job. These criteria address such questions as to what extent the desired changes in the job behaviors of the trainee are realized by the training program. If the goal of the training program is to increase production, the behavioral criterion assesses output before and after training. Other types of behavioral criteria are absenteeism, scrap rate, accidents, and grievances. All of these are objective criteria. They can be measured easily and have relatively clear meaning, as discussed in Chapter 3. But if the goal of the training program is to increase managers' sensitivity toward people with handicaps, "increased sensitivity" has to be translated into some objective behavioral criteria. Note that scores on learning criteria and on behavioral criteria do not always correspond to a great degree. Some people who perform well in training do not transfer their new knowledge or skills back to the job. This is particularly true with training programs aimed at changing attitudes or feelings.

Results criteria relate to the economic value of the training program to the company. Cascio (1989) developed a procedure to apply utility analysis to the assessment of training outcomes. One premise is if the training program has any effect, then the average job performance of the trained group should exceed that of the untrained group. Cascio proposed the use of a break-even analysis to determine that the economic value of the training program to the organization is greater than zero. Utility analyses are based upon a careful assessment of the costs associated with developing training, training materials, training time, and production losses. While such analyses are often difficult to perform, the failure to analyze training programs in dollars makes it more likely that training will be viewed as a cost rather than a benefit to the organization.

Collectively, behavioral and results criteria are called *external criteria*; they are evaluations external to the training program itself. Consideration of these four criteria sometimes produces different conclusions about the effectiveness of training than a judgment reached by just one or two criteria. For example, Campion and Campion (1987) compared two methods for improving a person's interview skills. An experimental group received multiple instruction techniques on improving their interview skills, while a control group engaged in self-study of relevant material. The results revealed that the experimental group performed better on reaction and learning criteria, but the two groups were equivalent with regard to behavioral and results criteria. Alliger and Janak (1989) concluded that training criteria are causally related; that is, attitudes toward training influence how much is learned and to what extent behavior is changed.

Saari, Johnson, McLaughlin, and Zimmerle (1988) examined the management training practices of 1,000 U.S. companies. Less than one-third conducted a needs assessment to determine the training needs of their managers. Relatively few companies attempted to evaluate training programs, and among those that did, most evaluations assessed only the participants' reactions to training. Goldstein (1978) illustrated the importance of assessing training effectiveness from multiple perspectives. He created some hypothetical complaints to show the many viewpoints by which the success of any training program can be judged:

> From a trainee: "There is a conspiracy. I just finished my training program. I even completed a pretest and a posttest. My posttest score was significantly better than the scores of my friends in the on-the-job control group. However, I lost my job because I could not perform the work."

> From a trainer: "There is a conspiracy. Everyone praised our training program. They said it was the best training program they ever attended. The trainees even had a chance to laugh a little. Now the trainees tell me that management will not let them perform their job the way we trained them."

> From an administrative officer in the company: "There is a conspiracy. My competition used the training program, and it worked for them. They saved a million. I took it straight from their manuals, and my employees still cannot do the job."

Each of these people asserted that the program did not have the intended effect. Goldstein (1991) says that the validity of any training program can be assessed along four dimensions:

1. *Training validity.* Did the trainees match the criteria established for them in the training program? This dimension is concerned with what Kirkpatrick (1976) referred to as internal criteria and addresses the extent to which the trainees mastered the training.
2. *Transfer validity.* Did the trainees match the criteria for success when they were back on the job? This dimension involves external criteria and addresses the extent to which employee performance on the job was enhanced by training.
3. *Intraorganizational validity.* Is the training program equally effective with different groups of trainees within the same organization? This dimension is concerned with the internal generalizability of the training, such as the effectiveness of sensitivity training for sales versus production workers in the same organization.
4. *Interorganizational validity.* Is the training program equally effective with different trainees in companies other than the one that developed the training program? This dimension involves the external generalizability of the training, such as the degree to which a training program that is successful for a manufacturing company would also be successful for a financial organization.

In a review of studies that examined the effectiveness of managerial training programs, Burke and Day (1986) concluded that managerial training is moderately effective in improving learning and job performance but found relatively little knowledge about the intra- and interorganizational validity of such programs. The question of training program success is not simple. One study that did address intraorganizational validity was reported by Morrow, Jarrett, and Rupinski (1997).

They concluded after a four-year study that managerial training had less effect and utility than sales/technical training. However, the results may be partly attributable to the greater difficulty of measuring the criteria of managerial job performance.

In the final analysis, the success of any training and development system is intimately tied to the culture of the organization. The organization sets the tone for the relative importance and need placed on enhancing the skills of its employees. Training and development activities are but a mirror of the organization's deeper values. Smith, Ford, and Kozlowski (1997) spoke to the need for *alignment* between the organization's culture and training initiatives. For example, a traditional authoritarian organization may not be supportive of individuals who attempt to take risks and try out new strategies. Mistakes and errors may be viewed as actions to be avoided rather than as opportunities from which to learn and develop. Also, given what we have discovered recently about the complexities of how and what we learn, our systems for evaluating learning should not be simplistic. Kraiger and Jung (1997) described the importance of linking training objectives to training evaluation criteria. Given the subtleties of how we learn, what we learn, and the duration of our learning, methods of assessing learning must be appropriately refined. Learning is the foundation of training and development. The recent advances we have made in understanding learning have their commensurate influences in our understanding of training and development.

CASE STUDY ◆ Train or Select?

The senior management staff at Barstow Industries faced an ongoing problem within the company. The company was large, employing approximately 11,000 people nationwide. Barstow hired a large number of people into their professional and scientific classification of employees: salespeople, engineers, accountants, and chemists. The management staff differed on the type of person to hire. About half the staff favored hiring people directly out of college and having the company train them in their jobs. The emphasis would be on training. The basic requirement was that the people had to be bright—bright enough to learn the job quickly. The other half of the staff favored hiring people with extensive job experience. There would be little need for training because the new employees had already demonstrated their ability to perform the job.

Both sides had good arguments. Those who favored the training approach argued that the company could save money on payroll costs because new, unproven employees could be hired at lower salaries than their experienced counterparts. Furthermore, by making the training company-specific, there was less chance the employees would be hired away by a competitor. It was also argued that the company had good training facilities, including trainers, that were resources the company should not underutilize.

Those who favored the selection of experienced employees proposed powerful counterarguments. They cited statistics showing that a sizable proportion of new college graduates don't last long with their first employer. They didn't want the company to act as a proving ground by weeding out the unsuccessful employees. Whatever increased salary costs were associated with hiring proven, experienced employees would be offset by their increased job performance. It was argued that their competitors could identify the "keepers," and Barstow would raid those companies' talent by offering a higher salary.

It was difficult to argue against the lower payroll costs the company would incur by hiring new, unproven people. But it was also difficult to argue with the better job performance and lower turnover obtained by hiring experienced employees. Every time it came to filling an open position the same arguments were presented by both sides. Individual managers in charge of filling positions within their departments had their own views on the issue, but it seemed there was always a person in authority above them who supported the other approach. Everyone seemed to believe there should be a uniform company position on the matter, but there certainly was no consensus on what the company should do. The only group that held a single view was the Human Resources Department, which was highly understandable because one of its major functions was to provide training. Everyone hoped the senior management staff would reach a decision shortly, but everyone also knew that many people would be unhappy with whatever decision was made.

Questions

1. What are some additional benefits and liabilities of hiring young employees and training them to fit a company's needs?
2. What are some additional benefits and liabilities of hiring experienced employees who have received most of their professional training elsewhere?
3. What are the benefits and liabilities of Barstow Industries staffing the organization using both approaches?
4. Do you think certain types of jobs (for example, sales) more readily lend themselves to one approach over the other? Why?
5. Give some examples of company-specific training and consider to what degree the training could be generalized to another company.

INFOTRAC ARTICLES

1. *Training & Development,* June 1997 v51 n6 p47(2)
   Virtual reality training takes off. Carol Gunther-Mohr
   Describes the nature of virtual reality training, which permits users to experience realistic, three-dimensional, interactive learning.
2. *Training & Development,* April 1998 v52 n4 p12(2)
   Eight steps to a sexual-harassment-free workplace. Herff L. Moore, Rebecca W. Gatlin-Watts, & Joe Cangelose
   Presents an eight-step training program based on behavioral modeling designed to decrease the likelihood of sexual harassment.
3. *Training & Development,* April 1998 v52 n4 p26(5)
   Big ideas for trainers in small companies. Sacha Cohen
   Discusses the value of training for small companies and presents useful suggestions for developing training programs.

4. *Training & Development*, March 1998 v52 n3 p10(2)
   A common standard for measuring training results. Laurie J. Bassi, Scott Cheney, & Daniel McMurrer
   Discusses a method that can be used to assess the effectiveness of training programs based on the use of standard criteria for evaluating results.

5. *Training & Development*, May 1998 v52 n5 p69(10)
   13 common mistakes using 360-degree feedback. Scott Wimer & Kenneth M. Nowack
   Presents and explains 13 mistakes companies make in implementing 360-degree feedback programs.

6. *Training & Development*, Feb 1998 v52 n2 p35(2)
   Global training's critical success factors. Cynthia L. Kemper
   Discusses the importance of possessing intellectual skills for conducting business in a global environment.

7. *Training & Development*, July 1996 v50 n7 p24(7)
   The new look of behavior modeling. Alice Pescuric & William C. Byham
   Discusses recent advances in behavior modeling as a training technique designed to develop skills and modify behavior.

8. *Training & Development*, Feb 1999 v53 i2 p12(3)
   Play "20 questions" to develop a successful mentoring program. Judith G. Lindenberger & Lois J. Zachary
   Proposes a plan for companies that are considering a mentorship program for developing the skills of their employees.

Performance Appraisal

MAJOR CHAPTER OBJECTIVES

- ◆ Understand the reasons organizations have performance appraisal systems.
- ◆ Know the sources of performance appraisal data and the associated limitations of each.
- ◆ Explain the purpose of rater training.
- ◆ Understand the bases of rater motivation.
- ◆ Understand self-appraisal and peer appraisal.
- ◆ Explain the use of performance appraisal interviews.

Employees continually have their job performance appraised, whether on a formal or an informal basis. Informal appraisals may be made from haphazard observation, memory, hearsay, or intuition. Alternatively, with a formal and rational system, appraisals are more accurate, fair, and useful to all concerned. This chapter deals with formal programs, methods, and techniques for appraising employee performance.

Before the discussion of performance appraisal, it should be noted that there is no clear understanding of what constitutes "performance," let alone how to appraise it. Campbell, McCloy, Oppler, and Sager (1993) asserted that the concept of performance is poorly understood. They stated that *performance* is to be distinguished from *effectiveness*. **Performance** is synonymous with behavior; it is what people actually do, and it can be observed. Performance includes those actions that are relevant to the organization's goals and can be measured in terms of each individual's proficiency (that is, level of contribution). **Effectiveness,** on the other hand, refers to the evaluation of the results of performance, and it is beyond the influence or control of the individual. Measures of effectiveness, while of major importance to the organization, are contaminated by factors over which the employee has little influence. An example of effectiveness is how many promotions an employee has had over a certain period of time—say, three years. The number of promotions a person has is affected by the availability of job openings to which one can be promoted and the qualifications of other candidates. Furthermore, it is the organization and not the individual that makes promotion decisions. Rewarding or punishing individuals on the basis of their effectiveness may be unfair and counterproductive. While there is a relationship between performance and effectiveness, the two concepts should not be confounded. The significance of the distinction is that appraisals of employee performance should be directed at job-related behaviors that are under the control of the employee.

Murphy and Cleveland (1995) believe that performance appraisals can help organizations in several ways. These factors are the primary reasons most organizations have formal performance appraisal systems. First, they can enhance the quality of organizational decisions ranging from pay raises to promotions to discharges. The purpose of the human resource function in an organization is to maximize the contributions of employees to the goals of the organization, and assessments of employee job performance can play a major role in accomplishing that function.

Second, performance appraisals can enhance the quality of individual decisions, ranging from career choices to the development of future strengths. Accurate performance feedback is an important component of success in training and provides critical input for forming realistic self-assessments in the workplace. Performance feedback is also a key to maintaining high levels of work motivation.

Third, performance appraisals can affect employees' views of and attachment to their organization. An organization's successful performance appraisal system may help to build employee commitment and satisfaction. Employees who believe that an organization's decisions are irrational or unfair are unlikely to develop a strong commitment to that organization.

Finally, formal performance appraisals provide a rational, legally defensible basis for personnel decisions. As discussed in Chapter 5, personnel decisions must

Table 7–1   *Employer and employee reasons for conducting appraisals*

Employer Perspective

1. Despite imperfect measurement, individual differences in performance make a difference.
2. Documentation of performance appraisal and feedback may be needed for legal defense.
3. Appraisal provides a rational basis for constructing a bonus or merit system.
4. Appraisal dimensions and standards can operationalize strategic goals and clarify performance expectations.
5. Providing individual feedback is part of a performance management process.
6. Despite the traditional individual focus, appraisal criteria can include teamwork and teams can be the focus of appraisal.

Employee Perspective

1. Performance feedback is needed and desired.
2. Improvement in performance requires assessment.
3. Fairness requires that differences in performance levels across workers be measured and have an impact on outcomes.
4. Assessment and recognition of performance levels can motivate improved performance.

SOURCE: From "Performance Appraisal in a Quality Context: A New Look at an Old Problem" by R. L. Cardy, 1998, in *Performance Appraisal* (p. 142), edited by J. W. Smither, San Francisco: Jossey-Bass.

be based on reason, not capriciousness. There must be a defensible explanation for why some employees are promoted, discharged, or receive differential pay raises compared to others. As will be discussed shortly, personnel decisions based on performance appraisals are subject to the same legal standards as tests. Both tests and performance evaluations are used as techniques in the personnel function. While performance appraisals may trigger discordant reactions from some employees, the alternative of making personnel decisions devoid of a rational basis is simply unacceptable. Cardy (1998) summarized employer and employee reasons for conducting appraisals, as shown in Table 7–1.

USING THE RESULTS OF PERFORMANCE APPRAISALS

The results of a performance appraisal program may be applied to many other management functions (see Figure 7–1). As discussed in Chapter 3, criteria are derived from job analysis procedures; the criteria, in turn, are the basis for appraisals. The major uses of performance appraisal information are described in the following paragraphs.

Personnel Training.   Perhaps the main use of performance appraisal information is for employee feedback; this is the basis for the person analysis discussed in the preceding chapter. Feedback highlights employees' strengths and weaknesses. Of

FIGURE 7–1   *Development of performance appraisal information and its applications*

course, the appraisal should pertain to job-related characteristics only. Deficiencies or weaknesses then become the targets for training. Training should involve only those areas where poor performance can be attributed to the individual and not to aspects of the work environment. The supervisor plays a key role in helping to develop the employee's skills. Although, by definition, performance appraisals are evaluative, in this context they serve more as diagnostic aids. Since some employees will not acknowledge their weaknesses, a supportive supervisor is more effective than one who is threatening or critical. More will be said about this later in the chapter.

Wage and Salary Administration.   Perhaps the second most common use of performance appraisals is to determine raises. Pay increases are often made, in part, on the basis of job performance. Appraisal programs can be designed so that there is a direct relationship between the evaluation and the size of the raise. For example, an employee who is judged to be performing in the top 10% of the workforce might get a 12% raise. Conversely, an employee who performs in the bottom 10% might get only a 2% raise.

Unfortunately, the "personnel development" and "salary administration" aspects of appraisal are often uncomfortable partners. Many employees attach far more meaning to raises because they are more immediate and real than revelations about weaknesses on the job. If the two functions are combined in the same appraisal, employees can become defensive. When admitting weaknesses means getting a smaller raise, personnel development may take a backseat.

In a classic article, Meyer, Kay, and French (1965) talked about the need for "split roles" for supervisors in conducting appraisals. One role is a counselor or coach in discussing employee development or performance improvement. The other is a judge in making salary decisions. Evidence shows that most supervisors cannot play both roles simultaneously. The problem may be addressed by having two appraisals—for example, one in January for employee development and the other in June for salary. Or the supervisor may handle development while the personnel department handles salary. Although both functions are important, it is customary practice that they not be conducted at the same time by the same person. However, some research by Prince and Lawler (1986) challenged the view that salary discussion hinders the developmental function of performance appraisal. The authors contended that employees prefer less ambiguity in the evaluation-to-reward connection; therefore, it may be advisable to combine the administrative and diagnostic functions of performance appraisal.

Placement.   Performance appraisal information is vital for placement decisions. New employees (such as management trainees) are often exposed to many tasks or jobs at first. Over a 12-month period, a trainee might have jobs in marketing, finance, and accounting. After being appraised in each, the trainee might be permanently assigned to that area where he or she performed best. By identifying the employee's strengths, performance appraisal indicates where the person's talents might best be used.

Promotions.   Promotions may be based on how well an employee performs on his or her current job. Appraisals identify the better-performing employees, and an employee who cannot perform well on his or her current job will not be considered for promotion. However, performance is not the sole determinant of promotion. Promotions are usually granted based on a combination of seniority and merit. If based strictly on seniority, there is nothing to ensure that competent people get promoted. Promotions based strictly on performance are more defensible, but most experts agree that experience in a job is also worth considering. Promotions have often served as the criterion in validating assessment center ratings.

Discharge.   Termination of employment must be predicated on just cause. A typical just cause is inadequate job performance, as determined through performance appraisal. It is also highly advisable for organizations to document the efforts made to enhance the employee's performance and that the decision to terminate employment was the organization's last resort. Many lawsuits stemming from performance appraisals allege the fired employee was the victim of a "wrongful discharge." In such cases the organization must demonstrate the fairness, job-relatedness, and accuracy of the performance appraisal process that led to the termination decision.

Personnel Research.   In many criterion-related validity studies, assessments of the criterion are derived from performance appraisals. Recall that the criterion is a measure of job performance, and that is what performance appraisals are supposed to measure. When I/O psychologists want to validate a new predictor test, they correlate scores with criterion measures, which are often exhumed from a company's performance appraisal files. Any selection device is only as good as the criterion it tries to predict, so the appraisal must be a relevant measure of job success. Research (e.g., Harris, Smith, & Champagne, 1995) has found that for the purpose of personnel research, specially constructed performance appraisal instruments yielded more useful and less biased information than evaluations originally collected for administrative purposes (for example, salary administration). Harris et al. recommended that more attention be given to the purposes behind performance appraisal, and how these purposes influence the quality and usefulness of the evaluation.

PERFORMANCE APPRAISAL AND THE LAW

Federal law on fair employment practices also pertains to performance appraisal. Unfair discrimination can occur not only on the predictor (test) side of the equation but also in the job behavior the test is trying to predict.

Malos (1998) stated that the importance of legal issues in performance appraisal has "skyrocketed" in recent years. He reviewed many court cases involving alleged discrimination and found that charges of discrimination were frequently related to the assessment of the employee's job performance. Charges of discrimination may be brought under the laws discussed in Chapter 5, including Title VII of the Civil Rights Act of 1964, the Civil Rights Act of 1991, the Age Discrimination in Employment Act (ADEA), and the Americans with Disabilities Act (ADA). Litigation can also result from charges of employer *negligence* (breach of duty to conduct appraisals with due care), *defamation* (disclosure of untrue unfavorable performance information that damages the reputation of the employee), and *misrepresentation* (disclosure of untrue favorable performance information that presents a risk of harm to prospective employees or third parties).

Malos synthesized the findings from many court cases involving performance appraisal and arrived at recommendations for employers regarding both the content and the process of performance appraisals. The *content* of performance appraisal refers to the criteria of job performance that are evaluated. Malos made the recommendations for legally sound performance appraisals listed in Table 7–2. Conducting the appraisals on job-related factors, usually derived from a job analysis, is particularly important. Werner and Bolino (1997) likewise found that

Table 7–2   *Content recommendations for legally sound performance appraisals*

Appraisal Criteria

- ◆ Should be objective rather than subjective
- ◆ Should be job-related or based on job analysis
- ◆ Should be based on behaviors rather than traits
- ◆ Should be within the control of the ratee
- ◆ Should relate to specific functions, not global assessments

SOURCE: From "Current Legal Issues in Performance Appraisal" by S. B. Malos, 1998, in *Performance Appraisal* (p. 80), edited by J. W. Smither, San Francisco: Jossey-Bass.

Table 7–3   *Procedural recommendations for legally sound performance appraisals*

Appraisal Procedures

- ◆ Should be standardized and uniform for all employees within a job group
- ◆ Should be formally communicated to employees
- ◆ Should provide notice of performance deficiencies and of opportunities to correct them
- ◆ Should provide access for employees to review appraisal results
- ◆ Should provide formal appeal mechanisms that allow for employee input
- ◆ Should use multiple, diverse, and unbiased raters
- ◆ Should provide written instructions for training for raters
- ◆ Should require thorough and consistent documentation across raters that includes specific examples of performance based on personal knowledge
- ◆ Should establish a system to detect potentially discriminatory effects or abuses of the system overall

SOURCE: From "Current Legal Issues in Performance Appraisal" by S. B. Malos, 1998, in *Performance Appraisal* (p. 83), edited by J. W. Smither, San Francisco: Jossey-Bass.

whether or not the company based its performance appraisals on criteria derived from job analyses was often a deciding factor in court rulings. Malos also made *procedural* recommendations for legally sound performance appraisals. These recommendations are presented in Table 7–3. Malos concluded by stating that as our economy continues to move toward a service and information emphasis, there will be the tendency to use subjective performance criteria, particularly at the professional and managerial levels. Also, more organizations are increasingly relying on multiple sources of evaluation (customers, subordinates, and peers). Both subjective criteria and untrained raters can lead to discrimination claims that are difficult to defend. It is recommended that when such criteria and raters are used, they should be used in conjunction with objective criteria and trained raters whose input is given greater weight.

SOURCES OF PERFORMANCE APPRAISAL INFORMATION

As stated in Chapter 3, job performance can be characterized by many criteria. Three different types of data are used: objective production data, personnel data, and judgmental data.

Objective Production Data

Using objective production data as an index of how well an employee is performing on the job is limited in its frequency and value. For a person in the job of a machine operator, job performance may be measured by counting the number of objects produced per day, per week, and so forth. Similarly, salespeople are appraised by assessing (counting) their sales volume over a given period. It is even possible to evaluate the performance of firefighters by counting the number of fires they extinguish.

Although each of these objective production measures has some degree of intuitive appeal, none is usually a complete measure of job performance. Two problems in particular affect each of these measures. First, we would like to assume that differences in performance across people reflect true differences in how well these people perform their jobs. Unfortunately, variability in performance can be due to factors beyond the individual's control. One machine operator may produce more because he or she works with a better machine. A salesperson might have a larger sales volume because his or her territory is better. Firefighters who put out few fires might be responsible for an area with relatively few buildings. This problem of variation in performance stemming from external factors should sound familiar: It represents a form of criterion contamination (a topic discussed in Chapter 3).

The second problem with objective performance measures is that they rarely tell the whole story. A machine operator who produces more objects per day but who also produces more defective objects should not be described as the "best." Quality may be as important as quantity, but this cannot be recorded in a simple count of objects produced. A salesperson spends a lot of time recruiting new customers, an aspect that must be weighed against simply making calls on established customers. Creating new customers can be as important as maintaining business with old ones. The sales volume might be lower at first, but in the long run, the new customers will increase total sales volume. Extinguishing fires is but one aspect of a firefighter's job; preventing fires is another one. The "best" firefighters conceivably may not have put out many fires but might have contributed heavily toward preventing fires in the first place. There is growing use of electronic performance monitoring (EPM) to assess the performance of workers engaged in computer-based tasks. An EPM system records the objective aspects of performance on computer-based tasks, such as volume and speed of entries (Lund, 1992). Research (Westin, 1992) has revealed that such systems are regarded as unfair and inaccurate assessments of work performance because they ignore the discretionary or judgmental component of work, which is inherent to all jobs. In short, all of these actual criteria suffer from criterion deficiency. They are deficient measures of the conceptual criteria they seek to measure.

Relevance of Objective Production Data.   For the jobs mentioned, objective production data have some relevance. It would be absurd to say that sales volume has no bearing on a salesperson's performance. The salesperson's job is indeed to sell. The issue is the degree of relevance. It is a mistake to give too much importance to objective production data in performance appraisal (see Field Note 1). This is sometimes a great temptation because these data are usually very accessible, but the meaning of those clear-cut numbers is not always so evident. Finally, for many jobs, objective performance measures do not exist or, if they do, they have little relevance to actual performance. Criterion relevance is a question of judgment. For some jobs, objective performance data are partially relevant measures of success; in many others, such relevance is lacking.

Personnel Data

The second type of appraisal information is personnel data, the data retained by a company's personnel office. The three most common indices of performance are absenteeism, turnover, and accidents. The critical issue with these variables is criterion relevance. To what extent do they reflect differences in job performance?

Absenteeism is probably the most sensitive measure of performance. In almost all jobs, employees who are often absent are judged as performing worse than others, all other factors being equal. Indeed, an employee can be fired for excessive absence. Most organizations have policies for dealing with absenteeism, which attests to its importance as a variable in judging overall performance. However, the measurement and interpretation of absenteeism are not clear-cut. Absences can be "excused" or "unexcused" depending on many factors pertaining to both the individual (for example, seniority) and the job (for example, job level). An employee who has ten days of excused absence may still be appraised as performing better than an employee with five days of unexcused absence. Whether the absence was allowed must be determined before performance judgments are made. Measuring absenteeism is a thorny problem, but it is seen as a highly relevant criterion variable in most organizations.

Turnover is also used to measure performance. It too has some measurement problems. Some turnover is voluntary (the employee quits); some is involuntary (the employee is fired). An employee who quit is probably appraised "better" than an employee who was fired. Some organizations will let an employee resign to improve his or her chances of getting another job. This clouds the value of turnover as a measure of performance. The attitude toward a chronic job-hopper has also changed over the years. Twenty years ago, job-hoppers were viewed with some suspicion at the management level; they seemed unstable and unable to hold a job for long. Today, however, job-hoppers are regarded more positively. Exposure to different jobs is taken to mean that they have more breadth of experience. This is

---

Field Note 1   *What Is "High" Performance?*

Usually we think of high performance as a positive score, a gain, or some improvement over the status quo. Conversely, when individuals perform "worse" than they did last year, it is tempting to conclude they didn't perform as well. However, such is not always the case. Performance must be judged in terms of what is under the control of the individuals being evaluated rather than those influences on performance that are beyond their control. There can be broad, pervasive factors, sometimes of an economic nature, that suppress the performance of everyone being judged. One example is in sales. If there is a general downturn in the economy

and products or services are not being purchased with the same frequency as in the previous year, sales could be down, for example, by an average of 15%. This 15% (actually −15%) figure would then represent "average" performance. Perhaps the best salesperson in the year had only a 3% drop in sales over the previous year. Thus, "good" performance in this situation is a smaller loss compared to some average or norm group. This example illustrates that there is always some judgmental or contextual component to appraising performance and that sole reliance on objective numbers can be misleading.

an example of how the same behavior (turnover) acquires different interpretations over time.

Accidents can be used as a measure of job performance but only for a limited number of jobs. Frequency and severity of accidents are both used as variables, as are accidents resulting in injury or property damage. Accidents are a more relevant criterion variable for blue-collar than for white-collar jobs. People who drive delivery trucks may be evaluated in part on the number of accidents they have. This variable can be contaminated by many sources, though. Road conditions, miles driven, time of day, and condition of the truck can all contribute to accidents. While relevance is limited to certain jobs, accidents can contribute greatly to appraisal. Companies often give substantial pay raises to drivers with no accidents and fire those with a large number.

Relevance of Personnel Data.   There is no doubt that factors such as absence, turnover, and accidents are meaningful measures of job performance. Employees may be discharged for excessive absences or accidents, and they may be rewarded for perfect attendance or a perfect safety record. However, as was the case with production data, personnel data rarely give a comprehensive picture of the employee's performance. Other highly relevant aspects of job performance often are not revealed by personnel data. It is for this reason that judgmental data are relied upon to offer a more complete assessment of job performance.

Judgmental Data

Judgmental data are commonly used for performance appraisal because finding relevant objective measures is difficult. Subjective assessments can apply to almost all jobs. Those who do the assessments are usually supervisors, but some use has also been made of self-assessment and peer assessment. A wide variety of measures have been developed, all intended to provide accurate assessments of how people are performing (Pulakos, 1997). These are the major methods used in performance appraisal:

1. Graphic rating scales
2. Employee-comparison methods
   a. Rank order
   b. Paired comparison
   c. Forced distribution
3. Behavioral checklists and scales
   a. Critical incidents
   b. Behaviorally anchored rating scale (BARS)
   c. Behavioral-observation scale (BOS)

Graphic Rating Scales.   **Graphic rating scales** are the most commonly used system in performance appraisal. Individuals are rated on a number of traits or factors. The rater judges "how much" of each factor the individual has. Usually performance is judged on a 5- or 7-point scale, and the number of factors ranges between 5 and 20. The more common dimensions rated are quantity of work, quality of work, practical judgment, job knowledge, cooperation, and motivation. Examples of typical graphic rating scales are shown in Figure 7–2.

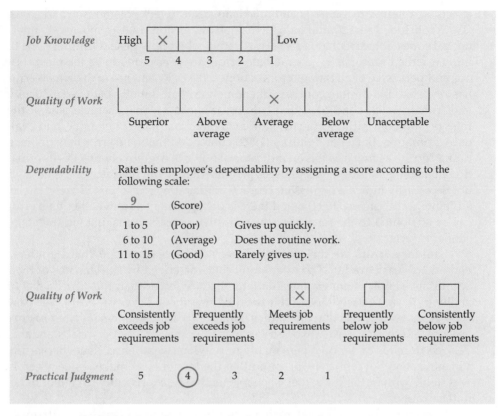

FIGURE 7–2   *Examples of graphic rating scales for various performance dimensions*

In making appraisals with rating scales, the rater may unknowingly commit errors in judgment. These can be placed into three major categories: halo errors, leniency errors, and central-tendency errors. All three stem from rater bias and misperception.

Halo errors are evaluations based on the rater's general feelings about an employee. The rater generally has a favorable attitude toward the employee that permeates all evaluations of this person. Typically, the rater has strong feelings about at least one important aspect of the employee's performance. This is then generalized to other performance factors, and the employee is judged (across many factors) as uniformly good or bad. The rater who is impressed by an employee's idea might allow those feelings to carry over to the evaluation of leadership, cooperation, motivation, and so on. This occurs even though the "good idea" is not related to the other factors.

Raters who commit halo errors do not distinguish among the many dimensions of employee performance. A compounding problem is that there are two types of halo. One type is truly a rating error and involves the failure to differentiate an employee's performance across different dimensions. The second type is giving uniformly consistent ratings to an employee when these ratings are in fact justified; that is, the employee truly performs well across many dimensions. These effects are referred to as *invalid* and *valid* halo, respectively. Solomonson and Lance (1997) concluded that a valid halo (actual job dimensions that are positively inter-related) does not affect halo rater error (raters who allow general impressions to influence their ratings). In general, halo errors are considered to be the most seri-ous and pervasive of all rating errors (Cooper, 1981). Recent research on halo error has revealed it is a more complex phenomenon than initially believed. Murphy and Anhalt (1992) concluded that halo error is not a stable characteristic of the rater or ratee, but rather is the result of an interaction of the rater, ratee, and eval-uative situation. Balzer and Sulsky (1992) contended that halo error may not be a rating "error" as much as it is an indicator of how we cognitively process informa-tion in arriving at judgments of other people. That is, the presence of a halo does not necessarily indicate there is inaccuracy in the ratings. In a related view, Lance, LaPointe, and Fisicaro (1994) noted there is disagreement as to whether halo error can be attributed to the rater or to the cognitive process of making judgments of similar objects.

Leniency errors are the second category. Some teachers are "hard graders" and others "easy graders," so raters can be characterized by the leniency of their appraisals. Harsh raters give evaluations that are lower than the "true" level of ability (if it can be ascertained); this is called *severity* or *negative leniency*. The easy rater gives evaluations that are higher than the "true" level; this is called *positive leniency*. These errors usually occur because the rater applies personal standards derived from his or her own personality or previous experience. Kane, Bernardin, Villanova, and Peyrefitte (1995) found that the tendency to make leniency errors was stable with individuals; that is, people tend to be consistently lenient or harsh in their ratings.

Central-tendency error refers to the rater's unwillingness to assign extreme—high or low—ratings. Everyone is "average," and only the middle (central) part of the scale is used. This may happen when raters are asked to evaluate unfamiliar aspects of performance. Rather than not respond, they play it safe and say the per-son is average in this "unknown" ability.

Even though we have long been aware of halo, leniency, and central-tendency errors, there is no clear consensus on how these errors are manifested in ratings. Saal, Downey, and Lahey (1980) observed that researchers define these errors in somewhat different ways. For example, leniency errors are sometimes equated with skew in the distribution of ratings; that is, positive skew is evidence of nega-tive leniency and negative skew of positive leniency. Other researchers say that an average rating above the midpoint on a particular scale indicates positive leniency. The exact meaning of central tendency is also unclear. Central-tendency errors oc-cur if the average rating is around the midpoint of the scale, but there is not much variance in the ratings. The amount of variance that separates central-tendency er-rors from "good" ratings has not been defined. Saal and associates feel that more precise definitions of these errors must be developed before they can be overcome. To help combat these errors, other appraisal methods have been developed, as dis-cussed next.

Employee-Comparison Methods. Rating scales provide for evaluating employees against some defined standard. With employee comparison methods, individuals are compared with one another; variance is thereby forced into the appraisals. Thus, the concentration of ratings at one part of the scale caused by rating error is avoided. However, all methods of employee comparison involve the question of whether variation represents true differences in performance or whether it creates a false impression of large differences when they are in fact small. There are three major employee-comparison methods: rank order, paired comparison, and forced distribution.

With the **rank-order method,** the rater ranks employees from high to low on a given performance dimension. The person ranked first is regarded as the "best" and the person ranked last as the "worst." However, because rank-order data have only ordinal-scale properties, we do not know how good the "best" is or how bad the "worst" is. We do not know the level of performance. For example, the Nobel Prize winners in a given year could be ranked in terms of their overall contributions to science. But we would be hard-pressed to conclude that the Nobel laureate ranked last made the worst contribution to science. Rank-order data are all relative to some standard, in this case excellence in scientific research. Another problem is that it becomes quite tedious and perhaps somewhat meaningless to rank order large numbers of people. What usually happens is that the rater can sort out the people at the top and bottom of the pile. However, for the rest with undifferentiated performance, the rankings may be somewhat arbitrary.

With the **paired-comparison method,** each employee is compared with every other employee in the group being evaluated. The rater's task is to select which of the two is better on the dimension being rated. The method is typically used to evaluate employees on a single dimension: overall ability to perform the job. The number of evaluation pairs is computed by the formula $n(n - 1)/2$, where n is the number of people to be evaluated. For example, if there are 10 people in a group, the number of paired comparisons is $10(9)/2 = 45$. At the conclusion of the evaluation, the number of times each person was selected as the better of the two is tallied. The people are then ranked by the number of tallies they receive.

A major limitation is that the number of comparisons made mushrooms dramatically with large numbers of employees. If 50 people are to be appraised, the number of comparisons is 1,225; this obviously takes too much time. The paired-comparison method is best for relatively small samples.

The **forced-distribution method** is most useful when the other employee-comparison methods are most limited—that is, when the sample is large. Forced distribution is typically used when the rater must evaluate employees on a single dimension, but it can also be used with multiple dimensions. The procedure is based on the normal distribution and assumes that employee performance is normally distributed. The distribution is divided into five to seven categories. Using predetermined percentages (based on the normal distribution), the rater evaluates an employee by placing him or her into one of the categories. All employees are evaluated in this manner. The method "forces" the rater to distribute the employees across all categories (which is how the method gets its name). Thus, it is impossible for all employees to be rated excellent, average, or poor. An example of the procedure for a sample of 50 employees is illustrated in Figure 7–3.

Some raters react negatively to this method, saying that the procedure creates artificial distinctions among employees. This is partly because the raters feel that

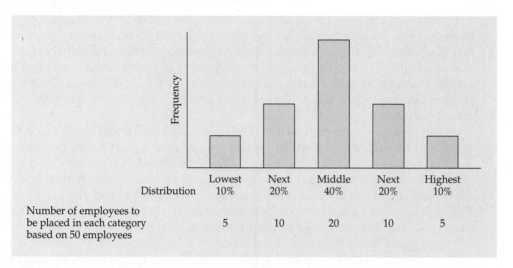

FIGURE 7–3   *The forced-distribution method of performance appraisal*

performance is not normally distributed but rather negatively skewed; that is, most of their employees are performing very well. The dissatisfaction can be partially allayed by noting that the lowest 10% are not necessarily performing poorly, just not as well as the others. The problem (as with all comparison methods) is that performance is not compared to a defined standard. The meaning of the differences among employees must be supplied from some other source.

Behavioral Checklists and Scales.   Most recent advances in performance appraisal involve behavioral checklists and scales. The key term is *behavior.* Behaviors are less vague than other factors. The greater the agreement on the meaning of the performance appraised, the greater the chance that the appraisal will be accurate. All of the methods in this category have their origin directly or indirectly in the critical-incidents method.

Critical incidents are behaviors that result in good or poor job performance. Anderson and Wilson (1997) noted that the critical-incident technique is flexible and can be used for performance appraisal as well as job analysis. Supervisors record behaviors of employees that greatly influence their job performance. They either keep a running tally of these critical incidents as they occur on the job or recall them at a later time. Critical incidents are usually grouped by aspects of performance: job knowledge, decision-making ability, leadership, and so on. The end product is a list of behaviors (good and bad) that constitute effective and ineffective job performance.

The original critical-incidents method did not lend itself to quantification (that is, a score reflecting performance). It was used to guide employees in the specifics of their job performance. Each employee's performance can be described in terms of the occurrence of these critical behaviors. The supervisor can then counsel the employee to avoid the bad and continue the good behaviors. For example, a negative critical incident for a machine operator might be "leaves machine running while unattended." A positive one might be "always wears safety goggles on the job." Discussing performance in such clear terms is more understandable than using such vague statements as "poor attitude" or "careless work habits."

Behaviorally anchored rating scales (BARS) are a combination of the behavioral-incident and rating-scale methods. Performance is rated on a scale, but the scale points are anchored with behavioral incidents. The development of BARS is time-consuming, but the benefits make it worthwhile. BARS are developed in a five-step process:

1. A list of critical incidents is generated in the manner discussed previously.

2. A group of people (usually supervisors—either the same people who generated the critical incidents initially or another group) clusters the incidents into a smaller set of performance dimensions (usually five to ten) that they typically represent. The result is a given number of performance dimensions, each containing several illustrative critical incidents.

3. Another group of knowledgeable people is instructed to perform the following task: The critical incidents are "scrambled" so that they are no longer listed under the dimensions described in step 2. The critical incidents might be written on separate note cards and presented to the people in random order. The raters' task is to reassign or retranslate all the critical incidents back to the original performance dimensions. The goal is to have critical incidents that clearly represent the performance dimensions under consideration. A critical incident generally is said to be retranslated successfully if some percentage (usually 50% to 80%) of the raters reassign it back to the dimension from which it came. Incidents that are not retranslated successfully (that is, there is ample confusion as to which dimension they represent) are discarded.

4. The people who retranslated the items are asked to rate each "surviving" critical incident on a scale (typically 7 or 9 points) of just how effectively or ineffectively it represents performance on the appropriate dimension. The ratings given to each incident are then averaged, and the standard deviation for each item is computed. Low standard deviations indicate high rater agreement on the value of the incident. Large standard deviations indicate low rater agreement. A standard deviation criterion is then set for deciding which incidents will be retained for inclusion in the final form of the BARS. Incidents that have a standard deviation in excess of 1.50 typically are discarded because the raters could not agree on their respective values.

5. The final form of the instrument consists of critical incidents that survived both the retranslation and standard deviation criteria. The incidents serve as behavioral anchors for the performance dimension scales. The final BARS instrument is a series of scales listed vertically (one for each dimension) and anchored by the retained incidents. Each incident is located along the scale according to its established rating. An example of BARS for patrol officer performance is shown in Figure 7–4. As can be seen, behaviors are listed with respect to what the employee is expected to do at various performance levels. For this reason, BARS are sometimes referred to as "behavioral expectation scales."

One of the major advantages of the method is unrelated to performance appraisal. It is the high degree of involvement of persons developing the scale. The participants must carefully examine specific behaviors that lead to effective

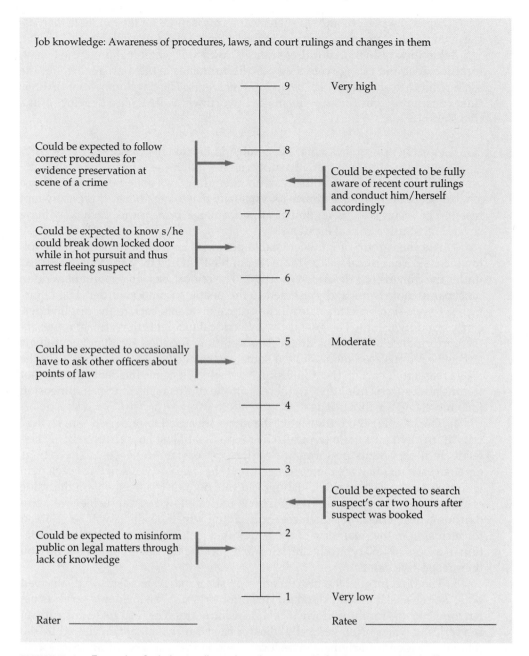

Job knowledge: Awareness of procedures, laws, and court rulings and changes in them

9 — Very high

Could be expected to follow correct procedures for evidence preservation at scene of a crime

8

Could be expected to be fully aware of recent court rulings and conduct him/herself accordingly

7

Could be expected to know s/he could break down locked door while in hot pursuit and thus arrest fleeing suspect

6

5 — Moderate

Could be expected to occasionally have to ask other officers about points of law

4

3

Could be expected to search suspect's car two hours after suspect was booked

Could be expected to misinform public on legal matters through lack of knowledge

2

1 — Very low

Rater _____

Ratee _____

FIGURE 7–4   *Example of a behaviorally anchored rating scale for appraising patrol officers*

SOURCE: From *Psychology of Work Behavior,* rev. ed. (p. 128), by F. J. Landy and D. A. Trumbo, 1980, Pacific Grove, CA: Brooks/Cole.

performance. In so doing, they may reject false stereotypes about ineffective performances. The method has face validity for both the rater and ratee and also appears useful for training raters. However, one disadvantage is that BARS are job specific; that is, a different behaviorally anchored rating scale must be developed for every job.

Another development in appraisal is the **behavioral-observation scale** (BOS). Like BARS, it is based on critical incidents. With BOS the rater must rate the employee on the frequency of critical incidents. The rater observes the employee over a certain period, such as a month. An example of a five-point critical-incident scale used in appraising salespeople, as provided by Latham and Wexley (1977), follows:

Knows the price of competitive products

Never	Seldom	Sometimes	Generally	Always
1	2	3	4	5

Raters evaluate the employees on several such critical incidents, recording how often they observed the behavior. The total score is the sum of all the critical incidents. The final step is to correlate the response for each incident (a rating of 1, 2, 3, 4, or 5) with the total performance score. This is called *item analysis*. It is meant to detect the critical incidents that most influence overall performance. Those incidents that have the highest correlations with the total score are the most discriminating factors in performance. They would be retained to develop criteria for job success.

Latham, Fay, and Saari (1979) suggested advantages to performance appraisals with BOS. First, like BARS, BOS are developed by those using the method for evaluation, who understand they are committed to using the scales. Second, BOS information can be used to teach new employees the behaviors most critical to the job. Finally, BOS are content valid; the aspects of performance appraised are derived directly from the job. The authors believe this satisfies the EEOC requirement that appraisal methods be job relevant.

Relevance of Judgmental Data.   The relevance of judgmental data in performance appraisal, like the relevance of any type of performance appraisal data, refers to the extent to which the observed data are accurate measures of the "true" variable being measured. The "true" variable can refer to a global construct, such as overall job performance, or a dimension of job performance, such as interpersonal relations ability. One method of assessing the relevance of judgmental data is to correlate them with performance appraisals from another method, such as objective production or personnel data. In studies that have conducted this type of analysis, the resulting correlations have been only moderate in magnitude. While these results may be interpreted to mean that judgmental data have only moderate relevance, the key question is whether the objective production data or the personnel data can be assumed to represent "true" ability. Those types of data might be just as incomplete or remotely relevant as judgmental data. Since we never obtain measures of the conceptual criterion (that is, "true" ability), we are forced to deal with imperfect measures that, not surprisingly, yield imperfect results. Research (e.g., Weekley & Gier, 1989) showed the existence of rater disagreement and halo error even among such expert raters as Olympic judges who were intensely trained to make accurate evaluations. DeNisi and Peters (1996) reported that instructing raters to keep a structured diary for continuous record keeping of performance (rather than using memory recall) produced more accurate assessments of the employees. Wagner and Goffin (1997) concluded that performance

"Barkley, I perceive my role in this institution not as a judge but merely as an observer and recorder. I have observed you to be a prize boob and have so recorded it."

appraisal ratings produced by behavioral-observation methods are no more accurate than those produced by employee comparison methods.

Borman (1978) had another approach to assessing the relevance of judgmental data. He made videotapes of two employment situations: a manager talking with a problem employee and a recruiter interviewing a job candidate. Sixteen videotapes were made, eight of each situation. Each tape showed a different degree of performance—for example, from a highly competent recruiter to a totally inept one. Similar degrees of performance were shown of the manager–subordinate meeting. Professional actors were used in the tapes. The same actor played the recruiter in all eight tapes, but a different actor played the new employee in each tape. Thus, the performance level (the "true" ability of the manager or recruiter) was "programmed" into the scripts.

Raters were asked to rate the performance of the manager and recruiter with a series of rating scales. The evaluations were correlated with the performance levels depicted. Correlations between ratings and levels of performance across several job dimensions (organizing the interview, establishing rapport, and so on) ranged from .42 to .97. The median was .69. Although this study used a simulation as opposed to actual job performance, it did show that various types of rating procedures are susceptible to differences in validity. The study also revealed that certain

Field Note 2 *Good Research Isn't Cheap*

Many times unexpected costs are associated with performance appraisal. Here is the story of one of the more unusual expenses I have ever encountered in a research study.

One of the uses of performance appraisal information is as a criterion of job performance. In turn, criteria of job performance may be used to validate selection tests. I had a colleague who needed to collect both performance appraisal (criterion) data and test score (predictor) data to develop a selection test battery for a company. He traveled to the company and had all the supervisors convene in the company cafeteria. He explained the nature of the performance ratings he wanted them to make. Then he explained that all their subordinates would be taking a 30-minute test, and the scores would be correlated with the supervisors' performance appraisal ratings, as is done in a concurrent criterion-related validity study. My colleague then asked the supervisors whether they wanted to take the same test their subordinates would be taking just to get a feel for what it was like. They agreed. He

passed out the test and informed them they would have 30 minutes to complete it. He wanted the testing procedure to be very exact, giving everyone precisely 30 minutes. His watch did not have a second hand, so he was about to ask if he could borrow someone else's watch, when he spied the company's microwave oven on the wall in the cafeteria. He went over to the microwave, set the timer for 30 minutes, told the supervisors to begin the test, and started the microwave.

About 20 minutes into the test, a terrible odor began to fill the cafeteria. Somebody noticed it was coming from the microwave. My colleague had failed to place anything into the microwave when he started it, so for 20 minutes the microwave cooked itself, ultimately suffering terminal meltdown. The microwave cost $800 to replace and is one of the more unusual test-validation expense items I have ever heard of. Incidentally, the test turned out to be highly predictive of the performance appraisal ratings, so the exercise was not a complete waste.

dimensions of performance are more accurately evaluated ("answering recruitee's questions," $r = .97$) than others ("reacting to stress," $r = .42$). Borman was led to conclude that raters are limited in their ability to appraise performance; they could not accurately evaluate the levels of "true" performance that were acted out in the scripts. He suggested a practical upper limit to validity that is less than the theoretical limit ($r = 1.0$) (see Field Note 2).

RATER TRAINING

Can you train raters to make better performance appraisals? The answer appears to be yes. Most rater-training studies seek to train appraisers to make fewer halo, leniency, and central-tendency errors. For example, Latham, Wexley, and Pursell (1975) randomly assigned 60 managers who appraised performance to one of these three groups:

- ◆ *Workshop group.* This group was shown videotapes on evaluating individuals. Members then discussed appraisal procedures and problems in making appraisals, with the intent of reducing rating errors.
- ◆ *Discussion group.* This group received training similar in content, but the main method was discussion.
- ◆ *Control group.* This group received no training.

Six months later, the three groups were "tested." They were shown videotapes of several hypothetical job candidates along with job requirements. The managers were asked to evaluate the candidates' suitability for the jobs in question. The groups showed major differences in the rating errors they made. The workshop group had no rating errors, and the control group performed the worst, making three types of errors.

Zedeck and Cascio (1982) considered the purpose for which performance appraisal ratings are made—merit raise, retention, and development—and found that training works better for some purposes than others. Training typically enhances the accuracy of performance appraisals as well as their acceptability to those who are being appraised.

However, not all research on rater training is positive. Bernardin and Pence (1980) reported that raters who were trained to reduce halo errors actually made less accurate ratings after training. This seems due to the fact that, as Bartlett (1983) noted, there are two types of halo; reduction of invalid halo increases accuracy, but reduction of valid halo decreases it. Hedge and Kavanagh (1988) concluded that certain types of rater training reduce classical rating errors such as halo and leniency but do not increase rating accuracy. This underscores the uncertain relationship between rating errors and accuracy because of our inability to know what "truth" is (Sulsky & Balzer, 1988). One type of rater training appears particularly promising. Frame-of-reference training (Sulsky & Day, 1992) involves providing raters with common reference standards (i.e., frames) by which to evaluate performance. Raters are shown vignettes of good, poor, and average performances and are given feedback on the accuracy of their ratings of the vignettes. The intent of the training is to "calibrate" raters so that they agree on what constitutes varying levels of performance effectiveness for each performance dimension. Research by Woehr (1994) and Day and Sulsky (1995) supported the conclusion that frame-of-reference training increases the accuracy of individual ratees on separate performance dimensions. In a meta-analytic review of rater training for performance appraisal, Woehr and Huffcutt (1994) examined the effectiveness of rater training methods on the major dependent variables of reduced halo error, reduced leniency error, and increased rating accuracy. The authors concluded that rater training has a positive effect on each dependent variable. However, the training strategies are differentially effective in addressing the aspect of performance ratings they are designed to meet.

RATER MOTIVATION

It is not unusual for the majority of employees in a company to receive very high performance evaluations. These inflated ratings are often interpreted as evidence of massive rater errors (i.e., leniency or halo) or a breakdown in the performance appraisal system. The typical organizational response to rating inflation is to make some technical adjustment in the rating scale format or to institute a new training program for raters. However, there is another explanation for rating inflation that is unrelated to rater errors.

Murphy and Cleveland (1995) posited that the tendency to give uniformly high ratings is an instance of adaptive behavior that is, from the rater's point of view, an eminently logical course of action. These deficiencies in ratings are more likely to be a result of the rater's *willingness* to provide accurate ratings than of the *capacity* to rate accurately. If the situation is examined from the rater's perspective, there are many sound reasons to provide inflated ratings.

First, there are typically no rewards from the organization for accurate appraisals and few if any sanctions for inaccurate appraisals. Official company policies often emphasize the value of good performance appraisals, but organizations typically take no specific steps to reward this supposedly valued activity. Second, the most common reason cited for rating inflation is that high ratings are needed to guarantee promotions, salary increases, and other valued rewards. Low ratings, on the other hand, result in these rewards being withheld from subordinates. Raters are thus motivated to obtain valued rewards for their subordinates. Third, raters are motivated to give inflated ratings because the ratings received by subordinates are a reflection of the *rater's* job performance (Latham, 1986). One of the duties of managers is to develop their subordinates. If managers consistently rate their subordinates as less than good performers, it can appear that the managers are not doing their jobs. Thus, high ratings make the rater look good and low ratings make the rater look bad. Fourth, raters tend to inflate their ratings because they wish to avoid the negative reactions that accompany low ratings (Klimoski & Inks, 1990). Negative evaluations typically result in defensive reactions from subordinates, which can create a very stressful situation for the rater. The simplest way to avoid unpleasant or defensive reactions in appraisal interviews is to give uniformly positive feedback (i.e., inflated ratings).

Kozlowski, Chao, and Morrison (1998) describe the process of "appraisal politics" in organizations. If there is a sense that most other raters are inflating their ratings of their subordinates, a good rater has to play politics to protect and enhance the careers of his or her own subordinates. To the extent that a rating inflation strategy actually enhances the prospects of the better subordinates, it may be interpreted as being in the best interests of the organization to do so. Kozlowski et al. stated: "Indeed, if rating distortions are the norm, a failure to engage in appraisal politics may be maladaptive" (p. 176). Supporting this conclusion, Jawahar and Williams (1997) meta-analyzed performance appraisals given for administrative purposes (e.g., promotions) versus developmental or research purposes. Their results showed that performance appraisals conducted for administrative purposes were one-third of a standard deviation higher than those obtained for development or research purposes. As these authors stated, performance appraisals will be much more lenient when those appraisals are "for keeps" (see Field Note 3).

There is no simple way to counteract a rater's motivation to inflate ratings. The problem will not be solved by just increasing the capability of raters. In addition, the environment must be modified in such a way that raters are motivated to provide accurate ratings. Murphy and Cleveland (1995) believe accurate rating is most likely to occur in an environment where the following conditions exist:

Field Note 3   Are High Ratings a "Problem"?

Research on performance appraisal ratings has typically regarded high ratings as reflecting some kind of error. This error then becomes the focus of corrective action, as methods (i.e., different rating techniques, rater training) are applied to produce lower evaluations. However, an examination of just the statistical properties of ratings, apart from the organizational context in which they are rendered, fails to capture *why* they occur. As recent research has revealed, managers who give high evaluations of their employees are behaving in an eminently reasonable fashion, not making errors, per se. Managers (or other supervisors) have a vested interest in the job performance of their subordinates. The subordinates are socialized and coached to exhibit desired behaviors on the job. Those who don't exhibit these behaviors are often dismissed.

Those who do are rewarded with social approval, if nothing more than being allowed to retain their jobs. The performance of subordinates is also regarded as a measure of the manager's own job performance. It is then logical for a manager to cultivate an efficient work group. Finally, managers often feel a sense of sponsorship for their employees. They want their employees to do well and have in fact often invested a sizable portion of their own time and energy to produce that outcome. Thus, when it comes time for a formal performance review of their subordinates, managers often respond by rating them highly. Rather than errors of judgment, the high evaluations could represent little more than the outcome of a successful socialization process designed to achieve that very outcome.

- Good and poor performance are clearly defined.
- Distinguishing among workers in terms of their levels of performance is widely accepted.
- There is a high degree of trust in the system.
- Low ratings do not automatically result in the loss of valued rewards.
- Valued rewards are clearly linked to accuracy in performance appraisal.

The authors know of organizations in which *none* of these conditions is met, but they don't know of any in which *all* of them are met. It is clear that we need more research on the organizational context in which performance appraisals are conducted. Mero and Motowidlo (1995) also reported findings that underscored the importance of the context in which ratings are made. They found that raters who are held accountable for their performance ratings make more accurate ratings than raters who are not held accountable. The problem of rating inflation will ultimately be solved by changing the context in which ratings are made, and not by changing the rater or the rating scale.

CONTEXTUAL PERFORMANCE

Borman and Motowidlo (1993) contended that individuals contribute to organizational effectiveness in ways that go beyond the activities that make up their jobs. They can either help or hinder efforts to accomplish organizational goals by doing many things that are not directly related to their main functions. However, these contributions are important because they shape the organizational or psychological context that serves as a catalyst for work. The authors argued that these contributions are a valid component of overall job performance, yet they transcend the assessment of performance in specific tasks.

Examples of contextual performance include the following:

- ◆ Persisting with enthusiasm and extra effort as necessary to complete one's own task activities successfully
- ◆ Volunteering to carry out task activities that are not formally part of one's own job
- ◆ Helping and cooperating with others
- ◆ Endorsing, supporting, and defending organizational objectives

Borman and Motowidlo believe that an accurate assessment of job performance must include such contextual factors as well as task performance. Motowidlo and Van Scotter (1994) found that both task performance and contextual performance contributed independently to overall performance in a sample of U.S. Air Force mechanics. Experience was more highly related to task performance than to contextual performance, while personality variables were more highly related to contextual performance than to task performance. Borman, White, and Dorsey (1995) concluded that supervisors weight contextual performance approximately as highly as task performance when making overall performance ratings. In general, it appears that knowledgeable raters are sensitized to the general contributions employees make in enhancing organizational welfare. Consideration of these contributions is as important in an overall evaluation as performance in the more narrow and specific behavior associated with task performance.

SELF- AND PEER APPRAISALS

Most research on judgmental performance appraisal deals with evaluations made by a superior (supervisor, manager). However, there is also information on the value of performance appraisals made by colleagues or peers. Self-evaluations have also been discussed. Our knowledge is somewhat limited, but these methods do offer added understanding of performance.

Self-Assessments

With **self-assessment,** as the term suggests, each employee appraises his or her own performance. The procedure most commonly used is some type of graphic rating scale. Meyer (1980) reported a study in which 92 engineers rated their own performance against their views of the performance of other engineers in the company. On average, each engineer thought he or she was performing better than 75% of the rest of the engineers in the study. Statistically, it is quite a trick to have 100% of the workforce be in the top 25% of job performers. This underscores the biggest problem with self-assessment: positive leniency. Most people have higher opinions of their own performance than others do.

Anderson, Warner, and Spencer (1984) demonstrated in a clever study just how prevalent and pervasive inflation bias is in self-assessments of ability. They asked applicants to rate their own abilities in real clerical tasks as well as in bogus tasks that sounded real but were nonsense. Some of the bogus tasks were "operating a matriculation machine," "typing from audio-fortran reports," and "circumscribing general meeting registers." The clerical applicants rated themselves high on the real tasks (where their ability was not verified) and also on the tasks that did not even exist! Steel and Ovalle (1984) found that there was less positive leniency in self-assessments when there was a high degree of feedback from supervisors. In other words, employees who get little feedback from their supervisors think more highly of their own abilities than employees who receive a lot of feedback. Mount (1984) found that managers evaluate themselves more leniently compared to both how they evaluate their supervisors and how their supervisors evaluate them. Bernardin, Hagan, Kane, and Villanova (1998) suggested that the reason for this pertains to perceptions of factors beyond the control of the individual. When we rate ourselves, we tend not to lower our own evaluations if we perceive that any shortcomings in our performance were beyond our control. However, when other people rate us, they tend to perceive us as being responsible for our performance.

Thornton (1980) reported that despite leniency problems, there are fewer halo errors with self-appraisals. People apparently recognize their own strengths and weaknesses and appraise themselves accordingly. Thornton also reported little agreement in most studies comparing self-assessments and supervisor assessments. Superiors do not evaluate employees in the same way that employees evaluate themselves. This does not mean that one appraisal is "right" and the other "wrong." It just means that the two groups do not agree in evaluating the same performance. Thornton suggested this may be healthy because it provides a basis for discussing differences and may foster an exchange of ideas. Campbell and Lee (1988) concluded that self-assessments were of greater value when used for developmental purposes rather than for administrative purposes. While they have documented value for developmental purposes, their frequency of use as a component of a performance appraisal process is approximately only 5% among U.S. companies (Atwater, 1998).

Peer Assessments

In **peer assessment,** members of a group appraise the performance of their fellows. According to Kane and Lawler (1978), three techniques are commonly used. One is *peer nomination,* in which each person nominates a specified number of group members as being highest on the particular dimension of performance. The second is *peer ratings,* in which each group member rates the others on a set of performance dimensions using one of several kinds of rating scales. The third technique is *peer ranking,* where each member ranks all others from best to worst on one or more performance dimensions.

The method's reliability is determined by assessing the degree of inter-rater agreement. Most studies report high reliabilities (coefficients in the .80s and .90s), indicating that peers agree about the job performance of group members. The validity of peer assessments is determined by correlating the peer assessments with criterion measures usually made later, such as who successfully completed a training program, who got promoted first, the size of raises, and so on. What is uncanny is that group members who have known one another a relatively short time (two to three weeks) can be quite accurate in their long-term predictions about one another. Validity coefficients are fairly impressive, commonly in the .40–.50 range. The peer nomination technique appears best in identifying people with extreme levels of attributes as compared to other members of the group. Peer ratings are the most applicable but have only marginal empirical support. It has been suggested that their use be limited to giving feedback to employees on how others perceive them. Relatively few data are available on the value of peer rankings, though they may be the best method for assessing overall job performance.

There is some evidence that peer assessments are biased by friendship (that is, employees evaluate their friends most favorably), but friendships may be formed on the basis of performance. Also, many work group members do not like to evaluate one another, so part of the method's success hinges on impressing participants with its value. Indeed, Cederblom and Lounsbury (1980) showed that lack of user acceptance may be a serious obstacle to this otherwise promising method. They found that a sample of college professors felt peer assessments were heavily biased by friendship. They thought peers would rate and be rated by their friends more favorably than would be justified. Problems with knowing the people to be rated and fostering a "mutual admiration society" caused the professors to question the value of peer assessment. They also felt that the method should be used for feedback, not for raises and promotions. Despite reluctance to use peer assessments for administrative decisions, research continues to support their predictive accuracy. Shore, Shore, and Thornton (1992) found peer assessments to be superior to self-assessments of job advancement.

Peer assessment, like self-assessment, is part of an overall performance appraisal system. The information generated cannot be isolated from information gained using other methods. Holzbach (1978) showed that superior, peer, and self-assessments all contribute information about performance. But information from each source was subject to halo errors. Borman (1974) showed that peers, superiors, and subordinates (if any) hold unique pieces of the puzzle that portrays a person's job performance. Thus, rather than having raters at just one level of the organization, it is better to have each level contribute the portion it is able to evaluate most effectively. Each performance dimension should be defined precisely enough to obtain the information unique to the relevant source. Overlap with dimensions better assessed by other sources should be avoided. The appraisal system should include compatible and mutually supporting segments. Each segment should be assigned the role to which it is best suited (Kane & Lawler, 1978). Performance appraisal should not be seen as simply selecting the best method. What is "best" varies with the use made of the information, the complexity of the performance appraised, and the people capable of making such judgments.

FEEDBACK OF APPRAISAL INFORMATION TO EMPLOYEES

In the final step of appraisal, the employee and his or her superior review and discuss the evaluation, usually referred to by the misnomer "performance appraisal interview." Performance was appraised before the interview; the interview is a means of giving the employee the results. Both superior and subordinate are usually very uneasy about the interview. Employees often get defensive about negative performance aspects. Superiors are often nervous about having to confront employees face to face with negative evaluations. However, for an appraisal system to be effective, interview objectives must be met with the same rigor as the other system objectives.

The interview typically has two main objectives. The first is reviewing major job responsibilities and how well the employee has met them. The second objective is future planning, or identifying goals the employee will try to meet before the next review. Both employee and superior should provide input in setting goals.

There has been much research on factors that contribute to success in meeting the two objectives of the interview. Feedback on job performance has two properties: information and motivation; that is, feedback can tell the employee how to perform better as well as increase his or her desire to perform well. Ilgen, Fisher, and Taylor (1979) showed that how the employee perceives the superior greatly influences his or her response to feedback. They feel that credibility and power are the most important traits here. *Credibility* is the extent to which the superior is seen as someone who can legitimately evaluate performance. It is enhanced when the superior is considered to have expertise about the employee's job and be in a position to evaluate performance. *Power* is the extent to which the superior can control valued rewards. Ilgen and associates believe that credibility and power influence (1) how well the employee understands feedback, (2) the extent to which the feedback is seen as correct, and (3) the willingness of the employee to alter behavior as suggested by the feedback.

Another area of research interest is nonverbal communication. **Nonverbal communication** refers to the messages we communicate without words. They are powerful and often unintended indicators of how we feel. It has been suggested that while we all can use words to deceive, our nonverbal communications reveal the truth about ourselves. Birdwhistell (1970) presented three major categories of nonverbal communication: *kinesics* (body movements such as eye contact, head nodding, posture, and gestures), *paralanguages* (such as saying "mm-hmm" or "un-huh"), and *proxemics* (the physical distance between people). We are just beginning to understand what role nonverbal behaviors play in organizational life.

DeMeuse (1987) concluded that the frequency of smiling and head nodding is related to overall performance evaluation. Smiling, approving, accepting people seem to receive higher evaluations than their more reserved counterparts. Research on proxemics indicates that distances of 4 to 5 feet seem most comfortable for many North Americans; greater distance is perceived as aloofness. Gifford, Ng, and Wilkinson (1985) reported that employment interviewers rated job applicants as having greater motivation and better social skills when the applicants smiled more, used hand gestures, dressed stylishly, and were talkative. People attribute meaning to these nonverbal cues, although the meaning may not accurately reveal the affective state of the cue sender. For example, if an employee slouches in the chair during the interview, the superior can interpret the behavior to mean the employee is indifferent or bored. The superior who does not smile during the meeting may be perceived by the employee as having a rejecting feeling about him or her. Both parties could be wrong in their attributions of meaning. The slouching employee may be very nervous, not bored. The unsmiling superior may only be trying to avoid the image that the interview is a lighthearted affair that should not be taken seriously. Sometimes nonverbal cues are seen as complementing the verbal message ("I got praised up and down, and he never quit smiling the whole time"). At other times, they may be a mixed signal ("I can't quite figure it out—he said I was doing great, but he didn't smile at me once").

Cederblom (1982) found that three factors consistently seem to produce effective performance appraisal interviews: the supervisor's knowledge of the subordinate's job and performance in it, the supervisor's support of the subordinate, and a welcoming of the subordinate's participation. However, just conducting a performance appraisal interview will not resolve all problems in evaluating subordinate performance. Ilgen, Peterson, Martin, and Boeschen (1981) found that even after the performance appraisal interview, subordinates and supervisors sometimes disagreed on the level of subordinate performance, with subordinates feeling their performance was at a higher level.

In a review of performance evaluations, Greenberg (1986) identified seven characteristics that contribute to employees' accepting their evaluations and feeling they were fair:

1. Solicitation of employee input prior to the evaluation and using it
2. Two-way communication during the appraisal interview
3. The opportunity to challenge/rebut the evaluation
4. The rater's degree of familiarity with the ratee's work
5. The consistent application of performance standards
6. Basing of ratings on actual performance achieved
7. Basing of recommendations for salary/promotions on the ratings

I fully concur with Greenberg's findings. My experience with effective performance appraisal systems underscores the importance of all of these characteristics and clearly reveals there is much more to performance evaluation than making a check mark on an appraisal instrument. Russell and Goode (1988) concluded that managers' reactions to performance appraisal systems are affected by their overall satisfaction with them (that is, their attitude toward the systems' ability to document the performance of their subordinates) and the appraisal's improvement value. Likewise, Dickinson (1993) found that the most important determinant of employee attitudes about performance appraisal is the supervisor. When the supervisor is perceived as trustworthy and supportive, attitudes about performance appraisal are favorable.

CONCLUDING COMMENTS

The topic of performance appraisal has attracted strong research interest among I/O psychologists over the past 30 years. However, the primary focus of the research has changed over time. Latham, Skarlicki, Irvine, and Siegel (1993) noted that earlier research on performance appraisal tended to address the psychometric properties of the various types of rating instruments. Such studies included the effects of rating scales on reducing rater errors and enhancing accuracy. More recent research has addressed the broader organizational context in which performance appraisals are conducted, including user reactions, perceptions of fairness, and how evaluations can be used to develop employees. Ilgen, Barnes-Farrell, and McKellin (1993) believe that the major problems facing performance appraisals are not rating scale construction or the cognitive processes raters use to make evaluations; rather, more attention should be given to the values and expectations generated by the social context in which raters find themselves. Factors such as the extent to which raters desire to be liked by ratees and beliefs about freedom to be open and honest in making evaluations are underresearched. Hauerstein (1998) asserted that many organizations are moving toward performance management rather than performance appraisal. The performance management perspective is that performance appraisal is a formal supervisory activity embedded in the larger context of conducting performance from day to day. For example, athletic coaches do not wait until after the season to evaluate players and give feedback to them. Thus, if managers openly and regularly discuss performance issues, then the yearly evaluation becomes little more than a formality.

CASE STUDY ◆ What Do You Do with Poor Performers?

Anita Douglass was the regional sales manager for a national chain of fitness centers. Her job was to direct a sales force that sold fitness center franchises to operators. The salesperson's job was to recruit responsible, ambitious people who would invest their own time and money in operating a center. Each operator would pay a franchise fee to the company. The company, in turn, would lease the building, supply all the equipment, and help with the financing, if needed. Sales throughout the nation were very strong, as there was a heavy demand for fitness training. Douglass's sales territory was second best in the nation. All her salespeople were doing very well, except two. Marty Crane and Julie Forester consistently failed to meet their sales goals. Both were running out of excuses and Douglass was running out of patience. Douglass was angry and embarrassed about their poor performance. She figured the only reason her boss hadn't inquired about Crane and Forester was because she could "bury" their performance in the overall performance of her sales territory. If these two salespeople had been at the top of the pile instead of the bottom, her sales territory would be number one in the nation.

Despite their common substandard performance, Douglass viewed the two salespeople somewhat differently. After Crane's first bad performance evaluation, she undertook additional training. Even though the extra training didn't seem to help, at least she tried. Crane seemed to be working hard but getting nowhere—described in her last performance review as "an ineffectual diffusion of energy," otherwise known as "spinning your wheels." Crane had a pleasing demeanor, which may have been part of her problem. Douglass thought that perhaps Crane was more concerned with having people approve of her than making a sale. Maybe Crane would perform better for the company in a job outside of sales, she thought.

Forester, on the other hand, seemed rather indifferent about failing to meet her sales goals and attributed her poor performance to everyone other than herself. If Forester ever worked up a sweat, it went unnoticed by Douglass. Forester conveyed the impression that the company was lucky to have her, although the reasons for this privilege were indiscernible. None of the other salespeople wanted to have anything to do with Forester. They wouldn't trade sales territories with her, and they didn't want Forester covering for them when they went on vacation.

Douglass thumbed through the personnel files of Crane and Forester. It was becoming increasingly difficult to justify not firing them. If only one of them got the axe, Douglass decided it would be Forester. Then Douglass caught herself in midthought. The performance of both these salespeople was equally bad. How could she justify keeping one and firing the other? Douglass surmised that the only difference between Crane and Forester was that she liked one more than the other. Douglass had the reputation of being tough but fair. She couldn't understand why this was becoming a difficult decision for her, and why she was considering being more charitable to Crane than to Forester.

Questions
1. What is it about Crane that makes Douglass view her differently from Forester?
2. Are these issues relevant in judging job performance? Should they matter?
3. If you were Douglass, what would you do with Crane and Forester?
4. Do you think Douglass's boss would be critical of Douglass for tolerating poor performance, or admire her for being patient with members of her staff?
5. What other information would you like to have before deciding whether Crane and Forester should be retained or fired?

INFOTRAC ARTICLES

1. *PC Work,* Sep 16, 1996 v13 n37 p64(1)
   Readers dislike Big Brother's gaze. Bill Machrone
   Results of a reader survey asking about the use of employee-monitoring software used to evaluate job performance.
2. *Across the Board,* Feb 1999 v36 i2 p51(2)
   The case for performance appraisals. Marilyn Moats Kennedy
   An article supportive of the value of performance appraisals for both employees and the company.
3. *Across the Board,* Feb 1999 v36 i1 p51(2)
   The case against performance appraisals. Marilyn Moats Kennedy
   An article that explains why there is resistance to and criticism of performance appraisals in organizations.
4. *Across the Board,* March 1998 v35 n3 p39(6)
   "C" players in an "A" world. Phyllis G. Doloff
   Discusses techniques that managers can use to elevate the job performance of "average" employees in a highly competitive work world.
5. *Working Woman,* June 1995 v20 n6 p54(1)
   Ratting on a colleague. Stephen M. Pollan & Mark Levine

Discusses how an employee should approach a supervisor regarding the poor performance of a peer.

6. *Across the Board*, June 1997 v34 n6 p53(2)
   "So how'm I doing?" Marilyn Moats Kennedy
   Discusses the attributes of constructive feedback on job performance that are most helpful to employees.

7. *Training & Development*, Oct 1997 v51 n10 p33(6)
   Taming the performance bell curve. Karen R. Adler & Paul M. Swiercz
   Presents the topic of "strategic performance evaluation," which links the life cycle of an organization to the evaluation of its employees.

8. *Hospitals & Health Networks*, Jan 5, 1996 v70 n1 p33(4)
   Report card daze. Jim Montague
   Describes a system of making public the performance evaluations of cardiac surgeons and the resulting effect on mortality rates for hospitals.

ORGANIZATIONAL
PSYCHOLOGY

Organizations and Work Teams

MAJOR CHAPTER OBJECTIVES

- ◆ Explain the three major theories of organization.

- ◆ Understand Mintzberg's theory of organizational structure.

- ◆ Explain downsizing and its effect on organizations.

- ◆ Describe the components of social systems: roles, norms, and culture.

- ◆ Understand the concept of work teams and their principles.

Many academic disciplines have contributed to the study of organizations, including I/O psychology, sociology, economics, and political science. Their contributions tend to differ in the specific constructs that are investigated. The most common I/O perspective is to examine individual behaviors and attitudes within an organizational context. A related topic of interest to I/O psychologists is how work groups function within organizations. Work groups may be examined in terms of how they are formed and how effectively they perform. Larger-scale analyses of organizations (most often conducted outside of I/O psychology) study the relationships between organizations as well as the relationship of organizations to larger social structures such as society.

Davis and Powell (1992) noted that the study of organizations is relatively recent, having begun in the 1950s. During that time period psychologists began to appreciate how much influence organizations exerted on the behavior of employees. It will be recalled from Chapter 1 that it wasn't until 1970 that the profession of "industrial" psychology officially became "industrial/organizational" psychology, thus defining the scope of I/O psychology as we know it today. Formal recognition of the *O* in I/O psychology compelled us to gain a better understanding of the social bases of behavior. This chapter will explain how two social concepts, organizations and work teams, influence and shape the behavior of their members. The concepts that will be examined (that is, the unit of analysis) shift from the individual to larger social collectivities. Included are various organizing concepts, ranging from the formal structure of an organization to the social dynamics of work groups.

THREE THEORIES OF ORGANIZATIONS

It is probably easier to state why organizations exist than to define what they are. In their simplest form, they exist as a vehicle for accomplishing goals and objectives; that is, **organizations** are collectivities of parts that cannot accomplish their goals as effectively if they operate separately. How one chooses to examine the organizing process produces the various schools of thought or theories about organizations. In my opinion there are three major schools of thought about organizations, with many variations and emphases (Scott, 1992): the classical, neoclassical, and systems theories of organization. These schools of thought take markedly different views of the same phenomenon.

Classical Theory

Classical theory, which emerged in the first few decades of the 20th century, focuses mainly on structural relationships in organizations. Classical theory begins with a statement of the basic ingredients of any organization and then addresses how the organization should best be structured to accomplish its objectives. There are four basic components to any organization.

1. *A system of differentiated activities.* All organizations are composed of the activities and functions performed in them and the relationships among these

activities and functions. A formal organization emerges when these activities are linked together.

2. *People.* Although organizations are composed of activities and functions, people perform tasks and exercise authority.
3. *Cooperation toward a goal.* Cooperation must exist among the people performing their various activities to achieve a unity of purpose in pursuit of their common goals.
4. *Authority.* Authority is established through superior–subordinate relationships, and such authority is needed to ensure cooperation among people pursuing their goals.

Given that four ingredients are the basis of any organization, classical theory addresses the various structural properties by which the organization should best reach its goals. Four major structural principles are the hallmarks in the history of organizational theory.

Functional Principle.   The **functional principle** is the concept behind division of labor; that is, organizations should be divided into units that perform similar functions. Work is broken down to provide clear areas of specialization, which in turn improves the organization's overall performance. Similar work activities are often organized into departments, which enhances coordination of activities and permits more effective supervision and a more rational flow of work. It is the functional principle that accounts for the grouping of work functions into such units as production, sales, engineering, finance, and so on; these labels describe the primary nature of the work performed within each unit. The functional principle relates to the horizontal growth of the organization—that is, the formation of new functional units along the horizontal dimension.

Scalar Principle.   The **scalar principle** deals with the organization's vertical growth and refers to the chain of command that grows with levels added to the organization. Each level has its own degree of authority and responsibility for meeting organizational goals, with higher levels having greater degrees. Each subordinate should be accountable to only one superior, a tenet referred to as the **unity of command.** Classical theorists thought the best way to overcome organizational fragmentation caused by division of labor was through a well-designed chain of command. Coordination among factions is achieved by people occupying positions of command in a hierarchy. Figure 8–1 shows a graphic representation of both the functional and scalar principles.

Line/Staff Principle.   One way to differentiate organizational work functions is by whether they are line or staff. **Line functions** have the primary responsibility for meeting the major goals of the organization, like the production department in a manufacturing organization. **Staff functions** support the line's activities but are regarded as subsidiary in overall importance to line functions. Typical staff functions are personnel and quality control. That is, while it is important to have good employees and to inspect products for their quality, the organization was not created to provide people with jobs or products to inspect. It was created to

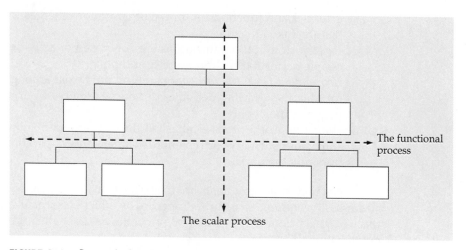

The functional process

The scalar process

FIGURE 8–1   *Pyramid of organization*

SOURCE: From *Organization Theory: A Structural and Behavioral Analysis* (p. 32) by W. G. Scott, T. R. Mitchell, and P. H. Birnbaum, 1981, Homewood, IL: Richard D. Irwin.

manufacture products (a line function), and personnel and quality control are but two staff functions designed to support this larger goal.

Span-of-Control Principle.   The **span-of-control principle** refers to the number of subordinates a manager is responsible for supervising. A "small" span of control is 2 subordinates; a "large" span of control might be 15. Large spans of control produce flat organizations (that is, few levels between the top and bottom of the organization); small spans of control produce tall organizations (that is, many levels). Figure 8–2 is a diagram showing how the span of control affects the shape of the organization.

Classical theory is credited with providing the structural anatomy of organizations. It was the first major attempt to articulate the form and substance of organizations in a comprehensive fashion. There is little that is "psychological" about this view of organizations; indeed, none of the classical organizational theorists were psychologists. The influence of psychology became apparent in neoclassical theory, the next school of thought. Nevertheless, although current organizational researchers regard classical theory as antiquated, its four principles are deeply ingrained in the real-life structure of organizations. Problems of line/staff relationships, number of organizational levels, division of labor, coordination, and spans of control are still of major concern. Further thinking about organizations occurred because organizations were more complex than the four classical principles suggested. This desire to add richness and realism to organizational theory gave rise to neoclassical theory.

Neoclassical Theory

Neoclassical theory was born in the 1950s, but its origins go back to the findings from the Hawthorne studies. It was identified with scholars who recognized the

Tall structure		Flat structure
X		X
X	X	X X X X X X X X X X
X X X X		
X X X X X X X X		
Levels.....4		Levels..... 2
Span 2		Span 10

FIGURE 8–2 *Span of control and organizational structure*

SOURCE: From *Organization Theory: A Structural and Behavioral Analysis* (p. 34) by W. G. Scott, T. R. Mitchell, and P. H. Birnbaum, 1981, Homewood, IL: Richard D. Irwin.

deficiencies in the classical school of thought. In fact, the name *neoclassical* connotes a modernization or updating of the original (classical) theory, while still acknowledging its contributions.

It is a misnomer to call **neoclassical theory** a "theory" because there really is no formal theory. Rather, it is a recognition of psychological/behavioral issues that question the rigidity with which the classical principles were originally stated. The neoclassicists examined the four major principles of classical theory and found evidence that challenged their apparent unassailability. This evidence was based primarily on either psychological research or an examination of real-life organizational problems.

The neoclassicists noted that while division of labor causes functional interdependence among work activities, it also depersonalizes these activities so that the individual finds little meaning in them. That is, people develop a sense of alienation from highly repetitive work, which ultimately results in dissatisfaction with their work. In turn, this dissatisfaction can result in decreased efficiency caused by lowered productivity and increased absence. In short, the neoclassicists argued for less rigid division of labor and for more "humanistic" work in which people derive a sense of value and meaning from their jobs.

The scalar principle was questioned on the grounds that other systems operate on people in organizations besides those imposed by formal superior—subordinate relationships. Individuals are influenced by interpersonal activities that extend well beyond those prescribed by the formal organizational structure. In short, although the scalar principle prescribes formal lines of authority, in reality many sources operating in an organization influence the individual.

The line/staff principle was perhaps the easiest for neoclassicists to challenge. The black-and-white theoretical distinction between line and staff functions is not always so clear in practice. Take, for example, the sales function. A manufacturing company's purpose is indeed to produce, but if it does not sell what it produces, the company cannot survive. What, then, is the sales function—a major line function or an ancillary staff function? The neoclassicists illustrated that many staff functions are critical to the success of the organization, so the value of the distinction between line and staff is not so great as originally proposed.

Finally, determining a satisfactory span of control seems far more complex than picking a number. The neoclassicists noted it depends on such issues as the supervisor's managerial ability (poor managers cannot supervise many subordinates) and the intensity of the needed supervision (one could effectively manage many more subordinates who do not require much direction than those who do require intensive direction). That is, such psychological factors as leadership style and capacity greatly influence the determination of effective spans of control.

The primary contribution of neoclassical theory was to reveal that the principles proposed by classical theory were not as universally applicable and simple as originally formulated. The neoclassicists drew heavily on behavioral research that revealed the importance of individual differences. They did not overtly reject classical theory. Rather than attempting to change the theory, they tried to make it fit the realities of human behavior in organizations. However, the neoclassicists were limited by commencing their conceptualization about organizations from the classical perspective. By the mid-1960s, it became apparent that an entirely new approach to thinking about organizations was necessary. Organizations were more complex than even the neoclassicists portrayed them; this led to the formation of a radically different school of thought called systems theory.

Systems Theory

Modern organization theory adopts a complex, dynamic view of organizations called the "systems approach." Systems theory had its origins in the biological sciences and was modified to meet the needs of organizational theory (Kast & Rosenzweig, 1972). **Systems theory** views an organization as existing in an interdependent relationship with its environment: "It is impossible to understand individual behavior or the activities of small groups apart from the social system in which they interact. A complex organization is a social system; the various discrete segments and functions in it do not behave as isolated elements. All parts affect all other parts. Every action has repercussions throughout the organization, because all of its elements are linked" (Scott, Mitchell, & Birnbaum, 1981, p. 44). In fact, the idea that all parts of the system are interdependent is the key to understanding the systems approach. All of the parts and their interrelatedness make up the "system," which is how the theory gets its name.

Systems theory asserts that an organizational system is composed of five parts.

1. *Individuals.* Individuals bring their own personalities, abilities, and attitudes with them to the organization, which influence what they hope to attain by participating in the system.
2. *Formal organization.* The formal organization is the interrelated pattern of jobs that provide the structure of the system.
3. *Small groups.* Individuals do not work in isolation but become members of small groups as a way to facilitate their own adaptability within the system.
4. *Status and role.* Status and role differences exist among jobs within an organization and define the behavior of individuals within the system.
5. *Physical setting.* This is the external physical environment and the degree of technology that characterizes the organization.

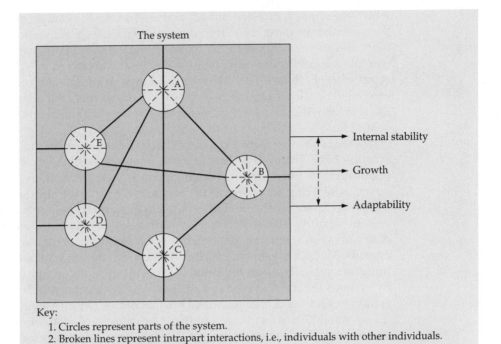

The system

Internal stability

Growth

Adaptability

Key:
  1. Circles represent parts of the system.
  2. Broken lines represent intrapart interactions, i.e., individuals with other individuals.
  3. Solid lines represent interpart interaction.
  4. Both the solid and broken lines are the processes that tie the parts of the system together.

FIGURE 8–3   *The framework of systems analysis*

SOURCE: From *Organization Theory: A Structural and Behavioral Analysis* (p. 48) by W. G. Scott, T. R. Mitchell, and P. H. Birnbaum, 1981, Homewood, IL: Richard D. Irwin.

Figure 8–3 illustrates the five parts of the system and their interrelatedness. Complex interactions exist among all parts of the system. Individuals interact to form small groups, members of the groups are differentiated by status and roles, the physical environment affects the behavior of individuals and groups, and all exist within the framework provided by the formal organization.

With all of these parts making up the system, it is necessary to have a means to provide coordination and linkage among them. Such functions are accomplished through communication and decision making; they permit the various parts of the system to "talk" to each other. Organizational communication occurs through a series of networks that often bear little resemblance to formal lines of authority. Similarly, decisions are often made in ways that deviate from formal lines of authority. That is, the reality of how organizations actually conduct themselves is usually quite different from the principles established by classical organizational theory. Also, the Achilles' heel of most large organizations is failure to communicate. This makes considerable sense, given the systems perspective of organizations, because communication is the means by which the system can be responsive to its environment.

Finally, systems theory instructs us that the parts and interactions of a system do not exist for themselves. Rather, they exist to meet the system's larger goals, which are stability, growth, and adaptability. A living organism has to be stable in the sense that its parts are harmoniously integrated. Growth reflects a sense of vitality and vigor. Adaptability is critical if the organism is to respond to environmental changes because adaptability enables the organism to survive in times of rapid change. Thus, a healthy, successful organization is not only "effective" in meeting its business objectives but also stable, growing, and adaptable. These are the characteristics of all living organisms, be they organizations, animals, plants, or societies.

Systems theory offers a radical departure from the classical and neoclassical schools of thought. Systems theory views organizations as any other form of living organism. The purpose of an organization is to reach stability, to grow, and to adapt, as all living organisms must do to survive. Note the abstractness of systems theory. There are no direct references to anything quite as simple as a span of control, for example. This abstractness is deliberate, for only at some degree of generality can one attempt to equate such diverse entities as organizations, plants, and animals. Modern organizational theorists believe that an understanding of something as complex as an organization requires the type of conceptualizations offered by systems theory. A systems perspective of organizations permits us to understand phenomena of organizational life that earlier theories would not permit.

Despite the distinctiveness of the three schools of thought on organizations, each school offered critical concepts that are of great relevance today. That is, these schools are more than historical milemarkers in the evolution of organizational theory. In particular, the concept of small groups from systems theory has been greatly amplified to provide a primary focal point of interest, the work team. The concept of work teams and their significance will be discussed later in this chapter.

ORGANIZATIONAL STRUCTURE

Mintzberg (1993) offered a comprehensive and lucid explanation of how organizations evolve to reach a certain form and shape. We refer to these characteristics as the "structure" or formal component of an organization. Various types of structure are possible, and organizations continuously seek to find a structure that is an optimal match to its environment. That is, the structure of an organization is an adaptive mechanism that permits the organization to function in its surroundings. Organizations that have maladaptive structures will ultimately cease to exist. Since individuals assume roles within organizations, individuals (most notably employees) feel the brunt of change caused by the continuing evolution of an organization's structure. It is in this regard that I/O psychology is involved in matters of organizational structure.

Coordinating Mechanisms

Mintzberg (1993) defined the **structure** of an organization as "the sum total of the ways in which its labor is divided into distinct tasks and then its coordination is achieved among these tasks" (p. 2). Although many structures are possible for an organization, relatively few are effective structures for a particular organization. Five coordinating mechanisms have been proposed to explain the fundamental ways in which organizations coordinate their work. These are considered the most basic elements of structure, the glue that holds organizations together.

1. *Mutual adjustment.* Mutual adjustment achieves coordination of work by the process of informal communication among employees. As the term implies, it is the process by which employees coordinate their efforts to produce an outcome. Two people paddling a canoe are an example of the mutual adjustment between individuals needed to propel the canoe through water.

2. *Direct supervision.* Direct supervision achieves coordination by having one person take responsibility for the work of others, issuing instructions to them and monitoring their actions. As an organization outgrows its simplest state, it turns to this second mechanism of coordination. In effect one brain coordinates several hands, such as the coxswain (stroke caller) of a six-person rowing crew.

3. *Standardization of work processes.* Work processes are standardized when the contents of the work are specified. The production assembly line of a manufacturing company is an example. A worker inserts a bolt into a holed piece of metal. There is only one action to perform, and there is no room for individual discretion as to how the work is performed. The work is designed in such a way that the same process is followed no matter who is performing the job.

4. *Standardization of work output.* Outputs are standardized when the results of the work—for example, the dimensions of the product or the performance—are specified. The fast-food industry is an example. A hamburger ordered from a particular fast-food vendor should look and taste the same whether it was purchased day or night, in July or December, or in Cleveland or San Diego. The work is designed in such a way that the same output is achieved irrespective of differences in time or location.

5. *Standardization of skills and knowledge.* Skills and knowledge are standardized when the kind of training required to perform the work is specified. In this case coordination is achieved before the work is undertaken. Organizations institute training programs for employees to standardize the skills needed to perform work, thereby controlling and coordinating the work. For example, there is rarely communication between an anesthesiologist and a surgeon while removing an appendix in an operating room. They need hardly to communicate because by virtue of their medical training they know what to expect of each other.

According to Mintzberg (1993), these five coordinating mechanisms manifest themselves in a rough order. As organizational work becomes more complicated, the means of coordination shifts from mutual adjustment to direct supervision. This is followed by standardization of work processes, then outputs, and finally skills. A person working alone has no need for any coordinating mechanisms. The addition of a second person requires the two individuals to adjust to each other. As the group gets larger, however, it becomes less able to coordinate informally. A need for leadership arises. Control of the work group passes to a single individual, as direct supervision becomes the favored coordinating mechanism. As the work becomes more involved, a transition occurs toward standardization. When the tasks are simple and routine, the organization relies on the standardization of the work processes themselves. However, increasingly complex work may preclude this, compelling the organization to turn to standardization of the outputs. In very complex work, the outputs often cannot be standardized either. Therefore, the organization must settle for standardizing the skills of the worker.

Organizations cannot rely on a single coordinating mechanism. Most use all five. A certain amount of direct supervision and mutual adjustment is always required. Contemporary organizations simply cannot exist without leadership and informal communication. In the most automated (that is, fully standardized) factory, machines break down, employees fail to show up for work, and schedules must be changed at the last minute. Supervisors must intervene, and workers must be free to deal with unexpected problems.

Classical organization theory emphasized both direct supervision and standardization as coordinating mechanisms. The concepts of span of control, line/staff, and unity of command characterize the components of an organization's *formal structure*. Frederick Taylor sought to achieve coordination through standardization, specifying the work operations (such as body movements and when to take work breaks) of pig-iron handlers and coal-shovelers. According to scholars in the beginning of the 20th century, organizational structure defined a set of official, standardized work relationships built around a tight system of formal authority.

However, neoclassical organizational theory revealed the significance of the most primary means of attaining coordination, mutual adjustment. That is, other activities take place among workers that are not in line with the official organizational structure. Thus, the presence of unofficial relationships within work groups (an *informal structure*) established that mutual adjustment serves as an important coordinating mechanism in all organizations. In fact, as will be seen in Chapter 13, the mechanism of standardization, a long-standing hallmark of formal organizational structure, was actually detrimental to the psychological and physical health of the worker. It was not until the creation of systems theory that a balance between the classical and neoclassical perspectives was attained and all five coordinating mechanisms were regarded as viable.

The Five Basic Parts of an Organization[1]

Consistent with systems theory, organizations are structured to define the interrelationships among the parts of the systems. Mintzberg proposed that all organizations consist of five basic parts, as shown in Figure 8–4.

1. *Operating core*. The operating core of the organization encompasses those members—the operators—who perform the basic work related directly to the production of products and services. The operators secure the inputs needed for production (buy the raw material), turn inputs into outputs (assemble individual

---

[1]Mintzberg (1993) noted that the number five reappears in the study of organizational structure (and is the basis of his book's title, *Structure in Fives*). While the number five is not magical, it is the number of concepts used to explain various aspects of organizational structure. The interested reader is encouraged to read the profound insights Mintzberg offered in his book about organizational structure.

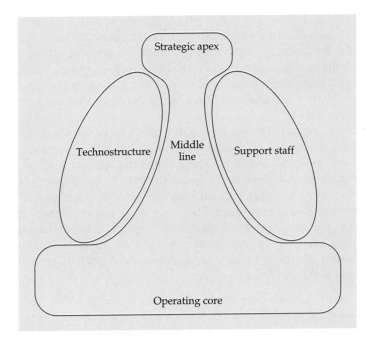

FIGURE 8–4   *The five basic parts of an organization*

SOURCE: From *Structure in Fives: Designing Effective Organizations* (p. 11) by H. Mintzberg, 1993, Englewood Cliffs, NJ: Prentice Hall.

parts into complete units), and distribute the outputs (sell the product). The operating core is the heart of every organization, the part that produces the essential outputs that keep it alive.

2. *Strategic apex.* The strategic apex is charged with ensuring that the organization serves its mission in an effective way. Here are found those people charged with *overall* responsibility for the organization: the president and any other top-level managers whose concerns are broad. The strategic apex plays the most important role in providing direction to the organization, serving as the organization's brain.

3. *Middle line.* The strategic apex is joined to the operating core by the chain of middle-line managers who have formal authority. This chain runs from the senior managers to the first-line supervisors, who have direct authority over the operators, and embodies the coordinating mechanism of direct supervision. In theory, one person—at the top of the strategic apex—can supervise all operators. In practice, direct supervision requires close personal contact between manager and operator, with the result that there is some limit to the number of operators any one manager can supervise (the span of control). An organizational *hierarchy* is built, as a first-line supervisor is put in charge of a number of operators to form a basic organizational unit. In turn, another manager is put in charge of a number of these units to form a higher-level unit, and so on. Eventually all the remaining units come under a single person at the strategic apex to form the whole organization.

4. *Technostructure.* In the technostructure are found the analysts who serve the organization by affecting the work of others. These analysts are removed from the

operating work flow. They may design the work, plan it, or train the people who do it, but they do not do it themselves. The technostructure is effective only when it can use its analytical techniques to make the work of others more effective. In general, the more standardization the organization uses to facilitate coordination, the more it relies on its technostructure. Standardization of skills plays a major role in coordinating the analysts' own work because analysts are typically highly trained specialists.

5. *Support staff*. The support staff exists to provide services that aid the basic mission of the organization and typically includes the mailroom, switchboard, security, and janitorial services. Many times the support staff is lumped together with the technostructure and labeled the "staff" (vis-à-vis the line/staff distinction). However, support units are decidedly different from the technostructure. The support staff is not directed toward giving advice; rather, their function is to perform. The support staff does not use a single coordinating mechanism. Each unit relies on whatever mechanism is most appropriate for itself, such as standardization of skills in the legal department and standardization of work processes in the cafeteria.

In many organizations decision-making power is highly centralized; that is, it flows from the strategic apex, down through the middle line of the hierarchy, to the operating core. Centralization is the tightest means of coordinating decision making in the organization. Decisions are made by one person and then implemented through direct supervision. However, there can exist strong pressures to decentralize, to push decision-making power down lower in the organizational hierarchy. Mintzberg (1993) cited three reasons. One is that not all of an organization's decisions can be understood at the strategic apex. Sometimes the necessary information just cannot be brought to the apex. People at the bottom of the hierarchy with the necessary knowledge end up having to defer to managers at the top who are out of touch with the immediate situation. Second is that decentralization allows the organization to respond quickly to local conditions. The transmission of information to the apex and back takes time, which may be critical. Third is that decentralization is a stimulus for motivation. The organization can attract and retain intelligent people only if it gives them considerable power to make decisions. Giving power to middle-line mangers trains them in decision making, which is an increasingly important skill as one moves up the organizational hierarchy. However, as Mintzberg cautioned, centralization and decentralization should not be treated as absolutes, but rather as two ends of a continuum. In reality most organizations manifest some of the properties of both, with one being more prominent.

Reorganizing and Downsizing

As was noted previously, the structure of an organization is its means of adapting to its environment. Accordingly, when the environment changes (for example, greater competition or regulatory control), it is common for the organization's structure to change in response. Earlier it was stated that the structure of an organization has a great impact on individuals (most notably its employees). Thus, an organization may choose to expand because of greater opportunities to sell its products or services. This necessitates hiring more employees at the operating core and middle-level management and typically more staff employees to serve their needs. It is also possible that as employees move up the organizational hierarchy, reporting relationships may change among the employees. These types of changes in the organizational structure are referred to as *reorganizing,* implying that the organization is reconfiguring itself to better adapt to its environment.

However, there is also another form of reorganization that greatly affects the lives of employees and involves the loss of jobs. The organization may believe it has too many employees to be effectively responsive to its environment. The most common cause for the decision to cut jobs is the conclusion the organization can "do more with less" (i.e., have greater efficiency with fewer employees). For most organizations the single largest expense is the wages and salaries paid to their employees. By eliminating jobs, they reduce costs. The work that was done by the departed employees will have to be performed by the remaining employees or through technical changes in work processes (e.g., automation). The terms given to this process of job loss include *downsizing, reduction-in-force,* and *right-sizing.* The term *right-sizing* implies that there is a size for the organization that is "right" or correct for its environment. It is not uncommon for large organizations to reduce their size by several thousand employees at one time (see Field Note 1).

Where do the eliminated jobs come from within an organization? All five parts of the organization are targeted, with the greatest losses typically coming from the middle line, technostructure, and support staff. Jobs can also be lost in the operating core, as jobs are automated or reassigned to other countries that pay lower wages. The strategic apex may be reduced, but generally the fewest job losses occur at this level. As noted previously, the support staff consists of such jobs as

---

Field Note 1   *Over-Downsizing*

Corporate downsizing has become a conventional response by contemporary organizations that find themselves burdened with economic inefficiencies. For most organizations the single biggest expense is the salaries and benefits paid to their employees. By eliminating jobs, they reduce payroll costs. By eliminating many jobs (4,000–10,000 jobs in some very large companies), they can save vast sums of money. But then comes the problem of getting all the work accomplished by the people who remain. The consequence of restructuring the organization may include greater use of computerization or automation of work, less oversight by supervisory/managerial personnel, greater use of overtime among hourly paid workers, and longer workweeks among salaried employees. These changes are brought about to make the organization operate more efficiently—lower cost per unit of production or service. While downsizing has forced organizations to operate with greater efficiency, some organizations are discovering they cannot reclaim the productive output they had achieved with a larger workforce. In short, the loss of jobs did not strengthen their economic position, rather it weakened it. Organizations that "over-downsized" are sometimes referred to as incurring "corporate anorexia"—a metaphor based on the medical condition of excessive refusal to eat. Some of these organizations are reestablishing a portion of the jobs they previously eliminated in their original quest to become more successful.

security personnel and cafeteria workers. Rather than an organization hiring their own employees to work in these jobs, organizations may contract (in effect, "rent") the services of these people through other organizations, such as a company that offers security guards or food preparers to other organizations. Contracting the services of these individuals is less costly to the organization than hiring their own employees to perform these services. Similar reductions occur in the technostructure. With fewer employees to advise (the primary function of the technostructure), there is less need for "advisers." In recent years the number of I/O psychologists working in organizations has decreased, while the number working for consulting firms has increased. In essence, organizations have reduced the number of jobs typically filled by I/O psychologists and in turn contract their services through consulting firms.

However, it is in the middle line where most of the job loss has occurred. It will be recalled that the middle line serves as a means of direct supervision for lower-level employees. How can an organization survive without the middle line? The answer lies in the coordinating mechanisms. Direct supervision is one of the five coordinating mechanisms. By eliminating much of the middle line, the coordinating mechanism shifts from direct supervision to standardization. The coordination that was formerly achieved through personal contact with a supervisor is now achieved through greater standardization of the work process, the output, or employee skills.

Another manifestation of reorganization through downsizing is larger spans of control. With larger spans of control, fewer managers are needed, the organizational hierarchy becomes smaller, and the shape of the organization becomes flatter. It is also common for decision making to become more decentralized following a downsizing. Figure 8–5 shows the top part of an organizational chart for a manufacturing company before downsizing. The company is structured to be organized by both function (production and sales) and location (California and Texas). There are small spans of control. Each person below the president has two subordinates. A total of 15 people are needed to staff this part of the organization with such a configuration. Figure 8–6 shows the same company following reorganization—in this case, downsizing. A total of eight jobs have been eliminated by this reorganization. The sales function has been consolidated into one job. The plant manager at each of the four locations now reports directly to the vice president. Each plant manager now also provides information directly to the sales manager (as indicated by the broken lines), but administratively the plant managers report to the vice president. The vice president now has a span of control of five. The jobs lost in this reorganization are one vice president, three sales managers, and the entire layer of (middle) managers.

What consequences might we expect from this reorganization? There would be less administrative control from the loss of managerial jobs. There would be greater pressure on the organization's parts to coordinate with each other because of the loss of direct supervision. There would probably be more stress placed on the surviving employees to work harder and find new ways to do the work of the employees whose jobs were eliminated. The organization would have fewer salary expenditures associated with the elimination of eight jobs. Eight people would be out of work.

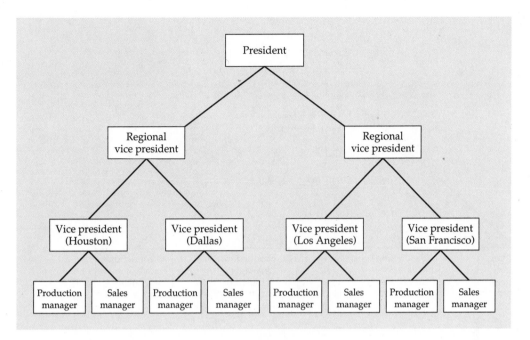

FIGURE 8–5   *Top part of organizational chart for manufacturing company before downsizing*

How would you feel if you lost your job because you were fired? Probably not very good, but in all likelihood you received some signals along the way that you were not performing satisfactorily. In turn, you probably had some control over whether you would change your job behavior. How would you feel if you lost your job because it was eliminated? You could have been an exemplary employee, but you lost your job through no fault of your own. *You* were not released, rather the *job* you were filling was eliminated to make the organization more efficient. The next chapter will examine the psychological reactions to downsizing, from the perspectives of both the survivors and those whose jobs were eliminated.

It was stated previously that organizational structure exerts a great influence on the lives of individuals. When organizations are expanding in size to better adapt to their environments, new jobs are created, leading to the recruitment, selection, training, and appraisal of new employees. When organizations are contracting in size, the overall social order of employment is altered. If, as a rule, organizations reduce the number of middle managers needed to run the business, these displaced middle managers will not simply find new jobs as middle managers in some other companies. Rather the *job* of middle manager is being reduced in frequency, necessitating holders of middle-management jobs to enter new jobs, not new positions in the same job family. This may necessitate professional retraining, learning new skills to fill jobs that continue to exist. Thus, issues of organizational structure affect not only I/O psychology but also the sociology of employment as well as the economics of across-occupational mobility.

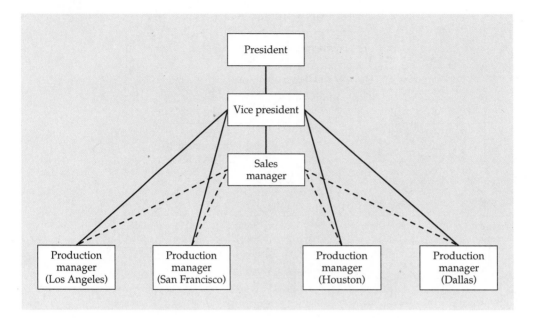

FIGURE 8–6   *Top part of organizational chart for manufacturing company after downsizing*

Although organizations are defined in large part by their structures, division of labor is not the only concept needed to understand the functioning of organizations. Organizations also have social systems that influence the conduct of their employees. Three components of social systems within organizations will be examined next.

COMPONENTS OF SOCIAL SYSTEMS

A **social system** is a structuring of events or happenings; it has no formal structure apart from its functioning. Physical or biological systems (cars or human beings) have structures that can be identified even when they are not functioning (electrical or skeleton structures); that is, they have both an anatomy and a physiology. There is no anatomy to a social system in this sense. When a social system stops functioning, no identifiable structure remains. It is hard for us to think of social systems as having no tangible anatomy because it is easier to understand concepts with concrete and simple components. Social systems do indeed have components, but they are not concrete. They are sometimes referred to as the *informal* component of an organization. We will examine three of them—roles, norms, and culture—while recognizing that they are abstract.

Roles

When an employee enters an organization, there is much for that person to learn: expected performance levels, recognition of superiors, dress codes, and time demands. Roles ease the learning process. **Roles** are usually defined as the expectations of others about appropriate behavior in a specific position. Each of us plays several roles simultaneously (parent, employee, club member, and so on), but the focus here will be on job-related roles.

Scott and associates (1981) listed five important aspects of roles. First, they are impersonal; the position itself determines the expectations, not the individual. Second, roles are related to task behavior. An organizational role is the expected behaviors for a particular job. Third, roles can be difficult to pin down. The problem is defining who determines what is expected. Since other people define our roles, opinions differ over what our role should be. How we see our role, how others see our role, and what we actually do may differ. Fourth, roles are learned quickly and can produce major behavior changes. Fifth, roles and jobs are not the same; a person in one job might play several roles.

We learn our role through a role episode, as Figure 8–7 shows. Group members have expectations about job performance, which they communicate either formally or by having the role occupant observe others in similar roles. In stage 3, the role occupant behaves as he or she believes is appropriate. If the behavior (stage 4) differs widely from the group's expectations (stage 1), the occupant gets feedback from the group regarding the discrepancy. This is intended to alter behavior toward group expectations. The role episode is ongoing. Expectations may change over time, as might the employee's behavior.

Another aspect is role differentiation. This is the extent to which different roles are performed by employees in the same subgroup. One person's job might be to maintain good group relations, such as a work-unit coordinator. His or her role might thus require providing emotional or interpersonal support to others. Another's role might be to set schedules, agendas, and meet deadlines; such a person is usually an administrator. When all the roles in a work group fit together like the parts of a puzzle, the result is a smoothly running, effective group. However, all parts may not fit together. The next chapter will examine the way some organizational pressures produce role problems.

Norms

Norms are shared group expectations about appropriate behavior. While roles define what is appropriate for a particular job, norms define acceptable group behavior. Roles differentiate positions; norms establish the behavior expected of everyone in the group, such as when employees take coffee breaks, how much they produce, when they stop for the day, and what they wear. Norms are unwritten rules that govern behavior. A no-smoking sign is not a norm but a formal written rule of behavior. If employees smoke despite the sign, there is a norm that sanctions such behavior in spite of the formal rule.

Norms have several important properties. First, there is "oughtness" or "shouldness"—that is, prescriptions for behavior. Second, norms are usually more obvious for behavior judged to be important for the group. A norm might exist for the time employees stop work before lunch, but there probably is no norm about what employees eat. Third, norms are enforced by the group. Much expected behavior is monitored and enforced through formal rules and procedures. With

FIGURE 8–7   *The role episode*

SOURCE: From *Organization Theory: A Structural and Behavioral Analysis* (p. 103) by W. G. Scott, T. R. Mitchell, and P. H. Birnbaum, 1981, Homewood, IL: Richard D. Irwin.

norms, group members regulate behavior. Sometimes formal rules and group norms clash. The no-smoking rule and the group norm sanctioning smoking are an example. Unless the organization imposes sanctions on smokers (that is, rule breakers), the group norm probably prevails. Finally, the degree that norms are shared and the degree that deviation is acceptable vary. Not all smokers might smoke in proscribed areas, and those who do not might be as accepted by the group as those who do.

There is a three-step process for developing and communicating norms. The norm must first be defined and communicated. This can be done either explicitly ("Here is the way we do things around here") or implicitly (the desired behavior is observed). Second, the group must be able to monitor behavior and judge whether the norm is being followed. Third, the group must be able to reward conformity and punish nonconformity. Conformity enhances the predictability of behavior within the group, which in turn promotes feelings of group cohesion.

Compliance with norms is enforced by positive reinforcement or punishment. Positive reinforcement can be praise or inclusion in group activities. Punishment can be a dirty look, a snide remark, or actual physical abuse. (Workers who exceeded the group norm for productivity in the Hawthorne studies were hit on the arm, which was called "binging.") Another form of punishment is exclusion from group activities. The group often tries to convince the nonconforming employee (referred to as a *deviant*) to change his or her behavior. The group tries to alter the

THE FAR SIDE   by Gary Larson

"Counterclockwise, Red Eagle! Always counterclockwise!"

SOURCE: "The Far Side" cartoon panel by Gary Larson is reprinted by permission of
Universal Press Syndicate.

deviant's opinion through increased communication, verbal or nonverbal. The clearer and more important the norm and the more cohesive the group, the greater the pressure. Eventually, the deviant either changes or is rejected. If rejected, the deviant becomes an *isolate*, and the pressure to conform stops. Because the group may need the isolate to perform work tasks, they usually reach a truce; the isolate is tolerated at work but excluded from group activities and relations. Obviously, the isolate can quit the job and try to find a better match between his or her values and a group.

Finally, norms are not always contrary to formal organization rules or independent of them. Sometimes norms greatly promote organization goals. For example, there may be a norm against leaving for home before a certain amount of work has been done. Although quitting time is 5:00 p.m., the group may expect employees to stay until 5:15 or 5:30 to finish a certain task. In this case, the deviant is one who conforms to the formal rule (that is, leaving at 5:00 p.m.) instead of the group norm. When group norms and organization goals are complementary, high degrees of effectiveness can result.

Organizational Culture

The concept of culture was originally proposed by anthropologists to describe societies, but we have also found it useful to describe organizations. **Culture** is the languages, values, attitudes, beliefs, and customs of an organization. As can be inferred, it represents a complex pattern of variables that, when taken collectively, gives each organization its unique "flavor." Several definitions of organizational culture have been proposed, but the most straightforward was offered by Deal and Kennedy (1982): "The way we do things around here."

Furnham and Gunter (1993) proposed three features of organizational culture. First, an organization's culture can often be traced to its founders. These people often possess dynamic personalities, strong values, and a clear vision of what the organization should look like. They play a big role in the initial hiring of employees, and their ideas and values are readily transmitted to new employees. Second, culture often develops out of an organization's experience with the external environment. Every organization must establish its own identity in its industry and in the marketplace where it operates. As it struggles to do so, it may find some values and practices are more effective than others. Third, culture develops from the need to maintain effective working relationships among employees. Depending on the nature of the organization's business and the characteristics of the types of people it must hire, different expectations and values develop.

Deeply ingrained within organizational culture are communication processes, for it is through communication that culture is transmitted. It is through interactions with long-time organizational members that new recruits are enculturated. This is how new members learn the language and appropriate behavior of the group, hear its stories and legends, and observe the organization's rites and rituals. Beyer and Trice (1987) believe the culture of an organization can best be understood by analyzing its tangible and visible rites. They refer to rites of passage (hiring and basic training), degradation (dismissal), renewal (organization development activities), conflict reduction (collective bargaining), and integration (office holiday party). New members must determine what is appropriate dress, how to arrange their office, and how much latitude they have in being on time for appointments and in meeting deadlines (Barnett, 1988). Culture may also be communicated through other channels, such as in-house memos, official policies, statements of corporate philosophy, and any other means of value expression (see Field Note 2).

Schein (1996) asserted that understanding the culture of an organization is critical to making sense of the behavior observed in the organization. A narrow description of behavior, divorced from the cultural context in which it occurs, is of limited value for understanding the organization. For example, Pratt and Rafaeli (1997) examined the types of clothes worn by members of a hospital staff to understand how the hospital views itself. They found that the manner of dress among the staff was symbolic of their sense of organizational identity. Furthermore, differing views among staff members about dress were deeply felt. The authors offered the following two quotes from nurses working in the hospital:

> Head nurse of a rehabilitation unit: "Patients who wear pajamas and see hospital garb around them think of themselves as sick. If *they and their caretakers wear*

street clothes, patients will think of themselves as moving out of the sick role and into rehabilitation. They will be ready for life outside the hospital. This is the rehab philosophy, and this is what makes this unit unique." [emphasis added]

Nurse on the evening shift of the same unit: "We are medical and health professionals. We do professional work. We take care of sick patients, we deal with their bodily fluids and get their slime all over us. So we should all look like medical professionals; *we should be dressed in scrubs.*" [emphasis added] (Pratt & Rafaeli, 1997, p. 862)

Schneider (1996) believes it is the people who populate the organization who most define its culture. That is, people (e.g., employees) are not actors who fill predetermined roles in an established culture, but rather it is the personalities, values, and interests of these people over time that make the organization what it is. Schneider (1987) proposed what he calls the attraction–selection–attrition (ASA) cycle. The ASA cycle proposes that people with similar personalities and values are drawn to (attraction) certain organizations and hired into these organizations (selection), and people who don't fit into the pattern of shared values eventually leave the organization (attrition). However, this process occurs over time, not immediately. There can also be differences among people in the organization in values that are not important. As in the example of the two nurses and their manner of dress, if dress is a deeply held value within the hospital unit, the ASA cycle would predict the attrition of one of the two nurses whose view is not accepted by the rest of the unit. In support of the hypothesis that organizations attract people

---

Field Note 2   *A Clear Message*

Organizational culture embraces the values and character of the organization. Sometimes the culture of an organization is communicated in a subtle way, and at other times the communication is loud and unambiguous. I have a client company that was founded about 90 years ago. It started through the efforts of one man who created the company when he was about 30 and served as the company's president until his death at age 80. The company manufactures world-class building supplies. Today its products are sold nationally, and the company employs about 3,000 people. The company was founded on the value of making the finest product in the market, for which it charges a high price. The marketing orientation is strictly top of the line—if you want the best, you think of them. The culture of the organization today follows the philosophy of the founder. The founder and his philosophy are so revered that the company turned his small office into something of a

shrine. Cordoned off with a thick velvet rope, the office is preserved as it was when the founder was leading the company. The office telephone, lamp, desk, chair, briefcase, and fountain pen are all period pieces. The decor of the office is not ostentatious or sumptuous, but rather understated elegance, like the company's products. A 1952 calendar is hanging on the wall. While the office is no longer in active use, it serves an extremely valuable purpose for the company. It is a constant reminder, a physical embodiment, of the person whose values continue to guide the company today, long after his death. The orientation for all new employees includes a visit to this office as a way of communicating the heritage of the company. It doesn't take long for anyone (including an outsider like me) to grasp what this company is all about. Sometimes you have to dig to unearth the culture of an organization. Not this one.

with relatively homogeneous personalities, Schneider, Smith, Taylor, and Fleenor (1998) found that organizations differ in the modal personality types of their employees. The authors speculate that organizations with different modal personalities may well differ in their organizational cultures and structures. The tendency for organizations to staff themselves and socialize their members in ways that promote a monolithic culture prompted Morgan (1997) to refer to organizations as "psychic prisons."

Summary of Social System Components

Organizations have physical structures, but these alone do not define organizations. The social fabric—norms, roles, and culture—is a significant influence on the conduct of organization members. These components are not tangible entities, but they are as much attributes of an organization as its size. Organizations differ in norms, roles, and culture. Norms influence behavior, increasing its consistency and predictability. Roles prescribe the boundaries of acceptable behavior and enhance conformity. These constructs help produce uniformity and consistency in individual behavior. This is necessary in part to ensure that all organizational members are pursuing common goals. Individuals give up some freedom when they join an organization, and these constructs represent ways through which freedom is limited. Organizations differ in culture just as individuals differ in personality. Similarly, just as certain personality types are better suited for some jobs, certain cultures foster certain behaviors. Together, these three constructs define an organization's social system; they are intangible but potent determinants of behavior.

WORK TEAMS

Historically, I/O psychologists have tended to make individuals the object of their attention. That is, we were concerned with finding the right person for the job, training the individual, and subsequently monitoring his or her performance on the job. While the existence of informal work groups was acknowledged in the Hawthorne studies, for the most part interest in groups was limited to social psychology. However, there is a growing trend in organizations to use work groups, not just individuals, as the organizing principle through which work is accomplished. Guzzo and Shea (1992) pointed to the growing use of project teams, focus groups, autonomous work groups, and multifunctional work teams by organizations. Such a perspective means groups are hired, trained, appraised, rewarded, promoted, and fired. Although formal group-oriented organizations are not yet the prevailing reality of organizational life, there are many indications we are moving in that direction (see Field Note 3). Accordingly, our knowledge of teams in organizations is growing rapidly (Guzzo & Dickson, 1996).

Guzzo (1995) noted that there is no real distinction between "groups" and "teams." Psychology has tended to use the term *groups*, as witnessed by the study of group dynamics and group processes. *Teams*, on the other hand, tend to describe groups that have a more narrow focus or purpose. Similar to Guzzo, both terms will be used interchangeably.

Groups are bounded social units that work within a larger social system—the organization. A group within an organization has identifiable membership (that is, members and nonmembers alike clearly know who is a member and who is not) and an identifiable task or set of tasks to perform. Tasks may include monitoring, producing, serving, generating ideas, and doing other activities. The group's work requires that team members interact by exchanging information, sharing resources, and coordinating with and reacting to one another in the course of accomplishing the group task. Furthermore, there is always some degree of interdependence among the teams in an organization; that is, the product of one team's efforts influences the conduct of another team.

Types of Teams

Larson and La Fasto (1989) proposed that there are three basic types of teams, each with a somewhat different objective.

Problem-resolution teams require each member of the team to expect that interactions among members will be truthful and embody a high degree of integrity. Each member must believe that the team will be consistent and mature in its approach to dealing with problems. The members must have a high degree of trust

---

Field Note 3   *Individualism Within Teams?*

The growing use of work teams by organizations may be aided by a transformation in the way we are enculturated in our society. Teamwork emphasizes deliberate cooperation, the sharing of mutual resources for collective gains, and sublimating individual interests. However, it is fair to ask to what degree these values and behaviors are nurtured by social institutions prior to our entering the work world.

Typically education stresses *individual*, not collective, accomplishment. In college, students are graded on the basis of their own academic performance. Some individuals do better than others. I am not aware of any professor who treats an entire class as one "team," yokes the assessment of each individual student to the overall performance of the class, and accordingly gives the same grade to all students in the class. It is individual students who graduate from college; one individual's name appears on the degree, not all the members of some team.

I have heard several individuals who are now functioning as team members in organizations describe the difficulties inherent in the individual-to-team member transition. New values and behaviors have to be learned, including mutual trust, interdependence, and a collective mentality. One new team member described how she had to overcome her reluctance to aid a fellow team member who was obviously struggling with an assignment. She said that if she had extended the same assistance to a fellow classmate during a college test, such behavior would have constituted "cheating." A behavior that two years earlier in one context would have warranted punishment is now encouraged and rewarded in another context. I am of the opinion that the successful implementation of work teams in organizations will be greatly ameliorated by increasing the exposure of individuals to contexts and situations where collective thinking and behavior are valued, particularly early in life. Indeed, Zhong-Ming (1997) reported that the collective mentality, which reflects the importance of people being equal and working together harmoniously, has facilitated the use of teams in China.

in a process of problem resolution that focuses on issues, rather than on predetermined positions or conclusions. The authors cite diagnostic teams at the Centers for Disease Control as an exemplar of this type.

Creative teams are responsible for exploring possibilities and alternatives, with the broad objective of developing a new product or service. A necessary feature of the team's structure is autonomy. For a creative team to function, it needs to have autonomy from systems and procedures as well as an atmosphere in which ideas are not prematurely quashed. Creative teams need to be insulated within the organizational structure in order to remain focused on the result to be achieved rather than on organizational processes. The IBM PC was developed by a creative team that endured many failures before arriving at a successful product. The design team needed protection from typical organizational pressures that reflect impatience with failure. The "incubation period" for the PC was many years and could not have been shortened by performance expectations imposed by others.

Tactical teams are responsible for executing a well-defined plan. To do so there must be high task clarity and unambiguous role definition. The success of tactical teams depends on a high degree of responsiveness from team members, a clear understanding of who does what, and a clear set of performance standards. An example of a tactical team is a police SWAT team or a cardiac surgical team. Each operational procedure must be well defined, and each task must be highly focused and very specific. Furthermore, the standards of excellence must be clear to everyone, and ways of measuring success or failure must be understood by the entire team. Table 8–1 lists the basic characteristics of the three major types of teams.

Decision Making in Teams

Decision making is a major activity contributing to team effectiveness. Morgan and Bowers (1995) identified four components of team decision making that serve as a useful model. These components are situation assessment, metacognition, shared mental models, and resource management. According to this model, team decision making begins with *situation assessment,* which refers to the detection and interpretation of cues to recognize the existence of a problem. *Metacognition* involves developing the definition of the problem and creating a strategy to solve it. This process leads to the development of *shared mental models,* or the ability of team members to develop a common understanding of the problem as well as a strategy for solving it. Finally, team decision making requires *resource management,* which is the efficient utilization of the team's skills and abilities in the execution of the task.

Guzzo (1995) asserted that decision making in teams is distinct from individual decision making. In teams, information is often distributed unequally among members and must be integrated. Choosing among alternatives is made more complicated by having to integrate the often-differing perspectives and opinions of team members. The integration process usually includes dealing with uncertainty, with the effects of status differences among members, and with the failure of one member to appreciate the significance of the information he or she holds. Ambiguity, compressed amounts of time, heavy workloads, and other factors may become sources of stress that affect the group's ability to perform its task.

Table 8–1   *Characteristics of the three types of teams*

Broad Objective	Dominant Feature	Process Emphasis	Example
Problem resolution	Trust	Focus on issues	Centers for Disease Control
Creative	Autonomy	Explore possibilities and alternatives	IBM PC team
Tactical	Clarity	Directive Highly focused tasks Role clarity Well-defined operational standards Accuracy	Cardiac surgery team

SOURCE: From *Teamwork* (p. 43) by C. E. Larson and F. M. La Fasto, 1989, Newbury Park, CA: Sage. Reprinted by permission of the publisher.

Hollenbeck, LePine, and Ilgen (1996) described the development of a multi-level theory of team decision making. The theory is called *multilevel* because effective team decision making is related to characteristics of the individuals who make up the team, pairs of people within the team, as well as how the team functions as a team. The theory is based on three concepts. The first is the degree to which team members are adequately informed about the issue they are evaluating. Teams can be well informed on some decisions but poorly informed on others. The general level of how well informed the team is on the issues they must address is *team informity.* Second, teams are composed of individuals who differ in their ability to make accurate decisions. That is, some individuals can make poor decisions, while others typically make highly accurate decisions. The concept of *staff validity* is the average of the individual team member's abilities to make accurate decisions. The final concept is *dyadic sensitivity.* A team leader must often listen to the differing opinions or recommendations of team members. The relationship between the leader and each team member is a dyad. The leader must be sensitive to weighing each team member's recommendation in reaching an overall decision. Thus, an effective decision-making team leader knows which member's opinion should be given more weight than others. The theory has been tested with computer-simulated military command-and-control scenarios in which the team is asked to decide on the level of threat posed by a series of unidentified aircraft. The results revealed that the three concepts of team informity, staff validity, and dyadic sensitivity explained more variance in team-level decision-making accuracy than other concepts. The authors concluded that getting accurate information, making accurate recommendations, and ensuring that these recommendations are incorporated into the team's overall decision are the core requirements for effective decision making in teams.

Principles of Teamwork

McIntyre and Salas (1995) conducted extensive research on U.S. Navy tactical teams and identified several principles of teamwork that are also relevant for other organizations that use teams. Five of the major principles are listed here.

Principle 1: Teamwork implies that members provide feedback to and accept it from one another. For teamwork to be effective, team members must feel free to provide feedback; that is, the climate within the group must be such that neither status nor power stands as an obstacle to team members' providing feedback to one another. Effective teams engage in tasks with an awareness of their strengths and weaknesses. When team leaders show the ability to accept constructive criticism, they establish a norm that this type of criticism is appropriate.

Principle 2: Teamwork implies the willingness, preparedness, and proclivity to back fellow members up during operations. Better teams are distinguishable from poorer teams in that their members show a willingness to jump in and help when they are needed, and they accept help without fear of being perceived as weak. Team members must show competence not only in their own particular area but also in the areas of other team members with whom they directly interact.

Principle 3: Teamwork involves group members collectively viewing themselves as a group whose success depends on their interaction. Team members must have high awareness of themselves as a team. Each member sees the team's success as taking precedence over individual performance. Members of effective teams view themselves as connected team members, not as isolated individuals working with other isolated individuals. Effective teams consist of individuals who recognize that their effectiveness is the team's effectiveness, which depends on the sum total of all team members' performance.

Principle 4: Teamwork means fostering within-team interdependence. Fostering team interdependence means the team adopts the value that it is not only appropriate but also essential for each team member (regardless of status within the team) to depend on every other team member to carry out the team's mission. Contrary to what may take place in the rest of the organization, interdependence is seen as a virtue—as an essential characteristic of team performance—not as a weakness.

Principle 5: Team leadership makes a difference with respect to the performance of the team. Team leaders serve as models for their fellow team members. If the leaders openly engage in teamwork—that is, provide and accept feedback and supportive behaviors—other team members are likely to do the same. Team leaders are vital and have tremendous influence on teams, and when team leaders are poor, so are the teams.

McIntyre and Salas (1995) believe these principles provide for a theory of teamwork. In their attempts to implement or improve team-based performance, organizations need to think specifically about how organization members can effectively serve in the capacity of team members. It requires the incorporation of a theory of teamwork into the organization's operating philosophy. Teamwork will take place within the organization to the extent that the organization fosters it and builds upon it.

Interpersonal Processes in Teams

The interpersonal processes in a team have been found to influence the overall performance of teams. Yeatts and Hyten (1998) identified several interpersonal characteristics that are endemic to the high-performing work teams they studied.

Communication.   In successful work teams, interpersonal communication is described as frank, continuous, and regular. Team members often meet briefly and informally to review the day's work. Formal, regularly scheduled weekly meetings are held to discuss team progress. When new information comes to a team member, it is often quickly disseminated among all team members. In high-performing groups, team members communicate problems they are having and freely solicit advice. They rarely "hold back" when it comes to revealing problems. In general, continuous and regular communication within a group results in the team quickly identifying resources that are inappropriate, that are likely to be insufficient to do the work, and that appear to be working best.

Conflict.   Conflict among members is unavoidable in any team. What matters is how the conflict is dealt with in the team, as well as the team's attitude about conflict. Conflict can be viewed either as something the group members actively seek to suppress or as an opportunity to learn from each other. Two types of conflict have been identified: beneficial and competitive. *Beneficial conflict* refers to situations where two or more members have opposing ideas and interests but are motivated to understand the views and interests of the other. The team members try to understand each other's perspective and seek to fashion a mutually satisfactory decision. Such experiences tend to strengthen their relationship, as they become more confident that future conflicts can also be resolved. On the other hand, in *competitive conflict* the disagreeing team members vigorously defend their respective positions and attempt to win over others. They look for weaknesses in each other's arguments as opposed to modifying their own conclusions. They may resort to using superior authority to impose their own solutions. Although not all conflict can be expressed in the beneficial form, Yeatts and Hyten found that high-performing work teams sought to diminish the manifestations of competitive conflict.

Cohesion.   *Cohesion* is the degree to which members of a team feel attracted to their team and are compelled to stay in it. Cohesion is based on two forms of attraction: attraction to the tasks of the team and to the members of the team. With high cohesion of either type, team members are more likely to ask for assistance or defer to others who have more talent with regard to the particular tasks being performed. Team-oriented cohesiveness facilitates decision making because the communication among team members is more open; that is, team members feel "safer" to express differing views and ideas. However, it is possible that once cohesive groups begin to achieve a sense of likemindedness or *groupthink* (a practice of agreeing with others rather than disagreeing), additional information important to decision making is likely to be rejected if it is regarded as weakening cohesion. Rewards that focus on team achievements are likely to enhance cohesiveness, whereas individual rewards encourage competition among team members, which weakens cohesiveness. Other teams and individuals within an organization often take notice of cohesive teams and sometimes express the desire to be members of a cohesive unit themselves. Cohesive teams have also been found to exert more influence in the running of the organization, compared with less cohesive teams.

Trust.   Yeatts and Hyten reported that we know less about trust than any of the other interpersonal processes in teams. *Trust* is defined as the belief that even though you have no control over another person's behavior toward you, that person will behave in a way that benefits you. Where trust is reported to be high, team members spend less energy worrying about what others are doing and thinking and more energy directly on doing the work. Furthermore, team members who trust one another are more willing to allow a more talented team member to perform tasks they are less skilled in doing. Team members who have low trust tend to believe that alternatives presented by others in making decisions are designed to benefit only certain members, rather than the team as a whole. In general, trust develops slowly within a team, even among teams with stable memberships. It is also the most fragile of the interpersonal processes. An individual who abuses the norms within a group can quickly destroy any trust with those whose trust was violated.

Yeatts and Hyten noted that these interpersonal processes are often highly interrelated in the workplace. High-performing teams often experience high levels of communication, constructive means of expressing conflict, cohesiveness, and trust among members of the team. While not all high-performing teams experience these interpersonal processes to the same degree, they are subtle yet enduring mechanisms for facilitating the functioning of the team.

Personnel Selection for Teams

Much of what I/O psychologists have learned about the selection of individuals into organizations is not wholly transferable to the selection of teams. Traditional job analytic methods identify the KSAs needed for individual job performance, yet these methods tend to be insensitive to the social context in which work occurs. Groups or teams, by definition, are social entities that interact in a larger social context. Klimoski and Jones (1995) believe that choosing team members on the basis of individual-task KSAs alone is not enough to ensure optimal team effectiveness. For example, Guzzo and Shea (1992) indicated that considerable interest has been shown in using the Myers-Briggs Type Indicator (which assesses cognitive style) to select team members. Successful teams also depend upon those characteristics of individual members that facilitate team functioning. Consideration should be given to such group process factors as learning ability, tolerance for stress, and risk-taking propensity.

Successful selection of team members requires identifying the best mix of personnel for effective team performance. Thus, the selection requirements for particular individuals may involve complementing the abilities that other individuals will bring to the task. Creating the right mix can also mean considering those factors that account for interpersonal compatibility. Establishing team requirements involves identifying and assessing the congruence among members with regard to personality and values. Prieto (1993) asserted that five social skills are particularly critical for an individual to enhance the performance of the group. Each individual must have these abilities:

1. Gain the group acceptance
2. Increase group solidarity

3. Be aware of the group consciousness
4. Share the group identification
5. Manage others' impressions of him or her

We are also learning about the relationship between personality variables and team effectiveness. Barry and Stewart (1997) reported that extraverts were perceived by other team members as having greater effect than introverts on group outcomes. Thus, individuals with more reserved personalities may be less successful in getting the team to accept their ideas and suggestions. A related finding was reported by Janz, Colquitt, and Noe (1997) pertaining to ability. They concluded that especially talented team members are likely to feel frustrated when they must work with lower ability individuals on interdependent tasks. The introverted team member with high ability may feel particularly vexed in influencing team processes and outcomes. Barrick, Stewart, Neubert, and Mount (1998) reported that extraversion and emotional stability are predictive of team performance and viability (the capacity of the team to maintain itself over time). In general these results suggest that individuals with outgoing and somewhat dominant personalities strongly influence the functioning of teams, yet a team composed of only such personality types may be thwarted by its own internal dynamics.

Training for Teams

The logic of team training is the same as the logic of individual training, although the mechanisms are somewhat different. The process begins with a job or task analysis, but one aimed at the functioning of teams. Salas and Cannon-Bowers (1997) described a team task analysis as an extension of traditional task analysis to tasks requiring coordination. SMEs are asked to provide information (e.g., ratings of difficulty, importance) on each task in which there is interdependency. The information obtained is then used to specify team training objectives and to develop realistic scenarios for practice.

The results of a team task analysis provide information about the knowledges, skills, and attitudes the team members must possess to be successful. Salas and Cannon-Bowers referred to these three as the *thinking, doing,* and *feeling* needed for the structure of team training, as shown in Figure 8–8. The identification of the criteria for team effectiveness serves to guide instructional activities in team training. The instructional activities focus on providing team members with shared mental models and knowledge structures. These activities are designed to foster common ways for team members to analyze information and make decisions. Cannon-Bowers and Salas (1997) postulated that the next decade will witness rapid growth in computer networking capabilities for team training purposes. Such technologies as video teleconferencing (or distance learning) permit team members who are physically dispersed to receive feedback on their performance. The evolution of these technologies allow for the creation of **virtual teams,** whose members communicate electronically and may never physically meet.

Much of what we know about team training has come, directly or indirectly, from military applications. The military has been responsible primarily for advanced training technologies (such as intelligent tutoring systems) as well as

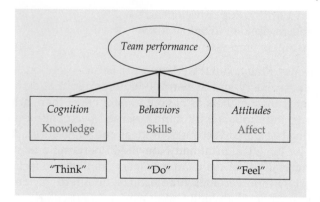

FIGURE 8–8 *The structure of team training*

SOURCE: Adapted from "Methods, Tools, and Strategies for Team Training" by E. Salas and J. A. Cannon-Bowers, 1997, in *Training for a Rapidly Changing Workplace*, edited by M. A. Quinones and A. Ehrenstein, Washington, DC: American Psychological Association.

strategies in team training, such as cross-training. The rationale behind cross-training is that exposure to and practice on other teammates' tasks should result in better team member knowledge about task responsibilities and coordination requirements. I/O psychologists working in military support roles have provided much of our knowledge of team training.

CONCLUDING COMMENTS

The conversion from an individual to a team perspective of work requires that we reexamine our knowledge about many facets of I/O psychology. In addition to team-based selection and team training, we have to learn more about the appraisal of team performance (e.g., Reilly & McGourty, 1998) and team pay (e.g., Reilly, in press). Furthermore, while some of our concepts might generalize directly from individuals to groups, some procedures might be incompatible (e.g., Campion, Papper, & Medsker, 1996). It will be recalled from the preceding chapter that one purpose of performance appraisal is to identify performance differences across individuals and to differentially reward them accordingly. If we strive for teamwork and a sense of unity across group members, we should then *not* differentially reward the "best" individual team members. We will have to develop appraisal and reward processes that treat all members of a group as a single entity, not as individuals. Organizations get what they reward. If they choose to appraise and reward individual job performance, then they should not decry a lack of teamwork and cooperation among their employees (Kerr, 1995). I believe I/O psychology should gird itself for the journey of understanding how work performed by teams requires insight into new psychological concepts, or existing concepts with unknown validity when generalized to groups.

CASE STUDY   ◆   Should We Use Work Teams?

Terry Porter was the founder and president of a small financial services company. The company was created about 10 years ago and has grown to 16 employees. The purpose of the company was to provide financial services such as billing, payment disbursement, collection, and record keeping to other organizations. Terry discovered there was a need to provide these services because larger companies were looking for less expensive ways to perform these needed business functions. The organizations could substantially downsize their accounting departments by contracting the work to other companies that specialized in this business. As other organizations increasingly contracted financial services to specialized firms, companies such as Terry's continued to prosper.

Business was growing at such a rate that Terry decided the time had come to consider changing the way the company was structured. Over the past few years, several new employees were hired as the workload grew. However, the additional employees seemed to create some problems of work flow coordination. Also, the potential for attaining greater business volume was evident, and what was needed was an organized method to obtain and service the new accounts. Terry contemplated reorganizing the staff into two work teams of seven employees each. Only Terry and the receptionist would not be a team member. The primary responsibility of one team member would be to recruit new business. Other team members would be involved in performing the mainstream functions of the business, which would be better coordinated by the assignment of specific roles. Terry further considered having each team target itself to the two different market segments of the business: manufacturing organizations and health-related services. In this way the company would be organized around the two major bases of business, and each team would have clearly defined objectives. The two teams would be called "Team Alpha" and "Team Beta," respectively. Their motto would be "There is no 'I' in our team."

Terry had never been involved with work teams before and had several concerns about how they operate. For example, Terry wasn't sure how to decide which employees would be assigned to each team. All the employees seemed to get along very well, but would the spirit of goodwill continue if they were divided? Would an unhealthy sense of competitiveness emerge between the two teams? Terry also didn't know how the employees would feel about such a reorganization. They all would have more specific duties and responsibilities compared to before. Terry also wondered about the use of special incentives for team performance. Should there be special incentives for recruiting the most new business? If so, the deck would be stacked in favor of Team Beta because of the greater growth of companies in the health-related services. Perhaps, Terry concluded, this would just make Team Alpha try harder.

The potential gains from using work teams seemed great, but Terry conceded that the conversion to work teams was perhaps more daunting than he originally believed.

Questions   1. What conditions or factors are driving the consideration of work teams?

2. What benefits do you think might flow to the company by creating work teams?

3. Could these same benefits be derived by *not* reorganizing into work teams? If so, how might this happen?

4. What are some other potential problems of Terry's company organizing into work teams?

5. Have you ever been a member of a team? What was your assessment of the benefits and liabilities of the team?

INFOTRAC ARTICLES

1. *Training & Development,* Sep 1996 v50 n9 p34(4)
   How to get your group to perform like a team. Ken Blanchard, Don Carew, & Eunice Parisi-Carew
   Discusses how groups can be differentiated from high-performing work teams and presents the benefits derived from effective teamwork.

2. *Training & Development,* Oct 1995 v49 n10 p22(8)
   Diverse teams: Breakdown or breakthrough? Lewis Brown Griggs & Lente-Louise Louw
   Describes four stages of development that diverse teams must traverse to encourage innovation, cooperation, and respect for differences within the team.

3. *Executive Female,* Sep–Oct 1997 v20 n5 p31(1)
   Is business casual here to stay?
   Discusses how casual dress codes in organizations may affect the culture, particularly as it relates to power.

4. *Human Relations,* Nov 1998 v51 i11 p1329(2)
   An introduction to the social psychology of insults in organizations. Yiannis Gabriel
   Discusses how individuals in organizations intentionally and unintentionally insult one another, and how insults contribute to the culture of the organization.

5. *Human Relations,* Dec 1998 v51 i12 p1425(1)
   Influence at work: A 25-year program of research. Frank Heller
   Describes a historically significant series of research studies on the use of power and influence within and by organizations.

6. *Training & Development,* Sep 1997 v51 n9 p34(6)
   Language, sex, and power: Women and men in the workplace. Richard Koonce
   An interview with a workplace communications expert who explains how men and women use language differentially in the workplace to assert power.

7. *Social Policy,* Summer 1998 v28 n4 p52(6)
   Fat and mean: The corporate squeeze of working Americans and the myth of managerial downsizing. Roy Metcalf
   Review of a book that offers an explanation of why organizations downsize and its effect on people.

8. *USA Today* (Magazine), June 1998 v126 n2632 p9(1)
   Understaffing is becoming a problem.
   Discusses the problems faced by organizations that have downsized their staff yet need more employees to perform work.

C H A P T E R

9

Organizational Attitudes and Behavior

MAJOR CHAPTER OBJECTIVES

◆ Explain the organizational attitudes of job satisfaction, job involvement, and organizational commitment.

◆ Understand the concept of organizational justice.

◆ Understand the concept of organizational citizenship behavior and its relationship to other concepts.

◆ Understand the concept of the psychological contract in employment and its changing nature.

◆ Explore the psychology of mergers and acquisitions.

◆ Explain antisocial behavior in the workplace, especially occupational homicide.

The preceding chapter examined several conceptual approaches to organizations, including their structure, configuration, and the social mechanisms that enable them to function. This chapter will examine various psychological concepts that have emerged within organizations. In particular, the focus will be on concepts that not only have theoretical value but also have been found to influence a wide array of practical matters relating to work behavior.

EMPLOYEE ATTITUDES

The chapter will begin with an examination of three important attitudes employees hold about their work: how satisfied they are with their job, how involved they are with their job, and how committed they are to their organization. Subsequent topics will expand on the psychological constructs that represent the domain of organizational attitudes and behavior.

Job Satisfaction

Job satisfaction refers to the degree of pleasure an employee derives from his or her job. Since our work is one of our major life activities, I/O psychologists have had a long-standing interest in job satisfaction. How employees feel about their jobs is highly variable. One hundred years ago employment conditions were, by today's standards, unacceptable. Work was often performed under unsafe conditions, hours of work were very long, there were no air-conditioned offices, and benefits we often take for granted today, such as paid vacations, medical insurance, and retirement contributions, did not exist. You might think that the employees of today, who enjoy favorable working conditions, would be highly satisfied with their jobs; however, such is not the case. Some employees derive great pleasure and meaning from their work, while others regard work as drudgery. Why is this so? The answer lies in individual differences in expectations and, in particular, the degree to which a job meets one's expectations. There are broad differences in what people expect from their jobs and thus broad reactions to them. As Hulin (1991) stated, "Jobs with responsibility may be dissatisfying to some because of the stress and problems that covary with responsibility; others may find responsibility a source of positive affect. Challenging jobs may be satisfying to some because of how they feel about themselves after completing difficult job assignments; others may find such self-administered rewards irrelevant" (p. 460). Why people differ in their preferences for job outcomes is posited to be related to their developmental experiences and levels of aspiration.

Research has revealed that people develop overall feelings about their jobs as well as about selected dimensions or facets of their jobs, such as their supervisor, coworkers, promotional opportunities, pay, and so on. I/O psychologists differentiate these two levels of feelings as *global job satisfaction* and *job facet satisfaction*, respectively. Considerable research has been devoted over the years to the measurement of job satisfaction. The two most widely used measures of job satisfaction are the Job Descriptive Index (Balzer, Smith, & Kravitz, 1990) and the

Minnesota Satisfaction Questionnaire (Weiss, Dawis, England, & Lofquist, 1967). A version of the Minnesota Satisfaction Questionnaire is shown in Figure 9–1.

The relationship between job satisfaction and important job-related criteria has been examined extensively. Three criteria will be presented: performance, turnover, and absence. The relationship between job satisfaction and job performance has been researched for over 40 years. The reason is obvious—ideally we would like to be both productive and happy in our work. However, the relationship between satisfaction and performance is not very strong. Iaffaldano and Muchinsky (1985) conducted a meta-analysis of studies that examined this correlation and reported the best estimate of their relationship to be .17. This correlation is not nearly as high as some scholars and practitioners would intuitively believe. Its implication is that organizational attempts to enhance both worker satisfaction and performance *simultaneously* will likely be unsuccessful. The reason is, for the most part, that the two concepts are only slightly related to each other. In fact, some organizational attempts to increase productivity (for example, cracking down on employees through tough supervisory practices) may decrease job satisfaction.

Turnover and absence are often referred to as *withdrawal behavior* because they reflect the employee withdrawing from a noxious employment condition, either temporarily (absence) or permanently (turnover). The relationship between how much you like your job and whether you withdraw from it has attracted considerable interest among I/O psychologists. In general, the research shows that the more people dislike their job, the more likely they are to quit. The magnitude of the satisfaction–turnover correlation, on average, is about −.40. However, this relationship is influenced by several factors, including the availability of other work. People would rather endure a dissatisfying job than be unemployed. Conversely, when alternative employment is readily available, workers are more likely to leave unsatisfying jobs (Carsten & Spector, 1987).

The correlation between job satisfaction and absence is considerably less, approximately −.25 (Johns, 1997). Absence from work can be caused by many factors that have nothing to do with how much you like your job, including transportation problems and family responsibilities. However, when researchers control for methodological issues in the design of research addressing this relationship (including whether the absence from work is paid or unpaid, and whether organizational sanctions are imposed on absent workers), a mild but consistent negative relationship emerges between the two. A practical implication of the finding is that if you like your job, you are more likely to make the extra effort needed to get to work (as when you have a cold) than if you are dissatisfied with your job.

How people feel about their jobs is also related to how they feel about their life in general. The link between work and family lives will be presented in Chapter 10.

Job Involvement

Job involvement refers to the degree to which a person identifies psychologically with his or her work and the importance of work to one's self-image. Brown (1996) asserted that people may be stimulated by and drawn deeply into their work, or they may be alienated from it mentally and emotionally. As others have noted, the

Ask yourself: How *satisfied* am I with this aspect of my job?

Very Sat. means I am very satisfied with this aspect of my job.

Sat. means I am satisfied with this aspect of my job.

N means I can't decide whether I am satisfied or not with this aspect of my job.

Dissat. means I am dissatisfied with this aspect of my job.

Very Dissat. means I am very dissatisfied with this aspect of my job.

On my present job, this is how I feel about ...	Very Dissat.	Dissat.	N	Sat.	Very Sat.
1. Being able to keep busy all the time	❑	❑	❑	❑	❑
2. The chance to work alone on the job	❑	❑	❑	❑	❑
3. The chance to do different things from time to time	❑	❑	❑	❑	❑
4. The chance to be "somebody" in the community	❑	❑	❑	❑	❑
5. The way my boss handles subordinates	❑	❑	❑	❑	❑
6. The competence of my supervisor in making decisions	❑	❑	❑	❑	❑
7. Being able to do things that don't go against my conscience	❑	❑	❑	❑	❑
8. The way my job provides for steady employment	❑	❑	❑	❑	❑
9. The chance to do things for other people	❑	❑	❑	❑	❑
10. The chance to tell people what to do	❑	❑	❑	❑	❑
11. The chance to do something that makes use of my abilities	❑	❑	❑	❑	❑
12. The way company policies are put into practice	❑	❑	❑	❑	❑
13. My pay and the amount of work I do	❑	❑	❑	❑	❑
14. The chances for advancement on this job	❑	❑	❑	❑	❑
15. The freedom to use my own judgment	❑	❑	❑	❑	❑
16. The chance to try my own methods of doing the job	❑	❑	❑	❑	❑
17. The working conditions	❑	❑	❑	❑	❑
18. The way my coworkers get along with each other	❑	❑	❑	❑	❑
19. The praise I get for doing a good job	❑	❑	❑	❑	❑
20. The feeling of accomplishment I get from the job	❑	❑	❑	❑	❑

FIGURE 9–1   *Minnesota Satisfaction Questionnaire (short form)*

SOURCE: From *Manual for the Minnesota Satisfaction Questionnaire* by D. J. Weiss, R. V. Dawis, G. W. England, and L. H. Lofquist , 1967, Minneapolis: Industrial Relations Center, University of Minnesota. Used by permission.

quality of one's entire life can be greatly affected by one's degree of involvement in, or alienation from, their work. Brown stated: "A state of involvement implies a positive and relatively complete state of engagement of core aspects of the self in the job, whereas a state of alienation implies a loss of individuality and separation of the self from the work environment" (p. 235). Some items from a job involvement questionnaire (Kanungo, 1982) are listed in Figure 9–2.

Research has shown a wide range of correlations between job involvement and other work-related constructs. Brown (1996) conducted a meta-analysis of studies that examined job involvement and reported an average correlation of .45

I consider my job to be very critical to my existence.

I am very much involved personally in my job.

Most of my personal life goals are job-oriented.

The most important things that happen in life involve work.

Work should be considered central to life.

Life is worth living only when people get absorbed in work.

FIGURE 9–2   *Sample items from a job involvement questionnaire*

SOURCE: From "Measurement of Job and Work Involvement" by R. N. Kanungo, 1982, *Journal of Applied Psychology, 67*, pp. 341–349.

with overall job satisfaction, .09 with performance, −.13 with turnover, and .53 with a personality dimension related to conscientiousness. These results suggest that job involvement is more strongly related to how people view their work and their approach to it and less related to how well they perform their jobs.

Organizational Commitment

Organizational commitment refers to the extent to which an employee feels a sense of allegiance to his or her employer. Allen and Meyer (1990) proposed three components to this construct. The *affective* component refers to the employee's emotional attachment to, and identification with, the organization. The *continuance* component refers to commitment based on the costs that the employee associates with leaving the organization. The *normative* component refers to the employee's feelings of obligation to remain with the organization. In essence, affective commitment reflects allegiance based on liking the organization, continuance commitment reflects allegiance because it is unlikely the person could get a better job elsewhere, and normative commitment reflects allegiance to the organization out of a sense of duty to be loyal.

Meyer (1997) asserted that in general organizational commitment reflects the employee's relationship with the organization and that it has implications for his or her decision to continue membership in the organization. Committed employees are more likely to remain in the organization than are uncommitted employees. Sample items from a questionnaire (Dunham, Grube, & Castaneda, 1994) measuring organizational commitment are listed in Figure 9–3.

Based on a meta-analysis by Brown (1996), the average correlation between organizational commitment and other work-related constructs is similar to the pattern found for job involvement, only stronger. The average correlations were: .53 with overall job satisfaction, .11 with performance, −.28 with turnover, and .67 with a personality construct similar to conscientiousness. Brown also estimated a correlation of .50 between job involvement and organizational commitment. The general pattern of results reveals that job satisfaction, job involvement, and organizational commitment are substantially correlated with each other but are only modestly correlated with performance and turnover. Thus, organizational

I really feel as if this organization's problems are my own.

This organization has a great deal of personal meaning for me.

Too much in my life would be disrupted if I decided I wanted to leave my organization now.

One of the major reasons I continue to work for this company is that leaving would require considerable sacrifice; another organization may not match the overall benefits I have here.

I think that people these days move from company to company too often.

I was taught to believe in the value of remaining loyal to one organization.

FIGURE 9–3   *Sample items from an organizational commitment questionnaire*

SOURCE: From "Organizational Commitment: The Utility of an Integrated Definition" by R. B. Dunham, J. A. Grube, & M. B. Castaneda, 1994, *Journal of Applied Psychology, 79*, pp. 370–380.

attitudes tend to be substantially intercorrelated. Performance is determined in part by ability and motivation, while turnover is determined in part by external economic variables. The linkage between organizational attitudes and behavior is thus moderated by factors beyond the control of the individual.

Historically, managerial and professional workers have exhibited a high degree of job involvement and organizational commitment. However, as seen in Chapter 8, it is these workers who often lose their jobs during downsizing and reorganization. The loss of work for these people is particularly painful because so much of their personal identity is defined by their work. The reactions of people who lose their jobs due to downsizing will be discussed later in this chapter.

ORGANIZATIONAL JUSTICE

Organizational justice is concerned with the fair treatment of people in organizations. It can be thought of as a more limited application of social justice, a concept that has been debated by philosophers for hundreds of years. In an organizational context there are always competing goals and objectives. A case in point is personnel selection. Job applicants are in the role of seeking to obtain employment with an organization. The organization, in turn, is in the role of offering employment to some applicants and denying the opportunity to others. The means by which this decision is made is an assessment of the applicants. Both the outcome of the selection decision (i.e., who is offered employment and who isn't) and the process (i.e., whether the assessment is rendered via a psychological test, interview, etc.) can be questioned in terms of fairness. That is, was a just and fair outcome reached through the use of just and fair methods? Organizational justice is a useful concept to examine a wide range of important organizational issues. Justice has been claimed to be "the first virtue of social institutions" (Rawls, 1971, p. 3). This section will examine the conceptual basis of organizational justice as well as its application in understanding behavior in organizations.

Distributive Justice

Justice has been conceptualized from two major perspectives. The first is called **distributive justice** and refers to the fairness of the outcomes, results, or ends achieved. Distributive justice, like all forms of justice, is heavily predicated upon values. These values are the rules or standards by which judgments of fairness are rendered. Three such rules have been identified as the basis for distributive justice: equity, equality, and need.

Equity.   The equity distribution rule suggests that people should receive rewards that are consistent with the contributions they make or bring to a situation. Consider a university that wants to award a financial scholarship to two students. Using the equity distribution rule, the university awards the scholarships to the two students judged most qualified on the basis of their abilities. These two individuals are judged to contribute the most to the university in terms of ability (as determined by high school grades, standardized test scores, etc.) so they are rewarded with the scholarship offers. In this case it is "fair" that the two most qualified students are offered the scholarships.

Equality.   The equality distribution rule suggests that all individuals should have an equal chance of receiving the outcome or reward, regardless of differentiating characteristics such as ability. The truest sense of the equality rule suggests random selection of the scholarship recipients rather than selection based on ability. Since universities don't award scholarships randomly, however, a modified equality rule must be used. In this example there are two scholarships, so the students are divided into two categories—for example, by gender. The university then offers a scholarship to the most qualified man and the most qualified woman. The "most qualified" consideration is derived from the equity rule, while the one man/one woman consideration is derived from the equality rule. In this case it is "fair" that one person from each gender is offered a scholarship.

Need.   The need distribution rule suggests that rewards should be distributed on the basis of individual need. The special consideration that the needy individual receives is thus perceived as fair. In the example the university assesses the financial needs of all the students and offers the scholarships to the two neediest students (irrespective of ability or gender). In this case it is "fair" that the two financially neediest students are offered the scholarships.

As you might imagine, there can be legitimate differences of opinion among people regarding which is the "fairest" rule to use in awarding these scholarships. One possible resolution might be to segment the scholarships—that is, to offer one based on ability and the other based on need. If the most academically qualified student is a woman, the other scholarship could be awarded to the financially neediest male student. With such a distribution the scholarships are awarded (in part) on the basis of equity, equality, and need. However, some people might say it is *unfair* to weight equity and need the same and that both scholarships should be awarded solely on the basis of need (or equity). Another person might say it is unfair to consider gender in such decisions—that the most qualified student and the neediest student should be offered the scholarships independent of gender.

These types of disagreements among people regarding what is fair (and unfair) about distributions are not at all uncommon. Since distribution rules are based on values, no rule is inherently right or wrong. Organizations typically address differences of opinion regarding distribution rules by seeking to gain consensus on which rule is the "fairest" to follow or by distributing different rewards by different rules. Leung (1997) reported a relationship between cultural orientations and reward allocation preferences. Some cultures, as typified by North America, tend to value *individualism* and are concerned more with individual interests, needs, and goals. Other cultures, as typified by Asia, tend to value *collectivism* and are concerned more with the interests, needs, and goals of ingroup members. Individualistic cultures prefer the equity rule because of the emphasis on competition and self-gain. Collectivist cultures prefer the equality rule because of the emphasis on solidarity, harmony, and cohesion. Kabanoff (1997) proposed that nations differ in their collective preferences for reward allocation strategies based upon the individualism/collectivism orientation. It is often difficult to reach consensus on fairness, and there can be far-reaching implications for organizations from differing views on what constitutes fairness in their practices (see Field Note 1).

Procedural Justice

The second major type of justice is **procedural justice,** which refers to the fairness of the means used to achieve the results. As the name suggests, it deals with the perceived fairness of the policies and procedures used to make decisions. In essence, the distinction between distributive and procedural justice is the difference between content and process that is basic to many of the philosophical approaches to the study of justice.

According to Folger and Greenberg (1985), there are two approaches to conceptualizing procedural justice. One emphasizes the role of the individual's "voice" in the process. Procedures are perceived to be more fair when affected individuals have an opportunity to either influence the decision process or offer input. The second approach emphasizes the structural components of the process, whereby procedural justice is a function of the extent to which procedural rules are satisfied or violated. These procedural rules suggest that decisions should be made consistently, without personal biases, with as much accurate information as possible, and with an outcome that could be modified. Also included in procedural justice is the treatment the individual receives during the process, reflecting issues of personal respect and the propriety of questions asked.

In applying the concept of procedural justice to a personnel selection system, for example, one could arrive at several components of what constitutes a "fair" selection process (Gilliland, 1993). Ideally the selection test should be job related (or more precisely from the applicant's view, face valid), should allow the candidate to demonstrate his or her proficiency, and should be scored consistently across applicants. Furthermore, candidates should receive timely feedback on their application for employment, should be told the truth, and should be treated respectfully in the assessment process. Note these procedural justice issues pertain to the selection process, not the outcome of whether the applicant is accepted or rejected (which is a matter of distributive justice). Greenberg (1990) graphically depicted the two major types of organizational justice and individual reactions to them, as shown in Figure 9–4.

Field Note I   What Is "Fair"?

What does it mean to be "fair"? Most certainly there are many ways to consider fairness, and I was party to one situation that evoked these multiple perspectives. A wealthy individual died and bequeathed $3,000,000 to a university to support students who attended the school. The university invested the $3,000,000 such that it earned 6% interest, or $180,000, per year. Thus, every year the university could grant $180,000 to students to support their education, without having to use the original $3,000,000 gift. The university formed a committee to determine the most fair way of dispersing the $180,000 per year. I was a member of that committee. Three distinct schools of thought emerged as to what constituted the "most fair" disbursement of money.

The first school of thought was to grant a financial award to the most academically talented applicants. As indexed by high school grades and standardized test scores, the "best" applicants were to receive the financial support. This university had highly reputable programs in engineering and agriculture, majors that typically attract more men than women. Because these programs attracted many of the most highly qualified applicants to the university, and because the vast majority of these applicants were men, the financial award recipients would be very heavily represented by men.

Proponents of the second perspective said the university sought to embrace all groups in society—across genders, racial groups, age groups, the physically disabled, and so on. Therefore, the financial support should be intentionally allocated to individual students who

represent the various groups. In this way the university would show its support for recruiting a diverse student body.

The third perspective was to allocate the money based upon financial need. It was proposed that the best use of the money would be to provide a vehicle for students to obtain a college education who could not otherwise afford it. Therefore, the recipients of the financial support would be the financially neediest students.

These were the three basic schools of thought on what was a "fair" strategy to disburse the money. I was struck not only by how different the recipients would be depending upon which strategy was followed, but also by the inherent plausibility of each strategy. That is, I felt each position had some intuitive appeal— each one made some sense to me. The three groups argued over such matters as the difference between a scholarship and financial aid, and what the intentions were of the deceased benefactor in disbursing his money. The final decision by the committee reflected a compromise—a (fair) resolution of conflicting standards of fairness. A portion of the funds were set aside to be allocated on the basis of need. The other funds would be allocated on the basis of academic ability, with members of the various groups being represented in the funding. It was not a decision the committee enthusiastically endorsed, but one it could live with.

If you had been on that committee, what position would you have taken in allocating the funds? Why do you think your position is the "most fair" one?

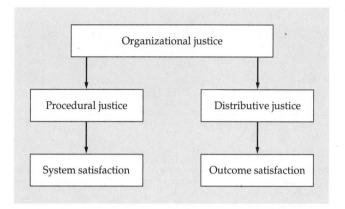

FIGURE 9–4   *Two major types of organizational justice and reactions to them*

SOURCE: Adapted from "Employee Theft as a Reaction to Underpayment Inequity: The Hidden Costs of Pay Cuts" by J. Greenberg, 1990, *Journal of Applied Psychology, 75,* pp. 567–568.

A Taxonomy of Justice Classes

Greenberg (1993) developed a taxonomy of justice classes based upon two factors. One is the type of justice, distributive or procedural. The second is the immediate focus of just action, structural or social. In the case of structural determinants, justice is sought by focusing on the context within which interaction occurs. In contrast, the social determinants of justice focus on the treatment of individuals. Thus, the act of following a prevailing rule of justice (e.g., distributing rewards equitably) is structurally fair, whereas the act of treating others in an open and honest fashion is socially fair. The taxonomy of justice classes is shown in Figure 9–5.

Systemic Justice.   **Systemic justice** is the variety of *procedural* justice that is accomplished via structural means. These structural means include making sure the decisions made (1) are consistent over people and time, (2) are based on accurate information, (3) represent the concerns of all parties, and (4) are compatible with prevailing moral and ethical standards. These are means of structuring the context to promote systemic justice.

Configural Justice.   **Configural justice** refers to the variety of *distributive* justice that is accomplished via structural means. It addresses the pattern of resource allocations perceived as fair under various circumstances. The allocation rules of equity, equality, and need are one illustration. These are all ways of structuring the context of reward allocations to achieve certain distributive patterns.

Informational Justice.   **Informational justice** refers to the social determinants of *procedural* justice. Informational justice may be sought by providing knowledge about procedures that demonstrate regard for people's concerns. People are given adequate accounts and explanations of the procedures used to determine desired outcomes. For explanations to be perceived as fair, they must also be recognized as genuine in intent (without any ulterior motives) and based on sound reasoning.

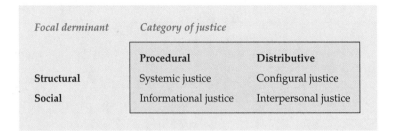

Focal derminant	*Category of justice*	
	Procedural	**Distributive**
Structural	Systemic justice	Configural justice
Social	Informational justice	Interpersonal justice

FIGURE 9–5   *Taxonomy of justice classes*

SOURCE: Adapted from "The Social Side of Fairness: Interpersonal and Informational Classes of Organizational Justice" by J. Greenberg, 1993, in *Justice in the Workplace: Approaching Fairness in Human Resource Management* (p. 83), edited by R. Cropanzano, Hillsdale, NJ: Erlbaum.

Because it is typically the open sharing of information that promotes this class of procedural justice, the term *informational* is used to identify it.

Interpersonal Justice.   **Interpersonal justice** refers to the social aspects of *distributive* justice. Interpersonal justice may be sought by showing concern for individuals regarding the outcomes they received. Ostensible displays of politeness and respect for citizens' rights enhance their perceptions of fair treatment by authorities, such as the police and the courts. Similarly, apologies enhance interpersonal justice because they involve expressions of remorse and serve to distance individuals from the negative effects of their actions. This social determinant of justice that deals with *outcomes* is different from justice dealing with *procedures*.

We conclude this section with how our knowledge of selected organizational issues has been aided by viewing them from the perspective of Greenberg's taxonomy of justice. The first organizational issue is performance appraisal. Greenberg (1986) proposed that beliefs about the fairness of a performance evaluation are based in part on the procedures used to make the evaluations. Greenberg asked participants in management training seminars to think of an incident in which they received either a particularly fair or unfair performance evaluation on the job. These identified incidents were subsequently rated by other managers regarding the factors that produced fair performance appraisals. Five procedural factors reflective of *systemic* justice were identified: (1) soliciting input from the ratee prior to the evaluation and using it, (2) two-way communication during the interview, (3) ability to challenge/rebut the evaluation, (4) the rater's familiarity with the ratee's work, and (5) the consistent application of standards. In keeping with Greenberg's class of systemic justice, these five factors may be used to structure the context of a performance appraisal to produce a fair evaluation.

A second study by Greenberg (1994) assessed the effectiveness of *informational* and *interpersonal* justice in promoting acceptance of a work site smoking ban. Two announcements of a work site smoking ban were made to employees of a large company. The announcements differed in the amount of information given about the need for the ban and the degree of interpersonal sensitivity shown for the personal impact of the ban. Some employees received a great deal of information about the reason for the smoking ban, while others received only the most cursory information. Furthermore, some employees received a personally sensitive message

("We realize that this new policy will be very hard on those of you who smoke. Smoking is an addiction, and it's very tough to stop. We are quite aware of this, and we do not want you to suffer"), while other employees received a message showing less personal concern ("I realize that it's tough to stop smoking, but it's in the best interest of our business to implement the smoking ban. And, of course, business must come first"). Immediately after the announcement, employees completed surveys on their acceptance of the ban. Although heavy smokers were least accepting of the ban, they showed the greatest incremental gain in acceptance after exposure to thorough information presented in a highly sensitive manner. By contrast, nonsmokers' acceptance of the ban was uniformly unaffected by the way it was presented to them. Regardless of how much they smoked, all participants recognized the procedural fairness associated with giving thorough information in a socially sensitive manner.

Perhaps the best illustration of Greenberg's fourth class of justice, *configural*, is the national debate on societal values in employment. Configural justice refers to how resources are allocated to achieve a fair outcome. The debate on societal values deals with whether the resource of jobs (or employment) is best allocated on the basis of equity or equality. Proponents of the equity rule of allocation argue that jobs should be filled strictly on the basis of ability, irrespective of such demographic groups as race, age, and gender. If selection of the most qualified applicants results in a distribution of jobs filled predominantly by members of one group, the equity rule would evince such an outcome as fair. Alternatively, the equality rule of allocation argues that society is composed of members of different groups based on race, age, and gender. Therefore, to be fair, the distribution of people holding jobs should be approximately equal to the distribution of people in society. Application of such a rule might require hiring someone who is a member of a certain race, age, or gender group with lesser ability than someone with greater ability from some other group. It is argued that all groups deserve a fair share of society's benefits, and jobs are among those benefits.

As others have observed (e.g., Gottfredson, 1994; Sackett & Wilk, 1994), discussions of technical issues in personnel selection (such as where to set the cutoff score on a test) are really superfluous to the larger issue of what objectives are guiding the offering of employment. If the objective is to pursue the equity rule of allocation of jobs, certain selection decisions are made. However, if the equality rule of allocation of jobs is followed, other selection decisions may be made. The societal debate about jobs and who fills them must squarely face issues of *configural* justice, with the realization that there is often more than one way to judge what is fair.

ORGANIZATIONAL CITIZENSHIP BEHAVIOR

The classic approach to thinking about a job is in terms of the tasks that make up the job. In fact, one purpose of job analysis (as described in Chapter 3) is to establish or identify these tasks. In turn, performance appraisal (as discussed in Chapter 7) is concerned with assessing how well employees perform the tasks that make up their jobs. However, organizational researchers have discovered that some employees contribute to the welfare or effectiveness of their organization by going beyond the duties prescribed in their jobs. That is, they give extra discretionary contributions that are neither required nor expected. The most frequently used term for this phenomenon is **organizational citizenship behavior.** It is also referred to as *prosocial organizational behavior* and *extra-role behavior.* Organ (1994) referred to a person who engages in organizational citizenship behavior as a "good soldier."

There appear to be several dimensions to citizenship behavior (Organ, 1988; Van Dyne, Graham, & Dienesch, 1994). Five dimensions are most frequently proposed by researchers:

1. *Altruism* (also called *helping behavior*) reflects willfully helping specific people with an organizationally relevant task or problem.
2. *Conscientiousness* refers to being punctual, having attendance better than the group norm, and judiciously following company rules, regulations, and procedures.
3. *Courtesy* is being mindful and respectful of other people's rights.
4. *Sportsmanship* refers to avoiding complaints, petty grievances, gossiping, and falsely magnifying problems.
5. *Civic virtue* is responsible participation in the political life of the organization. Civic virtue reflects keeping abreast of not only current organizational issues but also more mundane issues, such as attending meetings, attending to in-house communications, and speaking up on issues. It has been suggested that civic virtue is the most admirable manifestation of organizational citizenship behavior because it often entails some sacrifice of individual productive efficiency.

Employees who exhibit prosocial behavior are highly valued by their managers. Indeed, they should be because they contribute above and beyond the normal requirements and expectations of the job. An empirical study of performance evaluation revealed the degree to which citizenship behavior influences judgments of job performance. MacKenzie, Podsakoff, and Fetter (1991) examined three objective measures of weekly productivity relating to sales volume for a sample of insurance agents. Also obtained for these agents was an evaluation of their dimensions of organizational citizenship behavior as well as a managerial assessment of their overall job performance. The results indicated that the managers' subjective evaluations of the agents' job performance were determined as much by the agents' altruism and civic virtue as by the objective productivity levels. Podsakoff, Ahearne, and MacKenzie (1997) reported that altruism and sportsmanship had substantial effects on the overall quantity of performance of machine crews working in a paper mill, while altruism was related to the quality of performance.

It is reasonable to question the origins of organizational citizenship behavior; that is, are manifestations of such prosocial behavior a product of our individual dispositions (which are fairly immutable), or can organizations conduct themselves in ways that bring out such behavior in their employees? Research supports both the dispositional and situational antecedents of organizational citizenship behavior.

Support for dispositional antecedents comes from the Big 5 model of personality (as discussed in Chapter 4). Two of the Big 5 dimensions appear relevant to organizational citizenship behavior. One, agreeableness, pertains to the ease or difficulty one has in getting along with people, or how good-natured one is with respect to interpersonal relationships. The second, conscientiousness, pertains to reliability, dependability, punctuality, and discipline. Evidence indicates that some people, given selected aspects of their personality, are more likely to engage in organizational citizenship behaviors than others. As McNeely and Meglino (1994) noted, organizations can promote prosocial behavior by selecting applicants who have high scores on agreeableness and conscientiousness.

The second explanation for organizational citizenship behavior—situational antecedents—has at its basis the concept of organizational justice. It is proposed that if employees believe they are treated fairly, then they are more likely to hold positive attitudes about their work. Organ (1988) hypothesized that fairness perceptions may influence prosocial behavior by prompting employees to define their relationship with the organization as a social exchange. In exchange for being treated fairly, it is proposed that employees would engage in discretionary gestures of organizational citizenship behavior. However, to the extent that unfairness is perceived in the relationship, the tendency would be to recast the relationship as a more rigidly defined exchange. Thus, in a trusting relationship with the organization, the employee contributes more to the exchange than is formally required. However, to the degree the organization is perceived as lacking fairness, the employee retreats to contributing to the exchange only what he or she is obligated.

In a test of this proposition, Moorman (1991) examined the relationship between forms of organizational justice (distributive and procedural) and organizational citizenship behavior. A graphic portrayal of the relationship is presented in Figure 9–6. The figure reveals the relationship between organizational justice and prosocial behavior. It was proposed that employees engage in citizenship behavior because they perceive the organization to be fair (both distributively and procedurally). Moorman discovered that organizational citizenship behavior was related to perceptions of procedural justice but *not* distributive justice. Furthermore, the courtesy dimension of citizenship behavior was most strongly related to procedural justice. Employees who believed that their supervisors personally treated them fairly appeared to be more likely to exhibit citizenship behaviors.

The major implication of the study is that supervisors can directly influence employees' citizenship behavior. Employees' perception of justice was based on whether supervisors used procedures designed to promote fairness. Moorman concluded that if supervisors want to increase citizenship behavior among their employees, they should work to increase the fairness of their interactions with employees. Subsequent research has strengthened the conclusion of a reciprocal exchange between the employee and the organization. Organizations that are perceived as being equitable and that recognize desirable behavior in their employees reap the benefits of having employees engage in more citizenship behavior.

Research on citizenship behavior reflects the richness of examining workplace behavior from an organizational or social perspective. It is clear from the MacKenzie et al. (1991) study that evaluations of job performance cannot be divorced from the social context in which they occur. Citizenship behavior is related to perceptions of organizational justice and can be viewed as one dimension of

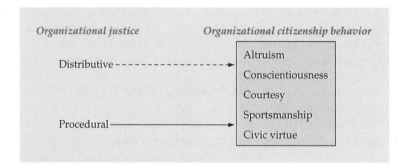

FIGURE 9–6   *Relationship between organizational justice and organizational citizenship behavior*

SOURCE: Adapted from "Relationship Between Organizational Justice and Organizational Citizenship Behaviors: Do Fairness Perceptions Influence Employee Citizenship?" by R. H. Moorman, 1991, *Journal of Applied Psychology, 76,* p. 849.

the social exchange between the employee and the organization. The next section will examine a related aspect of this social exchange, the psychological contract, and the effects of violating this contract.

THE PSYCHOLOGICAL CONTRACT

Rousseau (1995) described the **psychological contract** as the exchange relationship between the individual employee and the organization. It is not a formal written contract between the two parties but an implied relationship based on mutual contributions. The psychological contract is the employee's perception of the reciprocal obligations that exist within the organization. The employees have beliefs about the organization's obligations to them as well as their obligations to the organization. Thus, employees may believe the organization has agreed to provide job security and promotional opportunities in exchange for hard work and loyalty by the employee. The psychological contract is oriented toward the future. Without the promise of future exchange, neither party has incentive to contribute anything to the other and the relationship may not endure. The contract is composed of a belief that some form of a promise has been made and that the terms and conditions of the contract have been accepted by both parties.

Beliefs or perceptions regarding implied promises and acceptance are the basis of the psychological contract. Each party believes that both parties have made promises and that both parties have accepted the same contract terms (Rousseau, 1989). However, this does not necessarily mean that both parties share a common understanding of all contract terms. Each party believes only that they share the same interpretation of the contract. The psychological contract is made not once but rather is revised throughout the employee's tenure in the organization. The longer the relationship endures and the two parties interact, the broader the array of contributions that might be included in the contract. Rousseau and Parks (1993) found that employment itself is perceived as a promise (i.e., the implied contract of continued future employment) and that an employee's performance is perceived as a

Nature of Psychological Contract

Transactional   Relational

Antisocial behaviors	Indifferent social behaviors	Prosocial behaviors
Violence	Compliance	Conscientiousness
Threats		Sportsmanship
Negligence		Courtesy
Negativism		Civic virtue
		Altruism

Alienation   Commitment

FIGURE 9–7   *Relationship between the psychological contract and range of social behaviors*

SOURCE: Adapted from "'Till Death Do Us Part . . .': Changing Work Relationships in the 1990s" by J. M. Parks and D. L. Kidder, 1994, in *Trends in Organizational Behavior* (p. 120), edited by C. L. Cooper and D. M. Rousseau, New York: Wiley.

contribution (a way of paying for the promise). Robinson, Kraatz, and Rousseau (1994) examined how psychological contracts change over time. They found that during the first two years of employment, employees came to perceive that they owed less to their employer, while the employers in turn owed them more.

Rousseau suggested that psychological contracts lie along a continuum, ranging from the transactional to the relational. *Transactional contracts* are characterized by short time frames and specific obligations. Financial resources are the primary vehicle of exchange. *Relational contracts* are characterized by long-term relationships with diffuse obligations. Transactional contracts are predicated on total self-interest, whereas relational contracts implicitly acknowledge the value of the relationship itself, in which one party may put the immediate interests of the other party ahead of his or her own. At the relational end of the continuum, obligations are ambiguous and constantly evolving. These contracts are long term and exchange not only financial resources but also socioemotional resources such as loyalty and affiliation. Figure 9–7 shows the continuum of psychological contracts and the range of social behavior within an organization.

There is an element of power in all contracts. Power can be distributed either equally (i.e., symmetrically) between the two parties or unequally (i.e., asymmetrically). Asymmetrical power is most common in employment relationships. Power asymmetries affect the perceived voluntariness of the exchange relationship, dividing the two parties into contract makers (relatively powerful) and contract takers (relatively powerless). As contract takers, employees cannot easily exit the employment relationship. This may result in a perceived loss of control in the relationship, which is likely to intensify feelings of mistreatment and injustice when violations are perceived. Because the employer is the more powerful party, terms of the contract can be dictated to the less powerful employee, who must either accept them or exit the relationship.

Violation of the Psychological Contract

The psychological contract is violated when one party in a relationship perceives another as failing to fulfill promised obligations. Table 9–1 lists typical organizational violations of the psychological contract and related example quotes from employees. The failure of one party to meet its obligations to another can be expected to erode both the relationship and the affected party's belief in the reciprocal obligations of the two parties. Violations by an employer may affect not only what an employee feels he or she is owed by the employer, but also what an employee feels obligated to offer in return. Violation of a psychological contract undermines the very factors (e.g., trust) that led to emergence of a relationship. If the employer reneges on an implied promise, the employer's integrity is questioned. A violation signals that the employer's original motives to build and maintain a mutually beneficial relationship have changed or were false from the beginning. The psychological contract binds the employee and employer—a form of guarantee that if each does his or her part, then the relationship will be mutually beneficial. Thus, violations weaken the bond.

Shore and Tetrick (1994) posited three factors that determine the employee's reaction to violations of the psychological contract. The first is the type of psychological contract in effect. Violation of a primarily transactional contract, particularly of short duration, may be less intense and more amenable to correction than violation of long-standing relational contracts. Rousseau (1989) believes violation of a relational contract produces deep feelings equivalent to moral outrage. The second factor is the perceived magnitude of the violation. A minor violation probably induces the employee to seek to restore the contract—in effect, to resolve the perceived misunderstanding. However, a gross violation prompts the employee to focus on the emotional hurt of the violation, not its resolution. The third factor is the extent to which the employer is perceived as being directly responsible or accountable for the violation. If the organization is perceived as involuntarily breaking the psychological contract, the importance of the violation is less than if the organization is perceived as doing so voluntarily or deliberately. For example, if some employees lose their jobs because the organization is damaged by a natural disaster (e.g., a fire), the sense of violation is less than if the employer discharged the employees.

Morrison and Robinson (1997) proposed that two conditions give rise to violations of the psychological contract: reneging and incongruence. *Reneging* refers to when an agent or agents of the organization knowingly break a promise to the employee. In turn, there are two forms of reneging. One is caused by inability, where organizational agents find it impossible to fulfill promises they made at earlier times, such as a recruiter who promised rapid promotions. The other is caused by unwillingness, where agents do not want to fulfill specific terms of the employment agreement. The second condition, *incongruence*, occurs when the employee and agent(s) have different understandings about a promise.

Morrison and Robinson asserted that either reneging or incongruence may cause an employee to perceive an unmet promise compared to what he or she has actually received. The perception of this discrepancy serves as a trigger for the em-

Table 9–1   *Types of violations to the psychological contract*

Violation Type	Definition	Examples
Training/development	Absence of training or training experience not as promised	"Sales training was promised as an integral part of marketing training. It never materialized."
Compensation	Discrepancies in promised and realized pay, benefits, and bonuses	"Specific compensation benefits were promised. Either they were not given to me, or I had to fight for them."
Promotion	Promotion or advancement schedule not as promised	"I perceived a promise that I had a good chance of promotion to manager in one year. While I received excellent performance ratings, I was not promoted in my first year."
Job security	Promises not met regarding the degree of job security one could expect	"The company promised that no one would be fired out of the training program, that all of us were safe until placement. In return for this security we accepted lower pay. The company subsequently fired four people from the training program."
Feedback	Feedback and reviews inadequate compared to what was promised	"I did not receive performance reviews as promised."
People	Employer perceived as having misrepresented the type of people at the firm, in terms of things such as their expertise, work style, or reputation	"It was promised as dynamic and as having a challenging environment . . . rubbing elbows with some of the brightest people in the business . . . a lie. The true picture started to come out after the initial hype of working at one of the best 100 companies in the country had worn off."

SOURCE: Adapted from "Violating the Psychological Contract: Not the Exception but the Norm" by S. L. Robinson and D. M. Rousseau, 1994, *Journal of Organizational Behavior, 32,* pp. 245–259.

ployee to consider how well each of the parties has upheld its respective promises. A perceived breach of contract is more likely to result if the employee perceives that he or she has made contributions as promised, yet those contributions have not been reciprocated adequately.

What is the typical employee response to violations of the psychological contract? Robinson et al. (1994) found that psychological contracts become less relational and more transactional following violations. Employees turn away from the socioemotional aspects of work and focus on the monetary benefits of the relationship. This has the effect of increasing the psychological distance between the employee and the employer, making the contract more transactional. A sequential pattern of five employee responses to violations has been identified. The first is *voice:* The employee voices his or her concern over the violation and seeks to reinstate the contract. Dulebohn (1997) found that employees are somewhat reluctant to use formal mechanisms of voice because they fear that their use of voice mechanisms will expose them to subsequent reprisal by management. People who use formal voice mechanisms (grievance or appeal systems) often are labeled as organizational dissenters and experience retaliation. Instead, employees are more likely to use subtle influence tactics to affect procedural justice. If unsuccessful, voice is followed by *silence.* Silence connotes compliance with the organization, but a loss of commitment. Silence is followed by *retreat,* as indicated by passivity, negligence, and shirking of responsibility. *Destruction* may then occur, whereby the employees retaliate against the employer through theft, threats, sabotage, and in extreme cases, homicidal violence against individuals perceived as contributing to the violation. The topic of workplace violence will be discussed in greater detail later in this chapter. Finally, in the *exit* stage, the employees quit the organization or provoke the organization to dismiss them. Research has shown that justice perceptions exert a role in responses to violations of the psychological contract. In particular, procedural justice is of primary importance to employees whose relational contract was violated. The use of fair and equitable procedures by organizations can lessen the impact of the contract violation on the employee.

Pay is one of the most fundamental metrics of exchange between employer and employee, and a reduction in pay is regarded as a major violation of a psychological contract. Greenberg (1990) described a situation where, because of the loss of lucrative business relationships, a manufacturing company was forced to reduce its payroll by temporarily (for ten weeks) cutting wages by 15%. At one plant, the employees were explained the problem in great detail; they were shown respect and their questions were answered with sensitivity. At a second plant, the pay cut was simply announced to the employees, with no attempt to share expressions of remorse or apology. Greenberg reported that the employees of the second plant responded to their feelings of frustration and resentment by committing many more acts of theft against the employer, compared to employees at the first plant. The loss of income was no less at the first plant, but those employees perceived a greater sense of justice and fair play than their counterparts at the second plant.

Parks and Kidder (1994) noted at least three major underresearched issues regarding the psychological contract. First is the employer side of the contract and employer perceptions of violations by the employees. Most research has examined the contract from the employee's perspective (see Field Note 2). Second is what happens when the psychological contract is kept. It is unclear whether a contract becomes more relational as goodwill is enhanced by kept promises. Third, we don't know very much about whether, once violated, a psychological contract can be reinstated.

Next the chapter will examine one of the most fundamental violations of a psychological contract—the organization's decision to reduce employment through

Field Note 2   *Mutual Expectations*

The concept of the psychological contract can be extended from employees in a work organization to students in an educational organization. The psychological contract involves a set of mutual expectations that both parties in a relationship have for each other. What expectations do students have for their professors? Reasonable expectations might include that the professors are qualified to teach the subject matter, they will fairly evaluate the students' performance in class, and they harbor no personal bias against any students. Have you ever been in a class where one or more of these expectations were, in your opinion, unmet? If so, how did it affect your attitude toward the professor, the class, the school? If you felt the basic psychological contract between the students and the professor was violated, it is reasonable that your attitude and perhaps behavior (e.g., attendance, performance in class) were adversely affected. However, the psychological contract consists of *mutual* expectations—in this case, expectations the professors have of students. What expectations do professors have for their students? Reasonable expectations might include that the students want to learn, they will complete assignments on time, and they respect the institution of higher learning. Have you ever been in a class where it seemed the professor felt these expectations were violated by the students? If so, how did the professor respond to these perceived violations? The psychological contract applies to both parties in a relationship, but we know less about organizational expectations of their members than vice versa.

layoffs or downsizing. Such decisions demonstrate huge power differentials between employer and employee and involve the complete loss of control by the employee. As noted in the preceding chapter, downsizing affects thousands of employees annually and is changing the nature of the psychological contract as we know it.

INDIVIDUAL RESPONSES TO DOWNSIZING

As discussed in the preceding chapter, organizational downsizing has targeted middle-level managers and professional staffs as well as blue-collar employees. These developments are harbingers of fundamental change in the evolution and nature of organizational behavior. This section will examine downsizing from the perspective of individual employees, both those who have lost their jobs and the survivors (Kozlowski, Chao, Smith, & Hedlund, 1993).

There is an inherent paradox associated with downsizing. Downsizing is a deliberate organizational decision to reduce the workforce that is intended to improve organizational performance, yet it has a profound negative impact on the lives of individual employees. At the core of this paradox lies a challenge to a long-standing principle of work and employment—namely, that work can be structured in ways that are beneficial to both the individual and the organization. Downsizing emphasizes the cold and brutal reality that the goals of the individual and the goals of the organization need not necessarily align.

DILBERT   by Scott Adams

SOURCE: Dilbert ® reprinted by permission of United Feature Syndicate, Inc.

Terminated Personnel

The individuals most directly affected by downsizing are those who lose their jobs. Downsized employees face the immediate prospect of a loss of income. The amount of time employees have between hearing their jobs have been eliminated and the date of their termination is often a matter of weeks. There is often little time to search for a new job. Buss and Redburn (1987) reported that eight years after a plant closing, 27% of the affected workforce were still unemployed. Furthermore, those who do find some employment may only be able to obtain less attractive and lower-paying jobs. Individuals with skills that do not readily transfer outside of the organization and those with less education suffer greater financial losses.

Employment has a number of psychological benefits that are lost when an individual becomes unemployed. Individuals who lose their job suffer physical symptoms caused by the strain of unemployment. Some indicators of the stress of unemployment are headaches, stomach problems, and high blood pressure. Unemployed individuals have been found to exhibit patterns of learned helplessness, lower feelings of self-worth, and increased depression. Older, white-collar employees experience particularly acute feelings of betrayal by their organization, demoralization, and cynicism. Issues of stress and well-being will be discussed in greater detail in the next chapter.

Surviving Personnel

Although downsizing has more direct implications for the individuals who lose their jobs, employees who remain with the organization are also affected by downsizing strategies intended to make the organization run more efficiently. Survivors often respond with reduced trust and commitment because the organization broke its psychological contract with them (see Field Note 3). The reactions of these survivors to the downsizing process, as well as their reactions to the organization's treatment of terminated employees, can adversely affect future organizational effectiveness.

Surviving employees are still employed by the organization, but their conditions of employment may be different from before. In order to remain with the organization, some individuals may have to be demoted to lower-level jobs. This may be accompanied by a salary reduction as well. Other downsizing strategies targeted to reduce costs include job sharing, part-time schedules, and reduced hours. Although affected employees may experience a reduction in income, the experience is still less painful than the total loss of employment.

Brockner and Greenberg (1990) developed a conceptual model of survivor reactions to downsizing based upon organizational justice. Survivors may question whether the downsizing was a necessary response to an economic downturn, whether terminated employees were adequately forewarned, whether the rules used to choose those to be laid off were fair, and whether the organization provided "caretaking activities" (e.g., counseling, severance pay) to help individuals adjust to the job loss. Brockner, Davy, and Carter (1985) found that survivors felt guilt when a fellow worker was laid off, which resulted in increased productivity. However, survivors also feel less commitment to the organization and often seek employment with greater security elsewhere.

In addition to the impact on survivors individually, downsizing affects the functioning of groups. Krantz (1985) described the tendency for groups to engage in defensive behavior to relieve the stress of downsizing. The defensiveness manifests itself in a greater reluctance to be flexible and accommodating in performing group tasks. There is also evidence that work teams become more cohesive and resistant to change in response to environmental threats. Increased resistance to change can greatly impede the functioning of certain types of teams specifically created to be responsive to changing conditions.

Field Note 3   *The Loss of Resources*

To understand the impact of downsizing on the surviving members of an organization, consider an analogy: The employees of an organization are one of its resources (which is why they are often referred to as "human resources"). The organization uses these employees to accomplish its objectives. Individuals have resources as well. One resource that we all have in common is time. Every person has 24 hours in each day to accomplish his or her objectives. Organizational downsizing that results in the loss of 20% of the workforce is not unusual. How would you deal with a 20% loss in your time resources? That is, instead of a 24-hour day, your day has been "downsized" by 20% (or 5 hours) to become a 19-hour day. You still have to do everything you did before, you now just have 5 fewer hours in which to do it. How would you live your life differently? If you normally sleep 8 hours, would you now sleep only 3 hours? If you need 8 hours of sleep and have to continue working an 8-hour day, that leaves only 3 hours for everything else, including eating, transportation time, and recreation. Do you think you would feel stressed under these conditions? Do you think you might not be as fully committed to your activities under these conditions? While we all probably waste some time each day, it is questionable whether we waste 20% of it. Therefore, eliminating 20% of our day would not necessarily make us more efficient. It might compel us to use our time more wisely, but it would also exact a cost on us; that is, we would probably have to "give" on some other aspects of life. Such is the predicament faced by the survivors of organizational downsizing. They face increased pressure to perform the work that was once performed by a larger workforce.

Rather than staffing permanent employees, many organizations are making greater use of contingent (temporary) workers (Smither, 1995). Contingent workers perform particular tasks for a specific time period. The need for the services varies as a function of the organization's work flow. Contingent workers may work through temporary employment agencies that allocate their services to organizational clients in need of them. They are the modern-day industrial equivalent of migrant farm workers, people who obtain temporary employment by following the harvesting of crops across the nation. Contingent workers receive lower salaries than if they were permanent employees performing the same work, and they rarely receive fringe benefits such as medical insurance or pensions. Contingent workers are disproportionately young, female, and minority, who exemplify the transactional psychological contract. They have a short-term outlook on their involvement with an organization because the future holds no promise for them.

While contingent workers may increase organizational flexibility and decrease labor costs, there is a price to pay. The price is that workers exhibit fewer prosocial behaviors or, worse, engage in antisocial behaviors. Another common reaction of surviving employees after downsizing is to feel overworked. Schor (1992) reported that surviving employees often must take up the work slack from the terminated individuals. Additionally, they feel compelled to accept being overworked to ensure their own continued employment. These workers may in turn reassess their *own* psychological contracts and may perceive their own contracts as transactional, whether or not they were intended as such by the employer.

Downsizing has forced both organizations and individuals to reassess the nature of the employment relationship. One consequence has been an apparent increase in transactional psychological contracts, with the accompanying decrease in employees' sense of loyalty and commitment to their employer. It has been argued that downsizing is a necessary response to organizational structures that have become bloated and economically inefficient. Organizations that resist downsizing as a means of addressing their imperiled conditions risk their total demise (and the loss of even more jobs). However, downsizing has become bitter medicine for individuals as a treatment for organizational maladies. Its presence and frequency of use have prompted a major reassessment by I/O psychologists on long-held tenets regarding the nature of the employment relationship.

THE PSYCHOLOGY OF MERGERS AND ACQUISITIONS

One strategy organizations can use in response to environmental pressures is to become smaller—that is, to downsize. Another strategy is to become larger. But rather than just becoming a larger version of what the organization already is, organizations can choose to "marry" another organization as a way of increasing their size. The logic behind an organizational marriage is similar to that of the marriage of individuals; that is, the overall quality of life for both parties will be enhanced by the marriage. Organizational marriages encompass the concepts of mergers and acquisitions. The technical distinction between mergers and acquisitions is slim. A **merger** is the marriage or joining of two organizations of equal status and power. Their union is mutually decided. Both organizations think they will be more prosperous by their formal association with the other. An **acquisition** is the procurement of property (in this case, an organization) by another organization. The purchasing organization is in the dominant or more powerful role. Unlike a marriage of individuals, an acquisition can be a marriage between two organizations where only one party agrees to the new relationship. The dominant organization thus acquires an unwilling partner to enhance its financial status in what is called a **hostile takeover.** Other acquisitions are characterized by more friendly relations between the two organizations, but nevertheless the more powerful organization acquires the less powerful organization. The acquiring organization is referred to as the *parent*, and the organization being acquired is the *target*. For the purpose of this discussion, mergers and acquisitions will be portrayed as the combining of two companies, regardless of the difference in power between the two. There is relatively little research on this topic. What we do know applies mainly to the characteristics of the two organizations as they affect the quality of their marriage and the individual responses of employees to their organization being united with another.

Some characteristics of parent firms have been found to affect the way they implement the integration of the two companies (Hogan & Overmyer-Day, 1994). Two prominent issues are the parent's culture and the parent's arrogance toward the target. Some parent cultures are more likely than others to impose themselves on the target companies. Parent organizations with a strong consensus on beliefs and values, as well as strong socialization of their members into these beliefs and values, are particularly likely to attempt to impose them on targets. The unity of a parent's culture, as well as its tolerance for diversity, is related to how the parent treats the target. Some parent companies have been found to exhibit characteristics of arrogance and presumption—they "know what's best" for the target. Jemison and Sitkin (1986) proposed three types of organizational arrogance: interpersonal ("We're better than you"), cultural ("Our values, practices, and beliefs are superior"), and managerial ("Our administrative systems are better"). Arrogance influences parent managers to act condescendingly toward targets, increasing their tendencies to impose solutions and negatively affecting morale, turnover, and performance. Arrogance also increases target resistance to being integrated into the parent company. Buono and Bowditch (1989) suggested that the more important the target to the parent, the more likely the parent is to exert control over the target and thus increase the likelihood of conflict.

The elements of a target's culture pertaining to the identification of its heroes, leadership style, feelings of "family" among workers, and degree of mentoring among managers are likely sources of problems when integration is attempted. It has been suggested that management's attitude toward risk and the degree of responsibility for decision making are areas where cultural clashes are most evident. Each organization's ignorance of the other's culture appears to be responsible for the majority of problems faced when two organizations integrate. During negotiations between the two organizations, issues of *strategic fit* (that is, shared or complementary business strategies, financial goals) typically dominate the discussion. However, issues of *organizational fit* (that is, the compatibility of the cultures and the match between workforces) are often neglected.

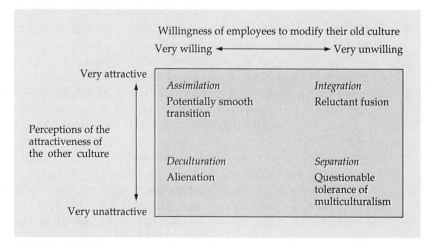

FIGURE 9–8   *Modes of interaction between two organizational cultures in mergers and acquisitions*

Cartwright and Cooper (1994) proposed two factors that account for the degree of success in merging two organizational cultures. One is the willingness of organizational members to modify their existing culture, and the second is the attractiveness of the "other" (parent or target) culture. These two factors result in four possible modes of interaction between organizational cultures, which are shown in Figure 9–8. The four modes reflect a harmonious blending of cultures (assimilation), a reluctant fusion of cultures (integration), the loss of cultural identity (deculturation), and the emergence of a multicultural organization (separation).

On an individual level, turnover is the most common behavioral outcome of mergers. Those individuals most likely to face involuntary removal are target employees situated near the top of the organizational hierarchy. Individuals in staff positions (for example, legal, human resources, accounting, and so forth) are most likely to face job loss because these functions are easily absorbed by the parent's operations. However, removal of key personnel from these functional specialties may create integration problems for the parent if the terminations are conducted too hastily or insensitively. Individuals in these high-level positions often possess knowledge of the target organization's culture or operations that could prove useful to the parent when implementing integration plans. If these positions are terminated too quickly by the new parent, it may communicate an undesirable message of corporate ruthlessness and callousness. The perceived lack of organizational justice can damage the image of the parent and increase resistance to integration.

Research has shown, however, that the majority of target employees who leave do so voluntarily. Baytos (1986) estimated that 50% to 75% of key managers from acquired organizations voluntarily leave the new organization within a few years of the merger. Many managers who quit their jobs cite a loss of managerial autonomy as a major reason for their decision to leave. The voluntary turnover of highly productive workers is considered by some as indicative of failure in the integration process. In cases where an acquisition is done in part to gain the skills and talents possessed by another company, the attrition of top performers undermines that goal.

The psychological response of employees to the announcement that their company has been acquired has been compared to the sense of loss experienced by a person following bereavement (Mirvis, 1985). As in models of individual bereavement, it is posited that employees pass through stages of grief beginning with disbelief and denial and followed by anger, emotional bargaining, depression, and finally acceptance. The loss of individuals' identification with their organization may produce stress associated with the loss as well as a nostalgic impulse in employees to hold on to what they have. Collective employee grief is likely to increase cohesiveness and resistance to change and make new cultures even more difficult to introduce.

It has been estimated that during the 1980s at least 25% of the U.S. workforce was affected by merger and acquisition activity (Fulmer, 1986). As with downsizing, I/O psychologists have little experience in dealing with how individuals respond to this type of organizational activity. In the past 10 to 15 years, we have had to address new aspects of organizational behavior about which we had little knowledge. The depth and magnitude of these issues on the psychology of work have had a profound impact on the profession of I/O psychology.

ANTISOCIAL BEHAVIOR IN THE WORKPLACE

Antisocial behavior in the workplace refers to a range of employee behaviors aimed at exacting revenge against the organization for some perceived injustice. Antisocial behavior includes lying, theft, sabotage, physical violence, and occupational homicide. It represents one of the more recent areas of research in organizational behavior.

Bies, Tripp, and Kramer (1997) described what they call the "thermodynamics of revenge" in organizations. It is predicated on the violation of two underlying concepts previously examined in this chapter: the psychological contract and organizational justice. There is typically a sparking event of one of two types. One is a violation of rules, norms, or promises by the organization. An organizational agent changes the rules or criteria of decision making after the fact to justify a self-serving judgment. The second is status or power derogation, such as destructive criticism or public ridicule intended to embarrass the employee. The employee then "heats up" and experiences anger and bitterness, often feeling a need to satisfy a burning desire for revenge. This is followed by a "cooling down" phase, which can take several forms. One is *venting*, in which the employee talks heatedly and animatedly to friends, "blows off steam," and has little or no intention of acting out his or her feelings. A second is *dissipation*, where the employee gives the harm-doer the benefit of the doubt and searches for plausible explanations for the harm-doer's behavior. A third form is *fatigue*, whereby employees maintain their negative feelings for long periods of time. These people do not forgive, forget, and let go. They often obsessively ruminate and express regret about not getting even with the harm-doer. The final form is *explosion*, which can manifest itself in the employee working harder to prove the critic wrong, mobilizing opposition to the harm-doer, or engaging in physical violence.

Skarlicki and Folger (1997) asserted that organizational agents, particularly managers and supervisors, play prominent roles in reducing employee desires to seek revenge. When managers and supervisors showed adequate sensitivity and concern toward employees, treating them with dignity and respect, the employees were willing to tolerate organizational violations of justice that would otherwise contribute toward retaliatory tendencies. Such retaliatory behaviors included deliberately damaging equipment or work processes, taking supplies home without permission, and wasting company material. Cropanzano and Greenberg (1997) discovered that workers who were treated in a disrespectful manner by their supervisor stole objects that were of no value to themselves, but were of value to their employer. Disrespectful treatment, adding insult to the injury of unfair treatment, encouraged people to retaliate against their employers. The employees sought to harm them in exchange for harming themselves, even if doing so did nothing more than even the score between them symbolically.

Violence in the Workplace

As Bies et al. (1997) noted, one of the responses to perceived violations of organizational justice is physical violence. Physical violence in the workplace is a growing epidemic. Prior to 1980 such terms as "violence in the workplace" and "occupational homicide" did not exist. The U.S. Department of Justice (1998) reported that annually there are over 150,000 violent workplace incidents. From these, more than 1,000 individuals were murdered on the job. The number of employees who killed their managers has doubled in the last decade. Bulatao and VandenBos (1996) reported that homicide is the leading cause of fatal occupational injuries in the retail trade, sales, service, managerial, and clerical occupations. Reporting statistics on crime has the subtle effect of making them appear somewhat dry and impersonal. The following are descriptions of specific acts of violence in the workplace (Mantell, 1994, pp. 2–4):

- ♦ A Tampa, Florida, man returned to his former workplace and shot three of his supervisors as they sat eating their lunches. He wounded two others before killing himself.
- ♦ A Sunnyvale, California, worker at a defense contractor shot and killed seven people in the office after a female coworker turned down his romantic advances.
- ♦ A woman in a Corona, California, hospital opened fire with a .38-calibre handgun, wounding a nurse and spraying the infant nursery with bullets.
- ♦ A terminated Woodlawn, Maryland, car mechanic came back to the garage and fired into a crowd of workers, killing two and wounding one.

It may be tempting to dismiss these accounts as somewhat sensationalized reporting of isolated events. However, it appears that the frequency and severity of workplace violence are escalating, both nationally and internationally. Kelleher (1996) described the breadth of the problem as follows: "If you are a gas station attendant, government employee, or retail store clerk, you have a higher probability of being murdered on the job than a police officer in your own community. If you are a secretary or clerk in an office, you are more likely to be murdered at work than a West Virginia miner is likely to be accidentally killed in an industry-related accident" (p. xi). Furthermore, Barling (1996) noted there are both primary and secondary victims of workplace violence—family members of primary victims plus coworkers who themselves were not violated but whose perceptions, fears, and expectations are changed as a result of being vicariously exposed to the violence.

A starting point to understanding the psychology of workplace violence is with the topic of aggression. Cox and Leather (1994) stated, "Human aggression is typically the product of interpersonal interactions wherein two or more persons become involved in a sequence of escalating moves and countermoves, each of which successively modifies the probability of subsequent aggression" (p. 222). Thus, aggressive acts are frequently the retaliatory response to a previous act or acts by the aggressor. A violent act is therefore conceptualized as a step in an integrated series of social acts. The retaliatory response can be understood in part by the concepts of organizational justice and the psychological contract.

Perpetrators of workplace violence often see themselves as victims of some injustice in the workplace. They may be particularly inclined to perceive the organization as having violated the principles of procedural justice. In fact, Johnson and Indvik (1994) posited that violation of the psychological contract is one of the leading causes of workplace violence. A term frequently associated with perpetrators of workplace violence is "disgruntled." Mantell (1994) reported that acts of physical violence are invariably preceded by indications of anger or betrayal, such as verbal threats or sullenness. Perpetrators seemingly want more from the organization in terms of personal identity and purpose than the organization can provide, and in turn they personalize a sense of rejection when their needs are unmet. They tend to see themselves as having their relationship (contract) with the organization violated, while accepting little or no responsibility for their own behavior. It also appears that perpetrators of violent workplace crimes often have maladaptive personalities and have experienced interpersonal conflict in other aspects of their lives.

The process of looking for systematic patterns among perpetrators of workplace violence has led to the identification of consistent characteristics among these individuals. A problem with this profile approach is that even though it may indeed describe perpetrators, the identified characteristics may also describe many other individuals. That is, many employees may "fit" the profile but in fact do *not* engage in workplace violence. For example, most employees whose jobs were downsized feel a sense of rejection and injustice, yet they do not commit violent acts. Hindsight or "postdiction" may give the impression that perpetrators were obvious candidates to commit such crimes and therefore should have been identified and deterred from their actions. Folger and Baron (1996) referred to the process of identifying which employees are likely to commit workplace violence as the "popcorn model." They state, "The employee who explodes violently and shoots his or her supervisor is akin to the first kernel of popcorn to explode. Obviously an observer might focus on trying to explain why this particular kernel exploded before all the others. Although all the popped kernels look similar to each other, a microscopic view or chemical assay might help reveal the extent to which each kernel is unique. Similarly, careful study of the individuals in a given workplace would reveal important differences with respect to various personal characteristics previously found to be related to aggression . . ." (p. 62). Despite the prevalence of workplace violence, its occurrence is still relatively rare in the total constellation of employed individuals. Therefore, the correct prediction of such events is far more problematic than "looking backward" after their occurrence.

Aggression is the product of both individual and situational factors. Among the situational factors identified are population density, noise, heat, and alcohol use. Both laboratory and field research on aggression (e.g., Geen, 1990) indicates that it becomes increasingly likely under conditions of perceived crowding, uncontrollable noise, and high ambient temperatures. However, the research on the relationship between alcohol use and aggression is most declarative. Pernanen (1991) posited that alcohol completely modifies one's ability to understand a social situation. Alcohol leads to both a narrowing of the situation at hand and a dampening of intellectual and verbal ability. Alcohol encourages an overinflated evaluation of one's sense of control, power, and mastery over the world. The inebriated individual may be led into aggression by both a biased interpretation of the situation and increased confidence in being able to cope by largely physical means (Cox & Leather, 1994). Many perpetrators of workplace violence were found to have consumed alcohol prior to their action.

Some researchers believe violence in the workplace is just part of the larger category of psychosocial hazards to which organizations must respond. Cox and Leather (1994) proposed three types of strategies organizations should adopt in dealing with complex hazards such as workplace violence:

- *Preventive strategies* (such as employee training) remove the hazard or reduce its impact on employees or their likelihood of exposure.
- *Reactive strategies* (such as formal organizational emergency plans) improve the organization's ability to recognize and deal with problems as they arise.
- *Rehabilitative strategies* (such as counseling) help employees cope with and recover from problems that exist.

Nicoletti and Spooner (1996) advocate organizational use of threat/violence assessment teams, who train managers to recognize and treat violent behaviors and who implement organized processes for reporting and responding to threats. Root and Ziska (1996) believe the need for such interventions is particularly acute during organizational downsizing.

Violence in the workplace is a complex phenomenon. Like drug use in the workplace, it spills over into other areas traditionally removed from I/O psychology. It remains to be seen how big a role we will play in addressing this topic. If primary emphasis is placed on the act (criminal violence) rather than on its location, then the role of I/O psychology will probably not be large. However, if such violence is examined primarily in terms of its location (the workplace), I anticipate that I/O psychology will be called upon to help understand and control this serious problem.

CONCLUDING COMMENTS

As was noted at the start of this chapter, organizational attitudes and behavior encompass a broad range of topics. Some scholars find it useful to view organizational concepts along a continuum, ranging from what is referred to as "micro to macro." The micro approach emphasizes the individual and his or her relationship with the organization. The psychological approach to the study of people in organizations falls into this perspective. For example, the psychological contract is defined in terms of an individual's expectations for the employment relationship. The macro approach examines organizational concepts from a broader perspective and reflects a sociological orientation to organizations. Mowday and Sutton (1993) believe the sociological perspective can offer new insights into concepts that have long been viewed from the individual perspective. For example, Pfeffer (1991) suggested that attitudes employees develop about the job can be construed as a consequence of social contagion processes, and emphasizes investigating who employees come into contact with in the organization.

It has also been suggested that researchers learn to distinguish between strong and weak organizational contexts in influencing behavior. That is, some behavior exhibited in organizations may be an extension or generalization of the same type of behavior individuals exhibit outside of a work context. Thus, we may be highly consistent in certain behaviors and demonstrate them irrespective of a work or home context. Other manifestations of behavior may be limited primarily to the organization. The importance of this distinction is evident when we consider violence in the workplace. Perhaps employees who commit criminal acts of violence in the workplace also commit aberrant behavior outside of the workplace. If such is the case, a comprehensive personnel selection system might be used to identify such people and limit their access to the organization. However, if otherwise well-adjusted people are driven to commit workplace violence because of perceived injustice and extreme stress, then a different course of action is warranted.

The next chapter will examine not only stress but also the process by which individuals attempt to balance the conflicts between work and home life. This work/home conflict in itself has been found to be a major source of stress for individuals.

CASE STUDY ◆ Where Should the Ax Fall?

Ted Simmons stared pensively at two personnel files. Simmons was the vice president of finance for Savannah Mills, a long-time business leader in the textile industry. Savannah Mills had endured another difficult year, as sales and profits were again lower than projected. Simmons had just returned from a staff meeting where he was told the company would be downsizing its staff as a way to reduce expenses. Simmons had to eliminate one of his two financial manager positions, and other job losses were to follow down the line in his department. In fact, all the major departments at Savannah Mills would face job losses, some more than others.

Simmons had the pleasure of working with two exemplary managers, and eliminating one of these jobs from the company would be extremely difficult and unpleasant. Warren Davis had been with the company for almost 25 years. He had devoted his entire career to Savannah Mills; he started working there after high school. His dedication and commitment to the company were almost legendary. He had earned a college degree on a part-time basis while holding a job at Savannah Mills, getting a bachelor's degree in general business. Whatever the company asked Davis to do, he did with vigor and good cheer. He willingly accepted assignments where the company needed him and always expressed sincere gratitude for the chance to be with Savannah Mills. His father had been an employee of the company for over 40 years when he retired, and the Davis children grew up playing on company-sponsored recreational teams. Warren Davis was also very active in the community, representing Savannah Mills on various civic projects. Davis was once referred to as a "walking billboard" for the company, so deep was his loyalty to the company that meant so much to him and his family.

The other manager was Barry Steele. Steele had a very different history than Davis. Steel was 29 and had been with Savannah Mills for five years. He had earned an MBA degree from a highly prestigious university in New England. Upon graduation, Steele had had many job offers but chose Savannah Mills because of its expressed intent to more strongly professionalize the financial operations at the company and to give Steele the opportunity to put his talents to work. Steele delivered on all the expectations of him and in fact exceeded these expectations. He revolutionized the company's system of managing financial assets through the use of automated control principles he had learned in graduate school. It was through Steele's shrewd assessments that Savannah Mills avoided even bigger financial losses, and he positioned the company to return to profitability. Steele was known as "the wonder kid" because of his accomplishments, but he never acted arrogant or pompous. He was not active in company or civic affairs, but quietly went about his business. If there was ever a young employee who seemed destined for a highly successful future with Savannah Mills, it was Steele.

Simmons faced a dreadful choice. He didn't have to fire one of his managers because poor job performance was not the issue. Rather, he had to choose to eliminate the job of a person whose contributions to the company were very positive. Simmons argued to the company president on the merits of keeping both managers. His arguments were to no avail because the issue was to reduce expenses, and all departments had to suffer the loss of good employees. Simmons felt this was one of the toughest calls he ever had to make, and no matter which way it went, the decision would speak loudly about what type of employee Savannah Mills valued the most.

Questions
1. Recall the concept of the psychological contract. What aspects of the contract are at issue in this case?
2. If Davis's job is eliminated, what message would that send to the other employees at Savannah Mills?
3. If Steele's job is eliminated, what message would that send to the other employees at Savannah Mills?
4. Recall the concept of organizational citizenship behavior. To what degree does this concept influence your thoughts about a just decision in this case?
5. If you were Simmons, whose job would you eliminate, and why?

INFOTRAC ARTICLES

1. *Electronic Design*, August 17, 1998 v46 n19 p1(1)
   Boosting job satisfaction by defining and pursuing worklife happiness. Lisa Hochgraf
   Discusses the complex and changing nature of job satisfaction and identifies factors that can lead to greater job satisfaction.

2. *Training & Development*, Sep 1977 v51 n9 p28(5)
   What to do about anger in the workplace? Helen Frank Bensimon
   Discusses violence in the workplace and the factors that are typically associated with its occurrence.

3. *Training & Development*, Nov 1997 v51 n11 p81(2)
   How to survive a corporate takeover. Mark S. Carley
   Discusses how to facilitate blending employees from the parent and target companies.

4. *Social Policy*, Summer 1996 v26 n4 p56(8)
   The new social contract: 10 suggestions for change. Gina Vega & James W. Lacey
   Discusses the concept of a contract between employees and employers and describes the evolution of a new psychological contract.

5. *Executive Female*, July–August 1996 v19 n4 p13(2)
   Workplace violence: What you should know. Joseph A. Kinney
   Initiates the topic of workplace violence by presenting a short true/false quiz about issues pertaining to its nature.

6. *Training & Development*, June 1997 v51 n6 p15(1)
   Feeling pigeonholed? Richard Koonce
   Discusses the subject of job satisfaction from the perspective of employees having their skills fully utilized at work.

7. *Across the Board*, Oct 1996 v33 n9 p41(6)
   Not made in heaven. David Nye
   Discusses the conflict between permanent and contingent workers, why the conflict can emerge, and ways to abate it.

8. *Training & Development*, March 1998 v52 n3 p32(6)
   The kept-on workforce. Beverly L. Kaye
   Discusses how an organization should respond to surviving employees of an organizational downsizing.

Stress and Well-Being at Work

MAJOR CHAPTER OBJECTIVES

◆ Explain the environmental influences on mental health.

◆ Understand the concept of mental health and identify developmental factors in mental health.

◆ Discuss the concept of work stress.

◆ Explain the basis of work/family conflict.

◆ Explore issues pertaining to dual-career families.

◆ Understand the psychological effects of unemployment.

Sigmund Freud was once asked what he thought a "normal" person should be able to do well. He is reported to have said "Lieben und Arbeiten" ("to love and to work"; Erickson, 1963, p. 265). Freud believed that it is through one's family that love-related needs are gratified and that work has a more powerful effect than any other aspect of human life to bind a person to reality. Therefore, Freud's call for a normal person to love and to work can be interpreted as an emphasis on work and family for healthy psychological functioning (Quick, Murphy, Hurrell, & Orman, 1992).

A person's work and occupational stature play a critical role in an individual's sense of identity, self-esteem, and psychological well-being. Work is the central and defining characteristic of life for most individuals. Work may have intrinsic value, instrumental value, or both. The intrinsic value of work is the value an individual finds in performing the work, in and of itself. The instrumental value of work is in providing the necessities of life and serving as a channel for the individual's talents, abilities, and knowledge.

It has been suggested that the split in a person's work and home identities dates back to the Industrial Revolution era. It was then that it became necessary for a person to leave the home and "go to work." However, work and home commitments need not necessarily be at odds with each other. Kanter (1977) proposed that knowledge of how tension and illness-producing features of one system, either work or family, can be used to understand a person's adjustment to the other system. It seems clear that most workers do not leave the pressures of the job behind when they leave work.

The purpose of this chapter is to examine a person's sense of well-being at work and to explain how work stress can threaten this well-being. Central to the discussion will be the balance between "love and work" needed for well-being and how work-related issues can lead to imbalance in this relationship.

ENVIRONMENTAL INFLUENCES ON MENTAL HEALTH

Warr (1987) proposed that a sense of well-being from work must first be understood in terms of the general environmental determinants of mental health. Warr identified nine of these determinants that can be viewed as the bases for psychological well-being.

1. *Opportunity for control.* The first determinant of mental health is assumed to lie in the opportunities an environment provides for a person to control activities and events. Mental health is enhanced by environments that promote personal control. Control has two main elements: the opportunity to decide and act in one's chosen way, and the potential to predict the consequences of action. Absence of the second element produces a specific form of uncontrollability—when a person has freedom to decide and act but cannot predict the outcomes. Not knowing the consequences of behavior, one cannot control what will happen.

2. *Opportunity for skill use.* A second feature is the degree to which the environment inhibits or encourages the utilization and development of skills. Restrictions on skill use may be of two kinds. First are those that prevent people from using skills they already possess, permitting instead only routine behaviors.

Second are restrictions on the acquisition of new skills, requiring people to remain at low levels of performance despite their potential for expanding into more complex activity.

3. *Externally generated goals.* The third feature assumed to underlie mental health is the presence of goals or challenges generated by the environment. An environment that makes no demands on a person offers no challenge and encourages no activity or achievement. Conversely, an environment that fosters the establishment and pursuit of goals is assumed to lead to activities that both intrinsically and through their consequences have a positive impact on mental health.

4. *Environmental variety.* Some environments generate goals and associated activities that are repetitive and invariant. Required repetitive activity is unlikely to contribute to mental health to the same degree as more diverse requirements, which introduce novelty and break up routine activity and location.

5. *Environmental clarity.* The fifth feature that underlies mental health is the degree to which a person's environment is clear. Clarity includes two components. First is feedback about the consequences of one's actions. Second is the clarity of role requirements and normative expectations about behavior, and the degree to which standards are explicit and accepted within one's environment.

6. *Availability of money.* Severely restricted access to money can give rise to many processes likely to impair mental health. The presence of money does not ensure mental health, but the absence of money often produces serious psychological problems. Poverty reduces the opportunity for personal control in one's life, which is a previously identified determinant of mental health.

7. *Physical security.* A seventh feature is a physically secure living environment. Environments need to protect a person against physical harm and to provide adequate security with respect to eating, sleeping, and residing. They also need to be reasonably permanent so that occupants can look forward to their continued presence.

8. *Opportunity for interpersonal contact.* Environments differ in the opportunities they provide for contact with other people. Such contact meets needs for friendship and reduces feelings of loneliness. Interpersonal contact also provides social support that is both emotional and instrumental (contributing to the resolution of problems through practical help and advice) in nature. Many goals can be achieved only through the interdependent efforts of several people. Membership in groups makes possible the establishment and attainment of goals that could not be realized by an individual alone.

9. *Valued social position.* The ninth aspect considered to be important is a position within a social structure that receives some esteem from others. Esteem is generated primarily through the value attached to activities inherent in a role and the contribution they make. Role membership also provides public evidence that one has certain abilities and meets certain social obligations. There is often widespread agreement about the level of esteem that derives from a particular position.

Warr (1987) recognized some overlap among these nine dimensions but felt that a recognition of each was necessary to understand how environments affect mental health. If one were interested in changing environments to enhance mental health, these nine features would be productive targets.

THE CONCEPT OF MENTAL HEALTH

Although nine environmental factors contributing to mental health have been examined, the concept itself has not yet been defined. This is in part because no single definition exists, and it is easier to understand the meaning of mental health by referencing its determinants. Societal standards contribute to the meaning of mental health (with many derived from contemporary Western society), as well as standards proposed by the medical profession regarding mental illness. We do not explore the varied contributions of these sources in conceptualizing mental health. Rather, we take an overall perspective of mental health as proposed by Warr (1987) and focus on its five major components.

1. *Affective well-being*. Affective well-being has two separate dimensions: pleasure and arousal. A particular level of pleasure may be accompanied by high or low levels of arousal, and a particular level of arousal may be either pleasurable or unpleasurable. Figure 10–1 portrays this two-dimensional model of affective well-being. A feeling of affective well-being derives from both dimensions. For example, "depressed" feelings are characterized by low status on each dimension (located in the bottom left-hand section of Figure 10–1), and "anxious" may be described as low status on pleasure and high status on arousal (in the top left-hand section). The highest levels of affective well-being are associated with the top right-hand section, reflecting high pleasure and high arousal. Terms such as "happy" and "full of energy" (from Figure 10–1) are indicative of high status on these two dimensions. In general, a person's affective well-being can be described in terms of the proportion of time spent in each of the four sections of Figure 10–1.

2. *Competence*. Good mental health is viewed partly in terms of acceptable degrees of success or competence in different spheres of activity, such as interpersonal relationships, problem solving, paid employment, and so on. The competent person has adequate psychological resources to deal with life's pressures. It has been suggested that good mental health becomes apparent only when a person faces adversity. A successful response to pressures requires having appropriate cognitive and psychomotor skills, as well as beliefs and opinions that are consistent with reality.

3. *Autonomy*. Autonomy refers to a person's ability to resist environmental influences and to determine his or her own opinions and actions. The tendency to strive for independence and self-regulation is a fundamental characteristic of a mentally healthy person. Autonomy is the tendency to feel and act on the assumption that one is influential rather than helpless in the face of life's difficulties. The contribution of autonomy to mental health appears to be given greater importance in Western than in Eastern societies.

4. *Aspiration*. The mentally healthy person is viewed as someone who engages with the environment. He or she establishes goals and makes active efforts to attain them. A raised aspiration level is reflected in high motivation, alertness to new opportunities, and a commitment to meet personal challenges. Conversely, low levels of aspiration are exhibited in reduced activity and an acceptance of the present state no matter how unsatisfactory it appears. In striving to achieve personal goals, one may face stressful situations, and indeed one may create them through

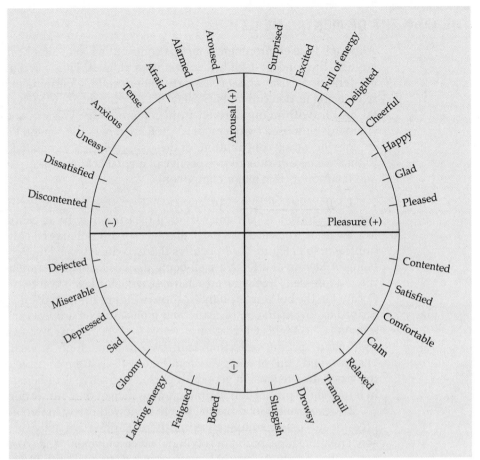

FIGURE 10–1   *Two-dimensional model of affective well-being*

SOURCE: From *Work, Unemployment, and Mental Health* by P. B. Warr, 1987, Oxford: Clarendon. Reprinted by permission.

pursuing difficult challenges. The importance of a raised aspiration level to good mental health is particularly clear in circumstances adverse to the individual, where the desire for change is likely to be viewed as central to a healthy response.

5. *Integrated functioning*. The final component of mental health is the most difficult to define and is most unlike the other four. Integrated functioning refers to the person as a whole. People who are psychologically healthy exhibit balance, harmony, and inner relatedness. Consider Freud's statement about love and work: It has been suggested that the healthy person is someone who can balance the importance of the two areas. Integrated functioning may also be considered across time, typically as a balance between accepted strain during difficult phases of goal attainment and relaxation during the intervening periods.

Warr's (1987) portrayal of mental health represents a comprehensive assessment of the major dimensions of psychological well-being. Competence, autonomy, and aspiration reflect aspects of a person's behavior in relation to the

Field Note I   *The Meaning of Work*

Why do people work? This seemingly simple question has been debated for centuries from many perspectives, including religion, economics, psychology, and philosophy. Early religious doctrine taught that work was a form of punishment for our original sin. Work was an obligation or duty toward building God's kingdom. Work was thus good, and hard work even better. Work was noble because of its taxing nature and because it is a hardship that strengthens our character. Religious teachings also emphasized work as a means of controlling and restraining our passions. Lack of work, or idleness, fosters unhealthy impulses, which deflect us from more admirable pursuits. Thus, work is thought of as an arduous process, deliberately filled with hardships, a means of facilitating our personal development. From an economic perspective, work provides us with the financial resources to sustain life and the aspiration to improve the quality of our material life. The most commonly accepted definition of work, the exchange of labor services for pay, clearly reflects an economic viewpoint. Work has psychological meaning as well, giving us a source of identity and union with other individuals, in addition to being a source of personal accomplishment. Work also has the effect of providing a temporal rhythm to our lives. Our work gives us our time structure—when we have to leave for work and when we are off work to pursue other activities. Finally, work even provides a philosophical explanation of our mission in life—to derive meaning from creating and giving service to others. As can be inferred, there is no one answer to the question of why we work, but its multiple meanings provide a basis to understand why work is so important.

environment and often determine a person's affective well-being. For example, an inability to cope with current difficulties (a form of low competence) may give rise to distress (an aspect of low affective well-being). Affective well-being has its roots in medical criteria; the person reports feeling well and also not being impaired psychologically or physically. Integrated functioning, however, deals with the multiple relationships among the four components and covers broader issues. The balance of this chapter will examine how work-related factors facilitate or inhibit psychological well-being as defined from this five-factor perspective (see Field Note 1).

WORK STRESS

Psychological disorders in the workplace have been identified among the ten leading work-related diseases and injuries in the United States (National Institute for Occupational Safety and Health, 1988). Ilgen (1990) stated, "The health of the work force is one of the most significant issues of our time" (p. 273). Recognition of the psychosocial risk of work has prompted research on medical, psychological, and behavioral stress. Pelletier (1977) reported that stress and psychosocial factors play a far more central role in chronic disorders than they do in acute and infectious diseases. As a consequence, both employees and organizations have become increasingly aware of the negative effects of work-related stress. A nationwide survey by the Northwestern National Life Insurance Company (1991) showed that nearly 46% of American workers felt that their jobs were very or somewhat stressful, whereas nearly 27% reported that their jobs were the single greatest source of stress in their lives. Almost 72% of those surveyed experienced frequent stress-related physical and mental problems.

A large amount of research has been conducted across many disciplines on work stress. Research has examined the causes, symptoms, and consequences of work stress, as well as interventions designed to reduce its effect on individuals. Furthermore, there is no agreed-upon definition of stress or how to conceptualize it. For example, not all work demands on individuals are undesirable. If they were, the preferred state of the individual would be inactivity, which we know to be untrue. People seek activity, including the kinds of activities that use abilities they value. However, some activities or situations produce undesirable effects such as emotional tensions, physical symptoms like sleep disorders, and decrements in job performance. Selye (1982) sought to distinguish "good stress" from "bad stress" by referring to them as "eustress" and "distress," respectively. The focus here will be primarily limited to distress as we seek to understand its negative effect on individuals.

A Model of Stress

Because of the many issues related to stress, researchers have proposed conceptual models of stress designed to integrate a diverse array of research findings. Many such models have been developed. A most useful model of stress in organizations has been developed by Kahn and Byosiere (1992), which will guide our discussion. The model presented in Figure 10–2 conceptualizes stress in organizations in terms of seven major categories. It should also be noted there are numerous linkages among the categories. This reflects one of the primary research findings about stress: There are complex associations among the antecedents of stress, individual differences in how people respond to stress, and the consequences of stress. A causal sequence is hypothesized to exist among these categories. Each of the seven categories presented in the model will be examined along with findings pertaining to the prevention of stress.

Organizational Antecedents to Stress. Research on the organizational antecedents to stress is generally directed toward understanding how broad-based and abstract factors induce stress. Brenner and Mooney (1983), for example, examined the relationship between economic conditions (such as economic growth, instability, and unemployment levels) and social indicators of health (such as diseases and death). The variables were examined in what are referred to as "lagged relationships"; that is, changes in economic conditions produce changes in health several years later. The authors examined the relationship between economic change and mortality in nine countries: Australia, Canada, England, Denmark, Finland, France, Germany, Sweden, and the United States. Unemployment and business failures predicted death from heart disease in eight of the nine countries, with a one-year to four-year lag, with controls for such variables as alcohol consumption. Kivimaki et al. (1997) reported on the worklives of employees in Finland when the national unemployment rate reached 18%. The loss of control in their lives (caused by the economy) added to psychosocial illnesses, which resulted in marked increases in absence.

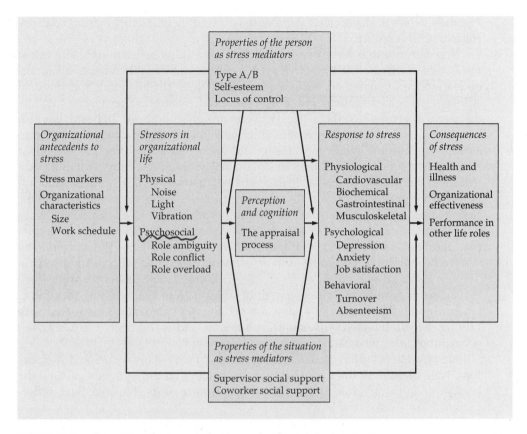

FIGURE 10–2   *Theoretical framework for the study of stress in organizations*

SOURCE: Adapted from "Stress in Organizations" by R. L. Kahn and P. B. Byosiere, 1992, in *Handbook of Industrial/Organizational Psychology* (p. 592), edited by M. D. Dunnette and L. M. Hough, Palo Alto, CA: Consulting Psychologists Press.

Cobb and Kasl (1977) conducted a longitudinal study on U.S. plant closings for the purpose of understanding the relationship between impending job loss and health. Workers in plants that did not close were compared to those in plants that were marked for closing. Five waves of data were collected over a two-year period, spanning the sequencing of events from rumor to actual job loss and (in most cases) reemployment. Psychological measures of health were collected along with self-reported information. The results showed that the threat of unemployment triggered some physiological changes long before actual job loss occurred and that most physical indicators returned to normal after new job stability was attained. For most people involuntary loss of a job was an event that generated stress, both directly and indirectly.

Stressors in Organizational Life.   The term *stressors* designates stimuli that are generated on the job and have negative consequences, physical or psychological, for significant proportions of people exposed to them. Kahn and Byosiere (1992) reduced the stressors to two major types. The first, *task content,* includes such dimensions as simplicity–complexity and monotony–variety. The second, *role* *properties*, refers to the social aspects of the job and includes supervisory relationships and role conflict.

Research findings have demonstrated relationships between ill health (most notably heart disease) and jobs that are characterized by highly repetitive, monotonous work and sustained vigilance (see Field Note 2). Shift work and physical stressors (such as cold, heat, and noise) also produce stress. These factors will be discussed in greater detail in Chapter 15 on working conditions. Ill health has also been associated with working in air-conditioned offices, a phenomenon referred to as the "sick building syndrome." Hedge, Erickson, and Rubin (1992) reported that sick building syndrome produces the following symptoms: sensory irritation; skin irritation; neurotoxic effects such as headaches, nausea, and drowsiness; and hyperactivity reactions such as runny eyes, runny nose, and asthma-like symptoms. Research has demonstrated that sick building syndrome is not caused solely by indoor pollutants but may be related to the electromagnetic fields from video display terminals, which attract irritating fibers and particles to the screens. The syndrome may be related to respiratory ailments associated with recirculated air. There is also a growing body of research (e.g., Soine, 1995; Stenberg & Wall, 1995) that suggests women are more susceptible than men to sick building syndrome. Other research (Hoffman, 1997) has examined the workplace stress associated with HIV disease on infected individuals, coworkers, and members of the caregiving occupations (e.g., medical personnel and counselors).

However, it is with regard to role properties that most organizational stressors have been identified. **Role conflict** refers to perceptual differences regarding the content of a person's role or the relative importance of its elements. Such differ-

---

Field Note 2 *Just Waiting Is Stressful*

Jobs that require sustained vigilance have been found to produce marked stress. Research on firefighters indicates that one of their major sources of stress is not responding to fire calls but waiting for a call to come in. The tension and anxiety associated with waiting to use their skills are often far more stress-inducing than responding to hazardous situations. A metropolitan fire department may get several calls per day, usually representing nonthreatening or mildly threatening situations, but occasionally involving large fires or hazardous materials. It is the continuous stream of relatively "minor" incidents that breaks the tedium associated with vigilance and reduces the level of job stress.

However, fire departments located at major airports (both commercial and military) face a somewhat different situation than their urban counterparts. Firefighters who work at airports may go several weeks without responding to any incident, but when an incident occurs it is invariably more threatening than rescuing a cat from a tree. Some military planes contain armaments that could explode in the event of a fire or crash landing. The potential loss of life in a commercial airline accident can be very high. When not responding to such potentially perilous situations, airport firefighters endure the stress of waiting for something dramatic to happen. The Greek writer Homer presaged airport firefighters as those who live "between Scylla and Charybdis"—two equally perilous alternatives, neither of which can be avoided without encountering and probably falling victim to the other.

ences occur between the individual and other people in a work group who do not hold the same role expectations. Role conflict generates negative affect, tension, and often physical symptoms on the part of the focal person. Conflict among the demands of different roles filled by the same individual can also occur. Such conflicts have been reported most often in occupations such as military service, police work, and teaching, where the compartmentalization of time between work and family cannot be easily or dependably arranged. **Role overload** is a variant of role conflict in which conflict is experienced as a necessity to compromise either quantity, time schedule, or quality. For example, consider a supervisor who says to an employee, "I want this report finished by tomorrow and I want it done well." There is conflict between the time deadline and the request for high-quality work. Findings from many studies reveal that overloaded individuals describe their work demands as excessive and their reactions as negative.

Perception and Cognition: The Appraisal Process.   The appraisal process seeks to explain that different people react differently to stressors that are objectively the same. Furthermore, the stressors encountered within organizations are often embedded in complex situations. Successful coping requires one to analyze both positive and negative features and to decide upon a course of action. Researchers have examined the stages through which individuals perceive and evaluate situations in assessing stress. Lazarus and Folkman (1984) proposed primary and secondary appraisal processes based on a temporal sequence. *Primary appraisal* consists of the initial determination that a stimulus (person, event, situation) is positive (benign), negative (stressful), or neither (irrelevant) in its implications for well-being. *Secondary appraisal* is a judgment about what can be done to minimize damage or maximize gain. The appraisal process may be cyclical as the individual takes into account a previous coping strategy or some new information.

The importance of the appraisal process as a predictor of stress outcomes is well illustrated by a study of patients who had undergone surgery for breast cancer (Vinokur, Threatt, Vinokur-Caplan, & Satariano, 1990). Neither the objective stage of the disease nor the extent of surgery predicted the person's appraisal of threat, but that appraisal was a major predictor of subsequent anxiety and depression. Other studies as well have indicated that appraisal plays a similar important role in predicting the outcome of job-generated stress.

Response to Stress.   Researchers have identified three major categories of possible responses to stress: physiological, psychological, and behavioral. The physiological responses included cardiovascular symptoms such as increased blood pressure and cholesterol level, biochemical measures such as catecholamines and uric acid, and gastrointestinal symptoms such as peptic ulcers. Faster heart rates have been reported under conditions of role conflict, ambiguity regarding future developments on the job, and overall reported stress at work. Levels of catecholamines change very rapidly and respond to a variety of stimuli. Unpredictability at work, loss of control over pace and method, and distracting noise have all been associated with increased levels of catecholamines. Air traffic controllers, for example, show significant associations between daily levels of cortisol secretion and work variables such as load and pace. Research on gastrointestinal symptoms has shown less consistent results compared to the other two types of physiological response.

Psychological responses to stress at work most typically involve affective variables, with job dissatisfaction being most common. Stress has also been found to influence more intense and aroused affective states such as anger, frustration, hostility, and irritation. More passive, but perhaps no less negative responses include boredom, burnout, fatigue, and depressed mood. The psychological effects of work-related stress have been found to produce lowered self-confidence and self-esteem.

Behavioral responses to stress at work have not been studied as frequently as psychological responses. However, five broad categories of behavioral responses have been examined: the work role (job performance, accidents, drug use at work), oppressive behavior at work (theft, purposeful damage), flight from the job (absenteeism, turnover), degradation of other life roles (spouse and child abuse), and self-damaging behaviors (alcohol and drug abuse). Some of the findings have not been studied extensively (such as drug use at work) and may be underreported for reasons of social acceptability or the avoidance of punishment. Dompierre and Lavoie (1994) reflected on the methodological and ethical difficulties of conducting research on work stress and family violence. Nevertheless, the research results indicate that work-generated stressors have behavioral effects that are manifested both on the job and away from it, and they impose substantial costs on organizations.

Consequences of Stress.   The consequences of stress typically affect the performance of the individual on the job and in other life roles. Other ramifications involve the health of the individual, as affected by prolonged exposure to physical stressors and through responses to recurrent psychological stressors. Researchers (Alfredsson & Theorell, 1983) in Sweden, for example, developed standardized measures of job characteristics for 118 occupational groups on a nationwide basis. Men in jobs characterized by high demand and low control (low autonomy) were at twice the risk for heart attacks compared with men in the same age range (40–54) employed in all other occupations. The authors concluded that the next step is to conduct field experiments and interventions to discover ways of reducing such sources of stress.

It is also highly plausible that nonwork stresses can affect attitudes and behavior at work. Research findings suggest such relationships are particularly evident for single-parent families and families in which both parents are employed. Research is also being conducted that shows the combined effects of work and nonwork stressors on health. Frankenhaeuser (1988), for example, showed that the characteristic elevation of catecholamine levels as the stresses of the workday accumulate are sharply reduced at the end of the workday for men, but for married, employed women the elevation persists until the household responsibilities are also fulfilled. Lowman (1996) presented a classification of mental disorders that are specifically work-related (i.e., not general mental disorders that carry over to the workplace). The classification includes patterns of undercommitment (underachievement and procrastination), patterns of overcommitment (obsessive-compulsive addiction to the workplace), anxiety in the work role, and work-related depression.

Properties of the Person as Stress Mediators. Individual differences in resistance to stress have long been recognized. Two personality characteristics have been clearly identified as mediating the effects of stress. The first is *personality type*. Type A is a personality type that intensifies the effects of various job stressors. Type A people walk, eat, and talk rapidly. They are aggressive and competitive and constantly feel under time pressure. Type B people are less concerned about time; they play for fun, not to win; and they can relax without guilt. Type A people have a higher standing pulse rate than Type B people and are twice as likely to develop heart disease. Barling and Boswell (1995) identified an irritability dimension to Type A behavior that adversely affects health and concentration. Wright (1988) concluded that Type A people have a high, possibly insatiable need for achievement. They experience early (no later than adolescence) success, which seems to breed a greater than usual sense of hope that striving efforts will eventually pay off. Type A individuals cannot control themselves when exposed to work-related stimuli. In assessing the proclivity of Type A individuals to feel stress from work, Wright said, "What is needed are ways of training ourselves and others to maintain diligence with pacing—that is, to run the race of life like a marathon and not a series of 100-yard dashes" (p. 13).

The second personality characteristic that mediates stress is *locus of control*. Locus of control differentiates people who believe that they themselves are primarily responsible for what happens to them from those who believe that major events in their lives are determined mainly by other people or forces beyond themselves. People whose locus of control is primarily internal respond to stress differently from those whose locus of control is external. Those who are internally oriented are more likely to take action against the source of the stress itself or to mitigate its effects in other ways. Those who are externally oriented are more likely to see effective actions as beyond their powers and thus endure rather than act. Some researchers have also identified a personality construct associated with the capacity to endure negative life events, including job stress. This personality construct has been called ego resilience or hardiness (Kinicki, McKee, & Wade, 1996).

Properties of the Situation as Stress Mediators. In addition to certain characteristics of individuals, certain properties of situations can mediate or buffer the effects of a stressor. The buffering effect reduces the tendency of organizational properties to generate specific stressors, alter the perceptions and cognitions evoked by such stressors, mediate the responses that follow the appraisal process, or reduce the health-damaging consequences of such responses. The primary variable hypothesized to provide this buffering effect is social support. Social support reduces the relationship between various job stressors and indicators of mental and physical health (anxiety, depression, and irritation). Social support does not reduce the relationship between job stressors and boredom or job dissatisfaction. Sutton and Kahn (1987) proposed three other situational variables as potential buffers against stress: (1) the extent to which the onset of a stressor is predictable, (2) the extent to which it is understandable, and (3) the extent to which aspects of the stressor are controllable by the person who must experience it. Of these three proposed relationships, the strongest support has emerged for the predictability of a stressor. If the occurrence of a stressful event can be predicted, its absence can also be predicted. Thus, the individual knows when it is safe to relax and need not maintain a constant state of vigilance or anxiety.

Prevention and Intervention

Employee at computer work-station performs finger exercises to relieve stress.
SOURCE: CNN

This final category is not part of the model of organizational stress proposed by Kahn and Byosiere (1992), but it does represent a major professional activity in stress management. For the most part stress management has been concerned more with reducing the effects of stress than reducing the presence of stressors at work. As a consequence, the major effort has been directed at increasing individual resistance to stressors generated at work.

Stress management initiatives that are directed at *preventing* stress may include on-site physical fitness, exercise, meditation, and time management programs. Ross and Altmaier (1994) reported a growing use of techniques designed to lower arousal to stressors, such as deep breathing, progressive muscle relaxation, biofeedback, and yoga. Stress *intervention* initiatives most typically involve counseling, social support groups, and employee assistance programs.

In general both the quality and quantity of research on the effectiveness of stress management programs fall short of research on other aspects of stress. Nevertheless, there are indications that stress management programs are successful. Those programs in stress management that have been rigorously evaluated show significant reductions in subjective work stress and psychophysiological indicators. Their effects on job satisfaction and performance are less clear.

WORK/FAMILY CONFLICT

As Thomas and Ganster (1995) described, over the past two decades the American family has undergone significant structural and functional changes. These changes have not been accompanied by equally dramatic shifts in organizational policies. Although there are still families in which the father works outside the home while the mother stays home to care for the house and the children, many companies continue to be guided by traditional workplace policies that were fashioned when that was the predominant pattern. Today's diverse workplace is increasingly populated with women, single parents, and dual-career couples. The potential for conflict and stress increases as most workers struggle with the demands of balancing paid employment and home responsibilities. A graphic representation of the critical issues associated with changing social conditions and work experiences is presented in Figure 10–3 (Barling & Sorenson, 1997).

Interest in family-related issues by I/O psychologists is relatively new, manifesting itself primarily in the past 15 years. For many years we tended to limit our focus to work-related issues (e.g., tasks, jobs, occupations, organizations) and left the subject of domestic matters (e.g., family) to other areas of professional study. However, I/O psychologists began to see legitimate linkages or connections between the two spheres of work and family and thus have expanded our areas of inquiry. It is also a topic of interest internationally. Watanabe, Takahashi, and

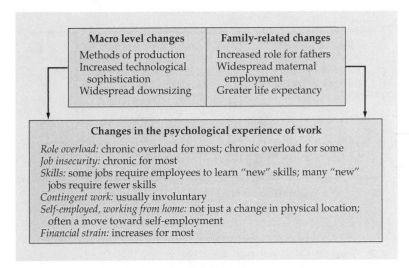

FIGURE 10–3   *Effects of social change on the experience of work*

SOURCE: From "Work and Family: In Search of a Relevant Research Agenda" by J. Barling and D. Sorenson, 1997, in *Creating Tomorrow's Organizations* (pp. 157–170), edited by C. L. Cooper and S. E. Jackson, New York: Wiley.

Minami (1997) discussed how Japanese families deal with work/family conflict. The following description was offered by a 35-year-old man:

> I am responsible for supporting my family. I leave home early in the morning and usually don't return until my kids are asleep. There is just no time for me to be with my kids. My only free time is on Sundays, but even then I may go play golf with my clients or colleagues. But you know, I don't do this for my own pleasure, but for my family. I think they [my wife and children] are grateful for the kind of life I am providing. Although I spend little time with my kids, I basically trust my wife when it comes to raising and educating them. (pp. 280–281)

The authors reported that the Japanese culture is finding it difficult to depart from their traditional view of men as the primary breadwinners while women stay home and raise children. However, they believe some Japanese families are moving away from the strict separation of male and female work/family roles.

Zedeck (1992) described the following three topics as targets of research in work/family conflict.

◆ *The effect of work on family.* This area examines what impact work factors have on family matters. To express this relationship in terms of research design, *work* is regarded as the independent variable, and *family* is the dependent variable. This perspective is most typical of I/O psychological research. A common finding is that aspects of work (such as job stress and work schedules) have negative effects on families.

◆ *The effect of family on work.* This perspective is the opposite of the former and generally focuses on how structural or developmental aspects of the family have an impact on work behavior. For example, some researchers have viewed family life as a "shock absorber" in that, if home life is positive, it blocks disappointment

DILBERT   by Scott Adams

SOURCE: Dilbert® reprinted by permission of United Feature Syndicate, Inc.

at work. Others view family responsibility as a major determinant of work absenteeism and tardiness.

◆ *The family–work interaction.* This third perspective views work and family as interacting and concludes that there is no simple or direct causal link between work and family matters. One view of the family–work interaction concerns the compatibility or incompatibility of family–work relationships and their impact on other processes, such as the transition between roles.

Regardless of which of these three perspectives is emphasized, researchers have offered conceptual models to explain the relationship between work and family. Three basic types of models have been proposed, and they represent different perspectives on how we fill both work and family roles.

◆ *Spillover model.* The spillover model asserts that there is similarity between what occurs in the work environment and what occurs in the family environment. It also proposes that a person's work experiences influence what he or she does away from work. It is assumed that attitudes at work become ingrained and carried over into home life, affecting a basic orientation toward the self and family members. In general, spillover is a notion of positive relationships between work and family variables such that an individual's satisfaction with work enhances family life.

◆ *Compensation model.* The compensation model is most often contrasted with the spillover model. It proposes an *inverse* relationship between work and family. It further assumes that individuals make differential investments of themselves in the two settings so that what is provided by one makes up for what is missing in the other. Thus, deprivations experienced in work are made up or compensated for in nonwork activities.

◆ *Segmentation model.* The segmentation model proposes that the work and nonwork spheres are distinct so that an individual can be successful in one without any influence on the other. The two spheres exist side by side and for all practical purposes are separated from each other. This separation, in type, space, or function, allows one to effectively compartmentalize one's life. The dominant view is that the family is the realm of intimacy and empathy, whereas the work world is impersonal and instrumental.

Barling (1990) observed a historical trend in when each of these three models was proposed. Barling concluded: (1) the suggestion that work and family affect each other had emerged by the 1930s; (2) the pervasive assumption during the 1950s was that work and family are independent; (3) by the 1970s the assumption was that work and family roles were intertwined; and (4) today there is considerable empirical evidence attesting to the overlap between work and family for most individuals.

However, none of the models clearly specifies the psychological processes by which work and family affect each other. Repetti (1987) addressed this shortcoming by proposing four processes through which work and family may be linked. One process is the direct transfer of mood from one sphere to another. Thus, if negative affect develops as a result of stressors in one sphere, it is subsequently transported to the other sphere. The second process is described through role conflict, which is based on the premise that people have limited supplies of physical, mental, and emotional resources and that work and family systems must strike a balance in their quest for such resources. The third process is a socialization process, whereby skills and values learned in one sphere, in which they are adaptive and functional, are applied in another setting. The fourth process is somewhat in opposition to the socialization process. Here the skills and values that assist functioning in one sphere do not generalize to the other. Repetti's processes underlying work–family linkages are primarily directed to the mechanisms of adaptation to stress and conflict.

Empirical tests of the three models have generally revealed some degree of support for each. Zedeck (1992) suggested the models need additional refinement and clarity to effectively assess their veracity. Among the unspecified questions underlying the models are these:

- Can more than one explanatory model be appropriate for the same individual? That is, can there be spillover for some aspects of the employing organization or family but compensation for others?
- If more than one model is applicable to an individual, can the models function simultaneously, or must they be sequential? That is, before there is compensation for some factors, do other factors need to have been spilled over?
- Do the models hold at different times or stages for individuals? Both work and family activities develop over time and pass through stages, such as initiation and maturity. What happens to the relationship between work and family if the stages of each are (or are not) synchronized?

Zedeck (1992) believes that reactions to work and nonwork are not totally stable but vary over time and conditions. Furthermore, the relationship is not the same across families. Friedman, Tucker, Neville, and Imperial (1996) offered this description of how the effects of domestic violence do not stay at home: "The battered woman who receives threatening calls or visits by her abuser at work, or who is suffering from the mental and physical bruises of the night before, is likely to have difficulty fulfilling her employer's expectations" (p. 153). However, as Adams, King, and King (1996) reported, the converse can also be true. They found that higher levels of family emotional support were associated with lower levels of family intervening with work. There also appear to be meaningful differences between men and women in the effect of work/family conflict on job and life satisfaction. Kossek and Ozeki (1998) reported a stronger correlation between work/family conflict and job satisfaction for women (−.35) than for men (−.29). Likewise, the correlation between work/family conflict and life satisfaction was stronger for women (−.42) than for men (−.32). Thus, there is a greater association for women than men in resolving issues of work/family conflict and feeling satisfaction.

Several researchers (e.g., Frone, Russell, & Cooper, 1992a) have proposed more specific models to address the relationship between work and family. One such model was developed by Howard (1992) and is presented in Figure 10–4. The model proposes that work and family are mirror images reflected along life's path. The two spheres are demarcated by the broad horizontal band that culminates in the hopeful expression of life satisfaction. The causal flow in Figure 10–4 is from left to right, beginning with individual characteristics and ultimately resulting in life satisfaction. In between are concepts pertaining to work and family experiences, involvement, and satisfaction. Howard conducted two major assessments of the model. One was of the model's *symmetry*, which meant that both work and family influences were comparable in affecting overall life satisfaction. The second assessment was the *consistency* of the relationship between work and family over the lifetime of the individual. The model was tested with a large sample of managers whose lives were followed over a 30-year period. Howard used a broad array of measures to assess the constructs in her study, such as stress, involvement, and satisfaction. The results revealed complex patterns between work and family over time. Work and family involvement were inversely related; greater absorption in work was accompanied by less involvement in the family. But work and family were found to move in the same direction at the crossroads of satisfaction and stress. Satisfaction with work generalized or spilled over into contentment with the family. However, the overall relationships between work and family were *not* found to be symmetrical, in that work involvement and satisfaction affected the family but the reverse was not true. Work had more influence on the family than vice versa. A similar conclusion was reached by Frone, Russell, and Cooper (1992b). The family may be as potent as work only when there is high stress. The opportunities that work provides encourage the development of new abilities. Involvement in the family domain can lead to satisfaction and a sense of peace; however, involvement in the work realm can escalate to even more work involvement and to neglect of the family domain. Left unchecked, the more work/less family spiral can lead to diminishing life returns or the phenomenon of career success and personal failure.

The managers in Howard's study were divided into four groups, based on high or low work involvement and high or low family involvement. Those managers who had advanced the farthest in the organizational hierarchy were characterized by high work involvement and low family involvement. Those managers who placed their families in the forefront paid a price in terms of advancement in management. The groups also differed in reports of opportunities missed in their career. The professionally successful high work–low family involvement group most often reported missed career opportunities, as if their desires for career challenge and success had become to some extent insatiable. The low work–low

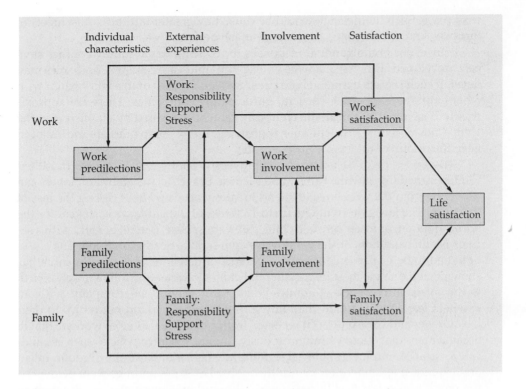

FIGURE 10–4 *Proposed model of work–family relationships*

SOURCE: Adapted from "Work and Family Crossroads Spanning the Career" by A. Howard, 1992, in *Work, Families, and Organizations* (pp. 70–137), edited by S. Zedeck, San Francisco: Jossey-Bass.

family involvement group was found to be the least adjusted, as they lacked the seriousness of purpose that would build commitments to either a career or family. In general, the results revealed that overall happiness in life can be attained through various combinations of work and family interests, and there is no one best approach to balancing work and family commitments.

Friedman and Galinsky (1992) noted some of the major changes in the labor force and how organizational efforts have had to change to recruit and retain a productive workforce. By the year 2000 about two-thirds of the new entrants into the workforce will be women, and about three-fourths of them will become pregnant at some point during their working years. More than half of these women will return to work before their child's first birthday. An estimated 20% of workers—mostly women—will be responsible for their aging parents. While women still perform most family tasks, 60% of men have wives who work.

The pressures of work and family are accelerating, and families, which already have borne the greater burden of conflicts experienced between home and work, can do little more to sustain the balance. Changes in the social pattern of worker participation have forced companies to make accommodations to their workers. These accommodations are directed toward reducing the conflict between home and family, which if unattended to, ultimately lead to lower efficiency in the workplace. Such inefficiency would be caused by greater tardiness, absenteeism, turnover, and stress-related decrements in job performance.

Four major organizational responses to reducing home/family conflict have been developed. The first is on-site or near-site child-care centers. Companies may develop such centers exclusively for their own employees or in a consortium with other employees for use by several participating companies. There are approximately 1,400 on-site or near-site child-care centers sponsored by employers in the United States. While their number is growing, many companies are too small to have the resources to provide such a center.

A second type of assistance to employees is family leave. In 1993 President Clinton signed into law the Family and Medical Leave Act, whereby employees can withdraw from the workforce to attend to family needs without risking the loss of their jobs. The law gives workers up to 12 weeks of unpaid leave each year for the birth, adoption, or foster care of a child; care for a spouse, parent, or child with a serious health condition; or the employee's own serious health condition. The law is designed to be of particular value to parents of newborn children. Research has shown that the single most important predictor of job retention following childbirth is the availability of job-guaranteed maternity leave. One company with an excellent leave policy found that only 5% of new mothers did not return to their jobs. Grover and Crooker (1995) reported from a national survey of workers that in organizations that offered family-responsive human resource policies such as child-care assistance, employees showed significantly higher organizational commitment and expressed less intention to quit their jobs. The same findings were evidenced for employees *without* children, which the authors interpreted as supporting the theory that offering assistance to employees in need symbolizes concern for employees and positively influences attachment to the organization.

While only a few hundred companies have responded to the elder-care needs of their employees, the number is likely to grow dramatically in the future. Caring for elderly relatives may be more complex than child care because it involves the coordination of a variety of social services, such as transportation, medical, legal, housekeeping, and personal services. Most of the companies that respond to employees' elder-care needs provide information and counseling about the array of available services. Some companies coordinate such services.

Finally, some use is being made of telecommuting—the arrangement to perform work at home. Such jobs often involve computer operations, but they need not be computer-based. The employees may perform work-at-home operations on an occasional basis to handle emergencies or planned-for family obligations. Companies carefully screen work-at-home candidates for initiative and ability to take responsibility, train participants, and often require regular time in the office to maintain communication. Parents who work at home acknowledge that this option does not preclude the need for child-care assistance. However, it does offer greater flexibility in balancing work and home obligations.

DUAL-CAREER FAMILIES

Balancing the demands of work and family can be an arduous task. Issues of adjustment can be further compounded when both partners have careers. Oakley

(1974) estimated that mothers with young children work an average of 77 hours per week in the home. Adding a career to that workload can create extraordinary pressures on both women and men to have fulfilling work and home lives.

Silberstein (1992) concluded that most dual-career couples have a work-oriented lifestyle prior to the birth of children. However, once there are children, the dual-career system undergoes a profound shift. The pragmatic demands of home life increase dramatically and cannot be postponed, rescheduled, or ignored. Both men and women attest that the arrival of children creates the greatest conflict between work and family. For the majority of both men and women, having children translates into fewer hours at work. However, the extent to which this occurred and the meanings of this shift differed for men and women. Karambayya and Reilly (1992), for example, reported that more women than men accommodated their careers to fit their families. The felt need to make an accommodation influenced the women's choice of a career (e.g., assuring a flexible schedule) or a work site. However, many women reported that their work environments were not willing or able to bend to the demands of family. Additionally, some women have described hostile reactions from work colleagues to pregnancies.

Men, on the other hand, tend to differentiate their feelings of conflict over family and career from their wives' feelings. This difference between husbands and wives stems from expectations in men that work is primarily for men and family is primarily for women. Silberstein (1992) offered the following statement from a man in his mid-30s:

> I have the suspicion that it's more difficult for a woman. If you're a traditional, career-oriented man, you're supposed to spend a lot of time in the office, and bring work home, and commute long distances. And the man has less time for the family, which is not a good thing, but that's how it is traditionally. Whereas for a woman, there's always the other side of the mirror, which is the woman who is at home, spending hours and hours with her children, and is always there when they need her. And that imposes some degree of guilt on a woman who is successful in her career. (p. 100)

Silberstein (1992) reported that the difference in the degree that wives and husbands accommodate their careers for children has become a central marital tension. Differential investment in career and family is the recurrent issue in arguments, and it demands constant renegotiation. In the dual-career marriage, both spouses arrive at their own definition of what is required for work success and what level of involvement in the family feels right. Each partner, therefore, argues from personal experience about the appropriate balance of work and family, whereas in the one-career marriage, the spheres of wife and husband are less comparable.

Dual-career couples often cite a lack of temporal control over their lives. There appears to be insufficient time to fulfill the obligations of both work and family. The creation of time schedules to coordinate activities can be facilitative, but adherence to the schedules can be a source of tension in itself. Other time-related issues pertain to the lack of personal time for individual activity (such as recreation or leisure) and coordinated social activities. Time constraints are also associated with reformulating role activities in the marriage, such as the division of domestic labor. The lack of time contributes to a couple's decision to seek external support services such as child care and assistance with household chores.

Field Note 3   *Recruitment of Dual-Career Couples*

The profusion of dual-career couples has spawned a new dimension in personnel recruitment. Dual-career couples are often reluctant to move unless there are meaningful jobs for both members. Organizations that seek to attract one member are at a strategic advantage if they can help secure a job for the other member. Some organizations, particularly in urban areas, have formed networks or alliances to help recruit dual-career couples. One member of the couple will work for one organization in the network, while the second member will work for another organization in the network. Organizations in the network represent various industries as a way to increase the likelihood of job placement.

It is rare that both members of the dual-career couple will get their first choice of a job in this fashion, but it does help to ensure they both will find something satisfactory. Participating organizations benefit as well by increasing the likelihood of sustained employment by the member. A major reason for turnover among dual-career couples is that one member can't find a good job. By forming a recruitment alliance, organizations enhance their own positions. The recruitment of dual-career couples through organizational alliances represents an unusual example of not only interorganizational but also interindustry cooperation.

In examining the benefits and costs of dual-career marriages, Silberstein (1992) reported that most marriages are aided by the self-fulfillment each spouse derives from the pursuit of a career. Each spouse experiences an independent source of self-esteem, and they benefit as a couple from the combined stimulation of each partner's work life (see Field Note 3). Both partners are also likely to feel that each is contributing in a similar fashion to the welfare of the marriage. However, the costs of dual careers are also considerable, with most sacrifices being associated with losses of time and energy. In particular, dual-career couples are likely to save the least amount of time and energy for their own personal relationship, after attending to the demands of work, children, and the managerial aspects of domestic life. This sentiment was expressed by a woman in her early 40s:

> I hesitate to use the analogy, but right now I feel we are more business partners than husband and wife. It's like we operate this small corporation together, but the intimate aspect is somewhat lacking. (Silberstein, 1992, p. 147)

THE PSYCHOLOGICAL EFFECTS OF UNEMPLOYMENT

As was discussed in Chapter 9, the possibility of job loss is a major concern for the contemporary worker. Thousands of employees lose their jobs annually through layoffs and organizational downsizing. Perilous economic conditions have resulted in large-scale job loss both domestically and globally. What have we learned about the meaning of work to individuals as a result of involuntary unemployment? This chapter will conclude with a discussion of the psychological effects of unemployment.

Jahoda (1981) asserted that being employed has both intended and unintended consequences for the individual. Earning a living is the most obvious intended consequence of employment, but the primary psychological meaning of work derives from the unintended or latent consequences. There are five important latent consequences of employment: (1) imposition of a time structure on the waking day, (2) regular shared experiences and contacts with people outside the nuclear family, (3) the linking of individuals to goals and purposes, (4) the definition of aspects of personal status and identity, and (5) the enforcement of activity. Jahoda claimed that these unintended consequences of employment "meet human needs of an enduring kind." Accordingly, when one is unemployed and is deprived of these functions, one's enduring human needs are unsatisfied. It is thus argued that employment is the major institution in society that reliably and effectively provides these supports to psychological well-being.

Fryer and Payne (1986) offered a somewhat different explanation for why unemployment is psychologically devastating based upon a loss of discretionary control. Their explanation is heavily tied to the loss of income associated with unemployment. Financial problems are an outstanding worry for most unemployed people, and lack of money is one of the underlying causes of problems in maintaining relationships. While the loss of adequate income is certain for most unemployed people, there is also uncertainty about how long the low income will persist. The poor resources of the unemployed cause them to have much less discretion or freedom to pursue various decision options, such as food or clothes to purchase. The act of choosing is severely restricted by unemployment. Attempting to solve problems with limited resources frequently means that the quality of the solution is poorer, which can engender a sense of failure and lowered self-esteem. Thus, the loss of financial resources limits choices, thereby enhancing feelings of limited control over one's life. In turn, lowered psychological health follows from this condition.

The explanations offered by both Jahoda (1981) and Fryer and Payne (1986) are represented in Warr's (1987) nine environmental factors needed for mental health (listed at the beginning of this chapter). A loss of employment has been found to trigger changes in eight of the nine environmental determinants of psychological well-being.

Wanberg (1997) reported that the act of job seeking can have a negative effect on mental health. Job search involves putting oneself on the line and dealing with feelings about being judged harshly, evaluated critically, and ultimately being rejected. Wanberg believes the best intervention programs for unemployed individuals incorporate exercises that promote feelings of self-esteem, optimism, and control as well as job-seeking skills.

The opportunity for control is clearly lessened by unemployment. Lack of success in job seeking, the inability to influence employers, and increased dependence on social welfare programs all reduce people's ability to control what happens to them. The opportunity to use skills is also likely to be reduced during unemployment. Occupational skills are generally not used during unemployment, although there may be opportunities to use certain skills in domestic activities. People who become unemployed from jobs that demand a high level of skill are likely to suffer a greater reduction in this feature than people whose previous employment required only limited skill. Unemployment reduces externally generated goals because fewer demands are placed on the individual. Since external demands are often linked to particular points (such as family meal times or the start of a workday), a general reduction in demands is often accompanied by a loss of temporal differentiation. Time markers that break up the day or week and indicate one's position in it are no longer as frequent or urgent.

An unemployed person loses variety by having to leave the house less often and also lacking the contrast between job and nonjob activities. Those domestic demands that impinge on the person are likely to be similar and unchanging from day to day, with standard routines and an absence of novelty. Environmental clarity is also likely to be reduced during unemployment. Information relating to the future permits planning within predictable time schedules and reduces the anxiety typically generated by uncertainty. Planning for the future is difficult in view of uncertainty about one's occupational or financial position in the months to come. Payment for work is at the heart of the employment contract, and the standard of living of almost all adults below retirement age is principally determined by income received from a job. Unemployment removes that income and in almost all cases has a serious and wide-ranging impact on the availability of money.

Physical security is usually associated with the availability of money. There appears to be a general need for some personal and private territory that contributes to a stable self-concept and enhanced well-being. Reduced income can give rise to loss of adequate housing or the threat that this will happen. The only determinant of mental health that appears primarily unaffected by unemployment is the opportunity for interpersonal contact. Younger and middle-aged unemployed individuals typically report no change in the amounts of interpersonal contact they have before and after job loss. Some research findings (e.g., Warr & Payne, 1983) indicated that social contacts even *increase* in frequency for these groups during unemployment. They report spending more time with neighbors and family members. However, older individuals (particularly women) report a reduction in social contacts after becoming unemployed, typically spending their days alone at home. On becoming unemployed, a person loses a socially approved role and the positive self-evaluations that go with it. The new position is widely felt to be of lower prestige, deviant, second rate, or not providing full membership in society. Even when social welfare benefits remove the worst financial hardships, there may be shame attached to receiving funds from public sources and a seeming failure to provide for one's family.

Based upon these assessments provided by Warr (1987), there is a strong linkage between unemployment and mental health. Work provides a sense of meaning and purpose to life, and the removal of that purpose lowers the quality of life. The next section will examine how unemployment affects four subgroups of the population: middle-aged men, women, teenagers, and the long-term unemployed.

Middle-Aged Men.   Research (e.g., Jackson & Warr, 1984; Warr & Jackson, 1985) has consistently revealed the negative impact of unemployment on the affective well-being of middle-aged men, especially those with families in need of financial support. The financial demands of middle-aged men are likely to be particularly great, as many of them have growing children in need of support. Middle-aged men's social position is also strongly affected by unemployment because they lose their valued role as providers for the family in addition to their positions as contributors to a work group. Their uncertainty about the future produces ambiguity that extends into the lives of all family members. Plans can be made less easily, and the future is less clearly predictable. Wanberg, Watt, and Rumsey (1996) found that older individuals who engaged in frequent job seeking were less likely to find work than younger individuals who engaged in frequent job seeking. Generally older, more experienced individuals command higher salaries, which decrease their employment prospects compared to younger individuals.

Women.   Historically, more men than women have been the subjects of unemployment research. Nevertheless, research indicates that the impact of unemployment on affective well-being is as negative for women as it is for men. The findings for women are somewhat complicated by marital status and role as a primary wage earner. Women who are unmarried or are primary wage earners respond to unemployment in a fashion similar to men. However, women who are married and are not primary wage earners may experience somewhat different responses to unemployment, as they do to employment. The primary differences involve the factors of esteem and externally generated goals. Esteem from one's social position does not always increase after a married woman gets a job. This depends both upon the nature of her employed role and upon the attitude taken by important people in her life. Married women whose domestic environments make few demands on them are likely to have their mental health enhanced by employment. In contrast, married women whose home environments are already very demanding are likely to suffer from the addition of job-related goals.

Leana and Feldman (1991) reported that women were not less traumatized by job loss than men, and there were no substantial differences between men and women in psychological and behavioral stress symptoms. There were differences, however, in how each group coped with the job loss. Men relied more on problem-focused activities such as job search, whereas women relied more on social support.

Teenagers.   The position of unemployed teenagers compared to middle-aged people is less problematic. Teenagers have relatively good opportunities for interpersonal contact, as they often maintain a network of friends and established patterns of leisure activities. Their financial requirements are generally less than those of older groups. Although unemployed teenagers experience the lack of valued social position that is common during unemployment at all ages, they may see themselves as members of a large group of unemployed youth who have been victimized by conditions beyond their control. Because of the widespread unemployment of teenagers, personal responsibility and social stigma are liable to be less strongly felt. Winefield, Tiggemann, and Winefield (1992), for example, reported that teenagers who gave externally based justifications for their unemployment displayed higher self-esteem and less hopelessness than those who gave internal justifications (i.e., they felt responsible for their unemployed status).

Despite these conditions, unemployment has a significant negative impact on teenagers' affective well-being. However, those components of mental health that explicitly involve behavior in social roles—autonomy, competence, and aspiration—appear to be of greatest concern. Gaining a job has special significance for adolescents, marking the end of childhood dependence and entry into the adult world. Independence is enhanced through the income provided by employment. Autonomy is thus retarded by joblessness after leaving school. The development of competence may also be inhibited, as new skills acquired from a job are denied to teenagers who fail to obtain paid work. There is also the fear that aspirations will be stunted as teenagers without paid work become adjusted to a relatively inactive life. The loss of aspiration in teenagers has generally not been supported by research, but the impact of teenage unemployment on autonomy and competence appears harmful.

The Long-Term Unemployed.   Warr (1987) reported that 40% of unemployed people in Britain had been continuously out of paid work for more than one year and 25% had been continuously unemployed for more than two years. Research has indicated that the impact of job loss on affective well-being is typically rapid. Further deterioration is likely in the period after job loss, until a plateau of poor mental health is reached between three and six months. This pattern is particularly marked for middle-aged men. The time frame for impaired mental health for unemployed teenagers appears to be longer. Winefield and Tiggemann (1990) reported that Australian teenagers did not exhibit substantially lower self-esteem or affective well-being after two years of unemployment compared to when they were students in school. However, after the third year of unemployment the mental health of the teenagers deteriorated markedly. Related findings were reported by Schaufeli and Van Yperen (1992) for a sample of Dutch teenagers. In general it appears that overall levels of mental health among the long-term unemployed are particularly low, and that their environments in terms of the nine features proposed by Warr (1987) remain chronically impoverished.

A closing note on the national origins of unemployment research is in order. It will be recalled from Chapter 2 that research topics in I/O psychology often emerge out of experience with practical problems. The vast majority of high-quality research on the psychological effects of unemployment has been conducted by international researchers, most notably in Great Britain (Warr) and Australia (Winefield). One reason for this is that unemployment rates are often higher in countries other than the United States. Warr (1987) also noted there are cultural differences in the availability of public money for the unemployed. For example, welfare benefits continue indefinitely in Great Britain and Australia, whereas in the United States substantial reductions occur after six or nine months. Furthermore, the long-term effects of unemployment and the costs associated with government subsidies have become the basis for legislative changes regarding welfare reform.

CONCLUDING COMMENTS

Work stress not only is a frequent problem for employees but also appears to be more and more accepted as part of the price individuals pay for employment. The fact that stress management programs are directed not at making work less stressful but at increasing our capacity to deal with stress suggests that few people believe stress can be eliminated or drastically reduced from work. As discussed in Chapter 9, one of the consequences of organizational downsizing is that fewer employees have to do the work that was once performed by a greater number of employees. The prevailing sentiment is that organizations are expected to do more (work) with less (resources). Technological advances (particularly relating to computer-based operations) have also accelerated the speed at which work is performed. These changes have the potential to diminish overall mental health by reducing autonomy or control and thus worker self-esteem (Locke, McClear, & Knight, 1996). In the evolution of work design, employees are becoming increasingly controlled by situational factors, as opposed to exerting control over their own work environments. As research on mental health and stress has revealed, the reduction in self-regulation (i.e., feeling "out of control") impairs psychological well-being (Murphy, Hurrell, & Quick, 1992). Rather than denying the reality of work stress or assuming no responsibility for it, organizations are becoming increasingly committed to addressing it. The annual health care costs in this country alone exceed $500 billion, with business paying about half the cost. The annual cost of stress-related illnesses to the American economy is estimated to be $150 billion (Joure, Leon, Simpson, Holley, & Frye, 1989). It is simply cheaper to promote healthful behavior than to pay the costs associated with not promoting it.

CASE STUDY ◆ Two Siblings, Two Lifestyles

Joe Vesco rarely got to see his older sister, Rita. Although they lived only 70 miles apart, their visits seemed limited to family holidays. Rita was 31, married, and had two boys, ages 6 and 3. She was a supervisor for a telemarketing company, overseeing the work of 15 sales agents. Rita put in long hours, typically 50–60 hours per week. She frequently worked until 8:00 P.M. because many sales calls were made in the early evening. She had a departmental sales quota to reach and also had to monitor the individual sales quotas of each of her agents. Work was very stressful. She also experienced considerable guilt and anxiety over how her work-life was affecting her family. Her husband picked the children up from day care and fed them dinner. The younger child was often asleep before Rita arrived home. She and her husband had discussed at length whether Rita should look for another job with more conventional hours. It always seemed to come down to money. They needed both incomes to maintain their family, and Rita's job paid particularly well. She was paid partly on commission, and because she frequently exceeded her department's sales quota, Rita received about 20% additional income over her base salary. No other job would pay as well.

Joe had a very different life. He was single, 24, and worked as a surveyor for the county. He had his own apartment, just recently purchased his first new car, and loved his independence. His job didn't pay very well, but the hours were stable. He left work every day at 4:30. Joe didn't worry about being fired or losing his job. The county employed only a few surveyors, and no one could remember anyone in his department ever being fired or laid off. It was a highly secure job, but not very challenging. Joe didn't think he would make a career out of the job, but for the present it suited him very well.

Joe and Rita got together at their parents' anniversary party. Joe hadn't seen Rita for quite some time and was surprised at how stressed out she looked. He remembered his sister as always being a stabilizing influence on him while they were growing up. She always seemed to be in control of her life. That apparent control, whether real or just imagined by Joe, was no longer evident. Rita complained about not being able to leave her work problems at work; she worried about her children while at work. She acknowledged taking medication to help her get to sleep, which had never been a problem before. Rita also talked about going back to smoking, after having given up cigarettes for almost seven years.

Joe reflected on his own life in comparison to his sister's. He didn't make nearly the money she did, but his biggest concern in life seemed to be which sporting event he would watch on TV when he came home from work. And car payments. Joe remembered his own mother always being home when he got back from school. He wondered how his nephews would respond to their mother's absence after school. Joe concluded that Rita was wondering the same thing.

Questions
1. What are the primary sources of work/family conflict in Rita's life?
2. To what degree does gender play a role in Rita's work/family conflict? Why?
3. What are the rewards and drawbacks for both Rita and Joe in the jobs they hold?
4. To what do you attribute the difference in lifestyle between Joe and Rita: age, gender, marital status, children, income?
5. Do you think Rita made a conscious choice to pursue her lifestyle, or do you think she was subtly drawn into it over time? What does your answer suggest about the nature of work/family conflict?

INFOTRAC ARTICLES

1. *Across the Board,* Oct 1997 v34 n9 p16(8)
   Soul searching: Looking for meaning in the workplace. A. J. Vogl
   Discusses the topic of spirituality in the workplace and explains its role in contributing to overall mental health.
2. *Net Statesmen & Society,* June 9, 1995 v8 n356 p26(2)
   Feel-bad factor. Paul Lashmar
   Discusses the link between increased job insecurity and decreased mental health among workers in Great Britain.
3. *Executive Female,* July–August 1995 v18 n4 p35(6)
   Till careers do us part. Michelle Harris
   A discussion of creative solutions several couples have found that allowed them to keep both marriage and family.
4. *Training & Development,* Nov 1997 v51 n11 p76(5)
   De-stress for success. Sacha Cohen
   Discusses strategies employees can follow to reduce stress in their worklives pertaining to career pressure, lack of sleep, heavy workloads, and so on.

5. *Success,* Jan 1998 v45 n1 p59(5)
   Is there sex after success?
   A discussion of how the hectic worklife of some successful business executives interferes with their sex lives.
6. *Across the Board,* Jan 1995 v32 n1 p11(2)
   The politics of couples. Marilyn Moats Kennedy
   Discusses issues associated with the same organization employing both members of a dual-career couple.
7. *Executive Female,* May–June 1996 v19 n3 p52(4)
   The trouble with husbands. Michele Morris
   Describes the responses of several women whose husbands lost their jobs and ways they have coped with their husbands' unemployment.
8. *Across the Board,* Feb 1999 v36 i2 p36(7)
   Workplace stress. James Krohe, Jr.
   Discusses three options organizations face in combating workplace stress: look for stress-relief methods, make people more tolerant of stress, and change the organization to make it less stressful.

Work Motivation

MAJOR CHAPTER OBJECTIVES

◆ Explain five critical concepts central to work motivation.

◆ Understand the conceptual basis and degree of empirical support for these work motivation theories: need hierarchy, equity, expectancy, reinforcement, and goal setting.

◆ Provide an overview and synthesis of the work motivation theories.

◆ Give practical examples of applying motivational strategies.

Motivation is not directly observable; it must be inferred. Motivational processes can be inferred from an analysis of a continuous stream of behaviors that are determined by both environment and heredity and are observed through their effects on personality, beliefs, knowledge, abilities, and skills.

Work motivation refers to the domain of motivational processes directed to the realm of work. Pinder (1998) offered this definition:

> **Work motivation** is a set of energetic forces that originate both within as well as beyond an individual's being, to initiate work-related behavior, and to determine its form, direction, intensity, and duration. (p. 11)

There are three noteworthy components to this definition. First, *direction* addresses the choice of activities we make in expending effort. That is, we might choose to work diligently at some tasks and not at others. Second, *intensity* implies we have the potential to exert various levels of effort, depending on how much we need to expend. Third, *duration* reflects persistence of motivation over time, as opposed to a one-time choice between courses of action (direction) or high levels of effort aimed at a single task (intensity). A comprehensive understanding of work motivation requires an integration of these concepts (see Field Note 1).

FIVE CRITICAL CONCEPTS IN MOTIVATION

It is relatively easy to misunderstand or confuse several concepts critical to work motivation. The distinctions among these concepts are not always discernable, or at the least they can become blurred. To help you differentiate them throughout the chapter, five critical concepts will be articulated next.

Field Note 1   *Three Dimensions of Motivation*

Motivation can be conceptualized along three dimensions: direction, intensity, and persistence. Each dimension has its associated issues and concerns. In an employment context, each dimension is highly relevant to both the organization and the individual. *Direction* pertains to those activities in life to which you direct your energy. Organizations want employees who will direct themselves to their work responsibilities, and many employees want jobs that will inspire their motivation and commitment. *Intensity* pertains to the amount of motivation that is expended in pursuit of an activity. Organizations want employees who will exhibit high levels of energy. Such people are often referred to as "self-starters" or "self-motivated" individuals, implying they bring a high level of energy to the job and do not require organizational inducements to work hard. Likewise, many employees hope to find jobs that are sufficiently appealing to invite large commitments of energy. The third dimension, *persistence*, pertains to sustained energy over time. It is concerned with how long the energy will be expended. Researchers know the least about this dimension, but it is the focus of more recent motivational theories. You can think of a career as an interrelated series of jobs through which individuals manifest their energies over a working lifetime. Organizations want employees who will persevere through good times and bad. Likewise, employees want jobs that will sustain their interests over the long haul. Each of the three dimensions of motivation has direct implications for both organizations and individuals.

Behavior. Behavior is the action from which we infer motivation. The behavior in question may be typing speed, firing a rifle at a target, or any of a broad constellation of human activities.

Performance. Performance entails some evaluation of behavior. The basic unit of observation is behavior, but coupled with the behavior is an assessment of the behavior as judged against some standard. Thus, if the behavior is typing 60 words per minute, a judgment can be made as to whether this *level of performance* is adequate or inadequate to hold a job. Thus, the behavior is appraised within some organizational context, and 60 words per minute might represent adequate performance in some jobs and inadequate performance in others. Most organizational theories tend to be concerned with performance, not just behavior. Performance, however, is determined by factors that transcend behavior.

Ability. Ability is one of three determinants of behavior. It is generally regarded as fairly stable within individuals and may be represented by a broad construct like intelligence or a more specific construct like physical coordination.

Situational constraints. Situational constraints are the second determinant of behavior. They are environmental factors and opportunities that facilitate or retard behavior (and ultimately performance). Examples include tools, equipment, procedures, and the like, which if present, facilitate behavior, and if absent, diminish it. If no situational constraints are present, it is possible to maximize behavior. Individual behavior manifests itself in some environmental or situational context that influences the conduct of behavior but is beyond the control of the individual.

Motivation. Motivation is the third determinant of behavior. You can think of ability as reflecting what you *can* do, motivation as what you *will* do (given your ability), and the situational constraints as what you are *allowed* to do. Each of the three components is critical to the manifestation of behavior. Maximum behavior is observed when a person has high ability, exhibits high motivation, and is in an environment that is supportive of such behavior. The judgment of "poor performance" could be attributed to four factors. First, the organization in which the behavior occurs may have high standards, which in another organization may result in a more positive evaluation of the behavior. Second, the individual may lack the needed ability to exhibit the desired behavior. (I was never very good at catching fly balls in baseball.) Third, the individual may lack the motivation to exhibit the desired behavior. (Countless hours of practice didn't seem to enhance my ball-catching behavior.) Fourth, the individual may lack the needed equipment or opportunity to exhibit the behavior. (An expensive new baseball glove didn't help either.)

WORK MOTIVATION THEORIES

Over the past 35 years there has been a profusion of work motivation theories. The theories offer markedly different explanations for the same aspect of human

FRANK AND ERNEST   by Bob Thaves

I THINK OF
MYSELF AS BEING
IN MOTIVATION
RESEARCH -- EVERY
MORNING I
WONDER WHY I
GO TO WORK.

SOURCE: Reprinted by permission of Newspaper Enterprise Association, Inc.

behavior. That is, work motivation theories have been proposed from environmental, social, dispositional, and cognitive perspectives. In the past five to ten years, however, attempts have been made to identify consistency in the psychological constructs that underlie the theories. As will be witnessed, certain psychological constructs coalesce more readily across theories than others.

Five different theories of work motivation will be presented here. They differ markedly in the psychological constructs that are hypothesized to account for motivation. Each theory will be presented in three sections: a statement of the theory, empirical tests, and an evaluation. At the conclusion of this presentation, there will be a discussion of points of convergence among the theories and the fundamental perspectives that have been taken in addressing work motivation.

Need Hierarchy Theory

Statement of the Theory.   One of the major theories of motivation was developed by Abraham Maslow. It is called the **need hierarchy theory.** Most of Maslow's writing was not concerned with work motivation. Only later in his career did he become interested in applications of his theory. Most of its uses were derived from other researchers' examinations of its relevance for organizations.

According to Maslow (1987), the source of motivation is certain needs. Needs are biological or instinctive; they characterize humans in general and have a genetic base. They often influence behavior unconsciously. What causes people to behave as they do is the process of satisfying these needs. Once a need is satisfied, it no longer dominates behavior, and another need rises to take its place. Need fulfillment is never ending. Life is thus a quest to satisfy needs.

Much of Maslow's theory identifies needs, but the second component explains how the needs relate to one another. Maslow proposed five types of needs: physiological, safety, social, self-esteem, and self-actualization. Physiological needs are the most basic; their fulfillment is necessary for survival. They include the need for air, water, and food. Safety needs include freedom from threat, danger, and deprivation. They involve self-preservation. Today most of our safety needs are met, but people experiencing disasters like hurricanes or riots have their safety needs threatened. Social needs include the desire for association, belonging, and companionship. These involve an individual's ability to exist in harmony with others.

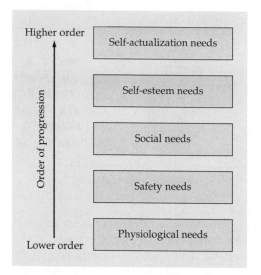

FIGURE 11–1   *Maslow's need hierarchy*

SOURCE: From *Motivation and Personality* (3rd ed.) by A. H. Maslow, 1987, New York: Harper & Row.

Self-esteem needs include self-confidence, recognition, appreciation, and the respect of one's peers. Satisfaction of these needs results in a sense of adequacy; their thwarting produces feelings of inferiority and helplessness. The last type of need is self-actualization, the best known and least understood in Maslow's scheme. Self-actualization is realization of one's full potential—in Maslow's words, "to become more and more what one is, to become everything that one is capable of becoming."

As mentioned, the second part of the theory concerns how these needs are related. According to Maslow, they exist in a hierarchy. At the base are the physiological needs, which must be met first and continuously. The remaining needs are placed in order, culminating with the highest need, self-actualization. Physiological and safety needs are referred to as basic needs; social, self-esteem, and self-actualization needs are higher-order needs. The need hierarchy theory is illustrated in Figure 11–1.

Maslow made these propositions about the need hierarchy:

- ◆ Behavior is dominated and determined by the needs that are unfulfilled.
- ◆ An individual will systematically satisfy his or her needs by starting with the most basic and working up the hierarchy.
- ◆ Basic needs take precedence over all those higher in the hierarchy.

The first proposition is fundamental: Once a need is fulfilled, it no longer motivates behavior. A hungry person seeks food, but once the hunger is satisfied, it does not dominate behavior. The second proposition involves fulfillment progression. A person progresses through the needs in order, moving on to the next one only after the preceding one has been fulfilled. We all spend our lives trying to fulfill these needs because, according to Maslow, only a small percentage of people have fulfilled the self-actualization need. Maslow also said this need can never be fully satisfied. The third proposition stresses that the needs basic to survival always have a higher priority.

Maslow's theory has several implications for work behavior. When pay and security are poor, employees will focus on those aspects of work necessary to fulfill their basic needs. As conditions improve, the behavior of supervisors and their relationship with the individual take on increased importance. Finally, with a much improved environment, the supervisor's role diminishes and the nature of the work reemerges. Work is now important in self-actualization and not in fulfilling basic needs.

The theory also predicts that as people move up in the management hierarchy, they are motivated by increasingly higher-level needs; thus, managers at various levels should be treated differently. Additionally, employees can be expected to always want more. The organization can never give enough in terms of individual growth and development. It is the nature of the self-actualization need that once it is activated and satisfied, it stimulates an even greater desire for satisfaction. Thus, it is a continuing source of motivation.

Empirical Tests of the Theory.   The ultimate test of any theory is empirical support, but a problem with Maslow's theory involves measuring the variables. Because he did not provide operational definitions of his variables, other researchers must measure them and test the theory.

Betz (1984) found mixed support for the theory. On the negative side, she found that need importance was not related to need deficiency. Yet, as the theory predicts, Betz found a positive correlation between need fulfillment and life satisfaction. Wahba and Bridwell (1976) reviewed all earlier research on Maslow's theory. They concluded that the theory has received little clear or consistent support. Some of Maslow's propositions were totally rejected; others received mixed or questionable support. The most support was for the importance of the basic needs; the least evidence was for the higher-level needs. The number of needs appeared questionable, as did the idea of fulfillment progression.

Evaluation of the Theory.   It is tempting to dismiss most of Maslow's theory, given the lack of support, but a few points suggest a more positive verdict. First, it is not a "theory" in the usual sense; Maslow did not propose testable hypotheses. As Wahba and Bridwell (1976) said, "Maslow's need hierarchy theory is almost a nontestable theory" (p. 234). It was based on logical and clinical insights into human nature rather than on research findings. Furthermore, Maslow did not discuss any guidelines for empirical tests of his theory. Many questions remain, and the way the theory is tested is open to interpretation. For example, what is the time span for the unfolding of the hierarchy? Is there a relationship between age and the need we are trying to satisfy? How does the shift from one need to another take place? Do people also seek to fulfill needs by going down the hierarchy? These questions are very important; they affect how we would use the theory in the work environment.

The theory's vagueness also leaves some nagging issues unanswered. According to Maslow, we systematically progress from one need to the next. Yet we all need to eat, drink, and breathe every day. We never really have our physio-logical needs satisfied. We try to fulfill our self-esteem needs even when our social needs are not fully satisfied. Rather than going through the hierarchy in stages, perhaps we attempt to satisfy all needs concurrently. Maslow did not deal with this speculation.

Pinder (1998) asked whether there is such a thing as a *hierarchy* of needs. There is evidence that different needs exist. However, there is much less empirical sup-port that these needs vary in their relative importance so consistently across indi-viduals that a generalizable hierarchy exists. Such a hierarchy ignores substantial differences among people at various stages in their lives. However, there are some consistencies among people at various life and career stages in the desires they ex-press on the job. It may be that a universal hierarchy of needs is not as valid as a need theory that takes individual and organizational circumstances into account.

Maslow's theory, a highly abstract statement about humankind, is far more philosophical than empirical. But his notion of self-actualization is well ingrained in the way we think about our mission in life. His writing has generated a great deal of thought about the nature of humankind in general. While Maslow's theory is deficient in explaining day-to-day behavior at work, his contributions to the field of psychology as a whole should not be ignored.

Equity Theory

Statement of the Theory.   Adams (1965) proposed a theory of work motivation drawn from the principle of social comparison. How hard a person is willing to work is a function of comparisons with the efforts of others. The theory has per-ceptual and social bases because motivation is a function of how a person sees himself or herself in comparison with others. Adams suggested that motivation has a social rather than biological origin.

Equity theory has four major parts:

1. Because it is a perceptually based theory, the individual perceives himself or herself in comparison with others. The person who does the perceiving is called *Person*.
2. It is postulated that Person compares himself or herself with another indi-vidual. This other person is called *Other*.
3. All of the assets Person brings to the job are the third component; collec-tively, these assets are referred to as *Inputs*. Inputs include Person's educa-tion, intelligence, experience, skill, seniority, effort level, health, and so on. They are anything of perceived value or importance that Person brings to the job.
4. All benefits Person derives from the job are the fourth component, collec-tively referred to as *Outcomes*. Outcomes include pay, benefits, working conditions, status symbols, seniority benefits, and so forth. They are those factors Person perceives as being derived from employment.

The theory states that Person forms a ratio of his or her inputs to outcomes and compares it with perceptions of Other's inputs/outcomes ratio. Adams assumes that people can quantify both their inputs and outcomes into common scale units.

For example, Person will consider all the inputs she brings to the job; let us say they total 50. Person will assess her outcomes in the same manner; again let us assume they total 50 units. Person's ratio is therefore 50:50. Person then compares her ratio with what she perceives Other is putting into his job and deriving in outcomes from it. Let us assume Person assesses Other's inputs and outcomes to be 50 units each. We now have two ratios as assessed by Person:

Person, 50:50   Other, 50:50

The equality of the ratios as perceived by Person represents *equity* (literally, "fair"). If Person perceives Other as deriving 200 units of outcomes from his job (due to more pay and higher status) but also contributing 200 units of inputs (due to more education and more experience), then this also represents equity to her. Other is getting more out of the job than Person but is also putting more into it; that is, 50:50 equals 200:200.

What happens if Person's ratio is different from Other's—that is, 50:50 versus 50:75? Both Person and Other are perceived as contributing the same amount of inputs (50 units), but Other is deriving more outcomes (75 units). According to Adams, this situation represents *inequity*, or "unfairness," in the sense that Person perceives Other to be getting more out of the job, although both are contributing the same number of inputs.

According to Adams, feelings of inequity cause tension, which Person will be motivated to reduce. The greater the inequity between Person and Other, the greater the tension and the greater the motivation to reduce it. Thus, for Adams, the source of motivation is feelings of tension caused by perceived inequity. Feelings of inequity are necessary for motivation to occur because if Person perceives herself as being in an equitable relationship with Other, she will not be motivated.

Adams proposed two types of inequity. *Underpayment* is when Person perceives herself as deriving fewer outcomes from a job than Other, when both are contributing comparable inputs. An example of underpayment inequity is

Person, 50:50   Other, 50:75

Overpayment is when Person perceives herself as deriving more outcomes from a job than Other, when both are contributing comparable inputs. An example of overpayment inequity is

Person, 50:75   Other, 50:50

Adams felt that people could alter their motivation levels in an attempt to bring feelings of inequity back into line. The drive to reduce the tension caused by inequity manifests itself in more or less effort being put into the job, which is a form of input. Adams said that how inequity is reduced is a function of the method of payment: hourly (wages determined per unit of time, such as $6 per hour) or piece rate (wages determined per unit of production, such as 25 cents per object).

Most research on equity theory was conducted in laboratory or field experiments. To test the theory, researchers induced feelings of overpayment and underpayment in the subjects by using the following types of manipulations: The experimenter, posing as a manager or supervisor of some fictitious company, placed an ad in a local newspaper announcing part-time job openings. At the employment interview, subjects (who did not know this was a psychology experiment) were told the job paid a certain hourly rate (such as $6 per hour) or piece rate (such as 25 cents per object produced). They then started work at this rate. After a few days the experimenter said, "We just received a large contract from the government, and we can now pay you more money. Starting tomorrow, you will make eight dollars per hour (or forty cents per object)." This manipulation was meant to induce feelings of overpayment. Subjects would be paid more for doing the same job. To induce feelings of underpayment, the experimenter said, "We have just experienced a major cutback in financial support due to the loss of a contract. Starting tomorrow, we can pay you only two dollars per hour (or fifteen cents per object)." These experimental instructions were given to some subjects but not others. Thus, some people would work at the "new" rate, and others would continue to work at the original rate. The first few days of employment were designed to set base rate expectations about the job. After this period, the amount of compensation for the same work went either up (in the overpayment condition) or down (in the underpayment condition). The question to be answered was, What would these people do as a result of feelings of inequity? Given two types of inequity (underpayment and overpayment) and two compensation systems (hourly and piece rate), four sets of hypotheses were proposed for how Person would reduce feelings of inequity:

- *Overpayment–hourly.* Subjects would try to reduce the inequity caused by overpayment by working harder or expending more effort. By increasing their inputs (effort level), they would reduce feelings of inequity. The increased effort was predicted to manifest itself in increased quantity or quality of production.
- *Overpayment–piece rate.* To reduce feelings of inequity, subjects would work harder as a means of increasing their inputs. However, if their increased effort resulted in greater output, the feelings of inequity would be magnified. Thus, subjects in this condition would produce fewer but higher-quality objects than before.
- *Underpayment–hourly.* Subjects would decrease their effort to accommodate the decrease in outcome. Decrements in product quantity and quality would result.
- *Underpayment–piece rate.* To compensate for the loss in pay, subjects would produce more but appreciably lower-quality objects.

Empirical Tests of the Theory.   A fairly large number of studies have tested some or all of the predictions made by equity theory. Researchers used both payment systems in studying the effects of inequity on performance of the interviewer. Certain groups of subjects were made to feel overpaid or underpaid; others were made to feel they were paid equitably. Most studies found that equity predictions held up best in the underpayment conditions. Also, the results of studies using hourly payment were stronger than those with piece-rate payment. These findings have important implications, which will be discussed shortly.

Table 11–1   *Modes of reducing inequity*

Behavioral modes of inequity reduction
1. Change inputs.
2. Change outcomes.
3. Get Other to change inputs or outcomes.
4. Quit job for more equitable one.

Cognitive modes of inequity reduction
1. Distort own inputs or outcomes.
2. Distort Other's inputs or outcomes.
3. Change comparison Other.

The original theory proposed that people expend more or less effort to reduce inequity. These are called *behavioral* ways of reducing inequity. As mentioned, one way to reduce inequity is to adjust the level of effort expended—changing one's inputs, as the theory postulates. A second way is to alter one's outcomes, such as asking for a raise if one feels underpaid. A third technique is to get Other to change his or her inputs or outcomes by using peer pressure to get Other to work faster or slower. Finally, if all else fails, Person can always quit a job if it is perceived as too inequitable.

Research has shown, however, that there are also *cognitive* ways to reduce inequity. By cognitive, we mean that a person does not have to "do" anything; rather, he or she reduces inequity through mental processes. One way is for Person to distort views of his or her inputs or outcomes. For example, Person could think, "I'm not really working that hard. After all, I spend a fair part of my day just talking to my friends." Outcomes could also be distorted in a similar way. A second technique is for Person to distort Other's inputs or outcomes; for example, "She really has to put up with a lot from her supervisor that I don't have to take." It has also been observed that, given the difficulty of making comparisons across jobs, the distortion of inputs (such as time and effort) is more common than the distortion of outcomes (such as salary increases and promotions). Finally, if a particular Other made Person feel inequitable, Person could always find a new Other for comparison. Equity theory does not state who that Other has to be. Research shows that the selection of Other can be oneself in a previous job, coworkers in the same organization, or people outside of one's own organization. The methods of reducing inequity (both behavioral and cognitive) are listed in Table 11–1.

Most experiments on equity theory have supported the predictions. Problems occur not because the theory is "wrong" but because hypotheses and predictions are not very precise. There are several ways of reducing inequity, and the theory does not specify which way will be chosen. A second problem involves time. Many experiments studied behavior for short periods, from ten minutes to 30 days. As with any motivation theory, we are interested in the long-term effects on behavior. Some of the implications of this will be addressed in the next section.

Evaluation of the Theory.   Numerous authors have expressed concern over both the theory's substance and implications. To date, the research on equity theory has addressed financial compensation, yet that is only one of many outcomes derived from a job. We know very little about the effects on motivation of manipulating other outcomes. Most studies have found fairly strong support for the underpayment predictions but less support for the overpayment ones. One consequence of inequity caused by underpayment is an increase in job dissatisfaction. We know that this is associated with increased absenteeism and turnover. We will have accomplished very little in the workforce if, in the name of increased motivation, people feel underpaid and then are absent from work or quit.

In theory, feelings of overpayment will cause a person to work harder to produce more or higher-quality products. However, research has shown that such feelings do not last very long. People seem to have a very high threshold for overpayment (that is, it takes a large increment for people to feel overpaid) but a low threshold for underpayment (that is, it takes a small decrement for people to feel underpaid). Given that feelings of overpayment are short-lived, an organization that doubled the wages of its employees every two months to make them feel consistently overpaid would soon be bankrupt. Huseman, Hatfield, and Miles (1987) suggested that individuals differ in their sensitivity to feeling over- or underrewarded. They believe that "benevolents" are employees who more likely feel a sense of being overrewarded than do "entitleds."

Finally, the whole issue of organizations deliberately manipulating their employees to induce feelings of inequity raises serious moral and ethical questions. Few employees would like to work for an organization that willingly made them experience inequity.

Research has shown that the principles of equity theory extend to nonmonetary outcomes. Greenberg (1988) examined employees who were randomly reassigned on a temporary basis to the offices of either higher-, lower-, or equal-status coworkers while their own offices were being remodeled. Relative to those workers reassigned to equal-status offices, those reassigned to higher-status offices raised their performance (a response to overpayment inequity) and those reassigned to lower-status offices lowered their performance (a response to underpayment inequity). Greenberg (1990) measured employee theft rates in manufacturing plants during a period in which pay was temporarily reduced by 15%. Compared with pre- and postreduction pay periods (or with control groups whose pay was unchanged), groups whose pay was reduced had significantly higher theft rates. When the bases for the pay cuts were thoroughly and sensitively explained to employees, feelings of inequity were lessened and the theft rate was reduced as well. In this study, the data supported equity theory's predictions regarding likely responses to underpayment.

The components of equity theory have been substantiated from research. It is evident that people do consider the inputs they bring to the job. "Equity theory assumes that people aggregate their perceived inputs into a sort of psychological total, representing the net value they believe they contribute to the job" (Pinder, 1998, p. 288). It is likewise true that people hold beliefs about the nature and quantity of the consequences or outcomes they receive as a result of doing their work. The process of social comparison is also valid because what we do is in part a product of what others around us do. Consistent with the concept of organizational justice, equity theory postulates that how hard a person is willing to work is in part determined by perceptions of what is fair or just (see Field Note 2). Indeed,

Field Note 2 *Equity Theory Applied to Baseball*

Most formal studies of equity theory have taken place in laboratory or field experiments. However, some researchers have used the tenets of equity theory to explain naturally occurring phenomena. Lord and Hohenfeld (1979) applied equity theory to explain the on-the-field performance of some major league baseball players.

A major league player signs a contract for a certain duration (say, three years) at a specified salary. At the end of the contract term, both the player and the team must negotiate a new contract. Sometimes the player and the team cannot agree on a new contract because the player feels he is worth more money than the team offers. In short, the player feels underpaid in comparison with what other players are receiving. In that case, the player may engage in a process known as "playing out his option"; that is, he will continue to play for the same team for one more year without a contract. This year is called the "option year." At the end of the option year, the player is free to sign with any other baseball team in the major leagues. However, during the option year, the player receives a lower salary than he did when he was under contract. There-

fore, his feelings of underpayment are intensified for two reasons. First, he feels he is worth more than he was being paid under the old contract. Second, he is paid even less than before during the option year.

According to equity theory, perceptions of underpayment should produce lower performance. Lord and Hohenfeld studied a sample of 23 baseball players who were unable to reach an agreement with their teams for a new contract and thus played out their option year. The authors selected four criteria of job performance: batting average, home runs, runs batted in, and runs scored. They compared the player's performance on these criteria before the option year with their performance during it. Equity theory would postulate that because the players felt underpaid, their performance on these four factors would be lower during the option year. The results supported the hypothesis for the first three performance indices but not for runs scored. The findings were consistent across the players, over time, and over the performance indices. They indicated that, at least in this sample, feelings of underpayment did produce lower job performance, as equity theory predicted.

the theoretical origins of procedural justice were based on the tenets of equity theory. There should be equity or fairness in the relationship between what you put into a job and what you get out of it, in comparison with other people. Problems with the theory from a motivational perspective pertain to how people deal with feelings of inequity or unfairness. Inequity need not always be resolved by expending greater effort, which cuts to the core of the theory.

Expectancy Theory

Statement of the Theory. **Expectancy theory** originated in the 1930s, but at that time it was not related to work motivation. Vroom (1964) brought expectancy theory into the arena of motivation research. In the past 35 years, expectancy theory has been one of the most popular and prominent motivation theories in I/O psychology. Since Vroom's formulation, several other researchers have proposed modifications. This section will not examine all variations but instead focus on key elements.

This is a cognitive theory. Each person is assumed to be a rational decision maker who will expend effort on activities that lead to desired rewards.

Individuals are thought to know what they want from work and understand that their performance will determine whether they get the rewards they desire. A relationship between effort expended and performance on the job is also assumed.

The theory has five major parts: job outcomes, valence, instrumentality, expectancy, and force.

Job outcomes. **Job outcomes** are things an organization can provide for its employees, such as pay, promotions, and vacation time. Theoretically, there is no limit to the number of outcomes. They are usually thought of as rewards or positive experiences, but they need not be. Getting fired or being transferred to a new location could be an outcome. Outcomes can also be intangibles like feelings of recognition or accomplishment.

Valence. **Valences** are the employee's feelings about the outcomes and are usually defined in terms of attractiveness or anticipated satisfaction. The employee generates valences; that is, he or she rates the anticipated satisfaction from (that is, ascribe a valence to) each outcome considered. Rating is usually done on a -10 to $+10$ scale. The individual can indicate whether an outcome has positive or negative valence. If the employee anticipates that all outcomes will lead to satisfaction, varying degrees of positive valence are given. If the employee anticipates that all outcomes will lead to dissatisfaction, varying degrees of negative valence are assigned. Last, if the employee feels indifferent about the outcomes, a valence of zero is given. The employee generates as many valences as there are outcomes.

Instrumentality. **Instrumentality** is defined as the perceived degree of relationship between performance and outcome attainment. This perception exists in the employee's mind. Instrumentality is like the word *conditional* and literally means the degree to which the attainment of a certain outcome is conditional on the individual's performance on the job. For example, if a person thinks that pay increases are totally conditional on performance, the instrumentality associated with that outcome (a pay raise) is very high. If a person thinks that being transferred is totally unrelated to job performance, the instrumentality associated with that outcome (a transfer) is very low. Like valences, instrumentalities are generated by the individual. He or she evaluates the degree of relationship between performance and outcome attainment on the job. Instrumentalities are usually thought of as probabilities (which therefore range from 0 to 1). An instrumentality of 0 means the attainment of that outcome is totally unrelated to job performance; an instrumentality of 1 means the attainment of that outcome is totally conditional on job performance. Just as there are as many valences as there are outcomes, there are as many instrumentalities as there are outcomes.

Expectancy. **Expectancy** is the perceived relationship between effort and performance. In some jobs there may seem to be no relationship between how hard you try and how well you do. In others there may be a very clear relationship: the harder you try, the better you do. Expectancy, like instrumentality, is scaled as a probability. An expectancy of 0 means there is no probability that an increase in effort will result in an increase in performance. An expectancy of 1 means an increase in effort will be followed by a corresponding increase in performance. As with the valence and instrumentality components, the individual generates the expectancy for his or her job. After thinking about the relationship between effort and job performance, the individual makes an assessment (ascribes an expectancy). Unlike the previous components, usually only one expectancy value is generated by the person to reflect the effort–performance relationship.

Force.   **Force,** the last component, is the amount of effort or pressure within the person to be motivated. The larger the force, the greater the hypothesized motivation. Mathematically, force is the product of valence, instrumentality, and expectancy, as expressed by this formula:

$$\text{Force} = E\left(\sum_{i=1}^{n} V_i I_i\right) \qquad\qquad \text{[Formula 11–1]}$$

The formula can be explained better with the aid of the information in Figure 11–2. The components that constitute expectancy theory—job outcomes (O), rated valences, instrumentalities, and expectancy—are presented for a hypothetical employee. To compute this individual's force, we multiply the valence for an outcome by its corresponding instrumentality and then sum these numbers. Therefore,

$$(7 \times .5) + (6 \times .3) + (2 \times .2) + (9 \times .8) = \sum_{i=1}^{4} V_i I_i = 12.9 \qquad \text{[Formula 11–2]}$$

We then multiply 12.9 by the listed expectancy of .75, which yields a force score of

$$E\left(\sum_{i=1}^{4} V_i I_i\right) = .75(12.9) = 9.7 \qquad\qquad \text{[Formula 11–3]}$$

This product—9.7—represents the amount of force within the person to be motivated. It is the end product of the information on valence, instrumentality, and expectancy.

Now that we have this force score, what do we do with it? Think of it as a predictor of how motivated a person is. As with any predictor, the next step is to correlate it with some criterion. Because the force score predicts effort, the criterion must also measure effort. The most common measure of effort is a subjective assessment, usually a rating: The individual renders a self-assessment of his or her effort, the individual's supervisor makes the judgment, or peer assessments are

Valences		Instrumentalities		Expectancy	
	Job outcomes		Performance	.75	Effort
7	O_1 Pay raise	.5			
6	O_2 Own office	.3			
2	O_3 Company car	.2			
9	O_4 Promotion	.8			

FIGURE 11–2   *An example of Vroom's expectancy theory*

used. For example, the number of hours spent studying each week has been used to predict the motivation of students. In one type of validation paradigm of expectancy theory, force scores and criterion measures of effort are calculated for a group of people. If the theory is valid, then the higher the person's force score, the greater the effort should be. The theory's validity is typically assessed by correlating the force scores with the criterion of effort. High correlations between the two variables would substantiate the theory; low correlations would disconfirm it. The validation process will be examined more closely in the next section.

Expectancy theory provides a rich rational basis for understanding motivation in a given job. Each component is a framework for analyzing the motivation process. First, we should consider the outcomes and their rated valences. If a person feels indifferent about the outcomes (a low valence), there is no reason to work hard to attain them. According to expectancy theory, therefore, the first ingredient for motivation is desired outcomes. Second, the person must believe that there is some relationship between job performance and attainment of outcomes (instrumentalities must be high). If a person wants the outcomes but does not see performance as a means of getting them, there is no link between what is done and what is wanted. Reward practices and the supervisor are crucial in establishing high instrumentalities. If a supervisor says, "Your performance has been very good lately; therefore, I will reward you with a raise [or promotion]," the individual will see that the attainment of a pay raise or a promotion is conditional on (instrumental to) good performance. Conversely, if a supervisor says, "We don't give pay raises or promotions on the basis of performance; we grant them only on the basis of seniority," the individual will not be motivated to perform well to attain these outcomes. Perhaps the only motivation will be to work hard enough not to be fired, so these outcomes would eventually be attained through increased service with the organization. When outcomes are made contingent on performance and the individual understands this relationship, expectancy theory predicts that job performance will be enhanced.

Finally, the notion of expectancy is crucial. People must see a relationship (an expectancy) between how hard they try and how well they perform. If expectancy is low, it will make no difference to them whether they work hard because effort and performance seem unrelated. When I first started college, I was a chemistry major. I desired certain outcomes (for example, good grades, a sense of accomplishment). I also realized that attaining these outcomes was conditional on my performance in classes. I had high valences for both the outcomes and the perceived high instrumentalities. However, after three agonizing semesters, my expectancy was near zero. It did not seem to matter how hard I tried; I just could not alter my (low) performance in chemistry classes. My overall motivation fell dramatically along with my performance, and I eventually chose a new major. In retrospect, I realize I lacked the abilities to perform well as a chemist. All the motivation I could muster would not lead to good performance.

The idea of expectancy also explains why some jobs seem to create high or low motivation. On assembly lines, the group performance level is determined by the speed of the line. No matter how hard a person works, he or she cannot produce any more until the next object moves down the line. The employee soon learns that he or she need only keep pace with the line. Thus, there is no relationship between individual effort and performance. Alternatively, sales jobs are characterized by high expectancy. Salespeople who are paid on commission realize that the harder they try (the more sales calls they make), the better their performance (sales volume). Expectancy theory predicts that motivation is highest in jobs with high expectancies.

In summary, expectancy theory is very good at explaining the components of motivation. It provides a rational basis on which to assess people's expenditure of effort.

Empirical Tests of the Theory.   Research has focused on the specific predictions the theory tries to make. One approach assumes the theory tries to distinguish the "most motivated" from the "least motivated" people in a group. With one force score derived for each person, the person with the highest score should be the most motivated and the person with the lowest score the least motivated. This type of approach is called an *across-subjects design* because predictions are made across people.

The second approach tests the theory differently. Here the theory assumes that each person is confronted with many tasks and then predicts on which tasks the person will work the hardest and on which he or she will expend the least effort. The theory is expanded to derive a force score for each task under consideration, and a criterion of effort is obtained for each. For each person, a correlation is computed between predictions of effort made by the theory and actual amounts of effort expended on the tasks. This type of approach is called a *within-subjects design*; predictions are made for each individual separately.

Validation studies generally find better predictions for the within-subjects design than the across-subjects design. Average validity coefficients for the across-subjects design are usually in the .30s to .40s, while average validity coefficients for within-subjects designs are usually in the .50s to .60s. The theory seems better at predicting levels of effort an individual will expend on different tasks than at predicting gradations of motivation across different people (Kennedy, Fossum, & White, 1983). These validity coefficients are quite impressive; they are generally higher than those reported for other motivation theories.

In a major study on incentive motivation techniques, Pritchard, DeLeo, and Von Bergen (1976) reported that a properly designed, successful program for motivating employees will have many of the attributes proposed by expectancy theory. Among the conditions they recommend for a program to be successful are the following:

◆ Incentives (outcomes) must be carefully sought out and identified as highly attractive.
◆ The rules (behaviors) for attaining the incentives must be clear to both those administering the system and those actually in it.
◆ People in the system must perceive that variations in controllable aspects of their behavior will result in variations in their level of performance and, ultimately, their rewards.

In somewhat different words, these three conditions for an effective incentive motivation program reflect the concepts of valence, instrumentality, and expectancy, respectively. The importance of having desired incentives is another way of stating that the outcomes should have high valence. The clarity of the behaviors needed to attain the incentives reflects the strength or magnitude of the instrumentalities. The ability to control performance through different expenditures of effort is indicative of the concept of expectancy. In short, expectancy theory contains the key elements of a successful incentive system as derived through empirical research. Although not all research on expectancy theory is totally supportive, the results have tended to confirm its predictions.

Evaluation of the Theory.   Expectancy theory is a highly rational and conscious explanation of human motivation. People are assumed to behave in a way that will maximize expected gains (attainment of outcomes) from exhibiting certain job behaviors and expending certain levels of effort. To the extent that behavior is not directed toward maximizing gains in a rational, systematic way, the theory will not be upheld. Whenever unconscious motives deflect behavior from what a knowledge of conscious processes would predict, expectancy theory will not be predictive. Research suggests that people differ in the extent to which their behavior is motivated by rational processes. This was quite apparent in one of my own studies (Muchinsky, 1977). I examined the extent to which expectancy theory predicted the amount of effort college students put into each of their courses. In a within-subjects design, the average validity of the theory for all students was .52; however, for individual students it ranged from −.08 to .92. Thus, the theory very accurately predicted the effort expenditure of some students but was unable to predict it for others. This supports the idea that some people have a very rational basis for their behavior, and thus the theory works well for them; others appear to be motivated more by unconscious factors, and for them the theory does not work well (Stahl & Harrell, 1981).

Van Eerde and Thierry (1996) conducted a meta-analysis of the expectancy theory of motivation. They concluded that the individual components of theory (valence, instrumentality, and expectancy—VIE) made as accurate predictions of criteria as did the complete multiplicative model. That is, the concepts measured by the theory are valid in predicting effort, but the VIE model does not enhance our understanding of motivation. On a practical level people do not go through life calculating VIE-based force scores, and at a conceptual level it appears equally untenable. However, the underlying concepts of expectancy theory provide one of the dominant explanations of work motivation in I/O psychology. As Pinder (1998) concluded, "At the very least [expectancy theory] is probably an accurate representation of how people form work-related intentions" (p. 359).

Reinforcement Theory

Statement of the Theory.   **Reinforcement theory** is one of the older approaches to motivation; what is novel is its application to industrial workers. Also referred to as *operant conditioning* and *behaviorism,* reinforcement theory has its origins in B. F. Skinner's work on the conditioning of animals. It was not until the 1970s, however, that I/O psychologists began to see some potential applications of reinforcement theory to the motivational problems of employees.

The theory has three key variables: stimulus, response, and reward. A **stimulus** is any variable or condition that elicits a behavioral response. In an industrial setting, a **response** is some measure of job performance, like productivity, absenteeism, or accidents. A **reward** is something of value given to the employee on the basis of the elicited behavioral response; it is meant to reinforce the occurrence of the desired response. Most attention has been paid to the response–reward connection. Based on research with animals, four types of response–reward connections or contingencies have been found to influence the frequency of the response:

- *Fixed interval.* The subject is rewarded at a fixed time interval, such as every hour. Those paid on an hourly basis can be thought of as being rewarded on a fixed-interval basis.
- *Fixed ratio.* The subject is rewarded for a fixed number of responses. For example, a real estate salesperson who gets a commission after each sale is rewarded on a fixed-ratio schedule. In this case the reward schedule is said to be continuous.
- *Variable interval.* The subject is rewarded at some time interval that varies. An example is fishing.
- *Variable ratio.* Reward is based on behavior, but the ratio of reward to response is variable. For example, a salesperson might sometimes be paid after each sale and at other times after two or three sales. The person is paid on the basis of the response (that is, making a sale), but the schedule of payment is not constant.

Advocates of reinforcement theory believe that the subject's motivation to respond can be shaped by manipulating these reinforcement schedules.

A number of authors have discussed the potential benefits and liabilities of using reinforcement theory as a basis for motivating employees. The theory entails placing the control of employee motivation in the organization's hands, since organizations can "regulate" the energy output of employees by manipulating reinforcement schedules. Most people would like to feel that they are in control of their own lives rather than being manipulated into certain behavior patterns by the organization. The issue of responsibility for controlling behavior is very sensitive because it involves ethical considerations of employee welfare. If employees work to exhaustion by mismanaging their efforts, they are responsible for their actions. However, if they are manipulated into expending excessive effort, they have been victimized by a force beyond their control, and the organization should be held responsible for their condition. Issues of ethical responsibility for behavior are not central to the theory, but they are important when it is applied in daily life. Whenever anything is "done" to someone by an outside agent, the question arises of whose values (the individual's or the agent's) are being optimized.

Empirical Tests of the Theory. Empirical tests of reinforcement theory have involved determining which schedule of reinforcement has the greatest effect on increasing the occurrence of the desired behavioral response. In a series of studies involving tree planters, Yukl and Latham (1975) and Yukl, Latham, and Pursell (1976) compared the effectiveness of various schedules of reinforcement. Some planters were paid on a fixed-interval schedule (hourly pay); others were paid based on the number of trees they planted. Employees paid on a ratio schedule were significantly more productive (planted more trees). Pritchard, Leonard, Von Bergen, and Kirk (1976) examined the effects of different payment schedules on employees' ability to pass self-paced learning tests of electrical knowledge. Some employees were paid a flat hourly wage, while others were paid according to the number of tests they passed. Two types of ratio payment schedules were used: fixed (the employee was paid after passing every third test) and variable (the employee was paid after passing a variable number). The results of the study are shown in Figure 11–3. Employees paid contingently (that is, based on their performance) passed 60% of the tests; those paid by the hour passed about 40%. Results showed no difference in test performance between fixed- and variable-ratio reinforcement schedules. Irrespective of the behavior in question, positive reinforcement, contingently applied, can effectively modify human behavior. Although there are some inconsistencies in results across differing schedules of reinforcement, the success of the theory depends on the appropriate use of positive reinforcement.

Research on reinforcement theory is not limited to measures of productivity. Pedalino and Gamboa (1974) described how the theory could be used to decrease absenteeism. They devised a plan whereby every employee who came to work on time was dealt one card from a poker deck. Each day the attending employees

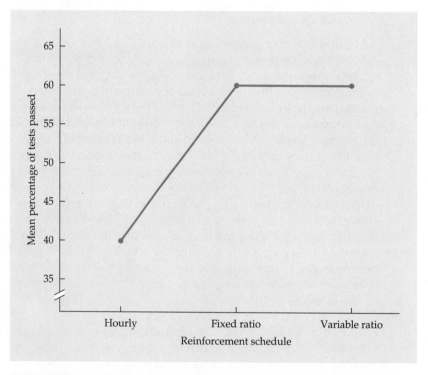

FIGURE 11–3 *Percentage of tests passed under different reinforcement schedules*

SOURCE: From "The Effect of Varying Schedules of Reinforcement on Human Task Performance" by R. D. Pritchard, D. W. Leonard, C. W. Von Bergen, and R. J. Kirk, 1976, *Organizational Behavior and Human Performance, 16*, p. 218.

were dealt a new card. At the end of the week, the employee with the best poker hand won $20. In this case the desired response (attendance) was reinforced through monetary reward. Attendance under this plan was higher than before the program was introduced.

Evaluation of the Theory.   Research clearly indicates that the principles of reinforcement theory do "work"; however, the theory suffers from some limitations in industrial settings. As Mawhinney (1975) noted, current applications of reinforcement theory tend to ignore individual differences in what are valued as rewards. In the Pedalino and Gamboa study, for example, it was assumed that all the employees were interested in playing poker and would respond positively to a gambling or lottery situation. Vast individual differences in preferences would have precluded the success of any such program. In addition, reinforcement has primarily been limited to studies of the quantity of production. We don't know very much about how the quality of performance is affected, the long-term

---

Field Note 3   *What Gets Rewarded?*

Reinforcement theory is premised on rewarding desired behavior. The stronger the link between the behavior and the reward, the greater the probability of the behavior. However, in an organizational context it is sometimes difficult to tie rewards to a particular behavior because many behaviors are typically elicited concurrently. It is thus possible to obscure the connection between the reward and the desired behavior, which decreases the probability of the behavior's occurring. In an extreme case everything gets turned around: The behaviors that organizations have tried to encourage are punished, and those that they have tried to discourage are actually rewarded. Kerr (1995) described how this can happen.

Orphanages are organizations created as residences for children before they are placed in private homes. Orphanages receive state funds to assist them in their operations. Since the primary goal of the orphanage is to place children in good homes, the way the orphanage is run should be directed toward this objective. However, such is not the case—the reward system created by the orphanage's management often drives the process in reverse for these reasons:

- The number of children enrolled in the orphanage often is the most important determinant of the size of its allocated budget.
- The number of children under the director's care affects the size of the support staff, which also is a determinant of the budget.
- The total organizational size largely determines the director's prestige at annual conventions, in the community, and so on.

Therefore, to the extent that staff size, total budget, and personal prestige are valued by the orphanage's executive personnel, it becomes rational for them to make it difficult for children to be adopted. Thus, the reward system reinforces the exact opposite of the behavior for which the orphanage was created—that is, the placement of children.

Vast amounts of research indicate that schedules of reinforcement can indeed motivate behavior to occur in certain patterns. However, the direction of that behavior is not always consistent with organizational goals.

effects of various reinforcement schedules, or people's attitudes toward such incentive methods.

The use of reinforcement theory in industry has both supporters and detractors. Advocates cite its wide applicability for solving problems. Its uses include reducing absence and turnover, enhancing productivity, and improving supervisory training. Emery Air Freight is one of the biggest reinforcement theory success stories. Emery reported $3 million in cost savings after adopting a system of positive reinforcement. Other companies have also reported successful applications. In a meta-analysis of reinforcement theory for task performance over a 20-year period, Stajkovic and Luthans (1997) reported an average of 17% improvement in task performance using the theory. Detractors of the theory cite possible ethical matters associated with the reinforcement of behavior. How ethical is it for an organization to use a payment system that increases productivity but may cause adverse side effects? Sweden has condemned piece-rate payment schedules because they cause tension and ultimately damage workers' mental and physical well-being. There is also evidence that workers in short-cycle, monotonous jobs prefer hourly rates to piece rates. They complain that piece-rate systems "control" them (or at least their behavior), which is the precise intent of the system. Despite these legitimate ethical concerns, reinforcement theory has a history of producing desired changes in work behavior. Unlike other motivational theories, its focus is not on the individual but on environmental factors that shape or modify behavior. While implementation problems exist, they address only the theory's applicability rather than its validity (see Field Note 3).

Goal-Setting Theory

Statement of the Theory.   **Goal setting** is a motivation theory based on the assumption that people behave rationally. The crux of the theory is the relationship among goals, intentions, and task performance. Its basic premise is that conscious ideas regulate a person's actions. Goals are what the individual is consciously trying to attain, particularly as related to future objectives.

According to Locke and Latham (1990), goals have two major functions: They are a basis for motivation and they direct behavior. A goal provides guidelines for a person deciding how much effort to put into work. Goals are intended behaviors; in turn, they influence task performance. However, two conditions must be met before goals can positively influence performance. First, the individual must be aware of the goal and know what must be accomplished. Second, the individual must accept the goal as something he or she is willing to work for. Goals can be rejected because they are seen as too difficult or too easy or because the person does not know what behaviors are needed to attain them. Acceptance of the goal implies the individual intends to engage in the behavior needed for goal attainment.

Locke and Latham's theory of goal setting states that more difficult goals lead to higher levels of job performance. The authors believe that commitment to a goal is proportional to its difficulty. Thus, more difficult goals engender more commitment to their attainment. Goals can also vary in specificity. Some goals are general (for example, to be a good biology student), and others are more specific (to get an A on the next biology test). The more specific the goal, the more concentrated the individual's effort in its pursuit and the more directed the behavior. It is also important for the person to receive feedback about task performance; this guides whether he or she should work harder or continue at the same pace.

Therefore, according to goal-setting theory, the following factors and conditions induce high motivation and task performance. Goals are behavioral intentions that channel our energies in certain directions. The more difficult and specific the goal, the greater is our motivation to attain it. Feedback on our performance in pursuit of the goal tells us whether our efforts are "on target." The source of motivation, according to goal setting, is the desire and intention to attain the goal; this must be coupled with the individual's acceptance of the goal. Rather than dealing with motivation as a product of innate needs, feelings of inequity, or schedules of reinforcement, goal setting assumes people set acceptable target objectives and then channel their efforts in pursuit of them. In particular, the emphasis in goal-setting theory is on the direction of behavior.

Empirical Tests of the Theory.   For the most part, empirical tests of the theory are quite supportive. As an example, Latham and Baldes (1975) studied truck drivers hauling logs to lumber mills. Their performance was studied under two conditions. First, drivers were told only to "do their best" in loading the trucks. After a time, they were told to set a specific, difficult goal of loading their trucks up to 94% of the legal weight limit. (The closer to the legal limit, the fewer trips were needed.) Each truck driver got feedback by means of a loading scale indicating tonnage. Figure 11–4 shows the drivers' performance over a 48-week period. At the onset of goal setting, performance improved greatly; however, the cause is not clear-cut. One explanation may be the effects of goal setting. Another could be a sense of competition among the drivers as to who could load the truck closest to the legal limit. (The decline in performance between the fourth and fifth blocks was due to the truck drivers' "testing" of management to gauge its reaction.) In any case, the study clearly showed that performance under goal setting was superior to the "do your best" condition.

Wright (1990), however, concluded that assigned goals produce greater increases in performance than self-set goals. Also, Hollenbeck, Williams, and Klein (1989) reported that commitment to difficult goals is higher when goals are stated publicly rather than privately. While variation does exist in terms of task behaviors and acceptance of goal setting, research indicates that goal setting produces better performance than the absence of goals or very general goals. As Latham and Marshall (1982) stated, the key issue appears to be not *how* a goal is set but *whether* the goal is set.

Evaluation of the Theory.   You should be struck by the elegance and simplicity of goal-setting theory. There are no references to innate needs, perceived instrumentalities, or comparison with others. As Latham and Locke (1991) observed, the goal-setting theory lies within the domain of purposefully directed action. The theory focuses on the question of why some people perform better on work tasks than others. If they are equal in ability and environmental conditions, then the cause must be motivational. The theory states that the simplest and most direct motivational explanation of why some people perform better than others is that they have

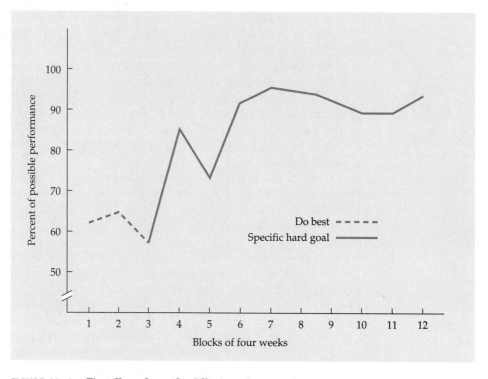

FIGURE 11–4   *The effect of specific, difficult goals on productivity*

SOURCE: From "The Practical Significance of Locke's Theory of Goal Setting" by G. P. Latham and J. J. Baldes, 1975, *Journal of Applied Psychology, 60,* p. 123.

different performance goals. The difficulty and specificity of the goal influence performance, as do the amount and nature of feedback. There are some differences in performance between goals that are assigned and some that are self-selected. Different types of people also prefer different types of goals, but it is clear that goal setting elicits better performance.

Why is goal setting an effective motivational strategy? Pinder (1998) offered several reasons. Goals direct attention and action. They identify the target of intended behavior, and if they are stated specifically (as is recommended), the focus of the person's effort becomes well defined. Similarly, the condition that goals be made difficult relates directly to the intensity and persistence components of the motivation concept. If a goal is difficult, it normally requires more effort, over a longer period of time, to be attained. One element of persistence is tenacity, which is the refusal to quit trying, despite obstacles, until the goal is achieved. Commitment is one factor that contributes to tenacity, as does the sheer difficulty of the goal itself. Goal setting requires the development of a task-related strategy. When people contemplate a goal, they must also consider means for its attainment, especially when the goal is seen as difficult. It may be that harder tasks are more likely to stimulate more strategy development than are easy tasks. Pinder believes it makes sense that the more specific the task goal, the more likely it is that people devise specific techniques to achieve it. Rousseau (1997) posited that goal setting is a form of self-management, where people can set their own goals and translate them into action. The acceptance of goals, when they are not self-set, is critical to their attainment. Thus, goal setting places people in control of their own behavior, which can itself serve as an incentive.

Goal setting seems to be generalizable as a theory of motivation. Its application is not limited to highly rational people, although it does assume that people follow through with their intentions. The theory has a cognitive basis: Employees must think about the goals they want to pursue; they must decide whether the goals are acceptable; they must understand what behaviors they have to exhibit to attain the goal; and they must know how to evaluate feedback on their progress. Research on feedback has shown that it is critical for optimal performance but that people differ in their ability to use the information provided. There is also evidence that goal setting is effective for groups. Thus, a work group can set a goal to decrease scrap rate, for example, or to increase productive output. Group goals can be more difficult to attain, however, because in many cases the success of the overall group depends on more than just the success of individual members. A basketball team may set a goal of winning a certain number of games in a season, but its success is determined by more than just the number of points scored by each player. Member coordination and integration must also be considered. One player might help the team by passing, another by rebounding, and the others by shooting.

Locke, Shaw, Saari, and Latham (1981) reviewed 12 years of goal-setting research studies and came to the following conclusion: 90% of the studies show that specific and challenging goals lead to higher performance than easy goals, "do your best" goals, or no goals. Goal setting was found to improve task performance when (1) subjects have sufficient ability, (2) feedback is provided on progress relative to goals, (3) rewards are given for goal attainment, (4) management is supportive, and (5) individuals accept assigned goals. Tubbs (1986) concluded that the concepts of goal difficulty, goal specificity, and participation in the goal-setting process were all supported by empirical research studies. However, the principles of goal setting were empirically supported more often in laboratory than in field studies. Tubbs also discovered that individuals are more willing to accept and work for an extremely difficult goal when they know that they will not have to do so for any extended period. In summary, the overall verdict on the value of goal setting as a theory of motivation is overwhelmingly positive.

Pritchard, Jones, Roth, Stuebing, and Ekeberg (1988) noted that most research on improving productivity through goal setting has studied relatively simple jobs with the individual as the unit of analysis. Because most jobs are more complex and given the interdependencies in work, they feel group-level intervention studies are needed. The authors studied work group productivity for nine months. They introduced a group-level intervention designed to enhance group productivity consisting of three parts: feedback, group goal setting, and incentives (time off from work). Group-level feedback was found to increase productivity by 50% over the baseline, and goal setting plus feedback increased productivity by 75% over the baseline. The combined effect of feedback, goal setting, and incentives increased productivity by 76% over the baseline. The study showed that the principles of goal setting, proven useful with individual performance, also hold for group performance.

OVERVIEW AND SYNTHESIS OF WORK MOTIVATION THEORIES

After studying the five theories of work motivation presented, one can reasonably ask whether any unifying themes run through them. Kanfer (1992) proposed that the theories can be examined along a continuum of their conceptual proximity to action. The endpoints of the continuum are distal (i.e., distant) and proximal (i.e., near) constructs. *Distal* constructs such as personality exert indirect effects on behavior. *Proximal* constructs begin with the individual's goals rather than with the factors that have shaped the individual's objectives. Figure 11–5 reveals the motivation constructs and associated theories arrayed along the distal/proximal continuum proposed by Kanfer.

At the extreme distal end is the construct of genetics/heredity. This chapter has not formally examined a genetics-based theory of motivation, but we are familiar with it from another area. It will be recalled that a contemporary interpretation of personality is represented in the Big 5 theory. One personality factor of considerable interest to I/O psychologists is conscientiousness because it is the basis for integrity tests. Another name for conscientiousness is "will to achieve" (Digman & Takemoto-Chock, 1981). This name implies that individuals who are attentive to detail, rule abiding, and honest also exhibit high ambition. Accordingly this view of motivation is that the capacity to be motivated is genetically determined, is an enduring component of one's personality, and can be assessed with a paper-and-pencil personality inventory.

Maslow's theory is predicated upon a universal set of basic human needs, arranged in a hierarchy, which all individuals have. Inter-individual differences in motivation are attributed to differences in the particular needs that people are trying to satisfy. Equity theory asserts there is a social component to motivation; that is, how hard we are willing to work is in part a function of how we perceive other people in our environment. Based on a social comparison of what other people are giving and getting, we assess how much effort we are willing to exert. Implicit in the equity theory is a sense of fairness (i.e., equity) or justice, which embeds this theoretical perspective of motivation in the same conceptual framework as that offered by the research on organizational justice.

As we continue down the continuum toward proximal constructs, there is increasing reliance on the assumption that people make conscious, deliberate, controllable choices about how much effort they choose to expend. This is the antithesis of a genetic/dispositional orientation toward motivation. Proximal theories are heavily predicated upon a cognitive explanation for motivation. Expectancy theory postulates that individuals are consciously aware of the results or outcomes they wish to attain, perceive relationships between their behavior and attaining those outcomes, and also perceive a relationship between their effort and their behavior. The theory elevates motivation to a conscious choice made by the individual. Goal-setting theory is another example of this orientation and offers motivation as an opportunity to engage in self-control or self-regulation. The capacity to control one's own life was noted in the preceding chapter as one of the determinants of mental health. Goal-setting theory postulates that one way we can take some control over our life is to decide how hard we are willing to work. Locke

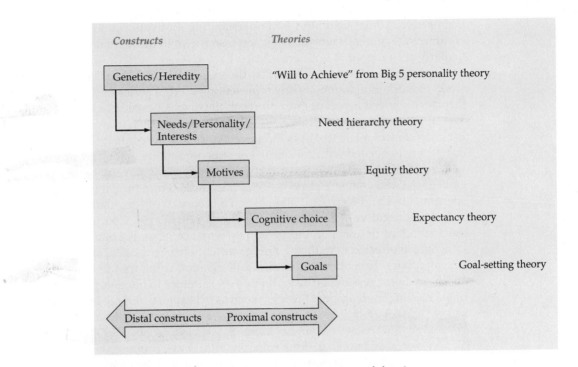

FIGURE 11–5   *A framework of motivation constructs and theories*

SOURCE: Adapted from "Work Motivation: New Directions in Theory and Research" by R. Kanfer, 1992, *International Review of Industrial and Organizational Psychology,* p. 4.

(1991) offered this description of how important individual choice or volition is in our lives:

> For example, people can choose . . . what their needs are and how to satisfy them; what values they should pursue and the validity of the values other people have told them to pursue; whether and how to apply their values to a specific situation; what goals to set, how to develop plans to reach them, and whether to commit to the goals and plans; what their performance capacity is for a specific task and how to raise it; what their performance means and who is responsible for it; the adequacy of their rewards and the relation of these rewards to their values; the causes of their affective reactions to their performance and rewards; and how to modify these reactions (e.g., by changing their performance or changing their value standards). (pp. 297–298)

As illustrated by the arrangement of motivational theories in Kanfer's framework, the array of explanations for motivation is based on consideration of the individual, ranging from genetic predisposition to individual conscious choice. Noticeably absent from Kanfer's framework is where reinforcement theory fits in. Reinforcement theory is predicated upon environmental factors that shape behavior through patterns of reward. The role of the individual, through either genetic makeup or cognitive processes, is not regarded as essential or necessary to understand motivation. Much current thinking in psychology asserts that the cognitive perspective is more insightful for understanding motivation, and believes the operant (reinforcement) perspective is too insensitive to individual differences, particularly with regard to volition.

It should also be noted that other theoretical advances are being made in the study of work motivation, mostly representing modifications or derivatives of the theories reviewed here. For example, from the dispositional perspective, Kuhl and Beckmann (1994) proposed a construct called *action control*. Individual differences in action control relate to dispositional tendencies in the context of an individual's cognitions associated with anticipated or ongoing activity. Persons who are high in action control direct their attention toward task resolution rather than internal emotional states unrelated to task accomplishment. From the cognitive choice perspective, Lord and Kernan (1989) posited a theory of self-regulation based on the notion of a negative (discrepancy-reducing) feedback loop. Comparisons between one's standard or goal and perceived performance result in cognitive and behavioral output directed at reducing discrepancies between the goal and the perceived state of affairs. This orientation toward motivation is referred to as *cybernetic control theory*. Some researchers (e.g., Klein, 1991) attempt to integrate the propositions of the existing motivational theories (such as expectancy and goal-setting theories) rather than formulate new theories. A general summary of the major theories of work motivation discussed in this chapter is presented in Table 11–2.

A few researchers (e.g., Erez & Earley, 1993) have proposed motivational concepts that originated in non-Western cultures but may be universally applicable. For example, Earley (1997) discussed the concept of *face* (as in "saving face") as a basis of social motivation. Face has been considered a predominantly Asian concept. Earley references face as the evaluation of a person based on self and external social judgments. Face does not lie completely within or outside the individual, as face is both given (by others) and claimed (by the self). Thus, the concept of face is grounded in a social exchange process involving self-presentation. It is proposed that our behavior is guided by efforts to regulate and enhance our self-image. Examples include the sense of prestige derived from a job title, living in an affluent neighborhood, and maintaining a certain physical appearance (e.g., "power dressing"). The loss of face is associated with shame and weakens the network of social relations of which we are all a part. Earley believes the concept of face is a useful framework for understanding our behavior within a social context. We are motivated to enhance face, and our actions can be judged as being instrumental for doing so. This perspective takes a decidedly social view of motivation and has no specific mechanistic tenets such as variable ratio schedules of reinforcement and perceived expectancies. It is most similar to equity theory, which is also based on a social comparison. Although it remains to be seen what role such concepts as face will play in the evolution of motivation theories, Earley's theory presents a cross-culturally based explanation for what is a timeless and boundaryless phenomenon—an understanding of our behavior.

Katzell and Thompson (1990) analyzed the vast body of research and theory on motivation and identified seven practices that can raise the level of motivation of people in work organizations:

1. Ensure that workers' motives and values are appropriate for the jobs on which they are placed.

Table 11–2   *Summary and evaluation of work motivation theories*

Theory	Source of Motivation	Empirical Support	Organizational Applicability
Need hierarchy theory	Unconscious, innate needs	Weak: Little support for proposed relationships among needs.	Very limited: Theory lacks sufficient specificity to guide behavior.
Equity theory	Drive to reduce feelings of tension caused by perceived inequity	Mixed: Good support for underpayment inequity; weak support for overpayment equity.	Limited: Social comparisons are made, but feelings of inequity can be reduced through means other than increased motivation.
Expectancy theory	Relationship among desired outcomes, performance–reward, and effort–performance variables	Moderate–strong: More strongly supported in within-subjects than across-subjects experiments.	Strong: Theory provides a rational basis for why people expend effort, although not all behavior is consciously determined as postulated.
Reinforcement theory	Schedule of reinforcement used to reward people for their performance	Moderate: Ratio reinforcement schedules evoke superior performance compared to interval schedules, but little difference exists among various ratio schedules.	Moderate: Contingent payment for performance is possible in some jobs, although ethical problems can be present in an attempt to shape employee behavior.
Goal-setting theory	Intention to direct behavior in pursuit of acceptable goals	Moderate–strong: Performance under goal-setting conditions is usually superior to conditions under which no goals are set.	Strong: Ability to set goals is not restricted to certain types of people or jobs.

2. Make jobs attractive and consistent with workers' motives and values.
3. Define work goals that are clear, challenging, attractive, and attainable.
4. Provide workers with the personnel and material resources that facilitate their effectiveness.
5. Create supportive social environments.
6. Reinforce performance.
7. Harmonize all these elements into a consistent sociotechnical system.

As can be inferred from the theories of work motivation presented in this chapter, no one theory strongly lends itself to all seven of these practices. However, each theory can be adequately directed to some of them, leaving us with the conclusion that each theory of work motivation offers something of value in understanding this most complex construct.

THE APPLICATION OF MOTIVATIONAL STRATEGIES

After several approaches to work motivation have been presented, it is almost inevitable to ask which theory has the greatest practical value or, perhaps more to the point, which theory will "work" for you. While there is no simple answer to this question, some practical guidelines are available to assist in the decision. Mitchell (1997) referred to this process as matching motivational strategies with varying organizational contexts.

Mitchell stated we must begin the process with some sort of problem recognition. Behavior has three main causal factors: motivation, ability, and constraints. The preferred point of origin in our analysis is constraints. In many cases, removal of constraints and situational obstacles is the appropriate action and may be far more effective than trying to enhance abilities or increase motivation. The lack of a needed piece of equipment (e.g., a computer) is an example of a situational obstacle.

If problems in behavior persist when situational constraints are removed, the next step is to examine abilities and skills—determine whether ability is an issue (e.g., have you exhibited the desired behavior in the past?). Perhaps you are seeking to behave in ways and in contexts for which you lack the needed abilities, and effort cannot compensate for lack of ability.

If lack of ability does not appear to be a major issue, the problem may have a major motivational component. However, there are several types of motivational problems. Apathy and boredom suggest an arousal problem. If you are working hard but not succeeding, directional processes may be misaligned. If you are not doing enough or following through, intensity and persistence should be the focus of attention.

Ideally there should be room in your environmental context for motivation to manifest itself. There may be organizational constraints that take precedence over inter- or intra-individual differences in motivation. For example, in assembly-line work the speed of the line determines the level of output. You cannot make the assembly line move faster by working harder, nor does the assembly line move faster for harder-working individuals. This type of organizational constraint must be absent for increases in motivation to result in increased performance.

After you have decided you have a motivational problem and have decided which motivational process (e.g., arousal, direction, intensity, persistence) is most involved, you still have a number of issues to consider. At this point Mitchell (1997) refers to the "match" between the motivational strategy you select and the organizational context you face. Organizational contexts differ in many ways—for example, the clarity of the performance criteria by which you will be judged, the frequency and nature of the feedback you receive about your behavior, whether your performance is judged on an individual or group basis, and so on. While goal setting is the most supportable and adaptable motivational strategy, it requires accurate and timely feedback. For example, if you set the goal of earning an A in a class but your grade is determined by one comprehensive exam at the end of the course, you will have received no formal feedback on your performance throughout the semester. Instead, you will have to rely on informal feedback as an internal sense of how well you are understanding the course material, which may be inaccurate. In such a case, reinforcement theory may provide you with a motivational incentive, such as rewarding yourself on a biweekly basis for reaching some level of mastery (e.g., doing well on a self-test). Expectancy theory can provide guidance on issues of direction and intensity, such as the perceived degree of association between how hard you try in a class and how well you perform. If the level of association is not high, do you have any insights about factors that determine the low level of association? That is, could you seek the assistance of the professor or a teaching assistant outside of class? Finally, if the class utilizes team projects, can team goals and team rewards be created? Can you use equity theory to judge the contributions (inputs) of other teams and their outcomes compared to your group?

There is probably no single, correct theory of motivation. Rather there are groups of theories that operate under different contexts, differentiated by such factors as simple versus complex tasks and short versus long time frames. Likewise, some motivational theories require fairly extensive self-management, such as having high self-awareness, obtaining feedback, determining strategies, and so on. Goal setting is one example. Other motivational theories are guided by less obtrusive mechanisms, such as innate needs. There are also individual differences in personality related to motivation. For example, Kanfer and Heggestad (1997) asserted that individuals differ in trait achievement. Persons high in trait achievement are more likely to pursue more challenging situations than persons low in trait achievement. By repeatedly engaging in challenging situations, persons high in trait achievement learn to better regulate their levels of motivation and to generalize this skill to other situations. Conversely, people with low trait achievement tend to avoid challenging situations and thus have fewer opportunities to develop motivational skills. Finally, Erez (1997) noted the importance of cultural differences in work motivation. Cultures differ in the extent to which they reward individual and collective achievement, which becomes yet another factor that promotes or inhibits motivation. In conclusion, work motivation has a multiplicity of causes and catalysts, and there are no simple solutions or "one correct way" to motivate an individual or group.

CASE STUDY ◆ What to Do with Harry?

Joe Collins, Production Manager of York Tool and Die Company, tapped Harry Simpson on the shoulder. "Harry," Collins said, "I'd like to talk to you in my office."

"Right now?" asked Simpson.

"Right now," Collins replied.

Simpson took off his safety goggles and put them on the rack. He was a line foreman, and it was unusual to be called away from his line. He figured it had to be something big; otherwise, Collins would have waited until break.

"Hey, Willie," Simpson yelled at his lead man, "cover for me, will you? I've got to talk to Joe."

Simpson walked into Collins's office and sat down. The look on Collins's face told him it wasn't going to be good news.

"Harry, I've known you for eight years," Collins began. "You've always kept your nose to the grindstone. You've been conscientious and diligent. I've had fewer problems with you than with most of the other foremen. But lately things have been different. You've come to work late five times in the past month. You've been late turning in your weekly production sheets. The scrap rate of your line has been going up, too. I was also told that Willie had to spend a lot of time breaking in the two new guys. That's your job. What's going on, Harry?"

Simpson shuffled his feet and cleared his throat. "I didn't realize these things were happening."

"You didn't know you were late?" Collins was incredulous."You've been coming to work at seven-thirty for eight years. When you punch in at seven-forty-five, you're late, and you know it."

"I don't know, Joe, I just haven't felt with it lately," Simpson explained. "Doris says I've been moping around the house a lot lately, too."

"I'm not here to chew you out, Harry," Collins replied. "You're a valuable man. I want to find a way to get you back in gear. Anything been bugging you lately?"

"Well, I've finally figured out I'm not going to make it to supervisor. At least not in the near future. That's what I've been working for all along. Maybe I've hit my peak. When Coleman made it to supervisor, I figured I'd be the next one up. But it never happened. I'm not sore—Coleman is a good man and he deserved it. I just feel kind of deflated."

"You're well respected by management, Harry, and your line thinks you're great, too. You've set a tough example to live up to. I want you to keep it up—we need people like you."

"I know I have an important job," said Simpson, "but I figure I can't get ahead anymore, at least not on how well I do my job. I guess it boils down to luck or something."

"What if I give you a new line to run?" Collins asked. "Would that give you a new challenge?"

"No, I wouldn't want that, Joe," replied Simpson. "I like my line, and I don't want to leave them."

"All right, Harry, but here's the deal," Collins stated. "I want you to cut back on the lateness, pronto. Get your production reports in on time, and watch the scrap. With the price of copper going up, we've got to play it tight. Oh, and give Willie a break. He's got enough to do. Does this sound okay to you?"

"Yeah," Simpson said. "You're only telling me to do what I'm supposed to be doing."

"Keep at it, Harry," Collins said with a smile. "In two more years, you'll get a ten-year pin."

Simpson got up to leave. "It won't pay the rent, but I'd like to have it."

Simpson walked back to the line. Willie looked up and saw him coming. "What'd Joe want?" Willie asked.

"Oh, nothing much," Simpson replied.

Willie knew Simpson was hiding something, and Simpson figured Willie knew what it was.

Questions   1. Which theory of motivation do you feel best explains Simpson's recent behavior?
2. What would equity theory have predicted about Simpson's behavior following Coleman's promotion?
3. In terms of expectancy theory, how would you describe Simpson's valence for a promotion and its instrumentality?
4. What psychological needs did Collins appeal to in talking to Simpson?
5. How might you use reinforcement theory to shape Simpson's behavior in the areas that need attention?

INFOTRAC ARTICLES

1. *Across the Board,* May 1998 v35 n5 p51(2)
   What makes people work hard? Marilyn Moats Kennedy
   A discussion of the broad range of factors that motivate employees to work harder.
2. *Women's Sports and Fitness,* Jan 1999 v2 i2 p82(1)
   On your mark, get set, goal!
   An application of goal-setting techniques by women in the areas of sport and fitness.
3. *Black Enterprise,* May 1998 v28 n10 p56(1)
   Pulling a rabbit out of a hat. Phaedra Brotherton
   A discussion of what organizations can do to keep their key employees motivated when financial rewards are limited.
4. *Across the Board,* Jan 1997 v34 n1 p9(2)
   Ultimate pay for performance. Geoffrey Loftus
   An article proposing that motivation can be enhanced and sustained by paying employees on a piece-rate basis.
5. *Across the Board,* Oct 1997 v34 n9 p13(2)
   As inequality grows . . . . Barbara Buell
   Discusses how the perceived pay of chief executive officers of companies creates a sense of inequity among the employees, which in turn has a negative impact on the organization.
6. *New Statesman (1996),* Jan 8, 1999 v128 i4418 p12(1)
   Women are pushy, men ambitious. Nicci Gerrard
   A discussion of gender differences in the social acceptability of being motivated and successful.
7. *The Futurist,* March–April 1997 v31 n2 p43(2)
   How to manage an X'er. Bob Losyk
   Recommendations for how organizations should attempt to motivate the generation of employees who are under the age of 30.
8. *Editor & Publisher,* Feb 25, 1995 v128 n8 p44(2)
   Ins and outs of employee stock ownership. Ed Carberry
   Discusses the use of employee stock ownership plans (ESOPs) to motivate employees in the newspaper business.

C H A P T E R

12

Leadership

MAJOR CHAPTER OBJECTIVES

◆ Explain the major topics of interest among
   leadership researchers.

◆ Describe the major theoretical approaches
   to the study of leadership: trait, behavioral,
   power and influence, situational,
   transformational and charismatic leadership,
   implicit leadership, and substitutes for
   leadership.

◆ Understand the points of convergence
   among leadership approaches.

◆ Discuss cross-cultural leadership issues.

◆ Discuss diversity issues in leadership.

When you think of leadership, many ideas come to mind. Your thoughts might relate to power, authority, and influence. Maybe you think of actual people—Washington, Lincoln, Kennedy, King—or what effective leaders do. In short, the concept of leadership evokes a multitude of thoughts, all of which in some way address the causes, symptoms, or effects of leadership.

This chapter will examine how I/O psychologists have tried to grapple with the multifaceted concept of leadership, particularly as it relates to behavior in the world of work. Research on leadership has been diverse because investigators have approached the concept from different perspectives. Some research has examined what strong leaders are like as people by looking at demographic variables, personality traits, skills, and so on. Without followers, there can be no leaders; accordingly, some research has examined leader–follower relations. Presumably "strong" leaders accomplish things that "weak" leaders do not; thus, other research is on the effects of leadership. An interesting question addresses contextual effects in leadership—for example, is leadership of a prison more demanding than that of a business organization? Thus, the situation in which leadership occurs has attracted much attention. Other areas of interest within the domain of leadership research have also been investigated. While such diversity of interest expands our basis of understanding, it also creates ambiguity as to exactly what leadership is all about.

Interest in leadership concerns the I/O practitioner as well as the scientist. In fact, leadership is one of the richer areas of interplay between the two; it has had a healthy influx of ideas from both camps. Identifying and developing leaders are major concerns of industry today. Companies often train their higher-level personnel in skill areas (interpersonal relations, decision making, planning) that directly affect their performance as leaders. In Greensboro, North Carolina, there is an organization called the Center for Creative Leadership whose purpose is to enhance, through training, the leadership abilities of key business personnel. Not surprisingly, the military is also greatly concerned with leadership. It sponsors a wide variety of research projects that have the potential for enhancing our understanding of this subject. In summary, the balance between the theory and practice of leadership is fairly even as a result of this dual infusion of interest.

MAJOR TOPICS IN LEADERSHIP RESEARCH

Because of the many facets of leadership, researchers have focused on selected areas. Six major categories of studies will be presented next.

Positional Power

Some investigators view leadership as the exercise of **positional power:** The higher the position in the organizational hierarchy, the more power the position has. In the leadership context, we are most concerned with legitimate power: the formal power given to a position. The positional power of a company president exceeds that of a manager; in turn, the manager has more power than a secretary. Viewing leadership in terms of positional power separates the person from the role. Little attention is given to the individual's attributes; most is aimed at the use of positional power. Organizational theorists use such terms as the power of the presidency and administrative clout, issues not really related to the people in such positions. Sometimes history judges leaders on their inability to use all the power their positions give them. Other leaders try to exceed the power granted their positions. In some countries leaders emerge by seizing power through military or political coups. According to this perspective, leadership is inherent in an organizational position based on the concept of power.

In the total spectrum of leadership research, a relatively small number of studies have been done on positional power. Many I/O researchers find it hard to separate leadership itself from the characteristics of people in leadership positions. But research on positional power has shown that some leadership issues transcend individual differences.

The Leader

Characteristics of individual leaders have been one of the most researched areas of leadership. Most leadership theories are based on understanding the differences among personal traits and behaviors. This is almost the opposite of the emphasis on positional power, which minimizes individual differences. Many early studies considered demographic and personality variables. Others studied what behaviors individual leaders exhibit that influence the judgment of whether they are strong or weak leaders. Statements like "Strong leaders radiate confidence" and "Weak leaders are indecisive" reflect the school of thought that stresses the importance of the leader in the leadership process. Research has been done on the selection of people into leadership positions; other research has been devoted to training people to enhance their leadership skills. The significance here is the focus on leader characteristics or behavior and their influence on others. This is a classic I/O psychology perspective, and it is the most popular in leadership research literature.

The Led

Another area of interest is the characteristics of the followers, or the led. This is quite a shift in emphasis from the preceding area, in that leadership is construed more in terms of who is led than who does the leading. Casual observation suggests that some people are easier for leaders to work with than others. Military leaders have long known that some groups of recruits are more responsive, cohesive, or productive. Teachers have noted variations among student classes. Industrial training directors have found differences among various trainee groups. We thus have evidence that a leader's performance is not the same across different groups of followers. We might label this class of studies "followership" research.

As an example, consider the case of a high school science teacher. The material may remain fairly constant over time, but the teacher's behavior may vary depending on the students. One year the teacher may have a class of bright, motivated students who quickly grasp the material. The teacher may respond by offering the class more advanced topics, laboratory experiments, or field trips. Another year the teacher could have students who have difficulty learning the material. The teacher may have to instruct at a slower pace, use more examples, and hold help sessions. Other variables are class size, disciplinary problems, and student backgrounds. Thus, attributes of the led (the students) as indexed by their intelligence, motivation, number, interpersonal harmony, and background would be examined as factors affecting the behavior of the leader (the teacher).

The Influence Process

Rather than focusing on either the leaders or the led, some researchers have found it instructive to examine the relationship or link between the two parties, particularly as they influence each other. Here researchers give their attention to the dynamics of this relationship, although they may also consider characteristics of both the leaders and the followers. In a general sense, what leaders "do" to a group is influence its members in the pursuit of some goal. Research on the influence process examines how this process is enacted.

The concept of influence entails how one person's actions affect another's. There are several methods of influence, including coercion, manipulation, authority, and persuasion. *Coercion* involves modifying behavior by force. *Manipulation* is a controlled distortion of reality, as seen by those affected. People are allowed to see only those things that will evoke the kind of reaction desired. In the case of *authority*, agents appeal to a mutual decision giving them the right to influence. *Persuasion* means displaying judgment in such a way that those exposed to it accept its value. Researchers study how these methods are used in leader–follower relations. As an example, Greene and Schriesheim (1980) studied two types of leader behavior: instrumental and supportive. In *instrumental* leadership a leader clarifies the group's goals. A *supportive* leader is friendly and considerate of others' needs. Greene and Schriesheim classified various work groups by size. The results showed that relatively small groups are most influenced by a supportive leader and that instrumental leadership works better in larger groups (perhaps because it brings order and structure to the group).

The Situation

Leadership research has also focused on the situation or context in which leader–group relations occur. The situation can greatly affect the types of behaviors a leader has to exhibit to be effective. Imagine the leader of a Boy Scout troop, the supervisor of a production crew, and the warden of a prison. Each faces a different situation. Research on situational factors has tried to identify how various contexts differ and what effect they have on leader behavior.

The context in which leadership occurs influences which type of leader behavior is called for. As an example, Green and Nebeker (1977) studied two types of leadership situations: one favorable and one unfavorable. In the favorable situation leaders emphasized interpersonal relations and were supportive of the group members. However, in the unfavorable situation the leaders became more task oriented and more concerned with goal accomplishment than with interpersonal relations. Green and Nebeker were able to show that different situations evoke different styles of leadership behavior.

Leader Emergence versus Leader Effectiveness

The final category considered here is emergence versus effectiveness of leaders. Some leadership researchers are interested in the dynamics of what causes leaders to emerge within a group. This emergence process can either be formal (that is, a person is designated to be the leader) or informal (that is, a person evolves as the leader of a group without having been so designated). Researchers examine such possible characteristics as the leader's age, gender, and physical appearance, or they consider verbal and nonverbal behaviors associated with the subsequent emergence. Also of possible interest might be the characteristics of the group from which the leader emerges. For example, Goktepe and Schneier (1989) reported in a study no difference in the proportion of men and women who emerged as leaders. However, group members with masculine gender-role characteristics emerged as leaders significantly more than those with feminine gender-role characteristics. In short, leader emergence is concerned with the process that results in someone's being regarded as the leader of a group.

Research on leader effectiveness is concerned with the performance of the leader. In this line of research, the characteristics of the leader (or the group) that are associated with evaluation of leader quality, and in establishing the criteria for effective leaders, are of interest. In the former case, effective leaders might be identified as possessing certain characteristics, such as verbal fluency, sensitivity, decisiveness, and so on. In the latter case, effective leadership might be regarded as success in task completion (that is, an effective leader gets the job done) or acceptance by the group (that is, an effective leader has group support). Issues associated with both leader emergence and leader acceptance have long been of interest to I/O psychologists.

Overview

Leadership researchers do not limit their studies or theories to just one of these six areas. A researcher interested in influence processes might consider in which situations influence attempts will be successful. Interest in leader traits may also include consideration of follower traits. My purpose in describing these areas is to highlight the major categories of leadership research and acknowledge their different units of analysis while realizing that the areas are not mutually exclusive. Table 12–1 summarizes the six major research areas and lists the types of topics and questions each area tends to address.

THEORETICAL APPROACHES TO LEADERSHIP

Several theoretical approaches have been developed to explain leadership. These orientations will be presented in terms of their dominant focus and contribution to

Table 12–1   *Research topics and associated issues in leadership research*

Research Topic	Unit of Analysis	Variables of Interest	Research Questions
Positional power	Organization roles and positions	Influence tactics; use of power	Under what conditions will organizations resort to strong influence attempts?
The leader	Individual leaders	Personality characteristics; leader behaviors	What traits and behaviors differentiate effective and ineffective leaders?
The led	Work groups and subordinates	Group size; experience of subordinates	What types of subordinates desire close supervision?
Influence process	Superior–subordinate interface	Receptivity to influence; nature of influence attempts	Under what conditions are leaders most susceptible to subordinate influence attempts?
The situation	Environment or context in which leadership occurs	Situational effects on leader behavior; factors defining favorable situations	How do various situations modify behavior?
Leader emergence versus effectiveness	Individual and/ or groups	Group dynamics and individual characteristics	How do individuals become recognized as leaders?

the study of leadership. Yukl and Van Fleet (1992) offered an expanded version of these approaches (and related issues) in their excellent review of leadership research.

The Trait Approach

The trait approach emphasizes the personal attributes of leaders. Early leadership theories attributed success to the possession of abstract abilities such as energy, intuition, and foresight. Some differences were found between leaders and nonleaders on selected traits, but for the most part the relationship between traits and leadership success did not reveal a particular set of universally relevant traits to be successful.

Advances in trait research led to a change of focus from abstract personality traits to specific attributes that can be related directly to behaviors required for effective leadership in a particular situation. This more directed approach revealed that some traits increase the likelihood of success as a leader, even though none of the traits guarantees success (Kirkpatrick & Locke, 1991). The relative importance of different traits for leader effectiveness appears to depend in part on the leadership situation.

Some individual traits that appear to be related to leadership success are high energy level, tolerance for stress, emotional maturity, integrity, and self-confidence. *High energy level* and *stress tolerance* help people cope with the hectic pace and demands of most leadership positions, frequent role conflicts, and the pressure to make important decisions without adequate information. Leaders with high emotional maturity and integrity are more likely to maintain cooperative relationships with subordinates, peers, and superiors. *Emotional maturity* means that a leader is less self-centered, has more self-control, has more stable emotions, and is less defensive. *Integrity* refers to a person's behavior being consistent with expressed values and that the person is honest and trustworthy. *Self-confidence* makes a leader more persistent in the pursuit of difficult objectives, despite initial problems and setbacks.

Motivation is another aspect of personality related to leader effectiveness. The classic research of McClelland and his colleagues (e.g., McClelland & Boyatzis, 1982) identified three leader motives: need for power, need for achievement, and need for affiliation. Someone with a high need for *power* enjoys influencing people and events and is more likely to seek positions of authority. Someone with a high need for *achievement* enjoys attaining a challenging goal or accomplishing a difficult task, prefers moderate risks, and is more ambitious in terms of career success. Someone with a high need for *affiliation* enjoys social activities and seeks close, supportive relationships with other people. Similar results were found in another study on managerial motivation conducted by Berman and Miner (1985).

A related line of research addresses leader skills, as opposed to the possession of personality traits, in the belief that skill is required to implement the traits in leadership roles. Three basic categories of skills have been proposed: technical, conceptual, and interpersonal. *Technical skills* include knowledge of work operations; procedures and equipment; and markets, clients, and competitors. *Conceptual skills* include the ability to analyze complex events and perceive trends, recognize changes, and identify problems. *Interpersonal skills* include an understanding of interpersonal and group processes, the ability to maintain cooperative relationships with people, and persuasive ability. In general, the research supports the conclusion that technical, conceptual, and interpersonal skills are necessary in most leadership positions. However, the relative importance of most specific skills probably varies greatly depending on the situation.

In general, the trait approach was dominant in the early days of leadership research, then fell out of favor for a long time, and only recently has regained some credibility through the recent advances in personality assessment. Traits offer the potential to explain why people seek leadership positions and why they act the way they do when they occupy these positions. It is now evident that some traits and skills increase the likelihood of leadership success, even though they do not ensure success. Despite this progress, the utility of the trait approach for understanding leadership is limited by the elusive nature of traits. Traits interact with situational demands and constraints to influence a leader's behavior, and this behavior interacts with other situational variables to influence group process variables, which in turn affect group performance. It is therefore difficult to understand how leader traits can affect subordinate motivation or group performance unless we examine how traits are expressed in the actual behavior of leaders. Emphasis on leadership behavior ushers in the next era of research on leadership.

The Behavioral Approach

The behavioral approach emphasizes what leaders actually do on the job and the relationship of this behavior to leader effectiveness. Two major lines of behavior research are (1) the classification of leadership behaviors into taxonomies and (2) the identification of behaviors related to criteria of leadership effectiveness.

A major question in behavior research is how to classify leadership behavior in a way that facilitates research and theory on leadership effectiveness. Early research conducted during the 1950s at Ohio State University sought to identify relevant aspects of leadership behavior and measure these behaviors with a questionnaire completed by subordinates of leaders. The results revealed that the subordinates perceived the behavior of their leader primarily in terms of two independent categories, one dealing with task-oriented behaviors (*initiating structure*) and the other with people-oriented behaviors (*consideration*). The questionnaire that resulted from this research, called the *Leader Behavior Description Questionnaire* (LBDQ), is a hallmark in the history of leadership research. Sample items from the LBDQ are presented in Table 12–2. The two-factor taxonomy of task-oriented and people-oriented behavior provided a good starting point for the conceptualization of leadership behaviors, but the two dimensions eventually proved too abstract for understanding how leaders handle the specific role requirements confronting them. More recent advances in the assessment of leadership from the behavioral perspective are evidenced in the *Leadership Practices Inventory* developed by Kouzes and Posner (1995). Further progress in behavior research required a shift in focus to more specific aspects of behavior. Yukl, Wall, and Lepsinger (1990) proposed an integrating taxonomy with 11 generic categories of behavior applicable to any leader. They asserted that their relative importance varies across situations, and they can be enacted in different ways in different situations. The taxonomy is presented in Figure 12–1, and the major purposes of the leadership behaviors are listed in Table 12–3.

An increasing amount of research has examined how specific types of leadership behavior are related to leader effectiveness. This research suggests that managerial effectiveness is predicted better by specific behaviors (e.g., clarifying, monitoring, and problem solving) relevant to the leadership situation than by broad measures such as initiating structure and consideration. Clarifying is the

Table 12–2   *Sample items from the Leader Behavior Description Questionnaire*

Structure	Consideration
1. He schedules work to be done.	1. He is friendly and approachable.
2. He emphasizes the meeting of deadlines.	2. He makes group members feel at ease when talking to them.
3. He lets group members know what is expected of them.	3. He does little things to make it pleasant to be a member of the group.

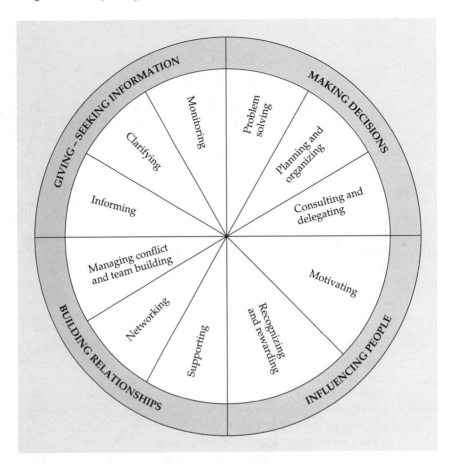

FIGURE 12–1   *Integrating taxonomy of leader behaviors*
SOURCE: From *Leadership in Organizations* (2nd ed.) (p. 129) by G. Yukl, 1989, Englewood Cliffs, NJ: Prentice Hall. Reprinted by permission.

primary component of initiating structure, and a number of studies have been conducted on the use of clarifying behavior by leaders (e.g., explaining responsibilities, assigning work, giving instructions, and setting priorities, deadlines, and standards). For example, setting specific challenging but realistic goals is an important component of providing clarification, and in the motivation literature there is ample evidence from field experiments that goal setting results in better performance than no goals or "do your best" instructions.

As was found in trait research, behavior research also suffers from a tendency to look for simple answers to complex questions. Most research on leadership effectiveness has focused on behaviors individually rather than how effective leaders use patterns of specific behaviors. It is likely that specific behaviors interact in complex ways and that leadership effectiveness cannot be understood unless these interactions are studied. For example, monitoring is useful for discovering problems, but unless something is done to solve problems when they are discovered, it will not contribute to the effectiveness of the leader. Delegating is unlikely to be effective unless the leader clarifies the subordinate's new responsibilities,

Table 12–3   *Major purposes of leadership behaviors in the integrating taxonomy*

Managerial Behavior	Internal Context	External Context
Networking	Good relations with subordinates	Good relations with peers, superiors, outsiders
Supporting	Good relations with subordinates, stress tolerance by subordinates	Good relations with peers, superiors, outsiders
Managing conflict and team building	Good relations with subordinates, group cohesiveness, cooperation among subordinates	Good relations with peers, superiors, outsiders
Motivating	Subordinate effort	Cooperation and support from peers, superiors, outsiders
Recognizing and rewarding	Subordinate effort and role clarity, good relations with subordinates	Cooperation and support from peers, superiors, outsiders
Planning and organizing	Unit efficiency and coordination	Adaptation to environment, external coordination
Problem solving	Stability of operations, unit efficiency and coordination	Adaptation to environment, external coordination
Consulting and delegating	Decision quality, subordinate effort	Decision quality and implementation
Monitoring	Detection of problems, evaluation of performance	Detection of problems and opportunities
Informing	Decision quality, unit efficiency and coordination	External coordination, enhance unit reputation
Clarifying	Role clarity, unit efficiency and coordination	External coordination

SOURCE: From *Leadership in Organizations* (2nd ed.) by G. Yukl, 1989, Englewood Cliffs, NJ: Prentice Hall. Reprinted by permission.

ensures that the subordinate accepts them, monitors progress in an appropriate way, and provides necessary resources.

Because of the growing realization of the importance of influencing others to attain goals, the next major direction in leadership research was to gain a better understanding of leader power and influence.

The Power and Influence Approach

The power possessed by a leader is important not only for influencing subordinates but also for influencing peers, superiors, and people outside the organization, such as clients and suppliers. Major questions in research on power include an identification of different types of power, an understanding of how different amounts and types of leader power are related to leadership effectiveness, and an understanding of how influence behavior is related to effective leadership.

Power and Leader Effectiveness.   Efforts to understand power usually involve distinctions among various forms of power. A classic power taxonomy was

DILBERT   by Scott Adams

SOURCE: Dilbert® reprinted by permission of United Feature Syndicate, Inc.

proposed by French and Raven (1960) that distinguished five types of power: reward, coercive, legitimate, expert, and referent.

1. *Reward power.* This is the capacity of an organization (or a member in a specified role) to offer positive incentives for desirable behavior. Incentives include promotions, raises, vacations, good work assignments, and so on. Power to reward an employee is defined by formal sanctions inherent in a superior's role.

2. *Coercive power.* The organization can punish an employee for undesirable behavior. Dismissal, docking of pay, reprimands, and unpleasant work assignments are examples. This capacity to punish is also defined by formal sanctions inherent in the organization.

3. *Legitimate power.* Sometimes referred to as *authority,* this means that the employee believes the organization's power over him or her is legitimate. Norms and expectations help define the degree of legitimate power. If a boss asks an individual to work overtime, this would likely be seen as legitimate, given the boss's authority. However, if a coworker makes the same request, it might be turned down. The coworker has no legitimate authority to make the request, although the individual might agree out of friendship.

4. *Expert power.* The employee believes that some other individual has expertise in a given area and that he or she should defer to the expert's judgment. Consultants are called on for help in handling problems because they are seen as experts in certain areas. The source of expert power is the perceived experience, knowledge, or ability of a person. It is not formally sanctioned in the organization. There are also differences in the perceived boundaries of expertise. One employee may be seen as the expert on using tools and equipment; others turn to him or her for help with technical problems. However, that expertise may not be seen as extending to other areas, like interpersonal relations.

5. *Referent power.* This is the most abstract type of power. One employee might admire another, want to be like that person, and want to be liked by him or her. The other worker is a referent, someone the employee refers to. The source of referent power is the referent's personal qualities. Cultural factors may contribute to these qualities. Younger people will often defer to an older person partly because age, per se, is a personal quality that engenders deference. Norms can also generate

Table 12–4   *Sources of leader power over subordinates and likely outcomes*

Source of Leader Influence	Type of Outcome		
	Commitment	Compliance	Resistance
Referent power	Likely* If request is believed to be important to leader	Possible If request is perceived to be unimportant to leader	Possible If request is for something that will bring harm to leader
Expert power	Likely* If request is persuasive and subordinates share leader's task goals	Possible If request is persuasive but subordinates are apathetic about task goals	Possible If leader is arrogant and insulting or subordinates oppose task goals
Legitimate power	Possible If request is polite and very appropriate	Likely* If request or order is seen as legitimate	Possible If arrogant demands are made or request does not appear proper
Reward power	Possible If used in a subtle, very personal way	Likely* If used in a mechanical, impersonal way	Possible If used in a manipulative, arrogant way
Coercive power	Very unlikely	Possible If used in a helpful, nonpunitive way	Likely* If used in a hostile or manipulative way

*Indicates most common outcome.
SOURCE: From *Leadership in Organizations* (2nd ed.) by G. Yukl, 1989, Englewood Cliffs, NJ: Prentice Hall. Reprinted by permission.

referent power. An employee may wish to identify with a particular group and will bow to the group's expectations.

Table 12–4 presents the five sources of power and their likely outcomes in dealing with subordinates. Yukl (1994) noted that the success of an influence attempt is a matter of degree. It produces three qualitatively distinct outcomes. *Commitment* describes an outcome in which an individual (the target) internally agrees with a request from another individual (the agent) and makes a great effort to carry out the request effectively. *Compliance* describes an outcome in which the target is willing to do what the agent asks but is apathetic rather than enthusiastic about it and makes only a minimal effort. *Resistance* describes an outcome in which the target person is opposed to the request, rather than merely indifferent about it, and actively tries to avoid carrying it out.

Research on legitimate power indicates that it is a daily influence on routine matters for managers in formal organizations (Yukl & Falbe, 1991). Research on positive reward behavior, which is based on reward power, finds that it has beneficial effects on subordinate satisfaction. Punishment, which is based on coercive power, can be used to influence the behavior of individuals who jeopardize the mission of the organization or threaten the leader's legitimate authority. Referent and expert power are used to make nonroutine requests and motivate commitment to tasks that require high effort, initiative, and persistence.

Some researchers have proposed that the manner in which power is exercised largely determines whether it results in enthusiastic commitment, passive compliance, or stubborn resistance. Effective leaders use combinations of power in a subtle fashion that minimizes status differentials and avoids threats to the self-esteem of subordinates. In contrast, leaders who exercise power in an arrogant and manipulative manner are like to engender resistance.

Organizations differ in the extent to which they use the various bases of power. Authoritarian managers rely on reward and coercive power. Managers with a participative style rely on expert and referent power. The military relies heavily on the legitimate power inherent in military rank. Stahelski, Frost, and Patch (1989) reported that university administrators use referent and expert power more than legitimate, reward, or coercive power to influence subordinates.

Ragins and Sundstrom (1989) examined gender differences in the use of power within organizations. They concluded that power seems to grow incrementally through the accumulation of multiple resources over the span of a career. For women, the path to power contains many impediments and barriers that can be characterized as an obstacle course. The path to power for men contains fewer obstacles that derive from their gender and may actually contain sources of support unavailable to their female counterparts.

Leader–Member Exchange Theory.   Graen and his associates (e.g., Dansereau, Graen, & Haga, 1975) proposed a theory of leadership based upon mutual influence, called leader–member exchange (LMX) theory. The theory postulates that leaders differentiate their subordinates in terms of (1) their competence and skill, (2) the extent to which they can be trusted (especially when not being watched by the leader), and (3) their motivation to assume greater responsibility within the unit. Subordinates with these attributes become members of what Graen calls the *in-group.* In-group members go beyond their formal job duties and take responsibility for completing tasks that are most critical to the success of the work group. In return, they receive more attention, support, and sensitivity from their leaders. Subordinates who do not have these attributes are called the *out-group;* they do the more routine, mundane tasks and have a more formal relationship with the leader. Leaders influence out-group members by using formal authority, but this is not necessary with in-group members. Thus, leaders and subordinates use different types and degrees of influence depending on whether the subordinate is in the in- or out-group. As expressed by Liden, Sparrowe, and Wayne (1997), "Quite simply, members who receive more information and support from the leader and who engage in tasks that require challenge and responsibility are expected to have more positive job attitudes and engage in more positive behaviors than members whose support is limited to what is required by the employment contract" (p. 60).

In a review of the theory, Dienesch and Liden (1986) concluded there are three psychological bases for the "exchange" between the superior and subordinate. *Personal contribution* refers to the perception of the amount, direction, and quality of work-oriented activity each member puts forth toward the mutual goals of the dyad. *Loyalty* is the expression of public support for the goals and personal character of the other members. *Affect* is the degree of liking members of the dyad have for each other. The authors refer to these three dimensions as the "currencies of exchange" within the dyad.

In a modification of LMX theory, the development of relationships in a leader–subordinate dyad was described in terms of a *life-cycle model* with three possible stages (Graen & Scandura, 1987). The relationship begins with an initial testing phase in which the leader and subordinate evaluate each other's motives, attitudes, and potential resources to be exchanged; changes in the role of the subordinate are negotiated through a series of mutually reinforcing behavior cycles. If the relationship proceeds to the second stage, the exchange arrangement is refined, and mutual trust, loyalty, and respect are developed. Some exchange relationships advance to a third (mature) stage, wherein exchange based on self-interest is transformed into mutual commitment to the mission and objectives of the work unit. Based on a meta-analytic review of LMX theory, Gerstner and Day (1997) concluded that the relationship an employee has with his or her supervisor is "a lens through which the entire work experience is viewed" (p. 840) and is not limited to leader–subordinate relations.

However, LMX theory has never been clear about the desirability of having sharply differentiated in-groups and out-groups. A sharply differentiated in-group is likely to create feelings of resentment and undermine team identification among subordinates who are excluded from the in-group (Yukl, 1989b). It is likely that effective leaders establish a special exchange relationship with all subordinates, not with just a few favorites. A leader can use some aspects of a special exchange, such as greater delegation of responsibility and sharing of administrative functions with a few subordinates, while also developing a relationship of mutual trust, support, respect, and loyalty with the other subordinates. It is not necessary to treat all subordinates exactly the same, but each should perceive that he or she is an important and respected member of the team rather than a "second-class citizen."

Influence Tactics.   A bridge between the power and behavior approaches is research on influence tactics. The choice of tactics for a particular influence attempt depends somewhat on the status of the target person and the objective of the influence attempt. The most common tactics are listed and defined in Table 12–5.

For example, pressure is used more in downward influence attempts than in lateral or upward influence attempts, consistent with the greater amount of positional power leaders have over subordinates than over peers or superiors. Some tactics such as ingratiation, rational persuasion, and personal appeals tend to be used more often in initial influence attempts, whereas other tactics such as pressure, exchange, and coalitions tend to be used more often in follow-up influence attempts after the agent has met initial resistance by the target (Yukl & Tracey, 1992).

Some tactics are more effective than others in gaining commitment, although the outcome of any influence attempt will likely depend in part on the specific situation, the relationship between agent and target, the agent's power over the target, and the perceived legitimacy and relevance of the agent's request. Yukl and Tracey reported that the most effective tactics for obtaining target commitment are rational persuasion, consultation, and inspirational appeals; the least effective tactics are pressure, coalition tactics, and legitimating tactics.

In conclusion, influence is a fundamental concept in leadership, and the power and influence approach appears to provide unique insights about the emergence and effectiveness of leadership. The conceptualization of power still remains somewhat unclear, however, because power may be construed as potential influence or

Table 12–5 *Definitions of influence tactics*

Rational Persuasion	The agent uses logical arguments and factual evidence to persuade the target that a proposal or request is viable and likely to result in the attainment of task objectives.
Inspirational Appeals	The agent makes a request or proposal that arouses target enthusiasm by appealing to target values, ideals, and aspirations, or by increasing target self-confidence.
Consultation	The agent seeks target participation in planning a strategy, activity, or change for which target support and assistance are desired, or is willing to modify a proposal to deal with target concerns and suggestions.
Ingratiation	The agent uses praise, flattery, friendly behavior, or helpful behavior to get the target in a good mood or to think favorably of him or her before asking for something.
Personal Appeals	The agent appeals to target feelings of loyalty and friendship toward him or her when asking for something.
Exchange	The agent offers an exchange of favors, indicates willingness to reciprocate at a later time, or promises a share of the benefits if the target helps accomplish a task.
Coalition Tactics	The agent seeks the aid of others to persuade the target to do something, or uses the support of others as a reason for the target to agree also.
Legitimating Tactics	The agent seeks to establish the legitimacy of a request by claiming the authority or right to make it, or by verifying that it is consistent with organizational policies, roles, practices, or traditions.
Pressure	The agent uses demands, threats, frequent checking, or persistent reminders to influence the target to do what he or she wants.

SOURCE: From *Leadership in Organizations* (3rd ed.) by G. Yukl, 1994, Englewood Cliffs, NJ: Prentice Hall. Reprinted by permission.

enacted influence. That is, power may be viewed as influence over the attitudes and behaviors of people or as influence over events. We need to learn more about the way power changes over time as a result of the leader's use and misuse of it.

The Situational Approach

The situational approach emphasizes the importance of contextual factors such as the leader's authority and discretion, the nature of the work performed by the leader's unit, the attitudes of subordinates, and the nature of the external environment. Situational research and theory fall into two major subcategories. One line of research treats leader behavior as a dependent variable; researchers seek to discover how the situation influences behavior and how much leader behaviors vary across different positions. The other line of research seeks to discover how situational variables moderate the relationship between leader attitudes (e.g., traits, behaviors) and measures of leader effectiveness. Fiedler (1996) believes it is critical to integrate situational components into an effective program of leadership training and development.

Path-Goal Theory.   According to path-goal theory (House, 1971), leaders motivate higher performance in subordinates by acting in ways that influence them to believe valued outcomes can be attained by making a serious effort. Aspects of the situation such as the nature of the task, the work environment, and subordinate attributes determine the optimal amount of each type of leader behavior for improving subordinate satisfaction and performance.

The theory states that a leader must be able to manifest four different styles of behavior, which have been derived from previous research on work behavior.

1. *Directive.* The leader provides specific guidelines to subordinates on how they perform their tasks. The leader should set standards of performance and provide explicit expectations of performance.
2. *Supportive.* The leader must demonstrate concern for subordinates' well-being and must be supportive of them as individuals.
3. *Participative.* The leader must solicit ideas and suggestions from subordinates and invite their participation in decisions that directly affect them (see Field Note 1).
4. *Achievement oriented.* A leader must set challenging goals, emphasize improvements in work performance, and encourage high levels of goal attainment.

Field Note 1 *Participation as Shared Power*

One leader style proposed by path-goal theory is participative leadership, which refers to allowing subordinates to participate in the decision-making process. I/O psychologists have had considerable difficulty figuring out the conditions under which this style is effective. Many factors seem to contribute to its success. We can start with the leader. Some individuals like to retain the decision-making authority inherent in their leadership roles. One basis for their feelings is that as leaders, they have more expertise than their subordinates, so why dilute the quality of the decision by delegating it to others? Some leaders solve this problem by giving subordinates the authority to make trivial decisions, or what is sometimes called "throwing them a bone."

Another problem is the subordinates. Most of us like to have our feelings solicited in matters that pertain to us, but there are wide individual differences. Some subordinates like to get involved in the fine-grained details of decisions, and others do not. Some subordinates resent having to make all sorts of decisions. If they are going to be burdened with the responsibility for making administrative decisions, then they want

the salary and title that traditionally come with it. When invited by the boss to participate in certain decisions, they are inclined to feel "That's your job, not mine." Willingness to participate is also moderated by the nature of the decision problem. Some problems are fair game for employee involvement, and others are not.

Finally, there are cross-cultural differences in the acceptance of participative leadership. A leading U.S. company once opened a production plant in Latin America. Using the latest leadership ideas from the United States, company officials invited the native employees to participate in a wide range of work-related decisions. Within a short period, turnover became exceedingly high. When the company investigated the cause of the turnover, it was shocked to learn its own management practices were primarily responsible. The employees interpreted management's participative style as evidence of its ignorance about running the plant. The employees were saying, in effect, "We're the workers, not management. If you don't know how to run your own plant, how do you expect us to know?" Effective use of the participative leadership style is more complex than you might think.

Effective leaders need all four of these styles, since each one produces different results. But when should a leader use which style? It depends on two types of situational factors. Some relate to subordinate characteristics, others to environmental factors. Leader behavior is motivating to the extent that it helps subordinates cope with environmental uncertainties or frustrations. What effect do these leader behaviors have? The leader can influence subordinates' perceptions of their jobs by (1) removing obstacles from the paths to the desired goals, (2) rewarding them for attaining their goals, and (3) helping them clarify paths to valued goals. Thus, the leader helps subordinates do the things that must be done to obtain the desired rewards.

However, path-goal theory has a number of conceptual limitations. The theory focuses on subordinate motivation as the explanatory process for the effects of leadership, and it ignores other explanatory processes, such as a leader's influence on the organization of work, resource levels, and skill levels. It has been suggested that greater empirical support would be found for the theory if some key propositions were stated in more narrowly defined behaviors, such as clarifying work roles, as opposed to the broader concept of initiating structure.

Cognitive Resources Theory.   Fiedler and Garcia (1987) proposed the cognitive resources theory of leadership. *Cognitive resources* are the leader's intelligence, technical competence, or job-relevant knowledge. The theory addresses how and under what conditions leaders should use their cognitive resources to lead their groups. Fiedler and Garcia proposed that when leaders employ directive behavior, are not under stress, and enjoy the support of their followers, they will make the most effective use of whatever cognitive resources they possess.

This theory focuses on unraveling the conditions for optimum use of leader abilities. The theory asserts that leaders have two general types of resources to help resolve problems: prior experience and intelligence. When a group is under stress because of the tense relationships between leaders and subordinates, leaders rely on prior experience in leading the group and do not make effective use of their intelligence. Fiedler believes that stress is a variable that can be managed effectively. Thus, through stress management, it is possible to increase the application of intelligence by leaders—that is, to make fuller utilization of cognitive resources. The theory postulates under which conditions leaders should draw more heavily on either prior experience or intelligence to solve leadership problems. Fiedler incorporated both situational and personal variables into this theory. We can think of cognitive resource theory as a specification of the process leaders should use in dealing with various types of situations to effectuate the success of the group.

In a test of the theory, Vecchio (1990) found that under stress, a leader's job-relevant experience (rather than intellectual ability) more strongly influences group performance. However, when the group is supportive of the leader, there is a stronger association between leader intelligence and group performance. In general, Yukl and Van Fleet (1992) stated that the theory is new with relatively little research conducted to assess it. However, some conceptual weaknesses also exist in the theory. For example, the intervening processes used to explain critical relationships are still incomplete, and likely differences among leaders in their reactions to stress are not recognized.

Transformational and Charismatic Leadership

Transformational leadership refers to the process of influencing major changes in the attitudes and assumptions of organization members and building commitment for major changes in the organization's objectives and strategies. Transformational leadership involves influence by a leader on subordinates, but the effect of the influence is to empower subordinates who also become leaders in the process of transforming the organization. Thus, transformational leadership is usually viewed as a shared process, involving the actions of leaders at different levels and in different subunits of an organization.

Charismatic leadership is defined more narrowly and refers to follower perception that a leader possesses a divinely inspired gift and is somehow unique and larger than life. Followers not only trust and respect the leader, but also idolize or worship the leader as a superhuman hero or spiritual figure (Bass, 1985). The indicators of charismatic leadership include a follower's trust in the correctness of the leader's beliefs, unquestioning acceptance of the leader, affection for the leader, and willing obedience. Thus, with charismatic leadership the focus is on an individual leader rather than on a leadership process that may be shared among multiple leaders.

Transformational Leadership. Bass (1998) defined transformational leadership in terms of the leader's effect on followers. Leaders transform followers by making them more aware of the importance and value of task outcomes, by activating their higher-order needs (in Maslow's sense), and by inducing them to transcend self-interest for the sake of the organization. As a result of this influence, followers feel trust and respect toward the leader, and they are motivated to do more than they originally expected to do.

Transformational leaders do more with colleagues and followers than set up simple exchanges or agreements. They behave in ways to achieve superior results by employing one or more of the four components of transformational leadership (Bass, 1998).

- *Idealized influence.* Transformational leaders behave in ways that make them role models for their followers. The leaders are admired, respected, and trusted. Followers identify with the leaders and want to emulate them; leaders are endowed by their followers with extraordinary capabilities, persistence, and determination.
- *Inspirational motivation.* Transformational leaders behave in ways that motivate and inspire those around them by providing meaning and challenge to their followers' work. Leaders get followers involved in envisioning attractive future states; they create clearly communicated expectations that followers want to meet.
- *Intellectual stimulation.* Transformational leaders stimulate their followers' efforts to be innovative and creative by questioning assumptions, reframing problems, and approaching old situations in new ways. New ideas and creative problem solutions are solicited from followers, who are included in the process of addressing problems and finding solutions.

◆ *Individualized consideration.* Transformational leaders pay special attention to each individual follower's needs for advancement and growth by acting as a coach or mentor. Followers and colleagues are developed to successively higher levels of potential. Individual differences of needs and desires are recognized, and the leader's own behavior demonstrates acceptance of these differences.

A leadership scale has been developed (the *Multifactor Leadership Questionnaire*) that assesses these components of transformational leadership. Research (e.g., Lowe, Kroeck, & Sivasubramaniam, 1996) has supported the construct validity of these components and has revealed that transformational leadership is strongly associated with work unit effectiveness. In particular, the idealized influence component is most strongly related to overall effectiveness. Bass (1997) asserted that these four components of transformational leadership transcend organizational and national boundaries and speak to the "universality of leadership."

Charismatic Leadership.   House (1977) proposed a theory that identifies how charismatic leaders behave, how they differ from other people, and the conditions under which they are most likely to flourish. As noted earlier, the theory specifies indicators of charismatic leadership that involve the attitudes and perceptions of followers about the leader. The theory also specifies leader traits that increase the likelihood of being perceived as charismatic, including a strong need for power, high self-confidence, and strong convictions. Some behaviors typical of charismatic leaders are (1) impression management to maintain follower confidence in the leader, (2) articulation of an appealing vision that defines the task in terms of ideological goals in order to build follower commitment, (3) communication of high expectations for followers to clarify expectations, and (4) expression of confidence in followers' ability to build their self-confidence.

Charismatic leaders are regarded as individuals who give their followers a vision of the future that promises a better and more meaningful life. Conger and Kanungo (1987) believe charismatic leaders are regarded as "heroes" who exhibit unconventional behaviors and transform people to share the radical changes they advocate. Manz and Sims (1991) added that such leaders should also be viewed as hero makers, and the spotlight should be on the achievements of the followers as well as the leaders. House, Spangler, and Woycke (1991) examined the personality and charisma of U.S. presidents and their effectiveness as leaders. The authors concluded that personality and charisma did make a difference in the effectiveness of the presidents. Gardner and Avolio (1998) identified the effective use of "staging" by charismatic leaders. Staging involves attention to the development and manipulation of symbols, including physical appearances, settings, props, and other artifactual displays. For example, a leader may stage a presentation by giving a speech in front of a building that has symbolic significance for the followers (see Field Note 2).

However, Hogan, Raskin, and Fazzini (1990) cautioned there is a "dark side" to charismatic leaders. Because they have excellent social skills, sometimes to the point of being charming, they are readily liked by their followers. But sometimes lurking behind the mask of likability is a person with pronounced adjustment problems. Only after these people fail in their leadership roles do we ever learn of their maladjustment, which was cleverly concealed by their ability to manipulate people to like them. Musser (1987) described the differences between positive and negative charismatics in terms of whether they seek to instill commitment to ideological goals or to themselves. Conger (1989) described the following problems that can occur with negative charismatics.

- They start grandiose projects to glorify themselves, and the projects are often unrealistic because of the leader's inflated self-assessment and unwillingness to seek and accept advice from others. They tend to ignore or reject evidence that a plan or strategy is encountering serious difficulties, thereby reducing the chance of correcting problems in time to avert a disaster.
- These leaders are willing to spend time in high visibility activities to promote a vision, but they are unwilling to spend the time necessary to guide and facilitate the implementation of a vision. They tend to vacillate between extremes of loose delegation when things are going well and overcontrolling behavior when trouble occurs with a project.
- They fail to develop competent successors. These leaders try to keep subordinates weak and dependent, and they remove people who have the leadership qualities of a potential successor. Thus, a leadership crisis is likely to occur when the leader dies or departs.

Field Note 2   *Use of Props by Leaders*

Current research has studied the use of props by leaders and the "staging" of activities designed to enhance communication effectiveness. Several examples of props have been used by U.S. political leaders. When Richard Nixon was Vice President of the United States, he was accused of inappropriately accepting gifts from people who wanted Nixon to use his influence on their behalf. In his defense Nixon appeared on television holding a cocker spaniel puppy named "Checkers." Nixon explained that he returned all the gifts he had received, except the dog, which he noted had become the family pet. The talk by Nixon while holding the dog became long remembered as "Nixon's Checkers speech."

When Dwight Eisenhower was President, he gave a speech on television to outline his philosophy of leadership. A camera was mounted above Eisenhower's head pointing downward at the top of his desk. Eisenhower pulled a piece of string out of his pocket, and then demonstrated that if the string were pulled, it would follow his fingers. But if the string were pushed, it would go nowhere. Equating the nation to the string, Eisenhower conveyed that he wanted to lead the nation to prosperity, not push it from behind.

Earl Butz was Secretary of Agriculture under President Nixon. Butz was scheduled to appear before a congressional committee to explain the financial budget of the Department of Agriculture. While seated before the committee, Butz pulled a loaf of sliced bread out from a paper bag. He proceeded to open the bread and stack the slices in various sized piles, demonstrating symbolically how the agriculture budget was allocated to various directives.

In these examples a dog, a piece of string, and a loaf of bread were used as props by the leaders to explain issues of considerable complexity. The props were remembered long after people had forgotten the content of the speeches.

In conclusion, both transformational and charismatic leadership theories identify the importance of leaders having a profound influence over their followers. Charismatic leadership theory tends to emphasize the characteristics of the leader, whereas transformational leadership theory tends to emphasize the processes by which the work group is transformed or developed.

The Implicit Leadership Theory

The previous theories of leadership presume that leadership is something that is really "out there," and the various theories are merely different ways to explain what it is. A radically different view is that leadership exists only in the mind of the beholder, usually the follower. It may be that "leadership" is nothing more than a label we attach to a set of outcomes; that is, we observe a set of conditions and events and make the attribution that leadership has occurred or exists. Implicit leadership theory regards leadership as a subjectively perceived construct rather than an objective construct. Implicit leadership theory is also referred to as the attribution theory of leadership and social information processing theory.

Lord and his associates have made the greatest contribution to this view of leadership. For example, Lord, Foti, and Phillips (1982) concluded that individuals hold conceptions of prototypic leaders (that is, what they think leaders are like) and then evaluate actual leaders according to their conceptions. People judged as "good" leaders are likely to be those whose actions and demeanors conform to the conception we hold. Thus, "effectiveness" in leadership is determined not objectively but through the confirmation of expectations. Phillips and Lord (1981) discovered that individuals develop global impressions of leader effectiveness and then use those global impressions to describe specific dimensions of leader behavior. Thus, individuals make confident judgments of behavior they have had no opportunity to observe, in much the same way halo error operates in performance appraisal. Meindl and Ehrlich (1987) discussed what they called "the romance of leadership" as it relates to assessments of organizational performance. In their study, subjects gave better evaluations to performance outcomes attributed to leadership factors than they gave to the same outcomes when they were attributed to nonleadership factors. The authors concluded that leadership has assumed a heroic, larger-than-life quality in people's minds. Meindl and Ehrlich believe leadership may serve a symbolic role, causing people to feel assured and confident that the fate and fortune of an organization are in good hands. Thus, the authors contend leadership may not account for as much of an organization's success as we believe, but "leadership" has a symbolic value in producing subordinate support, which may then paradoxically produce organizational effectiveness.

Implicit leadership theory poses a vexing dilemma for the assessment of leaders through questionnaires such as the LBDQ. We don't know if what these questionnaires measure is the actual behavior of the leader or the cognitive set of the rater. While Lord (1985) and Foti and Lord (1987) have proposed strategies to aid in the measurement of leaders, the issues raised by implicit leadership theory challenge the very foundation upon which most of our knowledge of leadership is based.

Substitutes for Leadership

Kerr and Jermier (1978) asked what it is that organization members need to maximize in seeking organizational and personal outcomes. They concluded that employees seek both guidance and good feelings from their work settings. Guidance usually comes from role or task structuring; good feelings may stem from any type of recognition. The authors feel that although these factors must be present, they do not necessarily have to come from a superior. Other sources may provide guidance and recognition as well. In these cases the need for formal leadership is diminished. The authors reference *substitutes for leadership* and highlight the point that a leader is merely a vehicle for providing these services. Indeed, some organizations have been experimenting with abandoning supervisor positions, leaving such traditional leadership roles in the hands of employees organized into special work teams. Podsakoff, MacKenzie, and Bommer (1996) reported that leaders and substitutes for leadership can simultaneously affect work groups. For example, leaders can create less need for formal supervision by carefully selecting employees who can function relatively independently. The authors concluded that such substitutes have very important effects on the work group, but they do not diminish the role of the leader.

There is evidence that the concept of leadership does not have to be vested in a formal position. Howell and Dorfman (1981) tested whether leader substitution can replace or "act in the place of" a specific leader. They examined whether having a closely knit cohesive work group and tasks that provide feedback concerning performance can take the place of a formal leader. The authors found partial support for the substitution of leadership, giving some credence to the idea that leadership need not always reside in a person. Pierce, Dunham, and Cummings (1984) provided further support for leader substitutes. They examined four environmental sources from which employees get structure and direction in how to perform their work: the job itself, technology, the work unit, and the leader. The authors found that only when the first three sources of structure were weak did the influence of the leader strongly affect employees. It seems that employees can derive typical leader qualities (that is, structure and direction) from inanimate sources in their environments, and that leadership functions need not be associated with someone in authority. It is thus possible to envision a successfully operating leaderless group in which the job itself provides direction in what to do (initiating structure) and the work group members support and tend to one another (consideration).

There is also evidence that some individuals are capable of directing themselves, a concept called *self-leadership.* Manz (1986) found that some employees could lead themselves if their values and beliefs were congruent with those of the organization (see Field Note 3). In summary, the research on substitutes for leadership suggests that leadership can be thought of as a series of processes or functions that facilitate organizational and personal effectiveness. These processes or functions need not necessarily emanate from a person in a formal leadership role but may be derived from characteristics of the work being performed by the group members.

Field Note 3 *Self-Leadership versus Self-Supervision*

The concept of self-leadership is related to many of the issues discussed in Chapter 8 on organizations and teams. Among them are the following.

The concept of organizational downsizing has resulted in broader spans of control and flatter organizational structures. As a consequence there is less direct supervision of employees because other control mechanisms must become operative to ensure that organizational goals are met. Small spans of control produce closer supervision but also additional layers in the organization's structure. Reducing the middle-management layer of organizations puts greater pressure on the other parts of the organization to accomplish what middle management once did—providing direction and control.

How might such direction and control be provided? One answer is through different organizing concepts, such as self-managed work teams. The work team provides a sense of direction or structure to the group's efforts and provides feedback and support to the team members. As the literature on substitutes for leadership has revealed, although structure and support are necessary for organizational functioning, they need not emanate from a formal leadership position.

It should also be recognized that today's workforce is more highly educated and trained than ever before. With education and training come the knowledges and skills the employee can bring to the task, lessening the need for a supervisor to tell employees what to do and to monitor their performance. Employees who know what needs to be done and have the resources to do it do not need extensive supervision.

Finally, do not equate supervision with leadership. One dimension of leadership is oversight or supervisory responsibilities. However, leadership entails more than just monitoring and directing others. It embraces a sense of vision, an understanding of how the organizational unit can function and even prosper in its environment. Leadership is more inclusive than supervision. Self-directed work teams ameliorate the need for direct supervision, but they do not obviate the need for organizational leadership.

POINTS OF CONVERGENCE AMONG APPROACHES

Despite the profusion of leadership approaches and related empirical findings, Yukl (1994) noted there is some convergence in the findings from different lines of leadership research. Yukl identified three consistent themes in the findings from leadership research.

Importance of Influencing and Motivating.   Influence is the essence of leadership. Much of the activity of leaders involves attempts to influence the attitudes and behaviors of people, including subordinates, peers, and outsiders. Motivating behavior includes a variety of social influence techniques for developing commitment to organizational objectives and compliance with requests. Much of the influence behavior of charismatic leaders falls into the motivating category, including inspiring commitment to new objectives and strategies, modeling exemplary behavior for followers to imitate, and appealing to values and aspirations.

Situational factors determine the importance of leader efforts to motivate subordinates. Leader influence on subordinate motivation is much less important when the task is intrinsically appealing. Motivation is more important for a very difficult task that frustrates and discourages subordinates. For these types of tasks, the subordinate's performance will suffer unless the leader intervenes to arouse enthusiasm and confidence.

Some of the traits and skills that predict leader effectiveness relate to the use of power. Leaders with high need for power and high self-confidence make more influence attempts. Self-confidence, persuasive ability, relevant expertise, and political insight facilitate the effectiveness of influence attempts. Interpersonal skills are necessary to articulate an appealing vision and persuade people of the need for change.

Importance of Maintaining Effective Relations.   Effective leaders establish cooperative relationships characterized by high levels of mutual trust and loyalty. The power research indicated the importance of referent power as a source of influence over the effect and commitment of subordinates. Referent power over subordinates is developed gradually over time as a result of dyadic social exchange processes in which the leader demonstrates trust and provides benefits to a subordinate while avoiding forms of influence that cause resentment. The behavior research found that subordinates are usually more satisfied with a leader who is friendly and helpful, shows trust and respect, and demonstrates concern for their needs and feelings. The situational research showed that the effects of leader behavior depend in part on the needs and values of subordinates. Supportive behavior is likely to have a stronger effect on subordinate satisfaction when the subordinate has a stressful, difficult task and lacks self-confidence.

Several of the traits and skills predictive of leadership effectiveness appear important for developing favorable relationships with subordinates, peers, and superiors. Relevant interpersonal skills include tact and diplomacy, listening skills, and social sensitivity. A leader with a positive regard for others is more likely to develop friendly relationships with people. Leaders who are preoccupied with personal ambition tend to do things that jeopardize relationships with people (e.g., betraying a trust or reneging on a promise in order to increase their personal gain).

Importance of Making Decisions.   Much of the activity of leaders involves decision making, but leaders seldom make important decisions at a single point in time, except for problem solving in response to immediate crises. In dealing with day-to-day decisions, effective leaders are guided by their long-term objectives and strategies.

People who effectively solve problems or develop successful strategies gain in status and power as a result. The reputation for expertise gained from successful decisions made in the past gives a person greater influence over subsequent decisions. Situational theories and research on group decision making suggest the conditions under which participation is most likely to improve the quality of a leader's decisions. The potential benefits from group decisions are greater for complex, important decisions than for routine ones. Participation results in better decisions when the participants have relevant information and clear ideas that the leader lacks, when they are willing to cooperate in finding a good solution, and when there is ample time for the participative process to be carried out.

Several of the traits and skills predictive of leadership effectiveness are relevant for decision making. Leaders with extensive technical knowledge and cognitive skills are more likely to make high-quality decisions. These skills are important for analyzing problems, identifying causal patterns and trends, and forecasting likely outcomes of different strategies for attaining objectives. Self-confidence and tolerance for ambiguity and stress help leaders cope with the responsibility for making major decisions on the basis of incomplete information.

CROSS-CULTURAL LEADERSHIP ISSUES

Because of the growing number of organizations that conduct international business, we are learning about cross-cultural issues in leadership. Much of our knowledge comes from situations where international managers are assigned to positions in the United States. Graen and Wakabayashi (1994) studied companies that have manufacturing plants located in both the United States and Japan, such as Toyota. These plants, which use Japanese organization methods and mostly American employees, require cross-cultural leadership to be successful. A *Japanese transplant* is a manufacturing plant owned by a Japanese parent company and located in a foreign country. Leadership presents special problems for Japanese transplants in the United States because of cultural differences between the two countries. Following are some of the problems found in Japanese transplants in the United States as identified by Graen and Wakabayashi:

1. *Language differences complicate communications and cooperation at managerial levels.* Very few domestic managers are able to interpret communications from the Japanese home office, and few Japanese managers can discuss abstract issues in English. Communication is therefore restricted to concrete issues without the benefit of any rationale or subtlety. The array of unresolved language problems keeps managers from confronting underlying cultural issues.

2. *Japanese managers and workers are shocked by what they perceive as American managers' seemingly underdeveloped sense of obligation to their company and coworkers.* Japanese managers often believe that American managers place their personal interests above those of the company and their coworkers. For example, one company launched a new product during deer hunting season and asked its hourly workers to postpone taking days off until the product launch was completed. The Japanese managers were pleased that absenteeism increased by only 5% for production workers, but they were aghast that absenteeism among American managers also increased by 5% during this period. The Japanese managers complained that the American managers should feel a stronger obligation to the company and lead the workers by setting a good example. This perceived underdeveloped sense of obligation makes it difficult for Japanese managers to trust or rely on domestic managers to perform critical tasks.

3. *American managers have difficulty with the absence of punishment for insubordination as an ideal.* According to the Japanese management principles, workers should not necessarily be punished for resisting a legitimate request by their managers. Instead, their philosophy considers the possibility that it is the manager who may be at fault for making a request that is resisted. Without insubordination as a punishable offense, a manager must develop a sense of obligation and

ownership in his or her workers through leadership development activities. Such activities build mutual obligations that render insubordination as superfluous.

4. *American managers see a lack of office perks as a loss of status.* The absence of status symbols such as private offices, reserved parking spaces, and management meeting rooms reduces the gulf between hourly workers and management. In addition, some companies require all plant management personnel to work on the shop floor at least one day per month and get their hands dirty. Though domestic managers understand at a conceptual level that such equal treatment helps reduce the social distance between hourly workers and managers, they feel the loss of status associated with a lack of perks at an emotional level. Compared to their cohorts in domestic companies, they feel that their situation is inferior and that they are not treated as well.

5. *American managers do not commit their entire career to a single company.* According to the authors, one of the most serious challenges Japanese transplants face is management mobility in the United States. Japanese transplants very carefully recruit and select domestic managers for home and staff functions. They hope that everyone hired will retire with the company. When domestic managers leave the transplant for another company, Japanese managers feel the loss doubly. First, they must repair their extensive networks by assuming the obligations of their departed peer and prepare for a new person to grow into the numerous company networks. This kind of adjustment is especially difficult for the Japanese leadership system because it is based on stable teams of committed managers. Second, many Japanese managers have difficulty accepting that a domestic manager can proclaim allegiance to a company and then leave within a year or two for another company—especially if it is a direct competitor.

Graen and Wakabayashi believe American and Japanese managers face different fears when confronted with a culture clash. The Americans fear that adopting the Japanese system could subvert traditional American values of individualism. Alternatively, the Japanese fear that adopting the American management system could undermine traditional Japanese values of teamwork. The authors pointed out that functional solutions to this dilemma can be reached when both parties are willing to learn each other's culture and work together to create a hybrid culture. Indeed, House, Wright, and Aditya (1997) and Bond and Smith (1996) contended that cultural differences in societies influence individual expectations and assumptions about their environment, attitudes toward others, and modes of social interaction. They proposed that cultural forces affect the kind of leader behavior that is usually accepted, enacted, and effective within an organization. This view of successful leadership being "culturally dependent" contrasts with the universality of leadership posited by transformational leadership theory.

DIVERSITY ISSUES IN LEADERSHIP

Hogan, Curphy, and Hogan (1994) questioned the role of leadership within organizations in the 21st century. They made the following observations. Historically, the typical American worker has been a White man with a high school education employed in a manufacturing job. Our knowledge of leadership largely focuses on how to lead that kind of person in those kinds of jobs in those kinds of organizations. Demographic trends suggest, however, that the national economy will shift from manufacturing to service jobs and that the workforce will become older, more diverse, and more female (Offerman & Gowing, 1990). The labor market for skilled workers will tighten, and there will be increased competition for talented personnel. As noted in Chapter 8, as organizations shrink, fewer middle managers will be needed, and the responsibilities of first-line managers will expand.

Chemers and Murphy (1995) noted that one explanation for gender differences in leadership is cultural. This view holds that because of their roles as family caretakers, women are socialized to be sensitive, nurturing, and caring. When they carry that socialization over into organizational roles, women are likely to be warmer, considerate, and democratic leaders. An alternative explanation proposed that observed differences in leadership style between men and women are more a function of biases in the observation process than the result of true differences. If we are more likely to notice and remember behaviors that are consistent with our categorical stereotypes, our observation of male and female leaders may be biased in attention, selection, memory, or recall. While minor differences may exist in leadership styles between men and women, our biases exaggerate the perception of these differences.

We do not have extensive knowledge on the best way to manage female and minority employees in service organizations. Moreover, we will likely have the same percentages of women and minorities in management as are currently in the workforce. Are there significant gender or cultural differences in leadership style, and will these styles be more or less effective for building teams in tomorrow's organizations? Eagly, Makhijani, and Klonsky (1992) provided some answers to these questions. They examined research on the evaluation of men and women who occupy leadership roles. While holding organizational characteristics constant and examining the gender of the leader, the research assessed whether people are biased against female leaders. Although the findings showed only a small overall tendency to evaluate female leaders less favorably than male leaders, this tendency was more pronounced under certain circumstances. Specifically, women in leadership positions were devalued relative to their male counterparts when leadership was carried out in stereotypically masculine styles, especially when this style was autocratic or directive. Also, the devaluation was greater when leaders occupied male-dominated roles and when the evaluators were women. In a meta-analysis of studies examining gender and effectiveness of leaders, Eagly, Karau, and Makhijani (1995) reported that the congruence of leadership roles with leaders' gender enhanced effectiveness. Men were more effective than women in roles that were defined in more masculine terms, and women were more effective than men in roles that were defined in less masculine terms.

CONCLUDING COMMENTS

In summary, although several approaches have been taken to understand leadership, the approaches agree in the conclusion that leadership is a vital process in directing work within organizations. There appear to be boundary conditions regarding when formal leadership is most effective as well as the processes leaders use to galvanize the members of their organizations. It is also insightful that current thinking about leadership considers leaders as not only heroes but also as hero makers. Thus, leadership need not be a phenomenon vested exclusively in upper-level positions, but rather is a contagious process that can manifest itself throughout all levels of an organization. Perhaps future research will be directed toward understanding the contagion of leadership.

CASE STUDY ◆ Which Direction Should We Follow?

Wayne LaPoe, president of Americom, studied his notes in preparation for the company's annual business planning and strategy meeting. It was at this meeting that most of the major goals for the next year would be set. As a diversified company in the communications field, Americom could go in several different directions. However, they basically boiled down to two possible avenues. One was to develop a wider range of products in anticipation of changing market needs. The other was to increase the sales and marketing of existing products. Each direction had its own champion within the company, and the decision of which path the company should take would be decided at the meeting where two executive vice presidents would state their cases.

Brandon McQuaid, vice president of Sales and Marketing, was a dominant force within the company. McQuaid stood 6 feet 4 inches tall, was perfectly trim, always appeared slightly tanned, and had an engaging smile and a resonant voice. He was impeccably dressed in the latest styles. He inspired tremendous loyalty among his staff. Always warm and gregarious, McQuaid was liked by everyone. It would be difficult not to like McQuaid, thought LaPoe. McQuaid had a knack for making everyone feel good about themselves, and he usually got a great deal of support for his ideas.

Ralph Pursell was vice president of Research and Development. An engineer by training, Pursell was about as different from McQuaid as night from day. Pursell was 5 feet 7 inches tall, at least 30 pounds overweight, and often appeared unkempt. No one ever accused Pursell of making a fashion statement. While his interpersonal skills were minimal, lurking behind his chubby face was the mind of a brilliant product designer. It was under his guidance in product development that Americom captured a huge share of the market in fiber optics. He was the most highly respected employee in the company. While some made snide remarks behind his back about his physical appearance, many employees realized they owed their jobs to Pursell's genius.

LaPoe anticipated how the planning meeting would go. He had seen it unfold the same way in past years. Pursell would make a pitch for developing some new products, using language that only he understood. The other executives in the room would simply take it on faith that Pursell knew what he was talking about. Then McQuaid would have his turn. Radiating confidence and optimism, McQuaid would soon have just about everyone eating out of his hand. He would argue that the company hadn't begun to scratch the surface in marketing Pursell's current trendsetting products. After 15 minutes of this charm, there would be a lot of smiling and head nodding in the room. When all was said and done, it was usually McQuaid's position that the management staff voted to adopt. Pursell would go back to his lab and wonder why the rest of the company didn't see things his way.

LaPoe questioned whether his management staff responded more to McQuaid's form than to Pursell's substance. He didn't want to alienate his staff by overturning their approval of McQuaid's position. Yet LaPoe wondered how much longer Pursell would continue to live with losing battles to McQuaid. LaPoe felt somewhat trapped himself. He needed the loyalty and commitment inspired by McQuaid, yet it was Pursell's ideas that McQuaid sold. LaPoe concluded that if it were possible to combine Pursell's technical ability with McQuaid's interpersonal skills, Americom would probably have a new president.

Questions
1. Is the management staff blinded by McQuaid's engaging leadership style, or is charm a legitimate component of leadership?
2. Should all leaders have strong interpersonal skills, or is someone like Pursell entitled to a leadership position on the basis of technical expertise?
3. If you were LaPoe, would you recommend that Pursell get some training in interpersonal skills and communication to enhance his credibility? Why, or why not?
4. Why are so many people at Americom "taken" with McQuaid? What does this suggest about why we accept people as leaders?
5. Is there a difference between having influence and being a leader? In what ways are these concepts related and unrelated?

INFOTRAC ARTICLES

1. *New Statesman (1996),* June 28, 1996 v125 n4290 p35(1)
   Merely importing East Asian work practices isn't enough. Peter Popham
   Discusses how leaders of industry in Great Britain want the Asian work ethic from their employees but are reluctant to adopt the Asian approach of giving employees responsibility.
2. *Journal of Sport Behavior,* Dec 1998 v21 i4 p387
   Leader member exchange theory and sport: Possible applications. Robert Case
   Discusses how the leader member exchange theory was applied to basketball teams based on a study of starters (the in-group) and nonstarters (the out-group).
3. *Training & Development,* May 1997 v51 n5 p58(14)
   How leaders develop leaders. Eli Cohen & Noel Tichy
   Discusses the importance of business leaders developing the skills of their subordinates to ensure the continued prosperity of their organizations.

4. *Training & Development*, Feb 1998 v52 n2 p12(2)
   The 10 commandments of team leadership. Kenneth E. Hultman
   Recommends 10 rules leaders should follow to maintain and enhance their team's effectiveness.
5. *Vital Speeches*, Jan 15, 1997 v63 n7 p202(4)
   Toward a female model: Leadership.
   A speech by a female CEO who describes the qualities female leaders bring to the workplace in addition to the traditional strengths of leaders.
6. *The Futurist*, Jan–Feb 1997 v31 n1 p68(1)
   Seven new principles on leadership. Donna C. L. Prestwood & Paul A. Schumann, Jr.
   Asserts that leadership is a path of personal growth reflecting a state of mind, not a position. Proposes seven principles of leadership that reflect this viewpoint.
7. *Across the Board*, Sep 1996 v33 n8 p28(5)
   The rush to leadership training. Louis S. Csoka
   Discusses that the need for leadership training has become more acute as society is in need of more leaders.
8. *Training & Development*, July 1995 v49 n7 p32(3)
   Leadership counts at Sears. Alan Perry & Dorothy Cottrell
   Describes a cost-effective method of leadership training used at Sears, Roebuck & Co. that has proven successful in developing a large and geographically dispersed workforce.

THE WORK ENVIRONMENT

Job Design and Organization Development: Creating High-Performance Organizations

MAJOR CHAPTER OBJECTIVES

◆ Explain the rationale of job design as reflected in job enlargement and job enrichment.

◆ Understand the logic and formulation of the job characteristics model.

◆ Discuss the rationale of organization development.

◆ Explain the concepts of the change agent, the client, and the intervention.

◆ Understand the concept of empowerment and why employees resist change.

◆ Discuss organizational culture change, Total Quality Management, and ISO 9000.

◆ Discuss values and ethics in organization development.

Organizations constantly try to maximize the "fit" between worker and workplace. The better the fit, the more likely the organization will be effective and run smoothly. Thus far, our discussion of increasing the fit has centered on the worker. Using the peg-and-hole analogy, we discussed finding new pegs that fit existing holes (personnel selection) or reshaping existing pegs for better fit (personnel training). However, the problem of fit can be approached by trying to change the shape of the hole. It is possible to change the workplace instead of, or in addition to, changing the worker. The overall goal is to create a high-performing organization, manifesting itself in greater productivity, lower cost, increased satisfaction, less turnover, and so on. However, change is never easy, and in fact it is often unwelcomed. The *status quo* is comfortable, and organizations must overcome resistance to change. The major reason for change in contemporary organizations is to achieve a competitive advantage in business operations. External pressures on organizations are the driving force to initiate change.

This chapter will examine two approaches to changing the workplace. One approach—job design—focuses on changing a job. The other approach—organization development—has a larger scope and involves more than just a job. The two approaches are related; some authors consider job design a part of organization development. However, organization development usually involves reorganizing many components of the workplace; job design has a narrower scope.

TO ALTER THE WORKER OR THE WORKPLACE?

The choice of whether to change the worker or the workplace is not easy. It is also not strictly an either/or choice; efforts to change the work environment may be made at the same time that workers themselves are being changed. Usually, though, there is more emphasis on changing one or the other. No magic formula can tell the I/O psychologist which side deserves more attention. This is a matter of professional judgment, best guided by the psychologist's experience with the organization.

The history of the organization's problems is usually the best place to begin. If a company has been successfully manufacturing a product or providing a service, it is better to replace a few workers who do not perform well than to revamp the entire organization. If large parts of the workforce have difficulty adjusting to work demands, personnel training may be the best method of raising skill levels to match organization needs. However, when problems seemingly reappear independent of who performs the work, thought must be given to altering the workplace. As a rule, it is more difficult to alter the workplace than the workers. Changing one part of an organization usually has intended as well as unintended effects on the rest of the organization.

Because organizations are designed to have interchangeable human parts, their life spans exceed the working life spans of employees. The complexities of personnel selection, placement, and training notwithstanding, the workplace is less alterable than the workforce. Successful organizations learn to alter both as conditions demand. This chapter will look at ways of changing the workplace, recognizing that the constant search for a good "fit" warrants giving attention to both sides of the relationship.

JOB DESIGN

Historical Overview

Job design originated in the early 1900s. Frederick Taylor believed that efficiency could be improved by carefully designing work to increase productivity. He advocated structuring jobs for simplification and standardization. **Simplification** means breaking down jobs into small tasks and then having each worker perform a small part of a total operation. A worker does the task repeatedly; the result is extreme specialization. For example, a job might be to connect two pieces of metal with a bolt. This is one part of an entire operation, and it might be repeated more than 100 times every hour. Other workers perform similar specialized tasks until the entire product is finally produced through the total efforts of all workers. The work process is also **standardized;** that is, the sequence of activities performed is the same.

Taylor's approach did improve productivity. Workers were able to produce more goods, lower skill levels were needed for these specialized tasks, and workers could be trained in less time. In the short run this approach resulted in economic efficiency. In Taylor's time, economic conditions were not good, jobs were relatively scarce, and people were grateful for whatever work they could get. However, this approach also produced problems. Workers rebelled at highly specialized, routine jobs. Monotony produced boredom, which, when coupled with lack of challenge and a sense of depersonalization, led to dissatisfaction. The behavioral consequences of work simplification are presented in Figure 13–1.

The dissatisfaction resulting from Taylor's approach showed itself in ways that decrease efficiency: lateness, absenteeism, turnover, stress, drug use, and sabotage. Over time, the problems were exacerbated by changing worker populations. At the turn of the century, workers were relatively uneducated and jobs were scarce; thus, workers were not very critical of their jobs. As workers became more educated and more jobs were available, workers were no longer content with jobs that provided little other than income. The economic gains of increased efficiency were offset by negative reactions to the simplified jobs. Indeed, Melamed, Ben-Avi, Luz, and Green (1995) have proposed that monotonous jobs produce a form of stress they believe relates to "underload"—an insufficient amount of stimulation on the job. Wong and Campion (1991), in turn, proposed that jobs should be designed to be in a mid-range of stimulation, neither too low nor too high in the demands placed on workers. In general, research on job design describes attempts to make jobs "better" by making them inherently motivating and satisfying to perform.

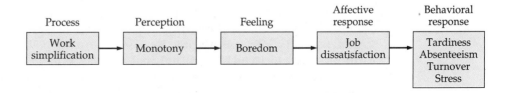

FIGURE 13–1   *Behavioral consequences of work simplification*

FRANK AND ERNEST   By Bob Thaves

Job Enlargement and Job Enrichment

In the 1940s and 1950s, organizations began to realize that the structure of jobs must focus on greater satisfaction of employee needs rather than specialization of work. During this time, two "job-change" strategies became popular: job enlargement and job enrichment. In theory the two are different; in practice they have a lot in common. **Job enlargement** means increasing the number and variety of tasks a worker performs. **Job enrichment** means increasing a worker's control over the planning and performance of a job and participation in setting organization policy. Job enlargement involves expanding the scope of a worker's job duties. An example is a production worker's responsibility for assembling several parts of a piece of equipment as opposed to one part. Job enrichment involves giving the worker more autonomy and decision-making power over when and how work operations are performed. At the core of both programs was the belief that motivation would be better if workers had more sense of achievement in their work.

Many early studies examined the effects of job enlargement and enrichment on worker behavior and attitudes. One can think of these as field studies: They compared on-site performance before and after job change. Several studies reported increases in either attitude or performance as a result of job design changes. However, the research was not of the best quality since it rarely used control groups. A company often introduced new technology along with changes in work operations. It was thus impossible to tell whether the changes in performance and attitude were due to changes in technology or to job design changes.

In 1959 Herzberg, Mausner, and Snyderman developed an approach to job design called *motivator-hygiene theory*. The theory proposed that the primary determinants of employee motivation and satisfaction are factors called *motivators*, which are intrinsic to the work itself, such as recognition, achievement, and responsibility. Dissatisfaction is caused by *hygiene* factors that are extrinsic to the work, such as salary, supervisory practices, and company policies. Herzberg's theory proposed that job changes will enhance motivation and productivity only to the extent that motivators are designed into work. Changes that address hygiene factors were expected to reduce dissatisfaction but not enhance motivation. As Oldham (1996) observed, the theory was not supported in a wide variety of studies. The research findings revealed that some aspects of the workplace can serve as both motivators and hygiene factors. The theory also did not provide for differences in how responsive people will be to jobs that contain many motivating factors. While Herzberg's theory was not empirically supported, it served a valuable purpose in propelling research on job design into a new era—the identification of specific job task attributes that have a positive effect on worker behavior.

Task Attributes

As the name suggests, *task attributes* are characteristics of the task components of jobs that influence worker behavior. In an early study, Turner and Lawrence (1965) identified six task attributes that they thought were related to satisfaction and attendance: variety, autonomy, required interaction, optional interaction, knowledge and skill required, and responsibility. They conducted interviews and made field observations of these six attributes for 47 different jobs. Each attribute was scaled to yield a score reflecting "how much" of it was present in each job. Jobs that scored high on these variables were positively correlated with high worker satisfaction and attendance. Yet a curious finding also emerged: This relationship held only for workers in factories in small towns and not for urban workers. Turner and Lawrence concluded that worker reactions to task attributes were influenced by cultural factors. This gave impetus to investigating what "types" of people respond most positively to redesigned jobs. The findings from such studies will be discussed shortly.

It was apparent that motivation was influenced by job structure. Furthermore, it seemed possible to design jobs to increase motivation. In this sense job design efforts can be viewed as attempts to increase motivation, as discussed in Chapter 11. Research studies produced evidence that jobs that provide variety, autonomy, identity, and feedback increased motivation among some employees. This manifested itself in greater organizational commitment and job involvement, as well as in increased attendance and job satisfaction.

It also became apparent that not all people responded in the same way. Why people differed in responses to jobs with comparable task attributes had to be explained. Researchers focused on the role of human needs in determining the "type" of job a person would want. It was thought that people trying to satisfy higher-order needs would want more stimulating jobs. They would thus respond more positively to enriched jobs. Jobs providing high levels of certain task attributes seemingly satisfied such needs.

Several scales were developed to identify people who would want an enriched job and would respond positively to (be more motivated by) it. Hackman and Oldham (1975) developed one such scale: the *Higher-Order Need Strength Questionnaire B.* The relative strength of growth needs is reflected in the choice of jobs characterized by opportunities for decision making, need for a variety of skills and abilities, freedom and independence, and factors such as high pay and fringe benefits, job security, and friendly coworkers. Results of studies testing the effect of these needs suggest that people with strong higher-order needs do derive more satisfaction from enriched jobs. However, not all research has been supportive. It appears that an individual's desire (need) to be challenged at work does affect reactions to an enriched job, but this alone does not account for all the variance.

Job Characteristics Model

Clearly, there has been no one theoretical explanation of why and how task attributes affect workers. The way jobs influence motivation could be partially explained by several existing theories, including Maslow's need hierarchy and expectancy theory. To integrate and synthesize much of the literature on this topic, Hackman and Oldham (1976) proposed a model to explain how jobs influence attitudes and behavior. Called the *job characteristics model*, it is probably the most researched explanation of job enrichment.

According to Hackman and Oldham, any job can be described by five core dimensions:

1. *Skill variety:* the number of different activities, skills, and talents the job requires
2. *Task identity:* the degree to which a job requires completion of a whole, identifiable piece of work—that is, doing a job from beginning to end, with visible results
3. *Task significance:* the job's impact on the lives or work of other people, whether within or outside the organization
4. *Autonomy:* the degree of freedom, independence, and discretion in scheduling work and determining procedures that the job provides
5. *Task feedback:* the degree to which carrying out the activities required results in direct and clear information about the effectiveness of performance

The second part of the model deals with the effect of the core job dimensions on the individual. They are said to influence three critical psychological states. The *experienced meaningfulness of work* is high when the job involves skill variety, task identity, and significance. The *experienced responsibility for work outcomes* is influenced mainly by the amount of autonomy. *Knowledge of results of work activities* is a function of feedback. According to the theory, high levels of the critical psychological states will lead to favorable personal and work outcomes, including high internal work motivation, work performance, satisfaction, and low absenteeism and turnover.

The final part of the Hackman and Oldham model is an individual difference variable called growth-need strength (GNS), which reflects a desire to fulfill higher-order needs. Like others before them, Hackman and Oldham felt that people with high needs for personal growth and development should respond more positively to jobs high on the core dimensions. Only people with high GNS should strongly experience the critical psychological states associated with such jobs. The entire job characteristics model is portrayed in Figure 13–2.

Hackman and Oldham developed an equation for indexing the potential of a job to motivate its holder. The equation is based on the five core dimensions. Hackman and Oldham refer to their index as the *motivating potential score* (MPS) and define it as

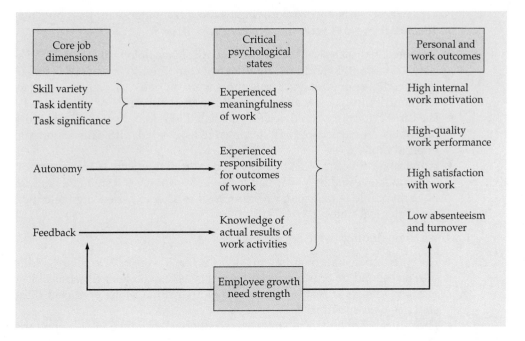

FIGURE 13–2   *The job characteristics model*

SOURCE: From "Motivation Through the Design of Work: Test of a Theory" by J. R. Hackman and G. R. Oldham, 1976, *Organizational Behavior and Human Performance, 16*, p. 256.

$$\text{MPS} = \frac{\text{Skill} + \text{Task} + \text{Task}}{3} \text{ variety } \text{ identity } \text{ significance} \times \text{Autonomy} \times \text{Feedback}$$

The first three core dimensions are averaged because they all contribute to the experienced meaningfulness of work, the first critical psychological state. The other two dimensions, autonomy and feedback, reflect the remaining critical states and thus are not averaged.

The job's motivating potential is very high when each component of the formula is high. Because the components are multiplied, low scores on any one yield a low motivating potential score. A score of zero on any of the major components (for example, a job completely lacking in autonomy) reduces the MPS to zero; the job has no potential for motivating incumbents.

Finally, as shown in Figure 13–2, the entire effect of the job characteristics model is moderated by the strength of growth need. Only employees who are trying to satisfy higher-order needs will respond favorably to a job high in motivating potential.

Empirical Tests of the Model.   A number of studies have tested the relationships and predictions of the model. Empirical support is mixed. Certain parts of the model are substantiated more than others.

Hackman and Oldham (1976) provided validation evidence for their own theory. In general, the results were moderately supportive:

- ◆ The core job dimensions related to the critical psychological states. Skill variety, task identity, and task significance combined to predict the level of perceived meaningfulness. The authors were thus able to identify those factors contributing to "meaningful work," a frequent desire of employees.
- ◆ The three critical psychological states related to selected personal and work outcomes. In particular, high levels were associated with satisfaction and internal motivation.
- ◆ Individual differences in GNS have a moderating effect, as Hackman and Oldham suggested. In particular, high-GNS employees were more likely to have favorable personal and work outcomes after experiencing the critical psychological states.

However, some findings were not supportive:

- ◆ The core dimensions of autonomy and feedback were not clearly related to the corresponding critical psychological states of experienced responsibility and knowledge of results. Some of the other dimensions predicted these states as well or better.
- ◆ The critical psychological states were only weakly related to absence and performance.

In general, the results showed that jobs high on the core job dimensions were associated with high levels of personal and work outcomes. Individuals with high GNS responded most favorably to these types of jobs. The importance of the intervening critical psychological states was not strongly supported.

Based on a review of over 200 studies that tested the model, Fried and Ferris (1987) arrived at three conclusions. First, research suggests the existence of multiple job characteristics, but it is not clear how many there are. Second, the linkage between the job characteristics and the critical psychological states is not as strong as originally hypothesized. Third, the personal and work outcomes specified in the model are indeed related to the job characteristics. The job design paradigm also has implications for other work-related concepts, such as pay.

More recently, Oldham (1996) proposed some needed research directions with the model. One involves the ongoing effects of job characteristics on individual needs and skills. Characteristics of a job can exert long-term influences on the people performing the job. Furthermore, it is also possible that the design of jobs might affect employees' GNS. For example, employees who work on simple jobs might experience chronic frustration, resulting in lowered GNS.

EFFECTIVENESS OF JOB REDESIGN PROGRAMS

Does job redesign "work"? Does it produce the intended positive outcomes? Since the number of studies on job enrichment has increased in recent years, we are now in a position to examine their cumulative findings. The major result of redesigned work appears to be an increase in job satisfaction. Loher, Noe, Moeller, and

Fitzgerald (1985) reported average correlations between scores on the five core job dimensions of the job characteristics model and reported job satisfaction of around .40. In other words, it seems that the more jobs are enriched (defined as higher scores on the core job characteristics), the more satisfied the people are who perform them. The research relating job characteristics to changes in job performance has produced mixed findings. Locke, Feren, McCaleb, Shaw, and Denny (1980) estimated that across all jobs there is a 17% improvement in productive output after enrichment. However, Griffin, Welsh, and Moorhead (1981) reported less supportive findings. Griffin and associates felt that poorly designed measures of job performance contribute to the ineffectiveness of some job enrichment programs.

What can we conclude about the effectiveness of job redesign? Probably the safest conclusion is that results vary depending on the criterion, and we cannot simply assume that such programs will have a common outcome. Most studies report mixed findings (improvements in some areas but not in others), but total failures have also been cited. Job redesign is complex; it is difficult to generalize findings across diverse situations. Differences can exist not only in redesign techniques but also in employees (age, experience, education, skill level) and workplace (jobs, organizations, union status). In trying to improve the worker/ workplace fit by changing the workplace, we should exercise the same caution and concern used in evaluating workers. Just as we know that a given test is not valid for hiring many different kinds of workers, we should also realize that a given job redesign technique will not always work for different jobs. Unfortunately, there are no universal procedures for selecting or modifying pegs or for reshaping holes.

ORGANIZATIONAL IMPLICATIONS OF JOB REDESIGN

As discussed in Chapter 8, organizations are complex systems composed of interdependent parts. If you alter one part of an organization, changes (often unanticipated) in other parts will likely ensue. As a simple example, suppose job redesign were successful in increasing the output of a production department. The organization would have to accommodate the growing supply of manufactured goods, which would create a warehousing and space problem. It would likely be pressured to increase the sale of these goods as the stockpile increased. If the sales department were successful, the responsibility of the accounting and bookkeeping departments would be increased. Thus, changes in production would have implications for the rest of the organization; such ripple effects are not at all uncommon. Organizations often do not understand the consequences of making changes in selected areas.

Furthermore, the multiple theoretical perspectives to job design have the potential for grossly differing organizational implications. As reported by Campion and Thayer (1985), jobs can be designed to increase psychological stimulation (make them more challenging to perform) or to decrease the likelihood of accidents and errors (make them simpler to perform). (This study is discussed more fully in Field Note 1.) Each approach to job design leads to different outcomes, and each approach has costs as well as benefits. Trade-offs are inevitable.

Field Note I When to Enrich?

The study by Campion and Thayer (1985) revealed a contradiction between two fundamental approaches to work design, both of which have a strong psychological heritage. The first approach is called the *human factors paradigm* (and will be presented in greater detail in Chapter 15). This approach emphasizes the design of work in terms of increasing efficiency. It typically involves designing tasks to avoid complicated movements, intensive decisions, and other factors that often lead to errors. In general, the human factors paradigm strives to maintain functional simplicity, forthrightness, and directness in task duties. The more complicated the system, the more things that can go wrong; thus, designers strive to keep things simple and straightforward. This philosophy tends to produce tasks that are easy to perform (with the ultimate goal of being "goof-proof") or at least as uncomplicated as possible.

The second approach is the *job enrichment paradigm;* it, too, seeks to enhance efficiency. However, its tack is very different from the human factors approach. The job enrichment paradigm seeks to provide a sense of challenge and stimulation. It is precisely because many jobs have been designed with simplicity in mind that they are perceived as boring and monotonous.

Thus, with a job enrichment approach, tasks are designed to provide some diversity of human response and, in the process, literally increase the variability in operator behavior—the very thing that the human factors paradigm seeks to minimize.

As Campion and Thayer discovered, these two approaches make almost polar-opposite recommendations for task design. Is there a middle-ground resolution to these conflicting views? Not directly. In the extreme, both approaches are dysfunctional. If every work task were designed to be so simple that it required no human thought or discretion, we would have created a very sterile and unappealing environment. On the other hand, when I get behind the wheel of my car, I am grateful that human factors psychologists have designed the steering mechanism such that when I want the car to turn left, I simply turn the wheel to the left. I would not want the steering mechanism "enriched" to the point where it would take simultaneous foot, knee, hand, and arm movements to get the car to turn left. In short, each approach has its place in work design, but there are occasions and situations in which it is not clear which paradigm should prevail.

Campion (1988) stated that a comprehensive theory of job design must be interdisciplinary. Psychological approaches strive to produce jobs that are stimulating and mentally demanding, but they may have the unintended consequences of increasing training times and creating staffing difficulties. The mechanistic approach errs in the other direction because jobs may be designed inadequately in terms of satisfaction and potential growth. Campion and McClelland (1991) experimentally redesigned jobs to examine the consequences. The enlarged jobs were better from a motivational perspective but worse from a mechanistic (engineering) perspective. The redesigned jobs had the benefits of greater job satisfaction, less boredom, and more chances of catching errors, but the costs were higher training requirements, higher basic skills, and higher compensable factors. Clegg and Wall (1990) found relatively poor mental health associated with workers performing jobs that had been simplified, but only for those who saw their work as not using their skills. Campion and Berger (1990) reported that jobs characterized by higher scores on the core job dimensions were associated with higher aptitudes and higher pay. When organizations want to make jobs more challenging, they should realize that they will need people with more talent and ability to perform them.

Increased employee talent will also demand more pay; more talented people are worth more. Schneider, Reichers, and Mitchell (1982) and Campion (1989) confirmed that elevating the core characteristics of jobs increased the aptitudes of individuals needed to perform the jobs successfully. Schneider and associates felt that some job-enrichment programs may fail because they increase the aptitude requirements beyond the levels incumbents possess. However, Campion and McClelland (1993) concluded that the trade-off between higher aptitude and higher wage levels need not be direct. They proposed a distinction between task enlargement and knowledge enlargement. Knowledge enlargement referred to adding requirements to the job for understanding procedures or rules relating to different products sold by the organization. Knowledge enhancement was found to increase employee motivation and satisfaction, but without the direct effect of escalating wage rates as found with task enlargement. Campion and McClelland were optimistic that jobs could be designed to enhance motivation and satisfaction, but they suggested that the effects of such efforts may take several years to manifest themselves.

ORGANIZATION DEVELOPMENT (OD)

The first part of this chapter dealt with job design: changing jobs to make them more motivating and meaningful for the worker. Job design is one way of improving organization effectiveness, but it is by no means the only way. Sometimes the problems facing organizations require solutions beyond making a job the unit of change. The topic of **organization development,** often referred to as simply OD, concerns the ways in which organizations can grow, change, and develop to function more effectively. This part of the chapter will examine OD.

What Is OD?

Definitions of OD tend to be rather long and cumbersome because it is a multifaceted concept that defies a simple yet accurate definition. One useful definition is by Huse and Cummings (1985), who defined OD as "a system-wide application of behavioral science knowledge to the planned development and reinforcement of organizational strategies, structures, and processes for improving an organization's effectiveness" (p. 2). Porras and Robertson (1992) indicated that most definitions of OD embody several themes. The *purpose* of OD is improvement in the organization's effectiveness, its ability to adapt, its self-renewing processes, and its development of new and creative organizational solutions. Its *scope* is overall organizational or systemwide change. Its *conceptual* underpinnings derive from behavioral science theory, research, and technology. Its *process* is planned, value-based, consultant-aided, and directed or supported by top management. Finally, its *targets* are the organization's culture, structure, strategy, and processes. As the foregoing suggests, OD is broadly based and ultimately designed to facilitate the organization's well-being.

The Need for OD

To understand why OD was invented requires some understanding of the social times and conditions through which it has evolved. The evolution of OD has been chronicled by Mirvis (1990).

In the 1950s theories of management and organization evolved out of a cold, sterile, and solely quantitative perspective to include the consideration of social, human factors. OD was born as an attempt to better understand the process of group dynamics. The preferred means of understanding group dynamics was through behavioral science training, also called the T-group ("T" for training). Individuals unknown to one another would come together with no set agenda, clear leadership, or established mode of operation. Their function was to learn about themselves and the dynamics of social interaction in an unstructured medium by creating their own rules and roles. The logic behind the T-group was that if people could learn to understand themselves and how groups operated, this knowledge could be applied to work organizations to enhance their effectiveness. However, it eventually became apparent that the capacity to enhance self-learning and effect change in a small group would not necessarily generalize to larger, more complex social systems as found in most organizations.

Although OD sought to humanize work at the group level, it was largely not successful in doing so. It took major social and economic changes to reroute the direction of OD. Such changes began to take place in the 1980s, as evidenced by massive organizational restructuring and downsizing. As discussed in Chapter 8, as the primary result of economic pressures caused by foreign competition, millions of jobs were eliminated. Organizations sought to staff themselves with fewer employees as a means of controlling costs. However, there is a psychological cost to treating employees as if they are highly disposable—the employees feel little in the way of loyalty and commitment to the organization. They develop feelings of self-interest and cynicism about trust in the workplace. Levinson (1994), in fact, described the failure of American corporations to adapt to changed economic circumstances as a social catastrophe. No organization can prosper in the long run without a committed workforce. It therefore fell to OD to reestablish the relationship between employees and organizations that culminates in sustained growth and development. Today OD is guided by attention to what some individuals regard as the "softer" sides of organizations—values, vision, culture, and integrity. Thus, OD is directed to the process of organizational transformation, transforming organizations to consider both the financial criteria of success and the social dynamics required to sustain such success. Not surprisingly there is a strong connection between OD and the concept of transformational leadership, as discussed in Chapter 12.

The driving mechanism behind OD is the manifestation of organizational *excellence* in its many forms. Organizations seek to attain excellence in the products they make, the services they provide, the customers they satisfy, and the individuals they employ. The concept of excellence is the unifying theme for integrating the facets of running an organization. The concept of organizational excellence as well as the OD practices used to pursue it will be examined later in this chapter.

Three Basic Concepts in OD

Three concepts are invariably evident in all OD literature: the change agent, the client, and the intervention. Each has been the subject of extensive investigation and is an integral part of any OD effort. Collectively, they are the ingredients of all OD programs.

The Change Agent.   The **change agent** (sometimes referred to as the *interventionist*) is the person who initiates the change. This is usually someone outside the organization (for example, a hired consultant), but occasionally it may be a person within it. The agent is usually involved in diagnosing and classifying problems, identifying courses of action, recommending change procedures, and in some cases actually implementing the changes.

Effective change agents should possess the following qualities: diagnostic ability, basic knowledge of behavioral science, empathy, knowledge of the theories and methods of their own disciplines, goal-setting ability, and problem-solving skills. Agents must strive to build trust among organization members; they must be seen as being sincerely concerned with improving the organization's well-being. Without this trust, organization members will resist attempts at change.

Also, the agent must intervene only to the extent required for effecting enduring solutions to the problem at hand. If the agent's role is to help the organization diagnose problems and plan strategies for improvement, he or she should not impose predetermined "solutions" with supposed "guaranteed" results. The change agent should never try to exceed the limits of his or her role; these should be mutually agreed on at the start of the program.

The Client.   The **client** is the recipient of the change effort. This may be an individual, a group, or possibly the entire organization. You might not think it would be a problem, but sometimes it is not exactly clear who the client is. For example, an organization may at first hire a consultant to diagnose why an important manager suffers from excessive role overload. The agreement may also include the consultant's offering strategies for alleviating the problem. In diagnosing the problem, the consultant discovers that the manager has assumed increasing responsibility because his or her subordinates are seen as incompetent. Rather than overseeing a poor job, the manager gradually assumes responsibility for doing it. At this point, there are three parties (besides the consultant) involved: the manager, the subordinates, and the organization employing these people.

To help people, an agent must interact with and influence them. If the agent's authority does not extend to interacting with subordinates, the real problem probably will not be resolved. Perhaps the true issue in the situation described is incompetent subordinates, but it could also be a manager who has distorted views of the quality of subordinates' work. Perhaps the manager is not good at delegating, irrespective of subordinates' merits. In this case how can the consultant help the client, and who in fact is the client? In practice, there may be more than one client. The manager may be the key client, but there may be various ancillary clients, all part of the total organization. Helping one client may conflict with enhancing the well-being of another. The agent must decide how the organization can best be helped, realizing that this is not always an easy decision.

The Intervention.   **Intervention** is what the change agent does on behalf of the client. The change agent can engage in a broad range of activities, such as the ones listed here:

- *Diagnostic activities:* to ascertain the state of the system, the status of a problem, the "way things are"
- *Intergroup activities:* to improve the effectiveness of interdependent groups
- *Education and training activities:* to improve skills, abilities, and knowledge
- *Coaching and counseling activities:* to work with people to help them define learning goals, learn how others see their behavior, and learn new behavior to see whether it helps in goal attainment
- *Life- and career-planning activities:* to enable individuals to focus on life and career objectives and how they might achieve them

Each of these categories includes many activities and exercises. They all use conceptual material and actual experience with the phenomenon being studied. Some are directed toward specific targets, problems, or processes. For example, intergroup activities are directed toward work teams; life-planning activities toward individuals. In general, interventions are structured activities in which selected units (target groups or individuals) engage in a series of tasks directed toward improving the organization.

A Model of Planned Organizational Change

As Porras and Robertson (1992) noted, in order to change an organization, one must understand at least three basic sets of variables. The first are those variables that can be manipulated or changed by OD intervention. The second are the outcomes intended by the change effort. Third are those variables that influence the degree to which the manipulated variables can alter the outcome variables.

Robertson, Roberts, and Porras (1993) have proposed a model to explain how organizations can be changed through OD intervention; it is illustrated in Figure 13–3.

Organizational Work Setting.   The work setting consists of four sets of characteristics. The first are the organizing arrangements, the structure, strategies, administrative systems, and reward systems of the organization. The second are the social factors, the organization's culture and management style. Third is the physical setting, the space configuration of the organization, interior design, and physical ambience. Technology is the fourth component and includes equipment, machinery, and work flow design. These four broad categories of organizational characteristics make up the internal work setting of the organization. The four categories affect one another such that the design of one influences the functioning of the others. Accordingly, a change in one factor usually results in changes in the

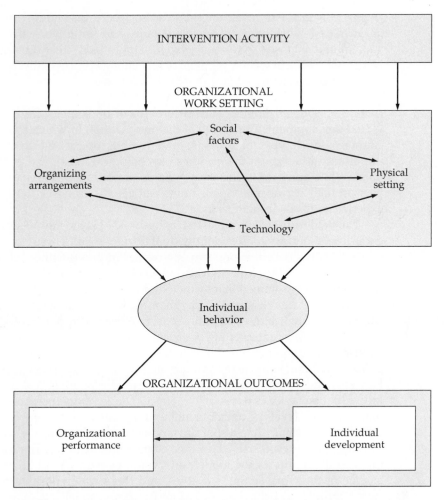

FIGURE 13–3   *A conceptual model of the dynamics of planned organizational change*

SOURCE: From "Dynamics of Planned Organizational Change: Assessing Empirical Support for a Theoretical Model" by P. J. Robertson, D. R. Roberts, and J. I. Porras, 1993, *Academy of Management Journal, 36,* p. 621. Reprinted by permission.

others. The interaction of the four categories affects the behavior of organizational members. If the different characteristics are congruent, they complement one another. If they are not aligned well, ineffectiveness is the likely result.

Individual Behavior.   The members of the organization are influenced by the work setting as it relates to their individual behavior. Changes in the work characteristics that produce seemingly incompatible demands (e.g., to perform very high quality work very rapidly) produce stress, which in turn leads to lower job performance, illness, or withdrawal from work. The first major outcome of OD is increased organizational performance.

Organizational Performance.   According to Porras and Robertson, if individual members work hard, take responsibility and initiative, learn their jobs well, and commit themselves to their jobs, it is more likely that the organization as a whole will perform well. A key goal of any change process must be to create work settings that promote and facilitate these behaviors.

Individual Development.   The second major outcome of OD is enhanced individual development. The nature of the organization in which a person works encourages some types of behavior and inhibits others, which in turn have an important influence on the person's psychological health and personal development. While much of the focus has been on organizations that have a negative impact on their members, organizations can also be designed to provide positive experiences for their members.

The final relationship indicated in Figure 13–3 is the mutual effect between organizational performance and individual development. These two outcomes affect each other, and over the long run one cannot improve without the other. The interdependence of the two is reflected in an observation by Mirvis (1988): "In OD of the 1960s, it was assumed that by developing people we could create healthier and more effective organizations. Today many advocate that we must develop organizations to create healthier and more effective people" (pp. 17–18).

The process of intervening in organizational systems, creating changes in organizational components that in turn result in changes in the work behaviors of organizational members, is the primary activity of OD (Porras & Robertson, 1992). However, individual behavioral change is not the singular goal of OD. Change in individual behavior is necessary to effect change in organizational outcomes. To maintain high levels of one outcome without correspondingly high levels of the other is not possible. In a test of the model shown in Figure 13–3, Robertson et al. conducted a meta-analysis of planned change interventions. The results supported the overall validity of the model. Interventions were found to generate positive change in the work setting variables, and there was a positive relationship between individual behavior change and organizational outcome change. Mixed support was found for changes in work settings influencing individual behavior changes. Robertson et al. believe their model provides useful insights into understanding which variables can be manipulated, the types of outcomes that result from OD interventions, and those variables that influence the linkage between organizational change and outcome attainment.

Typology of OD Interventions

Change agents deal with different kinds of clients (individuals, groups, total organizations), fill different roles, and direct their efforts to different problems. Consequently, researchers have tried to integrate the various OD interventions into a typology. A **typology** is a classification of types of things, usually in graphic form, used to promote a better understanding of relationships among them. In OD, typologies have classified interventions on such factors as role of the change agent, type of client, types of problems addressed, kinds of interventions, and so on. A typology of OD interventions is shown in Figure 13–4.

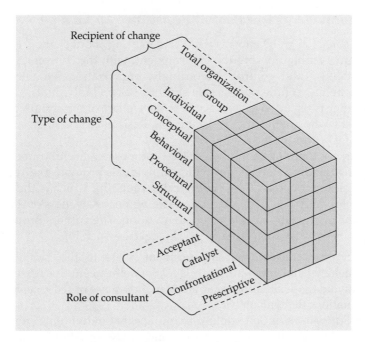

FIGURE 13–4   *Typology of organization development interventions*

A cube is created from the three dimensions of OD interventions. The first dimension is the recipient of the change effort: the client. Basically, agents try to change selected individuals, groups of workers, or entire organizations. The second dimension is the type or nature of change. This can be conceptual (new information or knowledge), behavioral (new skill), procedural (new policy or practice), or structural (including organization reporting relationships). The third dimension includes four roles of the change agent. In an acceptant role, the consultant offers passive support, permitting clients to explore problems and feelings in the presence of an accepting outsider. In a catalyst role, the consultant stimulates self-examination by providing feedback on the client's problems; in general, the agent functions as a catalyst for change. In the confrontative role, the consultant challenges client attitudes or procedures by asking probing questions, presenting discrepant data, and proposing alternatives that will motivate clients. Finally, in the prescriptive role, the consultant serves as an expert, controls the situation, and prescribes what should be done.

As researchers have commented, a change agent's intervention does not fit neatly into one of the boxes in the cube. In an intervention the key client may be an individual, but that person's relationship to a subgroup may also become an issue. Especially with the action-research model, changes may be sequential and incremental and may affect the way work is performed. Finally, during the intervention a consultant may support, stimulate, challenge, or direct the client, depending on the problem and stage of intervention. Nevertheless, a typology is often helpful in ordering the dimensions of a concept. You may find that Figure 13–4 serves such a purpose, recognizing that it is only an approximation and not a mirror of reality.

Overcoming Organizational Resistance to Change

At the core of any OD effort is the desire to bring about change. However, change introduces ambiguity into the environment, with the concomitant effects of less predictability and control. Accordingly, organizational members often resist change because of the undesirable effects it has on individuals. Yet, paradoxically the change is regarded as necessary for the welfare of the organization and thus its members, who are the ones resistant to it. Resistance to change is a major obstacle in any OD effort.

Dirks, Cummings, and Pierce (1996) proposed a useful framework for understanding the conditions under which individuals promote and resist change. It is based on the concept of **psychological ownership,** which is the feeling of being psychologically tied to an object and feeling possessiveness of that object. In this case, the organization is the object in question. The authors proposed three basic human needs that are related to psychological ownership:

♦ *Self-enhancement.* Self-enhancement refers to the individual's desire to achieve and maintain high levels of self-esteem. Individuals are likely to avoid those situations that threaten their sense of self-esteem and to seek situations that enhance it.

♦ *Self-continuity.* Self-continuity implies that individuals attempt to maintain stability of their self over time and across situations. Individuals actively seek those situations that confirm and preserve their sense of continuity and avoid those that do not.

♦ *Control and efficiency.* Individuals have a desire to maintain and demonstrate a sense of control and efficiency. Conditions that allow the individual to have a sense of control and to demonstrate efficiency are psychologically attractive, while those conditions that do not are unattractive.

Furthermore, Dirks et al. delineated three types of organizational change that influence the relationship between psychological ownership and the disposition to either accept or resist change:

♦ *Self-initiated versus imposed change.* With self-initiated change the individual undertakes change as a result of his or her own initiative and volition. Imposed change, on the other hand, is change initiated by others to which the individual is forced to react.

♦ *Evolutionary versus revolutionary change.* Evolutionary change involves incremental modifications to the organization, and as a consequence, it does not present a sudden alteration in the individual's understanding of, or relation to, the organization. In contrast, revolutionary change challenges the individual's understanding of the organization because the change alters the organization's existing structure.

♦ *Additive versus subtractive change.* Changes may add things to the organization or take them away. Examples of additive change are starting a program and enlarging a job. Conversely, a subtractive change is ending a program or downsizing.

The authors then proposed relationships among the concepts about accepting or rejecting attempts at change. It is proposed that individuals will promote

FIGURE 13–5   *Effect of psychological ownership or disposition toward change as influenced by type of change*

SOURCE: From "Psychological Ownership in Organizations: Conditions Under Which Individuals Promote and Resist Change" by K. T. Dirks, L. L. Cummings, and J. L. Pierce, 1996, in *Research in Organizational Change and Development*, Vol. 9 (pp. 1–24), edited by R. W. Woodman and W. A. Pasmore, Greenwich, CT: JAI Press.

change efforts under conditions that fulfill their needs for self-enhancement, self-continuity, and/or control and efficiency. Conversely, they will resist change efforts when it is perceived these needs will be frustrated by the change. Likewise, psychological ownership will be positively related to an individual's disposition toward change under conditions of self-initiated, evolutionary, and additive change. Conversely, psychological ownership will be negatively related to an individual's disposition toward change under conditions of imposed, revolutionary, and subtractive change. The relationship among these concepts is graphically portrayed in Figure 13–5.

Dirks et al. believe these concepts are critical to understanding why organizational change efforts are either accepted or resisted. The theoretical basis is a basic understanding of the self—namely, that people accept conditions that are perceived to enhance them. When employees feel a sense of psychological ownership of their organization, they have a vested interest in conditions that promote the organization and, in turn, themselves. Organizational change that is initiated from within, does not alter the fundamental identity of the relationship to the organization, and is perceived as adding to the reservoir of bonding between the individual and organization is most likely to be accepted. Change that threatens fundamental psychological needs derived from organizational membership are most strongly resisted. While it is not always possible to orchestrate how change occurs, we have some insights into why and how individuals react to change as they do.

EMPOWERMENT

Empowerment is a unifying concept that integrates several ideas addressed in this chapter and elsewhere. In a practical sense it is often stated as a goal or intended outcome of many organizational development efforts.

As the workforce has become more educated and skilled, there is the need to loosen some of the constraints organizations place on employees to control and monitor their actions. The need for organizational control systems such as close supervision, strict channels of communication, and chains of command evolved in part because of the perceived differentiation in ability levels between management and the workers. The classical perspective (emanating from the era of scientific management) was that management personnel generally had far more ability and insight into organizational issues than workers. The workers (or in Mintzberg's terminology, the operating core) were hired to perform the basic work that needed to be done, but they required mechanisms of control, or close supervision. As time passed and the workforce became more educated, it was no longer as necessary to closely control nonmanagerial personnel. It became feasible to push some of the traditional managerial responsibilities (such as decision making) down into the lower levels of the organization. This had the combined effect of giving traditional nonmanagerial personnel managerial-type powers and requiring fewer people in traditional managerial roles. The root meaning of *empowerment* rests with "power." By giving employees more power and distributing this power away from traditional managerial personnel, the downsizing or elimination of mid-level managerial jobs became possible. As we discussed in Chapter 8, most organizational downsizing has affected managerial-level positions. The power previously vested in these positions has been redistributed in part to the employees, thereby *empowering* them. Liden and Arad (1996) interpret empowerment as the psychological outcome of structural changes in the organization designed to provide power.

Spreitzer (1997) identified four general dimensions of empowerment.

1. *Meaning.* An individual feels a sense of meaning when an activity "counts" in his or her own value system. Empowered individuals derive personal significance from their work. They get "energized" about a given activity and thus become connected through a sense of meaning.
2. *Competence.* Empowered individuals have a sense of self-effectiveness or personal competence. They believe that they have not only the needed skills and abilities but also the confidence that they can perform successfully.
3. *Self-determination.* Self-determination is represented by behaviors that are initiated and regulated through choices as an expression of oneself, rather than behaviors that are forced by the environment. Empowered individuals have a sense of responsibility for and ownership of their activity.
4. *Impact.* Impact is the individual's belief that he or she can effect or influence organizational outcomes. Empowered individuals see themselves as "making a difference"—that is, providing the intended effects of their actions.

Spreitzer asserted that empowered individuals are more likely to be innovative, exert upward influence in the organization, and be effective in their jobs. Empowered individuals are more likely to challenge and question, rather than blindly follow, traditional role expectations. OD interventions are designed to enhance both effectiveness and personal satisfaction. The concept of empowerment provides a potentially useful framework for guiding the intervention. Thus, one outcome of a successful OD intervention is to empower the employees. However, this outcome is also dependent on the nature of the work performed by the organization and the ability levels of the employees. Kirkman and Rosen (1997) merged two contemporary approaches to organizational design: empowerment and the use of work teams. They identified the conditions that lead to *empowered work teams* and established that the four dimensions of individual-level empowerment have team-level analogs, which they called team meaningfulness, potency, team autonomy, and team consequences, respectively.

Empowerment integrates concepts from motivation, satisfaction, self-esteem, job performance, and organization development. It has the potential to synthesize diverse areas of scientific research on the experience of work. However, at the practical level it can be misunderstood and misused to justify organizational actions. Spreitzer offered this description of one organization she aided as an OD consultant:

> (T)he top management of one organization I worked with emphasized the need for greater employee empowerment as they approached an extensive organizational transformation. Employees were excited because they assumed employee empowerment meant more decision-making latitude and input into organizational decision making. Needless to say, significant conflict ensued when employees realized that top management equated empowerment with employee downsizing (i.e., fewer people in the organization meant that those remaining were by their definition "empowered"). Consequently, top management's approach to empowerment was actually experienced as disempowering by the organization's employees. (pp. 32–33)

MAJOR OD INTERVENTIONS

As noted, there are many intervention strategies for a consultant to draw on. It is beyond the present scope to describe all or even most of them. However, two OD interventions described next are representative of major types of initiatives in the field.

Organizational Culture Change

As discussed in Chapter 8, the culture of an organization embodies its values, beliefs, and attitudes and is the driving force behind its behavior. When the behavior or conduct of the organization no longer serves to attain its larger objectives, it becomes necessary for the organization to behave differently. A change in organizational behavior usually necessitates a change in the organization's culture. It is often difficult to bring about a change in organizational culture because it necessitates altering underlying values and beliefs that have long guided the organization. Although change is difficult to effect, several authors (e.g., Kotter & Heskett,

1992; Appelbaum & Batt, 1993) have identified the following critical features of the change process.

1. *A strong leader.* Perhaps the most important feature is a strong leader who can initiate and sustain the cultural change. Leaders must recognize that the environment and organizational members will exert significant energy to maintain the *status quo.* However, it is critical that leaders do not waiver from the plan for change. They must recognize that a vital component of their role is to influence others to examine prevailing assumptions and values. New approaches or perspectives often threaten or worry organizational members. Nevertheless, the leaders must perseverate in their endeavor with missionary zeal. Often the culture change is initiated by one strong leader at the helm, but other influential leaders emerge in the process.

2. *A clear vision of what needs to be done.* It is also critical that there be a sense of vision or direction as to where the organization is headed. It is not enough for a leader to provide intense energy to initiate the culture change. What must also be present is a shared belief in what the new culture will be like. The vision may arise from the values of the leader, or it may emerge out of a crisis that must be handled to save the business. The *process* of cultural change is more important than the *product.* Because change is continuously needed by organizations to adapt to their environments, the organization must develop some fluency in learning how to change. While moving from X to Y may be the initial object of attention, eventually the organization will also have to move from Y to Z.

The vision process entails not only charting the destination but also generating commitment from all organizational members to be players in the change process. The enrollment of all employees to cultivate change actively is often accelerated by a clear understanding of what will occur if change does not take place. It is not the case that leaders will "punish" employees who fail to participate, but rather the organization as a whole will suffer (most notably through the loss of jobs or the demise of the organization).

3. *Development of new work procedures.* It is necessary for the organization to develop new work procedures that buttress the new cultural values being espoused. If the organization does not "do" anything different besides verbally expressing its desire to do so, it will basically be "business as usual" within the organization. The organization must be prepared to "walk the talk" in the change process. New work procedures help to break the allegiance to old values from which the organization seeks to depart. These new work procedures may include the extensive use of teams. Moving to team-based operations necessitates major changes in organizational behavior, including communication, cooperation, and decision making, as well as new organizational policies pertaining to selection, training, and compensation. Another possible change in work procedures may be job redesign. In this case the employees will have the structure of their jobs altered, usually giving them greater decision-making authority over their work operations. Such new procedures for performing work provide a venue for organizational members to reframe their values, attitudes, and beliefs about the organization and what it is trying to accomplish. A failure to change how work is performed even though new values and beliefs have been expressed often results in "back-sliding." Back-

sliding is the return to the old ways of thinking and feeling, and ultimately behaving, from which the organization needs to evolve.

4. *An organization that is open to learn.* Everyone in the organization, from the leaders on down, must accept the fact that no one has all the answers. The organization must be prepared to go through periods of groping, grasping, and stumbling and to learn from these difficult times. Rather than viewing these occasions as representations of shortcomings in vision, intelligence, or fortitude, the organization must view itself as learning, adaptive, and growing. In so doing mistakes will be made. However, instead of viewing the mistakes as punishable offenses or signs of weakness, they should be regarded as part of a normal and healthy change process. Senge (1990) spoke to the need for "learning organizations," organizations that not only are comfortable with the growth process but also treat their members in a nurturing, as opposed to a sanctioning, manner. The organization must accept that good ideas and opportunities for growth can and do originate at all levels of the organization, not just from top management.

I heard a presentation by a chief executive officer (CEO) describing what it was like to change a major corporation. The company was a long-time leader in the aerospace industry. It had a long history of profitable years and great organizational prestige. The company then began to lose money because of foreign competition and other external pressures. Two previous CEOs tried and failed to change the culture of the company. Both had been long-time leaders of the company who were successively promoted into the CEO position. Both CEOs failed to change the organizational culture because in part they *were* the culture. Each person had been very influential within the company, and to change the organizational culture entailed "undoing" much of what they had already done.

The company's third attempt at a change in leadership brought in an outsider to the company, someone who was not steeped in its traditions and values. He encountered massive resistance on many fronts and hired two I/O psychologists to facilitate the change process. He successfully persuaded a few top executives to embrace his vision of the company, and the change process began—albeit slowly. The new CEO stated that the company was profitable not because of its actions, but in spite of them. They had relied on their esteemed industry reputation to get away with actions (such as not vigorously developing new products) that hurt them in the long run. When foreign competition increased, the "long run" became the "short run." There was still substantial resistance to the new vision, as some people claimed the company had endured downturns before. On those occasions the company had weathered the storms and eventually returned to economic prosperity. In short, some employees viewed the current crisis as but a temporary problem that would work itself out. It didn't.

Shortly thereafter a major unit of the company was sold off, affecting several hundred employees. Many were laid off by their new employer. This action got the attention of the remaining employees of the company, and the change process began in earnest. The company as a whole came to realize that the need for change wasn't just talk. Many changes began to occur in the way work was performed, particularly with regard to new product development and cost reductions. The company also began to change its self-image, going from self-assured smugness to being aware of its own vulnerability. The new CEO felt other changes would be in the offing but believed the company was more receptive to continued change after having overcome its inertia to change at all.

Total Quality Management

Total Quality Management (TQM) is a comprehensive approach to organization development that embraces not only behavioral concepts but also business strategy and the use of statistical information to aid in decision making. The principles of TQM were originally developed for manufacturing organizations but subsequently have been adapted to service organizations (including educational institutions) as well. In service organizations TQM is also referred to as Continuous Process Improvement.

The roots of TQM are varied and from multiple disciplines. From *psychology* is the emphasis on employee involvement in making operating decisions about the organization. That is, as research on participative decision making and leadership reveals, employees have expertise that can be accessed to improve organizational efficiency. Thus, effective decision making is rarely, if ever, a strictly top-down affair. From the field of *statistics* is the concept of statistical quality control. The American physicist W. Edwards Deming is credited with formulating the concept. It uses rudimentary statistical analyses to aid in understanding organizational processes. The most critical statistical index is variation, as discussed in Chapter 2. If an organization wants to provide a high-quality service or product, the quality should not vary across products; that is, consistency is regarded as a precursor of quality. For example, if a fast-food restaurant makes hamburgers that sometimes taste good and sometimes taste bad, there is too much variation in the quality. The hamburgers should taste the same all the time. In addition to reducing variation, the organization should strive to elevate the mean quality of the product. Thus, the goal is to produce hamburgers that always taste the same and always taste good. These two simple statistical concepts of reducing variation and raising the mean are the foundation of using statistical quality control to improve organizational performance. From *marketing* comes the idea that the primary focus of the organization is to satisfy its customers. Satisfied customers are the key to the retention and growth of business. Marketing research reveals that there can be differences between what customers really want from a product (e.g., a tasty hamburger) and what the organization believes its customers want (e.g., a hamburger delivered to the customer in less than 45 seconds). Customer service and satisfaction are the driving forces behind TQM. Finally, from the area of *business* comes the concept that all parts of the organization, including its overall mission, operating technology, support services, organizational culture, and employee training and rewards, must be aligned or work together to produce an effective outcome. For example, it would be dysfunctional for the organization to say it strives to produce a high-quality product yet train and reward employees to produce a large quantity of products irrespective of quality. Thus, TQM is the confluence of concepts and ideas from many disciplines that have been brought together to aid in the development and direction of organizations.

Lawler, Mohrman, and Ledford (1995) concluded that four factors are required in an effective system of employee involvement, upon which TQM is based. The first is the *sharing of information* about business performance, plans, and goals. It is impossible for employees to make good suggestions about how products and services can be improved without access to business information. It is also difficult for employees to alter their behavior in response to changing conditions and get feedback about the effectiveness of their performance. In the absence of business information, individuals are usually limited simply to carrying out prescribed tasks and roles in a relatively automatic way. Thus, it is imperative that relevant business information be shared at all levels of the organization and not be the sole province of upper management.

Second is the need for *developing knowledge*. It is critical that employees at all levels be involved in a continuous process of skill development. Without the proper skills, individuals cannot participate in a business and influence its direction. The skills of group decision making, team building, and leadership are critical because most employee involvement programs make use of meetings, interpersonal interactions, group problem solving, and influencing others.

The third factor needed is *rewarding organizational performance*. Basing rewards on organizational performance is one way to ensure that employees are involved in and care about the performance of their company. Individual incentive plans do not tie the individual into the overall success of the business; moreover, they can interfere with teamwork and problem solving. Team incentives can be supportive of employee involvement activities such as work teams and problem-solving groups. Profit sharing and employee stock ownership are widely used to link employees more closely to the success of the business and reward them for it.

The need for *redistributing power* is the fourth factor. Moving power downward in organizations often requires structural changes. Job enhancement and self-managed work teams involve a substantial change in the basic structure of the organization and are aimed at moving important decisions into the hands of individuals and teams performing the basic manufacturing or service work of the organization. Job enhancement programs are typically targeted at routine assembly and clerical jobs, while self-managed work teams are used in a broader array of jobs.

Lawler et al. noted that the effective utilization of employee involvement requires the simultaneous use of these four practices, not just the selective use of one or two of them. Interrelated patterns of mutually reinforcing practices are necessary to encourage and sustain employee behavior. Casual or fleeting use of these practices will be ineffectual and will not produce the sustained and systematic efforts needed to produce enduring organizational change.

Lawler et al. conducted a major study of organizations that have adopted TQM. A very high percentage (83%) of those companies report that their experience with TQM programs has been positive or very positive. Responses from their study are summarized in Table 13–1. It seems evident that organizational interest in TQM is not a passing fad or the "flavor of the month" panacea for organizational ills (see Field Note 2). The U.S. government annually grants the Malcolm Baldrige National Quality Award to the company that demonstrates the greatest advances in

Table 13–1   *Summary of responses to the question "Overall, how positive has your experience been with Total Quality Management?"*

	Response Percent
Very negative	0%
Negative	1%
Neither negative nor positive	16%
Positive	66%
Very positive	17%

SOURCE: Adapted from "Creating High Performance Organizations" (p. 75) by E. E. Lawler, S. A. Mohrman, and G. E. Ledford, 1995, San Francisco: Jossey-Bass. Reprinted by permission.

improving the quality of their products. Competition for the Baldrige Award is intense, and the recipients are highly regarded in the business community.

Reeves and Bednar (1994) noted that there is no universal definition of *quality;* rather, different definitions are appropriate under different circumstances. They believe there are organizational trade-offs in accepting one definition of quality over another. Despite multiple definitions of *quality,* Vaill (1982) identified eight defining characteristics of high-performing organizations that embody the principles of TQM. Vaill based his findings on a study of diverse organizations, including universities, a Coast Guard unit, hospitals, marching bands, drug rehabilitation agencies, and stock brokerages. The characteristics are listed in Table 13–2. It is these characteristics that all OD programs, directly or indirectly, try to develop in organizations.

Field Note 2   *Students as Customers?*

One of the underlying principles of Total Quality Management (TQM) is that the needs and preferences of the customer are of paramount importance. An organization's business strategy is directed toward satisfying the customer, which increases the likelihood of expanding the customer base as well as repeat business among current customers. For example, in the operation of a restaurant, food is prepared to the customers' specific preferences. The goal is to satisfy the customers by increasing their control over the final product. However, application of TQM principles in the field of medical practice is not so direct. A medical doctor does not regard patients as "customers," catering to their expressed needs. Rather the doctor controls the specific form of medical treatment the patient receives—for example, with regard to medication and surgery. In the field of medicine the patients put their faith and trust in the training and experience of the doctors to provide high-quality medical treatment. Now consider education. Are students more like "customers" (in the restaurant business) or "patients" (in the medical business)? Should educational institutions strive to please their students by giving them more control over the substance and delivery of educational programs? Or should students put their faith and trust in the training of the faculty to know what is in the students' best interests in providing high-quality education? There has been considerable interest in applying TQM principles to educational institutions, but there has also been controversy over how students are to be regarded.

Table 13–2   *Characteristics of high-performing organizations*

1. They are performing excellently against a known external standard.
2. They are performing excellently against what is assumed to be their potential level of performance.
3. They are performing excellently in relation to where they were at some earlier time.
4. They are judged by informed observers to be doing substantially better qualitatively than other comparable systems.
5. They are doing whatever they do with significantly fewer resources than it is assumed are needed.
6. They are perceived as exemplars of the way to do whatever they do, and this becomes a source of ideas and inspiration for others.
7. They are perceived to fulfill at a high level the ideals for the culture within which they exist; that is, they have mobility.
8. They are the only organization that has been able to do what they do at all, even though it might seem that what they do is not that difficult or mysterious a thing.

SOURCE: From "The Purposing of High-Performing Systems" by P. Vaill, 1982, *Organizational Dynamics*, 2 (2), pp. 23–39.

ISO 9000

A further extension of quality concepts in organizations is evidenced in the ISO 9000 quality systems standards by the International Organization for Standardization (ISO). ISO is a worldwide federation that links the standards of various national organizations. With the globalization of world product markets and especially the globalization of parts, components, and raw material, common international standards were introduced in 1987. ISO 9000 certifies organizations for using high-quality and standardized processes, systems, and products. A set of 23 quality standards are specified, including management responsibility, product inspection and testing, quality records, personnel training, and use of statistical methods. Without ISO 9000 certification, organizations that rely on supplies and services from international companies would have fewer opportunities to participate in global commerce. The goal of ISO 9000 is basically the same as TQM—to attain an improved level of quality and consistency of quality.

EMPIRICAL OD RESEARCH

Porras and Robertson (1992) reviewed 63 empirical research studies on OD over a 14-year period to assess the impact of interventions. They grouped the interventions into four categories: organizing arrangements, social factors, technology, and physical setting. *Organizing arrangements* included the creation of new committees, task forces, or work teams. *Social factors* most typically included team building and process consultation. *Technology* was most often represented by job redesign. Finally, the *physical setting* involved changes in office layout, such as from a closed-office (e.g., with partitions) to an open-office layout. The dependent variables were individual and organizational outcomes. The results of the study are presented in Figure 13–6. Two findings are evident. First, OD intervention resulted in no change more than half the time. Second, the percentage of studies reporting a negative change (i.e., the OD intervention produced negative outcomes) was very small.

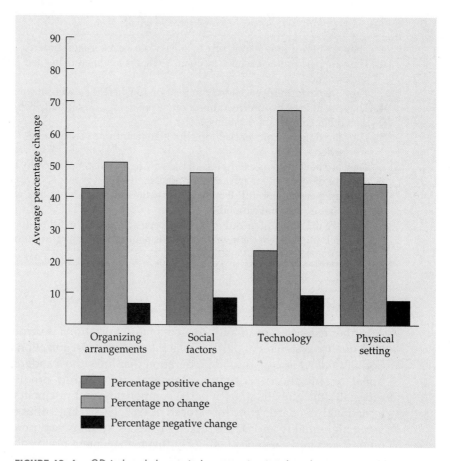

FIGURE 13–6   *OD-induced change in key organizational work setting variables*

SOURCE: From "Organizational Development: Theory, Practice, and Research" by J. I. Porras and P. J. Robertson, 1992, in *Handbook of Industrial and Organizational Psychology,* 2nd ed., Vol. 3 (p. 787), edited by M. D. Dunnette and L. M. Hough, Palo Alto, CA: Consulting Psychologists Press. Reprinted by permission.

These findings deserve two comments. First, given the problems of accurately measuring change, it is conceivable that at least some of the findings of no change may have been based on measures that were insensitive to the types of change occurring. Second, it is precisely because specific interventions, such as in technology, produce no change in outcomes that organizations have moved toward large-scale, multifaceted, comprehensive change efforts like TQM. One conclusion that may be drawn from this study is that singular OD interventions are not likely to produce large-scale changes in individual and organizational outcomes. This is not really surprising given that organizations tend to be resilient to change.

Macy and Izumi (1993) argued that to be successful, organizational change efforts must include systemwide design and transformation strategies. To significantly change and transform organizations, there must be change in the power, control systems, and decision making of the organization. Change efforts that start at the work site (office, plant, production line) are generally not as successful as those that start at the corporate level. TQM and other systemwide initiatives aimed at large-scale organizational change seemingly hold the greatest promise to be successful. There is also evidence (Rodgers & Hunter, 1996) suggesting that different conclusions can be drawn regarding the effectiveness of OD interventions depending on the criteria used to render the evaluations.

VALUES AND ETHICS IN OD

It is appropriate to end the discussion of OD with a section on values and ethics. Whenever change is deliberate, someone's value and beliefs are being acted on. The act of change itself is based on a value (that is, change is good or necessary). OD is saturated with values. Sometimes these are implicit, sometimes they are explicit, and sometimes they clash. The operative values include: cooperation is preferable to conflict, openness is preferable to suppression, and the level of trust and support in most groups and organizations is lower than necessary or desirable. Psychologists have long known that behavior manifests values. The behaviors of the change agent and client in an OD intervention are also guided by values. All parties involved should discuss their values before they consider possible choices. Some conflicts over strategies occur because participants disagree about fundamental values. Many times agreement is assumed when, in fact, it does not exist. A manager I knew preferred creating a feeling of competition among his subordinates to see who would come up with the best idea for a project. It would have been foolish to engage in team building to enhance intragroup cooperation when that value was not endorsed by the manager.

White and Wooten (1986) proposed a conceptual model to explain the domain of professional ethics. Ethics evolve from the intersection of four constructs: values, norms, science, and laws. The model is depicted in Figure 13–7, and the constructs are defined in Table 13–3. The model proposes that values, norms, science, and laws are necessary prerequisites for an ethical system to exist within a profession. Each of these constructs has significantly influenced the development of professional ethics.

Since OD is directed to planned organizational change, it is instructive to consider the ethics of change. Lippitt (1982) offered this observation:

> No person or group of persons, however empowered, can prevent change from occurring. At best, they can only hasten or delay it. More important, they can cope with change at all only if they are aware of its nature and probable effect. In this sense, those responsible for the management of our organizations are faced with extraordinary difficulties in being always correctly informed and situationally knowledgeable. Organizational changes faithfully reflect the needs and interests of some of the people, but not necessarily all of them; therefore, they inevitably produce inequities. Since everything is the result of a change, competent managers cannot afford to overlook any change whatsoever, because every change is a seed from which some part of tomorrow's organization will grow. (p. 385)

Given this inevitability, interventionists must confront the ethicality of change itself, particularly on organizational participants. As presented in the model shown in Figure 13–7, values play an integral role in the formation of any ethical

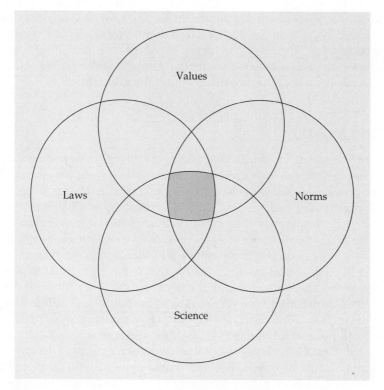

FIGURE 13–7   *The domain of professional OD ethics*

SOURCE: From *Professional Ethics and Practice in Organizational Development* (p. 73) by L. P. White and K. C. Wooten, 1985, New York: Praeger. © 1985 by Praeger Publishers. Reprinted by permission.

system. While it may be tempting to get caught up with the techniques associated with the latest intervention, the fundamental values that drive acceptance of the intervention must be articulated. For example, when an organization downsizes and 20% of the workforce lose their jobs, the consequences for the laid-off employees (as well as those who weren't) must be evaluated in terms of the values of fairness and justice. OD cannot be used blindly as a technique of change insensitive to the ethical consequences of its use.

The issue of ethics is also vitally important to the individual OD consultant. Like any professional working with people's lives, the OD consultant must have integrity. Conflicts can arise that directly involve ethical issues. One of the toughest decisions for a change agent is when to end a consultant/client relationship (White & Wooten, 1983). On the one hand, the consultant likes to "be there" to help; on the other, there comes a point when the client must break free of the consultant. If the consultant leaves the system too soon, the client may not have the internal resources to solve problems. If the consultant prolongs the relationship (all the while being paid a fee), he or she may create a state of being "needed" by the client to survive. When to end a relationship is a matter of professional judgment. No formula will provide the answer. While ethical matters are rarely black or white, they are the substance of the consultant's professional character (see Field Note 3).

Table 13–3   *Definitions of constructs used in describing professional OD ethics*

Values	Beliefs or ideals held by individuals or groups concerning what is good, right, desirable, or important in an idea, object, or action.
Norms	An idea, conceptualization, belief, or statement enforced by the sanctions of members of a group concerning their behavioral rules, patterns, and conduct, which is referenced in the form of what should be done, what ought to be done, what is expected, and the level of action or expectation under specific circumstances.
Science	A body of knowledge that is characterized by the use of the scientific method, which seeks out goal-oriented information through systematic, unified, and self-correcting processes.
Laws	A system of social rules, norms, or standards of behavior concerning the right and wrong of human conduct that is put in codes enforced by sanctions imposed through recognized authority.
Ethics	Concepts and standards held by individuals or groups concerning the values surrounding the rightness and wrongness of modes of conduct in human behavior and the result of human behavior or actions.

SOURCE: From *Professional Ethics and Practice in Organizational Development* (p. 75) by L. P. White and K. C. Wooten, 1985, New York: Praeger. © 1985 by Praeger Publishers. Reprinted by permission.

Field Note 3   *Limits of a Change Agent*

One of the assumptions behind OD is that change is beneficial and desirable. The client wants change, and the change agent leads the client through the change. But sometimes the client and the change agent don't see things the same way. As a change agent, I have been in a few situations where I felt the client should change in certain ways, but the client was unwilling. What happens then? Should you attempt to make someone change against their will? Is it unethical to make people change when you know they don't want to, even if it's "for their own good"? Just how far should a change agent go in attempting to bring about change when the client doesn't want it? I find this situation very frustrating. On the one hand, I recognize the need for clients to change (even though they don't and I can't convince them otherwise), but on the other hand, I know they invited me to help them and I can't abuse my invitation.

On three occasions in my work as an OD consultant I faced this dilemma. In all the cases I decided it would be unethical to push the clients to do something they didn't want to do, even though I felt it would be to their advantage to do so. All three cases turned out the same way. Each client eventually came back to me (within a two-year period) and basically said, "You were right. We should have listened to you but we didn't, and now we're ready to do it the way you recommended." While you might think this represents a happy ending, it is not so. During the interim the problems got much worse, and in two cases they got so bad I didn't know how I could help them. What would have worked two years earlier was no longer helpful. My attitude toward this situation remains the same. I believe I must respect the integrity of my clients' wishes, even though I may not agree with them. Despite the problems it sometimes produces, I still feel obligated not to manipulate or compel clients to move in directions against their will.

CASE STUDY ◆ How Do I Create Teamwork?

Alex Rowland gazed pensively out of his office, which overlooked the production area of his company. Seven years ago he had founded Microtechnics, Inc., a high-tech company that produced microchips for use in computers. Rowland, an engineer by training, prided himself on assembling one of the finest engineering design departments in his industry. He handpicked his people from the best universities in the country, gave them a free hand in product design, and paid them extremely well. While many companies feared losing their engineers to competitors, Rowland had the luxury of knowing many engineers were just waiting for a chance to join his company. In an industry where product quality and capacity were critical, Microtechnics was regarded as an industry leader in product design.

But all was not well. What was once the strongest asset of the company was bordering on becoming a liability. Rowland wondered whether he had created a monster. The problem was that the company was lagging far behind in production and in having its products hit the market at opportune times. The apparent cause was the Engineering Department, the very department that had put Microtechnics on the map. The engineers were very proud and territorial. They would not release a new product for production until they thought it was perfect down to the last detail. The engineers did not want the Production Department grabbing one of their "babies" until they were ready to release it. There was a constant struggle between the Engineering and Production Departments regarding the release of products for manufacturing and distribution. Although Rowland knew the value of superior products, he also knew that consumers paid for products, not great ideas, and if Microtechnics didn't put the product in the consumers' hands, soon there would be no Microtechnics. The Production Department repeatedly approached Rowland about missed production deadlines. Sales were way down because other companies were getting their products out the door first. They often lacked the quality of a Microtechnics product, but they still made great inroads into new markets by being there first. Microtechnics was developing a reputation of being the caboose in product delivery, and in a highly competitive industry its tardiness was killing it financially.

The Engineering Department viewed production workers as a bunch of bureaucrats, people who failed to understand the importance of superior workmanship. The engineers at Microtechnics had earned numerous patents on their products, and in the span of seven years had garnered three industry awards for product design. They were good, they knew it, everyone knew it. The problem was that Microtechnics wasn't just in the business of thinking up new products. It also had to produce them and get people to buy them.

Rowland stared out over a cup of coffee. He felt he was running two separate companies: one in engineering, the other in production. They certainly weren't working together. Rowland knew he couldn't kill the goose that laid his golden eggs. Without his engineers, his company would be nothing. But if he couldn't get his engineers to realize they were in the manufacturing business and to facilitate the production process, the company wouldn't stay in business. Rowland felt trapped. He couldn't live without his engineers, and he wasn't living too well with them. If he couldn't find a way to unite his company, he knew it wouldn't be long before he joined a long list of former company presidents who had great ideas but didn't know how to run a business.

Questions

1. What exactly is the problem facing Microtechnics?
2. What factors are reinforcing the way the Engineering Department is operating?
3. What intervention strategies might benefit Microtechnics, and how would you implement them?
4. Do you believe the situation at Microtechnics requires the involvement of a change agent external to the company, or should Rowland create a permanent job within the company to address this situation? Why do you feel as you do?
5. If the intervention strategy is successful, how would the operation of Microtechnics be conducted differently than it is now?

INFOTRAC ARTICLES

1. *Training & Development*, Oct 1995 v49 n10 p15(4)
   Scaling the wall of resistance.
   Explains why employees resist changing their behavior at work and offers reasons for the resistance.
2. *Training & Development*, May 1998 v52 n5 p63(5)
   Five conditions for high-performance cultures. W. Mathew Juechter, Caroline Fisher, & Randall J. Alford
   Discusses five conditions that must be present for organizations to undergo a successful organizational transformation.
3. *Training & Development*, Feb 1996 v50 n2 p37(5)
   Traveling through transitions. Bill Trahant & W. Warner Burke
   Discusses how to assess an organization's readiness for change, deal with employees' resistance to change, and measure the results of change programs.
4. *Training & Development*, August 1996 v50 n8 p9(3)
   Keeping quality alive. Brenda Lane Oliver
   Discusses steps that can be taken to increase the likelihood of success of total quality management (TQM) programs.
5. *Across the Board*, Jan 1997 v34 n1 p11 (2)
   Why empowerment is unworkable. Richard Koch & Ian Godden
   An article critical of the concept of empowerment in large organizations. It suggests that empowerment may be useful in only small- and medium-sized companies.
6. *Training & Development*, July 1997 v51 n7 p30(5)
   Developing internal consultants. R. Glenn Ray
   Discusses the importance of internal change agents as being instrumental for sustaining organizational change and development.

7. *Across the Board*, May 1996 v33 n5 p32(5)

   If you want people to buy-in to change, you have to sell them. Yes, sell them. John Guaspari

   Asserts that simply mandating change in organizations is not sufficient to produce change; it requires employees accepting and taking ownership of the change.

8. *Training & Development*, April 1996 v50 n4 p48(4)

   Accelerating change. Mary Buchel

   Proposes three techniques that organizations can use to facilitate organizational change.

Union/Management Relations

MAJOR CHAPTER OBJECTIVES

◆ Describe the nature and formation of a labor union.

◆ Explain the functions of a labor contract.

◆ Understand the strategies of impasse resolution in the collective bargaining process.

◆ Describe responses to impasse.

◆ Describe the nature of grievances and grievance arbitration.

◆ Discuss behavioral research on union/management relations.

Over the years, I/O psychologists have studied a broad range of topics relating to work. Strangely enough, one not often addressed is union/management relations. This area cannot be dismissed as "tangential" to work; for many organizations, union-related issues are among the most crucial. Many authors have observed that there is a great imbalance in I/O psychologists' interest between union and management problems. The two are not mutually exclusive, but I/O psychology seems more aligned with management. A listing of some of the professional activities of I/O psychologists testifies to this: managerial consulting, management development, use of assessment centers to identify those with management ability, and cross-cultural managerial issues. However, I/O psychologists have not spurned the advances of unions or been unreceptive to them. Shostak (1964) described the relationship as "mutual indifference." Unions appear reluctant to approach I/O psychologists for help in solving their problems. Rosen and Stagner (1980) think this is caused partly by the belief that I/O psychologists are not truly impartial and partly by reluctance to give outsiders access to union data.

The reasons for the unions' attitudes are not totally clear. One explanation is that the development of industrial psychology is closely tied to the work of Frederick Taylor. Criticisms of "Taylorism" have been raised by union workers; they see it as exploiting workers to increase company profits. There can be an adversarial relationship between unions and management, a "we/they" perspective. Unions may still see I/O psychologists as a partner of "them." Also, some factors may appear to place I/O psychologists more in the management camp. I/O psychologists are often placed in management-level positions. Management invariably sees the need for, explains the problems to, and pays the consultant. In short, I/O psychology has been more involved with management than with unions (to the point that some authors refer to I/O psychology as a "management tool"). This is most apparent in the conspicuous absence of psychological research on unions. A list of the major reasons unions distrust I/O psychologists was offered by Huszczo, Wiggins, and Currie (1984) and is presented in Table 14–1.

In the past several years interest in unions has increased. Whether the "thaw" will continue and grow remains to be seen. I suspect current interest stems from the realization that worker/workplace problems need not be dealt with from an either/or perspective. Unions and management can benefit from solving problems that affect them jointly. If our discipline is successful in overcoming its "promanagement" image, we can and will make greater inroads in understanding unions. Current research suggests that such changes are beginning (see Field Note 1).

This chapter will examine the nature of unions, the factors that influence union/management relations, recent research on unions, and how unionization affects many topics discussed earlier.

WHAT IS A UNION?

Unions are organizations designed to promote and enhance the social and economic welfare of their members. Basically, unions were created to protect workers from exploitation. Unions originally sprang from the abysmal working conditions in this country over 100 years ago. Workers got little pay, had almost no

TABLE 14–1   *Reasons unions distrust I/O psychologists*

They are associated with management.

They are associated with F. W. Taylor's scientific management (i.e., emphasis on efficiency, time and motion studies).

Unions are ignored in textbooks and journals of I/O psychology.

They are moralistic intellectuals who want social reform.

Methods (e.g., attitude surveys) have been used to avoid or beat union organizing attempts or to lower pay demands.

They are associated with job enrichment techniques that interfere with job classification and standards systems.

Methods of psychological testing emphasize differentiation among workers (hence, antisolidarity and antiseniority systems).

Many psychologists have not had work experience similar to union members', which causes suspicion and communication barriers.

SOURCE: From "The Relationship Between Psychology and Organized Labor: Past, Present, and Future" by G. E. Huszczo, J. G. Wiggins, and J. S. Currie, 1984, *American Psychologist, 39*, pp. 432–440.

Field Note 1   *Why Study Unions?*

I am of the opinion that unions have been given inadequate attention by educators. When the topic of labor unions comes up, students are more likely to have heard of Jimmy Hoffa (a union leader with reputed criminal connections) than Walter Reuther (a major contributor to organized labor). Why? There are probably many reasons, but one seems fundamental. Schools, colleges, and higher education in general are founded on scholarly intellectual values. They produce learned people, many of whom rise to become business leaders. Unions, on the other hand, got their start representing relatively uneducated workers, rank-and-file employees, rather than business leaders. Rightly or wrongly, unions have had the image of representing the "common man" in labor over the "privileged intellectuals." Some union leaders become suspicious and skeptical of the motives of formally educated people, feeling they are more likely to share values held by management.

Textbooks that offer more than a passing look at organized labor are rarely found in this country. It seems the "we/they" dichotomy between labor and management has also filtered down into textbook writing; unions simply are infrequently discussed in books. This book, in fact, is one of the few I/O psychology textbooks to devote a chapter to union/management issues. However, the anti-intellectual attitude that some unions hold is costing them in ways beyond exposure in education. Unions rarely hire outside professionals; they generally promote from within their own ranks. If you were an I/O psychologist who wanted to work full time for a union, I doubt you would have many employment possibilities. Furthermore, unions are currently experiencing a decline in membership, an unprecedented number of unions are being decertified, and unions are losing their effectiveness in negotiating for desired employment conditions. In short, I feel unions are in need of some fresh ideas. They could benefit from some OD-type interventions. But unless they are willing to look beyond their own ranks for expertise, I doubt that they (like any organization) will have sufficient internal strength to pull themselves up by the bootstraps. The paradoxical split between I/O psychology (the study of people at work) and labor unions (which represent a large portion of workers) has been detrimental to both parties.

job security, had no benefits, and, perhaps most important, worked under degrading and unsafe conditions. Unions gave unity and power to employees. This power forced employers to deal with workers as a group. Certain federal laws forced employers to stop certain activities (such as employing children) and engage in others (such as making Social Security contributions). Collectively, labor unions and labor laws brought about many changes in the workplace. Although the problems facing the North American worker today are not as severe as they were 75–100 years ago, unions continue to give a sense of security and increased welfare to their members (see Field Note 2).

Why do workers join unions? What can unions accomplish? According to several authors, unions have consistently contributed to the attainment of certain outcomes. Bok and Dunlop (1970) feel unions have made these contributions to worker welfare:

- They have increased wages; in turn, employers have raised the wages of some nonunion workers.
- They have bargained for and gotten benefits such as pensions, insurance, vacations, and rest periods.
- They have provided formal rules and procedures for discipline, promotion, wage differentials, and other important job-related factors. This has led to less arbitrary treatment of employees.

There are other reasons as well: Unions provide better communication with management, better working conditions, increased employee unity, and higher morale. Other authors cite social reasons, like belonging to a group with whom workers can share common experiences and fellowship. Thus, there are both economic and personal reasons for joining unions.

Field Note 2   *Is History Repeating Itself?*

In the early years of the 20th century, the use of child labor was prevalent in the United States, particularly in large cities. Children toiled for long hours (10–12 hours per day) in unsafe conditions (poor air to breathe, no heating or cooling) and for minuscule wages (pennies per hour) in what were called "sweat shops." Eventually state and federal labor laws were enacted to prohibit child labor. Then 80–90 years later some U.S. companies moved their production facilities to foreign countries where there are no child labor laws. In some factories children again work long hours in unsafe conditions for minuscule wages (less than $1.00 per hour). How do you feel about this practice? Should U.S. companies follow U.S. labor laws in foreign countries where the laws are much different, particularly with regard to child labor? Should social pressure (e.g., economic boycotts) be exerted against companies that use child labor? Some companies will argue that the reduced costs they incur by using child labor are passed on to consumers in the form of lower costs of the products. How should companies in particular and our society as a whole balance economic gain and social conscience? We are finding that history is repeating itself; the conditions that spawned labor laws in this country many years ago are now being exploited by some companies in foreign countries.

UNIONS AS ORGANIZATIONS

Approximately 20 million U.S. citizens belong to labor unions, representing about 25% of the nonagricultural workforce. In Canada membership is over 2 million. The largest labor union is the American Federation of Labor–Congress of Industrial Organizations (AFL-CIO). Other large unions are the United Auto Workers and the United Mine Workers. While historically unions were strongest among blue-collar employees, white-collar workers (particularly government employees and teachers) are now the dominant union base. In recent years there has been a decline in unionization as the number of service jobs has increased and the number of manufacturing jobs (a traditional union stronghold) has decreased.

Each union has a headquarters, but its strength is its many locals. A **local** may represent members in a geographic area (for example, all tollbooth collectors in Philadelphia) or a particular plant (for example, Amalgamated Beef Packers at Armour's Dubuque, Iowa, slaughterhouse). The local elects officials. If it is large enough, it affords some officials full-time jobs. Other officials are full-time company employees who may get time off for union activities. The shop, or union, steward has a union position equivalent to that of a company supervisor. The steward represents the union on the job site; he or she handles grievances and discipline. Usually the steward is elected by members for a one-year term.

A union represents an organization (for example, a labor organization) within another organization (the company). The local depends on the company for its existence. Large companies often have a multiunion labor force and thus multiple organizations within themselves. In this case the employer must deal with several collectively organized groups—for example, production workers, clerical workers, and truck drivers. Each union negotiates separately, trying to improve the welfare of its members. A large, multiunion employer is a good example of how organizations are composed of interdependent parts. Each union has a certain degree of power, which can influence the behavior of the total organization.

Union members pay membership dues, which are the union's chief resource. The union can also collect money for a strike fund, a pool members can draw from if they are on strike and do not get paid. (Strikes will be discussed in more detail shortly.) Unions use their funds to offer members such things as special group automobile insurance rates or union-owned vacation facilities. Unions are highly dependent on their members. Increased membership gives a union more bargaining clout, generates more revenue, and provides a greater range of services for members. Without members, a union cannot exist; indeed, declining membership can threaten its very survival.

THE FORMATION OF A UNION

When employees want to consider joining a union, they follow a standard procedure. First, they invite representatives to solicit union membership. Federal law allows organizers to solicit membership as long as this does not endanger employees' safety or performance. Solicitations usually occur over lunch or at break time. It is illegal for employers to threaten physically, interfere with, or harass organizers. It is also illegal to fire employees for prounion sentiments.

Both the union and the company typically mount campaigns on behalf of their positions. The union stresses how it can improve the workers' lot. The company's countercampaign stresses how well off the employees already are, the costs of union membership, and the loss of freedom. Then a federal agency, the National Labor Relations Board (NLRB), becomes involved. The NLRB sends a hearing officer to oversee the union campaign and monitor further developments.

Employees are asked to sign cards authorizing a union election. If fewer than 30% sign the authorization cards, the process ends. If 30% or more sign, an election is held to determine whether a union will represent the employees. The NLRB officer must determine which employees are eligible to be in the union and thus eligible to vote. Management personnel (supervisors, superintendents, and managers) are excluded. The hearing officer schedules the election, provides secret ballots and ballot boxes, counts the votes, and certifies the election. If more than 50% of the voters approve, the union is voted in. If the union loses the election, it can repeat the entire process at a later date. A union that loses a close election will probably do so.

Brief and Rude (1981) proposed that the decision to accept or reject a union is not unlike other choices facing an individual. Employees will support a union to the extent that it will get outcomes important to them without prohibitive costs. Over 50 years ago Bakke (1945) stated this most eloquently:

> The worker reacts favorably to union membership in proportion to the strength of his belief that this step will reduce his frustrations and anxieties and will further his opportunities relevant to the achievement of his standards of successful living. He reacts unfavorably in proportion to the strength of his belief that this step will increase his frustrations and anxieties and will reduce his opportunities relevant to the achievement of such standards. (p. 38)

DeCotiis and LeLouarn (1981) developed the model of the determinants of unionization shown in Figure 14–1. The work context includes employee reactions to work, organization climate, perceived organization structure, and supervision. Personal characteristics include age, gender, and race, as well as feelings of job satisfaction. The work context and personal characteristics determine union instrumentality—that is, the extent to which a union is seen as improving the employee's welfare. Instrumentality affects the employee's attitude toward unions; in turn, this affects the employee's intent to vote for a union. The actual vote is determined by the sequence shown in the model. DeCotiis and LeLouarn were able to explain over 54% of the variance in perceptions of union instrumentality with the concepts in their model.

Summers, Betton, and DeCotiis (1986) found that union instrumentality can be lowered when different unions are competing for the right to represent employees. They discovered that employees are likely to take antiunion information more seriously if its source is another union rather than management. Premack and Hunter (1988) carefully studied the unionization decision by means of elaborate statistical methods. They concluded that some employees hold strong attitudes about unions, both pro and con, and their attitudes are usually not altered one way

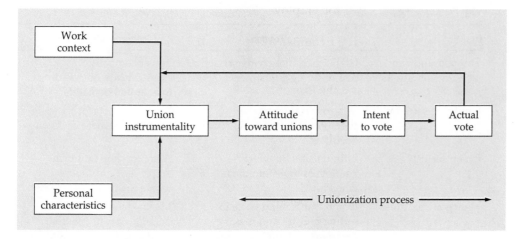

FIGURE 14–1   *A model of the determinants of the unionization process*

SOURCE: From "A Predictive Study of Voting Behavior in a Representation Election Using Union Instrumentality and Work Perceptions" by T. A. DeCotiis and J. Y. LeLouarn, 1981, *Organizational Behavior and Human Performance*, 27, p. 109.

or the other during the course of the organizing campaign. However, other employees are uncertain about their attitudes toward unions, and their attitudes can be altered by the behavior of both parties during the organizing campaign. Premack and Hunter noted that these employees' votes are critical to the outcome of the election because most union representation elections are decided by a small number of votes.

THE LABOR CONTRACT

Once a union is recognized, its officials are authorized to negotiate a **labor contract.** This is a formal agreement between union and management, specifying conditions of employment over a set period.

Both sides prepare a preliminary list of what they want included; the union presents its demands and the employer its offers. The union tends to ask for more than it knows it can get; management tends to offer less. While both sides seek a satisfactory agreement, they often resort to bombast, which is a hallmark of such negotiations. Union officials may allege that management is making huge profits and taking advantage of workers. Management may allege that malicious union leaders have duped the good workers and that their policies may force the company into bankruptcy. Over time, both sides usually come to an agreement; the union often gets less than it wanted and management gives more. When agreement is not reached (an impasse), other steps are taken, as will be discussed.

Contract negotiations take place between two teams of negotiators. The union side typically consists of local union officials, shop stewards, and perhaps a representative of the national union. Management usually fields a team of a few personnel and production managers, who follow preset guidelines. The contract contains many articles; there are also many issues to bargain over. The issues can

TABLE 14–2 *Typical bargaining issues and positions taken by union and management*

Issue	Union's Position	Management's Position
Compensation and working conditions	Higher pay, more fringe benefits, cost-of-living adjustments	Lower company expenditures, not yielding to all union demands
Employee security	Seniority is the basis for promotions, layoffs, and recall decisions	Merit or job performance is the basis for these decisions
Union security	A union shop in which employees must join the union when hired	An open shop in which employees can choose to join the union
Management rights	Union wants more voice in setting policies and making decisions that affect employees	Management feels certain decisions are its inherent right and does not want to share them with the union
Contract duration	Shorter contracts	Longer contracts

generally be classified into five categories: compensation and working conditions, employee security, union security, management rights, and contract duration. Table 14–2 gives examples of these issues and the positions typically taken by each side.

In the process each bargaining team checks with its members to see whether they will compromise on the initial positions. Each side may be willing to yield on some points but not others. Eventually they reach a tentative agreement. Union members then vote on the contract. If they approve it, the contract is ratified and remains in effect for the agreed-on time (typically two to three years). If members reject the contract, further negotiation is necessary.

Whether a contract will be ratified typically depends on industry practices, community practices, and recent trends. If the union represents truck drivers and a critical issue is wages, the union will collect data needed to judge the proposal: what other companies in the industry pay truck drivers, what other companies in the community pay them, and whether prices and wages are rising or falling. Stagner and Rosen (1965) classically referred to the area of compromise as the *bargaining zone*; this is illustrated in Figure 14–2. Both parties must move toward a compromise without exceeding their tolerance limits; this is the point beyond which the contract will be unacceptable. If both parties reach a compromise within their expectations, there will be agreement. If, however, one side exceeds its tolerance limit, the proposed contract will not be acceptable.

Both sides will use whatever external factors are available to influence the contract in their favor. If there is high unemployment and the company could replace workers who go on strike, management has an advantage. If the company does much of its business around Christmas, the union may choose that time to negotiate a contract, knowing the company can ill afford a strike then. Each side looks for factors that will bolster its position.

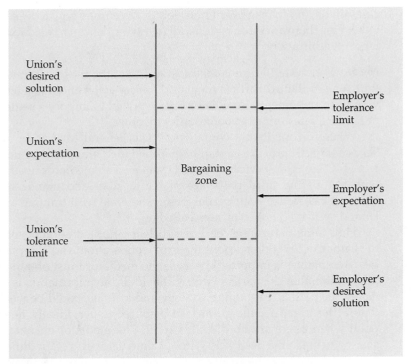

FIGURE 14–2 *Desires, expectations, and tolerance limits that determine the bargaining zone*

SOURCE: From *Psychology of Union-Management Relations* (p. 96) by R. Stagner and H. Rosen, 1965, Belmont, CA: Wadsworth. Reprinted by permission of the publisher. Brooks/Cole Publishing Company, Pacific Grove, California.

Collective Bargaining and Impasse Resolution

Whether the bargaining process runs smoothly often depends on to the parties' approaches. Pruitt (1993) distinguished between distributive and integrative bargaining postures. *Distributive bargaining* is predominant in the United States. This assumes a win/lose relationship; whatever the employer gives the union, the employer loses, and vice versa. Because both sides are trying to minimize losses, movement toward a compromise is often painful and slow.

The alternative is *integrative bargaining*. Both sides work to improve the relationship while the present contract is in effect. Contract renewal is not seen as the time and place for confrontation. Instead, both parties seek to identify common problems and propose acceptable solutions that can be adopted when the contract expires.

These bargaining postures are not formally chosen; rather, they are implied by behavior in the workplace. While it is not always a strict either/or decision, distributive bargaining is far more characteristic of union/management relations than is integrative bargaining.

What happens if the two parties cannot reach an agreement? In some cases the labor contract may stipulate what will be done if an impasse is reached. In other cases union and management must jointly determine how to break the impasse. In either case there are three options, all involving third parties: mediation, fact-finding, and arbitration.

Mediation.   **Mediation** is the most used yet the most informal third-party option. A neutral third party (a mediator) assists union and management in reaching voluntary agreement. A mediator has no power to impose a settlement; rather, he or she facilitates bringing both parties together.

Where do mediators come from? The Federal Mediation and Conciliation Service (FMCS) provides a staff of qualified mediators. An organization may contact FMCS for the services of such a person. The mediator need not be affiliated with FMCS; any third party acceptable to labor and management may serve. Generally, however, both parties prefer someone with training and experience in labor disputes, so FMCS is often called on.

How a mediator intervenes is not clear-cut. Mediation is voluntary; thus, no mediator can function without the trust, cooperation, and acceptance of both parties. Acceptance is important because the mediator must obtain any confidential information that the parties have withheld. If the information is used indiscriminately, the parties' bargaining strategy and leverage could be weakened. The mediator tries to reduce the number of disputed issues; ideally, he or she reaches a point where there are no disputes at all. The mediator encourages information sharing to break the deadlock. Without a mediator, it is often difficult for parties to "open up" after assuming adversary roles. The mediator facilitates the flow of information and progression toward compromise. If the mediator is unsuccessful, both parties may engage in the next phase: fact-finding.

Fact-Finding.   **Fact-finding** is more formal than mediation. A qualified mediator may also serve as a fact finder, but his or her role is different. In fact-finding the third party reviews the facts, makes a formal recommendation to resolve the dispute, and makes the recommendation public. It is presumed that if the recommendation is public, the parties will be pressured to accept it or use it for a negotiated settlement. However, fact-finding has not produced the desired pressure. Public interest is apparently aroused only when a strike threatens or actually imposes direct hardship on the public.

Fact-finding may be most useful when one party faces internal differences and needs recommendations from an expert to overcome opposition to a settlement. There appears to be a difference in the effectiveness of fact-finding between private- and public-sector employers. In the public sector fact-finding has met with limited success. Parties learn that rejecting a fact-finding recommendation is not politically or economically costly, so they are unlikely to value the opinion of the fact finder. In the private sector fact-finding can be helpful primarily because the final technique of settlement (arbitration) is strongly opposed by unions and management. However, fact-finding is not used very often in the private sector.

Arbitration.   **Arbitration** is the final and most formal settlement technique. Both parties must abide by the decision of the neutral third party. "Final and binding" is usually associated with arbitration. The use of arbitration may be stipulated in the labor contract; it may also be agreed on informally. This is called *interest* *arbitration* because it involves the interests of both parties in negotiating a new contract.

Arbitrators must have extensive experience in labor relations. The American Arbitration Association (AAA) maintains the standards and keeps a list of qualified arbitrators. Arbitrators listed by AAA often also serve as mediators listed by FMCS. Effective mediators, fact finders, and arbitrators all need the same skills. What distinguishes the services is the clout of the third party.

There are many forms of interest arbitration. With *voluntary arbitration*, the parties agree to the process. It is most common in the private sector in settling disputes that arise while a contract is still in effect. *Compulsory arbitration* is legally required. It is most common in the public sector.

There are other types of arbitration. With *conventional arbitration*, the arbitrator creates the settlement he or she deems appropriate. In *final-offer arbitration*, the arbitrator must select the proposal of either union or management; no compromise is possible. For example, suppose the union demands $8 per hour, and the company offers $7. In conventional arbitration the arbitrator could decide on any wage but would probably split the difference and decide on $7.50. In final-offer arbitration the arbitrator must choose the $7 or the $8. An additional variation also holds for final-offer arbitration: The arbitrator may make the decision on a total package. He or she chooses the complete proposal of either the employer or the union on all issues. The decision may also be made on an issue-by-issue basis. In this case the arbitrator might choose the employer wage offer but select the union demand on vacation days. Decisions on voluntary versus compulsory arbitration, conventional versus final-offer arbitration, and total-package versus issue-by-issue arbitration are determined by law for public-sector employers and by mutual agreement in the private sector (see Field Note 3).

Interest arbitration is more common in the public sector. Historically, the private sector has been opposed to outside interference in resolving labor problems that are "private" affairs. Thus, private-sector employers will readily seek the advice of a mediator but shun strategies that require certain courses of action. The public sector, however, is quite different. Strikes in the public sector (for example, police) can have devastating effects on the general public. Since they are often prohibited by law, other means of settlement (fact-finding, arbitration) are used. Some public-sector employees have gone on strike (sometimes legally but usually illegally), but strikes are more often the outcome of impasses in the private sector.

Responses to Impasse

Consider the situation in which union and management cannot resolve their disputes. They may or may not have used a mediator. Assume the private sector is involved because mediation, fact-finding, and arbitration might be required in the public sector. What happens if the two parties cannot agree?

In collective bargaining both sides can take actions if they are not pleased with the outcome. These actions are weapons with which to bring about favorable settlements. What the union can do is to strike. Union members must vote for a strike. If members support a strike and no settlement is reached, they will stop work at a particular time. That point is typically the day after the current contract expires.

Taking a strike vote during negotiations brings pressure on management to agree to union demands.

The right to strike is a very powerful tool. The losses from a long strike may be greater than the concessions made in a new contract. Also, unions are skilled in scheduling their strikes (or threatening to do so) when the company is particularly vulnerable (such as around Christmas for the airline industry). If employees do strike, the company is usually closed down completely. There may be limited production if management performs some jobs. It is also possible to hire workers to replace those on strike. These replacements are called "scabs." Given the time it takes to recruit, hire, and train new workers, replacements will not be hired unless a long strike is predicted.

While a strike hurts management, it is unpleasant for the workers as well. Since they are not working, they do not get paid. The employees may have contributed to a strike fund, but such funds usually pay only a fraction of regular wages. A strike is the price employees pay to get their demands. It sometimes also limits their demands. By the time a union faces a strike, it is usually confronted with two unpalatable options. One is to accept a contract it does not like; the other

---

Field Note 3   *Overuse of Arbitration?*

Interest arbitration can be a seductively simple means of resolving impasses—so simple, in fact, that some people fear it is overused. Let us say the union wants a 50-cents-per-hour pay increase and management offers 10 cents per hour. Both sides believe from past experience that an arbitrator would likely split the difference between the two, settling on 30 cents per hour. It has been suggested that the more arbitration is used to resolve impasses and the more splitting that occurs, the more likely it is that parties will not bargain seriously between themselves; that is, they will opt for the effortless remedy, arbitration. Thus, the parties will disregard the mediation and fact-finding stages and go directly to arbitration. Arbitration becomes an addictive response to impasse; this phenomenon has been labeled the "narcotic effect" of arbitration.

How do you weaken the narcotic effect of arbitration? One solution is to have arbitrators not split the difference in making decisions. Arbitrators are free to fashion whatever decisions they think are fair. Splitting the difference is often perceived as the fairest thing to do, and it increases the acceptability of the arbitrator for future cases because neither party will have received preferential treatment. Thus, with each split decision, the narcotic effect becomes stronger. One way to weaken the narcotic effect is to prohibit split decisions, which is what happens in final-offer arbitration. Here, the arbitrator is bound to accept either the 50-cents or 10-cents position and not any figure over, under, or in between. Given this, it has been hypothesized that negotiators will offer more serious, reasonable proposals, knowing the alternative is to have an arbitrator choose one position over the other. An absurd offer would never get chosen. In total-package, final-offer arbitration the arbitrator must choose the entire package of either the union or management, which tends to drive both parties into compromise. The alternative version of issue-by-issue, final-offer arbitration produces its own type of split decisions; that is, since there can be no within-issue splits, the arbitrator splits between issues. Thus, the union position is accepted on one issue and management's position on another. The creation of total-package, final-offer arbitration is presumed to have greatly decreased reliance on arbitration for impasse resolution.

TABLE 14–3   *Union and company alternatives and related consequences*

Company	Union
Alternative 1	
Perceived consequences of giving in to union demands	Perceived consequences of accepting company counteroffer
1. Lessening investor returns	1. Losing membership support
2. Losing competitive standing	2. Losing status within union movement
3. Setting bad precedent	3. Setting bad precedent
4. Avoiding costly strike	4. Avoiding costly strike
5. Avoiding government and public ill will	5. Avoiding government and public ill will
Alternative 2	
Perceived consequences of refusing to accede to union demands	Perceived consequences of sticking to original demands
1. Due to potential strike, lessening investor return	1. Proving strength and determination of union to members
2. Due to potential strike, losing competitive standing	2. Due to potential strike, losing member income
3. Losing government and public good will	3. Due to potential strike, losing member support
4. Maintaining company prerogatives	4. Losing government and public good will
5. Breaking union power	5. Teaching company a "lesson"

SOURCE: Adapted from *Psychology of Union-Management Relations* (p. 103) by R. Stagner and H. Rosen, 1965, Belmont, CA: Wadsworth. Reprinted by permission of the publishers, Brooks/Cole Publishing Company, Pacific Grove, California.

is to strike. Employees may seek temporary employment while they are on strike, but such jobs are not always available. On the basis of labor economists' studies of the costs of strikes to both employees and employers, it is safe to say that strikes rarely benefit either party. Sometimes the company suffers the most; in other cases the union does. There are rarely any "winners" in a strike. Stagner and Rosen (1965) listed the consequences for both union and management in accepting each other's alternatives, particularly as they relate to a strike (see Table 14–3).

One study examined some of the dynamics associated with strikes. Stagner and Effal (1982) looked at the attitudes of unionized automobile workers at several times, including when contracts were being negotiated, during an ensuing strike, and seven months after the strike ended. The authors found that union members on strike (1) had a higher opinion of the union and its leadership than before the strike, (2) evaluated the benefit package more highly after the strike, (3) became more militant toward the employer during the strike, and (4) reported more willingness to engage in union activities. The results of this study support predictions based on theories of conflict and attitude formation.

Management is not totally defenseless in the case of a strike. If it anticipates a strike, it might boost production beforehand to stockpile goods. Most public-sector employees, on the other hand, perform services, and services cannot be stockpiled. This is one reason strikes are illegal in some parts of the public sector.

THE WIZARD OF ID   by Brant Parker and Johnny Hart

SOURCE: The Wizard of Id by Brant Parker and Johnny Hart. By permission of Johnny Hart and Creators Syndicate, Inc.

Sometimes a strike uncovers information about the quality of the workforce. When one company replaced strikers with temporary help, new production records were set. In this case the strike revealed a weakness in the employees.

A strike is not the only option available to the union. Work *slowdowns* have also been used. Workers operate at lower levels of efficiency. They may simply put out less effort and thus produce less, or they may be absent to reduce productivity. Since strikes are illegal in the police force, police officers who are dissatisfied with their contracts may call in sick en masse with what has become known as the "blue flu." Such tactics can exert great pressure on management to yield to union demands.

Sabotage is another response to impasse in negotiations. Stagner and Rosen (1965) described a situation in which factory production was increased from 2,000 to 3,000 units per day by modifying a drill press. However, wages were not increased, and workers resented it. They found that bumping the sheet metal against the drill would eventually break the drill. Then the employee handling the drill would have to wait idly for a replacement. By some curious accident, average production continued at around 2,000 units per day. However, management got the "message." While sabotage is not a sanctioned union activity like a strike, it is a way of putting pressure on management to accept demands.

Management also has a major tactic to get the union to acquiesce. It is called a *lockout* and is considered the employer's equivalent of a strike. The company threatens to close if the union does not accept its offer. Employees cannot work and thus "pay" for rejecting the employer's offer. A threatened lockout may cause a majority of workers to pressure a minority holding out against a contract issue. Like strikes, lockouts are costly to both the company and the union, and they are not undertaken lightly. They are management's ultimate response to an impasse.

Before this section ends, note that strikes, slowdowns, sabotage, and lockouts represent failures in the collective bargaining process. These actions are taken because a settlement was not reached. Like most responses to frustration, they are rarely beneficial in the long run. Some unions may want to "teach the company a lesson"; some companies want to break a union. But both parties have a symbiotic relationship. A company cannot exist without employees; without a company, employees have no jobs. Collective bargaining reflects the continual tussle for power, but neither side can afford to be totally victorious. If a union exacts so many concessions that the company goes bankrupt, it will have accomplished nothing. As Estey (1981) put it, "Labor does not seek to kill the goose that lays the golden eggs; it wants it to lay more golden eggs, and wants more eggs for itself" (p. 83).

If management drives employees away by not making enough concessions, it will not have a qualified workforce. Industrial peace is far more desirable for all parties than warfare. Conflict can provide opportunities for change and development; if conflict gets out of hand, it can be devastating. Union/management relations are not all typified by infighting and power plays. Nothing unites opposing factions faster than a common enemy. Because the United States was losing some economic battles to foreign competition, some union/management relations became far more integrative. For example, unions in the auto industry have given up some concessions gained before the current contract expired. The industry, in turn, used the money saved to become more competitive. By remaining solvent, the industry continued to provide jobs. Both management and labor could pursue some common goals. Collective bargaining is a delicate process. Neither side should lose sight of the total economic and social environment, even though short-term, narrow issues are often at the heart of disputes.

Grievances

Collective bargaining is mainly directed toward resolving disputes over new labor contracts; however, disputes also occur over contracts that are in effect. No matter how clearly a labor contract is written, disagreements invariably arise over its meaning or extent. Developing a clear and precise contract involves writing skills in their highest form. Despite the best intentions of those involved, events occur that are not covered clearly in a labor contract. For example, companies often include a contract clause stating that sleeping on the job is grounds for dismissal. A supervisor notices that an employee's head is resting on his arms and his eyes are closed. The supervisor infers the employee is asleep and fires him. The employee says he was not sleeping but felt dizzy and chose to rest for a moment rather than risk falling down. Who is right?

If the supervisor dismissed the employee, the employee would probably file a **grievance,** or formal complaint. The firing decision can be appealed through a grievance procedure, which is usually a provision of a labor contract. First, the employee and supervisor try to reach an understanding. If they do not, the shop steward represents the employee in negotiating with the supervisor. This is often done whether or not the steward thinks the employee has a "case"; above all, the steward's job is to represent union members. If it is not resolved, the case may then be taken to the company's director of industrial relations, who hears testimony from both sides and issues a verdict. This may be a compromise—such as the employee keeps his or her job but is put on probation. The final step is to call in an arbitrator. He or she examines the labor contract, hears testimony, and renders an opinion. This process is called rights or grievance arbitration; it involves the rights of the employee. The labor contract usually specifies that union and management share the cost of arbitration, which may be $2,000 per hearing. This is done to prevent all grievances from being routinely pushed to arbitration. Each side must believe it has a strong case before calling in an arbitrator.

The arbitrator must be acceptable to both sides; this means he or she must be seen as neither prounion nor promanagement. The arbitrator may decide in favor of one side or issue a compromise decision. The decision is final and binding. If an arbitrator hears many cases in the same company and repeatedly decides in favor of one side, he or she may become unacceptable to the side that always loses. Articles of the labor contract that are repeated subjects of grievance (due mainly to ambiguous language) become prime candidates for revision in the next contract.

Think of grievances as a somewhat contaminated index of the quality of union/management relations. In general, when the working relationship is good, there are fewer grievances. However, as Gordon and Miller (1984) noted, in some organizations work problems are resolved informally between the conflicting parties and never develop into formal grievances. While formal grievances are usually indicative of conflict, their absence does not always reflect a problem-free work environment. Also, the more ambiguous the labor contract, the more likely conflicts will ensue. A poorly written or inconsistently interpreted contract invites grievances. There can be much grievance activity in a recently unionized organization; employees use grievances to "test" management's knowledge of the labor contract (Muchinsky & Maassarani, 1981). Particularly in the public sector, where collective bargaining is relatively new, government employees are expected to act as "management" even though they have little or no training in dealing with labor. This can contribute to errors in contract administration. Gordon and Bowlby (1989) found employees were more likely to file a grievance when management actions against them were perceived as a threat and when the employee attributed the discipline to a manager's personal disposition (animus toward the worker). Employees were less likely to file a grievance when they perceived managers as simply following rules that required punishment for the specific worker behavior.

Employee concern over capricious management decisions is one of the major reasons employees opt for union representation. Fryxell and Gordon (1989) reported that the amount of procedural justice afforded by a grievance system was the strongest predictor of employee satisfaction with a union. Gordon and Bowlby (1988) also challenged the dictum that grievances are best resolved at the lowest step of the grievance process. Grievants who won their cases at higher levels of the grievance process showed greater faith in the fairness and perceived justice of the dispute resolution process. Klaas (1989) reported that at higher levels in the grievance process managers were influenced by the grievant's work history as documented in their performance appraisals, even when that history was not relevant to evaluating the merits of the grievance. Olson-Buchanan (1996) found that, consistent with procedural justice, employees who had access to a grievance system were more willing to continue working for the organization. Consistent with the equity theory of motivation, employees who had a basis for dispute had lower objective job performance and were less willing to continue working for the organization.

In conclusion, while there is much publicity about strike-related issues, union members feel the union's highest priority should be better ways of handling grievances. Unions serve many purposes; however, the most pressing need they fill seems to be ensuring fair treatment in employment. Of course, this is a primary reason that unions appeal to workers.

INFLUENCE OF UNIONS ON NONUNIONIZED COMPANIES

Even if they do not have unionized employees, companies are still sensitive to union influence. Companies that are unresponsive to employees' needs invite unionization. A nonunion company that wants to remain so must be receptive to its workers' ideas and complaints. If a company can satisfy its employees' needs, a union is unnecessary; that is, the company does voluntarily what a labor union would force it to do. A given community or industry often has a mix of union and nonunion companies. If unionized employees get concessions from management on wages, benefits, hours, and so on, these become reference points for nonunionized employees. Thus, for example, a nonunion company may feel compelled to raise wages to remain competitive. If a labor contract calls for formal grievance procedures, a nonunion company may well follow suit. Workers are aware of employment conditions in other companies, which gives them a frame of reference for judging their own. If a company does not offer comparable conditions, employees may see a union as a means of improving their welfare. This is not to say that nonunion companies must offer identical conditions. There are costs associated with a union (for example, dues); a nonunion company might set wages slightly lower than those paid in a unionized company so the net effect (higher wages minus dues) is comparable. What economists call the "union/nonunion wage differential" has been the subject of extensive research. Jarrell and Stanley (1990) reported that the union/nonunion wage differential varied with the national unemployment rate and ranged from 8.9% to 12.4%.

Although a prudent nonunion employer keeps abreast of employment conditions in the community and the industry, a company cannot act to keep a union out "at all costs." There is powerful labor relations legislation. Many laws (like the National Labor Relations Act) were enacted to prohibit unfair practices on both sides. For example, an employer cannot fire a worker just because he or she supports a union. The history of labor relations is full of cases of worker harassment by unions or management to influence attitudes toward unionization. But both sides can suffer for breaking the law.

BEHAVIORAL RESEARCH ON UNION/MANAGEMENT RELATIONS

Thus far this chapter has examined the structure of unions, collective bargaining, and various issues in union/management relations. For the most part, psychological issues have not been discussed. With the exception of grievances, there is little behavioral research on union/management relations. However, over the past few years, interest in this area has increased. We are beginning to see an interdisciplinary approach to topics that historically were treated with parochialism (Brett, 1980). This section will examine research on union/management relations with a strong behavioral thrust.

Employee Support for Unions

Numerous studies have dealt with why employees support a union, particularly with regard to personal needs and job satisfaction. Feuille and Blandin (1974) sampled the attitudes toward unionization of over 400 college professors at a university experiencing many financial and resource cutbacks. The items measured satisfaction with areas like fairness of the university's personnel decisions, adequacy of financial support, representation of faculty interests in the state legislature, and salary. The professors were also asked to rate their inclination to accept a union. Professors who were dissatisfied with employment conditions were much more likely to support a union. Respondents also were consistent in their attitudes toward a union and their perceptions of its impact and effectiveness. Proponents of a union saw it as an effective way of protecting employment interests and as having a positive impact. In general, results indicated that unionization is more attractive as employment conditions deteriorate.

Using a similar research design and sample, Bigoness (1978) correlated measures of job satisfaction, job involvement, and locus of control with disposition to accept unionization. Bigoness also found that feelings of dissatisfaction correlated with acceptance of unionization. In particular, dissatisfaction with work, pay, and promotions each correlated at .35 with attitude toward unionization. Additionally, unionization was more appealing to people who were less involved in their jobs and had an external locus of control. Combining all independent variables in a multiple regression equation, Bigoness accounted for over 27% of the variance in attitudes toward unionization.

Hamner and Smith (1978) examined union activity in 250 units of a large organization. In half the units there had been some union activity; in the other half no activity was reported. Using an immense sample of over 80,000, the authors found that employee attitudes predicted the level of unionization activity. The strongest predictor was dissatisfaction with supervision. Schriesheim (1978) found that prounion voting in a certification election was positively correlated with dissatisfaction; also, dissatisfaction with economic facets was more predictive than dissatisfaction with noneconomic factors. Furthermore, research by Youngblood, DeNisi, Molleston, and Mobley (1984) and Zalesny (1985) showed the importance of two other factors in union support. The first factor is attitude toward collective bargaining in general. The more acceptable unions in general are to a person, the more likely he or she will vote for unionization. The second factor is attitude toward unions as instrumental in enhancing worker welfare. Employees may not be satisfied with their employment conditions, but they may feel that unions can do little to aid them.

These studies all show that dissatisfaction with employment conditions is predictive of support for unionization. The more satisfied workers are, the less likely they are to think a union is necessary or that it can improve their welfare. These results are not surprising. They reveal the types of dissatisfaction associated with a disposition toward unions. Some authors tout the social benefits of unions (for example, association with similar people), but it is mainly the perceived economic advantages that give unions their appeal. Not all support for unions, however, is based on dissatisfaction with economic conditions. Hammer and Berman (1981) found that the faculty at one college wanted a union mainly because they distrusted administrative decision making and were dissatisfied with work content. Prounion voting was motivated by the faculty's desire for more power in dealing with the administration.

Union Influence

What influence do unions have on enhancing employee welfare? Various studies have produced somewhat different conclusions. Gomez-Mejia and Balkin (1984) found that samples of unionized and nonunionized college teachers were equally satisfied with all job facets except pay; unionized faculty were more satisfied with their wages. Carillon and Sutton (1982) found a strong positive relationship between union effectiveness in representing teachers and their reported quality of worklife. Allegedly, college administrators fear that faculty unionization will affect organization effectiveness. Cameron (1982) dealt with this in 41 colleges; faculty were unionized in 18 colleges and nonunionized in 23. Cameron proposed nine indices of effectiveness for a college, involving student academic development, faculty and administrator satisfaction, and ability to acquire resources. Nonunionized colleges were significantly more effective on three of the nine indices; unionized colleges were not significantly more effective on any. Cameron also collected attitude data from faculty members on four factors relating to their work. These results are presented in Figure 14–3. Faculty power and "red tape" were seen as increasing since unionization; collegiality was seen as decreasing. The study revealed some major differences in the effectiveness of union and nonunion colleges; however, the cause was not determined. Unionization may "cause" colleges to be less effective, which would be a strong argument against unions. However, the less effective colleges may turn to unions for improvement, which is obviously an argument supporting unionization. As discussed in Chapter 2, causality is difficult to determine. Raelin (1989) suggested that the literature on this topic indicates that less effective colleges turn to unions in an attempt to restore their professional status, although it is questionable whether a union by itself can return an established profession to its status prior to perceived deprofessionalization.

Fullagar, Gallagher, Gordon, and Clark (1995) tested the proposition that new organizational members are socialized to consider joining a union. There are two types of socialization. The first is *institutional,* which refers to the collective and formal practices organizations use to provide newcomers with a common set of experiences and information to elicit standardized responses. In contrast, *individual* socialization practices are idiosyncratic and informal. Individual socialization is informal in that learning takes place on the job through interactions with other organizational members. Fullagar et al. found that individual socialization practices had a positive impact on both affective and behavioral involvement in the union. However, institutional socialization practices were shown to be either ineffective or counterproductive. The practical implications are that important interactions occur between union officials and new members in developing new members' affective attachment to the union and later participation in union activities. Informal and individual socialization tactics may be undertaken by active or interested rank-and-file members and not necessarily by union stewards. Institutional socialization efforts (e.g., an orientation program to the union) seemingly are more effective in increasing awareness, whereas individual socialization efforts are more effective in producing involvement (Fullagar, Clark, Gallagher, & Gordon, 1994).

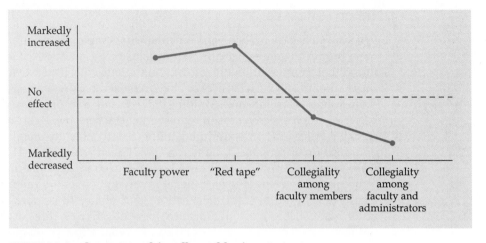

FIGURE 14–3   *Perceptions of the effects of faculty unionization*

SOURCE: From "The Relationship Between Faculty Unionism and Organizational Effectiveness" by K. Cameron, 1982, *Academy of Management Journal, 25,* p. 13.

Dispute Settlement

As you might imagine, I/O psychologists have examined the process by which disputes are settled in both laboratory and field settings. As in some other areas of I/O research, the generalizability of laboratory findings in this area is somewhat limited. Gordon, Schmitt, and Schneider (1984) feel the value of laboratory studies is to prepare people for undertaking actual collective bargaining in the future and to help develop questionnaires for later field use in dispute settlement. They noted that the limitations of laboratory and field research on dispute settlement are the classic ones discussed in Chapter 2. There is questionable generalizability from laboratory studies, and field studies fail to identify causal relationships.

There have been several studies on mediation and arbitration as means of settling disputes. Bazerman and Neale (1982) asked whether strategies of personnel selection and training can improve negotiating effectiveness. They proposed selecting negotiators on the basis of their ability to take a broad perspective on problems and training them not to be overconfident about effecting a resolution. The authors found that training increased the number of concessions negotiators were willing to make and concluded that it may be a useful tool in dispute settlement. Neale (1984) determined that when the costs of arbitration are high, negotiators are more likely to reach a resolution on their own before they resort to arbitration. However, when cost is not much of an issue, they are more likely to accept arbitration. Researchers have also discovered the behavioral implications of the different types of arbitration. Starke and Notz (1981) reported that subjects who anticipated final-offer arbitration were closer to agreement at the conclusion of their bargaining than subjects who anticipated conventional arbitration. In fact, Grigsby and Bigoness (1982) concluded that final-offer, conventional, total-package, and issue-by-issue arbitration all produced different bargaining outcomes even though they are all variations of the same resolution process (arbitration). These behavioral studies on dispute settlement have enhanced our understanding in ways that traditional labor economic research has been unable to do. In fact, Brett, Goldberg, and Ury (1990) discussed how I/O psychologists can be used to resolve disputes. They proposed that a dispute-system designer organize procedures in a low- to high-cost sequence and work with parties to help them acquire new motivation, negotiation skills, and recourses to new procedures. The individual may even recommend changes in the broader organization that will facilitate the success of a dispute resolution system.

Commitment to the Union

The concept of employee commitment to a union addresses the notion of dual allegiance: Can a person be loyal to both a labor union and the employing company? For several years, researchers have examined the antecedents of both union and company commitment.

Our understanding of union commitment was enhanced through a major study by Gordon, Philpot, Burt, Thompson, and Spiller (1980). These authors developed a questionnaire for measuring commitment that was completed by more than 1,800 union members. Responses were factor analyzed, and union commitment was found to be composed of four dimensions: loyalty, responsibility to the union, willingness to work for the union, and belief in unionism. The research had at least two major benefits for unions. First, unions could use the questionnaires to assess the effect of their actions and estimate solidarity, especially before negotiations. Second, the research revealed the importance of socialization to new union members. The authors felt that union commitment increases when both formal and informal efforts are made to involve a member in union activities soon after joining. Coworker attitudes and willingness to help are crucial to the socialization process. Improving the socialization of new members improves their commitment, which is one index of union strength. In a follow-up study by Ladd, Gordon, Beauvais, and Morgan (1982), the questionnaire was administered to nonprofessional and professional members of a white-collar union. The results were the same as those from the original study despite the sample differences, although other researchers arrived at somewhat different conclusions (Friedman & Harvey, 1986). Klandermans (1989) found the scale useful for understanding unionism in Holland.

Mellor (1990) studied membership decline in 20 unions. The unions with the greatest decline in membership showed the strongest commitment to the union by the surviving members. Members in locals with more severe losses expressed a greater willingness to participate in future strikes. Fullagar and Barling (1989) reported that union loyalty was best predicted by union instrumentality, extrinsic job dissatisfaction, and early socialization experiences with unions. The authors proposed that greater union loyalty resulted in more formal participation in union activities. In a study of dual allegiance, Margenau, Martin, and Peterson (1988) found that satisfied workers felt allegiance to both the company and the union, whereas dissatisfied workers showed allegiance only to the union.

Tetrick (1995) proposed that union commitment occurs in a context of organizational rights that are provided by the union as well as organizational citizenship behaviors on the part of union members. Tetrick stated that the degree of commitment to the union can be understood in terms of the psychological contract between the employee and the organization, and the role the union plays in maintaining this relationship. Sverke and Kuruvilla (1995) identified two dimensions that explain why employees are committed to a union. The first is *instrumentality*, the perceived value or usefulness associated with union membership. The second is *ideology*, the individual's acceptance and support of the ideals or principles upon which labor unions are based. Sverke and Sjoberg (1995) developed a typology of union members' commitment to the union based on these two dimensions, as shown in Figure 14–4. Each dimension (instrumentality and ideology) is divided into two levels, high and low, resulting in a four-cell classification model. As shown in Figure 14–4, the *alienated member* is the noncommitted member who is likely to be nonparticipative and who might intend to withdraw membership. The *instrumental member* can be expected to retain membership and to support union activities directed at improving wages and working conditions. Members committed primarily because of their prounion ideology (*ideological members*) support and take part in union activities, such as attending meetings. The *devoted member* category, representing members with high degrees of commitment on both dimensions, is postulated to contain the most active union members. Other forms of union participation activities include holding office, serving on union committees, and voting in elections (Kelloway, Catano, & Carroll, 1995).

Finally, Gordon and Ladd (1990) provided a cautionary note about professional ethics to researchers studying dual allegiance. They said researchers should be fully aware of the reasons that either the union or the company would encourage research on allegiance. I/O psychologists should not allow themselves to be "used" by either side to further their own aims by conducting such research.

I/O PSYCHOLOGY AND INDUSTRIAL RELATIONS

Hartley (1992) proposed that there are many areas where I/O psychology might contribute to the field of industrial relations. These include many of the issues already examined, including why workers join unions, dispute settlement, and dual commitment. Four traditional I/O topics will be examined from a labor union perspective: personnel selection, training, leadership development, and employee involvement.

Personnel Selection.   In both union and nonunion companies, management determines the knowledge, skills, and abilities needed to fill jobs. The personnel office usually determines fitness for employment in lower-level jobs. For higher-level jobs, responsibility is spread through various units of the company. However, in a union company the labor contract may stipulate that those hired for jobs represented by the union must join the union after a probationary period. This is a **union shop**; the employee has no choice about joining.[1] In other unionized com-

---

[1]However, currently 21 states have "right to work" laws prohibiting compulsory union membership as a condition of continued employment.

Ideological commitment to the union

	High	Low
High	Devoted member	Instrumental member
Low	Ideological member	Alienated member

Instrumental commitment to the union

FIGURE 14–4   *Typology of union commitment*

SOURCE: Adapted from "Union Membership Behavior: The Influence of Instrumental and Value-Based Commitment" by M. Sverke and A. Sjoberg, 1995, in *Changing Employment Relations* (pp. 229–254), edited by L. E. Tetrick and J. Barling, Washington, DC: American Psychological Association.

panies the employee has the choice of joining a union; these are **agency** or **open shops.** However, considerable pressure can be brought on an employee to join. In many cases, it is to the employee's advantage to join the union for the benefits and protection it affords.

Union influence in personnel selection can affect both applicants and companies. Those who do not endorse unions (or who are uncertain about them) may not apply for jobs in unionized companies. Obviously, the applicant pool for unionized companies is smaller if such feelings are widespread. The extent of this problem varies with antiunion sentiment and availability of other jobs.

Union influence can also work in reverse. One company I know of prides itself on remaining nonunionized. It believes unionization is encouraged by employees who have prior union experience, and therefore it carefully screens job applicants for union membership. Those who have been members are not considered (however, they are not told why). The company wants applicants with the talent needed, but it places a higher priority on avoiding unions. Whether the company can continue this without adversely affecting the quality of the workforce will depend on the job openings and the number of applicants for employment with the company. Thus, from the perspectives of both the applicants and the company, unions can and do ultimately influence who gets hired.

Personnel Training.   One area in which unions have direct and significant influence is personnel training. One of the oldest forms of training is apprenticeship, and unions have a long history of this kind of training, especially in trades and crafts. Apprenticeship is governed by law; at the national level, it is administered by the Department of Labor. The Bureau of Apprenticeship and Training works closely with unions, vocational schools, state agencies, and others. According to the U.S. Department of Labor (1994), there are more than 475 apprenticed occupations employing over 280,000 apprentices. Apprentices go through a formal program of training and experience. They are supervised on the job and are given the facilities needed for instruction. There is a progressive wage schedule over the course of apprenticeship, and the individual is well versed in all aspects of the trade.

Most apprentice programs are in heavily unionized occupations (construction, manufacturing, transportation); thus, unions work closely with the Bureau of Apprenticeship and Training. For example, Figure 14–5 shows the cooperation among various organizations and agencies in the carpentry trade. Although not all unions are involved in apprentice programs, the linkage between unions and apprenticeship is one of the oldest in the history of American labor.

Leadership Development.   Often employees elected to leadership roles within their unions (e.g., shop stewards) or within the organization (e.g., supervisors) have had little developmental instruction in how to behave in a position of leadership. Several studies used the tenets of procedural justice as a basis to explain the concept of organizational fairness. Cole and Latham (1997) used a development exercise to teach supervisors to take effective disciplinary action with employees. The supervisors were placed into either a training group or a control group. Following simulated role-playing exercises derived from organizational incidents, both unionized employees and disciplinary subject matter experts (managers, union officials, and attorneys) rated the trained supervisors higher on disciplinary fairness than the supervisors in the control group. Skarlicki and Latham (1996) examined whether training union officers in the skills necessary for implementing principles of organizational justice would increase citizenship behaviors on the part of members of a labor union. The results showed that three months after training, the perceptions of union fairness among members whose leaders were in the training group were higher than among members whose leaders were in the control group. Skarlicki and Latham (1997) taught shop stewards methods of procedural justice using cases based on organizational incidents. The training improved knowledge of what constitutes fairness and may result in fewer grievances among employees regarding alleged unfairness in work. These examples illustrate how concepts such as procedural justice and organizational citizenship behavior can be used to improve the quality of leadership in organizations with labor unions.

Employee Involvement.   Employee involvement embraces some of the newer management concepts such as employee ownership of companies, employee profit-sharing plans, self-managed work teams, and Total Quality Management. It is reasonable to question whether the increased interest in workers' participation in management has resulted in a reduction of "we/they" attitudes on the part of employees. Kelly and Kelly (1991) concluded that employees express positive attitudes toward particular innovations (self-managed work groups) but that these attitudes are specific to the innovation and do *not* generalize to broader "we/they" attitudes and the industrial relations climate. Kelly and Kelly believe that the proper conditions have not been present for fostering broader cooperative attitudes. They note that attitudes are more likely to change where there is a perception of personal choice and control, but economic conditions and management directives have not provided the conditions to generate employee perceptions of

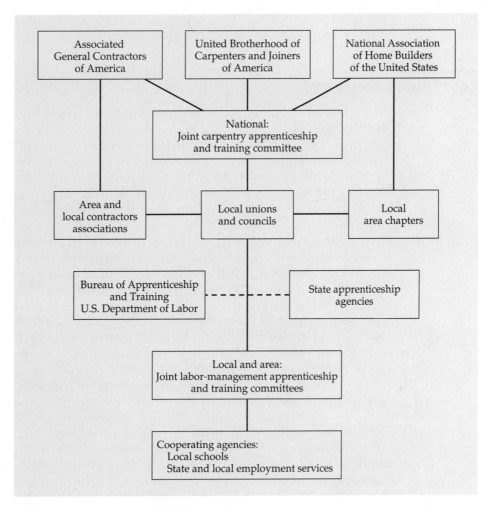

FIGURE 14–5 *Cooperation among unions, industry, and government in the apprenticeship system of the carpentry trade*

SOURCE: From *Apprenticeship: Past and Present* (p. 25) by U.S. Department of Labor, 1994, Washington, DC: U.S. Government Printing Office.

choice and control. That is, there is a perception among workers that management has been compelled because of economic pressures to try new concepts that reduce the power differential between workers and management. Given that, the amount of sincere trust between workers and management is insufficient to increase the cooperation between parties in some companies. In a related vein, Fields and Thacker (1992) examined changes in union and organizational commitment after the implementation of a joint union-management quality-of-worklife program. The results indicated that company commitment among unionized workers increased only when participants perceived the program as successful, but union commitment increased irrespective of the perception of the program's success. In general, it appears that while unionized employees recognize the benefits of employee involvement programs, participation in them does not mean the boundaries between union and management are less well defined.

CONCLUDING COMMENTS

The role of labor unions in the service and industry sectors of the U.S. economy has changed over the years. The high-water mark of union influence and power was in the 1930s and 1940s. American labor unions have steadily lost membership and influence since the 1970s. Masters (1997) believes unions are at the crossroads in their evolution. Masters notes that three traditional objectives are pursued by unions. The first is to bargain collectively with employers, gaining favorable wages and job conditions for unionized workers. The second is political activity, which is regarded by some scholars as the most prominent objective of European labor unions. Political activity is intended to lead to laws favorable to unions and their members. As such, some labor scholars contend that unions have been more influential in Europe than in the United States because of their greater political and ideological orientation. The third objective is organization activities that generate new members and increased revenues in the form of dues. Each objective adds to the overall strength of the union. Masters asserted that unions must devote more financial and human resources to strengthen their own organizations and reaffirm their value in society. One path of the crossroads faced by unions leads to rejuvenation, while the other path leads to irrelevance.

As a science, I/O psychology can benefit from examining topics from a union perspective, in addition to the more traditional management perspective. A case in point is violence in the workplace. The management perspective tends to emphasize detecting workers who are likely candidates to exhibit antisocial behavior. The union perspective, according to King and Alexander (1996), is to place the issue of workplace violence into the total context of workplace safety and health. The workers cite precursors to violence at the work site, such as production pressures, stress, long hours, forced overtime, and fears of plant shutdown or job loss. Furthermore, it is often evidence regarding what needs to be done to alleviate the problems witnessed on the job that leads to outbreaks of fights and threats on the job site. Unions claim that management is unwilling to respond to the work conditions that are precursors to violence, while the management perspective is to weed out those job candidates who will respond negatively to those conditions. In my opinion, both perspectives have merit, and it is this type of creative interplay between the two views that increases our chances of better understanding the issue of workplace violence.

CASE STUDY   ◆   Should We Let in a Labor Union?

Carl Dwyer and Ann Stovos were faculty members at Springdale College. The college had been in existence for about 30 years, and Dwyer had been on the staff almost since the beginning. Stovos was a relative newcomer, just completing her third year as a faculty member. For the past two years, there had been talk about unionizing the faculty. Much of the interest was sparked by two events. First, the college had experienced financial cutbacks due to low enrollment. Without tuition revenue, it was facing hardships paying the faculty. As a result, six teaching positions had been eliminated. The faculty understood the college's financial problems, but they felt cutbacks should be made in other areas, like some administrative positions. The faculty was also critical of how the college determined which teaching positions were eliminated. The other event was that for the third year in a row, the faculty were given only a 5% raise. Other colleges in the state were giving bigger raises, and some of the Springdale faculty felt they were getting the short end of the stick.

Various union representatives had been on campus; there was enough support for a representation election to be held in about a month. The faculty really seemed divided. Some openly supported a union, some were openly opposed, but the majority did not voice their sentiments. Dwyer was opposed to the idea of collective bargaining; Stovos supported it. Since they were officemates, the topic came up quite often. On this particular day, they were discussing whether the goals of unions were compatible with the goals of higher education.

Dwyer began the conversation: "I just don't think there is any place in a college for burly picketers carrying placards and threatening to beat up anyone who crosses the picket line. A college is a place for quiet, scholarly thought, an opportunity to teach interested students and to contemplate some of the deeper values. I've been here since we had only five buildings and a staff of twenty. I don't want to see this place turned into a playground for skull crushers."

"You've been watching too many movies, Carl," Stovos replied. "No one is going to turn Springdale into a battlefield. I want the same things you do. I didn't come here to be physically intimidated. I wouldn't like that any more than you do. But I also want to be treated fairly by the administration. I'd like some security from arbitrary decisions. There's nothing immoral about that, is there?"

"Do you think a union can prevent layoffs and get us twenty-five percent yearly raises?" Dwyer asked facetiously.

"No, I don't," Stovos countered, "but a union can force the drafting of fair and equitable policies if layoffs have to occur. And if everyone else is getting ten percent raises, maybe they can help us there, too. A union won't work miracles, but it can help prevent injustice."

"You don't understand, Ann. A college is not a factory. Different ideals run a college. It's not profit but scholarship. We have to foster a climate for inquisitive minds, learning, and personal growth. If I were interested only in making a buck, I wouldn't have become a college professor," Dwyer replied.

"Whether you like it or not, Carl, we are employees like all other working people. What's wrong with trying to ensure fair treatment at work? We have bills to pay and families to support just like everyone else. I don't understand why a college is somehow 'different' from all other employers."

"That's the problem in a nutshell," Dwyer rejoined. "A college is not just an employer, and we don't just have jobs. We have careers, and the success of our careers depends on an environment that supports what we are trying to do. Union organizers, picket lines, labor contracts, and mediators have no place in a college."

"I don't see why a college is somehow 'immune' from having to treat its employees fairly like every other employer. What makes a college so special?" Stovos asked.

"Twenty years ago—ten years ago, even—the very thought of a union would have been absurd. The fact that we're now considering one is just proof the quality of education in this country is going downhill. I can just see it now: 'Sorry, class, this is our last meeting. I'm going on strike Monday,'" Dwyer fumed. He got up from his desk, grabbed his coat and hat, and headed off for a meeting.

Stovos shot back, "I suppose you'd feel better if you met your class for the last time because you were one of the ones whose position got eliminated."

Dwyer didn't answer, but he slammed the door on the way out.

Questions

1. Do you feel that Dwyer is correct in believing a union would interfere with the goals of higher education?
2. What benefits does Stovos see from unionization?
3. Do you believe that some organizations, because of their purpose and goals, should not have unionized employees? If so, which ones, and why?
4. Do you think the respective lengths of time that Dwyer and Stovos have spent at the college are related to their attitudes? Why, or why not?
5. When you think of unions, what thoughts come to mind? Why do you feel as you do?

INFOTRAC ARTICLES

1. *The Humanist*, Sep–Oct 1997 v57 n5 p41(2)
   The future of unions. John Buell
   An article highly supportive of the value of labor unions for protecting workers.
2. *Dollars & Sense*, Sep–Oct 1998 n219 p16(5)
   Rank and file teamsters fight for labor's future. Dan la Botz
   As reflected in the results of a major union election, the International Brotherhood of Teamsters will decide which of two conflicting models of unionism will be adopted.
3. *Washington Monthly*, July–August 1995 v27 n7–8 p26(6)
   The case for unions. Sean Reilly
   Discusses the benefits of labor unions for providing fair wages, working conditions, and benefits for workers.
4. *Dollars & Sense*, Sep–Oct 1998 n219 p22(3)
   How Yale workers defied union busting. Andrea Cole
   Discusses the long-running conflict between Yale University and two local labor unions, and the results of a recent labor dispute.
5. *Canadian Dimension*, Sep–Oct 1997 v31 n5 p30(3)
   "A McUnion with that?" Christian Huot
   Discusses an attempt by employees of McDonald's, an antiunion company, in Quebec, Canada, to create a union, the only one of the 12,700 McDonald's in the United States and Canada.
6. *Nursing Homes*, March 1997 v46 n3 p23(2)
   How to avoid (or decertify) a union. Stephen J. Cabot

Describes the interest labor unions have in representing nursing home employees and recommends tactics to weaken the appeal of unions to employees.

7. *PC Week,* Oct 28, 1996 v13 n43 pA1(2)

Unionizing the nerds. Stanley Holmes

Describes the attempts of labor organizers to represent employees in the technology industry, which has only 3% union workers compared to 15% in the national workforce.

8. *Reason,* May 1998 v30 n1 p4(3)

Unions forever? Virginia Postrel

Suggestions are made for unions to re-create themselves in a new image to be more responsive to the social conditions of employees.

Ergonomics and Work Conditions

MAJOR CHAPTER OBJECTIVES

◆ Describe ergonomic approaches to work design.

◆ Explain psychological approaches to accident reduction.

◆ Identify physical stressors in the workplace.

◆ Understand how alternative work schedules influence worker attitudes and behavior.

◆ Describe the impact of alcoholism and drug abuse in the workplace.

As mentioned in Chapter 1, **ergonomics** (or human factors psychology) is the study of the interface between individuals and their work environment. The *environment* may be a work tool or piece of equipment or the spatial surroundings in which work is conducted. Ergonomics has experienced remarkable growth as a profession in the past ten years, as many aspects of society are recognizing the contributions of this area to improve the quality of our lives.

Howell (1993) views ergonomics as being responsive to social changes, as witnessed by increased computerization, automation, and information display. Reschetyuk (1992) and Haigh (1993) described the growing interest in the design of products for individuals 50 years of age and older, the fastest growing segment of the population. An evaluation of research conducted in gerontology (aging) indicates deterioration of vision and hearing, hand function, and mental abilities in older populations. They recommend the use of ergonomic research findings to guide designers in the specifications of products that are functional, efficient, safe, and attractive to older and younger users alike. Reschetyuk referred to the study of product design for older populations as "gero-ergonomics." However, ergonomics is not limited strictly to issues of product design. Annett (1994) described the application of ergonomic principles to sports science, and in particular the role of mental imagery in enhancing motor skills. Becker and Steele (1995) noted that organizations are making increased use of teams in conducting business operations, yet most offices still are designed for individual use. The authors described a variety of office-space layouts that facilitated teamwork and made the physical design of the workplace congruent with its organizing principles. Wang (1993) discussed recent trends in ergonomics in China, including their close link to economic and social reform. Kaplan (1995) suggested that the field of ergonomics has become more sensitive to culturally appropriate user applications for varied work environments worldwide. As in most areas of I/O psychology, ergonomics is influenced by cross-cultural factors, primarily pertaining to user acceptability. Finally, Damos and Parker (1996) noted that because of advances in the treatment of HIV, increased numbers of individuals infected with HIV are remaining in the workforce longer. They believe ergonomists will be called upon soon to modify the work environment or job to allow these individuals to remain productive.

People work under a broad array of conditions. For example, most people work indoors, but some work outdoors. Some jobs require exposure to intense heat, cold, and noise; others offer temperate conditions. Many people work from 8:00 a.m. to 5:00 p.m., but other hours are also common. Some jobs involve a high risk of injury or illness; others have low risk. How do these different conditions affect attitudes and behavior? What have I/O psychologists learned about responses to different working conditions? This chapter is also devoted to examining how work conditions affect the employee.

Research in these areas has been conducted in a wide range of professions. Although I/O psychology has made many contributions, so have engineering, physiology, and medicine. Engineers have designed tools, equipment, and work procedures to minimize employee stress and fatigue. Physiologists have studied the effects of heat, cold, noise, and other forms of physical stress on the human body. Physicians studying industrial medicine have examined the relationship between certain illnesses and types of work, such as black lung disease among coal miners and cancer among asbestos workers. Thus, research on working conditions and employee behavior is interdisciplinary. Many of the questions addressed extend beyond I/O psychology, but our profession is a primary contributor to the area.

ERGONOMIC APPROACHES TO WORK DESIGN

The ergonomic perspective to achieving person/environment congruence is to hold the individual as a constant and mold the work environment to the person. The theory behind ergonomics is that environments are more malleable than people; thus, the environment is adapted to the limitations and qualities of people. Personnel selection and training approaches take the opposite perspective; that is, people are either selected or developed to fit the environment. In reality, of course, successful person/environment fits require a combination of all three approaches.

Grandjean (1986) presented four major objectives of ergonomics:

- To fit the demands of work to the efficiency of people to reduce stress
- To design machines, equipment, and installations so that they can be operated with great efficiency, accuracy, and safety
- To work out proportions and conditions of the workplace to ensure correct body posture
- To adapt lighting, air-conditioning, noise, and so on to suit people's physical requirements

The *environment* includes a wide variety of physical situations—the physical conduct of work, equipment design, workplace layout—in short, the arena in which people operate. When I/O psychologists speak of an environment (that is, a machine or work site) as having been "ergonomically designed," we mean it was developed or designed with special regard for its impact on the operator's physical or psychological well-being (see Field Note 1). Imada (1990) recommended that ergonomics be assigned to top management as a method of reducing costs and increasing the user appeal of products.

Three fundamental paradigms guide the ergonomic analysis and design of work. These paradigms are the anthropometric, biomechanical, and physiological bases of work design. Each will be briefly explained in the following sections, and illustrative examples of work design from each paradigm will be presented.

Anthropometric Approach

Anthropometry is the study of people's physical dimensions. It includes the measurement of human body characteristics, such as size, breadth, girth, and distance between anatomical points. Anthropometrists take a large number of measurements (for example, the distance between shoulder and elbow, between the eyes, and so forth) on individuals to create a sizable database. The measurements are categorized by demographic variables such as gender, age, and ethnicity because of their relationship to the variables being measured. That is, men are typically physically bigger than women, our bodies change shape as we get older, and

Caliper

Anthropometer

FIGURE 15–1   *Two instruments used to assess body measurements*

SOURCE: From *Engineering Physiology: Physiologic Bases of Human Factors/Ergonomics* by K. H. Kroemer, H. J. Kroemer, and K. E. Kroemer-Elbert, 1986, New York: Elsevier.

different races have differing physical proportions. Figure 15–1 shows two instruments used to make body measurements: a caliper and an anthropometer. With descriptive statistics such as percentiles, researchers calculate major points in the distribution of anthropometric data. Thus, we can describe individuals according to their body characteristics compared to their norm group. For example, a person who is at the 80th percentile in height but the 30th percentile in weight has a tall, slender build.

The compilation of anthropometric measurements becomes the basis for equipment design, used in either work or leisure. Countless examples abound for the application of anthropometric measures. The size of the keys on a keyboard and the spacing between the keys were determined through anthropometry. Men with stubby fingers sometimes have difficulty typing because most keyboards were designed for people with smaller hand features. Figure 15–2 shows ten hand/object couplings. The size of the object would be designed in accordance with anthropometric data about people's hands. The width of airline and theater seats were similarly determined from the measures on the associated relevant body parts. The leisure industry has drawn heavily on anthropometric data to determine the sizes of football helmets, golf clubs, tennis racquets, and so forth.

The military also makes great use of anthropometrics. Because people in the military come in a broad range of sizes, weapons and equipment have to be designed to accommodate individual differences. I once heard an ergonomist comment on the problems of designing an adjustable monitor screen and chair that could accommodate operators (either male or female) who were in the 10th percentile in height and 90th percentile in weight, or vice versa. Thus, this system had to be workable (that is, a readable screen and a comfortable chair) for people who were short and heavy, tall and thin, or anything in between.

There are also civilian, commercial applications of anthropometrics. For example, Roebuck (1995) described the development of a system for the photographic recording of body silhouettes and for applying computer analysis techniques to develop flat clothing patterns from body outlines. The customer enters a booth where a side-view and a front-view photograph are taken. The resulting outline contours are then matched as closely as possible to one of a series of standard silhouettes. A computer analysis of differences then estimates the necessary deviations from the standard flat clothing patterns to fit the individual. The suit or other clothing is thus custom-tailored to the individual.

Biomechanical Approach

Biomechanics is defined as the application of mechanical principles (such as levers and forces) to the analysis of body-part structure and movement. Whereas anthropometrics is utilized in equipment design, biomechanics helps determine the physical movements required in work. Furthermore, as opposed to body measurements, biomechanics is concerned with the effect of movement and force on human muscles, tendons, and nerves. Its focus is how the conduct of work affects these body parts and, in turn, the best way to design work to minimize stress, pain, or fatigue.

Biomechanics entails the use of complex sensing instruments to measure the effects of movements on the body. For example, there are instruments that measure how much force your arms can exert as a function of the angle of your elbow, how much stress is applied to your shoulders as a function of the position of your arms, and so on. Extensive use is also made of motion pictures and video recorders that focus on close-up views of the body at work. Through this information, biomechanics provides a way to design work that is most compatible with the physical limits of the human body.

The biomechanical approach to work design goes well beyond the domain of psychology into such disciplines as physics and human anatomy. As such,

---

Field Note 1   *Ergonomics and the Space Program*

The field of ergonomics is experiencing a rejuvenation. About 35 years ago our nation's interest in the space program triggered a large outpouring of interest in ergonomics. Designing space capsules that could be operated by an astronaut captivated a great deal of attention. In one space flight the astronauts were instructed to flip a switch "up" to conduct some flight operation. Upon doing so the capsule began to shake violently, so the astronauts flipped the switch "down," contrary to what they were supposed to do. The capsule's operation returned to normal, and no one knew what went wrong. Then someone figured it out. In the weightlessness of space, the astronauts happened to be floating upside-down at the time. Thus, the "up" and "down" positions of the switch were reversed from their vantage point. This was a condition no one on gravity-bound Earth had anticipated when the system was designed.

The military has been a continual user of ergonomic research, but after our nation's interest in the space program began to wane, there was a concomitant reduction of interest in ergonomics. Now that trend appears to be reversing again. With the boom in high-tech equipment, such as computers, copiers, and electronic recreational products, there is renewed interest in designing these products from a human perspective—that is, to be "user friendly," a phrase reflecting an ergonomic orientation. There are a growing number of jobs for psychologists in the field of ergonomics. What the space program did for ergonomics in the 1960s is being re-created by the high-tech companies of the 1990s.

1. Finger Touch: One finger touches an object without holding it.

2. Palm Touch: Some part of the inner surface of the hand touches an object without holding it.

3. Finger Palmar Grip (Hook Grip): One finger or several fingers hook(s) onto a ridge, or handle. This type of finger action is used where thumb counterforce is not needed.

4. Thumb-Fingertip Grip (Tip Grip): The thumb tip opposes one fingertip.

5. Thumb-Finger Palmar Grip (Pinch or Plier Grip): Thumb pad opposes the palmar pad of one finger (or the pads of several fingers) near the tips. This grip evolves easily from coupling #4.

6. Thumb-Forefinger Side Grip (Lateral Grip) or Side Pinch: Thumb opposes the (radial) side of the forefinger.

7. Thumb-Two-Finger Grip (Writing Grip): Thumb and two fingers (often forefinger and index finger) oppose each other at or near the tips.

8. Thumb-Fingertips Enclosure (Disk Grip): Thumb pad and the pads of three or four fingers oppose each other near the tips (object grasped does not touch the palm). This grip evolves easily from coupling #7.

9. Finger-Palm Enclosure (Collet Enclosure): Most, or all, of the inner surface of the hand is in contact with object while enclosing it.

10. Power Grasp: The total inner hand surface is grasping the (often cylindrical) handle which runs parallel to the knuckles and generally protrudes on one or both sides from the hand.

FIGURE 15–2   *Ten couplings between hand and object*

SOURCE: From *Engineering Physiology: Physiologic Bases of Human Factors/Ergonomics* by K. H. Kroemer, H. J. Kroemer, and K. E. Kroemer-Elbert, 1986, New York: Elsevier.

biomechanics is an interdisciplinary approach to designing work; as its very name suggests, it is a fusion of mechanical principles and living organisms. The research methods of this approach also depart considerably from those of traditional I/O psychology. For example, Viano, Lau, Asbury, and King (1989) studied the effects of simulated automobile accidents on chest and pelvic injuries by subjecting un-embalmed cadavers to blunt lateral impacts. In many ways the biomechanical approach to work design is the classic human-factors perspective: the design of the physical requirements of work to be compatible with the capabilities and limitations of the human body.

Physiological Approach

The **physiological** approach to work design focuses on the underlying systemic aspects of the body, such as circulation, respiration, and metabolism. From this perspective, work is designed with regard to such parameters as oxygen flow, blood flow, heart rate, and blood pressure. As is characteristic of ergonomics in general, there is extensive reliance on measurement—in this case, the measurement of the body's physiological responses. Rather than speaking about such issues as muscle fatigue and back strain, physiologists address the specific neurochemical conditions that produce the symptoms of fatigue and strain. Therefore, "work" is thought of in terms of the flow of nerve impulses, sugar metabolism, and acid secretion.

Figure 15–3 is a good illustration of the physiological perspective. Pictured are three ways to carry a satchel and their associated oxygen consumptions. Carrying the satchel as a backpack consumes the smallest amount of oxygen (and thus energy). Carrying the satchel slung over the shoulder consumes 82% more energy. Finally, carrying the satchel as a briefcase uses the most energy. We can also use Figure 15–3 to compare the anthropometric, biomechanical, and physiological approaches to work design. Anthropometrics would seek to design the satchel to be approximately equal to the width of a person's back, biomechanics would consider the strain caused by the satchel on the body, and physiologists would address themselves to energy depletion.

Another example of the physiological perspective is in the analysis of the causes of muscle fatigue. Muscle fatigue is caused by the production of lactic acid at a faster rate than oxygen can be delivered through the circulatory system. Energy is provided as nutrients from food are burned with oxygen (aerobic) and without (anaerobic). Most oxygen is delivered to the muscle cells from the circulatory system, with blood flow to the muscles matching the muscular demands for oxygen after a few minutes of work. By measuring the amount of oxygen a person uses during work, researchers can calculate the amount of aerobic metabolism taking place. Thus, work tasks that require moderate or heavy effort are designed to keep the demands low enough to permit aerobic metabolism to supply the necessary energy. If the demands exceed what aerobic metabolism can provide, the anaerobic metabolic system helps produce energy but also produces lactic acid in the process. Hence, it is common for workers in jobs requiring intense bursts of energy (such as firefighters) to experience fatigue quickly. Work designers therefore

100%   182%   241%

FIGURE 15–3   *Effect of effort on energy consumption for three ways of carrying a school satchel*

SOURCE: From "Carrying of School Bags by Children" by M. S. Malhotra and J. Sengupta, 1965, *Ergonomics, 8,* p. 56.

try to distribute the intensity and duration of peak energy demands to reduce these fatigue-producing conditions. In jobs where intense energy bursts are unavoidable, equipment may help ease the energy demand or backup personnel may permit adequate recovery. Markowitz (1989) compared a sample of firefighters who fought a large polyvinyl chloride (a dangerous chemical) fire with an unexposed sample. The results suggested a strong relationship between psychological distress experienced shortly after a toxic exposure event and longer-term symptoms. Lim, Ong, and Phoon (1987) examined heart rate and urinary catecholamine levels as stress indicators among firefighters. The results suggested that stress levels were higher on work shifts where there were no fires, indicating that boredom and anxiety contribute to stress.

The physiological perspective approaches work design from the most molecular level. Like biomechanics, it embraces scientific methods not usually found in the more traditional areas of I/O psychology. Because all work activities have an inherent physiological basis, this perspective is particularly well adapted to studying all types of jobs. With the recent advances in computerization, many people now make use of video display terminals (VDTs) in their jobs. A growing body of literature suggests that extensive use of VDTs leads to visual strain and physical discomfort in the neck and shoulder area (Stellman, Klitzman, Gordon, & Snow, 1987). Grandjean (1987) examined the physiological effects of VDTs on vision as a function of various characteristics of VDTs, such as brightness, contrast, and flicker. He reported definite relationships between photometric characteristics and physiological responses, and recommends that VDTs be designed from an ergonomic perspective as well as a purely mechanical one. Grandjean also studied the effects of hand placements and positions, and believes they contribute to operator efficiency and satisfaction. He believes the VDT workstation has become the launch vehicle for ergonomics in the office world.

Overview

The anthropometric, biomechanical, and physiological approaches to work design are simply three ways to modify the environment to accommodate people's characteristics and limitations. While each approach has its own distinctive focus, they are not mutually exclusive. Anthropometric information can be of great help in the design of work from a biomechanical perspective. However, think of these approaches as three tacks researchers have found useful to modify the environment to fit people in the conduct of work. Anthropometrics relies on a descriptive inventory of bodily measurements, biomechanics examines major body parts and movements in terms of mechanical principles, and the physiological perspective deals with the effect of work on the body's fundamental systems.

HUMAN/COMPUTER INTERACTIONS IN THE WORKPLACE

It is estimated that the majority of all U.S. workers will deal daily with a computer by the year 2000. Computers greatly affect the lives of blue-collar and white-collar workers alike. Freese (1987) stated that technology is driven to its limits to automate as completely as possible. The rest that cannot (yet) be done by technical means or is uneconomical to do with machines is being left to humans. He feels computerization is a major ethical concern for the blue-collar sector of the workforce. Turnage (1990) argued that technological innovation will not be adopted (and thus will not improve productivity) readily unless due regard is given to the users of technology. She proposed the concept of "high tech/high touch"—whenever technology is introduced there must be a counterbalancing human response (such as high touch) or else the technology is rejected. Turnage argued that sophisticated technology will not work unless the proper balance is struck between human and machine systems.

Computers are also being used to conduct a form of performance appraisal called **computer-aided monitoring.** Computer-aided monitoring provides continuous assessment of an employee's performance, sometimes on a minute-by-minute basis. Chalykoff and Kochan (1989) found that management views such monitoring as a way to develop the employee and gauge the quality of work. However, some employees feel they are being spied on, and the monitoring tends to provide negative, not positive, feedback. Larson and Callahan (1990) found that computer-aided monitoring serves as a cue to signal the perceived importance of a task, which in turn affects the amount of effort devoted to it. Also, some employees regard computer-aided monitoring as a major source of job stress.

Parsons and Kearsley (1982) addressed the issue of division of labor between humans and a growing segment of the workforce: robots. They recommended studying the relationship between humans and robots with regard to not only performance and output but also human/robot communication, job satisfaction, and organizational impact. Chao and Kozlowski (1986) found that low-skill workers reacted negatively toward the implementation of robots, perceiving them largely as threats to their job security. High-skill workers reacted more positively toward robots, perceiving their implementation as opportunities to expand their skills. Research on the human/robot interface may become the Hawthorne studies of the future, and Shenkar (1988) considers robotics to be one of the major challenges facing I/O psychology in the future.

SAFETY AND ACCIDENTS

Industrial safety and accidents are among the oldest concerns in I/O psychology, dating back to the early 1900s. One of the first responsibilities of psychologists was to develop safer working conditions. Engineers also contributed greatly, particularly in equipment design and plant layout. Although we have made big strides in improving work safety, industrial accidents still are a major concern. Loughlin, Hepburn, and Barling (1995) reported alarming statistics about industrial safety. Every year 100,000 workers in the United States are killed or die of work-related accidents or diseases, 400,000 are disabled, and 6 million are hurt at work. A U.S. worker is five times more likely to die than a Swedish worker, and three times more likely to die than a Japanese worker.

Researchers in different disciplines address the problem of industrial accidents from many perspectives, but all are concerned with reducing frequency and severity. I/O psychologists focus on individual characteristics associated with accidents and investigate traditional approaches (personnel selection, work design, and training) in accident reduction. Industrial hygienists view occupational diseases as consequences of recurring events or accidents. Safety engineers see accidents as results of a sequence of acts or events with undesirable consequences, such as personal injury, property damage, or work interruption.

Accidents and injuries are not the same. Injury is the consequence of an accident, but many "no-injury" accidents also occur. Although psychologists are concerned with accidents whether or not they result in injury, they generally pay more attention to those accidents involving injuries. In an attempt to make people more aware of the likelihood of accidents, researchers have computed the objective probability of incurring an accident as a function of, for example, miles driven, trips taken, and so on. However, Sheehy and Chapman (1987) found that an increase in the objective probability of an accident seems to generate a proportional denial of its likelihood (that is, perceived probability) among people, thereby mitigating its ability to sensitize people to its occurrence.

Furthermore, when accidents and injuries do occur, there is often a strong impetus to assign blame for their occurrence and to search out their cause. As Senders and Moray (1991) noted, it is often very difficult to identify a single cause of accidents, particularly those involving human error. Reason (1994) reported that only recently has the medical profession been open to acknowledging physician error in mishaps to patients. Reason stated, "This new spirit of *glasnost* has led to an increasing number of fruitful research partnerships between doctors (particularly anesthetists) and human factor specialists" (p. vii). In short, social, legal, and political forces often retard our ability to understand the causes of human error, which in themselves are inherently difficult to identify.

Safety Legislation

State and federal laws protect the welfare of the worker. The major one is the Occupational and Safety Health Act (OSHA), which became effective in 1971. OSHA was meant to integrate federal and state legislation under a federal program establishing uniform codes, standards, and regulations. The purpose of the act is "to assure, as far as possible, every working woman and man in the nation safe and healthful working conditions, and to preserve our human resources." To accomplish this, there are provisions for safety and health standards, research, information, and education and training in occupational safety and health.

OSHA is comprehensive, covering such things as record keeping, inspection, compliance, and enforcement of safety standards. It lists over 5,000 safety and health standards, including the density of particles in the air and the height at which a fire extinguisher is to be mounted. Some critics suggest that the act is too concerned with trivial standards that burden employers without really protecting workers. Others consider OSHA one of the most important and influential pieces of legislation ever enacted. The law provides for safety inspections and fines for noncompliance. Trained officers conduct over 100,000 inspections annually. Companies can be fined for maintaining improper safety records and for willfully violating standards. In 1987 financial penalties totaling over $3 million, the largest sum ever levied against an employer, were proposed against a beef-packing plant for having more than 100 serious safety violations.

Other laws involving safety (for example, Workers' Compensation) exist, but none of them has the far-reaching impact of OSHA. It has given new status and responsibility to safety and health practitioners. OSHA has increased concern among employers and unions over safety and health problems, as well as compliance

---

Field Note 2 *Occupational Disease Among Nuclear Power Plant Workers*

Work-related injuries and diseases are often associated with particular occupations—for example, black lung disease and emphysema among coal miners, and carpal tunnel syndrome among bank tellers. However, we are now learning of certain occupational diseases associated with selected geographic areas. The nuclear industry in the former Soviet Union is one example. While under communism, the Soviet Union did not often share or reveal information about its nuclear industry. After the fall of communism and the emergence of *glasnost* (a spirit of openness), Western countries began to learn about their nuclear industry. The incidence of cancer among nuclear power plant workers in the former Soviet Union is several times higher than among their counterparts in Western countries.

The higher incidence of cancer is attributed to less stringent safety standards and fewer inspections in the nuclear power plants. Nuclear energy is derived in part from plutonium, an *extremely* dangerous element that causes horrific diseases with the slightest exposure. Nuclear power plant workers, through exposure, developed plutonium poisoning, which in turn produced cancer. Alcoholism was also high among Soviet workers in general, which further increased the risk of work-related mishaps for nuclear power plant workers. The downfall of the former Soviet Union enhanced our understanding of the linkage between two areas of study we would not normally associate with each other: occupational disease and geopolitics.

with safety regulations. Has OSHA been effective in enhancing industrial safety? Cascio (1998) noted that OSHA has been the subject of controversy since its inception. Investigations by Congress have found that OSHA has made few lasting reductions in lost workdays or injury rates. However, because of OSHA and other agencies concerned with industrial safety, we know more about dangerous workplace substances such as vinyl chloride, PCBs, and asbestos. As a result, companies have taken at least the initial actions needed to protect workers from them (see Field Note 2).

Psychological Approaches to Reducing Accidents

Cooper (1998) described the domino theory of accident causation to demonstrate the influence of management, as shown in Figure 15–4. This model takes the view that poor management control creates either poor personal factors (e.g., lack of appropriate training) or poor job factors (e.g., unguarded machinery). In combination, these two factors lead to either unsafe acts or unsafe conditions. These cause an incident that leads to losses related to people, property, or production processes.

This book has stressed three approaches to achieving a better fit between worker and workplace. The first is based on individual differences and involves selecting people who have the characteristics thought necessary or desirable for specified work demands. This is the *personnel selection approach*, the analog of "finding the right pegs to fit the holes." The second approach is to train people in the necessary skills, knowledge, or attitudes. This is the *personnel training approach*, the analog of "reshaping the pegs to fit the holes." The third approach is modifying the workplace to provide a better match with abilities and characteristics. This is the ergonomic or *work design approach*, the analog of "reshaping the holes to fit the pegs." These approaches are all used to reduce industrial accidents, an area whose criterion is a safer work environment. Given that 50%–80% of all accidents are attributable to human error (Spettell & Liebert, 1986), an examination of accidents from a human perspective is most reasonable. This section will examine in some detail I/O research on achieving greater person/environment congruence.

Personnel Selection Approach

The personnel selection approach is the search for individual differences that are predictive of accidents. This paradigm has proceeded along two paths: group prediction and individual prediction. Group prediction (also called actuarial prediction) has been remarkably successful in forecasting accidents. It is the basis on which insurance companies operate, and it works as follows. Based on hundreds of thousands of cases from national samples, insurance companies calculate the probability of automobile-driving accidents as a function of many variables, such as age, gender, marital status, and so on. From a purely statistical standpoint, it is calculated that young (under 25), single, male drivers are more likely to have accidents than are persons with other characteristics. Therefore, the cost of the insurance sold to members of various cohorts is adjusted to reflect their differential likelihood of having an accident. In the extreme case, an insurance company might

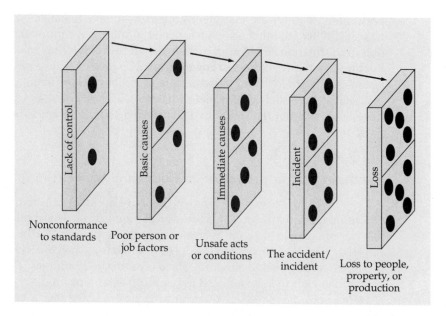

FIGURE 15–4   *Domino theory of accident causation*

SOURCE: From *Improving Safety Culture* by D. Cooper, 1998, Chichester: Wiley. © 1998 John Wiley & Sons Ltd.
Reprinted by permission.

refuse to cover people who have extremely high probabilities for accidents. As you can imagine, these demographic categories cover millions of people nationwide and are very coarse groupings. Consequently, insurance companies, being highly competitive, seek additional predictors of accidents to refine their assessments (and thus lower the cost of insurance). For example, if you are a college student with a B or better grade point average, you are a member of a group that has fewer accidents than less academically accomplished students. Accordingly, the cost of your insurance can be reduced somewhat. Some companies offer cost reductions for nonsmokers, infrequent drivers (that is, 7,500 miles per year or less), and graduates of driver education classes. These variables have been found to be predictive of fewer accidents on an actuarial basis.

The second avenue of the personnel selection approach to accidents is individual prediction. Here predictions are made on the likelihood of certain individuals having accidents. This is the approach that I/O psychologists would most likely use. Beirness (1993) examined research findings pertaining to the role of personality factors in driving behavior and accidents in an attempt to relate driving style to lifestyle. Six broad dimensions of personality appeared to be strongly and consistently correlated with accidents: thrill seeking, impulsiveness, hostility/anger, emotional instability, depression, and loss of control. High levels of these personality factors predispose individuals to high-risk driving situations and/or to react to situations in the driving environment that place them at high risk. Personality factors were found to account for 10%–20% of the variance in accidents and up to 35% of the variance in risky driving. Gabany, Plummer, and Grigg (1997) identified gender differences in an inventory designed to understand why drivers speed. Men were more likely than women to speed for reasons of ego gratification, while women were more likely than men to speed because of time pressure and the disdain of driving.

Research on the value of personality tests to predict accidents has yielded some encouraging findings. For example, Hansen (1989) developed personality scales from the MMPI assessing a state of distractibility that was correlated with accidents in a sample of chemical workers. Hilakivi and colleagues (1989) examined the validity of a personality test to select drivers for the Finnish military. The personality factors of impulsivity, adventurousness, naiveté, and excessive trustfulness correlated with motor vehicle accidents.

In the personnel selection approach, variables predictive of accidents may be used to hire people for jobs having high accident risk. People may be hired for transportation jobs (chauffeurs, bus drivers, pilots) and jobs that have a high risk (handling hazardous chemicals) based on their likelihood of having accidents.

Ergonomic Approach

Designing a safer work environment is one of the oldest and most important objectives of ergonomists or engineering psychologists. This section will review a few examples of their work.

Many industrial workers use tools in carrying out their jobs. If the tools are not designed with the limitations of the human body in mind, injuries can result. A common work-related injury is carpal tunnel syndrome, a painful injury to the wrist. It occurs frequently in people whose jobs require extensive finger and hand movements. Figure 15–5 shows three ergonomically designed knives for meat cutting and packing jobs that reduce the stress on the wrists, particularly with extended use.

Voevodsky (1974) described a study that tried to reduce the number of times taxicabs are struck from behind. Cab drivers often stop faster than drivers behind them anticipate. Voevodsky installed yellow warning lights on the trunks of 343 cabs. These lights began to blink when the cab slowed down. The rate of blinking was proportional to the rate of deceleration; faster blinking implied more rapid deceleration. A control group of 160 cabs was not fitted with the lights. After ten months, accident statistics on the two groups of cabs were compared. On three major performance dimensions (number of rear-end collisions, cost of repairs, and injuries to cab drivers), the experimental cabs outperformed the control cabs. The size of the difference was impressive: Accidents with the experimental cabs were reduced by over 60%, while the statistics on the control cabs were unchanged during the study. To see whether the differences were due simply to greater caution on the part of the drivers of the experimental cabs, comparisons were made of front-end collisions. No significant differences were found between experimental and control cabs. The author thus concluded that the cab drivers did not change their driving, but the motorists behind them had.

This study is a good example of the ergonomic approach to safety. The researcher modified the equipment used, and the changes resulted in fewer accidents and injuries. Engineering psychology has shown that performance can be improved by designing the workplace to complement human skills, be it muscle use or reaction time.

FIGURE 15–5 *The handles on these knives are designed to utilize the larger muscle groups of the forearm and upper arm. This design also allows an improved power grip that can reduce grip force.*
SOURCE: Courtesy of The Saunders Group.

Personnel Training Approach

As discussed in Chapter 6, personnel training involves more than selecting a method to improve skills. It also involves creating an atmosphere that supports training and rewards trained persons for improvement. The personnel training approach to safety involves everything discussed about other types of training and represents a major approach in reducing accidents. As in all training, employees must be motivated. With safety training, employees must have a reason for behaving safely. Training is thus directed toward making safety a desirable outcome.

All training programs are conducted in a climate that places some degree of importance on training. In some organizations training may be highly valued; in others it may be treated with only mild interest. Dedobbeleer and Beland (1991) reported that an effective safety climate was one in which management had a strong commitment to safety and the workers were heavily involved in safety issues. Janssens, Brett, and Smith (1995) examined variations in the relationships among constructs that affect the perceptions of worker safety in U.S., France, and Argentine plants of the same division of a multinational organization, all having the same corporate-wide safety policy. Management's concern for safety had the least effect on accidents in France and the greatest effect in Argentina. The authors proposed that cultural differences in managerial style and decision making across the three plants contributed to the variation in how workers perceived the company's safety policy.

Adams-Roy, Knap, and Barling (1995) reported that although the workers themselves may believe that safety is their primary job-related concern, the prevailing opinion is that management does not share this concern. A commonly held belief is that despite the suffering and potential long-term effects of injuries on the workers themselves, as well as the financial cost and loss of productivity borne by the organization, employees and managers still do not regard organizational health and safety as a serious or significant issue. The authors cited a senior executive who worked for 30 years in the asbestos industry to illustrate this view. The executive stated that middle- and lower-level managers at a major manufacturer continued to endanger the health of both workers and customers even after senior management had recognized the critical health and safety implications for the industry. The executive also stated that denial of health and safety issues became part of the corporate culture and that this blunder eventually not only cost thousands of lives but also destroyed an entire industry. Further evidence of the importance of managerial support for occupational safety was provided by Simard and Marchand (1997). They found that work group cooperation and the supervisor's approach to safety management were the primary determinants of safe workplace behaviors. The results suggested that managerial actions in developing a participative approach to safety management can substantially support a culture that is attentive to safety.

Employees quickly pick up cues on the importance of safety in an organization. Scrap or waste on the floor, unprotected wires, and failure to wear hard hats contradict bulletin-board posters saying "Safety First." Organizational attitudes toward safety are conveyed by what people do. Studies show that management behavior and attitudes affect both employee feelings about safety and accidents.

Other studies have documented the value of safety training. Reber, Wallin, and Chhokar (1984) developed checklists of safe and unsafe behaviors at work. Employees were asked to set hard but attainable goals for improved safety performance. They were shown slides of the safe and unsafe behaviors, identified by means of the checklists, and were instructed to select the safe behaviors in conducting their jobs. Their safety performance was fed back to them, giving them knowledge of their results on the job. The training produced a 54% reduction in lost-time injuries. McAfee and Winn (1989) reviewed 24 studies that examined the use of positive incentives and feedback to improve safety and decrease accidents in industry. All studies found that incentives and feedback were successful in improving safety conditions and reducing accidents.

An interesting common denominator of all these safety training studies is that they focused on positive (safe) behavior rather than railing against violations of safety rules (negative behavior). That is, they all conclude that training should be directed toward promoting safe behavior rather than eradicating unsafe behavior.

Overview

Organizations need not limit themselves to one approach to reducing accidents. In fact, Peters (1991) suggested the prudent organization should adopt a comprehensive program using multiple approaches together. Each approach has its own merits; when used in combination, they improve the likelihood of reducing accidents. Hollenbeck, Ilgen, and Crampton (1992) recommended the use of a comprehensive system of multiple approaches to reduce the frequency of lower-back disability, a widespread phenomenon that has dramatic impacts on employer costs. Research indicates that some variables are useful for predicting which people are most likely to have accidents. To the extent that these differences can be reliably predicted, organizations can be staffed with people who exhibit safe behavior. The engineering psychology approach entails modifying the tools, equipment, and machinery to eliminate unsafe conditions. Machines must be designed to complement human skills and limitations. The training approach is based on the belief that safety skills, like all skills, can be improved through training. This approach stresses the importance of creating an environment conducive to safety and of acquiring the knowledge and skills needed to reduce accidents. Each method approaches safety from a different perspective, but all have proved effective in reducing accidents.

Despite all the advances made in recent years in equipment, tools, machinery, and technology in general, safety is not totally a technical issue. It is primarily a people issue. Smith, Cohen, Cohen, and Cleveland (1978) identified seven factors that were found to differentiate low-accident from high-accident companies. These factors are listed in Table 15–1. Note how many relate to people. While the topic of safety certainly transcends individual differences and the value of technical advances in equipment design should not be underestimated, the ultimate responsibility for maintaining a safe work environment rests with people. Cohen (1977) cogently summarized this point when he said, "Maximally effective safety programs in industry will be dependent on those practices that can successfully deal with 'people' variables" (p. 168). The world's best seat belts will save no lives if people won't wear them or find ways to circumvent their use (see Field Note 3).

Field Note 3 *Safety Gambles in a Coal Mine*

As I mentioned in Chapter 6, I spent some time studying miners of bituminous coal. I discovered that the miners occasionally felt compelled to take some major risks that could result in accidents and fatal injuries. Here is what happened.

The machinery used to extract coal from the ground was electrically powered. Down on the mine floor (several hundred feet below the surface), miners operated tremendously powerful machinery that required large amounts of electrical current. The current was supplied by a cable that was attached to the rear of the machinery. In much the same way that an upright vacuum cleaner is moved over a carpet, the mining equipment was moved back and forth over the mine floor to extract the coal from the coal face.

The miners were supposed to mount the electrical cable on hooks elevated above the mine floor. But because there were organizational pressures to extract the coal from the ground as quickly as possible, the miners sometimes took a "shortcut" and left the cables on the mine floor. Mounting the cables on hooks would take time away from their work, so they skipped this step to save time and be more productive. Why was this important? If we return to the vacuum cleaner analogy, when you are pushing and pulling the vacuum across the carpet, sometimes you may inadvertently back it over the attached electrical cord. However, nothing happens because the vacuum is not heavy enough to slice through the cord and thus give you an electrical shock. Mining equipment, on the other hand, is very heavy (several tons) and could easily cut into the power cable. This is precisely what could happen to the miners. When moving the machinery back and forth, the operator inadvertently could run over the power cable trailing on the mine floor, which would send several thousand volts of electricity into the machinery, thus electrocuting the operator. The miners told me that as they became more experienced in operating the machinery, they "kind of got the feel" for where the cables were and would not back over them. However, should they have ever "missed" in their judgments, a lethal injury would have awaited them.

TABLE 15–1 *Characteristics of successful safety programs*

1. Greater management commitment and involvement in safety programs
2. A more humanistic approach in dealing with employees, stressing frequent positive contact and interaction
3. Better employee selection procedures
4. More frequent use of lead workers versus supervisors to train employees
5. A much greater degree of housekeeping and general plant cleanliness
6. Better plant environment qualities
7. Lower turnover and absenteeism among a more stable workforce

SOURCE: From "Characteristics of Successful Safety Programs" by M. J. Smith, H. H. Cohen, A. Cohen, and R. J. Cleveland, 1978, *Journal of Safety Research, 10,* pp. 5–15.

PHYSICAL STRESSORS IN THE WORKPLACE

As discussed in Chapter 10, stress is highly complex and multifaceted. Some causes of stress are work demands, role pressures, and organization characteristics. Chapter 10 discussed how role pressures contribute to stress. This chapter will examine how work demands (noise, heat, and cold) and some organization characteristics (most notably, work hours) contribute. There are wide individual differences associated with perceptions of stress; that is, one person may feel stressed by a hectic schedule, while another may enjoy the challenge and variety. Any stimulus (for example, work pace, noise, role pressure) that elicits a stress response is a **stressor.** Stressors associated with the physical conditions of work elicit fairly consistent stress responses. However, the degree of stress is often moderated by individual differences.

Noise

Noise is defined as unwanted sound. Before the effects of noise on performance are discussed, one must understand the characteristics of sound. Two physical characteristics are frequency and intensity; their psychological counterparts are pitch and loudness. Sound emanates in waves. If the sound is "pure" (like a tuning fork), a graph of the wave looks like a sine (sinusoidal) curve. Low-frequency sounds have fewer wave repetitions per unit of time than high-frequency sounds do. In fact, the number of waves per second is the frequency. Frequency is usually measured in cycles per second (cps) or Hertz (Hz). Impure sounds have more complex wave patterns because they are composed of differing frequencies. The psychological analog of frequency is pitch; we recognize this by saying that a tenor has a different pitch than a soprano.

The intensity of sound is usually measured in decibels (dB) and reflects differences in sound energy. The decibel scale is constructed so that a change of 10 dB means a tenfold change in sound power. Differences in frequency are represented by differences in waves per second; differences in intensity are represented by differences in the height of the waves. "Loud" sounds have more intensity than "soft" sounds. Figure 15–6 shows various sounds and corresponding decibel values.

Specific Noise Sources

50 hp siren (100 ft.)

Jet takeoff (200 ft.)

Riveting machine

Cutoff saw
Pneumatic peen hammer
Textile weaving plant

Subway train (20 ft.)
Pneumatic drill (50 ft.)
Freight train (100 ft.)

Vacuum cleaner
Speech (1 ft.)
Large transformer (200 ft.)

Soft whisper (5 ft.)

Decibels

140
130
120
110
100
90
80
70
60
50
40
30
20
10
0

FIGURE 15–6   *Decibel levels for various sounds*
SOURCE: From *Handbook of Noise Measurement* (8th ed.) by
A. P. Petersen and F. E. Gross, 1978, New Concord, MA:
GenRad.

The Effects of Noise.

It is difficult to say definitely what effect noise has on performance because "performance" has been examined in many contexts. Some aspects of performance are more affected by noise than others. Noweir (1984) examined the effects of noise (80–99 dB) on employees in three textile mills. Employees with high noise exposure (above 90 dB) had more disciplinary actions, accidents, and absenteeism and less productivity than employees with less noise exposure. Noise appeared to affect the quality of work, as reflected by disciplinary actions for material damage, and was particularly evident for spinning operations involving vigilance. Sundstrom, Town, Rice, and Osborn (1994) reported that in a field study of office workers, 54% said they were bothered by noise, especially by people talking and telephones ringing. Increasing dissatisfaction with the work environment was directly related to increasing noise.

There are no simple relationships between noise and human performance. Noise adversely affects performance on some tasks but not on others. Additionally, some people are more sensitive to noise than others. To the extent that I/O psychologists can (1) identify tasks whose performance is impaired by noise and (2) identify people sensitive to noise, steps can be taken to improve the worker/ workplace fit. Headphones and soundproof construction materials can be used in jobs subject to interference from noise. People can be hired based on their sensitivity to noise. As stated, with differences in both jobs and people, the I/O psychologist's job is to get as good a match as possible between abilities and work requirements.

Hearing Loss from Work.   Employees exposed to intense noise over long periods of time usually lose a portion of their hearing. If the noise is of a particular frequency, partial or complete hearing loss to tones of that frequency is quite possible. Extreme noise over the full spectrum of frequencies may cause a general hearing decrease.

To protect workers in noisy jobs (like airline ground employees, construction workers, and data processors) from hearing loss, companies provide headphones or earplugs. Many labor contracts specify that not wearing such safety equipment is grounds for dismissal. Some companies also approach the problem of noise stress through personnel selection, hiring partially or totally deaf people for noisy jobs.

Noise stress is a major concern for some companies. Noisy equipment may have to be reengineered or housed in special areas to lessen disruption. Special ear protection has been devised that eliminates the intensity of unwanted noise while still permitting communication among workers. Employees suffering from work-related hearing impairment are eligible for special compensation from employers; some victims of hearing loss have sued employers for not providing safe working conditions. Fortunately, the risk of hearing impairment is slight in most jobs, but in those where it is a problem, corrective measures are necessary.

Heat

Discomfort from heat is not due to only high temperatures. Adjustment to heat is a function of three variables: air temperature, humidity, and airflow. High temperatures, high humidity, and a lack of airflow are most uncomfortable. Some research indicates that humidity may be the most important variable in determining discomfort. With high temperature and humidity, rapid air movement can make the situation tolerable. Because the sensation of heat cannot be measured adequately by simply recording air temperature, other indices have been developed. One index used in enclosed environments is the wet-bulb globe temperature (WBGT), which takes into account the effects of humidity in combination with air temperature. The WBGT is a more sensitive index of discomfort than simple air temperature.

Heat stress is a problem not only for those who work outdoors but also for people who work around furnaces, boilers, dryers, and other heat-producing equipment. Heat stress can greatly decrease the productivity of those doing strenuous work. Workers lose stamina because their bodies are taxed by the combination of heat and physical exertion. However, heat stress can also impair performance in tasks requiring little physical effort, even those limited to mental skills. For example, Fine and Kobrick (1978) compared the performances of individuals working on problem-solving tasks under different heat-stress conditions. The treatment group

THE FAR SIDE   by Gary Larson

"You know, we're just not reaching that guy."

SOURCE: © 1982. Reprinted by permission of Universal Press Syndicate.

worked at 95°F and 88% humidity; the control group worked at 70°F and 25% humidity. Performance was monitored for seven hours. The results are shown in Figure 15–7. The number of errors made by the treatment group was considerably greater, and the extent of the difference became greater over time.

Organizations are aware of the effects of heat, and they spend a lot of money to cope with the problem. Central air-conditioning is a standard feature of most new office buildings. Dehumidifiers are installed where humidity may affect performance or damage sensitive equipment (like computers). Industrial fans are often installed to draw off the heat (and noxious fumes) associated with some types of manufacturing. However, in many cases the climate cannot be controlled or modified, as in outdoor work. In such cases workers may be allowed more rest breaks or may be relieved by other crews. Given rising energy costs, it is increasingly expensive to maintain ideal climates.

Cold

Both mental and physical tasks are affected by cold; however, there is evidence that people can adapt to cold over time. Prolonged exposure constricts blood

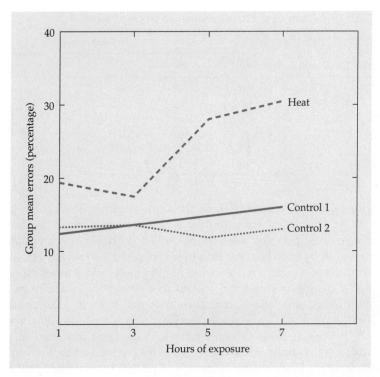

FIGURE 15–7 *Mean percentage of errors in cognitive tasks for a group working under heat and for two control groups*

SOURCE: From "Effects of Altitude and Heat on Complex Cognitive Tasks" by B. J. Fine and J. L. Kobrick, 1978, *Human Factors, 20*, pp. 115–122. Copyright 1978 by The Human Factors Society, Inc.

vessels, which reduces blood flow to the skin surface and reduces skin temperature. Under such conditions, exposed skin and extremities (fingers and toes) become numb. Under more extreme conditions, total body temperature is lowered. Manual performance is adversely affected by lowered body temperature, even when hands are kept warm. Similar results have been reported for tasks that require concentration. In attempting to explain this, Fox (1967) suggested that cold causes other stimuli to compete for the individual's attention. Cooling of the extremities, with the resulting threat of injury, distracts the worker from the task at hand, thus lowering performance. In particular, tasks that require fine finger dexterity are more susceptible to impairment from the cold than grosser types of manual activity. Enander (1987) found that exposure to moderate cold decreased manual dexterity but had no effects on simple reaction time.

With outdoor activities, wind chill can be a major factor affecting workers. The wind chill index provides a means for making a quantitative comparison of combinations of temperature and wind speed. Table 15–2 shows the cooling effects of combinations of certain temperatures and wind speeds derived from the index, these being expressed as equivalent temperatures. An equivalent temperature refers to the sensation of cold and wind. For example, an air temperature of 10°F

TABLE 15–2   *Cooling effects of temperature and wind speed*

Wind Speed (mph)	Air Temperature (°F)					
	40	*20*	*10*	*0*	*−10*	*−30*
Calm	40	20	10	0	−10	−30
5	37	16	6	−5	−15	−36
10	28	4	−9	−21	−33	−46
20	18	−10	−25	−39	−53	−67
30	13	−18	−33	−48	−63	−79
40	10	−21	−37	−53	−69	−85

Special clothing is needed for working under extremely cold conditions.

SOURCE: CNN

with a 20-mph wind produces the same cooling sensation as a temperature of −25°F under calm wind conditions. Extreme cold produced by a wind chill increases numbness and reaction time (Ellis, 1982). However, visual performance (as measured by speed or precision in responding) is generally not impaired by exposure to cold. Continued exposure to extremely cold temperatures produces frostbite, a danger encountered by outdoor workers, especially in the Midwest. In midwestern states the temperature may get down to −20°F, and with the strong 30–40-mph wind that blows across the plains, the wind chill temperature can reach −70°F. Special clothing and footwear have been designed to protect workers. Additionally, some workers receive extra compensation for working in the cold. Fortunately, few indoor jobs involve exposure to extremely cold temperatures.

Multiple Stressors

Stressors do not always exist in isolation. If they occur jointly, a worker must contend with their additive or interactive effects. For example, if the noise level and the heat level each decrease performance by 10%, the combined effect of a hot, noisy workplace may reduce performance by 20%. These two stressors have an additive effect. However, in some cases, stressors have an interactive effect; their combined effect may exceed the sum of the independent effects.

I recall an episode from a job analysis that illustrates the effect of multiple stressors. A construction worker described his job in the summer as being "hot and noisy." I wanted to observe him at work. He was using a pneumatic air drill to remove street pavement, and the temperature was 90°F. However, the heat radiating off the pavement made the temperature at street level over 110°F. The noise from a pneumatic drill (at a range of about 15 feet) was over 100 dB. After observing this worker for about five minutes and taking notes on his job duties, I felt faint and nauseated from the heat and noise. While the construction worker could perform under those conditions, I could not. I found the noise worse than the heat, but the combined effect made me abandon my efforts. I also learned that simple descriptive phrases like "hot and noisy" mean different things to different people.

From a practical standpoint, stressors that occur in combination create a far more dangerous work environment than stressors in isolation. Attempts to minimize the effects of one stressor may compound the effects of the other. While protective headgear can reduce noise, the extra covering can increase the effects of heat. Headgear for protecting a worker from cold may also impair hearing and cause accidents. Action taken to minimize stressor effects must not make the worker vulnerable to other potential hazards.

Fatigue

Fatigue is quite elusive, yet it is a major symptom of poor worker/workplace fit. There are several kinds of fatigue, and they all have physiological and psychological characteristics. The I/O psychologist studies fatigue in order to eliminate as many of its effects, particularly on performance and satisfaction, as possible.

The symptoms of fatigue include tiredness, diminished willingness to work, and boredom. *Fatigue* is a physiological phenomenon, or a reduction in performance capability that can be restored by rest. In contrast, *boredom* is a psychological phenomenon, or a reduction in mental performance capability that is the result of monotony. Fatigue is not synonymous with being bored or tired; such feelings may be short-lived and can be "cured" by a diversion or a night's sleep. Fatigue is more generalized and enduring. Also, distinguishing various kinds of fatigue is difficult because of interrelated effects.

Several authors have attempted to isolate different kinds of fatigue; there seem to be four major varieties. The most distinct type is *muscular fatigue,* caused by prolonged and demanding physical activity. This is associated with biochemical changes and is an acute pain in the muscles. *Mental fatigue* is more closely aligned with feelings of boredom associated with monotonous work. *Emotional fatigue* results from intense stress and is generally characterized by dulled emotional responses. Finally, *skills fatigue* is associated with decreased attention to certain tasks. With skills fatigue, standards of accuracy and performance become progressively lower. The decline is thought to be a major cause of accidents, particularly involving automobiles and airplanes.

All four kinds of fatigue are associated with neurochemical changes in the blood. The changes create an inhibiting system in the body that works against our arousal system. The inhibiting system tends to retard our normal functioning, so that mentally, physically, and emotionally we operate in a more subdued fashion. That is, our physiological mechanisms protect us from some previous form of overstimulation that precipitated the fatigue. Our ability to react normally in job contexts is impaired when we suffer from fatigue. In particular, both our sense of timing and vigilance are often diminished. Timing involves the precise coordination of integrated behaviors into a pattern or sequence. Typing on a keyboard and driving a car are two examples. Vigilance refers to alertness in monitoring and responding to critical stimuli in the environment. Reading the text material to be typed and paying attention to traffic, road conditions, and pedestrians are examples of vigilance. Individuals can more readily endure the effects of fatigue in jobs that require little timing or vigilance, but these components are critical to the conduct of many jobs.

I/O psychologists are concerned with all four types of fatigue, but their response to each is different. Muscular fatigue is best dealt with through new work procedures so people will not overexert themselves. Procedures may involve redesigning a piece of equipment or finding other, less strenuous ways to perform the task. Mental fatigue is addressed through job redesign that attempts to make work more stimulating and challenging. However, as discussed in Chapter 13, individuals differ in what they think is boring. Emotional fatigue is usually caused by factors external to the workplace. However, an increasing number of organizations provide counseling services for employees because their performance can be affected by problems either within or outside the workplace. Skills fatigue is a major concern for those in jobs with a small margin for error. For a pilot or air traffic controller, the consequences of lower standards can be severe and tragic. Such employees are continually monitored for skills fatigue and given time off when necessary.

People differ in their susceptibility to fatigue, and jobs differ in inducing fatigue. I/O psychologists still have much to learn about fatigue, particularly its treatment and prediction. Kumar (1994) proposed a conceptual model of muscle fatigue based on four job demands: strength required, frequency-duration of exposure, recovery time from exposure, and range of required motion. Kumar believes the model will be useful in explaining work-related injuries caused by overexertion.

WORK SCHEDULES

Shift Work

Not all employees work from 8:00 a.m. to 5:00 p.m., Monday through Friday. The nature of the services performed may necessitate other schedules. Police officers, firefighters, and telephone operators provide 24-hour-a-day service. In industrial manufacturing, some technology requires constant monitoring and operation. It isn't practical to shut off furnaces, boilers, and chemical process operations at 5:00 p.m. just because workers go home. In those cases it is advantageous to have different shifts work around the clock. About 25% of all working hours in the United States are estimated to be "nontraditional." Psychologists have become interested in how different hours (or shift work) affect employee attitudes and behavior.

There are no uniform shift-work hours; companies use different shifts. Usually a 24-hour day is divided into three 8-hour work shifts, like 7:00 a.m.–3:00 p.m. (day shift), 3:00 p.m.–11:00 p.m. (swing or afternoon shift), and 11:00 p.m.–7:00 a.m. (night shift). Some companies have employees work just one shift, but workers generally don't like the swing and night shifts, so many firms rotate the shifts. Employees may work two weeks on the day shift, two weeks on the swing shift, and then two weeks on the night shift. A shift workweek need not be Monday through Friday. Also, there may be an uneven number of days off between shifts, like two days off after the swing shift and three after the night shift.

Thierry and Meijman (1994) identified the 11 aversive characteristics of shift work that are listed in Table 15–3. Their effects are more strongly aversive in some patterns of shift work than in others. Shift workers experience many problems in physiological and social adjustment. Most physiological problems are associated with interruptions of the circadian rhythm; that is, our bodies are "programmed" for a certain time cycle (Aschoff, 1978). Because shift work interrupts the cycle of

TABLE 15–3   *Aversive characteristics of shift work*

Characteristic	Definition	Inconveniences
Regularity	Mean number of changes in the starting times of working periods during the week	Unrest, nervous complaints, constipation
Periodicity	Weekly mean of the sum of the accumulated number of successive night shifts plus half of the number of accumulated successive afternoon shifts	Sleeping problems, fatigue, stomach and intestinal complaints
Load per shift	Mean shift length in hours	Fatigue, feelings of overload
Load per week	Mean weekly working time in hours	Fatigue, feelings of overload
Opportunity to rest at night	Mean weekly number of hours off work between 11:00 p.m. and 7:00 a.m.	Sleeping problems, insomnia, fatigue, nervous complaints
Predictability	Cycle time in weeks	Planning/coordination problems
Opportunity for household and family tasks	Weekly mean number of hours off work from Monday through Friday between 7:00 a.m. and 7:00 p.m.	Frustration of partner/ parental role, complaints on limitation of household tasks
Constancy of opportunity for household and family task	Variation coefficient of weekly opportunity for household and family tasks	Lack of continuity in partner/parental role and in household tasks
Opportunity for evening recreation	Mean weekly number of hours off work from Monday through Friday between 7:00 p.m. and 11:00 p.m.	Lack of continuity in partner role, limitation of social and recreational activities
Opportunity for weekend recreation	Half of the number of days off work during the weekend per week	Limitation of social and recreational activities
Constancy of opportunity for weekend recreation	Variation coefficient of the number of days off during the weekend per week	Lack of continuity in social and recreational activities

SOURCE: From "Time and Behavior at Work" by H. Thierry and T. Meijman, 1994, in *Handbook of Industrial and Organizational Psychology*, Vol. 4 (p. 360), edited by H. C. Triandis, M. D. Dunnette, and L. M. Hough, Palo Alto, CA: Consulting Psychologists Press. Reprinted by permission.

eating, sleeping, and working, workers often complain of lack of sleep, fatigue, constipation, irritability, and appetite loss. Meers, Maasen, and Verhaagen (1978) reported that the health of a sample of shift workers declined during the first six months of shift work; the decline became more pronounced after four years.

Because most people work during the day and sleep at night, shift workers also have social problems. They often experience difficulties with children, marital relationships, and recreation. Frost and Jamal (1979) reported that shift workers experienced less need fulfillment, were more likely to quit their jobs, and participated in fewer voluntary organizations. Jamal (1981) reported similar findings; workers on fixed work schedules were better off than workers on rotating schedules in terms of mental health, job satisfaction, and social participation.

Shift workers make up a relatively small proportion of the population; they are thus forced to fit their schedules to the rest of society. Dunham (1977) made the interesting point that many social problems would be alleviated by increasing shift work. Society would then make more concessions to the needs of shift workers. Changes might be made in such things as hours of television broadcasting, restaurant service, recreational services, and hours of business operation (banks, supermarkets, gas stations, and the like). In fact, convenience food stores and automated bank machines derive much of their business from employees who work nontraditional hours.

Research indicates that shift work has a strong influence on the lives of people who perform it. As long as certain industries require 24-hour-a-day operations, psychologists will continue searching for ways to improve this particularly difficult person/environment fit. Social problems may be lessened by changing some existing patterns in the community; however, physiological problems will be more difficult to overcome. Monk, Folkard, and Wedderburn (1996) noted that shift workers must face three enduring conditions of *biochronology:* (1) human beings and society are diurnal (awake in the day, asleep in the night), (2) daylight has a cueing effect to initiate wakefulness, and (3) the circadian system is slow to adjust to night work. Any organizational or social policy designed to assist shift workers must address these conditions.

At least one major source of physiological difficulty is the rotation of workers across shifts. If workers were assigned to a fixed shift (day, swing, or night), their behavior would be consistent, which would help them adjust to the circadian rhythm. Some people prefer to work afternoons or nights, so part of the solution may be personnel selection. Workers could choose a shift; if enough workers of the appropriate skill level were placed in the shift of their choice, that would meet both individual and organizational needs. Barton (1994) found that the physical and psychological health of nurses was better if they worked a fixed night shift than if they engaged in night work as part of a rotating-shift schedule. Smith, Reilly, and Midkiff (1989) developed a scale to predict morningness based on circadian rhythms. They concluded that the scale could be used to select workers for the night shift based on their preference for evening activities. Indeed, Jamal and Jamal (1982) found that employees who worked a fixed shift had better mental and physical health than employees on a rotating shift. Rotating shift work seems particularly difficult to adjust to. There is also evidence (Knauth, 1996) that backward rotation (from day to night to afternoon shifts) is more difficult to adjust to than forward rotation (from day to afternoon to night). Totterdell, Spelten, Smith, Barton, and Folkard (1995) reported that nurses felt worse (on such measures as alertness, calmness, moodiness, etc.) on a rest day following a night shift rather than a day shift. The findings attest to the costs of fatigue and adjustment to and from a nocturnal work routine. In fact, Freese and Okonek (1984) reported that some people who have reached the emotional, mental, and physical breaking point because of rotating shift work are told by their physicians to find jobs with traditional work hours. Costa (1996) estimated that 20% of workers have to leave shift work in a short time because of serious disturbances; those remaining show different and varying levels of adaptation and tolerance. Tepas (1993) concluded that organizations should design educational programs for shift workers and their families to better prepare them for the demands imposed by this work schedule. Kogi (1996) proposed that organizations devote substantial resources to occupational health services that support shift workers.

Flexible Working Hours

One variation in work schedules is flexible working hours, popularly known as **flextime.** According to Gottleib, Kelloway, and Barham (1998), 73% of U.S. employers offer flextime to their workers. The main objective of flextime is to create an alternative to the traditional, fixed working schedule by giving workers some choice in arrival and departure times. The system is usually arranged so that everyone must be present during certain designated hours ("coretime"), but there is latitude in other hours ("flexband"). For example, coretime may be 9:00 a.m. to 3:00 p.m., and flexband may be 6:00 a.m. to 6:00 p.m. Some employees may start working at 9:00 a.m. and work until 6:00 p.m., some may end at 3:00 p.m. by starting at 6:00 a.m.; others work any combination in between. Problems with family commitments, recreation, second jobs, commuting, and stress may be alleviated by flexible working hours. Lateness is virtually eliminated since the workday begins with arrival. Workers can be late only if they arrive after coretime has begun.

In general, the findings on flextime appear quite positive; at least no very adverse effects have yet been reported. The variables examined include satisfaction, productivity, absence, and turnover. Some studies reported more positive results than others. Golembiewski and Proehl (1978) summarized the findings of several studies on flextime; they reported that worker support for adoption or continuation of flextime across nine samples of workers ranged from 80% to 100%. It thus appears that many employees are highly receptive to the idea. Hicks and Klimoski (1981) found that employees did not become more satisfied with their work after flextime was adopted. Nevertheless, they reported other benefits like easier travel and parking, less interrole conflict, more feelings of control in the work setting, and more time for leisure activities.

Narayanan and Nath (1982) examined the impact of flextime at two organizational levels: lower-level and professional employees. They concluded that flextime primarily benefited lower-level employees by giving them more flexibility in their schedules. For professional employees, the flextime system merely formalized the already existing informal system they had with the company. Ralston (1989) found flextime was especially helpful for working mothers and dual-career couples, two growing segments of the workforce. In a six-year study of flextime, Dalton and Mesch (1990) reported large reductions in employee absenteeism compared to a control group on regular hours. However, the rate of turnover in the two groups was equivalent.

While there is ample evidence that flextime benefits individuals (Gottlieb et al., 1998), it is quite possible it could be detrimental to the functioning of teams. If employees must work as a team, the individualized schedules that flextime permits may limit the continuity of the team. However, we need additional research to address this issue. For the present, flextime appears to be highly beneficial in accommodating the scheduling needs of individual employees.

Compressed Workweek

Employees traditionally have worked 8 hours a day, five days a week, for a 40-hour workweek. Some employees work 10 hours a day for four days, popularly known as the "4/40." Gottlieb et al. (1998) reported that 21% of U.S. employers have compressed workweeks.

There are several obvious advantages to a compressed workweek for both the individual and the organization. Individuals have a three-day weekend, which gives them more recreation time, the chance to work a second job, more time for family life, and so on. Organizations have fewer overhead costs because they are open one day less per week. However, the possible drawbacks include worker fatigue, fewer productive hours, and more accidents.

In a major review of 4/40, Ronen and Primps (1981) reached some conclusions based on many studies. It has a positive effect on home and family life as well as on leisure and recreation. There appears to be no change in employee job performance. Finally, there are mixed results with regard to absenteeism, but worker fatigue definitely increases. A few studies have been reported on reactions to a 12-hour shift, typically noon to midnight and then midnight to noon. The results are mixed. Breaugh (1983) reported that nurses on 12-hour shifts experienced substantial fatigue associated with the longer hours. However, the midnight-to-noon shift felt more out of phase with physiological and social rhythms than did the noon-to-midnight shift. Pierce and Dunham (1992) reported significant improvements in work schedule attitudes, general affect, and fatigue in a sample of police officers who switched from a rotating 8-hour shift work schedule to a fixed 12-hour schedule. Duchon, Keran, and Smith (1994) examined underground miners who switched from an 8-hour to a 12-hour schedule. The miners reported improved sleep quality with the new schedule, while fatigue had either no change or slight improvement. The findings from such studies may be influenced by the variety of jobs examined in the research.

Conversion to a compressed workweek is not simply a matter of worker preference. Organizations are limited in altering their work schedules by the services they provide and other factors. For example, a compressed workweek is not viable if customer service must be provided five days a week. The success of organizations that provide services depends partially on accessibility. Dunham, Pierce, and Castaneda (1987) cautioned against blanket support for the 4/40; its success depends on the type of organization and the people in it.

Telecommuting

Telecommuting is an arrangement in which an employee works at home, in a satellite office, or at a customer's location for part or all of the workweek. When they are not in the central office, telecommuters communicate with their co-workers and managers by phone, computer modem, and fax. A similar arrangement is an electronic office created through the use of computers and computer networks (Finholt, 1997). Its significance is that it allows people to work together independent of time or location. Thus, the workplace is no longer a specific physical location. An impromptu office can spring up anywhere with employees working at home, in public places, or while traveling. Because "telework" is performed independently, telecommuters must be engaged in work that involves at least some autonomous tasks.

According to Gottleib et al. (1998), employees who work at home need a proper work setting for their comfort, safety, and productivity, including sufficient lighting, office furnishings, and equipment. Telecommuters need to have strong work habits and the ability to discern when to stop work and turn their attention to personal matters. Telework is particularly well suited to employees who are self-disciplined and self-directed. They must also be employees who have earned their manager's trust through good performance.

Telecommuting is appealing because it eliminates long-distance commuting to work, employees do not have to keep their children in day care centers, and employees have flexibility to schedule their own daily work. However, telework does not eliminate the need for child-care services because it is rarely possible to combine job responsibilities and the care of young children at home. In order to meet deadlines and complete tasks that they are not able to finish during the typical workday, some telecommuters work unpaid overtime hours in the evening at home. Isolation from colleagues is often cited as a significant cost of telework. When employees are "out of the loop," they can miss opportunities for taking on new assignments, competing for vacant positions, networking, and following new developments. Gottleib et al. reported that approximately 19% of U.S. employers have some arrangement for telecommuting.

ALCOHOLISM AND DRUG ABUSE IN THE WORKPLACE

Alcoholism and drug abuse are global problems, affecting all arenas of life. Moore (1994) offered this concise statement: "Alcohol and work. This has always been an uneasy relationship. Genius may be fired by wine. More commonplace talent is often fired because of it" (p. 75). Due to the sensitivity and confidentiality of substance abuse, we do not have a very strong research foundation on which to base our knowledge. That is, it is difficult to collect reliable and valid data on substance abuse, given the delicacy of the issue. What follows is a brief overview of some of the major dimensions of this complex social problem.

The term **substance abuse** covers a broad array of substances but usually includes alcohol, prescription drugs, and illegal drugs. Some people include tobacco (both smoking and chewing). Most of our knowledge is limited to alcoholism and illegal drugs. It has been estimated that there are over 10 million alcoholic American workers. Tyson and Vaughn (1987) reported that approximately two-thirds of the people entering the workforce have used illegal drugs. Four to 5 million people in the United States use cocaine monthly. The frequency of marijuana use is much higher. Every year $50 billion is spent on cocaine in the United

States—the same amount that companies spend annually on substance abuse programs for their employees. By any reasonable standard, substance abuse is a major problem in industry today.

Although I/O psychologists may approach the topic of substance abuse from several perspectives, a primary area of concern is performance impairment—that is, the extent to which substance abuse contributes to lower job performance. Experts in employee assistance programs estimate that as much as 50% of absenteeism and on-the-job accidents are related to drugs and alcohol use. Drug addiction also contributes to employee theft to support a habit. Thus, we have some knowledge about how substance abuse affects the more global performance criteria of absence, accidents, and theft. Our knowledge of the effects of substance abuse on skill decay is more tentative. Much of what we know is based on industrial accidents in which alcohol or drug use was confirmed. It is also very difficult to make categorical statements about "drugs" in general because of their variety, duration of effects, and interactive properties with other substances. We do know that cognitive skills such as vigilance, monitoring, reaction time, and decision making are adversely affected by many kinds of drugs. We do not know whether these drugs simply lengthen the amount of time needed to perform these cognitive functions, or whether they cause attention to be focused on irrelevant or competing stimuli. Jobs involving the use of these skills in areas like the transportation industry (for example, pilots and railroad engineers) have regrettably contributed to our knowledge through tragic accidents. Some drugs (such as anabolic steroids) have been found to enhance aspects of physical performance (most notably, strength and speed), but their long-term effects can be very harmful to the individual.

Hollinger (1988) concluded that the employees most likely to work under the influence of alcohol or other drugs are men younger than 30 and that the likelihood of their (or other employees') doing so increases when they feel unhappy about their jobs and socialize frequently with coworkers off the job. Trice and Sonnenstuhl (1988) found not only that employees seek relief from the effects of job stress with alcohol, but also that organizational subcultures establish norms for alcohol use. That is, employees may be expected to consume alcohol after work with their coworkers if there is a norm that encourages such behavior. Harris and Trusty (1997) reported that international cultural norms are less disparaging of alcohol use in work contexts than U.S. norms are, asserting that alcohol use is "part and parcel of business life" (p. 309). They cited that 5% of German employees are estimated to be alcoholics and 10% are at risk of becoming alcohol abusers. Alcohol abuse is an epidemic among workers in the former Soviet Union.

Stein, Newcomb, and Bentler (1988) believe that drug involvement and its adverse consequences are facets of a lifestyle that includes more than drug use only. They feel we must appreciate the diverse range of life areas affected by drug use and not treat drug use as an isolated or singular problem in the individual. Bruno (1994) reported that in Italy drug dependence does not limit a person's right to keep a job, even if employees perform tasks dangerous to their own or others' safety. To safeguard others, federal laws require employers to reassign such employees to other tasks. The introduction of drug testing in the workplace in Italy has been delayed because it appears to imply a conflict between the organization's right to safeguard its interest and the individual's right to privacy.

Economic issues are also salient to drug use. Bennett, Blum, and Roman (1994) noted that organizations typically address the problem of drug use at work in two ways. The first is drug testing, designed to exclude drug users from the workplace. The second is Employee Assistance Programs (EAPs). EAPs started mostly after World War II to rehabilitate veterans who came home with alcohol abuse problems. Drug abuse treatment was added to the EAP programs mainly after the Vietnam War for veterans returning with drug problems. Currently EAPs address all kinds of adjustment, stress, and family problems faced by workers. Such programs are mandated by the federal government for all employees who receive over a specified amount of federal funding. Bennett et al. found that organizations in geographic areas with high unemployment rates are more likely to use pre-employment drug testing, while work sites with low turnover more often provide an EAP.

Finally, Normand, Lempert, and O'Brien (1994) offered some staggering estimates of the annual financial costs of alcohol and drug abuse to society. Estimates were based on four factors: the costs of treatment, lowered work productivity, the lost income that would have been earned by individuals who die prematurely from substance abuse, and crime-related costs. The total estimated cost of alcohol abuse is $70 billion; the total estimated cost of drug abuse is $44 billion.

It is very difficult for I/O psychologists to conduct high-quality research on substance abuse. Alcohol or drugs can be administered in an experimental setting only under the most restrictive conditions, given ethical concerns. Reliance on self-report measures are problematic, given issues of social desirability and accuracy. There are also civil and legal issues associated with drug testing, both in this country and internationally, particularly pertaining to the constitutional rights of individuals to submit to drug testing. As with most complex social problems, researchers and scholars from many professions (such as pharmacology, toxicology, law, and genetics) must take an interdisciplinary approach to addressing these issues. While I/O psychologists will contribute only a small piece of the total picture, I envision our efforts as concentrated in two traditional areas: individual assessment and performance measurement. Perhaps in 20 years an evaluation of working conditions may also include the propensity of certain jobs to induce substance abuse and the likelihood your coworker is under the influence of drugs or alcohol. Whether we are ready for it or not, I believe society will expect I/O psychologists to provide information on problems our predecessors could scarcely have imagined.

CASE STUDY ◆ Will Life Ever Get Back to Normal?

Janet Ryder sat at her kitchen table reading the entertainment section of the local newspaper. A movie was playing that she had heard a lot about, and she was hoping it would stay in town for at least two weeks. Her husband, Mark, had recently changed jobs and was now working for St. Regis Aluminum, a large manufacturer of lightweight metal products. The company worked shifts, and Mark was starting a two-week stint on the night shift. Neither Janet nor Mark had any previous experience with shift work, and the switch from conventional hours was difficult for both of them.

Janet tried to plan their family life around Mark's changing hours, but she couldn't get the hang of it. Little things kept cropping up that had never been a problem before. For example, the boy next door had been taking trumpet lessons for about two months. He would practice after school. Janet heard the notes straining from the trumpet, but after a while the sounds seemed to blend in with the rest of the neighborhood noise, and she could ignore them. When Mark was sleeping in the afternoon, the noise of the trumpet often woke him up. They had two arguments about whether they should call the boy's mother and ask that he practice at another time.

Yesterday there had been a sale on roast beef, which was one of their favorite dinners. Janet liked to fix a fancy dinner when there was something special to eat. However, with Mark's schedule, she had to "time" special meals when he worked the day shift. While Mark might be ready to sit down to a full meal at 7:00 a.m. after working the night shift, Janet couldn't quite handle either fixing it or eating it after just getting up. The roast beef would sit in the freezer, waiting for a time when they both could enjoy it.

It was also awkward for their friends. They had been in a biweekly poker club that met on Friday nights. They got together with some other couples at 8:00, and the party would break up around midnight. When Mark worked afternoons, there was no way they could play. When he worked the night shift, they would have to leave at 10:00, just when things were going great. Only when he worked the day shift could they make it. Now they played in the poker club about once every two months, and their friends got another couple to sub for them.

Janet started to feel guilty about feeling sorry for herself. It had been no bargain for Mark either. The weekend the long-awaited Custom Boat and Trailer Show arrived in town, Mark was working the swing shift. He got to visit the show for about half an hour before he had to leave for work. It seemed that on Saturdays and Sundays, just when he found something he liked to do, it was time to go to the plant.

Their 10-year-old son Billie wandered into the kitchen. Billie was holding a Little League schedule in his hand. "Mom," he said, "in three weeks there's the regional tournament in Union City. Will you and Dad make it to my game?"

Janet got up and checked Mark's work schedule, which was posted on the cupboard. "I can make it, Billie, but Dad will be working the afternoon shift that week," Janet said.

Billie looked downcast. "I never get to see Dad very much any more," he said, as he slowly walked out of the kitchen.

Questions
1. Think of Chapter 10 on work stress. Do you see any relationship between work and nonwork satisfaction for shift workers?
2. What other disruptions in family life might you predict for the Ryder family as a result of shift work?
3. Are there things St. Regis Aluminum could do to alleviate some of the problems of shift workers? What are they?
4. Are there things the community could do to make life easier for shift workers? What are they?
5. How long would you guess it takes for a family to get into the "rhythm" of shift work?

INFOTRAC ARTICLES

1. *Executive Female*, July–August 1995 v18 n4 p70(4)
   How do I make a flexible schedule work? Anna Sobkowski, Michelle Mendes, Suzanne Curley, Deborah Swiss, & Valerie McQuat
   Discuss the concept of flexible work schedules from the perspectives of two employees, one manager, and one consultant.

2. *The Progressive*, Dec 1995 v59 n12 p29(2)
   "They killed my son." One father fights for safety in the workplace. Discusses a fatal job accident that occurred in a company that had a history of OSHA safety violations.

3. *Training & Development*, Feb 1996 v50 n2 p20(8)
   Making telecommuting work. George M. Piskurich
   Discusses the benefits and weaknesses of telecommuting and recommends issues to consider in undertaking a system of telecommuting.

4. *Computer Life*. Feb 1998 v4 n2 p116(3)
   Wrist assured. Laurel Merlino
   Discusses how computer users may develop a repetitive stress injury, most commonly represented by tendinitis, carpal tunnel syndrome, and back pain.

5. *USA Today* (Magazine), April 1997 v125 n2623 p13(1)
   "Psychonomics" is the new buzzword.
   Describes the extension of ergonomics into "psychonomics"—how consumers demand products that are simple to operate and can do many things.

6. *Nursing Homes*, June 1995 v44 n5 p13(5)
   Shift work: Its challenges and management. Ruth R. Alward
   Discusses the problems caused by shift work in the health care industries and recommends strategies for coping with it.

7. *Alcohol Health & Research World*, Summer 1996 v20 n3 p162(8)
   Alcohol's role in work-force entry and retirement. Paul M. Roman and J. Aaron Johnson
   Describes the pattern of alcohol consumption over the lifespan and its effects at various stages of a career.

8. *Public Health Reports*, Sep–Oct 1995 v110 n5 p593(7)
   Prevalence and consequences of smoking, alcohol use, and illicit drug use at five worksites. Michael T. French, Gary A. Zarkin, Tyler D. Hartwell, & Jeremy W. Bray.
   Results of a study designed to help employers identify the extent of substance abuse problems in their work sites and specific areas to target for possible intervention.

The Changing Nature of Work

MAJOR CHAPTER OBJECTIVES

- ◆ Understand why emotions in the workplace, adaptability, and genetic influences on work behavior will be potent individual-level factors affecting I/O psychology in the future.

- ◆ Understand why technology, groups at work, and lifelong learning will be potent work-level factors affecting I/O psychology in the future.

- ◆ Understand why global economic competition, social values, and time will be influential societal-level factors affecting I/O psychology in the future.

This final chapter is intended to provide a glimpse into the future rather than a capstone summary of the past. It will examine how the nature of work is changing and how these changes are influencing I/O psychology.

Change is inevitable and unavoidable. However, the rate of change can vary from slow to fast, and change can exhibit continuity or discontinuity. It appears that as a society we are in the midst of rapid change of a highly discontinuous nature. As Havel (1994) expressed it, "Many things indicate we are going through a transitional period, when it seems that something is on the way out and something else is painfully being born. It is as if something were crumbling, decaying and exhausting itself, while something else, still indistinct, were arising from the rubble" (p. 27). Discontinuous change implies the past is no longer a guide to the future. According to Drucker (1993), every few hundred years in Western civilization a sharp transformation creates a very different world. We are in the middle of a transformation that is not yet complete. A primary cause of the discontinuous change is the tremendous growth in knowledge produced by higher levels of education, new technologies, and increased research. This burst of knowledge causes social systems to adapt in fits and starts rather than through a steady stream of continuous change.

Three major dimensions of change affecting I/O psychology will be examined—those pertaining to individuals, work, and society. In turn, each dimension will be represented by three illustrative exemplars. In particular, consideration is given to how these dimensions of change influence the conduct of I/O psychology, as described in the preceding chapters of this book.

INDIVIDUAL DIMENSIONS

If the world of work is going through tumultuous change, it most certainly will influence the type of individuals who will prosper in this new environment. It will also influence the attributes of individuals organizations find desirable and how job applicants will be assessed.

Emotions in the Workplace. Throughout the history of the scientific study of work, researchers have tended to use a paradigm or approach that is guided by "rationality." Thus, the experience of work is often portrayed through reasoned, analytic concepts, as witnessed by task statements, job specifications, goal objectives, and the like. However, as anyone who has ever worked can attest, "emotions are an integral and inseparable part of everyday organizational life" (Ashforth & Humphrey, 1995, p. 98). Employees are, first and foremost, people, and it is the feeling and expression of emotions that make us human. Elation, gratification, and pride are among the more meaningful positive feelings we derive from our work. However, work can also produce feelings of fear and sadness, as well as the "nasty" emotions of anger, jealousy, and envy. Recently I/O psychologists have come to recognize that emotions influence work-related behaviors, and they accept emotions as a legitimate topic of research.

Arvey, Renz, and Watson (1998) proposed that (1) emotions are common in the workplace and it is futile to ignore emotions or attempt to eliminate them,

(2) emotions produce both positive and negative work outcomes, and (3) people have stable individual differences in their predispositions to experience certain emotions and in the intensity and duration of their expressed and displayed emotions. A person may consistently become angry instead of sad in a variety of situations where either emotion could be elicited. The stable patterns of emotional responses (i.e., individual differences in emotionality) may enable us to predict both the individual's emotional responses to job demands and the resulting behaviors that may affect job performance. The authors also proposed that work performance can be improved by matching people and jobs in terms of emotionality.

George and Brief (1996) asserted that there is an association between emotions and moods in the workplace. Both are based on feelings, but it is the intensity of the feeling that distinguishes moods from emotions. *Emotions* are normally associated with specific events and are relatively intense. Because of their intensity, emotions interrupt cognitive thought processes and behaviors. *Moods,* on the other hand, are typically day-to-day feelings that provide an affective context for thought processes and behaviors without necessarily interrupting them or demanding attention. George and Brief proposed that emotions and moods provide a basis to understand work motivation, as feelings help determine the causes of actions people take.

In general, recognizing emotions in the workplace reestablishes "workers" as people first, who assume several roles in life, one of which is in an employment context. Given the centrality of work in our lives and the omnipresence of our emotions, this emerging interest is a long-overlooked area of fusion.

Adaptable Employees.   Adaptability is a personality construct that relates to a willingness to embrace new situations, one of the Big 5 personality factors. Personality assessment is experiencing renewed popularity in I/O psychology because it can predict the "will do" component of behavior; ability tests assess the "can do" component (Katzell, 1994).

Associated with the ability to adapt to new situations is the ability to adapt to, and relate to, other people. With a growing shift to the use of teams, it is becoming increasingly important to staff organizations with employees who have effective relational skills. Relational skills include communication, interpersonal relating, conflict resolution, and influencing capabilities. Quite apart from team-based work, organizations want employees who are responsible and conscientious and can get along with their coworkers. Dunn, Mount, Barrick, and Ones (1995) found that managers considered general mental ability and conscientiousness to be the most important attributes related to applicants' hirability. Furthermore, emotional stability, conscientiousness, and agreeableness were the most important attributes relating inversely to insubordination, rule infractions, and theft. It will be recalled that integrity tests measure these attributes. It is therefore reasonable that a selection test battery should include an assessment of both the "can do" (intelligence) and the "will do" (personality) constructs. It is a matter of debate among I/O psychologists whether the selection test battery should assess just these two constructs, or whether additional constructs should be assessed as well. What is agreed upon is that an employee's ability to adapt to change and to relate well to others is becoming as critical to successful job performance as the needed cognitive ability.

Genetic Influences on Work Behavior.   Psychology has long been captivated by the nature/nurture debate—the relative degrees to which heredity and the environment influence behavior. For at least the past 40 years, the nurture or environmental perspective has predominated the thinking in psychology. That is, by carefully crafting our environment (such as by providing certain educational experiences for children), we can fashion a society where all people have a high likelihood of attaining selected outcomes, such as good health or satisfying employment. However, recently the pendulum is starting to swing back to the importance of genetic or heredity influences on behavior. That is, because of our individual genetic compositions, we are *not* all equally likely to attain selected outcomes. As Arvey and Bouchard (1994) stated, "biology is back" as an explanation for behavior. Recently researchers have identified genetic structures that account for a wide range of conditions, including obesity and alcoholism.

Arvey and Bouchard described genetic influences on work behavior and the extent to which genetics will play a role in I/O psychology. They presented a descriptive model of how genetic and environmental factors influence concepts important to I/O psychology, as shown in Figure 16–1. As can be seen in the model, genetic differences across individuals are hypothesized to influence such factors as job choice, job performance, how we feel about our work, how we perceive our work environment, our length of service on a job, and our level of income. Research has identified work situations where individuals with certain genetic makeups are at risk when exposed to radiation and/or certain chemicals. Commercially available tests exist to detect genetic conditions such as sickle-cell anemia, cystic fibrosis, and polycystic kidney disease. Future tests for cancer and hypertension are likely. In addition, methods have been developed to detect a person's susceptibility to environmental work hazards, as well as methods to determine whether a worker's chromosomes have been altered by conditions in the workplace.

Genetic studies offer us new insights into serious work problems, such as stress. Research indicates that life stress can be divided into two types of causing factors: controllable and uncontrollable. Genetic research has shown that the capacity to control stress has high heritability. However, a critical question is whether organizations should use such information for screening, selection, and placement purposes. Ethical issues abound in this area that have yet to be resolved from a practical standpoint. Among them is the precision of measurement of genetic factors, and the likelihood of misclassifying individuals. This is the same issue that applies to the use of psychological tests in making selection decisions. Are the consequences of making true and false positive and negative decisions any different when using genetic tests versus psychological tests? A more extreme ethical concern applies to altering a person's genetic structure through such procedures as gene splicing, gene transfer, and gene replacement. Such interventions are currently being discussed and implemented in medical settings.

It appears we are entering an era where there is growing recognition of the importance of genetic factors in influencing behavior, including in the workplace. It remains to be seen what its degree of impact will be across the full spectrum of concepts studied by I/O psychologists. However, if indeed "biology is back" as an explanation of work behavior, I/O psychologists will have to adjust to the discontinuous change in our own thinking caused by this perspective.

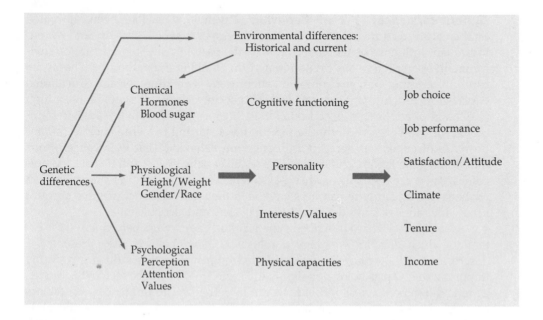

FIGURE 16–1   *Model of genetic and environmental variables and their influence on traditional I/O psychology constructs*

SOURCE: From "Genetics, Twins, and Organizational Behavior" by R. D. Arvey and T. J. Bouchard, Jr., 1994, in *Research in Organizational Behavior,* Vol. 16 (p. 55), edited by B. M. Staw and L. L. Cummings, Greenwich, CT: JAI Press.

WORK DIMENSIONS

Perhaps more than any other dimension, change is affecting the very nature of how work is performed. These changes in work are profound and reverberate throughout the complete domain of I/O psychology.

Technology.   Van der Spiegel (1995) asserted that advances in information technologies (computers and communication systems) are the driving forces behind major changes in how we work. Only a few decades ago computers were accessible to only a privileged few, mainly engineers and scientists. The microprocessor and the personal computer now give a large portion of the population access to new information technologies. As we move into the next century, the emergence of portable systems such as cellular phones, faxes, notebook computers, personal digital assistants, and pen-based computers will provide multimedia capabilities to the user independent of space or time. Van der Spiegel believes that in the not too distant future we will see the emergence of instruments that can understand natural language instructions and make intelligent decisions. The information technologies will have an impact on office space and facility usage. It may become more efficient to work at home for several days where one can work uninterrupted using a personal desktop that provides access to the same resources that are available in the office.

These new technologies are posited to change not only the knowledge, skills, and abilities (KSAs) of individual workers, but also the manner in which we think of KSAs. Davis (1995) suggested that organizations develop differences in their competencies—that is, organizations have their own unique KSAs. Organizational competencies include the sum of knowledge possessed collectively by all employees in the organization. These competencies, particularly core competencies used to coordinate diverse production skills and integrate multiple technologies, have a strategic advantage. Unlike physical assets that deteriorate over time, knowledges grow with use. Hesketh and Bochner (1994) believe that massive technological changes are compelling individuals and organizations to become *multiskilled*, increasing their flexibility to adapt to their dynamic environments. The new information technologies are the driving mechanism behind the changes in the way work is conducted, and the corresponding talents of individuals and organizations needed to adapt to these changes.

Groups at Work.   Katzell (1994) regards the use of groups or teams as a primary vehicle for conducting work as one of the major "meta-trends" in contemporary I/O psychology. Interest in groups began with the Hawthorne studies, and the current explosion of interest in work groups will undoubtedly continue. Two targets of interest in work groups identified by Katzell are: (1) the effect of the group on its individual members and (2) the work group as a productive entity. The following discussion includes representative issues from these areas of interest.

Although the performance of groups is generally superior to the average performance of its individual members, it is often less than that of the best individual worker in tasks that can be performed by individuals. This is partly a consequence of the loss of motivation among individual members. The loss of motivation among some group members has been attributed to "social loafing," a phenomenon where some individuals in a work group slacken their performance in the belief that other group members will accelerate their own performance. However, the group's influence on the individual can also be positive. Groups can help members learn effective skills and behaviors by providing role models. Katzell believes that I/O psychology is in a position to create conditions that generate positive and avoid negative consequences of group membership.

The issue of selecting the ideal mix of individuals in a work group has been approached in terms of ability, personality, and attitude. However, successful group composition appears to be influenced by the kind of tasks the group performs. For example, heterogeneity in members' personalities typically facilitate performance when the task emphasizes group problem solving and creativity, but not when the task involves performance using available knowledge and skills. Likewise, the degree of autonomy accorded the team has attracted interest. We do not yet know the boundaries of its effectiveness, and whether there are cross-cultural differences in its acceptability. The issue of team development embraces enhancing the collective skills of the team as a team, and not just the skills of the individual members. Most of our knowledge from training and development applies to individuals, not groups. This issue pertains to what researchers refer to as the "unit of analysis" and reminds us that findings derived from one unit (e.g., the individual) do not necessarily generalize to another unit (e.g., the group).

Katzell believes that I/O psychology will be heavily influenced by the movement toward team-based work operations. We have much to learn about the degree to which our knowledge base developed on individuals concerning such matters as recruitment, selection, placement, training, performance appraisal, motivation, and leadership extends to work groups.

Lifelong Learning.   The conventional view is that learning is acquired by formal education during the years through college, followed by a relatively brief period of on-the-job learning. Following this phase of knowledge and skill acquisition, you set about "doing" your job, and for the most part your learning days are over. This model of learning (and living) is being replaced by an ethic that emphasizes learning throughout the individual's lifetime. Failure to follow this model will render you more susceptible to job loss and increasingly likely to have difficulty gaining re-employment. The changing nature of the psychological contract between employer and employee requires the individual to assume a greater responsibility for career development. Organizations are now far less likely to offer the implicit promise to provide career advancing opportunities. Organizations are increasingly becoming "vendors of employment" as opposed to incubators of individual professional growth. Consider the following message found posted on the bulletin board of a plant experiencing widespread layoffs (as reported by Hall & Mirvis, 1995):

> We can't promise you how long we'll be in business.
> We can't promise you that we won't be bought by another company.
> We can't promise that there'll be room for promotion.
> We can't promise that your job will exist until you reach retirement age.
> We can't promise that the money will be available for your pension.
> We can't expect your undying loyalty and we aren't sure we want it. (p. 326)

Hall and Mirvis believe that workers will have to change jobs, companies, and even careers over their lifetimes. Workers who cannot adapt to this kind of change will likely plateau in their worklives or simply be ushered out of the organization. This shift puts a premium on learning how to adapt to new situations. It will become increasingly important for workers to be immersed in a wide variety of professional experiences. The authors assert it is fruitless to try to predict exactly which skills will be required in a given organization in the future. Rather, organizations should encourage employees to learn how to learn so they are capable of gaining job-specific skills as the need becomes apparent. Hall and Mirvis refer to the process of continuous development as "learning a living."

While the general blueprint for such a new system is evident for both individuals and organizations, it is not clear whether both parties have the capability to deliver what is needed. At the individual level we do not know whether people can learn to be adaptable. Is adaptability a characteristic of the individual that is relatively fixed, or can it be developed? Can we measure the ability to be adaptable, and would it predict how people will cope with organizations restructuring and rapid job movement? At the organizational level we need to identify what company practices really help people adapt and learn to learn. In order to become proficient learning centers, companies have to tailor training and work assignments to people's learning styles and set up systems of advanced skill certification, mentoring, and so forth. These are daunting assignments for organizations that are not accustomed to functioning as learning centers. Despite these issues, it is clear that one consequence of continuous change is the need to enhance our capability of responding to it. For that reason lifelong learning is posited as a critical adaptive mechanism for both individuals and organizations.

SOCIETAL DIMENSIONS

Societal dimensions of change are broad-based forces that shape both individuals and organizations. Although they are abstract in nature, their influence can be direct and potent.

Economic Competition.   Cascio (1995) stated that wars—World Wars I and II, Korea, Vietnam, and the Persian Gulf—were the driving forces behind geopolitical development in the 20th century. However, in the 21st century economic forces will rule. The competition that is normal and inevitable among nations will be acted out not in war but in commerce. The weapons will be growth rates, investments, trade blocs, and imports and exports.

These changes reflect the impact of globalized product and service markets. In the 1960s only 7% of the U.S. economy was exposed to international competition. By the 1980s that number exceeded 70%. Merchandise exports have risen by 50% since 1986, and every $1 billion in U.S. merchandise that is exported generates approximately 20,000 new jobs. Free-market enterprise in the former Soviet Union will further intensify economic competition. The competition for business has resulted in a worldwide need for a highly skilled workforce. Nations are judged in economic surveys by the quality of their public education, secondary schooling, on-the-job training, and computer literacy. There is thus a global need for a broad, technically literate labor pool.

Changes in the global economy have had profound impacts on jobs in the United States. Over 7 million jobs have been lost permanently since 1987. As a rule companies do not downsize because they are losing money, but rather to strategically improve themselves. Cascio stated that we are moving from an economy where there are many hard-working people to one where there are fewer, smarter-working people. Jobs aren't being lost temporarily because of an economic recession; rather they are being eliminated permanently as a result of new technology, improved machinery, and new ways of organizing work.

Carnevale (1995) aptly summarized how economic issues have transformed the work world:

> Something happened on the way to the second century of American economic dominance. The globalization of wealth and technology created a whole new economic ball game with new rules and an expanded set of competitive standards. . . . In addition, the globalization of competition assures that if Americans don't deliver on the new competitive standards, someone else will, and that someone else is likely to be a foreign worker in Europe or Asia. The new economy requires profound changes in American institutions. (pp. 238–239)

Although economic issues have always been a driving influence in our society, they have never attained the dominance they now possess. Increased globalization of society has ensured that no country is immune from its effects.

Values. The issue of values, particularly values that guide our society, has been hotly debated over the past decade. Values are the basis of legislation and judicial decisions that have profound impacts on our lives. Conflicting values in society regarding such issues as abortion and the separation of church and state generate intense reactions among partisan supporters. Values also pervade employment matters, especially what is meant by "fairness." There are conflicting standards of fairness in employment, standards that seemingly do not lend themselves to a widely endorsed middle ground or compromise position. It has been argued that as a society we do *not* necessarily need a singular concept of fairness and thus a reduction in conflict. That is, open discourse on differing viewpoints that are strongly held is one of the hallmarks of a vibrant and healthy society. However, an alternative view is that if there is not some fusion or coalescence among differing societal values, we will be continuously embroiled in the conflict such divergent values produce.

Although there are many ways to conceptualize the conflict about values in employment, a useful framework is the distinction between the standards of equity and equality in social justice. The *equity* standard stems from the position that individuals differ in a wide variety of attributes like intelligence and physical strength. When these attributes are judged critical for performance in societal roles, it is acceptable to base membership in these roles on the attributes. Thus, one role in society is to maintain the security and welfare of its members, as witnessed by police and firefighter jobs. If the attribute of strength is judged critical to performance in this role, it is acceptable to select members of police and fire departments, in part, on the basis of physical strength. Because not all individuals are equally strong, some individuals will be judged more suitable for police and firefighter jobs than others.

The *equality* standard of fairness is predicated upon minimizing differences in individuals, thus ensuring that all individuals in society are treated the same or equally. For example, we all have the same opportunity to vote in an election, and each person's vote counts the same as any other person's vote. Voting is an institution whereby individuals can have a voice in matters that affect their welfare. Another institution affecting individual welfare is employment. It is through employment that we earn a living as well as have the opportunity to better ourselves in life. Accordingly, the opportunity for employment should be extended equally to all members of society.

It is at this point where the two standards of social fairness, equity and equality, frequently clash. The basis for the clash is that the attributes that differentiate individuals (such as strength) are not equally distributed across all the groups in society. That is, there are *group* differences in the attributes that are used to determine individual membership in employment. Members of society can be grouped in several ways, but one major grouping factor is gender. In the case of physical strength, there is a pronounced difference between men and women, with men (as a group) being physically stronger than women (as a group). Thus, it might be reasonable to conclude that if men are physically stronger than women, and if physical strength is an attribute needed to be a firefighter, then men are more suited to be firefighters than women. Thus, because of a difference between the two genders with regard to an attribute, men and women have an *unequal* opportunity to assume membership in the role of firefighter in our society.

Proponents of the equity standard of fairness argue that male-populated fire departments merely reflect the reality that men are stronger than women. Proponents of the equality standard of fairness argue that it is not fair, for a variety of reasons. One is that although men are stronger than women, the strongest men are not necessarily the best firefighters. A certain amount of strength may be required, but greater amounts of strength beyond that threshold are unrelated to job performance. Thus, women are not as strong as men, but they may be "strong enough" to perform the job of firefighter. Another reason is although strength is important to being a firefighter, many other attributes such as judgment are also important, which women possess to the same degree as men. Therefore, women shouldn't be disproportionately excluded from the job of firefighter because of one attribute. Third, it can be argued that with the advent of technical advances in firefighting equipment, the equipment exerts the force needed on the job, not the human body. Thus, the manual aspects of firefighting that require physical strength can be done through technological advances in equipment design, which women can operate as proficiently as men. And fourth, not all jobs in the fire department require the same degree of physical strength. Jobs such as radio dispatcher, fire truck driver, and paramedic within the fire department are less physically demanding than other jobs. Women are as able as men to meet the demands of these types of jobs in the fire department.

While counterarguments can be raised for each of these issues, the clash between the equity and equality standards of fairness with regard to gender and physical strength are evident. The same arguments can be extended to other classifications of societal groups, such as race and age, and the unequal distribution of attributes across these groups. The dilemma is how to be fair to groups that are unequal in selected attributes yet equally deserving of the societal benefits of employment.

Over the past 30 years the pendulum has swung between the equity and equality perspectives. Despite strident claims by proponents of each perspective regarding the "correctness" of their position, the reality is that both perspectives are manifestations of social justice. Whatever the next iteration in societal preference for these two positions will be, it will continue to have a major impact on I/O psychology. As a scientific discipline, psychology focuses on how we differ as individuals, which has the effect of gravitating us more toward the equity perspective of justice. However, the philosophic underpinnings of law seem to lean toward the equality perspective of justice. I/O psychology will continue to operate at the cusp of the interplay between these two standards of justice. We will also be compelled to be responsive to the implications of their dictates in the workplace.

Time.   A resource possessed by all is time. Each of us has 24 hours in a day, each day, to live our lives. Many resources (both financial and natural) have been the object of inquiry, but we are about to enter an era in which time will be a focal point of our attention.

There are many manifestations of our interest in time, both scientific and practical. Katzell (1994) asserted that time is one of the major meta-trends in I/O psychology. He pointed to research findings indicating that the accuracy of predictive relationships change over time. Some aspects of behavior are more predictable in the immediate future than in the distant future. Other aspects of behavior may not be immediately evident but will manifest themselves over time. One can view these relationships in terms of the specific constructs being measured, or by examining the temporal-based developmental process. Time should also be considered in the issues of career development and motivation. In particular, researchers have examined the stages of a career over time, and they are questioning how the new economic order will affect these stages. While most theories of motivation have typically addressed "how much" motivation a person will exhibit in the pursuit of a goal, more recent research is addressing "how long" a person will perseverate in the pursuit of a goal. Also of interest is how time affects group formation. I/O psychologists are becoming more attuned to time as a prominent issue that affects many other constructs. As Katzell (1994) noted, "Paying more attention to consistencies and changes over time contributes to a better understanding of various subjects of interest, and thereby to more effective ways of dealing with them" (p. 8).

Another manifestation of an interest in time is the identification of a personality construct that reflects our preferred use of time. *Serial monochronicity* refers to the pattern of preferring to start and complete one major task before moving on to another. *Polychronicity* is the pattern of preferring to attend to multiple tasks simultaneously. Preferred patterns of time utilization are posited to be predictive of performance in jobs that demand the individual to be responsive to overlaying waves of stimuli from divergent sources.

Time and time management have attracted growing interest as factors that affect the quality of life. Among the memorable statements about the importance of time in our lives are these:

> "How many people on their deathbed wish they'd spent more time at the office?"
> "Time is gone forever, once spent, and is the ultimate equal opportunity employer."

Covey, Merrill, and Merrill (1994) asserted that time-based issues are the leading causes of stress in life. As a way to reduce stress they advocate partitioning issues according to their importance and urgency. They recommend we do not confuse the two, as important but nonurgent issues do not require the same type or speed of response as do important and urgent issues. Covey et al. believe that stress reduction through time management does not involve "working harder" or "working smarter" but being cognizant of the principles that guide our behavior. Although we cannot control events in our lives, we can control how we appraise them and respond to them. Wright (1997) proposed that researchers can gain a better understanding of organizational issues by regarding time as an explanatory concept.

The foregoing discussion is not meant to imply that I/O psychologists have been oblivious to time as an issue in our lives. Rather it reflects expanding one's focus from the particular substantive concepts of interest to include the temporal framework in which they are evidenced. It is also likely that a recognition of time as a precious resource will grow among researchers, as we seek ways to cultivate this universal resource. Time is not a *fungible* resource, a resource that can readily be traded or exchanged for another. While we can trade money for goods, we cannot trade money for time. It is anticipated that time will be a critical variable on the research agenda of many scientific disciplines in the 21st century.

CONCLUDING COMMENTS

The axiom that "the best predictor of the future is the past" may have to be modified in the next century, at least as it applies to I/O psychology. A few caveats or modifiers may be in order, such as "The best predictor of the future is the very recent past." Also, we would be advised to pay close attention to emerging trends. The concept of discontinuous change indicates that the future may look very little like the past. Forces of change are operating with such intensity and velocity that it is indeed very difficult to predict the future, more so now than ever before. This chapter has outlined some of the major dimensions of change in individuals, work, and society. I/O psychology will continue to address human behavior in the work world, and in that sense our mission and purpose as a discipline will not waver. We have much to gain by all that we have learned in the past. However, it seems we will no longer be allowed the luxury of prolonged deliberation over relatively static events and conditions. The pace of change in employment issues will require adaptive responses to mixes of individual, work, and societal factors that are cascading at an accelerated speed.

INFOTRAC ARTICLES

1. *Training & Development*, April 1998 v52 n4 p41(3)
   The future: Two views. Haidee E. Allerton
   The results of an interview with two authors about the future of work and its effect on career planning.
2. *International Labour Review*, Nov–Dec 1996 v135 n6 p615(8)
   Work and usefulness to the world. Robert Castel
   Discusses the meaning of work from a social perspective and how changing conceptions of the employment relationship can ultimately be harmful for society.
3. *International Labour Review*, Nov–Dec 1996 v135 n6 p665(10)
   Work and training: A blurring of the edges. Francoise Favennevc-Hery
   An examination of the linkage between training and work from a social perspective and the nature of that relationship in the future.
4. *Training & Development*, Oct 1998 v52 n10 p26(8)
   Train your brain. Jennifer J. Salopek
   An interview with Daniel Goleman, one of the leading authorities on emotional intelligence, in which he describes the importance of understanding emotions in the work world.
5. *American Scientist*, Jan–Feb 1995 v83 n1 p68(11)
   Self-conscious emotions. Michael Lewis

A discussion of how such emotions as guilt, shame, and pride develop. It proposes that even complex emotions may begin to develop early in childhood.

6. *Technology Review,* Oct 1996 v99 n7 p63(1)

Lifelong what? Samuel C. Florman

Argues that successful lifelong learning must include not only upgrading technical knowledge and skills but also examining one's own life.

7. *Training & Development,* August 1996 v50 n8 p36(5)

The state of lifelong learning. Cynthia Pantazis

Discusses how policy makers and legislators should modify laws to enhance the creation of a national workforce development system that promotes lifelong learning.

8. *Executive Female,* March–April 1996 v19 n2 p44(6)

Women's work is never done *c.* 1996. Perri Capell, Virginia Gordon, & Blanche Marker

Describes how advances in technology (laptops, e-mail, voice mail, etc.) permit us to perform many tasks at once ("multitasking"), thus increasing our productive efficiency, but can also make us feel overwhelmed.

Ackerman, P. L. (1987). Individual differences in skill learning: An integration of psychometric and information processing perspectives. *Psychological Bulletin, 102,* 3–27.

Ackerman, P. L. (1992). Predicting individual differences in complex skill acquisition: Dynamics of ability determinants. *Journal of Applied Psychology, 77,* 598–614.

Ackerman, P. L., & Heggestad, E. D. (1997). Intelligence, personality, and interests: Evidence of overlapping traits. *Psychological Bulletin, 121,* 219–245.

Ackerman, P. L., & Kanfer, R. (1993). Integrating laboratory and field study for improving selection: Development of a battery for predicting air traffic controller success. *Journal of Applied Psychology, 78,* 413–432.

Adair, J. G. (1984). The Hawthorne effect: A reconsideration of the methodological artifact. *Journal of Applied Psychology, 69,* 334–345.

Adams, G. A., King, L. A., & King, D. W. (1996). Relationships of job and family involvement, family social support, and work–family conflict with job and life satisfaction. *Journal of Applied Psychology, 81,* 411–420.

Adams, J. S. (1965). Inequity in social exchange. In L. Berkowitz (Ed.), *Advances in experimental social psychology* (Vol. 2, pp. 267–299). New York: Academic Press.

Adams-Roy, J. E., Knap, M. A., & Barling, J. (1995). Commitment to organizational health and safety in management training. In L. E. Tetrick & J. Barling (Eds.), *Changing employment relations* (pp. 133–144). Washington, DC: American Psychological Association.

Adler, N. J., Doktor, R., & Redding, S. G. (1986). From the Atlantic to the Pacific century: Cross-cultural management reviewed. *Journal of Management, 12,* 295–318.

Alfredsson, L., & Theorell, T. (1983). Job characteristics of occupations and myocardial infarction risk: Effect of possible confounding factors. *Social Science and Medicine, 17,* 1497–1503.

Allen, N. J., & Meyer, J. P. (1990). The measurement and antecedents of affective, continuance, and normative commitment to the organization. *Journal of Occupational Psychology, 63,* 1–18.

Alley, W. E. (1994). Recent advances in classification theory and practice. In M. G. Rumsey, C. B. Walker, & J. H. Harris (Eds.), *Personnel selection and classification* (pp. 431–442). Hillsdale, NJ: Erlbaum.

Alliger, G. M., & Janak, E. A. (1989). Kirkpatrick's levels of training criteria: Thirty years later. *Personnel Psychology, 42,* 331–342.

Alliger, G. M., Tannenbaum, S. I., Bennett, W., Traver, H., & Shotland, A. (1997). A meta-analysis of the relations among training criteria. *Personnel Psychology, 50,* 341–358.

American Psychological Association. (1992). Ethical principles of psychologists and code of conduct. *American Psychologist, 47,* 1597–1611.

American Psychological Association. (1993). Profile of Division 14 members: 1993. Report prepared by the Office of Demographic, Employment, and Educational Research, American Psychological Association, Washington, DC.

Americans with Disabilities Act. (1990). P.L. 101–336, 104 Statute 327, 26 July.

Anderson, C. C., Warner, J. L., & Spencer, C. C. (1984). Inflation bias in self-assessment examinations: Implications for valid employee selection. *Journal of Applied Psychology, 69,* 574–580.

Anderson, J. R. (1985). *Cognitive psychology and its implications* (2nd ed.). New York: Freeman.

Anderson, L., & Wilson, S. (1997). Critical incident technique. In D. L. Whetzel & G. R. Wheaton (Eds.), *Applied measurement methods in industrial psychology* (pp. 89–112). Palo Alto, CA: Consulting Psychologists Press.

Annett, J. (1994). The learning of motor skills: Sports science and ergonomic perspectives. *Ergonomics, 37*, 5–16.

Appelbaum, E., & Batt, R. (1993). *High-performance work systems*. Washington, DC: Economic Policy Institute.

Argyris, C. (1968). Some unintended consequences of rigorous research. *Psychological Bulletin, 70*, 185–197.

Argyris, C. (1996). Actionable knowledge: Design causality in the service of consequential theory. *Journal of Applied Behavioral Science, 32*, 390–406.

Arthur, W., & Bennett, W. (1995). The international assignee: The relative importance of factors perceived to contribute to success. *Personnel Psychology, 48*, 99–114.

Arvey, R. D. (1986). Sex bias in job evaluation procedures. *Personnel Psychology, 39*, 315–335.

Arvey, R. D., & Bouchard, T. J., Jr. (1994). Genetics, twins, and organizational behavior. In B. M. Staw & L. L. Cummings (Eds.), *Research in organizational behavior* (Vol. 16, pp. 47–82). Greenwich, CT: JAI Press.

Arvey, R. D., & Campion, J. E. (1982). The employment interview: A summary and review of recent research. *Personnel Psychology, 35*, 281–322.

Arvey, R. D., Landon, T. E., Nutting, S. M., & Maxwell, S. E. (1992). Development of physical ability tests for police officers: A construct validation approach. *Journal of Applied Psychology, 77*, 996–1009.

Arvey, R. D., Passino, E. M., & Lounsbury, J. W. (1977). Job analysis results as influenced by sex of incumbent and sex of analyst. *Journal of Applied Psychology, 62*, 411–416.

Arvey, R. D., Renz, G. L., & Watson, T. W. (1998). Emotionality and job performance: Implications for personnel selection. In G. R. Ferris (Ed.), *Research in personnel and human resources management* (Vol. 16, pp. 103–147). Stamford, CT: JAI Press.

Aschoff, J. (1978). Features of circadian rhythms relevant to the design of shift schedules. *Ergonomics, 21*, 739–754.

Ashforth, B. E., & Humphrey, R. H. (1995). Emotions in the workplace: A reappraisal. *Human Relations, 48*, 97–125.

Atwater, L. E. (1998). The advantages and pitfalls of self-assessment in organizations. In J. W. Smither (Ed.), *Performance appraisal* (pp. 331–369). San Francisco: Jossey-Bass.

Austin, J. T., & Villanova, P. (1992). The criterion problem: 1917–1992. *Journal of Applied Psychology, 77*, 836–874.

Bakke, E. W. (1945). Why workers join unions. *Personnel, 22*, 37–46.

Baldwin, T. T., & Ford, J. K. (1988). Transfer of training: A review and directions for future research. *Personnel Psychology, 41*, 63–105.

Baldwin, T. T., & Magjuka, R. J. (1991). Organizational training and signals of importance: Effects of pre-training perceptions on intentions to transfer. *Human Resource Development, 2*(1), 25–36.

Baldwin, T. T., Magjuka, R. J., & Loher, B. T. (1991). The perils of participation: Effects of choice of training on trainee motivation and learning. *Personnel Psychology, 44*, 51–66.

Baldwin, T. T., & Padgett, M. Y. (1993). Management development: A review and commentary. In C. L. Cooper & I. T. Robertson (Eds.), *International review of industrial and organizational psychology* (Vol. 8, pp. 35–85). London: Wiley.

Balzer, W. K., Smith, P. C., & Kravitz, D. E. (1990). *User's manual for the JDI and J16 scales*. Bowling Green, OH: Bowling Green State University.

Balzer, W. K., & Sulsky, L. M. (1992). Halo and performance appraisal research. *Journal of Applied Psychology, 77*, 975–985.

Barling, J. (1990). *Employment, stress and family functioning*. Chicester: Wiley.

Barling, J. (1996). The prediction, experience, and consequence of workplace violence. In G. R. VandenBos & E. Q. Bulatao (Eds.), *Violence on the job* (pp. 29–50). Washington, DC: American Psychological Association.

Barling, J., & Boswell, R. (1995). Work performance and the achievement striving and impatience-irritability dimensions of Type A behavior. *Applied Psychology: An International Review, 44*, 143–153.

Barling, J., & Sorenson, D. (1997). Work and family: In search of a relevant research agenda. In C. L. Cooper & S. E. Jackson (Eds.), *Creating tomorrow's organizations* (pp. 157–170). New York: Wiley.

Barnett, G. A. (1988). Communication and organizational culture. In G. M. Goldhaber & G. A. Barnett (Eds.), *Handbook of organizational communication*. Norwood, NJ: Ablex.

Barrett, G. V., Alexander, R. A., & Doverspike, D. (1992). The implications for personnel selection of apparent declines in predictive validities over time: A critique of Hulin, Henry, and Noon. *Personnel Psychology, 45*, 601–617.

Barrett, G. V., Caldwell, M. S., & Alexander, R. A. (1985). The concept of dynamic criteria: A critical reanalysis. *Personnel Psychology, 38*, 41–56.

Barrick, M. R., & Mount, M. K. (1991). The big five personality dimensions and job performance: A meta-analysis. *Personnel Psychology, 44*, 1–26.

Barrick, M. R., Stewart, G. L., Neubert, M. J., & Mount, M. K. (1998). Relating member ability and personality to work-team processes and team effectiveness. *Journal of Applied Psychology, 83*, 377–391.

Barry, B., & Stewart, G. L. (1997). Composition, process, and performance in self-managed groups: The role of personality. *Journal of Applied Psychology, 82*, 62–78.

Bartlett, C. J. (1983). What's the difference between valid and invalid halo? Forced-choice measurement without forcing a choice. *Journal of Applied Psychology, 68*, 218–226.

Barton, J. (1994). Choosing to work at night: A moderating influence on individual tolerance to shiftwork. *Journal of Applied Psychology, 79*, 449–454.

Bartram, D. (1993). Emerging trends in computer-assisted assessment. In H. Schuler, J. L. Farr, & M. Smith (Eds.), *Personnel selection and assessment* (pp. 267–288). Hillsdale, NJ: Erlbaum.

Bashore, T. R., & Rapp, P. E. (1993). Are there alternatives to traditional polygraph procedures? *Psychological Bulletin, 113,* 3–22.

Bass, B. M. (1985). *Leadership and performance beyond expectations.* New York: Free Press.

Bass, B. M. (1997). Does the transactional-transformational leadership paradigm transcend organizational and national boundaries? *American Psychologist, 52,* 130–139.

Bass, B. M. (1998). *Transformational leadership.* Mahwah, NJ: Erlbaum.

Baumgartel, H., & Jeanpierre, F. (1972). Applying new knowledge in the back-home setting: A study of Indian managers' adaptive efforts. *Journal of Applied Behavioral Science, 8,* 674–694.

Baytos, L. (1986). The human resource side of acquisitions and divestitures. *Human Resource Planning, 9,* 167–175.

Bazerman, M. H., & Neale, M. A. (1982). Improving negotiation effectiveness under final offer arbitration: The role of selection and training. *Journal of Applied Psychology, 67,* 543–548.

Becker, B., & Gerhart, B. (1996). The impact of human resource management on organizational performance: Progress and prospects. *Academy of Management Journal, 39,* 779–801.

Becker, F., & Steele, F. (1995). *Workplace by design: Managing the high-performance workscape.* San Francisco: Jossey-Bass.

Becker, T. E., & Colquitt, A. L. (1992). Potential versus actual faking of a biodata form: An analysis along several dimensions of item type. *Personnel Psychology, 45,* 389–406.

Beirness, D. J. (1993). Do we really drive as we live? The role of personality factors in road crashes. *Alcohol, Drugs, and Driving, 9,* 129–143.

Benjamin, L. T. (1997). Organized industrial psychology before Division 14: The ACP and the AAAP (1930–1945). *Journal of Applied Psychology, 82,* 459–466.

Bennett, G. K. (1980). *Test of mechanical comprehension.* New York: Psychological Corporation.

Bennett, N., Blum, T. C., & Roman, P. M. (1994). Pressure of drug screening and employee assistance programs: Exclusive and inclusive human resource management practices. *Journal of Organizational Behavior, 15,* 549–560.

Ben-Shakhar, G., Bar-Hillel, M., Bilu, Y., Ben-Abba, E., & Flug, A. (1986). Can graphology predict occupational success? Two empirical studies and some methodological ruminations. *Journal of Applied Psychology, 71,* 645–653.

Berman, F. E., & Miner, J. B. (1985). Motivation to manage at the top executive level: A test of the hierarchic role-motivation theory. *Personnel Psychology, 38,* 377–391.

Bernardin, H. J., & Cooke, D. K. (1993). Validity of an honesty test in predicting theft among convenience store employees. *Academy of Management Journal, 36,* 1097–1108.

Bernardin, H. J., Hagan, C. M., Kane, J. S., & Villanova, P. (1998). Effective performance management. In J. W. Smither (Ed.), *Performance appraisal* (pp. 3–48). San Francisco: Jossey-Bass.

Bernardin, H. J., & Pence, E. C. (1980). Effects of rater training: Creating new response sets and decreasing accuracy. *Journal of Applied Psychology, 65,* 60–66.

Betz, E. L. (1984). Two tests of Maslow's theory of need fulfillment. *Journal of Vocational Behavior, 24,* 204–220.

Beyer, J. M., & Trice, H. M. (1987). How an organization's rites reveal its culture. *Organizational Dynamics, 15,* 5–24.

Bies, R. J., Tripp, T. M., & Kramer, R. M. (1997). At the breaking point. In R. A. Giacalone & J. Greenberg (Eds.), *Antisocial behavior in organizations* (pp. 18–36). Thousand Oaks, CA: Sage.

Bigoness, W. J. (1978). Correlates of faculty attitudes toward collective bargaining. *Journal of Applied Psychology, 63,* 228–233.

Bingham, W. V. (1917). Mentality testing of college students. *Journal of Applied Psychology, 1,* 38–45.

Binning, J. F., & Barrett, G. V. (1989). Validity of personnel decisions: A conceptual analysis of the inferential and evidential bases. *Journal of Applied Psychology, 74,* 478–494.

Birdwhistell, R. L. (1970). *Kinesics and context.* Philadelphia: University of Pennsylvania Press.

Black, J. S., & Mendenhall, M. (1990). Cross-cultural training effectiveness: A review and theoretical framework for future research. *Academy of Management Review, 15,* 113–136.

Blum, M. L., & Naylor, J. C. (1968). *Industrial psychology: Its theoretical and social foundations.* New York: Harper & Row.

Bobko, P. (1994). Issues in operational selection and classification systems: Comments and commonalities. In M. G. Rumsey, C. B. Walker, & J. H. Harris (Eds.), *Personnel selection and classification* (pp. 443–456). Hillsdale, NJ: Erlbaum.

Bobko, P., & Karren, R. (1979). The perception of Pearson product moment correlations from bivariate scatterplots. *Personnel Psychology, 32,* 313–326.

Boehm, V. R. (1980). Research in the "real world"—A conceptual model. *Personnel Psychology, 33,* 495–504.

Bok, D., & Dunlop, J. (1970). *Labor and the American community.* New York: Simon & Schuster.

Bommer, W. H., Johnson, J., Rich, G. A., Podsakoff, P. M., & MacKenzie, S. B. (1995). On the interchangeability of objective and subjective measures of employee performance: A meta-analysis. *Personnel Psychology, 48,* 587–605.

Bond, M. H., & Smith, P. B. (1996). Cross-cultural social and organizational psychology. *Annual Review of Psychology, 47,* 205–235.

Borman, W. C. (1974). The rating of individuals in organizations: An alternative approach. *Organizational Behavior and Human Performance, 12,* 105–124.

Borman, W. C. (1978). Exploring upper limits of reliability and validity in performance ratings. *Journal of Applied Psychology, 63,* 135–144.

Borman, W. C. (1982). Validity of behavioral assessment for predicting military recruiter performance. *Journal of Applied Psychology, 67,* 3–9.

Borman, W. C. (1991). Job behavior, performance, and effectiveness. In M. D. Dunnette & L. M. Hough (Eds.), *Handbook of industrial and organizational psychology* (2nd ed., Vol. 2, pp. 271–326). Palo Alto, CA: Consulting Psychologists Press.

Borman, W. C., Hanson, M. A., & Hedge, J. W. (1997). Personnel selection. *Annual Review of Psychology, 48,* 299–337.

Borman, W. C., & Motowidlo, S. J. (1993). Expanding the criterion domain to include elements of contextual performance. In N. Schmitt & W. C. Borman (Eds.), *Personnel selection in organizations* (pp. 71–98). San Francisco: Jossey-Bass.

Borman, W. C., White, L. A., & Dorsey, D. W. (1995). Effects of ratee task performance and interpersonal factors on supervisor and peer performance in ratings. *Journal of Applied Psychology, 80,* 168–177.

Bramel, D., & Friend, R. (1981). Hawthorne, the myth of the docile worker, and class bias in psychology. *American Psychologist, 36,* 867–878.

Brand, C. (1987). The importance of general intelligence. In S. Modgil & C. Modgil (Eds.), *Arthur Jensen: Consensus and controversy.* New York: Falmer.

Breaugh, J. A. (1983). The 12-hour work day: Differing employee reactions. *Personnel Psychology, 36,* 277–288.

Brenner, M. H., & Mooney, A. (1983). Unemployment and health in the context of economic change. *Social Science and Medicine, 17,* 1125–1138.

Brett, J. M. (1980). Behavioral research on unions and union management systems. In B. M. Staw & L. L. Cummings (Eds.), *Research in organizational behavior* (Vol. 2). Greenwich, CT: JAI Press.

Brett, J. M., Goldberg, S. B., & Ury, W. L. (1990). Designing systems for resolving disputes in organizations. *American Psychologist, 45,* 162–170.

Brett, J. M., Tinsley, C. H., Janssens, M., Barsness, Z. I., & Lytle, A. L. (1997). New approaches to the study of culture in industrial/organizational psychology. In P. C. Earley & M. Erez (Eds.), *New perspectives on international industrial/organizational psychology* (pp. 75–129). San Francisco: New Lexington Press.

Brief, A. P., & Hayes, E. L. (1997). The continuing "American dilemma": Studying racism in organizations. In C. L. Cooper & D. M. Rousseau (Eds.), *Trends in organizational behavior* (Vol. 4, pp. 89–106). London: Wiley.

Brief, A. P., & Motowidlo, S. J. (1986). Prosocial organizational behavior. *Academy of Management Review, 11,* 710–725.

Brief, A. P., & Rude, D. E. (1981). Voting in a union certification election: A conceptual analysis. *Academy of Management Review, 6,* 261–267.

Brockner, J., Davy, J., & Carter, C. (1985). Layoffs, self-esteem, and survivor guilt: Motivational, affective, and attitudinal consequences. *Organizational Behavior and Human Decision Processes, 36,* 229–244.

Brockner, J., & Greenberg, J. (1990). The impact of layoffs on survivors: An occupational justice perspective. In J. Carroll (Ed.), *Applied social psychology and organizational settings* (pp. 45–75). Hillsdale, NJ: Erlbaum.

Brown, B. K., & Campion, M. A. (1994). Biodata phenomenology: Recruiters' perceptions and use of biographical information in resume screening. *Journal of Applied Psychology, 79,* 897–908.

Brown, S. P. (1996). A meta-analysis and review of organizational research in job involvement. *Psychological Bulletin, 120,* 235–255.

Bruno, F. (1994). Drug and alcohol problems in the workplace in Italy. *Journal of Drug Issues, 24,* 697–713.

Bryan, W. L. (1904). Theory and practice. *Psychological Review, 11,* 71–82.

Bryan, W. L., & Harter, N. (1897). Studies in the physiology and psychology of the telegraphic language. *Psychological Review, 4,* 27–53.

Bryan, W. L., & Harter, N. (1899). Studies of the telegraphic language. *Psychological Review, 6,* 345–375.

Bulatao, E. Q., & VandenBos, G. R. (1996). Workplace violence: Its scope and the issues. In G. R. VandenBos & E. Q. Bulatao (Eds.), *Violence on the job* (pp. 1–24). Washington, DC: American Psychological Association.

Buono, A. F., & Bowditch, J. L. (1989). *The human side of mergers and acquisitions: Managing collision between people, cultures, and organizations.* San Francisco: Jossey-Bass.

Burke, M. J., & Day, R. R. (1986). A cumulative study of the effectiveness of managerial training. *Journal of Applied Psychology, 71,* 232–246.

Buss, T. F., & Redburn, F. S. (1987). Plant closings: Impacts and responses. *Economic Development Quarterly, 1,* 170–177.

Camara, W. J., & Schneider, D. L. (1994). Integrity tests: Facts and unresolved issues. *American Psychologist, 49,* 112–119.

Cameron, K. (1982). The relationship between faculty unionism and organizational effectiveness. *Academy of Management Journal, 25,* 6–24.

Campbell, D. J., & Lee, C. (1988). Self-appraisal in performance evaluation: Development versus evaluation. *Academy of Management Review, 13,* 302–314.

Campbell, J. P. (1990a). An overview of the Army selection and classification project. *Personnel Psychology, 43,* 231–240.

Campbell, J. P. (1990b). The role of theory in industrial and organizational psychology. In M. D. Dunnette & L. M. Hough (Eds.), *Handbook of industrial and organizational psychology* (2nd ed., Vol. 1, pp. 39–74). Palo Alto, CA: Consulting Psychologists Press.

Campbell, J. P. (1996). Group differences and personnel decisions: Validity, fairness, and affirmative action. *Journal of Vocational Behavior, 49,* 122–158.

Campbell, J. P., McCloy, R. A., Oppler, S. H., & Sager, C. E. (1993). A theory of performance. In N. Schmitt & W. C. Borman (Eds.), *Personnel selection in organizations* (pp. 35–70). San Francisco: Jossey-Bass.

Campion, J. E. (1972). Work sampling for personnel selection. *Journal of Applied Psychology, 56,* 40–44.

Campion, M. A. (1988). Interdisciplinary approaches to job design: A constructive replication with extensions. *Journal of Applied Psychology, 73,* 467–481.

Campion, M. A. (1989). Ability requirement implications of job design: An interdisciplinary perspective. *Personnel Psychology, 42,* 1–24.

Campion, M. A. (1991). Meaning and measurement of turnover: Comparison of alternative measures and recommendations for research. *Journal of Applied Psychology, 76,* 199–212.

Campion, M. A., & Berger, C. J. (1990). Conceptual integration and empirical test of job design and compensation relationships. *Personnel Psychology, 43,* 525–554.

Campion, M. A., & Campion, J. E. (1987). Evaluation of an interviewee skills training program in a natural field experiment. *Personnel Psychology, 40,* 675–691.

Campion, M. A., Cheraskin, L., & Stevens, M. J. (1994). Career-related antecedents and outcomes of job rotation. *Academy of Management Journal, 37,* 1518–1542.

Campion, M. A., & McClelland, C. L. (1991). Interdisciplinary examination of the costs and benefits of enlarged jobs: A job design quasi-experiment. *Journal of Applied Psychology, 76,* 186–198.

Campion, M. A., & McClelland, C. L. (1993). Follow-up and extension of the interdisciplinary costs and benefits of enlarged jobs. *Journal of Applied Psychology, 78,* 339–351.

Campion, M. A., Palmer, D. K., & Campion, J. E. (1997). A review of structure in the selection interview. *Personnel Psychology, 50,* 655–702.

Campion, M. A., Papper, E. M., & Medsker, G. J. (1996). Relations between work team characteristics and effectiveness: A replication and extension. *Personnel Psychology, 49,* 429–452.

Campion, M. A., & Thayer, P. W. (1985). Development and field evaluation of an interdisciplinary measure of job design. *Journal of Applied Psychology, 70,* 29–43.

Cannon-Bowers, J. A., & Salas, E. (1997). A framework for developing team performance measures in training. In M. T. Brannick, E. Salas, & C. Prince (Eds.), *Team performance assessment and measurement: Theory, methods, and applications* (pp. 45–62). Mahwah, NJ: Erlbaum.

Cardy, R. L. (1988). Performance appraisal in a quality context: A new look at an old problem. In J. W. Smither (Ed.), *Performance appraisal* (pp. 132–162). San Francisco: Jossey-Bass.

Carillon, J. W., & Sutton, R. I. (1982). The relationship between union effectiveness and the quality of members' worklife. *Journal of Occupational Behavior, 3,* 171–179.

Carling, P. (1994). Reasonable accommodations in the workplace for persons with psychiatric disabilities. In S. M. Bruyere & J. O'Keeffe (Eds.), *Implications of the Americans with Disabilities Act for psychology* (pp. 103–136). New York: Springer.

Carlson, R. E. (1968). Employment decisions: Effect of mode of applicant presentation on some outcome measures. *Personnel Psychology, 21,* 193–207.

Carnevale, A. P. (1995). Enhancing skills in the new economy. In A. Howard (Ed.), *The changing nature of work* (pp. 238–251). San Francisco: Jossey-Bass.

Carson, K. P., Becker, J. S., & Henderson, J. A. (1998). Is utility really futile? A failure to replicate and an extension. *Journal of Applied Psychology, 83,* 84–96.

Carsten, J. M., & Spector, P. E. (1987). Unemployment, job satisfaction, and employee turnover: A meta-analytic test of the Muchinsky model. *Journal of Applied Psychology, 72,* 374–381.

Cartwright, S., & Cooper, C. L. (1994). The human effect of mergers and acquisitions. In C. L. Cooper & D. M. Rousseau (Eds.), *Trends in organizational behavior* (pp. 47–62). New York: Wiley.

Cascio, W. F. (1976). Turnover, biographical data, and fair employment practice. *Journal of Applied Psychology, 61,* 576–580.

Cascio, W. F. (1982). *Applied psychology in personnel management* (2nd ed.). Reston, VA: Reston.

Cascio, W. F. (1989). Using utility analyses to assess training outcomes. In I. L. Goldstein (Ed.), *Training and development in organizations* (pp. 63–88). San Francisco: Jossey-Bass.

Cascio, W. F. (1993). Assessing the utility of selection decisions: Theoretical and practical considerations. In N. Schmitt & W. C. Borman (Eds.), *Personnel selection in organizations* (pp. 310–340). San Francisco: Jossey-Bass.

Cascio, W. F. (1995). Whither industrial and organizational psychology in a changing world of work? *American Psychologist, 50,* 928–939.

Cascio, W. F. (1998). *Managing human resources* (5th ed.). New York: McGraw-Hill.

Cascio, W. F., Alexander, R. A., & Barrett, G. V. (1988). Setting cutoff scores: Legal, psychometric, and professional issues and guidelines. *Personnel Psychology, 41,* 1–24.

Cascio, W. F., & Phillips, N. F. (1979). Performance testing: A rose among thorns? *Personnel Psychology, 32,* 751–766.

Castellow, W. A., Wuensch, K. L., & Moore, C. H. (1990). Effects of physical attractiveness of the plaintiff and defendant in sexual harassment judgments. *Journal of Social Behavior and Personality, 15,* 547–562.

Cederblom, D. (1982). The performance appraisal interview: A review, implications and suggestions. *Academy of Management Review, 7,* 219–227.

Cederblom, D., & Lounsbury, J. W. (1980). An investigation of user acceptance of peer evaluations. *Personnel Psychology, 33,* 567–580.

Chalykoff, J., & Kochan, T. A. (1989). Computer-aided monitoring: Its influence on employee job satisfaction and turnover. *Personnel Psychology, 42,* 807–834.

Chao, G. T., & Kozlowski, S. W. (1986). Employee perceptions on the implementation of robotic manufacturing technology. *Journal of Applied Psychology, 71,* 70–76.

Chao, G. T., Walz, P. M., & Gardner, P. D. (1992). Formal and informal mentorships: A comparison on mentoring functions and contrast with nonmentored counterparts. *Personnel Psychology, 45,* 619–636.

Chapanis, A., Garner, W. R., & Morgan, C. T. (1949). *Applied experimental psychology.* New York: Wiley.

Chemers, M. M., & Murphy, S. E. (1995). Leadership and diversity in groups and organizations. In M. M. Chemers, S. Oskamp, & M. A. Costanzo (Eds.), *Diversity in organizations: New perspectives for a changing workforce* (pp. 157–188). Thousand Oaks, CA: Sage.

Childs, A., & Klimoski, R. J. (1986). Successfully predicting career success: An application of the biographical inventory. *Journal of Applied Psychology, 71,* 3–8.

Clegg, C., & Wall, T. (1990). The relationship between simplified jobs and mental health: A replication study. *Journal of Occupational Psychology, 63,* 289–296.

Cleveland, J. N., & Kerst, M. E. (1993). Sexual harassment and perceptions of power: An under-articulated relationship. *Journal of Vocational Behavior, 42,* 49–67.

Clifford, J. P. (1994). Job analysis: Why do it, and how should it be done? *Public Personnel Management, 23,* 321–338.

Cobb, S., & Kasl, S. V. (1977). *Termination: The consequence of job loss.* U.S. Department of Health, Education and Welfare. Washington, DC: U.S. Government Printing Office.

Cohen, A. (1977). Factors in successful occupational safety programs. *Journal of Safety Research, 9,* 168–178.

Cohen, D. J. (1990, November). What motivates trainees? *Training and Development Journal,* 91–93.

Cole, N. D., & Latham, G. P. (1997). Effects of training in procedural justice on perceptions of disciplinary fairness by unionized employees and disciplinary subject matter experts. *Journal of Applied Psychology, 82,* 699–705.

Collins, J. M., & Muchinsky, P. M. (1993). An assessment of the construct validity of three job evaluation methods: A field experiment. *Academy of Management Journal, 36,* 895–904.

Collins, J. M., & Schmidt, F. L. (1993). Personality, integrity, and white collar crime: A construct validity study. *Personnel Psychology, 46,* 295–311.

Conger, J. A. (1989). *The charismatic leader: Behind the mystique of exceptional leadership.* San Francisco: Jossey-Bass.

Conger, J. A., & Kanungo, R. N. (1987). Toward a behavioral theory of charismatic leadership in organizational settings. *Academy of Management Review, 12,* 637–647.

Conley, P. R., & Sackett, P. R. (1987). Effects of using high-versus low-performing job incumbents as sources of job analysis information. *Journal of Applied Psychology, 72,* 434–437.

Cooper, D. (1998). *Improving safety culture.* Chichester: Wiley.

Cooper, W. H. (1981). Ubiquitous halo. *Psychological Bulletin, 90,* 218–244.

Cornelius, E. T., DeNisi, A. S., & Blencoe, A. G. (1984). Expert and naive raters using the PAQ: Does it matter? *Personnel Psychology, 37,* 453–464.

Costa, G. (1996). The impact of shift and night work on health. *Applied Ergonomics, 27,* 9–16.

Costa, P. T. (1996). Work and personality: Use of the NEO-PI-R in industrial/organizational psychology. *Applied Psychology: An International Review, 45,* 225–241.

Covey, S. R., Merrill, A. R., & Merrill, R. R. (1994). *First things first.* New York: Simon & Schuster.

Cox, T., & Leather, P. (1994). The prevention of violence at work: Application of a cognitive behavioral theory. In C. L. Cooper & I. T. Robertson (Eds.), *International review of industrial and organizational psychology* (Vol. 9, pp. 213–245). London: Wiley.

Cronshaw, S. F. (1997). Lo! The stimulus speaks: The insider's view of Whyte and Latham's "The futility of utility analysis." *Personnel Psychology, 50,* 611–616.

Cropanzano, R., & Greenberg, J. (1997). Progress in organizational justice: Tunneling through the maze. In C. L. Cooper & I. T. Robertson (Eds.), *International review of industrial and organizational psychology* (Vol. 12, pp. 317–372). Chichester: Wiley.

Cunningham, M. R., Wong, D. T., & Barbee, A. P. (1994). Self-presentation dynamics on overt integrity tests: Experimental studies of the Reid Report. *Journal of Applied Psychology, 79,* 643–658.

Daft, R. L. (1983). Learning the craft of organizational research. *Academy of Management Review, 8,* 539–546.

Dalton, D. R., & Mesch, D. J. (1990). The impact of flexible scheduling on employee attendance and turnover. *Administrative Science Quarterly, 35,* 370–387.

Damos, D. L., & Parker, E. S. (1996). Methodological issues in the study of HIV+ individuals. *Applied Ergonomics, 27,* 165–170.

Daniel, M. H. (1997). Intelligence testing. *American Psychologist, 52,* 1038–1045.

Dansereau, F., Graen, G., & Haga, W. (1975). A vertical dyad linkage approach to leadership in formal organizations. *Organizational Behavior and Human Performance, 13,* 46–78.

Davis, D. D. (1995). Form, function, and strategy in boundaryless organizations. In A. Howard (Ed.), *The changing nature of work* (pp. 112–138). San Francisco: Jossey-Bass.

Davis, G. F., & Powell, W. W. (1992). Organization–environment relations. In M. D. Dunnette & L. M. Hough (Eds.), *Handbook of industrial and organizational psychology* (2nd ed., Vol. 3, pp. 315–375). Palo Alto, CA: Consulting Psychologists Press.

Day, D. V., & Sulsky, L. M. (1995). Effects of frame-of-reference training and information configuration on memory organization and rater accuracy. *Journal of Applied Psychology, 80,* 158–167.

Deadrick, D. L., & Madigan, R. M. (1990). Dynamic criteria revisited: A longitudinal study of performance stability and predictive validity. *Personnel Psychology, 43,* 717–744.

Deal, T., & Kennedy, A. (1982). *Corporate cultures.* Reading, MA: Addison-Wesley.

DeCotiis, T. A., & LeLouarn, J. Y. (1981). A predictive study of voting behavior in a representation election using union instrumentality and work perceptions. *Organizational Behavior and Human Performance, 27*, 103–118.

Dedobbeleer, N., & Beland, F. (1991). A safety climate measure for construction sites. *Journal of Safety Research, 22*, 97–103.

DeMeuse, K. P. (1987). Employee nonverbal cues: Their effects on the performance appraisal process. *Journal of Occupational Psychology, 60*, 207–216.

DeNisi, A. S., & Peters, L. H. (1996). Organization of information in memory and the performance appraisal process: Evidence from the field. *Journal of Applied Psychology, 81*, 717–737.

Dickinson, T. L. (1993). Attitudes about performance appraisal. In H. Schuler, J. L. Farr, & M. Smith (Eds.), *Personnel selection and assessment* (pp. 141–162). Hillsdale, NJ: Erlbaum.

Dienesch, R. M., & Liden, R. C. (1986). Leader-member exchange model of leadership: A critique and further development. *Academy of Management Review, 11*, 618–634.

Digman, J. M., & Takemoto-Chock, N. K. (1981). Factors in the natural language of personality: Re-analysis and comparison of six major studies. *Multivariate Behavioral Research, 16*, 149–170.

Dipboye, R. L. (1990). Laboratory vs. field research in industrial and organizational psychology. In C. L. Cooper & I. T. Robertson (Eds.), *International review of industrial and organizational psychology* (Vol. 5, pp. 1–34). London: Wiley.

Dipboye, R. L. (1997). Structured selection interviews: Why do they work? Why are they underutilized? In N. Anderson & P. Herriot (Eds.), *International handbook of selection and assessment* (pp. 455–473). Chichester: Wiley.

Dirks, K. T., Cummings, L. L., & Pierce, J. L. (1996). Psychological ownership in organizations: Conditions under which individuals promote and resist change. In R. W. Woodman & W. A. Pasmore (Eds.), *Research in organizational change and development* (Vol. 9, pp. 1–24). Greenwich, CT: JAI Press.

Dompierre, J., & Lavoie, F. (1994). Subjective work stress and family violence. In G. P. Keita & J. J. Hurrell (Eds.), *Job stress in a changing workforce* (pp. 213–228). Washington, DC: American Psychological Association.

Dossett, D. L., & Hulvershorn, P. (1983). Increasing technical training efficiency: Peer training via computer-assisted instruction. *Journal of Applied Psychology, 68*, 552–558.

Dotlich, D. L. (1982, October). International and intracultural management development. *Training and Development Journal, 36*, 26–31.

Dovidio, J. F., & Gaertner, S. L. (1996). Affirmative action, unintentional racial biases, and intergroup relations. *Journal of Social Issues, 52*, 51–75.

Drakely, R. J., Herriot, P., & Jones, A. (1988). Biographical data, training success, and turnover. *Journal of Occupational Psychology, 61*, 145–152.

Dreher, G. F., & Ash, R. A. (1990). A comparative study of mentoring among men and women in managerial, pro-

fessional, and technical positions. *Journal of Applied Psychology, 75*, 539–546.

Dreher, G. F., Ash, R. A., & Hancock, P. (1988). The role of the traditional research design in underestimating the validity of the employment interview. *Personnel Psychology, 41*, 315–328.

Drucker, P. F. (1993). *Post-capitalist society.* New York: Harper.

Duchon, J. C., Keran, C. M., & Smith, T. J. (1994). Extended workdays in an underground mine: A work performance analysis. *Human Factors, 36*, 258–268.

Dulebohn, J. H. (1997). Social influences in justice evaluations of human resources systems. In G. R. Ferris (Ed.), *Research in personnel and human resources management* (Vol. 15, pp. 241–292). Greenwich, CT: JAI Press.

Dunham, R. B. (1977). Shift work: A review and theoretical analysis. *Academy of Management Review, 2*, 626–634.

Dunham, R. B., Grube, J. A., & Castaneda, M. B. (1994). Organizational commitment: The utility of an integrated definition. *Journal of Applied Psychology, 79*, 370–380.

Dunham, R. B., Pierce, J. L., & Castaneda, M. B. (1987). Alternative work schedules: Two field quasi-experiments. *Personnel Psychology, 40*, 215–242.

Dunn, W. S., Mount, M. K., Barrick, M. R., & Ones, D. S. (1995). Relative importance of personality and general mental ability in managers' judgments of applicant qualifications. *Journal of Applied Psychology, 80*, 500–509.

Dunnette, M. D. (1993). My hammer or your hammer? *Human Resource Management, 32*, 373–384.

Dunnette, M. D., & Hough, L. M. (Eds.) (1990). *Handbook of industrial and organizational psychology* (2nd ed., Vol. 1). Palo Alto, CA: Consulting Psychologists Press.

Eagly, A. H., Karau, S. J., & Makhijani, M. G. (1995). Gender and the effectiveness of leaders: A meta-analysis. *Psychological Bulletin, 117*, 125–145.

Eagly, A. H., Makhijani, M. G., & Klonsky, B. G. (1992). Gender and the evaluation of leaders: A meta-analysis. *Psychological Bulletin, 111*, 3–22.

Earley, P. C. (1997). Doing an about-face: Social motivation and cross-cultural currents. In P. C. Earley & M. Erez (Eds.), *New perspectives on international industrial/organizational psychology* (pp. 243–255). San Francisco: New Lexington Press.

Earley, P. C., & Randel, A. E. (1997). Culture without borders: An individual-level approach to cross-cultural research in organizational behavior. In C. L. Cooper & S. E. Jackson (Eds.), *Creating tomorrow's organizations* (pp. 59–74). New York: Wiley.

Ebel, R. L. (1972). *Essentials of educational measurement.* Englewood Cliffs, NJ: Prentice Hall.

Eby, L. T. (1997). Alternative forms of mentoring in changing organizational environments: A conceptual extension of the mentoring literature. *Journal of Vocational Behavior, 51*, 125–144.

Ellis, H. D. (1982). The effect of cold on the performance of serial choice reaction time and various discrete tasks. *Human Factors, 24*, 589–598.

Enander, A. (1987). Effects of moderate cold on performance of psychomotor and cognitive tasks. *Ergonomics, 30*, 1431–1445.

England, P. (1992). *Comparable worth: Theories and evidence.* Hawthorne, NY: Aldine de Gruyter.

Equal Employment Opportunity Commission. (1980). Discrimination because of sex under Title VII of the Civil Rights Act of 1964, as amended; adoption of interim interpretive guidelines. *Federal Register, 45*, 25024–25025.

Erez, M. (1994). Toward a model of cross-cultural industrial and organizational psychology. In H. C. Triandis, M. D. Dunnette, & L. M. Hough (Eds.), *Handbook of industrial and organizational psychology* (2nd ed., Vol. 4, pp. 559–608). Palo Alto, CA: Consulting Psychologists Press.

Erez, M. (1997). A culture-based model of work motivation. In P. C. Earley & M. Erez (Eds.), *New perspectives on international industrial/organizational psychology* (pp. 193–242). San Francisco: New Lexington Press.

Erez, M., & Earley, P. C. (1993). *Culture, self-identity, and work.* New York: Oxford University Press.

Erickson, E. H. (1963). *Childhood and society* (2nd ed.). New York: Norton.

Estey, M. (1981). *The unions: Structure, development, and management* (3rd ed.). New York: Harcourt Brace Jovanovich.

Fagenson, E. A. (1989). The mentor advantage: Perceived career/job experiences of proteges versus non-proteges. *Journal of Organizational Behavior, 10*, 309–320.

Farr, J. L., & Tesluk, P. E. (1997). Bruce V. Moore: First president of Division 14. *Journal of Applied Psychology, 82*, 478–485.

Ferdman, B. M. (1992). The dynamics of ethnic diversity in organizations: Toward integrative models. In K. Kelly (Ed.), *Issues, theory, and research in industrial/organization psychology* (pp. 339–384). Amsterdam: North Holland.

Ferguson, L. W. (1962). *The heritage of industrial psychology.* Hartford, CT: Finlay.

Fetterman, D. M. (1998). Ethnography. In L. Bickman & D. J. Rog (Eds.), *Handbook of applied social research methods* (pp. 473–504). Thousand Oaks, CA: Sage.

Feuille, P., & Blandin, J. (1974). Faculty job satisfaction and bargaining sentiment: A case study. *Academy of Management Journal, 17*, 678–692.

Fiedler, F. E. (1996). Research on leadership selection and training: One view of the future. *Administrative Science Quarterly, 41*, 241–250.

Fiedler, F. E., & Garcia, J. E. (1987). *New approaches to leadership: Cognitive resources and organizational performance.* New York: Wiley.

Fields, M. W., & Thacker, J. W. (1992). Influence of quality of work life on company and union commitment. *Academy of Management Journal, 35*, 439–450.

Fine, B. J., & Kobrick, J. L. (1978). Effects of altitude and heat on complex cognitive tasks. *Human Factors, 20*, 115–122.

Fine, S. (1989). *Functional job analysis scales: A desk aid* (rev. ed.). Orlando, FL: Dryden.

Finholt, T. A. (1997). The electronic office. In C. L. Cooper & D. M. Rousseau (Eds.), *Trends in organizational behavior* (Vol. 4, pp. 29–42). London: Wiley.

Fitzgerald, L. F., Drasgow, F., Hulin, C. L., Gelfand, M. J., & Magley, V. J. (1997). Antecedents and consequences of sexual harassment in organizations: A test of an integrated model. *Journal of Applied Psychology, 82*, 578–589.

Flanagan, M. F., & Dipboye, R. L. (1981). Research settings in industrial and organizational psychology: Facts, fallacies, and the future. *Personnel Psychology, 34*, 37–47.

Fleishman, E. A., & Quaintance, M. K. (1984). *Taxonomies of human performance.* Orlando, FL: Academic Press.

Folger, R., & Baron, R. A. (1996). Violence and hostility at work: A model of reactions to perceived injustice. In G. R. VandenBos & E. Q. Bulatao (Eds.), *Violence on the job* (pp. 51–86). Washington, DC: American Psychological Association.

Folger, R., & Greenberg, J. (1985). Procedural justice: An interpretive analysis of personnel systems. In K. Rowland & G. Ferris (Eds.), *Research in personnel and human resources management* (Vol. 3, pp. 141–183). Greenwich, CT: JAI Press.

Ford, J. K., Quinones, M., Sego, D., & Speer, J. (1991). *Factors affecting the opportunity to use trained skills on the job.* Paper presented at the 6th annual conference of the Society for Industrial and Organizational Psychology, St. Louis.

Foti, R. J., & Lord, R. G. (1987). Prototypes and scripts: The effects of alternative methods of processing information on rating accuracy. *Organizational Behavior and Human Decision Processes, 39*, 318–340.

Fox, W. F. (1967). Human performance in the cold. *Human Factors, 9*, 203–220.

Frankenhaeuser, M. (1988). Stress and reactivity patterns at different stages of the life cycle. In P. Pancheri & L. Zichella (Eds.), *Biorhythms and stress in physiopathology of reproduction.* Washington, DC: Hemisphere.

Freeberg, N. E. (1976). Criterion measures for youth-work training programs: The development of relevant performance dimensions. *Journal of Applied Psychology, 61*, 537–545.

Freeman, R. E. (1990). Ethics in the workplace: Recent scholarships. In C. L. Cooper & I. T. Robertson (Eds.), *International review of industrial and organizational psychology* (Vol. 5, pp. 149–168). London: Wiley.

Freese, M. (1987). Human–computer interaction in the office. In C. L. Cooper & I. T. Robertson (Eds.), *International review of industrial and organizational psychology* (Vol. 2, pp. 117–165). London: Wiley.

Freese, M., & Okonek, K. (1984). Reasons to leave shiftwork and psychological and psychosomatic complaints of former shiftworkers. *Journal of Applied Psychology, 69*, 509–514.

French, J. R. P., & Raven, B. (1960). The basis of social power. In D. Cartwright & A. F. Zander (Eds.), *Group dynamics* (2nd ed.). Evanston, IL: Row & Peterson.

Fretz, B. R., & Mills, D. H. (1980). *Licensing and certification of psychologists and counselors*. San Francisco: Jossey-Bass.

Fried, Y., & Ferris, G. R. (1987). The validity of the job characteristics model: A review and meta-analysis. *Personnel Psychology, 40,* 287–322.

Friedman, D. E., & Galinsky, E. (1992). Work and family issues: A legitimate business concern. In S. Zedeck (Ed.), *Work, families, and organizations* (pp. 168–207). San Francisco: Jossey-Bass.

Friedman, L., & Harvey, R. J. (1986). Factors of union commitment: The case for a lower dimensionality. *Journal of Applied Psychology, 71,* 371–376.

Friedman, L. N., Tucker, S. B., Neville, P. R., & Imperial, M. (1996). The impact of domestic violence on the workplace. In G. R. VandenBos and E. Q. Bulatao (Eds.), *Violence on the job* (pp. 153–162). Washington, DC: American Psychological Association.

Frone, M. R., Russell, M., & Cooper, M. L. (1992a). Antecedents and outcomes of work–family conflict: Testing a model of the work–family interface. *Journal of Applied Psychology, 77,* 65–78.

Frone, M. R., Russell, M., & Cooper, M. L. (1992b). Prevalence of work–family conflict: Are work and family boundaries asymmetrically permeable? *Journal of Organizational Behavior, 13,* 723–729.

Frost, P. J., & Jamal, M. (1979). Shift work, attitudes and reported behaviors: Some association between individual characteristics and hours of work and leisure. *Journal of Applied Psychology, 64,* 77–81.

Fryer, D., & Payne, R. (1986). Being unemployed: A review of the literature on the psychological experience of unemployment. In C. L. Cooper & I. Robertson (Eds.), *International review of industrial and organizational psychology* (Vol. 1, pp. 235–278). London: Wiley.

Fryxell, G. E., & Gordon, M. E. (1989). Workplace justice and job satisfaction as predictors of satisfaction with union and management. *Academy of Management Journal, 32,* 851–866.

Fullagar, C., & Barling, J. (1989). A longitudinal test of a model of the antecedents and consequences of union loyalty. *Journal of Applied Psychology, 74,* 213–227.

Fullagar, C., Clark, P. F., Gallagher, D. G., & Gordon, M. E. (1994). A model of the antecedents of early union commitment: The role of socialization experiences and steward characteristics. *Journal of Organizational Behavior, 15,* 517–533.

Fullagar, C., Gallagher, D. G., Gordon, M. E., & Clark, P. F. (1995). Impact of early socialization on union commitment and participation: A longitudinal study. *Journal of Applied Psychology, 80,* 147–157.

Fulmer, R. (1986). Meeting the merger integration challenge with management development. *Journal of Management Development, 5,* 7–16.

Furnham, A., & Gunter, B. (1993). Corporate culture: Definition, diagnosis and change. In C. L. Cooper & I. T. Robertson (Eds.), *International review of industrial and organizational psychology* (Vol. 8, pp. 234–261). London: Wiley.

Gabany, S. G., Plummer, P., & Grigg, P. (1997). Why drivers speed: The Speeding Perception Inventory. *Journal of Safety Research, 28,* 29–36.

Gardner, W. L., & Avolio, B. J. (1998). The charismatic relationship: A dramaturgical perspective. *Academy of Management Review, 23,* 32–58.

Garvin, D. A. (1986). Quality problems, policies, and attitudes in the United States and Japan: An exploratory study. *Academy of Management Journal, 29,* 653–673.

Geen, R. G. (1990). *Human aggression*. London: Open University Press.

George, J. M., & Brief, A. P. (1996). Motivational agendas in the workplace: The effects of feelings on focus of attention and work motivation. In B. M. Staw & L. L. Cummings (Eds.), *Research in organizational behavior* (Vol. 18, pp. 75–109). Greenwich, CT: JAI Press.

Gerhart, B., & Milkovich, G. T. (1992). Employee compensation: Research and practice. In M. D. Dunnette & L. M. Hough (Eds.), *Handbook of industrial and organizational psychology* (2nd ed., Vol. 3, pp. 481–569). Palo Alto, CA: Consulting Psychologists Press.

Gerstner, C. R., & Day, D. V. (1997). Meta-analytic review of leader–member exchange theory: Correlations and construct issues. *Journal of Applied Psychology, 82,* 827–844.

Ghiselli, E. E., & Brown, C. W. (1955). *Personnel and industrial psychology*. New York: McGraw-Hill.

Gifford, R., Ng, C. F., & Wilkinson, M. (1985). Nonverbal cues in the employment interview: Links between applicant qualities and interviewer judgments. *Journal of Applied Psychology, 70,* 729–736.

Gilliland, S. W. (1993). The perceived fairness of selection systems: An organizational justice perspective. *Academy of Management Review, 18,* 694–734.

Goktepe, J. R., & Schneier, C. E. (1989). Role of sex, gender roles, and attraction in predicting emergent leaders. *Journal of Applied Psychology, 74,* 165–167.

Goldberg, S. L., Mastaglio, T. W., & Johnson, W. R. (1995). Training in the close combat tactical trainer. In R. J. Seidel & P. R. Chatelier (Eds.), *Learning without boundaries: Technology to support distance/distributed learning* (pp. 119–133). New York: Plenum.

Goldstein, I. L. (1978). The pursuit of validity in the evaluation of training programs. *Human Factors, 20,* 131–144.

Goldstein, I. L. (1980). Training in work organizations. *Annual Review of Psychology, 31,* 229–272.

Goldstein, I. L. (1991). Training in work organizations. In M. D. Dunnette & L. M. Hough (Eds.), *Handbook of industrial and organizational psychology* (2nd ed., Vol. 2, pp. 507–619). Palo Alto, CA: Consulting Psychologists Press.

Goldstein, I. L. (1993). *Training and organizations: Needs assessment, development and evaluation.* Pacific Grove, CA: Brooks/Cole.

Goldstein, I. L., & Gilliam, P. (1990). Training system issues in the year 2000. *American Psychologist, 45,* 134–143.

Goldstein, I. L., Zedeck, S., & Schneider, B. (1993). An exploration of the job analysis–content validity process. In N. Schmitt & W. C. Borman (Eds.), *Personnel selection in organizations* (pp. 3–34). San Francisco: Jossey-Bass.

Goleman, D. (1995). *Emotional intelligence.* New York: Bantam.

Goleman, D. (1998). *Working with emotional intelligence.* New York: Bantam.

Golembiewski, R. T., & Proehl, C. W. (1978). A survey of the empirical literature on flexible workhours: Character and consequences of a major innovation. *Academy of Management Review, 3,* 837–853.

Gomez-Mejia, L. R., & Balkin, D. B. (1984). Faculty satisfaction with pay and other job dimensions under union and nonunion conditions. *Academy of Management Journal, 27,* 591–602.

Gomez-Mejia, L. R., Page, R. C., & Tornow, W. W. (1982). A comparison of the practical utility of traditional, statistical, and hybrid job evaluation approaches. *Academy of Management Journal, 25,* 790–809.

Gordon, M. E., & Bowlby, R. L. (1988). Propositions about grievance settlements: Finally, consultation with grievants. *Personnel Psychology, 41,* 107–124.

Gordon, M. E., & Bowlby, R. L. (1989). Reactance and intentionality attributions as determinants of the intent to file a grievance. *Personnel Psychology, 42,* 309–330.

Gordon, M. E., & Ladd, R. T. (1990). Dual allegiance: Renewal, reconsideration, and recantation. *Personnel Psychology, 43,* 37–69.

Gordon, M. E., & Miller, S. J. (1984). Grievances: A review of research and practice. *Personnel Psychology, 37,* 117–146.

Gordon, M. E., Philpot, J. W., Burt, R. E., Thompson, C. A., & Spiller, W. E. (1980). Commitment to the union: Development of a measure and an examination of its correlates. *Journal of Applied Psychology, 65,* 479–499.

Gordon, M. E., Schmitt, N., & Schneider, W. G. (1984). Laboratory research on bargaining and negotiations: An evaluation. *Industrial Relations, 23,* 281–233.

Gottfredson, L. S. (1994). The science and politics of race norming. *American Psychologist, 49,* 955–963.

Gottlieb, B. H., Kelloway, E. K., & Barham, E. (1998). *Flexible work arrangements.* Chichester: Wiley.

Gough, H. G. (1984). A managerial potential scale for the California Psychological Inventory. *Journal of Applied Psychology, 69,* 233–240.

Graen, G. B., & Scandura, T. A. (1987). Toward a psychology of dyadic organizing. In B. M. Staw & L. L. Cummings (Eds.), *Research in organizational behavior* (Vol. 9, pp. 175–208). Greenwich, CT: JAI Press.

Graen, G. B., & Wakabayashi, M. (1994). Cross-cultural leadership making: Bridging American and Japanese diversity for team advantage. In H. C. Triandis, M. D. Dunnette, & L. M. Hough (Eds.), *Handbook of industrial and organizational psychology* (2nd ed., Vol. 4, pp. 415–446). Palo Alto, CA: Consulting Psychologists Press.

Grandjean, E. (1986). *Fitting the task to the man: An ergonomic approach.* London: Taylor & Frances.

Grandjean, E. (1987). *Ergonomics in computerized offices.* London: Taylor & Frances.

Green, S. G., & Nebeker, D. M. (1977). The effects of situational factors and leadership style on leader behavior. *Organizational Behavior and Human Performance, 19,* 368–377.

Greenberg, J. (1986). Determinants of perceived fairness of performance evaluations. *Journal of Applied Psychology, 71,* 340–342.

Greenberg, J. (1988). Equity and workplace status: A field experiment. *Journal of Applied Psychology, 73,* 606–613.

Greenberg, J. (1990). Employee theft as a reaction to underpayment inequity: The hidden costs of pay cuts. *Journal of Applied Psychology, 75,* 561–568.

Greenberg, J. (1993). The social side of fairness: Interpersonal and informational classes of organizational justice. In R. Cropanzano (Ed.), *Justice in the workplace: Approaching fairness in human resource management* (pp. 79–103). Hillsdale, NJ: Erlbaum.

Greenberg, J. (1994). Using socially fair treatment to promote acceptance of a work site smoking ban. *Journal of Applied Psychology, 79,* 288–297.

Greenberg, J., & Scott, K. S. (1996). Why do workers bite the hands that feed them? Employee theft as a social exchange process. In B. M. Staw & L. L. Cummings (Eds.), *Research in organizational behavior* (Vol. 18, pp. 111–156). Greenwich, CT: JAI Press.

Greene, C. N., & Schriesheim, C. A. (1980). Leader–group interactions: A longitudinal field investigation. *Journal of Applied Psychology, 65,* 50–59.

Grether, W. F. (1968). Engineering psychology in the United States. *American Psychologist, 23,* 743–751.

Griffin, R. W., Welsh, A., & Moorhead, G. (1981). Perceived task characteristics and employee performance: A literature review. *Academy of Management Review, 6,* 655–664.

Grigsby, D. M., & Bigoness, W. J. (1982). Effects of mediation and alternative forms of arbitration on bargaining behavior: A laboratory study. *Journal of Applied Psychology, 67,* 549–554.

Grover, S. L., & Crooker, K. J. (1995). Who appreciates family-responsive human resource policies: The impact of family-friendly policies on the organizational attachment of parents and non-parents. *Personnel Psychology, 48,* 271–288.

Guion, R. M. (1998). *Assessment, measurement, and prediction for personnel decisions.* Mahwah, NJ: Erlbaum.

Guion, R. M., & Gottier, R. F. (1965). Validity of personality measures in personnel selection. *Personnel Psychology, 18,* 135–164.

Gunter, B., Furnham, A., & Drakeley, R. (1993). *Biodata: Biographical indicators of business performance*. London: Routledge.

Gutek, B. A. (1985). *Sex and the workplace*. San Francisco: Jossey-Bass.

Guzzo, R. A. (1995). Introduction: At the intersection of team effectiveness and decision making. In R. A. Guzzo & E. Salas (Eds.), *Team effectiveness and decision making in organizations* (pp. 1–8). San Francisco: Jossey-Bass.

Guzzo, R. A., & Dickson, M. W. (1996). Teams in organizations: Recent research on performance and effectiveness. *Annual Review of Psychology, 47*, 307–338.

Guzzo, R. A., Jette, R. D., & Katzell, R. A. (1985). The effects of psychologically based intervention programs on worker productivity: A meta-analysis. *Personnel Psychology, 38*, 275–291.

Guzzo, R. A., & Shea, G. P. (1992). Group performance and intergroup relations in organizations. In M. D. Dunnette & L. M. Hough (Eds.), *Handbook of industrial and organizational psychology* (2nd ed., Vol. 3, pp. 269–313). Palo Alto, CA: Consulting Psychologists Press.

Hackman, J. R., & Oldham, G. R. (1975). Development of the Job Diagnostic Survey. *Journal of Applied Psychology, 60*, 159–170.

Hackman, J. R., & Oldham, G. R. (1976). Motivation through the design of work: Test of a theory. *Organizational Behavior and Human Performance, 16*, 250–279.

Hahn, D. C., & Dipboye, R. L. (1988). Effects of training and information on the accuracy and reliability of job evaluations. *Journal of Applied Psychology, 73*, 146–153.

Haigh, R. (1993). The aging process: A challenge for design. *Applied Ergonomics, 24*, 9–14.

Hall, D. T., & Mirvis, P. H. (1995). Careers as lifelong learning. In A. Howard (Ed.), *The changing nature of work* (pp. 323–381). San Francisco: Jossey-Bass.

Hall, G. S. (1917). Practical relations between psychology and the war. *Journal of Applied Psychology, 1*, 9–16.

Hall, G. S., Baird, J. W., & Geissler, L. R. (1917). Foreword. *Journal of Applied Psychology, 1*, 5–7.

Hammer, T. H., & Berman, M. (1981). The role of noneconomic factors in faculty union voting. *Journal of Applied Psychology, 66*, 415–421.

Hamner, W. C., & Smith, F. J. (1978). Work attitudes as predictors of unionization activity. *Journal of Applied Psychology, 63*, 415–421.

Handbook of human engineering data. (1949). Medford, MA: Tufts College and United States Naval Training Devices Center.

Haney, W. (1981). Validity, vaudeville, and values: A short history of social concerns over standardized testing. *American Psychologist, 36*, 1021–1034.

Hansen, C. P. (1989). A causal model of the relationship among accidents, biodata, personality, and cognitive factors. *Journal of Applied Psychology, 74*, 81–90.

Harmon, L. W. (1991). Twenty years of the *Journal of Vocational Behavior*. *Journal of Vocational Behavior, 39*, 297–304.

Harrell, T. W. (1992). Some history of the Army General Classification Test. *Journal of Applied Psychology, 77*, 875–878.

Harris, M. M. (1989). Reconsidering the employment interview: A review of recent literature and suggestions for future research. *Personnel Psychology, 42*, 691–726.

Harris, M. M., Smith, D. E., & Champagne, D. (1995). A field study of performance appraisal purpose: Research-versus administrative-based ratings. *Personnel Psychology, 48*, 151–160.

Harris, M. M., & Trusty, M. L. (1997). Drug and alcohol programs in the workplace: A review of recent literature. In C. L. Cooper & I. T. Robertson (Eds.), *International review of industrial and organizational psychology* (Vol. 12, pp. 289–316). New York: Wiley.

Hartley, J. F. (1992). The psychology of industrial relations. In C. L. Cooper & I. T. Robertson (Eds.), *International review of industrial and organizational psychology* (Vol. 7, pp. 201–243). London: Wiley.

Harvey, R. J. (1991). Job analysis. In M. D. Dunnette & L. M. Hough (Eds.), *Handbook of industrial and organizational psychology* (2nd ed., Vol. 2, pp. 71–163). Palo Alto, CA: Consulting Psychologists Press.

Harvey, R. J., & Lozada-Larsen, S. R. (1988). Influence of amount of job descriptive information on job analysis rating accuracy. *Journal of Applied Psychology, 73*, 457–461.

Hattrup, K., Rock, J., & Scalia, C. (1997). The effects of varying conceptualizations of job performance on adverse impact, minority hiring, and predicted performance. *Journal of Applied Psychology, 82*, 656–664.

Hauerstein, N. M. (1998). Training raters to increase the accuracy of appraisals and the usefulness of feedback. In J. W. Smither (Ed.), *Performance appraisal* (pp. 404–444). San Francisco: Jossey-Bass.

Havel, V. (1994, July 8). The new measure of man. *The New York Times*, p. A27.

Hawk, R. H. (1967). *The recruitment function*. New York: AMACOM.

Hazer, J. T., & Highhouse, S. (1997). Factors influencing managers' reactions to utility analysis: Effects of SD_y, method, information frame, and focal intervention. *Journal of Applied Psychology, 82*, 104–112.

Hedge, A., Erickson, W. A., & Rubin, G. (1992). Effects of personal and organizational factors on sick building syndrome in air-conditioned offices. In J. C. Quick, L. R. Murphy, & J. J. Hurrell (Eds.), *Stress and well-being at work* (pp. 286–298). Washington, DC: American Psychological Association.

Hedge, J. W., & Kavanagh, M. J. (1988). Improving the accuracy of performance evaluations: Comparison of three methods of performance appraisal training. *Journal of Applied Psychology, 73*, 68–73.

Heilman, M. E. (1996). Affirmative actions' contradictory consequences. *Journal of Social Issues, 52*(4), 105–109.

Heilman, M. E., Block, C. J., & Lucas, J. A. (1992). Presumed incompetent? Stigmatization and affirmative action efforts. *Journal of Applied Psychology, 77*, 536–544.

Heilman, M. E., & Herlihy, J. M. (1984). Affirmative action, negative reaction? Some moderating considerations. *Organizational Behavior and Human Performance, 33*, 204–213.

Heilman, M. E., McCullough, W. F., & Gilbert, D. (1996). The other side of affirmative action: Reactions of nonbeneficiaries to sex-based preferential selection. *Journal of Applied Psychology, 81*, 346–357.

Heilman, M. E., Simon, M. C., & Repper, D. P. (1987). Intentionally favored, unintentionally harmed? Impact of sex-based preferential selection in self-perceptions and self-evaluations. *Journal of Applied Psychology, 72*, 62–68.

Hemphill, H., & Haines, R. (1997). *Discrimination, harassment, and the failure of diversity training.* Westport, CT: Quorum.

Herzberg, F., Mausner, B., & Snyderman, B. (1959). *The motivation to work.* New York: Wiley.

Hesketh, B., & Bochner, S. (1994). Technological change in a multicultural context: Implications for training and career planning. In H. C. Triandis, M. D. Dunnette, & L. M. Hough (Eds.), *Handbook of industrial and organizational psychology* (2nd ed., Vol. 4, pp. 191–240). Palo Alto, CA: Consulting Psychologists Press.

Hess, H. F. (1977). Entry requirements for professional practice of psychology. *American Psychologist, 32*, 365–368.

Hicks, W. D., & Klimoski, R. J. (1981). The impact of flexitime on employee attitudes. *Academy of Management Journal, 24*, 333–341.

Hilakivi, I., Veilahti, J., Asplund, P., & Sinivuo, J. (1989). A sixteen-factor personality test for predicting automobile accidents of young drivers. *Accident Analysis and Prevention, 21*, 413–418.

Hoffman, C. C., & Thornton, G. C. (1997). Examining selection utility where competing predictors differ in adverse impact. *Personnel Psychology, 50*, 455–470.

Hoffman, M. A. (1997). HIV disease and work: Effect on the individual, workplace, and interpersonal contexts. *Journal of Vocational Behavior, 51*, 163–201.

Hoffman, P. J. (1980). On the establishment of an appropriate length for the EPPP. *Professional Psychology, 11*, 784–791.

Hofmann, D. A., Jacobs, R., & Baratta, J. E. (1993). Dynamic criteria and the measurement of change. *Journal of Applied Psychology, 78*, 194–204.

Hogan, E. A., & Overmyer-Day, L. (1994). The psychology of mergers and acquisitions. In C. L. Cooper & I. T. Robertson (Eds.), *International review of industrial and organizational psychology* (pp. 247–281). London: Wiley.

Hogan, J. (1991a). Physical abilities. In M. D. Dunnette & L. M. Hough (Eds.), *Handbook of industrial and organizational psychology* (2nd ed., Vol. 2, pp. 753–831). Palo Alto, CA: Consulting Psychologists Press.

Hogan, J. (1991b). Structure of physical performance in organizational tasks. *Journal of Applied Psychology, 76*, 495–507.

Hogan, J., & Brinkmeyer, K. (1997). Bridging the gap between overt and personality-based integrity tests. *Personnel Psychology, 50*, 587–600.

Hogan, J., & Hogan, R. (Eds.). (1990). *Business and industry testing: Current practices and reviews.* Austin, TX: Pro-Ed.

Hogan, J., Hogan, R., & Busch, C. M. (1984). How to measure service orientation. *Journal of Applied Psychology, 69*, 167–173.

Hogan, R. T. (1991). Personality and personality measurement. In M. D. Dunnette & L. M. Hough (Eds.), *Handbook of industrial and organizational psychology* (2nd ed., Vol. 2, pp. 873–919). Palo Alto, CA: Consulting Psychologists Press.

Hogan, R., Curphy, G. J., & Hogan, J. (1994). What we know about leadership: Effectiveness and personality. *American Psychologist, 49*, 493–504.

Hogan, R. T., & Hogan, J. (1992). *Hogan Personality Inventory.* Tulsa, OK: Hogan Assessment Systems.

Hogan, R., Hogan, J., & Roberts, B. W. (1996). Personality measurement and employment decisions: Questions and answers. *American Psychologist, 51*, 469–477.

Hogan, R., Raskin, R., & Fazzini, D. (1990). The dark side of charisma. In K. E. Clark & M. B. Clark (Eds.), *Measures of leadership.* West Orange, NJ: Leadership Library of America.

Hogan, R., & Sinclair, R. (1996). Intellectual, ideological, and political obstacles to the advancement of organizational service. *Journal of Applied Behavioral Science, 32*, 378–389.

Hollander, E. P. (1965). Validity of peer nominations in predicting a distant performance criterion. *Journal of Applied Psychology, 49*, 434–438.

Hollenbeck, J. R., Ilgen, D. R., & Crampton, S. M. (1992). Lower back disability in organizational settings: A review of the literature from a human resource management view. *Personnel Psychology, 45*, 247–278.

Hollenbeck, J. R., LePine, J. A., & Ilgen, D. R. (1996). Adapting to roles in decision-making teams. In K. R. Murphy (Ed.), *Individual differences and behaviors in organizations* (pp. 300–333). San Francisco: Jossey-Bass.

Hollenbeck, J. R., Williams, C. R., & Klein, H. J. (1989). An empirical examination of the antecedents of commitment to difficult goals. *Journal of Applied Psychology, 74*, 18–23.

Hollinger, R. C. (1988). Working under the influence (WUI): Correlates of employees' use of alcohol and other drugs. *Journal of Applied Behavioral Science, 24*, 439–454.

Hollinger, R., & Clark, J. (1983). *Theft by employees.* Lexington, MA: Lexington Books.

Holzbach, R. L. (1978). Rater bias in performance ratings: Superior, self-, and peer assessments. *Journal of Applied Psychology, 63*, 579–588.

Hom, P. W., & Griffeth, R. W. (1995). *Employee turnover.* Cincinnati, OH: South-Western.

Honts, C. R. (1991). The emperor's new clothes: Application of polygraph tests in the American workplace. *Forensic Reports, 4*, 91–116.

House, R. J. (1971). A path-goal theory of leader effectiveness. *Administrative Science Quarterly, 16*, 321–338.

House, R. J. (1977). A 1976 theory of charismatic leadership. In J. G. Hunt & L. L. Larson (Eds.), *Leadership: The cutting edge.* Carbondale, IL: Southern Illinois University Press.

House, R. J., Spangler, W. D., & Woycke, J. (1991). Personality and charisma in the U.S. presidency: A psychological theory of leader effectiveness. *Administrative Science Quarterly, 36*, 364–396.

House, R. J., Wright, N. S., & Aditya, R. N. (1997). Cross-cultural research on organizational leadership: A critical analysis and a proposed theory. In P. C. Earley & M. Erez (Eds.), *New perspectives on international industrial/organizational psychology* (pp. 535–625). San Francisco: New Lexington Press.

Howard, A. (1990). *The multiple facets of industrial-organizational psychology.* Arlington Heights, IL: Society for Industrial and Organizational Psychology.

Howard, A. (1992). Work and family crossroads spanning the career. In S. Zedeck (Ed.), *Work, families, and organizations* (pp. 70–137). San Francisco: Jossey-Bass.

Howard, A., & Lowman, R. L. (1985). Should industrial/organizational psychologists be licensed? *American Psychologist, 40*, 40–47.

Howell, J. P., & Dorfman, P. W. (1981). Substitutes for leadership: Test of a construct. *Academy of Management Journal, 24*, 714–728.

Howell, W. C. (1993). Engineering psychology in a changing world. *Annual Review of Psychology, 44*, 231–263.

Howell, W. C., & Cooke, N. J. (1989). Training the human information processor: A review of cognitive models. In I. L. Goldstein (Ed.), *Training and development in organizations* (pp. 121–182). San Francisco: Jossey-Bass.

Hulin, C. (1991). Adaptation, persistence, and commitment in organizations. In M. D. Dunnette & L. M. Hough (Eds.), *Handbook of industrial and organizational psychology* (2nd ed., Vol. 2, pp. 445–505). Palo Alto, CA: Consulting Psychologists Press.

Hulin, C. L., Henry, R. A., & Noon, S. L. (1990). Adding a dimension: Time as a factor in the generalizability of predictive relationships. *Psychological Bulletin, 107*, 328–340.

Hunt, D. M., & Michael, C. (1983). Mentorship: A career training and development tool. *Academy of Management Review, 8*, 475–485.

Hunter, J. E. (1986). Cognitive ability, cognitive aptitudes, job knowledge, and job performance. *Journal of Vocational Behavior, 29*, 340–362.

Hunter, J. E., & Hunter, R. F. (1984). Validity and utility of alternative predictors of job performance. *Psychological Bulletin, 96*, 72–98.

Hunter, J. E., & Schmidt, F. L. (1990). *Method of meta-analysis: Correcting error and bias in research findings.* Newbury Park, CA: Sage.

Hunter, J. E., & Schmidt, F. L. (1996). Cumulative research knowledge and social policy formation: The critical role of meta-analysis. *Psychology, Public Policy, and Law, 2*, 324–347.

Huse, E. F., & Cummings, T. G. (1985). *Organizational development and change* (3rd ed.). St. Paul, MN: West.

Huseman, R. C., Hatfield, J. D., & Miles, E. W. (1987). A new perspective on equity theory: The equity sensitivity construct. *Academy of Management Review, 12*, 222–234.

Huszczo, G. E., Wiggins, J. G., & Currie, J. S. (1984). The relationship between psychology and organized labor: Past, present and future. *American Psychologist, 39*, 432–440.

Iacono, W. G., & Lykken, D. T. (1997). The validity of the lie detector: Two surveys of scientific opinion. *Journal of Applied Psychology, 82*, 426–433.

Iaffaldano, M. T., & Muchinsky, P. M. (1985). Job satisfaction and performance: A meta-analysis. *Psychological Bulletin, 97*, 251–273.

Ilgen, D. R. (1990). Health issues at work: Opportunities for industrial/organizational psychology. *American Psychologist, 45*, 273–283.

Ilgen, D. R., Barnes-Farrell, J. L., & McKellin, D. B. (1993). Performance appraisal process research in the 1980s: What has it contributed to appraisals in use? *Organizational Behavior and Human Decision Processes, 54*, 321–368.

Ilgen, D. R., Fisher, C. D., & Taylor, M. S. (1979). Motivational consequences of individual feedback on behavior in organizations. *Journal of Applied Psychology, 64*, 349–371.

Ilgen, D. R., Peterson, R. B., Martin, B. A., & Boeschen, D. A. (1981). Supervisor and subordinate reactions to performance appraisal sessions. *Organizational Behavior and Human Performance, 28*, 311–330.

Imada, A. S. (1990). Ergonomics: Influencing management behavior. *Ergonomics, 33*, 621–628.

Impara, J. C., & Plake, B. S. (1998). *The thirteenth mental measurements yearbook.* Lincoln, NE: Buros Institute of Mental Measurements.

Jackson, P. R., & Warr, P. B. (1984). Unemployment and psychological ill-health: The moderating role of duration and age. *Psychological Medicine, 14*, 605–614.

Jackson, S. E., & Schuler, R. S. (1990). Human resource planning. *American Psychologist, 45*, 223–239.

Jahoda, M. (1981). Work, employment, and unemployment: Values, theories and approaches in social research. *American Psychologist, 36*, 184–191.

Jamal, M. (1981). Shift work related to job attitudes, social participation, and withdrawal behavior. A study of nurses and industrial workers. *Personnel Psychology, 34*, 535–548.

Jamal, M., & Jamal, S. M. (1982). Work and nonwork experiences of employees on fixed and rotating shifts: An empirical assessment. *Journal of Vocational Behavior, 20*, 282–293.

Janssens, M., Brett, J. M., & Smith, F. J. (1995). Confirmatory cross-cultural research: Testing the viability of a corporation-wide safety policy. *Academy of Management Journal, 38*, 364–382.

Janz, B. D., Colquitt, J. A., & Noe, R. A. (1997). Knowledge worker team effectiveness: The role of autonomy, interdependence, team development, and contextual support variables. *Personnel Psychology, 50*, 877–904.

Jarrell, S. B., & Stanley, T. D. (1990). A meta-analysis of the union–nonunion wage gap. *Industrial and Labor Relations Review, 44*, 54–67.

Jawahar, I. M., & Williams, C. R. (1997). Where all the children are above average: The performance appraisal purpose effect. *Personnel Psychology, 50,* 905–925.

Jemison, D. B., & Sitkin, S. B. (1986). Corporate acquisitions: A process perspective. *Academy of Management Review, 11,* 145–163.

Jenkins, J. G. (1946). Validity for what? *Journal of Consulting Psychology, 10,* 93–98.

Johns, G. (1994). How often were you absent? A review of the use of self-reported absence data. *Journal of Applied Psychology, 79,* 574–591.

Johns, G. (1997). Contemporary research on absence from work: Correlates, causes, and consequences. In C. L. Cooper & I. T. Robertson (Eds.), *International review of industrial and organizational psychology* (Vol. 12, pp. 115–173). Chichester: Wiley.

Johnson, P. R., & Indvik, J. (1994). Workplace violence: An issue of the nineties. *Public Personnel Management, 23,* 515–523.

Jones, N. (1994). The alcohol and drug provisions of the ADA: Implications for employers and employees. In S. M. Bruyere & J. O'Keeffe (Eds.), *Implications of the Americans with Disabilities Act for psychology* (pp. 151–168). New York: Springer.

Joure, S. A., Leon, J. S., Simpson, D. B., Holley, G. H., & Frye, R. L. (1989, March). Stress: The pressure cooker of work. *The Personnel Administrator, 34,* 92–95.

Kabanoff, B. (1997). Organizational justice across cultures: Integrating organization-level and culture-level perspectives. In P. C. Earley & M. Erez (Eds.), *New perspectives on international industrial/organizational psychology* (pp. 676–712). San Francisco: New Lexington Press.

Kagitcibasi, C., & Berry, J. W. (1989). Cross-cultural psychology: Current research and trends. *Annual Review of Psychology, 40,* 493–531.

Kahn, R. L., & Byosiere, P. B. (1992). Stress in organizations. In M. D. Dunnette & L. M. Hough (Eds.), *Handbook of industrial and organizational psychology* (2nd ed., Vol. 3, pp. 571–650). Palo Alto, CA: Consulting Psychologists Press.

Kane, J. S., Bernardin, H. J., Villanova, P., & Peyrefitte, J. (1995). Stability of rater leniency: Three studies. *Academy of Management Journal, 38,* 1036–1051.

Kane, J. S., & Lawler, E. E. (1978). Methods of peer assessment. *Psychological Bulletin, 85,* 555–586.

Kanfer, R. (1992). Work motivation: New directions in theory and research. In C. L. Cooper & I. T. Robertson (Eds.), *International review of industrial and organizational psychology* (Vol. 7, pp. 1–53). London: Wiley.

Kanfer, R., & Ackerman, P. L. (1989). Motivation and cognitive abilities: An integrative/aptitude–treatment interaction approach to skill acquisition. *Journal of Applied Psychology, 74,* 657–690.

Kanfer, R., & Heggestad, E. D. (1997). Motivational traits and skills: A person-centered approach to work motivation. In B. M. Staw & L. L. Cummings (Eds.), *Research in organizational behavior* (Vol. 19, pp. 1–56). Greenwich, CT: JAI Press.

Kanter, R. M. (1977). *Work and family in the United States: A critical review and agenda for research and policy.* New York: Russell Sage Foundation.

Kanungo, R. N. (1982). Measurement of job and work involvement. *Journal of Applied Psychology, 67,* 341–349.

Kaplan, A. (1964). *The conduct of inquiry.* New York: Harper & Row.

Kaplan, M. (1995). The culture at work: Cultural ergonomics. *Ergonomics, 38,* 606–615.

Karambayya, R., & Reilly, A. H. (1992). Dual earner couples: Attitudes and actions restructuring work for family. *Journal of Organizational Behavior, 13,* 585–601.

Kast, F. E., & Rosenzweig, J. E. (1972). General systems theory: Applications for organization and management. *Academy of Management Journal, 15,* 444–465.

Katzell, R. A. (1994). Contemporary meta-trends in industrial and organizational psychology. In H. C. Triandis, M. D. Dunnette, & L. M. Hough (Eds.), *Handbook of industrial and organizational psychology* (2nd ed., Vol. 4, pp. 1–89). Palo Alto, CA: Consulting Psychologists Press.

Katzell, R. A., & Austin, J. T. (1992). From then to now: The development of industrial-organizational psychology in the United States. *Journal of Applied Psychology, 77,* 803–835.

Katzell, R. A., & Guzzo, R. A. (1983). Psychological approaches to productivity improvement. *American Psychologist, 38,* 468–472.

Katzell, R. A., & Thompson, D. E. (1990). Work motivation: Theory and practice. *American Psychologist, 45,* 144–153.

Keinan, G., & Eilat-Greenberg, S. (1993). Can stress be measured by handwriting analysis? The effectiveness of the analytic method. *Applied Psychology: An International Review, 42,* 153–170.

Kelleher, M. D. (1996). *New arenas for violence: Homicide in the American workplace.* Westport, CT: Praeger.

Kelloway, E. K., Catano, V. M., & Carroll, A. E. (1995). The nature of member participation in local union activities. In L. E. Tetrick & J. Barling (Eds.), *Changing employment relations* (pp. 333–348). Washington, DC: American Psychological Association.

Kelly, J. E., & Kelly, C. (1991). "Them and us": Social psychology and "The new industrial relations." *British Journal of Industrial Relations, 29,* 25–48.

Kelman, H. C. (1972). The rights of the subject in social research: An analysis in terms of relative power and legitimacy. *American Psychologist, 27,* 989–1016.

Kennedy, C. W., Fossum, J. A., & White, B. J. (1983). An empirical comparison of within-subjects and between-subjects expectancy theory models. *Organizational Behavior and Human Performance, 32,* 124–143.

Kerr, S. (1995). On the folly of rewarding A, while hoping for B. *Academy of Management Executive, 9,* 7–14.

Kerr, S., & Jermier, J. M. (1978). Substitutes for leadership: Their meaning and measurement. *Organizational Behavior and Human Performance, 22,* 375–403.

King, J. L., & Alexander, D. G. (1996). Unions respond to violence on the job. In G. R. VandenBos & E. Q. Bulatao (Eds.), *Violence on the job* (pp. 315–326). Washington, DC: American Psychological Association.

Kinicki, A. J., McKee, F. M., & Wade, K. H. (1996). Annual review, 1991–1995: Occupational health. *Journal of Vocational Behavior, 49*, 190–220.

Kirk, R. E. (1996). Practical significance: A concept whose time has come. *Educational and Psychological Measurement, 56*, 746–759.

Kirkman, B. L., & Rosen, B. (1997). A model of work team empowerment. In W. A. Pasmore and R. W. Woodman (Eds.), *Research in organizational change and development* (Vol. 10, pp. 131–168). Greenwich, CT: JAI Press.

Kirkpatrick, D. L. (1976). Evaluation of training. In R. L. Craig (Ed.), *Training and development handbook* (2nd ed.). New York: McGraw-Hill.

Kirkpatrick, S. A., & Locke, E. A. (1991). Leadership: Do traits matter? *Academy of Management Executive, 5*(2), 48–60.

Kivimaki, M., Vahtera, J., Thomson, L., Griffiths, A., Cox, T., & Pentti, J. (1997). Psychosocial factors predict employee sickness absence during economic decline. *Journal of Applied Psychology, 82*, 858–872.

Klaas, B. S. (1989). Managerial decision making about employee grievances: The impact of the grievant's work history. *Personnel Psychology, 42*, 53–68.

Klandermans, B. (1989). Union commitment: Replications and tests in the Dutch context. *Journal of Applied Psychology, 74*, 869–875.

Kleiman, L. S., & Faley, R. H. (1988). Voluntary affirmative action and preferential treatment: Legal and research implications. *Personnel Psychology, 41*, 481–496.

Klein, H. J. (1991). Further evidence on the relationship between goal setting and expectancy theories. *Organizational Behavior and Human Decision Processes, 49*, 230–257.

Kleinmann, M. (1993). Are rating dimensions in assessment centers transparent for participants? Consequences for criterion and construct validity. *Journal of Applied Psychology, 78*, 988–993.

Klimoski, R. J., & Brickner, M. (1987). Why do assessment centers work? The puzzle of assessment center validity. *Personnel Psychology, 40*, 243–260.

Klimoski, R. J., & Inks, L. (1990). Accountability forces in performance appraisal. *Organizational Behavior and Human Decision Processes, 45*, 194–208.

Klimoski, R., & Jones, R. G. (1995). Staffing for effective group decision making: Key issues in marketing people and teams. In R. A. Guzzo & E. Salas (Eds.), *Team effectiveness and decision making in organizations* (pp. 291–332). San Francisco: Jossey-Bass.

Klimoski, R. J., & Palmer, S. N. (1994). The ADA and the hiring process in organizations. In S. M. Bruyere & J. O'Keeffe (Eds.), *Implications of the Americans with Disabilities Act for psychology* (pp. 37–84). New York: Springer.

Klimoski, R. J., & Strickland, W. J. (1977). Assessment centers—Valid or merely prescient? *Personnel Psychology, 30*, 353–361.

Kluger, A. N., & DeNisi, A. (1996). The effects of feedback interventions on performance: A historical review, a meta-analysis, and a preliminary feedback intervention theory. *Psychological Bulletin, 119*, 254–284.

Kluger, A. N., Reilly, R. R., & Russell, C. J. (1991). Faking biodata tests: Are option-keyed instruments more resistant? *Journal of Applied Psychology, 76*, 889–896.

Knauth, P. (1996). Designing better shift systems. *Applied Ergonomics, 27*, 39–44.

Kogi, K. (1996). Improving shift workers' health and tolerance to shiftwork: Recent advances. *Applied Ergonomics, 27*, 5–8.

Komaki, J. L. (1986). Toward effective supervision: An operant analysis and comparison of managers at work. *Journal of Applied Psychology, 71*, 270–279.

Koppes, L. L. (1997). American female pioneers of industrial and organizational psychology during the early years. *Journal of Applied Psychology, 82*, 500–515.

Kossek, E. E., & Ozeki, C. (1998). Work–family conflict, policies, and the job–life satisfaction relationship: A review and directions for organizational behavior–human resources research. *Journal of Applied Psychology, 83*, 139–149.

Kotter, J. P. (1988). *The leadership factor.* New York: Free Press.

Kotter, J. P., & Heskett, J. L. (1992). *Corporate culture and performance.* New York: Free Press.

Kouzes, J. M., & Posner, B. Z. (1995). *The leadership challenge.* San Francisco: Jossey-Bass.

Kozlowski, S. W., Chao, G. T., & Morrison, R. F. (1998). Games raters play: Politics, strategies, and impression management in performance appraisal. In J. W. Smither (Ed.), *Performance appraisal* (pp. 163–208). San Francisco: Jossey-Bass.

Kozlowski, S. W., Chao, G. T., Smith, E. M., & Hedlund, J. (1993). Organizational downsizing: Strategies, interventions, and research implications. In C. L. Cooper & I. T. Robertson (Eds.), *International review of industrial and organizational psychology* (Vol. 8, pp. 263–331). London: Wiley.

Kraiger, K., & Jung, K. M. (1997). Linking training objectives to evaluation criteria. In M. A. Quinones & A. Ehrenstein (Eds.), *Training for a rapidly changing workplace* (pp. 151–176). Washington, DC: American Psychological Association.

Kram, K. E., & Isabella, L. A. (1985). Alternatives to mentoring: The role of peer relationships in career development. *Academy of Management Journal, 28*, 110–132.

Krantz, J. (1985). Group processes under conditions of organizational decline. *Journal of Applied Behavioral Science, 21*, 1–17.

Kravitz, D. A., Harrison, D. A., Turner, M. E., Levine, E. L., Chaves, W., Brannick, M. T., Denning, D. L., Russell, C. J., & Conrad, M. A. (1997). *Affirmative action: A review of psychological and behavioral research.* Bowling Green, OH: Society for Industrial and Organizational Psychology.

Kroemer, K. H., Kroemer, H. J., & Kroemer-Elbert, K. E. (1986). *Engineering physiology: Physiologic bases of human factors/ergonomics.* New York: Elsevier.

Kuhl, J., & Beckmann, J. (Eds.). (1994). *Volition and personality: Action- and state-oriented modes of control.* Gottingen, Germany: Hogrefe.

Kumar, S. (1994). A conceptual model of overexertion, safety, and risk of injury in organizational settings. *Human Factors, 36,* 197–209.

Ladd, R. T., Gordon, M. E., Beauvais, L. L., & Morgan, R. L. (1982). Union commitment: Replication and extension. *Journal of Applied Psychology, 67,* 640–644.

Lance, C. E., LaPointe, J. A., & Fisicaro, S. A. (1994). Tests of three causal models of halo rater error. *Organizational Behavior and Human Decision Processes, 57,* 83–96.

Landy, F. J. (1992). Hugo Münsterberg: Victim or visionary? *Journal of Applied Psychology, 77,* 787–802.

Landy, F. J., & Trumbo, D. A. (1980). *Psychology of work behavior* (rev. ed.). Pacific Grove, CA: Brooks/Cole.

Landy, F. J., & Vasey, J. (1991). Job analysis: The composition of SME samples. *Personnel Psychology, 44,* 27–50.

Landy, F. L. (1997). Early influences on the development of industrial and organizational psychology. *Journal of Applied Psychology, 82,* 467–477.

Larson, C. E., & La Fasto, F. M. (1989). *Teamwork.* Newbury Park, CA: Sage.

Larson, J. R., Jr., & Callahan, C. (1990). Performance monitoring: How it affects work productivity. *Journal of Applied Psychology, 75,* 530–538.

Latham, G. P. (1986). Job performance and appraisal. In C. L. Cooper & I. T. Robertson (Eds.), *International review of industrial and organizational psychology* (Vol. 1, pp. 117–155). London: Wiley.

Latham, G. P., & Baldes, J. J. (1975). The practical significance of Locke's theory of goal setting. *Journal of Applied Psychology, 60,* 122–124.

Latham, G. P., Fay, C. H., & Saari, L. M. (1979). The development of behavioral observation scales for appraising the performance of foremen. *Personnel Psychology, 32,* 299–311.

Latham, G. P., & Finnegan, B. J. (1993). Perceived practicality of instructional, patterned, and situational interviews. In H. Schuler, J. L. Farr, & M. Smith (Eds.), *Personnel selection and assessment* (pp. 41–56). Hillsdale, NJ: Erlbaum.

Latham, G. P., & Kinne, S. B. (1974). Improving job performance through training in goal setting. *Journal of Applied Psychology, 59,* 187–191.

Latham, G. P., & Locke, E. A. (1991). Self-regulation through goal-setting. *Organizational Behavior and Human Decision Processes, 50,* 212–247.

Latham, G. P., & Marshall, H. A. (1982). The effects of self-set, participatively set, and assigned goals on the performance of government employees. *Personnel Psychology, 35,* 399–404.

Latham, G. P., & Saari, L. M. (1979). The application of social learning theory to training supervisors through behavioral modeling. *Journal of Applied Psychology, 64,* 239–246.

Latham, G. P., Skarlicki, D., Irvine, D., & Siegel, J. P. (1993). The increasing importance of performance appraisals to employee effectiveness in organizational settings in North America. In C. L. Cooper & I. T. Robertson (Eds.), *International review of industrial and organizational psychology* (Vol. 8, pp. 87–132). London: Wiley.

Latham, G. P., & Wexley, K. N. (1977). Behavioral observation scales for performance appraisal purposes. *Personnel Psychology, 30,* 255–268.

Latham, G. P., Wexley, K. N., & Pursell, E. D. (1975). Training managers to minimize rating errors in the observation of behavior. *Journal of Applied Psychology, 60,* 550–555.

Lawler, E. E. (1982). Strategies for improving the quality of work life. *American Psychologist, 37,* 486–493.

Lawler, E. E., Mohrman, S. A., & Ledford, G. E. (1995). *Creating high performance organizations.* San Francisco: Jossey-Bass.

Lazarus, R. S., & Folkman, S. (1984). *Stress, appraisal, and coping.* New York: Springer.

Leana, C. R., & Feldman, D. C. (1991). Gender differences in responses to unemployment. *Journal of Vocational Behavior, 38,* 65–77.

Leung, K. (1997). Negotiation and reward allocations across cultures. In P. C. Earley & M. Erez (Eds.), *New perspectives on international industrial/organizational psychology* (pp. 640–675). San Francisco: New Lexington Press.

Levine, E. L., Ash, R. A., Hall, H., & Sistrunk, F. (1983). Evaluation of job analysis methods by experienced job analysts. *Academy of Management Journal, 26,* 339–347.

Levine, E. L., Sistrunk, F., McNutt, K. J., & Gael, S. (1988). Exploring job analysis systems in selected organizations: A description of process and outcomes. *Journal of Business and Psychology, 3,* 3–21.

Levinson, H. (1994). Why the behemoths fell: Psychological roots of corporate failure. *American Psychologist, 49,* 428–436.

Lewandowsky, S. (1993). The rewards and hazards of computer simulations. *Psychological Science, 4,* 236–243.

Liden, R. C., & Arad, S. (1996). A power perspective of empowerment and work groups: Implications for human resources management research. In G. R. Ferris (Ed.), *Research in personnel and human resources management* (Vol. 14, pp. 205–251). Greenwich, CT: JAI Press.

Liden, R. C., Sparrowe, R. T., & Wayne, S. J. (1997). Leader–member exchange theory: The past and potential for the future. In G. R. Ferris (Ed.), *Research in personnel and human resources management* (Vol. 15, pp. 47–120). Greenwich, CT: JAI Press.

Lim, C. S., Ong, C. N., & Phoon, W. O. (1987). Work stress of firemen as measured by heart rate and catecholamine. *Journal of Human Ergology, 16,* 209–218.

Lippitt, G. L. (1982). *Organizational renewal: A holistic approach to organizational development* (2nd ed.). Englewood Cliffs, NJ: Prentice Hall.

Lobel, S. A. (1993). Sexuality at work: Where do we go from here? *Journal of Vocational Behavior, 42,* 136–152.

Locke, E. A. (1991). The motivation sequence, the motivation hub, and the motivation core. *Organizational Behavior and Human Decision Processes, 50,* 288–299.

Locke, E. A. (Ed.). (1985). *The generalizability of laboratory experiments: An inductive study*. Lexington, MA: D.C. Heath.

Locke, E. A., Feren, D. B., McCaleb, V. M., Shaw, K. N., & Denny, A. T. (1980). The relative effectiveness of four methods of motivating employee performance. In K. Duncan, M. Gruneberg, & D. Wallis (Eds.), *Changes in working life*. New York: Wiley.

Locke, E. A., & Latham, G. P. (1990). *A theory of goal setting and task performance*. Englewood Cliffs, NJ: Prentice Hall.

Locke, E. A., McClear, K., & Knight, D. (1996). Self-esteem and work. In C. L. Cooper & I. T. Robertson (Eds.), *International review of industrial and organizational psychology* (Vol. 11, pp. 1–32). Chichester: Wiley.

Locke, E. A., Shaw, K. N., Saari, L. M., & Latham, G. P. (1981). Goal setting and task performance: 1969–1980. *Psychological Bulletin, 90*, 125–152.

Loher, B. T., Noe, R. A., Moeller, N. L., & Fitzgerald, M. P. (1985). A meta-analysis of the relation of job characteristics to job satisfaction. *Journal of Applied Psychology, 70*, 280–289.

Lombardo, M. M., & McCauley, C. D. (1988). *The dynamics of management derailment* (Tech. Report No. 134). Greensboro, NC: Center for Creative Leadership.

London, M., & Bray, D. W. (1980). Ethical issues in testing and evaluation for personnel decisions. *American Psychologist, 35*, 890–901.

London, M., Smither, J. W., & Adsit, D. J. (1997). Accountability: The Achilles' heel of multisource feedback. *Group & Organization Management, 22*, 162–184.

Lord, R. G. (1985). An information processing approach to social perceptions, leadership, and behavioral measurement in organizations. In B. M. Staw & L. L. Cummings (Eds.), *Research in organizational behavior* (Vol. 7, pp. 87–128). Greenwich, CT: JAI Press.

Lord, R. G., Foti, R. J., & Phillips, J. S. (1982). A theory of leadership organization. In J. G. Hunt, U. Sekaran, & C. Schriesheim (Eds.), *Leadership: Beyond establishment views*. Carbondale: Southern Illinois University.

Lord, R. G., & Hohenfeld, J. A. (1979). Longitudinal field assessment of equity effects in the performance of major league baseball players. *Journal of Applied Psychology, 64*, 19–26.

Lord, R. G., & Kernan, M. C. (1989). Application of control theory to work settings. In W. A. Herschberger (Ed.), *Volitional action* (pp. 493–514). Amsterdam: Elsevier.

Loughlin, C. A., Hepburn, C. G., & Barling, J. (1995). Changing future managers' attitudes toward occupational health and safety. In L. E. Tetrick & J. Barling (Eds.), *Changing employment relations* (pp. 145–162). Washington, DC: American Psychological Association.

Lowe, K. B., Kroeck, K. G., & Sivasubramaniam, N. (1996). Effectiveness correlates of transformational and transactional leadership: A meta-analytic review of the MLQ literature. *Leadership Quarterly, 7*, 385–425.

Lowman, R. L. (1996). Work dysfunctions and mental disorders. In K. R. Murphy (Ed.), *Individual differences and behavior in organizations* (pp. 371–415). San Francisco: Jossey-Bass.

Lowman, R. L. (Ed.). (1998). *The ethical practice of psychology in organizations*. Washington, DC: American Psychological Association.

Lubinski, D., & Dawis, R. V. (1992). Aptitudes, skills, and proficiencies. In M. D. Dunnette & L. M. Hough (Eds.), *Handbook of industrial and organizational psychology* (2nd ed., Vol. 3, pp. 1–59). Palo Alto, CA: Consulting Psychologists Press.

Lund, J. (1992). Electronic performance monitoring: A review of research issues. *Applied Ergonomics, 23*, 54–58.

Lyness, K. S., & Thompson, D. E. (1997). Above the glass ceiling: A comparison of matched samples of female and male executives. *Journal of Applied Psychology, 82*, 359–375.

Mabe, P. A., & West, S. G. (1982). Validity of self-evaluation of ability: A review and meta-analysis. *Journal of Applied Psychology, 67*, 280–296.

MacKenzie, S. B., Podsakoff, P. M., & Fetter, R. (1991). Organizational citizenship behavior and objective productivity as determinants of managerial evaluations of salespersons' performance. *Organizational Behavior and Human Decision Processes, 50*, 123–150.

Macy, B. A., & Izumi, H. (1993). Organizational change, design and work innovation: A meta-analysis of 131 North American field studies—1961–1991. In W. A. Pasmore & R. W. Woodman (Eds.), *Research in organizational change and development* (Vol. 7, pp. 235–313). Greenwich, CT: JAI Press.

Mael, F. A. (1991). A conceptual rationale for the domain and attributes of biodata items. *Personnel Psychology, 44*, 763–792.

Mael, F. A., Connerly, M., & Morath, R. A. (1996). None of your business: Parameters of biodata invasiveness. *Personnel Psychology, 49*, 613–650.

Mahoney, T. A. (1983). Approaches to the definition of comparable worth. *Academy of Management Review, 8*, 14–22.

Malhotra, M. S., & Sengupta, J. (1965). Carrying of school bags by children. *Ergonomics, 8*, 55–60.

Malos, S. B. (1998). Current legal issues in performance appraisal. In J. W. Smither (Ed.), *Performance appraisal* (pp. 49–94). San Francisco: Jossey-Bass.

Mantell, M. (1994). *Ticking bombs: Defusing violence in the workplace*. Burr Ridge, IL: Irwin.

Manz, C. C. (1986). Self-leadership: Toward an expanded theory of self-influence. *Academy of Management Review, 11*, 585–600.

Manz, C. C., & Sims, H. P. (1991). Superleadership: Beyond the myth of heroic leadership. *Organizational Dynamics, 19*(4), 18–35.

Margenau, J. M., Martin, J. E., & Peterson, M. M. (1988). Dual and unilateral commitment among stewards and rank-and-file union members. *Academy of Management Journal, 31*, 359–376.

Markowitz, J. S. (1989). Long-term psychological distress among chemically exposed firefighters. *Behavioral Medicine, 15*, 75–83.

Martin, S. L., & Terris, W. (1991). Predicting infrequent behavior: Clarifying the impact on false-positive rates. *Journal of Applied Psychology, 76,* 484–487.

Martocchio, J. J., & Baldwin, T. T. (1997). The evolution of strategic organizational training: New objectives and research agenda. In G. R. Ferris (Ed.), *Research in personnel and human resources management* (Vol. 15, pp. 1–46). Greenwich, CT: JAI Press.

Martocchio, J. J., & Harrison, D. A. (1993). To be there or not to be there: Questions, theories, and methods in absenteeism research. In G. R. Ferris (Ed.), *Research in personnel and human resources management* (Vol. 11, pp. 259–329). Greenwich, CT: JAI Press.

Marx, R. D. (1982). Relapse prevention for managerial training: A model for maintenance of behavior change. *Academy of Management Review, 7,* 433–441.

Marx, R. D., & Karren, R. K. (1988). *The effects of relapse prevention training and interactive follow-up on positive transfer of training.* Paper presented at the National Academy of Management Meeting, Anaheim.

Maslow, A. H. (1987). *Motivation and personality* (3rd ed.). New York: Harper & Row.

Masters, M. F. (1997). *Unions at the crossroads: Strategic membership, financial, and political perspectives.* Westport, CT: Quorum.

Matarazzo, J. D. (1987). There is only one psychology, no specialties, but many applications. *American Psychologist, 42,* 893–903.

Mateer, F. (1917). The moron as a war problem. *Journal of Applied Psychology, 1,* 317–320.

Mathieu, J. E., Tannenbaum, S. I., & Salas, E. (1990). *A causal model of individual and situational influences on training effectiveness measures.* Paper presented at the 5th annual conference of the Society for Industrial and Organizational Psychology, Miami.

Mawhinney, T. C. (1975). Operant terms and concepts in the description of individual work behavior: Some problems of interpretation, application, and evaluation. *Journal of Applied Psychology, 60,* 704–712.

Maxwell, J. A. (1998). Designing a qualitative study. In L. Bickman & D. J. Rog (Eds.), *Handbook of applied social research methods* (pp. 69–100). Thousand Oaks, CA: Sage.

Mayfield, E. C. (1972). Value of peer nominations in predicting life insurance sales performance. *Journal of Applied Psychology, 56,* 319–323.

McAfee, R. B., & Winn, A. R. (1989). The use of incentives/feedback to enhance workplace safety: A critique of the literature. *Journal of Safety Research, 20,* 7–19.

McCall, M. W., & Bobko, P. (1990). Research methods in the service of discovery. In M. D. Dunnette and L. M. Hough (Eds.), *Handbook of industrial and organizational psychology* (2nd ed., Vol. 1, pp. 381–418). Palo Alto, CA: Consulting Psychologists Press.

McClelland, D. C., & Boyatzis, R. E. (1982). Leadership motive pattern and long term success in management. *Journal of Applied Psychology, 67,* 737–743.

McCormick, E. J., & Jeanneret, P. R. (1988). Position analysis questionnaire (PAQ). In S. Gael (Ed.), *The job analysis handbook for business, industry, and government* (Vol. 2, pp. 825–842). New York: Wiley.

McCrae, R. R., & Costa, P. T. (1987). Validation of the five-factor model of personality across instruments and observers. *Journal of Personality & Social Psychology, 56,* 586–595.

McCrae, R. R., & Costa, P. T. (1997). Personality trait structure as a human universal. *American Psychologist, 52,* 509–516.

McIntyre, R. M., & Salas, E. (1995). Measuring and managing for team performance: Lessons from complex environments. In R. A. Guzzo & E. Salas (Eds.), *Team effectiveness and decision making in organizations* (pp. 9–45). San Francisco: Jossey-Bass.

McNeely, B. L., & Meglino, B. M. (1994). The role of dispositional and situational antecedents in prosocial organizational behavior: An examination of the intended beneficiaries of prosocial behavior. *Journal of Applied Psychology, 79,* 836–844.

Meers, A., Maasen, A., & Verhaagen, P. (1978). Subjective health after six months and after four years of shift work. *Ergonomics, 21,* 857–859.

Meindl, J. R., & Ehrlich, S. B. (1987). The romance of leadership and the evaluation of organizational performance. *Academy of Management Journal, 30,* 91–109.

Melamed, S., Ben-Avi, I., Luz, J., & Green, M. (1995). Objective and subjective work monitoring: Effects on job satisfaction, psychological distress, and absenteeism in blue-collar workers. *Journal of Applied Psychology, 80,* 29–42.

Mellor, S. (1990). The relationship between membership decline and union commitment: A field study of local unions in crisis. *Journal of Applied Psychology, 75,* 258–267.

Mero, N. P., & Motowidlo, S. J. (1995). Effects of rater accountability on the accuracy and the favorability of performance ratings. *Journal of Applied Psychology, 80,* 517–524.

Messick, S. (1995). Validity of psychological assessment: Validation of inferences from persons' responses and performances as scientific inquiry into score meaning. *American Psychologist, 50,* 741–749.

Meyer, H. H. (1980). Self-appraisal of job performance. *Personnel Psychology, 33,* 291–296.

Meyer, H. H., Kay, E., & French, J. R. P., Jr. (1965). Split roles in performance appraisal, *Harvard Business Review, 43,* 123–129.

Meyer, J. P. (1997). Organizational commitment. In C. L. Cooper & I. T. Robertson (Eds.), *International review of industrial and organizational psychology* (Vol. 12, pp. 175–228). Chichester: Wiley.

Michalak, D. F. (1981). The neglected half of training. *Training and Development Journal, 35,* 22–28.

Mintzberg, H. (1993). *Structure in fives: Designing effective organizations.* Englewood Cliffs, NJ: Prentice Hall.

Mirvis, P. H. (1985). Negotiations after the sale: The roots and ramifications of conflict in an acquisition. *Journal of Organizational Behavior, 6,* 65–84.

Mirvis, P. H. (1988). Organization development: Part I—An evolutionary perspective. In W. A. Pasmore & R. W. Woodman (Eds.), *Research in organizational change and development* (Vol. 2, pp. 1–57). Greenwich, CT: JAI Press.

Mirvis, P. H. (1990). Organizational development: Part II—A revolutionary perspective. In W. A. Pasmore & R. W. Woodman (Eds.), *Research in organizational change and development* (Vol. 4, pp. 1–66). Greenwich, CT: JAI Press.

Mirvis, P. H., & Seashore, S. E. (1979). Being ethical in organizational research. *American Psychologist, 34,* 766–780.

Mitchell, T. R. (1985). An evaluation of the validity of correlation research conducted in organizations. *Academy of Management Review, 10,* 192–205.

Mitchell, T. R. (1997). Matching motivational strategies with organizational contexts. In B. M. Staw & L. L. Cummings (Eds.), *Research in organizational behavior* (Vol. 19, pp. 57–149). Greenwich, CT: JAI Press.

Monahan, C. J., & Muchinsky, P. M. (1983). Three decades of personnel selection research: A state-of-the-art analysis and evaluation. *Journal of Occupational Psychology, 56,* 215–225.

Monk, T. H., Folkard, S., & Wedderburn, A. I. (1996). Maintaining safety and high performance on shiftwork. *Applied Ergonomics, 27,* 17–23.

Mook, D. G. (1983). In defense of external invalidity. *American Psychologist, 38,* 379–387.

Moore, D. A. (1994). Company alcohol policies: Practicalities and problems. In C. L. Cooper & S. Williams (Eds.), *Creating healthy work organizations* (pp. 75–96). Chichester: Wiley.

Moorman, R. H. (1991). Relationship between organizational justice and organizational citizenship behaviors: Do fairness perceptions influence employee citizenship? *Journal of Applied Psychology, 76,* 845–855.

Moreland, J. L., Eyde, L. D., Robertson, G. J., Primoff, E. S., & Most, R. B. (1995). Assessment of test user qualifications. *American Psychologist, 50,* 14–23.

Morgan, B. B., Jr., & Bowers, C. A. (1995). Teamwork stress: Implications for team decision making. In R. A. Guzzo & E. Salas (Eds.), *Team effectiveness and decision making in organizations* (pp. 262–290). San Francisco: Jossey-Bass.

Morgan, G. (1997). *Images of organizations.* Thousand Oaks, CA: Sage.

Morgeson, F. P., & Campion, M. A. (1997). Social and cognitive sources of potential inaccuracy in job analysis. *Journal of Applied Psychology, 82,* 627–655.

Morrison, E. W., & Robinson, S. L. (1997). When employees feel betrayed: A model of how psychological contract violation develops. *Academy of Management Review, 22,* 226–256.

Morrison, R. F., & Brantner, T. M. (1992). What enhances or inhibits learning a new job? A basic career issue. *Journal of Applied Psychology, 77,* 926–940.

Morrow, C. C., Jarrett, M., & Rupinski, M. T. (1997). An investigation of the effect and economic utility of corporate-wide training. *Personnel Psychology, 50,* 91–119.

Moses, J., Hollenbeck, G. P., & Sorcher, M. (1993). Other people's expectations. *Human Resource Management, 32,* 283–298.

Motowidlo, S. J., Hanson, M. A., & Crafts, J. L. (1997). Low-fidelity simulations. In D. L. Whetzel & G. R. Wheaton (Eds.), *Applied measurement methods in industrial psychology* (pp. 241–260). Palo Alto, CA: Consulting Psychologists Press.

Motowidlo, S. J., & Van Scotter, J. R. (1994). Evidence that task performance should be distinguished from contextual performance. *Journal of Applied Psychology, 79,* 475–480.

Mount, M. K. (1984). Psychometric properties of subordinate ratings of managerial performance. *Personnel Psychology, 37,* 687–702.

Mowday, R. T., & Sutton, R. I. (1993). Organizational behavior: Linking individuals and groups to organizational contexts. *Annual Review of Psychology, 44,* 195–229.

Muchinsky, P. M. (1975). Consumer installment credit risk: A need for criterion refinement and validation. *Journal of Applied Psychology, 60,* 87–93.

Muchinsky, P. M. (1977). A comparison of within- and across-subjects analyses of the expectancy-valence model for predicting effort. *Academy of Management Journal, 20,* 154–158.

Muchinsky, P. M. (1979). The use of reference reports in personnel selection: A review and evaluation. *Journal of Occupational Psychology, 52,* 287–297.

Muchinsky, P. M. (1993). Validation of intelligence and mechanical aptitude tests in selecting employees for manufacturing jobs. *Journal of Business and Psychology, 7,* 373–382.

Muchinsky, P. M. (1994). What is the shape of the distribution of job performance (and what difference does it make)? *International Journal of Selection and Assessment, 2,* 255–258.

Muchinsky, P. M., & Maassarani, M. A. (1981). Public sector grievances in Iowa. *Journal of Collective Negotiations, 10,* 55–62.

Mumford, M. D., & Peterson, N. G. (1999). The O*NET content model: Structural considerations in describing jobs. In N. G. Peterson, M. D. Mumford, W. C. Borman, P. R. Jeanneret, & E. A. Fleishman (Eds.), *An occupational information system for the 21st century: The development of O*NET* (pp. 21–30). Washington, DC: American Psychological Association.

Mumford, M. D., & Stokes, G. S. (1992). Developmental determinants of individual action: Theory and practice in applying background measures. In M. D. Dunnette & L. M. Hough (Eds.), *Handbook of industrial and organizational psychology* (2nd ed., Vol. 3, pp. 61–138). Palo Alto, CA: Consulting Psychologists Press.

Münsterberg, H. (1913). *Psychology and industrial efficiency.* Boston: Houghton Mifflin.

Murphy, K. R. (1996). Individual differences and behavior in organizations: Much more than *g.* In K. R. Murphy (Ed.), *Individual differences and behavior in organizations* (pp. 3–30). San Francisco: Jossey-Bass.

Murphy, K. R. (1997). Meta-analysis and validity generalization. In N. Anderson & P. Herriot (Eds.), *International handbook of selection and assessment* (pp. 323–342). Chichester: Wiley.

Murphy, K. R., & Anhalt, R. L. (1992). Is halo error a property of the rater, ratees, or the specific behaviors observed? *Journal of Applied Psychology, 77*, 494–500.

Murphy, K. R., & Cleveland, J. N. (1995). *Understanding performance appraisal: Social, organizational, and goal-based perspectives.* Thousand Oaks, CA: Sage.

Murphy, K. R., Osten, K., & Myors, B. (1995). Modeling the effects of banding in personnel selection. *Personnel Psychology, 48*, 61–84.

Murphy, K. R., Thornton, G. C., & Prue, K. (1991). Influence of job characteristics on the acceptability of employee drug testing. *Journal of Applied Psychology, 76*, 447–453.

Murphy, L. L., Conoley, J. C., & Impara, J. C. (1994). *Tests in print IV.* Lincoln, NE: Buros Institute of Mental Measurements.

Murphy, L. R., Hurrell, J. J., & Quick, J. C. (1992). Work and well-being: Where do we go from here? In J. C. Quick, L. R. Murphy, & J. J. Hurrell (Eds.), *Stress and well-being at work* (pp. 331–347). Washington, DC: American Psychological Association.

Murray, H. A., & MacKinnon, D. W. (1946). Assessment of OSS personnel. *Journal of Consulting Psychology, 10*, 76–80.

Murrell, A. J., & Jones, R. (1996). Assessing affirmative action: Past, present, and future. *Journal of Social Issues, 52*(4), 77–92.

Musser, S. J. (1987). *The determination of positive and negative charismatic leadership.* Unpublished manuscript, Messiah College, Grantham, PA.

Napoli, D. S. (1981). *The architects of adjustment: The history of the psychological profession in the United States.* Port Washington, NY: Kennikat.

Narayanan, V. K., & Nath, R. (1982). Hierarchical level and the impact of flextime. *Industrial Relations, 21*, 216–230.

National Institute for Occupational Safety and Health. (1988). *Proposed national strategies for the prevention of leading work-related diseases and injuries—Psychological disorders.* Washington, DC: U.S. Department of Health and Human Services.

Neale, M. A. (1984). The effects of negotiation and arbitration cost salience on bargainer behavior: The role of the arbiter and constituency in negotiator judgment. *Organizational Behavior and Human Performance, 34*, 97–111.

Nickels, B. J. (1994). The nature of biodata. In G. S. Stokes, M. D. Mumford, & W. A. Owens (Eds.), *Biodata handbook: Theory, research, and use of biographical information in selection and performance prediction* (pp. 1–16). Palo Alto, CA: Consulting Psychologists Press.

Nicoletti, J., & Spooner, K. (1996). Violence in the workplace: Response and intervention strategies. In G. R. VandenBos & E. Q. Bulatao (Eds.), *Violence on the job* (pp.

267–282). Washington, DC: American Psychological Association.

Nilsen, D., & Campbell, D. P. (1993). Self-observer rating discrepancies: Once an overrater, always an overrater? *Human Resource Management, 32*, 265–282.

Noe, R. A. (1988). An investigation of the determinants of successful assigned mentoring relationships. *Personnel Psychology, 41*, 457–480.

Noe, R., & Ford, J. K. (1992). Emerging issues and new directions for training research. In K. Rowland & G. Ferris (Eds.), *Research in personnel and human resource management* (Vol. 10, pp. 345–384). Greenwich, CT: JAI Press.

Normand, J., Lempert, R. O., & O'Brien, C. P. (Eds.). (1994). *Under the influence? Drugs and the American workforce.* Washington, DC: National Academy Press.

Normand, J., Salyards, S. D., & Mahoney, J. J. (1990). An evaluation of preemployment drug testing. *Journal of Applied Psychology, 75*, 629–639.

Northwestern National Life Insurance Company. (1991). *Employee burnout: America's newest epidemic.* Minneapolis: Author.

Noweir, M. H. (1984). Noise exposure as related to productivity, disciplinary actions, absenteeism, and accidents among textile workers. *Journal of Safety Research, 15*, 163–174.

Oakley, A. (1974). *The sociology of housework.* New York: Pantheon.

Offerman, L. R., & Gowing, M. K. (1990). Organizations of the future. *American Psychologist, 45*, 95–108.

O'Keeffe, J. (1994). Disability, discrimination, and the Americans with Disabilities Act. In S. M. Bruyere & J. O'Keeffe (Eds.), *Implications of the Americans with Disabilities Act for psychology* (pp. 1–14). New York: Springer.

Oldham, G. R. (1996). Job design. In C. L. Cooper & I. T. Robertson (Eds.), *International review of industrial and organizational psychology* (Vol. 11, pp. 33–60). London: Wiley.

Olson-Buchanan, J. B. (1996). Voicing discontent: What happens to the grievance filer after the grievance? *Journal of Applied Psychology, 81*, 52–63.

Ones, D. S., & Viswesvaran, C. (1998). Gender, age, and race differences on overt integrity tests: Results across four large-scale job applicant data sets. *Journal of Applied Psychology, 83*, 35–42.

Ones, D. S., Viswesvaran, C., & Reiss, A. (1996). Role of social desirability in personality testing for personnel selection: The red herring. *Journal of Applied Psychology, 81*, 660–679.

Ones, D. S., Viswesvaran, C., & Schmidt, F. L. (1993). Comprehensive meta-analysis of integrity test validities: Findings and implications for personnel selection and theories of job performance. *Journal of Applied Psychology, 78*, 679–703.

Organ, D. W. (1988). *Organizational citizenship behavior: The good soldier syndrome.* Lexington, MA: Lexington Books.

Organ, D. W. (1994). Organizational citizenship behavior and the good soldier. In M. G. Rumsey, C. B. Walker, & J. H. Harris (Eds.), *Personnel selection and classification* (pp. 53–68). Hillsdale, NJ: Erlbaum.

Ostroff, C., & Ford, J. K. (1989). Assessing training needs: Critical levels of analysis. In I. L. Goldstein (Ed.), *Training and development in organizations* (pp. 25–62). San Francisco: Jossey-Bass.

Overton, R. C., Harms, H. J., Taylor, L. R., & Zickar, M. J. (1997). Adapting to adaptive testing. *Personnel Psychology, 50,* 171–185.

Overton, R. C., Taylor, L. R., Zickar, M. J., & Harms, H. J. (1996). The pen-based computer as an alternative platform for test administration. *Personnel Psychology, 49,* 455–464.

Parks, J. M., & Kidder, D. L. (1994). "Till death do us part . . .": Changing work relationships in the 1990s. In C. L. Cooper & D. M. Rousseau (Eds.), *Trends in organizational behavior* (Vol. 1, pp. 111–136). New York: Wiley.

Parsons, H. M., & Kearsley, G. P. (1982). Robotics and human factors: Current status and future prospects. *Human Factors, 24,* 535–552.

Pedalino, E., & Gamboa, V. U. (1974). Behavior modification and absenteeism. *Journal of Applied Psychology, 59,* 694–698.

Pelletier, K. (1977). *Mind as healer, mind as slayer: A holistic approach to preventing stress disorders.* New York: Delacorte.

Pernanen, K. (1991). *Alcohol in human violence.* London: Guilford Press.

Peters, R. H. (1991). Strategies for encouraging self-protective employee behavior. *Journal of Safety Research, 22,* 53–70.

Petersen, A. P., & Gross, F. E. (1978). *Handbook of noise measurement* (8th ed.). New Concord, MA: GenRad.

Peterson, N. G., & Jeanneret, P. R. (1997). Job analysis. In D. L. Whetzel & G. R. Wheaton (Eds.), *Applied measurement methods in industrial psychology* (pp. 13–50). Palo Alto, CA: Consulting Psychologists Press.

Peterson, N. G., Mumford, M. D., Borman, W. C., Jeanneret, P. R., & Fleishman, E. A. (Eds.). (1999). *An occupational information system for the 21st century: The development of the O*NET.* Washington, DC: American Psychological Association.

Pfeffer, J. (1991). Organization theory and structural perspectives on management. *Journal of Management, 17,* 789–803.

Phillips, J. S., & Lord, R. G. (1981). Causal attribution and prescriptions of leadership. *Organizational Behavior and Human Performance, 28,* 143–163.

Pickard, C. O. (1945). Absentee control plans. *Personnel Journal, 23,* 271–276.

Pierce, C. A., & Aguinis, H. (1997). Using virtual reality technology in organizational behavior research. *Journal of Organizational Behavior, 18,* 407–410.

Pierce, C. A., Byrne, D., & Aguinis, H. (1996). Attraction in organizations: A model of workplace romance. *Journal of Organizational Behavior, 17,* 5–32.

Pierce, J. L., & Dunham, R. B. (1992). The 12-hour work day: A 48-hour, four-day week. *Academy of Management Journal, 35,* 1086–1098.

Pierce, J. L., Dunham, R. B., & Cummings, L. L. (1984). Sources of environmental structuring and participant responses. *Organizational Behavior and Human Performance, 33,* 214–242.

Pinder, C. C. (1998). *Work motivation in organizational behavior.* Upper Saddle River, NJ: Prentice Hall.

Ployhart, R. E., & Ryan, A. M. (1998). Applicants' reactions to the fairness of selection procedures: The effects of positive rule violations and time of measurement. *Journal of Applied Psychology, 83,* 3–16.

Podlesny, J. A., & Truslow, C. M. (1993). Validity of an expanded-issue (Modified General Question) polygraph technique in a simulated distributed-crime-roles context. *Journal of Applied Psychology, 78,* 788–797.

Podsakoff, P. M., Ahearne, M., & MacKenzie, S. B. (1997). Organizational citizenship behavior and the quantity and quality of work group performance. *Journal of Applied Psychology, 82,* 262–270.

Podsakoff, P. M., MacKenzie, S. B., & Bommer, W. H. (1996). Meta-analysis of the relationship between Kerr and Jermier's substitutes for leadership and employee job attitudes, role perceptions, and performance. *Journal of Applied Psychology, 81,* 380–399.

Porras, J. I., & Robertson, P. J. (1992). Organizational development: Theory, practice, and research. In M. D. Dunnette & L. M. Hough (Eds.), *Handbook of industrial and organizational psychology* (2nd ed., Vol. 3, pp. 719–822). Palo Alto, CA: Consulting Psychologists Press.

Pratt, M. G., & Rafaeli, A. (1997). Organizational dress as a symbol of multilayered social identities. *Academy of Management Journal, 40,* 862–898.

Premack, S. L., & Hunter, J. E. (1988). Individual unionization decisions. *Psychological Bulletin, 103,* 223–234.

Prieto, J. M. (1993). The team perspective in selection and assessment. In H. Schuler, J. L. Farr, & M. Smith (Eds.), *Personnel selection and assessment* (pp. 221–234). Hillsdale, NJ: Erlbaum.

Prince, J. B., & Lawler, E. E. (1986). Does salary discussion hurt the developmental performance appraisal? *Organizational Behavior and Human Decision Processes, 37,* 357–375.

Pritchard, R. D., DeLeo, P. J., & Von Bergen, C. W. (1976). A field experimental test of expectancy-valence incentive motivation techniques. *Organizational Behavior and Human Performance, 15,* 355–406.

Pritchard, R. D., Jones, S. D., Roth, P. L., Stuebing, K. K., & Ekeberg, S. E. (1988). Effects of group feedback, goal setting, and incentives on organizational productivity. *Journal of Applied Psychology, 73,* 337–358.

Pritchard, R. D., Leonard, D. W., Von Bergen, C. W., & Kirk, R. J. (1976). The effect of varying schedules of reinforcement on human task performance. *Organizational Behavior and Human Performance, 16,* 205–230.

Pruitt, D. G. (1993). *Negotiation in social conflict*. Pacific Grove, CA: Brooks/Cole.

Pulakos, E. D. (1997). Ratings of job performance. In D. L. Whetzel & G. R. Wheaton (Eds.), *Applied measurement methods in industrial psychology* (pp. 291–318). Palo Alto, CA: Consulting Psychologists Press.

Pulakos, E. D., Borman, W. C., & Hough, L. M. (1988). Test validation for scientific understanding: Two demonstrations of an approach to studying predictor–criterion linkages. *Personnel Psychology, 41*, 703–716.

Pulakos, E. D., & Schmitt, N. (1995). Experience-based and structured interview questions: Studies of validity. *Personnel Psychology, 48*, 289–308.

Pursell, E. D., Dossett, D. L., & Latham, G. P. (1980). Obtaining valid predictors by minimizing rating errors in the criterion. *Personnel Psychology, 33*, 91–96.

Pynes, J. E., & Bernardin, H. J. (1989). Predictive validity of an entry-level police officer assessment center. *Journal of Applied Psychology, 74*, 831–833.

Quick, J. C., Murphy, L. R., Hurrell, J. J., & Orman, D. (1992). The value of work in the risk of distress and the power of prevention. In J. C. Quick, L. R. Murphy, & J. J. Hurrell (Eds.), *Stress and well-being at work* (pp. 3–13). Washington, DC: American Psychological Association.

Quinn, R. E., & Lees, P. L. (1984). Attraction and harassment: Dynamics of sexual politics in the workplace. *Organizational Dynamics, 13*(2), 36–46.

Quinones, M. A. (1995). Pretraining context effects: Training assignment as feedback. *Journal of Applied Psychology, 80*, 226–238.

Raelin, J. A. (1989). Unionization and deprofessionalization: Which comes first? *Journal of Organizational Behavior, 10*, 101–115.

Rafaeli, A., & Klimoski, R. J. (1983). Predicting sales success through handwriting analysis: An evaluation of the effects of training and handwriting sample content. *Journal of Applied Psychology, 68*, 212–217.

Ragins, B. R., & Cotton, J. L. (1991). Easier said than done: Gender differences in perceived barriers to gaining a mentor. *Academy of Management Journal, 34*, 939–951.

Ragins, B. R., & McFarlin, D. B. (1990). Perceptions of mentor roles in cross-gender mentoring relationships. *Journal of Vocational Behavior, 37*, 321–339.

Ragins, B. R., & Sundstrom, E. (1989). Gender and power in organizations: A longitudinal perspective. *Psychological Bulletin, 105*, 51–88.

Raju, N. S., Burke, M. J., Normand, J., & Langlois, G. M. (1991). A new meta-analytic approach. *Journal of Applied Psychology, 76*, 432–446.

Ralston, D. A. (1989). The benefits of flextime: Real or imagined? *Journal of Organizational Behavior, 10*, 369–374.

Rawls, J. (1971). *A theory of justice*. Cambridge, MA: Harvard University Press.

Reason, J. T. (1994). Foreword. In M. S. Bogner (Ed.), *Human error in medicine* (pp. vii–xv). Hillsdale, NJ: Erlbaum.

Reber, R. A., Wallin, J. A., & Chhokar, J. S. (1984). Reducing industrial accidents: A behavioral experiment. *Industrial Relations, 23*, 119–125.

Ree, M. J., Earles, J. A., & Teachout, M. S. (1994). Predicting job performance: Not much more than g. *Journal of Applied Psychology, 79*, 518–524.

Reeves, C. A., & Bednar, D. A. (1994). Defining quality: Alternatives and implications. *Academy of Management Review, 19*, 419–445.

Reilly, R. R. (In press). *Team pay: Establishing reward systems*. Thousand Oaks, CA: Sage.

Reilly, R. R., & McGourty, J. (1998). Performance appraisal in team settings. In J. W. Smither (Ed.), *Performance appraisal* (pp. 244–277). San Francisco: Jossey-Bass.

Repetti, R. L. (1987). Linkages between work and family roles. *Applied Social Psychology Annual, 7*, 98–127.

Reschetyuk, A. L. (1992). The working ability of aging workers. *Gerontology & Geriatrics Education, 13*, 91–102.

Rhodes, S. R., & Steers, R. M. (1990). *Managing employee absenteeism*. Reading, MA: Addison-Wesley.

Robertson, I. T., & Kandola, R. S. (1982). Work sample tests: Validity, adverse impact and applicant reaction. *Journal of Occupational Psychology, 55*, 171–183.

Robertson, P. J., Roberts, D. R., & Porras, J. I. (1993). Dynamics of planned organizational change: Assessing empirical support for a theoretical model. *Academy of Management Journal, 36*, 619–634.

Robinson, S. L., Kraatz, M. S., & Rousseau, D. M. (1994). Changing obligations and the psychology contract: A longitudinal study. *Academy of Management Journal, 37*, 137–152.

Robinson, S. L., & Rousseau, D. M. (1994). Violating the psychological contract: Not the exception but the norm. *Journal of Organizational Behavior, 15*, 245–259.

Rodgers, R., & Hunter, J. E. (1996). The methodological war of the "Hardheads" versus the "Softheads." *Journal of Applied Behavioral Science, 32*, 189–208.

Roebuck, J. A. (1995). *Anthropometric methods: Designing to fit the human body*. Santa Monica, CA: Human Factors and Ergonomics Society.

Roethlisberger, F. J., & Dickson, W. J. (1939). *Management and the worker*. Cambridge, MA: Harvard University Press.

Ronen, S. (1989). Training the international assignee. In I. L. Goldstein (Ed.), *Training and development in organizations* (pp. 417–454). San Francisco: Jossey-Bass.

Ronen, S., & Primps, S. B. (1981). The compressed work week as organizational change: Behavioral and attitudinal outcomes. *Academy of Management Review, 6*, 61–74.

Root, D. A., & Ziska, M. D. (1996). Violence prevention during corporate downsizing: The use of a people team as context for the critical incident teams. In G. R. VandenBos & E. Q. Bulatao (Eds.), *Violence on the job* (pp. 353–366). Washington, DC: American Psychological Association.

Rosen, H., & Stagner, R. (1980). Industrial/organizational psychology and unions: A viable relationship? *Professional Psychology, 11*, 477–483.

Ronen, S. (1997). Personal reflections and projections: International industrial/organizational at a crossroads. In P. C. Earley & M. Erez (Eds.), *New perspectives in industrial/organizational psychology* (pp. 715–731). San Francisco: New Lexington Press.

Rosenthal, R. (1991). *Meta-analytic procedures for social research* (2nd ed.). Newbury Park, CA: Sage.

Rosnow, R. L. (1997). Hedgehogs, foxes, and the evolving social contract in psychological science: Ethical challenges and methodological opportunities. *Psychological Methods, 2,* 345–356.

Ross, R. R., & Altmaier, E. M. (1994). *Intervention in occupational stress.* London: Sage.

Rouillier, J. Z., & Goldstein, I. L. (1990). *The determination of positive transfer of training climate through organizational analysis.* Unpublished manuscript.

Rousseau, D. M. (1989). Psychological and implied contracts in organizations. *Employee Responsibilities and Rights Journal, 2,* 121–139.

Rousseau, D. M. (1995). *Psychological contracts in organizations.* Thousand Oaks, CA: Sage.

Rousseau, D. M. (1997). Organizational behavior in the new organizational era. *Annual Review of Psychology, 48,* 515–546.

Rousseau, D. M., & Parks, J. M. (1993). The contracts of individuals and organizations. In B. M. Staw & L. L. Cummings (Eds.), *Research in organizational behavior* (Vol. 15, pp. 1–43). Greenwich, CT: JAI Press.

Ruback, R. B., & Innes, C. A. (1988). The relevance and irrelevance of psychological research. *American Psychologist, 43,* 683–693.

Rumsey, M. G., Walker, C. B., & Harris, J. H. (Eds.). (1994). *Personnel selection and classification.* Hillsdale, NJ: Erlbaum.

Russell, J. S., & Goode, D. L. (1988). An analysis of managers' reactions to their own performance appraisal feedback. *Journal of Applied Psychology, 73,* 63–67.

Rynes, S. L. (1993). Who's selecting whom? Effects of selection practices on applicant attitudes and behavior. In N. Schmitt & W. C. Borman (Eds.), *Personnel selection in organizations* (pp. 240–274). San Francisco: Jossey-Bass.

Rynes, S. L., & Milkovich, G. T. (1986). Wage surveys: Dispelling some myths about the "market wage." *Personnel Psychology, 39,* 71–90.

Rynes, S. L., Orlitzky, M. O., & Bretz, R. D. (1997). Experienced hiring versus college recruiting: Practices and emerging trends. *Personnel Psychology, 50,* 309–340.

Rynes, S., & Rosen, B. (1995). A field survey of factors affecting the adoption and perceived success of diversity training. *Personnel Psychology, 48,* 247–270.

Saal, F. E., Downey, R. G., & Lahey, M. A. (1980). Rating the ratings: Assessing the psychometric quality of rating data. *Psychological Bulletin, 88,* 413–428.

Saari, L. M., Johnson, T. R., McLaughlin, S. D., & Zimmerle, D. M. (1988). A survey of management training and education practices in U.S. companies. *Personnel Psychology, 41,* 731–744.

Sackett, P. R., & Larson, J. R., Jr. (1990). Research strategies and tactics in industrial and organizational psychology. In M. D. Dunnette & L. M. Hough (Eds.), *Handbook of industrial and organizational psychology* (2nd ed., Vol. 1, pp. 419–489). Palo Alto, CA: Consulting Psychologists Press.

Sackett, P. R., & Wanek, J. E. (1996). New developments in the use of measures of honesty, integrity, conscientiousness, dependability, trustworthiness, and reliability for personnel selection. *Personnel Psychology, 49,* 787–829.

Sackett, P. R., & Wilk, S. L. (1994). Within-group norming and other forms of score adjustment in psychological testing. *American Psychologist, 49,* 929–954.

Salas, E., & Cannon-Bowers, J. A. (1997). Methods, tools, and strategies for team training. In M. A. Quinones & A. Ehrenstein (Eds.), *Training for a rapidly changing workplace* (pp. 249–280). Washington, DC: American Psychological Association.

Salgado, J. F. (1997). The five factor model of personality and job performance in the European Community. *Journal of Applied Psychology, 82,* 30–43.

Salovey, P., & Mayer, J. D. (1990). Emotional intelligence. *Imagination, Cognition, and Personality, 9,* 185–211.

Schaufeli, W. B., & Van Yperen, N. W. (1992). Unemployment and psychological distress among graduates: A longitudinal study. *Journal of Occupational and Organizational Psychology, 65,* 291–305.

Schein, E. H. (1996). Culture: The missing concept in organizational studies. *Administrative Science Quarterly, 41,* 229–240.

Schippman, J. S., Prien, E. P., & Katz, J. A. (1990). Reliability and validity of in-basket performance measures. *Personnel Psychology, 43,* 837–859.

Schmidt, F. L. (1991). Why all banding procedures in personnel selection are logically flawed. *Human Performance, 4,* 265–278.

Schmidt, F. L., & Hunter, J. E. (1978). Moderator research and the law of small numbers. *Personnel Psychology, 31,* 215–232.

Schmidt, F. L., & Hunter, J. E. (1980). The future of criterion-related validity. *Personnel Psychology, 33,* 41–60.

Schmidt, F. L., & Hunter, J. E. (1981). Employment testing: Old theories and new research findings. *American Psychologist, 36,* 1128–1137.

Schmidt, F. L., & Hunter, J. E. (1995). The fatal internal contradiction in banding: Its statistical rational is logically inconsistent with its operational procedures. *Human Performance, 8,* 203–214.

Schmidt, F. L., Hunter, J. E., McKenzie, R. C., & Muldrow, T. W. (1979). Impact of valid selection procedures on work-force productivity. *Journal of Applied Psychology, 64,* 609–626.

Schmit, M. J., & Ryan, A. M. (1993). The big five in personnel selection: Factor structure in applicant and nonapplicant populations. *Journal of Applied Psychology, 78,* 966–974.

Schmitt, N., Gooding, R. Z., Noe, R. D., & Kirsch, M. (1984). Meta-analyses of validity studies published between

1964 and 1982 and the investigation of study characteristics. *Personnel Psychology, 37,* 407–422.

Schmitt, N., & Landy, F. J. (1993). The concept of validity. In N. Schmitt & W. C. Borman (Eds.), *Personnel selection in organizations* (pp. 275–309). Palo Alto, CA: Consulting Psychologists Press.

Schneider, B. (1987). The people make the place. *Personnel Psychology, 40,* 437–454.

Schneider, B. (1996). When individual differences aren't. In K. R. Murphy (Ed.), *Individual differences and behaviors in organizations* (pp. 548–572). San Francisco: Jossey-Bass.

Schneider, B., Goldstein, H. W., & Smith, D. B. (1995). The ASA framework: An update. *Personnel Psychology, 48,* 747–773.

Schneider, B., Reichers, A. E., & Mitchell, T. M. (1982). A note on some relationships between the aptitude requirements and reward attributes of tasks. *Academy of Management Journal, 25,* 567–574.

Schneider, B., Smith, D. B., Taylor, S., & Fleenor, J. (1998). Personality and organizations: A test of the homogeneity of personality hypothesis. *Journal of Applied Psychology, 83,* 462–470.

Schneider, K. T., Swan, S., & Fitzgerald, L. F. (1997). Job-related and psychological effects of sexual harassment in the workplace: Empirical evidence from two organizations. *Journal of Applied Psychology, 82,* 401–415.

Schor, J. (1992). *The overworked American.* New York: Basic Books.

Schriesheim, C. A. (1978). Job satisfaction, attitudes toward unions, and voting in a union representation election. *Journal of Applied Psychology, 63,* 548–552.

Schuler, H. (1993). Social validity of selection situations: A concept and some empirical results. In H. Schuler, J. L. Farr, & M. Smith (Eds.), *Personnel selection and assessment* (pp. 11–26). Hillsdale, NJ: Erlbaum.

Schwab, D. P., & Wichern, D. W. (1983). Systematic bias in job evaluation and market wages: Implications for the comparable worth debate. *Journal of Applied Psychology, 68,* 60–69.

Scott, W. D. (1903). *The theory of advertising.* Boston: Small, Maynard.

Scott, W. D. (1908). *The psychology of advertising.* New York: Arno Press.

Scott, W. D. (1911a). *Increasing human efficiency in business.* New York: Macmillan.

Scott, W. D. (1911b). *Influencing men in business.* New York: Ronald Press.

Scott, W. G., Mitchell, T. R., & Birnbaum, P. H. (1981). *Organization theory: A structural and behavioral analysis.* Homewood, IL: Richard D. Irwin.

Scott, W. R. (1992). *Organizations: Rational, natural, and open systems* (3rd ed.). Englewood Cliffs, NJ: Prentice Hall.

Seashore, S. E., Indik, B. P., & Georgopoulos, B. S. (1960). Relationship among criteria of job performance. *Journal of Applied Psychology, 44,* 195–202.

Selye, H. (1982). History and present status of the stress concept. In L. Goldberger & S. Breznitz (Eds.), *Handbook of stress* (pp. 7–17). New York: Free Press.

Senders, J. W., & Moray, N. P. (1991). *Human error: Cause, prediction, and reduction.* Hillsdale, NJ: Erlbaum.

Senge, P. (1990). *The fifth discipline: The art and practice of the learning organization.* New York: Doubleday/Currency.

Seymour, G. O., Stahl, J. M., Levine, S. L., Ingram, J. L., & Smith, R. F. (1994). Modifying law enforcement training simulators for use in basic research. *Behavior Research Methods, Instruments, & Computers, 26,* 266–268.

Shadish, W. R. (1996). Meta-analyses and the explanation of causal mediating processes: A primer of examples, methods, and issues. *Psychological Methods, 1,* 47–65.

Sheehy, N. P., & Chapman, A. J. (1987). Industrial accidents. In C. L. Cooper & I. T. Robertson (Eds.), *International review of industrial and organizational psychology* (Vol. 2, pp. 201–227). London: Wiley.

Shenkar, O. (1988). Robotics: A challenge for occupational psychology. *Journal of Occupational Psychology, 61,* 103–112.

Shore, L. M., & Tetrick, L. E. (1994). The psychological contract as an explanatory framework in the employment relationship. In C. L. Cooper & D. M. Rousseau (Eds.), *Trends in organizational behavior* (Vol. 1, pp. 91–110). New York: Wiley.

Shore, T. H., Shore, L. M., & Thornton, G. C. (1992). Construct validity of self- and peer evaluations of performance dimensions in an assessment center. *Journal of Applied Psychology, 77,* 42–54.

Shostak, A. B. (1964). Industrial psychology and the trade unions: A matter of mutual indifference. In G. Fisk (Ed.), *The frontiers of management psychology.* New York: Harper & Row.

Silberstein, L. R. (1992). *Dual-career marriage: A system in transition.* Hillsdale, NJ: Erlbaum.

Silvester, J., & Chapman, A. J. (1997). Asking "why" in the workplace. In C. L. Cooper & D. M. Rousseau (Eds.), *Trends in organizational behavior* (Vol. 4, pp. 1–14). London: Wiley.

Simard, M., & Marchand, A. (1997). Workgroups' propensity to comply with safety rules: The influence of micro-macro organizational factors. *Ergonomics, 40,* 172–188.

Siskin, B. R. (1995). Relation between performance and banding. *Human Performance, 8,* 215–226.

Skarkicki, D. P., & Folger, A. (1997). Retaliation in the workplace: The roles of distributive, procedural, and interactional justice. *Journal of Applied Psychology, 82,* 434–443.

Skarlicki, D. P., & Latham, G. P. (1996). Increasing citizenship behavior within a labor union: A test of organizational justice theory. *Journal of Applied Psychology, 81,* 161–169.

Skarlicki, D. P., & Latham, G. P. (1997). Leadership training in organizational justice to increase citizenship behavior within a labor union: A replication. *Personnel Psychology, 50,* 617–654.

Smith, C. S., Reilly, C., & Midkiff, K. (1989). Evaluation of three circadian rhythm questionnaires with suggestions for an improved measure of morningness. *Journal of Applied Psychology, 74,* 728–738.

Smith, E. M., Ford, J. K., & Kozlowski, S. W. (1997). Building adaptive expertise: Implications for training design strategies. In M. A. Quinones & A. Ehrenstein (Eds.), *Training for a rapidly changing workplace* (pp. 89–118). Washington, DC: American Psychological Association.

Smith, M. J., Cohen, H. H., Cohen, A., & Cleveland, R. J. (1978). Characteristics of successful safety programs. *Journal of Safety Research, 10,* 5–15.

Smith, M., Farr, J. L., & Schuler, H. (1993). Individual and organizational perspectives on personnel procedures: Conclusions and horizons for future research. In H. Schuler, J. L. Farr, & M. Smith (Eds.), *Personnel selection and assessment* (pp. 333–351). Hillsdale, NJ: Erlbaum.

Smither, J. W. (1995). Creating an internal contingent workforce: Managing the resource link. In M. London (Ed.), *Employees, careers, and job creation.* San Francisco: Jossey-Bass.

Smither, J. W., Reilly, R. R., Millsap, R. E., & Pearlman, K. (1993). Applicant reactions to selection procedures. *Personnel Psychology, 46,* 49–76.

Society for Industrial and Organizational Psychology, Inc. (1987). *Principles for the validation and use of personnel selection procedures* (3rd ed.). College Park, MD: Author.

Soine, L. (1995). Sick building syndrome and gender bias: Imperiling women's health. *Social Work in Health Care, 20,* 51–65.

Solomonson, A. L., & Lance, C. E. (1997). Examination of the relationship between true halo and halo error in performance ratings. *Journal of Applied Psychology, 82,* 665–674.

Spector, P. E., Brannick, M. T., & Coovert, M. D. (1989). Job analysis. In C. L. Cooper & I. T. Robertson (Eds.), *International review of industrial and organizational psychology* (Vol. 4, pp. 281–328). London: Wiley.

Spettell, C. M., & Liebert, R. M. (1986). Training for safety in automated person–machine systems. *American Psychologist, 41,* 545–550.

Spool, M. D. (1978). Training programs for observers of behavior: A review. *Personnel Psychology, 31,* 853–888.

Spreitzer, G. M. (1997). Toward a common ground in defining empowerment. In W. A. Pasmore & R. W. Woodman (Eds.), *Research in organizational change and development* (Vol. 10, pp. 31–62). Greenwich, CT: JAI Press.

Spreitzer, G. M., McCall, M. M., & Mahoney, J. D. (1997). Early identification of international executive potential. *Journal of Applied Psychology, 82,* 6–29.

Spychalski, A. C., Quinones, M. A., Gaugler, B. B., & Pohley, J. (1997). A survey of assessment center practices in organizations in the United States. *Personnel Psychology, 50,* 71–90.

Sredl, H. J., & Rothwell, W. J. (1987). *Professional training roles and competencies* (Vol. II). Amherst, MA: HRD Press.

Stagner, R. (1981). Training and experiences of some distinguished industrial psychologists. *American Psychologist, 36,* 497–505.

Stagner, R. (1982). Past and future of industrial/organizational psychology. *Professional Psychology, 13,* 892–903.

Stagner, R., & Effal, B. (1982). Internal union dynamics during a strike: A quasi-experimental study. *Journal of Applied Psychology, 67,* 37–44.

Stagner, R., & Rosen, H. (1965). *Psychology of union–management relations.* Belmont, CA: Wadsworth.

Stahelski, A. J., Frost, D. E., & Patch, M. E. (1989). Use of socially dependent bases of power: French and Raven's theory applied to workgroup leadership. *Journal of Applied Psychology, 19,* 283–297.

Stahl, M. J., & Harrell, A. M. (1981). Modeling effort decisions with behavioral decision theory: Toward an individual differences model of expectancy theory. *Organizational Behavior and Human Performance, 27,* 303–325.

Stajkovic, A. D., & Luthans, F. (1997). A meta-analysis of the effects of organizational behavior modification on task performance, 1975–1995. *Academy of Management Journal, 40,* 1122–1149.

Standards for educational and psychological testing. (1985). Washington, DC: American Psychological Association.

Starke, F. A., & Notz, W. W. (1981). Pre- and post-intervention effects of conventional versus final offer arbitration. *Academy of Management Journal, 24,* 832–850.

Steel, R. P., & Ovalle, N. K. (1984). Self-appraisal based upon supervisory feedback. *Personnel Psychology, 37,* 667–686.

Steel, R. P., & Rentsch, J. R. (1997). The dispositional model of job attitudes revisited: Findings of a 10-year study. *Journal of Applied Psychology, 82,* 873–879.

Stein, J. A., Newcomb, M. D., & Bentler, P. M. (1988). Structure of drug use behaviors and consequences among young adults: Multitrait-multimethod assessment of frequency, quantity, work site, and problem substance abuse. *Journal of Applied Psychology, 73,* 595–605.

Steiner, D. D., & Gilliland, S. W. (1996). Fairness reactions to personnel selection techniques in France and the United States. *Journal of Applied Psychology, 81,* 134–141.

Stellman, J. M., Klitzman, S., Gordon, G. C., & Snow, B. R. (1987). Work environment and the well-being of clerical and VDT workers. *Journal of Occupational Behavior, 8,* 95–114.

Stenberg, B., & Wall, S. (1995). Why do women report "sick building symptoms" more often than men? *Social Science and Medicine, 40,* 491–502.

Sternberg, R. J. (1997a). The concept of intelligence and its role in lifelong learning and success. *American Psychologist, 52,* 1030–1057.

Sternberg, R. J. (1997b). *Thinking styles.* Cambridge, UK: University of Cambridge.

Stokes, G. S., Mumford, M. D., & Owens, W. A. (Eds.). (1994). *Biodata handbook: Theory, research, and use of biographical* information in selection and performance prediction. Palo Alto, CA: Consulting Psychologists Press.

Stone, D. L., & Kotch, D. A. (1989). Individuals' attitudes toward organizational drug testing policies and practices. *Journal of Applied Psychology, 74,* 518–521.

Strasser, S., & Bateman, T. S. (1984). What we should study, problems we should solve: Perspectives of two constituencies. *Personnel Psychology, 37,* 77–92.

Streufert, S., Pogash, R. M., Roache, J., Gingrich, D., Landis, R., Severs, W., Lonardi, L., & Kantner, A. (1992). Effects of alcohol intoxication on risk taking, strategy, and error rate in visuomotor performance. *Journal of Applied Psychology, 77,* 515–524.

Sulsky, L. M., & Balzer, W. K. (1988). Meaning and measurement of performance rating accuracy: Some methodological and theoretical concerns. *Journal of Applied Psychology, 73,* 497–506.

Sulsky, L. M., & Day, D. V. (1992). Frame-of-reference training and cognitive categorization: An empirical investigation of rater memory issues. *Journal of Applied Psychology, 77,* 501–510.

Summers, T. P., Betton, J. H., & DeCotiis, T. A. (1986). Voting for and against unions: A decision model. *Academy of Management Review, 11,* 643–655.

Sundstrom, E., Town, J. P., Rice, R. W., & Osborn, D. P. (1994). Office noise, satisfaction, and performance. *Environment & Behavior, 26,* 195–222.

Sutton, R. I., & Kahn, R. L. (1987). Prediction, understanding, and control as antidotes to organizational stress. In J. W. Lorsch (Ed.), *Handbook of organizational behavior.* Englewood Cliffs, NJ: Prentice Hall.

Sverke, M., & Kuruvilla, S. (1995). A new conceptualization of union commitment: Development and test of an integrated theory. *Journal of Organizational Behavior, 16,* 505–532.

Sverke, M., & Sjoberg, A. (1995). Union membership behavior: The influence of instrumental and value-based commitment. In L. E. Tetrick & J. Barling (Eds.), *Changing employment relations* (pp. 229–254). Washington, DC: American Psychological Association.

Sweetland, R. C., & Keyser, D. J. (Eds.). (1991). *Tests: A comprehensive reference for assessments in psychology, education, and business* (3rd ed.). Kansas City, MO: Test Corporation of America.

Tangri, S. S., Burt, M. R., & Johnson, L. B. (1982). Sexual harassment at work: Three explanatory models. *Journal of Social Issues, 38*(4), 33–54.

Tannenbaum, S. I., & Yukl, G. (1992). Training and development in work organizations. *Annual Review of Psychology, 43,* 399–441.

Taylor, F. W. (1911). *The principles of scientific management.* New York: Harper.

Tenopyr, M. L. (1996). The complex interactions between measurement and national employment policy. *Psychology, Public Policy, and Law, 2,* 348–362.

Tepas, D. I. (1993). Educational programmes for shiftworkers, their families, and prospective shiftworkers. *Ergonomics, 36,* 199–209.

Tetrick, L. E. (1995). Developing and maintaining union commitment: A theoretical framework. *Journal of Organizational Behavior, 16,* 583–595.

Tett, R. P., Jackson, D. N., & Rothstein, M. (1991). Personality measures as predictors of job performance: A meta-analytic review. *Personnel Psychology, 44,* 703–742.

Tharenou, P. (1997). Managerial career advancement. In C. L. Cooper & I. T. Robertson (Eds.), *International review of industrial and organizational psychology* (Vol. 12, pp. 39–94). New York: Wiley.

Tharenou, P., Latimer, S., & Conroy, D. (1994). How do you make it to the top? An examination of influences on women's and men's managerial advancement. *Academy of Management Journal, 37,* 899–931.

Thierry, H., & Meijman, T. (1994). Time and behavior at work. In H. C. Triandis, M. D. Dunnette, & L. M. Hough (Eds.), *Handbook of industrial and organizational psychology* (2nd ed., Vol. 4, pp. 341–413). Palo Alto, CA: Consulting Psychologists Press.

Thomas, D. A. (1990). The impact of race on managers' experiences of developmental relationships (mentorship and sponsorship): An intra-organizational study. *Journal of Organizational Behavior, 11,* 479–492.

Thomas, D. A. (1993). Racial dynamics in cross-race developmental relationships. *Administrative Science Quarterly, 38,* 169–194.

Thomas, K. W., & Tymon, W. G., Jr. (1982). Necessary properties of relevant research: Lessons from recent criticisms of the organizational sciences. *Academy of Management Review, 7,* 345–352.

Thomas, L. T., & Ganster, D. C. (1995). Impact of family-supportive work variables on work–family conflict and strain: A control perspective. *Journal of Applied Psychology, 80,* 6–15.

Thompson, D. E., & Thompson, T. A. (1982). Court standards for job analysis in test validation. *Personnel Psychology, 35,* 865–874.

Thornton, G. C., III. (1980). Psychometric properties of self-appraisals of job performance. *Personnel Psychology, 33,* 263–272.

Tornow, W. W. (1993). Perceptions or reality: Is multiperspective measurement a means or an end? *Human Resource Management, 32,* 221–230.

Totterdell, P., Spelten, E., Smith, L., Barton, J., & Folkard, S. (1995). Recovering from work shifts: How long does it take? *Journal of Applied Psychology, 80,* 43–57.

Tracey, J. B., Tannenbaum, S. I., & Kavanagh, M. J. (1995). Applying trained skills on the job: The importance of the work environment. *Journal of Applied Psychology, 80,* 239–252.

Triandis, H. C. (1975). Culture training, cognitive complexity, and interpersonal attitudes. In R. Brislin, S. Bochner,

& W. Lonner (Eds.), *Cross-cultural perspectives on learning* (pp. 39–77). Beverly Hills, CA: Sage.

Triandis, H. C. (1994). Cross-cultural industrial and organizational psychology. In H. C. Triandis, M. D. Dunnette, & L. M. Hough (Eds.), *Handbook of industrial and organizational psychology* (2nd ed., Vol. 4, pp. 103–172). Palo Alto, CA: Consulting Psychologists Press.

Triandis, H. C. (1995). A theoretical framework for the study of diversity. In M. M. Chemers, S. Oskamp, & M. A. Costanzo (Eds.), *Diversity in organizations* (pp. 1–36). Thousand Oaks, CA: Sage.

Triandis, H. C., Kurowski, L. L., & Gelfand, M. J. (1994). Workplace diversity. In H. C. Triandis, M. D. Dunnette, & L. M. Hough (Eds.), *Handbook of industrial and organizational psychology* (2nd ed., Vol. 4, pp. 769–827). Palo Alto, CA: Consulting Psychologists Press.

Trice, H. M., & Sonnenstuhl, W. J. (1988). Drinking behavior and risk factors related to the work place: Implications for research and practice. *Journal of Applied Behavioral Science, 24,* 327–346.

Tubbs, M. E. (1986). Goal setting: A meta-analytic examination of the empirical evidence. *Journal of Applied Psychology, 71,* 474–483.

Turnage, J. J. (1990). The challenge of new workplace technology for psychology. *American Psychologist, 45,* 171–178.

Turnage, J. J., & Muchinsky, P. M. (1984). A comparison of the predictive validity of assessment center evaluations versus traditional measures in forecasting supervisory job performance: Interpretive implications of criterion distortion for the assessment paradigm. *Journal of Applied Psychology, 69,* 595–602.

Turner, A. N., & Lawrence, P. R. (1965). *Industrial jobs and the worker: An investigation of response to task attributes.* Cambridge, MA: Harvard University Press.

Tyson, P. R., & Vaughn, R. A. (1987, April). Drug testing in the work place: Legal responsibilities. *Occupational Health and Safety,* 24–36.

Tziner, A., & Dolan, S. (1982). Validity of an assessment center for identifying future female officers in the military. *Journal of Applied Psychology, 67,* 728–736.

U.S. Civil Service Commission. (1977). *Instructions for the Factor Evaluation System.* Washington, DC: U.S. Government Printing Office.

U.S. Department of Justice. (1998). *Bureau of Justice Statistics Special Report on Workplace Violence 1992–1996.* Washington, DC: The Bureau.

U.S. Department of Labor. (1994). *Apprenticeship: Past and present.* Washington, DC: U.S. Government Printing Office.

U.S. Department of Labor, Employment, and Training Administration. (1991). *Dictionary of occupational titles* (4th ed.). Washington, DC: U.S. Government Printing Office.

Vaill, P. (1982). The purposing of high-performing systems. *Organizational Dynamics, 2*(2), 23–39.

Van De Water, T. J. (1997). Psychology's entrepreneurs and the marketing of industrial psychology. *Journal of Applied Psychology, 82,* 486–499.

Van der Spiegel, J. (1995). New information technologies and changes in work. In A. Howard (Ed.), *The changing nature of work* (pp. 97–111). San Francisco: Jossey-Bass.

Van Dyne, L., Graham, J. W., & Dienesch, R. M. (1994). Organizational citizenship behavior: Construct redefinition, measurement, and validation. *Academy of Management Journal, 37,* 765–802.

Van Eerde, W., & Thierry, H. (1996). Vroom's expectancy models and work-related criteria: A meta-analysis. *Journal of Applied Psychology, 81,* 575–586.

Van Velsor, E., Ruderman, M. N., & Young, D. P. (1991). *Enhancing self objectivity and performance on the job: The role of upward feedback.* Paper presented at the 6th annual conference of the Society of Industrial and Organizational Psychology, St. Louis.

Varca, P. E., & Pattison, P. (1993). Evidentiary standards in employment discrimination: A view toward the future. *Personnel Psychology, 46,* 239–258.

Vecchio, R. P. (1990). Theoretical and empirical examination of cognitive resource theory. *Journal of Applied Psychology, 75,* 141–147.

Viano, D. C., Lau, I. V., Asbury, C., & King, A. I. (1989). Biomechanics of the human chest, abdomen, and pelvis in lateral impact. *Accident Analysis and Prevention, 21,* 553–574.

Vinokur, A. D., Threatt, B. A., Vinokur-Caplan, D., & Satariano, W. A. (1990). The process of recovering from breast cancer in younger and older patients. *Cancer, 65,* 1242–1254.

Viswesvaran, C., & Schmidt, F. L. (1992). A meta-analytic comparison of the effectiveness of smoking cessation methods. *Journal of Applied Psychology, 77,* 554–566.

Voevodsky, J. (1974). Evaluation of a deceleration warning light for reducing rear-end automobile collisions. *Journal of Applied Psychology, 59,* 270–273.

Vroom, V. H. (1964). *Work and motivation.* New York: Wiley.

Wagner, R. K. (1997). Intelligence, training, and employment. *American Psychologist, 52,* 1059–1069.

Wagner, S. H., & Goffin, R. D. (1997). Differences in accuracy of absolute and comparative performance appraisal methods. *Organizational Behavior and Human Decision Processes, 70,* 95–103.

Wahba, M. A., & Bridwell, L. T. (1976). Maslow reconsidered. A review of research on the need hierarchy theory. *Organizational Behavior and Human Performance, 15,* 212–240.

Wallace, S. R. (1965). Criteria for what? *American Psychologist, 20,* 411–417.

Wanberg, C. R. (1997). Antecedents and outcomes of coping behaviors among unemployed and reemployed individuals. *Journal of Applied Psychology, 82,* 731–744.

Wanberg, C. R., Watt, J. D., & Rumsey, D. J. (1996). Individuals without jobs: An empirical study of job-seeking behaviors and reemployment. *Journal of Applied Psychology, 81,* 76–87.

Wang, Z. (1993). Editorial: Strategies for ergonomics in developing countries. *Ergonomics, 36,* 597–599.

Wanous, J. P., Sullivan, S. E., & Malinak, J. (1989). The role of judgment calls in meta-analysis. *Journal of Applied Psychology, 74,* 259–264.

Warr, P. B. (1987). *Work, unemployment, and mental health.* Oxford: Clarendon.

Warr, P. B., & Jackson, P. R. (1985). Factors influencing the psychological impact of prolonged unemployment and of re-employment. *Psychological Medicine, 15,* 795–807.

Warr, P. B., & Payne, R. L. (1983). Social class and reported changes in behavior after job loss. *Journal of Applied Social Psychology, 13,* 206–222.

Watanabe, S., Takahashi, K., & Minami, T. (1997). The emerging role of diversity and work–family values in a global context. In P. C. Earley & M. Erez (Eds.), *New perspectives on international industrial/organizational psychology* (pp. 276–318). San Francisco: New Lexington Press.

Webster, J., & Starbuck, W. H. (1988). Theory building in industrial and organizational psychology. In C. L. Cooper & I. T. Robertson (Eds.), *International review of industrial and organizational psychology* (Vol. 3, pp. 93–138). London: Wiley.

Weekley, J. A., & Gier, J. A. (1989). Ceilings in the reliability and validity of performance ratings: The case of expert raters. *Academy of Management Journal, 32,* 213–222.

Weekley, J. A., & Jones, C. (1997). Video-based situational testing. *Personnel Psychology, 50,* 25–49.

Weisinger, H. (1998). *Emotional intelligence at work.* San Francisco: Jossey-Bass.

Weiss, D. J., Dawis, R. V., England, G. W., & Lofquist, L. H. (1967). *Manual for the Minnesota Satisfaction Questionnaire.* Minneapolis: Industrial Relations Center, University of Minnesota.

Weiss, D. J., & Vale, C. D. (1987). Adaptive testing. *Applied Psychology: An International Review, 36,* 249–262.

Weiss, H. M. (1990). Learning theory and industrial and organizational psychology. In M. D. Dunnette, & L. M. Hough (Eds.), *Handbook of industrial and organizational psychology* (2nd ed., Vol. 1, pp. 171–221). Palo Alto, CA: Consulting Psychologists Press.

Werner, J. M., & Bolino, M. C. (1997). Explaining U.S. court of appeals decisions involving performance appraisal: Accuracy, fairness, and validation. *Personnel Psychology, 50,* 1–24.

Westin, A. F. (1992). Two key factors that belong in a macroergonomic analysis of electronic monitoring: Employee perceptions of fairness and the climate of organizational trust or distrust. *Applied Ergonomics, 23,* 35–42.

Wherry, R. J. (1957). The past and future of criterion evaluation. *Personnel Psychology, 10,* 1–5.

Whetten, D. A., & Cameron, K. S. (1991). *Developing management skills* (2nd ed.). New York: HarperCollins.

Whetzel, D. L., & McDaniel, M. A. (1997). Employment interviews. In D. L. Whetzel & G. R. Wheaton (Eds.), *Applied measurement methods in industrial psychology* (pp. 185–206). Palo Alto, CA: Consulting Psychologists Press.

White, L. P., & Wooten, K. C. (1983). Ethical dilemmas in various stages of organizational development. *Academy of Management Review, 8,* 690–697.

White, L. P., & Wooten, K. C. (1986). *Professional ethics and practice in organizational development.* New York: Praeger.

Whyte, G., & Latham, G. (1997). The futility of utility analysis revisited: When even an expert fails. *Personnel Psychology, 50,* 601–610.

Wigdor, A. K., & Sackett, P. R. (1993). Employment testing and public policy: The case of the General Aptitude Test Battery. In H. Schuler, J. L. Farr, & M. Smith (Eds.), *Personnel selection and assessment* (pp. 183–204). Hillsdale, NJ: Erlbaum.

Williams, C. R., & Livingstone, L. P. (1994). Another look at the relationship between performance and voluntary turnover. *Academy of Management Journal, 37,* 269–298.

Williams, K. M., & Crafts, J. L. (1997). Inductive job analysis. In D. L. Whetzel & G. R. Wheaton (Eds.), *Applied measurement methods in industrial psychology* (pp. 51–88). Palo Alto, CA: Consulting Psychologists Press.

Williams, L. K., Seybolt, J. W., & Pinder, C. C. (1975). On administering questionnaires in organizational settings. *Personnel Psychology, 28,* 93–103.

Williamson, L. G., Campion, J. E., Malos, S. B., Roehling, M. V., & Campion, M. A. (1997). Employment interview on trial: Linking interview structure with litigation outcomes. *Journal of Applied Psychology, 82,* 900–912.

Winefield, A. H., & Tiggemann, M. (1990). Employment status and psychological well-being: A longitudinal study. *Journal of Applied Psychology, 75,* 455–459.

Winefield, A. H., Tiggemann, M., & Winefield, H. R. (1992). Unemployment distress, reasons for job loss and causal attributions for unemployment in young people. *Journal of Occupational and Organizational Psychology, 65,* 213–218.

Woehr, D. J. (1994). Understanding frame-of-reference training: The impact of training on the recall of performance information. *Journal of Applied Psychology, 79,* 524–534.

Woehr, D. J., & Huffcutt, A. I. (1994). Rater training for performance appraisal: A quantitative review. *Journal of Occupational and Organizational Psychology, 67,* 189–205.

Wong, C., & Campion, M. A. (1991). Development and test of a task level model of motivational job design. *Journal of Applied Psychology, 76,* 825–837.

Wright, L. (1988). The Type A behavior pattern and coronary artery disease: Quest for the active ingredients and the elusive mechanism. *American Psychologist, 43,* 2–14.

Wright, P. M. (1990). Operationalization of goal difficulty as a moderator of the goal difficulty–performance relationship. *Journal of Applied Psychology, 75*, 227–234.

Wright, T. A. (1997). Time revisited in organizational behavior. *Journal of Organizational Behavior, 18*, 201–204.

Yeatts, D. E., & Hyten, C. (1998). *High-performing self-managed work teams*. Thousand Oaks, CA: Sage.

Yost, E. (1943). *American women of science*. New York: Stokes.

Youngblood, S. A., DeNisi, A. S., Molleston, J. L., & Mobley, W. H. (1984). The impact of work environment, instrumentality beliefs, perceived labor union image, and subjective norms on union voting intentions. *Academy of Management Journal, 17*, 576–590.

Yukl, G. (1989a). *Leadership in organizations* (2nd ed.). Englewood Cliffs, NJ: Prentice Hall.

Yukl, G. (1989b). Managerial leadership: A review of theory and research. *Journal of Management, 15*, 251–289.

Yukl, G. (1994). *Leadership in organizations* (3rd ed.). Englewood Cliffs, NJ: Prentice Hall.

Yukl, G., & Falbe, C. M. (1991). The importance of different power sources in downward and lateral relations. *Journal of Applied Psychology, 76*, 416–423.

Yukl, G. A., & Latham, G. P. (1975). Consequences of reinforcement schedules and incentive magnitudes for employee performance: Problems encountered in an industrial setting. *Journal of Applied Psychology, 60*, 294–298.

Yukl, G. A., Latham, G. P., & Pursell, E. D. (1976). The effectiveness of performance incentives under continuous and variable ratio schedules of reinforcement. *Personnel Psychology, 29*, 221–232.

Yukl, G., & Tracey, J. B. (1992). Consequences of influence tactics used with subordinates, peers, and bosses. *Journal of Applied Psychology, 77*, 525–535.

Yukl, G., & Van Fleet, D. D. (1992). Theory and research on leadership in organizations. In M. D. Dunnette & L. M. Hough (Eds.), *Handbook of industrial and organizational psychology* (2nd ed., Vol. 3, pp. 147–197). Palo Alto, CA: Consulting Psychologists Press.

Yukl, G., Wall, S., & Lepsinger, R. (1990). Preliminary report on validation of the management practices survey. In K. E. Clark & M. B. Clark (Eds.), *Measures of leadership* (pp. 223–238). West Orange, NJ: Leadership Library of America.

Zalesny, M. D. (1985). Comparison of economic and noneconomic factors in predicting faculty vote preference in a union representation election. *Journal of Applied Psychology, 70*, 243–256.

Zedeck, S. (1992). Introduction: Exploring the domain of work and family careers. In S. Zedeck (Ed.), *Work, families, and organizations* (pp. 1–32). San Francisco: Jossey-Bass.

Zedeck, S., & Cascio, W. F. (1982). Performance appraisal decisions as a function of rater training and purpose of the appraisal. *Journal of Applied Psychology, 67*, 752–758.

Zedeck, S., Outtz, J., Cascio, W. F., & Goldstein, I. L. (1995). Why do "testing experts" have such limited vision? *Human Performance, 8*, 179–190.

Zeidner, J., & Johnson, C. D. (1994). Is personnel classification a concept whose time has passed? In M. G. Rumsey, C. B. Walker, & J. H. Harris (Eds.), *Personnel selection and classification* (pp. 377–410). Hillsdale, NJ: Erlbaum.

Zhong-Ming, W. (1997). Effective team management and cooperative decisions in Chinese organizations. In C. L. Cooper & D. M. Rousseau (Eds.), *Trends in organizational behavior* (Vol. 4, pp. 61–72). London: Wiley.